普通高等教育"十一五"国家规划教材

美英报刊导读
（第二版）

How to Read & Understand English
Newspapers & Magazines

(Second Edition)

周学艺　编著

北京大学出版社
PEKING UNIVERSITY PRESS

图书在版编目(CIP)数据

美英报刊导读/周学艺编著. —2版. —北京：北京大学出版社，2010.9
ISBN 978-7-301-17809-6

Ⅰ.美… Ⅱ.周… Ⅲ.英语－阅读教学－高等学校－自学参考资料 Ⅳ.H319.4

中国版本图书馆 CIP 数据核字(2010)第 183155 号

书　　　名：	美英报刊导读(第二版)
著作责任者：	周学艺　编著
责 任 编 辑：	李　颖
标 准 书 号：	ISBN 978-7-301-17809-6/H·2643
出 版 发 行：	北京大学出版社
地　　　址：	北京市海淀区成府路 205 号　100871
网　　　址：	http：//www.pup.cn
电　　　话：	邮购部 62752015　发行部 62750672　编辑部 62765014
	出版部 62754962
电 子 信 箱：	evalee1770@sina.com
印　　刷　者：	河北滦县鑫华书刊印刷厂
经　　销　者：	新华书店
	730 毫米×980 毫米　16 开本　28.25 印张　510 千字
	2003 年 7 月第 1 版　2010 年 9 月第 2 版
	2019 年 9 月第 3 次印刷
定　　　价：	56.00 元

未经许可，不得以任何方式复制或抄袭本书之部分或全部内容。
版权所有，侵权必究
举报电话：(010)62752024　电子信箱：fd@pup.pku.edu.cn

前　言

　　报刊或新闻语言,形式多样,并不局限于报刊。从广义讲,凡是提供信息的媒体,诸如电视、广播、互联网,乃至谈论时局或国际关系的专著等等,使用的语言,其实大同小异,无妨统统包括进去。

　　形式如此多姿多彩,内容就更加琳琅满目,美不胜收了。举凡政治、经济、外交、军事、金融等等,都可以一股脑装进这个大筐里去。

　　在全球化,信息化的今天,我堂堂中华,成为名副其实的世界大国,举世瞩目,早已融入外部世界了,想分也分不开。人们要学会站在全球的高度,分析问题,见微知著,捕捉先机。国际风云,瞬息万变。一场远在美国的次贷危机,捅了大祸,迅速蔓延全球,酿成百年不遇的经济灾难,殃及人人,对整个国际格局,必将产生深远影响。非典、甲流、"9·11"事件,莫不如此,只是程度有所不同罢了。如此看来,及时通过报刊、广播、电视、互联网,掌握信息,不仅是学好英语的最好帮手,简直成了生活必需品,快要赶上阳光、空气与水了。

　　因此,可以说报刊英语是一面时代的镜子,无所不包,无时不在,无孔不入。集当代英语之大成,开明日英语之先河。

　　现代英语始于 16 和 17 世纪 Shakespeare works 和 the first edition of the King James Bible 的出版。报刊出现在 18 世纪初叶。1702 年,英国伦敦出版了第一份日报,名叫 The Daily Courant。1704 年,北美第一份周刊 Boston News-letter 创刊。就古英语转变成现代英语而言,现代文学起了重要的推动作用,报刊也功不可没,如 Time 就自称是现代英语的代表。

　　形势变了,反映现实的语言也在紧跟紧追。近几十年来,人类生活节奏加快,在报刊等媒体推动下,英语一直在朝着简明的方向走。著名语言学家和几位美国民主党总统都一直在或曾经推动过 plain English,现在报刊走在这个运动的前列。其代表人物之一是 Newsweek 国际版主编 Fareed Zakaria,所写文章言简意赅。此外,每年出现千把新词,多是报刊带头使用,其中不少可以根据构词法,大体猜出来,但更多的是熟词新义,处处有陷阱,一不小心便会出错。

　　改革开放,对外交往频繁,报刊英语火起来了,形势喜人。同时,大量英语电影、电视连续剧的光盘,涌进课堂,不少从经典名著改编而来,成为学习英美文学的有力帮手。回想当年上大学学英语的情景,恍如隔世。

　　报刊用语的一个显著特点是不断标新立异,力求走在当代语言的最前列。

正如编者在第一版"前言"所说:"阅读美英报刊可以扩大视野,增长知识,学习现代语言……是迅速提高英文水平、增长涉外业务才干的另一条重要途径。"是推动英语向前发展的火车头。"如能与教授文学作品相结合,两头一起抓,相信教学效果会更理想。"

《美英报刊导读》,英文名是 *How To Read & Understand English Newspapers & Magazines*。顾名思义,这本书应该理论联系实际,要求作者写出一本有启发性、指导性、研究性、系统性的著作来。对我而言,这简直是项艰巨而难以完成的任务。原因有二:一是以往的英语系只重视文学。报刊英语,在人们眼里,不过是些急就章(journalism is literature in a hurry),赶写出来的大路货,质量不高,上不了台面。何况当年国外广播叫敌台,外刊外报全是大毒草,是犯大忌的,躲都躲不过来,还谈什么学习,更不用说有这方面的研究成果可资借鉴,连这种参考书都没有。好在本人改革开放后受到北大老前辈治学精神的熏陶和鼓舞,使我一直能在普及英文报刊阅读这块田园里耕耘着。二是无师承。本人几十年来都是摸着石头过河,只求能看懂报刊上的有些文章。平时虽然也注意积累资料,且其数量可观,然而却消化不了,不会在这方面从事系统而严密的研究。

报刊绝非只是消息报道,看似简单,其实包罗万象,名堂不少,时刻花样翻新,当初连国外出版的最新版字典与工具书也帮不上忙。稍微马虎大意,便会望文生义,闹笑话,出洋相。好在本人经过二三十年勤奋努力,摸爬滚打,才悟出些门道来。

1987年,编注第一套报刊文选,接着主编三种文选及导读,出了两部报刊词典,二十多年来,初步形成一套系列丛书,奉献在有志学习英语报刊的读者面前。

这套丛书,承蒙广大读者错爱。上海外国语大学新闻学院还把第一版《导读》列为考研必读书,《英语文摘》(*English Digest*)月刊干脆拨出宝贵篇幅连载。但本人有自知之明,并不满足于这点微薄成绩,打算跳出报刊框框,为我国整个外刊英语教学,略尽绵薄。

关于报刊阅读理解究竟难在何处,编者既对一些名牌大学没有上过报刊课的毕业生作过调查,又从实际出发,重新审视自己自1987年编注报刊文选及后来主编的教材和参考书。为了紧跟时代步伐,又将2005年至2008年的 *Newsweek* 基本翻看了一遍。思考一下该书第一版所写有哪些章节读者能受益,哪些有改进的必要。这样为第二版的重编打下基础。

基于上述报刊引领语言的认识,第二版丰富了"语言"和"读报知识",两者糅合在一起,这是与第一版的最大不同之处。优点是初入门者能在不知不觉中既学到了文化知识,又增加了词汇量,扩大了词义面。在语言部分,编者试图对有些词语追溯其源及用于何处、在不同的场合作何解释加以讲解。如"改朝换代产生和流行的词语"和"党语和党争用语初探"等就是如此。在"学习方法"一章里，探讨了一些学习方法，词汇的记忆及定义之道等。此外，为使读者对有些词语理解得透，情况了解得更深，在有的章节里还配以图片和漫画。

为使读者读懂报刊和掌握报刊用语的特点，本书除了一般语言解说外，还增加了"跟踪语言的变化和发展"，对"读懂标题"和"报刊语言主要特点"进行了总结。这两章节是编者试图在系统性和理论性上有所提高，这是读懂报刊和提高报刊语言遣词用字敏感性的关键。不过，编者总结的是指导读报的理论，还是管椎之见或谬论，尚待读者评判指正。

上世纪 70 年代初，周总理曾指出："外语教学有个基本功。……基本功包括三个方面：政治思想、语言本身和各种文化知识。"那么什么是读报基本功呢？在语言方面，大学高年级学生开始学习读报，他们掌握的基本词语是不够应付的，首先要扩大常见词的词义面，增加词汇量，并了解报刊语言主要特点；在文化知识方面，要掌握本书在"读报知识"一章里的那些核心知识，并能学以致用。这就是本人认为的基本功。夯实了基础，他们不但可以不必为读懂报刊犯愁，且终身受益。当然也得紧跟形势，了解 What's going in the world，做到与时俱进。

美英报刊涵盖其国内外大事，各类题材无所不包，对初读报学生而言，有点像是一本一大堆难题的天书。读懂文章要求有广泛的语言知识和各种文化知识。报刊不如文学语言那样深刻含蓄，但读一份报刊与读一本一般文学作品相比，文化知识面则要求更广，这是许多词语难以理解的一个重要原因。所以，同仁们普遍认为，读懂报刊的关键是掌握各类分析语言的文化背景知识，当然这是指语言基本功已过关的读者，否则压根儿读不了报。

第二版对美英"读报知识"作了重点介绍，并结合例句、语篇进行说明，尤其还对两国政治作了较详细的对比。否则下列问题便难以回答：

1. United States President Barack Obama, a member of the Democratic Party, was endorsed or supported by some members of the Republican Party and by some political figures holding conservative views in the 2008 election. Just as in the 1980s many Democrats became known as "Reagan Democrats," **in 2008 Republicans who supported Barack Obama became known as "Obama Republicans," or "Obamacans." The word "Obamacon" was also used during the campaign, for conservatives who expressed support for Obama.** (Wikipedia)

为什么说"The word 'Obamacon' was also used."？虽然此段的前面句子和后面的"for conservatives who..."已经作了阐明，但要深究它与 Obamacan 从广义、狭义讲有何相同和异同？这可能还要再看书才能透懂。克林顿获胜为何只有 Clinton Republican 而不再加上 Clinton conservative？

2. 为何美国竞选的名言是："All politics is personal."而英国选举时候选人主要靠政党？

3. majority party 在英美议会有何相同和异同？为什么英国有执政党和反对党，而美国却常常没有真正意义上的执政党和反对党，只有 the party in/out of the White House？

现在是信息爆炸的时代，信息不等于知识。学生在课本上只是学了知识，能否将所学知识用于实际，这是检验其是否真正掌握知识的试金石。上述三题能否仅凭上网就能回答得了呢？如果不透彻了解美国两党、两派（自由派和保守派）的不同理念是回答不了第一个问题的。不知道美英政体有别，就难以回答第二和第三个问题。

本书将"政治名言的理解与翻译"和"对号入座式单词转换翻译的弊病"置于读报知识后，是基于不少名言的理解与翻译不但是语言问题，文化知识也极其重要，否则许多问题便似懂非懂，理解不透。此外，"读报经验教训谈"对帮助和鼓励初学者或许有益，而"编书谈"看似有些离题，因本书的读者群不同，对有志于此业者可作参考，以待更多新人出现。这部分正是应一些有志青年教师的要求补写的。

本书的目的在于突破阅读理解难点，所以重点突出语言解说、读报知识、语言的变化与发展、报刊用语的特点及政治名言的理解与翻译这些章节上。这是与新闻系教师所写以写作为重点的书不同。

《导读》与其他三种报刊文选课本——《美英报刊文章选读》（上下册）（第四版）（正文内简称《上下册》四版）和《美英报刊文章阅读》（精选本）（第四版）（简称《精选本》四版）和其《学习辅导》（第四版）（简称《学习辅导》四版）及《大学英语报刊文选》（非英语专业高年级用书）（简称《大学》）——相辅相成，相得益彰。《导读》中有的章节以一些文选课文作阅读理解习题。讲授文选课的教师可视具体情况将《导读》内容充实到课堂教学当中，引导学生在阅读报刊文章时发现、总结报刊语言特点，认识语言演变规律，还可以结合具体语言实际，介绍相关的翻译技巧。

《美英报刊导读》是一本实用的书，适合大学英语、新闻和涉外专业的高年级学生、研究生使用，也适于青年教师及对英文报刊有兴趣者自修之用。相信他们读完全书后，定会对当代英语的认识、理解能力和翻译水平提高一步。

本书所引的例句绝大部分都是编者经年累月从读外刊、编教科书和词典里撷取的，小部分吸收了他人的研究成果。书里有个别例句由于一时找不到出处而难以注明，恕已不是故意剽窃他人成果。特此说明。

在编书过程中得一些好友和同仁的帮助。这里我尤其要提到挚友马宗师先生,他不但是资深的国际问题研究员,还是高级翻译家,懂得多种外文,尤其精通中英两种语言。他一贯给予我慷慨帮助,这次也不例外。在此,特别要对他表示由衷的谢忱和敬意。嘉兴学院的赵林教授、北京信息学院的郭丽萍副教授、天津外国语大学的曲莉老师、编辑李颖女士都曾给予我帮助。在此,我一并表示谢意。此外,我还要说明,由于我女儿周蓓和女婿石磊在我编书关键的最后四个多月时间里提供了良好的"后勤"支持,才使我得已完成书稿。

"取法乎上,仅得其中"。只有高标准,严要求,才能拿出点像样的东西,对得住读者。但毕竟编者年已逾古稀,且身患顽疾,深感在编书的过程中力不从心,书中肯定会存在不少缺点和谬误,恳请方家不吝赐教。

周学艺
北京西山养心园
广州汇景新城
E-mail:zhou_xueyi@sina.com

目 录

第一章　报刊、新闻、文体、体裁及政治倾向性等 (1)

第一节　美英主要报刊和通讯社简介 (1)

一、美国报纸 (1)
1. The New York Times (2)
2. The Washington Post (2)
3. Los Angeles Times (4)
4. USA Today (4)
5. The Wall Street Journal (5)
6. International Herald Tribune (5)
7. The Christian Science Monitor (5)

二、美国新闻期刊 (6)
1. Time (6)
2. Newsweek (6)
3. U. S. News & World Report (6)
4. Reader's Digest (7)
5. Fortune (7)
6. Business Week (7)
7. Far Eastern Economic Review (7)

三、英国报纸 (8)
1. The Times (8)
2. Financial Times (10)
3. The Guardian (10)
4. The Daily Telegraph (10)
5. The Independent (10)
6. The Sun (11)
7. The Daily Mirror (11)

四、英国新闻期刊 (11)
1. The Economist (11)

  2. The Spectator ……………………………………………… (12)
  3. New Statesman …………………………………………… (12)
 五、美英通讯社 ………………………………………………… (12)
  1. AP ………………………………………………………… (12)
  2. UPI ………………………………………………………… (12)
  3. Bloomberg News ………………………………………… (12)
  4. Dow-Jones Newswires …………………………………… (12)
  5. Reuters …………………………………………………… (13)
  6. PA ………………………………………………………… (13)
  7. 其他通讯社 ……………………………………………… (13)
第二节 新闻、电头及导语 ………………………………………… (14)
 一、何谓 News …………………………………………………… (14)
 二、新闻的价值 ………………………………………………… (16)
 三、电头(Dateline) ……………………………………………… (16)
 四、消息导语(Lead)种种 ……………………………………… (17)
  1. 重要性 …………………………………………………… (17)
  2. 作用 ……………………………………………………… (17)
  3. 形式多样 ………………………………………………… (17)
  4. 报道手法翻新 …………………………………………… (18)
第三节 文体与体裁 ………………………………………………… (19)
 一、文体 ………………………………………………………… (19)
  1. 新闻体 …………………………………………………… (19)
  2. 综合体 …………………………………………………… (19)
  3. 实用文体 ………………………………………………… (19)
  4. 文学文体 ………………………………………………… (19)
 二、新闻体裁 …………………………………………………… (20)
  1. 消息(News) ……………………………………………… (20)
  2. 特写(Feature) …………………………………………… (22)
  3. 社论和评论(Editorial & Commentary) ……………… (24)
第四节 报刊的政治倾向性 ………………………………………… (27)
 一、立场 ………………………………………………………… (27)
 二、党派属性 …………………………………………………… (28)
 三、惯用套路 …………………………………………………… (29)
  1. 直接灌输,巧妙暗示 …………………………………… (29)

2. 预定角色，刻意误导 …………………………………… (29)

　　3. 媒体政府，高度默契 …………………………………… (29)

　　4. 利用媒体，颠倒黑白 …………………………………… (30)

　四、用词 ……………………………………………………………… (30)

　五、对我国媒体的影响 ……………………………………………… (31)

　六、擦亮眼睛，提高警惕 …………………………………………… (31)

第二章　语言 …………………………………………………………… (32)

　第一节　扩大若干常见词的词义面 ……………………………… (36)

　　一、Agenda ……………………………………………………… (36)

　　二、Challenge …………………………………………………… (38)

　　三、Community ………………………………………………… (39)

　　四、Dimension ………………………………………………… (41)

　　五、Establishment ……………………………………………… (43)

　　六、Interest ……………………………………………………… (45)

　　七、Ironically …………………………………………………… (46)

　　八、Presence …………………………………………………… (47)

　　九、Story ………………………………………………………… (51)

　　十、Technical/Technically ……………………………………… (53)

　第二节　改朝换代产生和流行的词语 …………………………… (56)

　　一、美国 ………………………………………………………… (56)

　　　1. 从奥巴马狂看新词 ……………………………………… (56)

　　　2. F. 罗斯福任期 …………………………………………… (59)

　　　3. 杜鲁门任期 ……………………………………………… (59)

　　　4. 艾森豪威尔任期 ………………………………………… (60)

　　　5. 肯尼迪任期 ……………………………………………… (60)

　　　6. L. 约翰逊任期 …………………………………………… (61)

　　　7. 尼克松任期 ……………………………………………… (61)

　　　8. 福特任期 ………………………………………………… (62)

　　　9. 卡特任期 ………………………………………………… (62)

　　　10. 里根任期 ……………………………………………… (63)

　　　11. 老布什任期 …………………………………………… (64)

　　　12. 克林顿任期 …………………………………………… (64)

　　　13. 小布什任期 …………………………………………… (65)

二、英国 ··· (66)
　　　　1. 从希思到卡拉汉首相任期(1970—1979) ································· (67)
　　　　2. 从撒切尔夫人到梅杰首相任期(1979—1997) ····························· (68)
　　　　3. 从布莱尔到布朗首相任期(1997—2010) ································· (70)
　　　　4. 保守党和自由民主党组成联合政府(2010年5月—　　) ···················· (71)
　第三节　党语和党争用语初探 ··· (72)
　　一、党语与党争用语之异同 ·· (72)
　　二、党争用语产生的原因 ·· (73)
　　三、党争用语种种 ·· (74)
　　　　1. 竞选口号和人身攻击 ·· (74)
　　　　2. 社会政策和主张 ·· (75)
　　　　3. 经济政策和主张等 ·· (77)
　　　　4. 战争、战俘和窃听政策等 ·· (78)
　　四、党争用语的目的和用词特点 ·· (79)
　第四节　外交用语 ··· (82)
　　一、外交分类用语 ·· (82)
　　　　1. 官方外交 ·· (82)
　　　　2. 非官方外交 ·· (83)
　　二、美国对外政策及用语 ·· (83)
　　三、对华外交政策及用语 ·· (84)
　　四、其他外交用语 ·· (85)
　第五节　军事用语 ··· (87)
　　一、美国军队的建制及预算 ·· (87)
　　二、二战和越战产生和流行的词语 ·· (88)
　　三、第一次伊拉克战争 ·· (88)
　　四、阿富汗战争和第二次伊战 ·· (89)
　　五、新战略产生的词语 ·· (89)
　　六、对华和俄罗斯的政策 ·· (90)
　　七、行话和委婉语 ·· (91)
　　八、其他 ·· (91)
　第六节　社会用语 ··· (92)
　　一、争民权,反越战,新词生 ·· (92)
　　二、女权运动 ·· (92)
　　三、反正统文化运动 ·· (92)

四、多元文化运动 …………………………………… (93)
　　五、社会问题出新词 ………………………………… (94)
　　六、造词能力 ………………………………………… (94)
第七节　经济用语 ………………………………………… (96)
　　一、从次贷危机到经济衰退或危机 ………………… (96)
　　二、金融和经济危机的祸根 ………………………… (97)
　　三、出招应对，G20 开会 …………………………… (98)
　　四、金融危机催生新词 ……………………………… (98)
第八节　法律用语 ………………………………………… (101)
　　一、一般法律用语 …………………………………… (101)
　　二、新词和一度流行的时髦词 ……………………… (103)
　　三、易误解词语 ……………………………………… (103)
　　四、其他 ……………………………………………… (104)
第九节　科技用语 ………………………………………… (105)
　　一、科技新语不断 …………………………………… (105)
　　二、造词能力出众 …………………………………… (106)
　　三、旧词引申出新义 ………………………………… (107)
第十节　跟踪语言的变化和发展 ………………………… (109)
　　一、词义变化多奇妙 ………………………………… (109)
　　　1. Defining Moment …………………………… (109)
　　　2. Launch Window ……………………………… (111)
　　　3. Orwellian 添新义 …………………………… (112)
　　　4. Cowboy 新解 ………………………………… (114)
　　二、词义变化溯根源 ………………………………… (115)
　　　1. 从具体到抽象和从抽象到具体 …………… (115)
　　　2. 从泛指到特指 ……………………………… (116)
　　　3. 名词的变化 ………………………………… (116)
　　　4. 词性的变化 ………………………………… (116)
　　　5. 从某一领域转用于另一领域 ……………… (116)
　　　6. 时代变化 …………………………………… (117)
　　三、语言的弃旧换新 ………………………………… (118)
　　四、语言语法创新 …………………………………… (120)
　　　1. 语言的发展 ………………………………… (120)
　　　2. 语法的变化和发展 ………………………… (121)

第三章　广告与漫画 (124)

第一节　广告(Advertisement) (124)

一、广告内容和语言特色 (124)

二、广告的分类 (124)

　　1. 竞选广告 (124)

　　2. 商业类 (126)

　　3. 公益类 (129)

第二节　漫画 (130)

一、种族歧视 (130)

二、财经类 (130)

三、阿富汗和伊拉克战争 (131)

　　1. 失败 (131)

　　2. 虐囚丑闻 (131)

四、社会百态 (132)

五、国际 (134)

第四章　读懂标题和报刊用语主要特点 (138)

第一节　读懂标题 (138)

一、标题特点 (138)

　　1. 缩略词 (138)

　　2. 短字 (139)

　　3. 省略 (142)

　　4. 时态 (143)

二、情况与知识 (145)

三、具有文学功底 (145)

第二节　报刊语言主要特点 (146)

一、简约 (146)

　　1. 修辞手段 (147)

　　2. 词性转化 (147)

　　3. 构词手法 (147)

　　4. 句法上的简约 (148)

二、时尚 (150)

　　1. 语言上的时尚 (150)

2. 语法的时尚 …………………………………………… (151)
三、创新 ………………………………………………………… (151)
　　1. 新词新义如潮涌 ……………………………………… (151)
　　2. 语法、句法结构的变化发展 ………………………… (152)
四、修词色彩浓,常引经据典;用语新颖别致,形象生动 …… (152)
　　1. 引经据典,成语典故多 ……………………………… (152)
　　2. 标题常运用各种修辞手段 …………………………… (153)
　　3. 用语新颖别致,形象生动活泼 ……………………… (157)
五、图文配合,交相辉映 ……………………………………… (158)
　　1. 吸引读者 ……………………………………………… (158)
　　2. 真实又节省篇幅 ……………………………………… (158)
　　3. 释疑解惑 ……………………………………………… (159)
　　4. 图表漫画语言简炼、形象生动、幽默等特点得到体现 … (160)
六、程式化 ……………………………………………………… (161)
　　1. 常用套语(conventional phrases) ………………… (161)
　　2. 报道程式 ……………………………………………… (161)
七、其他特点 …………………………………………………… (161)
　　1. 外来语多 ……………………………………………… (161)
　　2. 被动语态较多 ………………………………………… (162)
　　3. 俚语、行话多 ………………………………………… (162)
　　4. 即兴造词 ……………………………………………… (162)

第三节　报刊语言弊病 ………………………………………… (163)
　一、用词出格多 ……………………………………………… (163)
　二、陈词多 …………………………………………………… (163)
　三、不看对象行话多 ………………………………………… (163)
　四、加缀构词滥 ……………………………………………… (163)
　五、求新弄巧成拙多 ………………………………………… (163)
　六、任意扩大词义 …………………………………………… (164)
　七、赘词多 …………………………………………………… (164)
　八、省略过度 ………………………………………………… (165)
　九、避免重复用词过头,反而用词不当 …………………… (166)
　十、标题编排令人生疑 ……………………………………… (166)
　十一、体例不统一 …………………………………………… (166)
　十二、语言尤其是背景知识错误屡见不鲜 ………………… (167)

第四节 常见时髦语 (168)
　　一、政治领域 (168)
　　二、经济和其他领域 (171)

第五节 常见借喻词和提喻词 (172)
　　一、常用借喻法 (172)
　　　　1. 常见借喻法 (172)
　　　　2. 另类借喻法 (173)
　　二、提喻法 (173)
　　三、一词数义 (173)
　　四、常见借喻和提喻词一览 (174)

第六节 常见委婉语 (176)
　　一、社会领域委婉语 (176)
　　二、政治领域 (177)

第七节 常用套语 (179)
　　一、报道、评析常用套语 (179)
　　二、消息来源常用套语 (180)

第五章 读报知识 (182)

第一节 美国 (183)
　　一、国名 (183)
　　二、简况 (184)
　　三、联邦政府 (185)
　　　　1. 组织机构 (185)
　　　　2. 国务院＝中国国务院或外交部吗 (186)
　　　　3. Dept of War＝Dept of Defense 吗 (186)
　　　　4. Deputy Secretary＝Under Secretary 吗 (186)
　　四、三权分立,各自为政 (187)
　　　　1. 何谓三权分立 (187)
　　　　2. 制衡制的理论基础 (187)
　　五、总统 (189)
　　　　1. 继任顺序(order of succession) (189)
　　　　2. 何谓总统制(Presidential System) (189)
　　　　3. 帝王总统(imperial president/presidency) (189)
　　　　4. 总统梦 (190)

六、总统选举 (192)
1. 两党制 (193)
2. 两个阶段 (193)
3. 选举团的作用 (193)
4. 选举人票与普选票不一致咋办 (194)
5. 参选总统资格 (194)
6. 选举：金钱政治，富人游戏 (195)
7. 527组织兴起 (196)
8. 奥巴马算是第几位总统 (197)

七、国会 (198)
1. Bicameral Congress (198)
2. Divided Government (198)
3. 与总统较量的权力 (198)
4. 两院议员的身价 (199)
5. 副总统有投票权吗 (199)
6. 何谓 Majority or Minority Party (199)
7. 有哪些重要官职 (199)

八、国会选举 (200)
1. 何谓 Congressional Election (200)
2. 何谓 Midterm Election (201)
3. off-year/off-off year/special election(s) (201)

九、国会是 Bureaucratic Empire 吗 (202)

十、国会是"Rich Man's Club" (204)

十一、总统与国会 (205)
1. 总统与国会是何关系 (205)
2. 府会倾轧为哪般 (206)
3. 谁占上风 (208)
4. 谁播下斗争的种子 (209)
5. State of the Union message 与国会的关系 (210)

十二、司法机构 (211)
1. 司法机关为何不如总统和国会"出风头" (211)
2. 高法裁决震动大 (211)
3. 裁决有利于普通百姓吗 (212)
4. The Supreme Court Follows the Election Results (212)

5. 法院和高院法官 ……………………………………………… (213)

十三、州政府(State Government) ………………………………… (214)
　　1. 组成与联邦政府相似吗 ……………………………………… (214)
　　2. 州议会英文名称种种 ………………………………………… (215)

十四、市政府(City Government) ………………………………… (215)
　　1. 何谓 Mayor-Council form/system …………………………… (215)
　　2. 何谓 Commission form/system ……………………………… (215)
　　3. 何谓 City-Manager form/system …………………………… (216)

十五、其他地方政府(Other Local Governments) ………………… (216)
　　1. 各州是否都设县 ……………………………………………… (216)
　　2. Parish 和 Borough＝County 吗 ……………………………… (216)
　　3. Commissioner 是 Dogcatcher 吗 …………………………… (216)
　　4. Mayor 是"镇长"吗 …………………………………………… (217)

十六、政党 ………………………………………………………… (217)
　　1. 民主党和共和党 ……………………………………………… (217)
　　2. 政党起何作用 ………………………………………………… (217)
　　3. 两党演变轨迹 ………………………………………………… (217)
　　4. 各自代表哪些阶层 …………………………………………… (218)
　　5. 理念不同的代表人物 ………………………………………… (219)
　　6. 松散的组织 …………………………………………………… (221)
　　7. 两党党徽——Donkey & Elephant …………………………… (221)
　　8. 理念不同,用词各异 ………………………………………… (222)
　　9. 第三党及其运动 ……………………………………………… (222)

十七、美式自由派和保守派 ……………………………………… (223)
　　1. 何谓 Liberals & Conservatives ……………………………… (223)
　　2. 两派区别何在 ………………………………………………… (223)
　　3. 两党与两派有何关系 ………………………………………… (224)
　　4. 党内有派 ……………………………………………………… (225)
　　5. 何谓 Neocon …………………………………………………… (225)
　　6. 两派之分说端详 ……………………………………………… (226)

十八、骷髅会 ……………………………………………………… (230)
　　1. Order of Skull and Bones 是何组织 ………………………… (230)
　　2. 在政界有何势力 ……………………………………………… (230)

十九、院外游说群体 ……………………………………………… (231)

  1. 何谓"Lobby" …………………………………………… (231)
  2. 谁开创了 Lobbying …………………………………… (232)
  3. Lobbyists 何其多 ……………………………………… (232)
  4. 为谁帮腔 为谁忙 ……………………………………… (233)
  5. 为何叫"Third House" ………………………………… (233)
  6. 何谓"K Street" ………………………………………… (234)
  7. 政坛丑闻何其多 ……………………………………… (234)
  8. 第五产业 ……………………………………………… (235)
二十、竞选活动委员会（PAC） ……………………………………… (235)
  1. 为谁服务 ……………………………………………… (235)
  2. 创建目的 ……………………………………………… (236)
  3. PAC 与议员的关系 …………………………………… (236)
二十一、宗教 ………………………………………………………… (236)
  1. 政治影响大 …………………………………………… (236)
  2. 教会与国家 …………………………………………… (237)
  3. 宗教题材常见诸报端 ………………………………… (237)
  4. 基督教的三大教派 …………………………………… (238)
  5. 犹太教 ………………………………………………… (239)
  6. 势力无孔不入 ………………………………………… (239)
  7. 政教"貌离神合" ……………………………………… (240)
  8. 接受和物色总统候选人 ……………………………… (242)
二十二、价值观 ……………………………………………………… (244)
  1. 何谓 values …………………………………………… (244)
  2. 各行各业都有价值观 ………………………………… (244)
  3. 共和党不离口的道德和家庭价值观 ………………… (244)
  4. 两党候选人同打一张牌 ……………………………… (245)
二十三、电影分级制 ………………………………………………… (247)
  1. 影片为何分级 ………………………………………… (247)
  2. 共分几级 ……………………………………………… (247)
二十四、电视节目 …………………………………………………… (248)
  1. D.L.S.V. 指何内容 …………………………………… (248)
  2. 节目分几类几档 ……………………………………… (249)
第二节　英国 ………………………………………………………… (251)
 一、国名 …………………………………………………………… (251)

二、简况 …………………………………………………… (251)

三、体制与宪法 …………………………………………… (251)

四、联合王国政府组织机构 ……………………………… (253)

五、权力的分配 …………………………………………… (254)

六、国王 …………………………………………………… (254)
  1. 权力和影响 ………………………………………… (254)
  2. 产生方式 …………………………………………… (254)
  3. 王位继承酝酿改革 ………………………………… (255)

七、行政机构——内阁 …………………………………… (255)

八、政府行政部门及官职 ………………………………… (255)
  1. 政府部门和大臣名称多不同 ……………………… (255)
  2. 大臣分几类几等　各司何责 ……………………… (256)
  3. 易混清的官职 ……………………………………… (256)

九、内阁种种 ……………………………………………… (257)
  1. 何谓"Responsible Government" ………………… (257)
  2. 何谓"Shadow Cabinet" …………………………… (257)
  3. 何谓"Caretaker Government" …………………… (257)
  4. 何谓"Coalition Government" ……………………… (258)

十、立法机构——议会 …………………………………… (258)
  1. 议会制是何种政体 ………………………………… (258)
  2. 议会制的英文种种表达 …………………………… (258)
  3. 为何政府的中心是议会 …………………………… (258)
  4. 议会分几院　各司何职 …………………………… (259)

十一、议会选举——大选 ………………………………… (259)
  1. 议会选举是全体议员的选举吗 …………………… (259)
  2. 采用何种选举制 …………………………………… (259)
  3. 为何议会选举即大选 ……………………………… (260)

十二、议会有哪些重要官职　(Party)Whip 有何职责 …… (260)
  1. 贵族院 ……………………………………………… (260)
  2. 平民院 ……………………………………………… (260)
  3. 何谓 One-/Two-/Three-/Four-line Whip ………… (262)

十三、司法机构 …………………………………………… (262)

十四、地方政府(Local Government) …………………… (262)
  1. 英格兰分哪三类政府机构 ………………………… (263)

2. 威尔士、苏格兰和北爱尔兰议会独立于英国政府吗 …………(263)
十五、政党 ……………………………………………………………(264)
　　1. 工党和新工党(Labour & New Labour) …………………(264)
　　2. 保守党 ……………………………………………………(265)
　　3. 自由民主党 ………………………………………………(266)
十六、英国君主制的废留之争…………………………………………(266)
　　1. 反对君主制会动摇民族意识的基础 ……………………(267)
　　2. 君主制与英国历史密不可分 ……………………………(267)
　　3. 英国人不喜欢共和制 ……………………………………(267)
　　4. 国王比总统更能代表国家形象 …………………………(267)
　　5. 君主比总统更能凝聚人心 ………………………………(268)
　　6. 伊丽莎白二世已成为民族精神和道德价值观的代表 …(268)
　　7. "统而不治"成优点 ………………………………………(268)
　　8. 有助于维持大国地位和促进经济发展 …………………(268)
　　9. 王室有严格的家规 ………………………………………(268)
　　10. 王权面临改革而非废止 …………………………………(268)
十七、何谓英联邦(The Commonwealth) …………………………(269)
　　1. 由哪些成员国组成　与英女王有何关系 ………………(269)
　　2. 联邦是何组织　英能主宰吗 ……………………………(269)
十八、英美特殊关系(Anglo-American Special Relationship) ……(270)
　　1. 英国为何要维持这种关系 ………………………………(270)
　　2. 谁首创这一关系 …………………………………………(270)
　　3. 美欧对英各有何期待 ……………………………………(271)
　　4. 国内外政要有何评论 ……………………………………(271)
　　5. 英国无外交 ………………………………………………(271)

第三节　英美政治比较…………………………………………………(273)
　一、国家体制形式不同 ………………………………………………(273)
　二、政体有别 …………………………………………………………(273)
　三、国王与总统 ………………………………………………………(274)
　四、首相与总统 ………………………………………………………(274)
　　1. 产生方式迥异 ……………………………………………(274)
　　2. 与议会关系有别 …………………………………………(274)
　　3. 行政权分大小 ……………………………………………(274)
　　4. 任期长短各别 ……………………………………………(275)

5. 助手顾问班子规模大小有别 (275)
  五、议会(Parliament & Congress) (275)
    1. 两院制各有千秋 (275)
    2. 议席多寡讲究各异 (275)
    3. 官职名称不尽相同 (276)
    4. 官职不能相互套用 (276)
    5. 政党督导或领袖能否兼职有别 (276)
    6. 重大法案通过与否 政府和议会影响各异 (276)
    7. (Party) Whip 权力大小不等 (277)
  六、内阁(Cabinet) (277)
    1. 内阁组成、作用和成员背景有别 (277)
    2. 两码事的 Shadow Cabinet 和 Kitchen Cabinet (278)
  七、大选(General Election) (278)
    1. 覆盖的面大小各别 (278)
    2. 总统首相选举大相径庭 (278)
    3. 政党作用有别 (278)
    4. 定期与否分得清 (279)
  八、政党 (279)
    1. 政党组织分松紧 (279)
    2. 领袖地位各高低 (279)
    3. 竞选策略有区别 (279)
    4. 党纪有无显异同 (280)
    5. 属性强调见轻重 (280)
    6. 政策主张不尽同 (281)
    7. 在朝在野境遇异 (281)
    8. 竞选：政党作用大小殊 (281)
    9. 左派右派 (281)
 第四节 其他方面的读报知识 (283)
  一、各国体制形形色色 (283)
  二、议会名称林林总总 (283)
  三、人名背后文章多 (284)
    1. 绰号、简称常成拦路虎 (284)
    2. 政策思想藏人名 (285)
    3. 公司品牌人名见 (286)

4. 性格抱负人心显 …………………………………………(287)
　　　5. 名人经历蕴玄机 …………………………………………(287)
　　　6. 作品人物寓意深 …………………………………………(290)
　四、地名里头有名堂 ……………………………………………(290)
　　　1. 地名作喻词不少见 ………………………………………(290)
　　　2. 地名暗喻贫富 ……………………………………………(290)
　五、地名面前防陷阱 ……………………………………………(291)
　　　1. 地域划分有讲究 …………………………………………(291)
　　　2. 国名相似易混淆 …………………………………………(291)
　　　3. 首都多了区分难 …………………………………………(292)
　六、时间弄清休马虎 ……………………………………………(293)
　　　1. 何谓"Chronology of World Events" ……………………(293)
　　　2. 时代背景知识对读报有何重要意义 ……………………(293)
　　　3. "Octobet"和"November"在美国何年有何意义 ………(294)
　　　4. "April 15"有啥蹊跷 ……………………………………(295)
　　　5. 联邦财政年度预算始末于何时 …………………………(296)
　七、美英等国情治机构知多少 …………………………………(296)
　　　1. 美国 ………………………………………………………(297)
　　　2. 英国 ………………………………………………………(298)
　　　3. 苏联 ………………………………………………………(299)
　　　4. 俄罗斯 ……………………………………………………(299)
　　　5. 法国 ………………………………………………………(299)
　　　6. 以色列 ……………………………………………………(299)
　八、重要"智库"(Think Tank) ………………………………(300)
　　　1. 有些公司、基金会等是何机构　有何作用 ……………(300)
　　　2. 五花八门的智库 …………………………………………(301)
　九、重要国际组织(Major International Organizations) ………(302)

第六章　翻译 …………………………………………………………(305)

　第一节　政治名言的理解与翻译 ………………………………(305)
　　一、对译论的看法 ……………………………………………(305)
　　二、常见诸报端 ………………………………………………(305)
　　三、读报刊,紧跟语言的变化和发展 ………………………(306)
　第二节　对号入座式单词转换翻译的弊病 ……………………(324)

一、Politics/Political ……………………………………………（324）
　　二、Culture/Cultural ……………………………………………（328）
　　三、Resources ……………………………………………………（330）

第七章　学习方法 ……………………………………………（333）

第一节　网络和读报工具书 ………………………………（333）
　　一、读报工具书重要性 …………………………………………（333）
　　二、学会利用工具书 ……………………………………………（334）
　　三、勤上网和查词典 ……………………………………………（335）
　　　1. 职位不明 …………………………………………………（335）
　　　2. 望文生义 …………………………………………………（335）
　　四、报刊、网络和词典也出错 …………………………………（337）
　　　1. 报刊背景知识不明 ………………………………………（337）
　　　2. 报刊语言错误 ……………………………………………（338）
　　　3. 网络粗心错字多 …………………………………………（339）
　　　4. 美英词典要区分 …………………………………………（339）
　　　5. 行话专业词典来当家 ……………………………………（339）

第二节　词语学习记忆法 …………………………………（341）
　　一、学习法 ………………………………………………………（341）
　　二、名师指点记忆法 ……………………………………………（342）
　　三、词根的重要性 ………………………………………………（344）

第三节　词义之确定及辨析 ………………………………（346）
　　一、词义之确定举例 ……………………………………………（346）
　　　1. 从文内阐释求解 Decommissioning ……………………（346）
　　　2. 靠同位语帮忙 Wheels Within Wheels …………………（347）
　　　3. 用对比法索义 Commercial Business/Industry …………（348）
　　　4. 向背景知识问路 Anti-Government 等 …………………（349）
　　　5. 紧跟形势解 Madonna 跟 Mogadishu 之对比 …………（351）
　　二、报刊用词辨析 ………………………………………………（351）
　　　1. Above politics 与 Nonpartisan …………………………（351）
　　　2. Avalanche 与 Clean Sweep, Landslide (Victory), Tidal Wave 和 Tide ……（352）
　　　3. Nonperson 与 Unperson …………………………………（353）
　　　4. Jail 与 Prison ……………………………………………（353）
　　　5. Elector 与 Voter 和 Presidential Elector ………………（354）

    6. Rome Correspondent 与 Roman Correspondent ……………… (354)
    7. Prime Minister, Premier 和 Chancellor …………………………… (354)
    8. Law Lord 与 Law Lords ……………………………………………… (354)
    9. Lord Commissioner 与 Lords Commissioners …………………… (354)
    10. Armed Force 与 Armed Forces …………………………………… (354)
    11. National Emblem 与 National Symbol …………………………… (354)
    12. Confidential 与 Secret, Top Secret 和 Royal …………………… (354)
    13. Ticket 与 Slate …………………………………………………… (354)
    14. Tax Credit 与 Tax Deduction …………………………………… (355)
    15. Neutral Nation 与 Neutralist Nation, Nonaligned Country
        和 Uncommitted Nation …………………………………………… (355)
    16. Solicitor 与 Barrister 和 Sergeant-at-Law ……………………… (355)
    17. Informer 与 Informant …………………………………………… (355)
    18. Limdis 与 Exdis 和 Nodis ………………………………………… (355)
    19. Need-To-Know 与 Eyes Only 和 Compartmentalization ……… (355)
    20. Spree Killer 与 Serial Killer ……………………………………… (355)
    21. Preference Poll 与 Trial Heat …………………………………… (356)
    22. Police agent 与 Police officer …………………………………… (356)
    23. Disinformation 与 Misinformation 和 Black Propaganda ……… (356)
    24. Chairman 和 Leader ……………………………………………… (356)
第四节　读报经验教训谈……………………………………………… (357)
  一、文章和期刊的难易决定阅读的先后顺序 ……………………… (357)
  二、泛读、精读和"死读" …………………………………………… (358)
  三、带着问题读书看报 ……………………………………………… (359)
  四、带着问号读书看报 ……………………………………………… (360)
  五、有关科研的几点看法 …………………………………………… (362)
  六、教训 ……………………………………………………………… (364)
第五节　编书谈………………………………………………………… (365)
  一、选材与课文 ……………………………………………………… (366)
    1. 趣味性和知识性是选材的首要标准 …………………………… (366)
    2. 题材新颖多样, 信息量大, 覆盖面广 ………………………… (367)
    3. 课文要有种种体裁 ……………………………………………… (367)
    4. 选材内容配合国策, 与时共进 ………………………………… (368)
    5. 选材内容等要平衡 ……………………………………………… (368)
    6. 课文尽量配有图表或漫画 ……………………………………… (368)

7. 编排合理 …………………………………………………… (369)
　　　8. 讲政治 ……………………………………………………… (369)
　二、词汇 ………………………………………………………………… (369)
　　　1. New Words 的范畴 ………………………………………… (369)
　　　2. 以英文定义为主 …………………………………………… (369)
　　　3. 看懂全文再下定义 ………………………………………… (370)
　　　4. 拓展学生的词汇面和词义面 ……………………………… (370)
　　　5. 注音一致，拼写有异 ……………………………………… (371)
　　　6. 用通用的缩略词表明词性等 ……………………………… (371)
　三、注释原则 …………………………………………………………… (371)
　　　1. 当注必注，不避难题 ……………………………………… (371)
　　　2. 注释精当，不画蛇添足 …………………………………… (374)
　　　3. 具有启发性、指导性和研究性 …………………………… (375)
　　　4. 扩大学生语汇量和语义面 ………………………………… (376)
　　　5. 讲政治 ……………………………………………………… (376)
　　　6. 标志清楚，体例统一 ……………………………………… (376)
　四、注释与语言解说和读报知识介绍相辅相成 …………………… (376)
　　　1. 语言解说举例 ……………………………………………… (377)
　　　2. 读报知识举例 ……………………………………………… (377)
　五、设计 Pre-Reading Questions 的要求和目的 …………………… (377)
　六、提 Questions 的要求及技巧 ……………………………………… (378)
　七、设计 Vocabulary Building 之技巧 ……………………………… (378)
　八、课文导读 …………………………………………………………… (378)
　　　1. 写导读三要素 ……………………………………………… (378)
　　　2. 不当的典型 ………………………………………………… (379)
　　　3. 好范例 ……………………………………………………… (379)
　九、报刊课考试的若干建议 …………………………………………… (381)
　十、学会校对 …………………………………………………………… (383)
　十一、建议开设报刊语言班 …………………………………………… (383)
　十二、教训 ……………………………………………………………… (384)

附录 …………………………………………………………………… (385)

Ⅰ. 报刊从业人员常用术语 …………………………………………… (385)
Ⅱ. 美国选举常用词语 ………………………………………………… (387)

- Ⅲ. 外事人员常用词语 …………………………………………… (389)
- Ⅳ. 宗教词语 ……………………………………………………… (390)
- Ⅴ. 间谍行话 ……………………………………………………… (392)
- Ⅵ. 美国历任总统一览 …………………………………………… (393)
- Ⅶ. 英国历任国王一览 …………………………………………… (396)
- Ⅷ. 英国历任首相一览 …………………………………………… (397)
- Ⅸ. 美英司法系统一览 …………………………………………… (400)
- Ⅹ. 美英军衔一览 ………………………………………………… (403)
- Ⅺ. 美国地图 ……………………………………………………… (405)
- Ⅻ. 英国地图 ……………………………………………………… (406)

参考书目 ………………………………………………………………… (407)
索引 ……………………………………………………………………… (409)

第一章 报刊、新闻、文体、体裁及政治倾向性等

第一节 美英主要报刊和通讯社简介

读报先要了解美英报刊基本情况。下面介绍的报刊均属于个人、家族、报业集团所有,办报理念、方针、立场各异。美英报刊有大报和小报(tabloid)之分,指质量高低与开张大小无关。读报还要分析其政治、立场、用词特点。这些是入门的第一步。

随着科技进步,网络走俏,报刊跟风,纷纷出网络版,与电视、广播、互联网争夺市场,恰好说明新闻英语的范围更广,时间性更强,更值得我们好好学习,做到与时俱进。不过据皮尤研究中心(Pew Research Center)今年调查发现,网络的竞争虽然削弱了报纸的销量,但六成以上的新闻仍来源于报纸,谷歌和其他网站的不少新闻抄袭于报纸的文章,旨在吸引更多读者,卖出更多广告。此处本人顺便借报刊介绍和上段皮尤研究中心的调查发表一点看法。我们读一份大报与在网上浏览看报感觉有所不同,前者林林总总题材和体裁的文章历历在目,犹如看一本小说或戏剧等文学作品,给人一种整体或全面的感觉,且随时随地可读,也较舒服;后者却无此优点。难怪现在仍有成千上万美英人既上网也看报。

美国和英国的日报总数约两千多家,各种期刊达一万余种(title),其中绝大多数是地方性报纸和专业、商业消费类期刊,全国性大报和其他类杂志为数不多。下面简要介绍若干在美英国内外有影响的报刊。报刊发行量,有的引用世界报业协会 2008 年 6 月发表的数字,有的根据 Wikipedia(维基百科)2009 年的统计。随着经济等情况的变化,销量也会随之生变。

一、美国报纸

美国报纸大体上可分为两种类型:通俗类小报,面向一般市民;大报讲究质量,力求吸引知识界。小报为了迎合读者兴趣、追求轰动效应。编辑读到天灾人祸、谋杀、罢工的新闻稿,挖空心思配上煽动情绪的标题,结果降低了质量,忽视了社会责任,为了营利,对公益事冷漠,却对性、暴力、明星私生活则尽情渲染,配以大量图片,以招引读者,发行量虽大,对重大问题却缺乏深远影响。至于严肃而高质量的大报,销量不及小报,影响力却大。它们常批评政府,监督官员,被誉为"民主制度守护神"。美国多数大报还有一个特点——维护国家利益,相对轻

视党派利益。共同点是狠抓社论、采编和国际大事,对经济效益绝不忽视。

1. The New York Times

The New York Times《纽约时报》,1851年创刊。属苏兹贝格(Sulzberger)家族所有。其大楼前有大广场,称为"时报广场"。同《华盛顿邮报》和《洛杉矶时报》并列美国最有影响的三大报。它内容充实,资料齐全,拥有一批名记者,位居榜首。在评选优秀报纸的民意测验中,曾多次夺冠,获美国最高新闻奖——普利策奖(The Pulitzer Prizes)最多。2003年假新闻而出丑,一度面临困境。但敢于承认错误,吸取教训,东山再起,2009年竟获五项普奖,成为媒体最大赢家。2010年不敌《华盛顿邮报》,只斩获三项大奖。订户遍及国内外。为了招徕更多客户,该报于2001年发行电子版。

《纽约时报》一贯标榜客观公正,座右铭是,"刊登一切适合刊登的新闻",也即不漏掉任何一条要闻。常用较大篇幅刊登政府重要文件和领导人讲话,但也不时发表一些批评政府政策的报道和评论,披露一些内幕和机密。例如,1971年刊登"五角大楼文件"(The Pentagon Papers),透露越南战争隐情,举国哗然。虽有"执美国舆论之牛耳"之说,但与政府关系密切,不时透露官方消息、报道和评述的国际新闻,基本上反映美国政府外交政策动向。与东部权势集团渊源较深,刊登自由派人士文章较多,被称为"自由派重镇"。有的评论界人士认为,该报政治上应属"中间偏左",2004年大选中与《华盛顿邮报》一道力挺民主党总统候选人克里(John Kerry)便是明证。

《纽约时报》是美国和其他国家领袖人物和高级知识分子必读的报纸。据世界报业协会的数据,该报日发行量约100多万份。在美国日报发行量的排行榜上,名列第三。

近年来,其版面的"导读索引框"(Inside)原来放在头版,突出当日要闻数则,标明何部何版。接着是News Summary(新闻提要),说明在A部的第二版。再下面是将这天报纸内容分为5部(Sections)。现在改变了原来多年的导读版面和内容。举2009年5月6日Wednesday刊登为例,"Inside"已置于第二版,并改为"Inside The Times",其内容也发生了变化,只相当以前的"News Summary"。令人不解的是头版也有与其相同的International, New York, National ... 等分类,只是具体的新闻不同。这种改动,反而不如原来的简明,难道两个"导读"不是重复吗?《华盛顿邮报》的"Inside"仍在头版,不同的是,其内容只是突出几则要闻,而无其他消息和索引。

2. The Washington Post

The Washington Post《华盛顿邮报》,1877年创刊。注重报道国会消息,号称"国会议员和政府官员早餐桌上少不了的报纸"。2010年,该报大出风头,竟超越《纽约时报》,揽下四项普奖。

第一章 报刊、新闻、文体、体裁及政治倾向性等

美国评论家认为,《华盛顿邮报》疾恶如仇、热情似火,比《纽约时报》富于攻击性,自由主义色彩也比《纽约时报》更浓烈。该报是民主橱窗里的一项重要装饰,历史超过百年。最初几十年只是挣扎求存,缺乏鲜明个性,忽而走大报路线,忽而向小报靠拢。忽冷忽热,不仅争取不到读者,反而赤字累累,换了不少主人。这些报人私心太重,在民主、共和两党之间东张西望,希望捞些政治油水。

1933年,《华盛顿邮报》终于遇到了救星。纽约银行家迈耶买下了该报,广告电话响个不停,报童的叫声像小云雀,八方英豪纷纷归来,好一幅兴旺景象。

1946年,迈耶将报纸交给女婿菲利普·格雷厄姆。1961年,格买下《新闻周刊》后,如虎添翼,声望从此紧追《纽约时报》。

1963年,菲利普自杀。凯瑟琳·格雷厄姆(Katharine Graham)继承夫志,聘奇才布莱德利任编辑,自1965年迄今,始终信誉不衰。在她任期内,尼克松被水门丑闻(Watergate)冲垮,副总统阿格纽因索贿倒台,俄亥俄众议员海斯假公济私被揭发,韩国收买国会议员而震惊国会(Koreagate)。

《华盛顿邮报》属格雷厄姆(Graham)家族所有,2001年去世的董事长兼发行人凯瑟琳·格雷厄姆是美国新闻界女强人。据称,美国政要、名流以及外国使节、王宫贵族,当时竞相与她攀交情。

《华盛顿邮报》在近年美国日报发行量的排行榜上,名列第五,平日发行量60多万份。《邮报》还出版小开张的全国性周末版(The *Washington Post National Weekly Edition*),发行量多于平日版。

3. Los Angeles Times

Los Angeles Times《洛杉矶时报》,1881年创刊。号称美国最有影响的三大报之一,是西部老大。处理国际新闻迅速、完整、深入,全球新闻同行公认为是一家最优秀的报纸。在全球22个重要据点均设有记者站。

该报已有一百年历史。第一阶段,是共和党台柱。上世纪50年代,曾因竭力支持尼克松竞选总统,引起美国政界重视,一跃成为全国有影响的大报。1964年,《洛杉矶时报》转而支持温和的共和党人。最近20年,该报像《纽约时报》、《华盛顿邮报》一样,走向"政治独立",至少表面上不偏向任何一党一派。有的评论家认为,该报自由派色彩较浓。先前属洛克菲勒家族所有,后被芝加哥论坛报集团收购。销量名列第四,发行量近80万份。

4. USA Today

USA Today《今日美国报》,由甘内特报业集团(Gannet Co.,Inc)于1983年创办,是美国唯一的全国性日报,因为其他报纸都冠以 New York、Washington 和 Los Angles 等地方色彩的字眼。它利用通信卫星在全美各地同时印刷和发行。它的出版一鸣惊人,在美国报业史上写下新的一页。彩虹的套色让人精神

一振；别具匠心的头条选择给全美各报灌输了编辑新概念；不仅巧妙总结当日要闻，更对未来进行展望。这份报纸每期56版，分为新闻、经济、体育、生活四组，正中美国人的心坎，其体育版遥遥领先全美各报。

《今日美国报》编排丰富多彩，图文并茂，报道翔实而不浮夸，文章短小，文字简练，报道面宽，信息量大。原以国内新闻为主，较少刊载国际新闻，为迎合大众化趣味一味模仿电视。为此，它付出了巨大的经济代价，现在已改变这一倾向。发行量退居第二，日发行量达188万份。

5. The Wall Street Journal

The Wall Street Journal《华尔街日报》，创刊于1889年。Wall指御敌之城墙，并非人名。社址在美国金融中心纽约市华尔街附近，原先由美国主要财政金融新闻出版企业集团"道-琼斯公司"（Dow-Jones & Company, Inc.）出版，现已转卖给媒体大亨默多克。其财经新闻迅速，带权威性，没有一家美国报纸可望其项背，是金融企业家必读报纸。此外，还向传统新闻领域伸展触须，经常发表在政治、外交等方面别有见地的文章。日发行量达202万份，比《纽约时报》和《华盛顿邮报》加在一起的总量还多，2009年竟跃居排名第一。

次年，默多克壮心不已，招揽人才，着手全面扩大版面内容，全彩印刷，使该报以保守派报业为代表，挑战自由派观点为主的《纽约时报》。有评论称这场大战最终可能两败俱伤。

该报原与香港《南华早报》（*South China Morning Post*）、日本《经济新闻》及新加坡和马来西亚的《海峡时报》（*The Straits Times*）合股，在香港出版《亚洲华尔街日报》（*The Wall Street Journal Asia*），行销亚洲各地。

6. International Herald Tribune

International Herald Tribune《国际先驱论坛报》，早先于1963年由《华盛顿邮报》与《纽约时报》及原来的《纽约先驱论坛报》（*The New York Herald Tribune*）联手在巴黎出版，行销欧亚各地。后来由前两家合办，并发行亚洲版。《纽约时报》于2002年买下《华盛顿邮报》全部股份，一家独办，其网站现称为the Global Edition of the New York Times。该报在欧亚影响很大，许多国家如韩国、日本和德国等英文报纸都与其合作。

这份报纸供在海外工作的美国人和讲英语的移民阅读。读者群包括作家、亿万富翁和政策制定者，影响远远超过发行量。

7. The Christian Science Monitor

The Christian Science Monitor《基督教科学箴言报》，1908年在美国波士顿创刊，由美国基督教教会创始人艾娣（Mary Eddy）（1821—1910）任社长。旨在抑制黄色报刊。此处Christian science指基督教旨，科学一词系误译将错就错，

改不过来了。

这是一份精编精写、品位极高的特殊报纸。有宗教背景,却非宗教宣传品。历来少登犯罪及灾祸等消息,一贯拒绝烟酒广告,以示忠于教义。该报寻常以抢新闻为目标,以新闻专栏见长。其国际专栏,仿佛置身哈佛讲堂,听历史学者以平静的语调,将一件件国际事件剖析得丝丝入扣,没有夸张的形容,没有仇恨的煽动,不伤害任何人,自然让人由衷敬服。

《基督教科学箴言报》以往常入选美国十大名报。因资金不足,1989年不得不缩减版面,削减栏目,影响力大不如前。1976年由大报改小开张报纸,我国读者看到的是该报的国际版(World Edition)周报。2009年4月起仅出网络版。

二、美国新闻期刊

1. Time

Time《时代》周刊,1923年创刊于纽约,由时代出版公司(Time Inc.)出版。原本是供没有时间天天读报的忙人阅读的,刊名应译为《时间》,寓意"时间就是金钱",work against time 是抢时间,争分夺秒。时代、年代多用复数。但《时代》念起来响亮顺口,约定俗成,便叫开了。它是美国三大新闻周刊中最成功的一家,影响大,每期发行量340万份。除发行国内版、军队版、大学生版外,还发行国外版。国外版又分欧洲版、亚洲版和拉丁美洲版。

《时代》周刊以报道精彩、及时,分析问题深刻和文字新颖取胜,自称是"现代英文的代表"。每期除综述一周国内外重大时事外,还对经济、科技、音乐、文教、宗教、艺术、人物、书刊、体育等方面的新闻精选整理,综合分析和评述,并配以插图和背景材料分类刊出,使之较一般报纸报道更具有深度,但又不是这些方面专业性杂志,旨在让没有时间天天读报的"忙人"了解世事。政治上较保守,倾向于共和党。

2. Newsweek

Newsweek《新闻周刊》,创刊于1933年,曾属华盛顿邮报公司,为格雷厄姆家族所有,因而在重大政治问题上,这两家立场基本相同。因此外资金亏损,该公司于2010年下半年被迫卖给新东家。

《新闻周刊》除了名记者综述一周重大事件和报道、评论白宫新闻外,还聘请其他国家的名记者撰写专栏评论。版面与竞争对手《时代》周刊相仿,但文字较通俗易懂一些。再则,新词后往往加释义,对我们而言,是它的一大优点。发行量在三大新闻周刊中位居首位,每期发行量400多万份。除发行国内版外,还有大西洋(即欧洲)版和太平洋(即亚洲)版。

3. U. S. News & World Report

U. S. News & World Report《美国新闻与世界报道》,周刊,1948年由 *The*

United States News, *World Report* 和 *U.S.Weekly* 三家刊物合并而成,在华盛顿出版,是仅次于《时代》周刊和《新闻周刊》的美国第三大新闻周刊,着重登载美国政治、经济、军事和国防问题等综合性报道与评论,专题报道美国国内问题和对官方人物的访问是其一大特色。政治立场倾向保守。文字较上述两家周刊浅显易懂。每期发行量约150万份。

4. Reader's Digest

Reader's Digest《读者文摘》,创刊于1922年。号称资本主义世界发行量最大的月刊。用英、德、法、西、意、日、汉、阿拉伯等17种语言在几十个国家和地方出版。在美国发行量为1,000万份,居美国各杂志之首。美国以外发行量为2,800多万份。它是美国中产阶级爱看的一份杂志,政治上反映美国保守派的观点。

《读者文摘》原以摘取书刊的报道为主,现在文摘只占60%,其余为本刊或特邀记者所写文章。编辑方针是"每月从一流杂志选出文章去粗取精力求紧凑,兴味永存"。每期内容广泛,从国内外政治、社会、科学到生活琐事,无所不包。体裁活泼,有小说、散文、日记、小品、游记等。另一特色是利用文末到处补白,插以警语、箴言、座右铭、笑话等。此外,为了帮助读者扩大词汇量,还辟有"Word Power"栏,独具一格。

5. Fortune

Fortune 前译《幸福》杂志,现译《财富》,创刊于1930年,由时代公司在芝加哥出版。原为月刊,1978年改为双周刊。以丰富专业知识为背景,对各行各业经营做深入研究报道,极具权威性。尤其是每年5月第一周刊登的美国企业500强排行榜(The Fortune 500)、8月第二周刊登的外国企业500强排行榜(The Fortune 500 Outside the U.S.)、外国50家最大的银行排行榜(The Largest Banks Outside the U.S.)及全球50家最大的工业公司排行榜(The Largest Industrial Companies in the World)最具权威性。此外,有时还发表一些有分量的外交及军事方面的文章。每期发行量近500万份。

6. Business Week

Business Week《商业周刊》,创刊于1929年。属 The McGraw-Hill Companies 所有。面向全世界,每期发行约97万多份。总部设在纽约,是美国著名财政企业杂志。国内版主要报道和评论美国的商业、经济、金融、贸易、企业经营和管理等方面,同时也报道一些世界经济和商业动态,以及美国公司海外活动。1980年创办国际版,栏目与国内版类似,以海外经济为主。

7. Far Eastern Economic Review

Far Eastern Economic Review《远东经济评论》,周刊,创办于1946年,在香港出版。1997年香港回归中国后,业主易人,由道-琼斯公司(Dow-Jones &

Company, Inc.)出版。主要报道和评论远东国家和地区的经济,但也发表政治、军事等方面文章。语言较《时代》周刊等浅显易懂。每期发行约20万份,订户主要是该地区的公司,其次是投资和关注远东地区的美欧公司。

三、英国报纸

英国报刊发行与美国不尽相同,受内外财团控制的大报业集团的报纸占全英发行量的90%,这些大集团以往又都是集中在伦敦市中心的"舰队街"(Fleet Street,其实从未有舰队,应音译为"弗利特街")。因此,Fleet Street 常用来借喻"伦敦或英国报界或新闻界"。现在为了改善发行和促进海外销售,有的已迁往伦敦其他地区或外地城市,甚至海外,如《卫报》就在德国发行国际版,《金融时报》直接在德国、美国和日本等国印刷发行。现在英国各报纷纷缩成中、小开张,并不意味着都变成通俗类小报,这是两个概念。星期日各大报都单独出版,报名加上"Sunday",以示区别。

英国报纸按内容和风格分为 quality/popular/mid-market papers,"质量类"报纸是严肃性的全国性日报,即大报或高级报纸,编辑水平高,面向受过较高教育的上层和中产阶级人士。*Daily Express*《每日快报》、*Daily Mail*《每日邮报》、*Daily Mirror*《每日镜报》、*Daily Star*《每日明星报》和 The Sun《太阳报》都是"通俗类"小报,消息不如 quality papers 那样严肃可靠,往往追求轰动效应。如《太阳报》就以登载英国王室成员和政界人士的桃色新闻和美女照片而著称。发行量居首位。读者基本是工人阶级和中产阶级。"中间市场类"指介于这两者之间的报纸。英国人读书看报成癖,报多,发行量按人口比例也很大。

1. The Times

The Times《泰晤士报》,创刊于1785年,是英国一家历史最悠久的报纸,也是在西方最有影响的一家大报。读者为统治阶级、高级知识分子和工商、金融界人士。虽标榜"独立",采取中间立场,其实政治观点保守,常支持保守党的政策和主张。英国有所谓"当权派读《泰晤士报》"一说。该报的"读者来信栏"(Letters to the Editor)办得特别出色,许多知名人士在这个非正式论坛高谈阔论,对舆论有很大影响,大都代表当权派观点。

《泰晤士报》在世界各地派有记者,以较大篇幅报道和评论国际、国内重大新闻。过去曾由于内容过分严肃,不符合一般读者的趣味,因而发行量下降,利润锐减。1978年底曾因劳资纠纷和经济问题停刊一年之久。1981年,英国九大报业集团之一的国际新闻社(News International)老板、美籍澳大利亚媒体大王鲁伯特·默多克(Rupert Murdoch)从加拿大财阀肯尼思·汤姆森(Kenneth Thomson)手中买下该报。

该报有几种以周刊形式出版的副刊，其中《泰晤士报文学副刊》(*Times Literary Supplement*)被认为是英国最有影响的一家文学周刊，刊载的文章和书评具有权威性。

《泰晤士报》2008年日发行量40多万份，在英国质量类报纸中排名第五。星期日无报，由《星期日泰晤士报》(*The Sunday Times*)补缺。《泰晤士报》俗称 *The London Times* 和 *The Thunderer*。在美国又称 *The London Times* 或 *The Times of London*，以区别于《纽约时报》和《洛杉矶时报》也简称 *The Times*。

2．Financial Times

Financial Times《金融时报》，1888年创刊，由皮尔逊父子公司所属的金融时报集团出版，是英国资本家喉舌，也是世界上有代表性的一家金融商情报纸。在英国有"大老板们读《金融时报》"一说。各国政府、大企业家、银行以及大学、研究机构均重视该报的报道与评论。据近几年评价统计，在英国前10家质量高和发行量大的日报中名列榜首。在1999年的世界评比中，竟高于《纽约时报》而名列第一。政治上支持保守党。

《金融时报》着重报道财政、金融和工商等方面的消息、问题研究和动向。有时攻击英国政府的金融政策，因而往往影响官员的金融思想。它是英国每天提供伦敦股票交易所全部行情的唯一日报，也刊登有政治、文化等方面的文章与评论，特别重视国际消息，派驻海外的记者100多名，超过西方国家各大报包括《纽约时报》在内，曾一度引领西方乃至全球性商业报纸。2009年4月，日发行量为42万多份，多年来，称雄英国质量类报纸。

3．The Guardian

The Guardian《卫报》，创刊于1821年，原名《曼彻斯特卫报》(*The Manchester Guardian*)。上世纪50年代末，迁至伦敦，去掉"Manchester"这一带有地方色彩的字眼，同《泰晤士报》、《每日电讯报》和《金融时报》构成英国质量类报纸的"四巨头"。英国有"想当官，《卫报》翻"一说。该报支持工党，立场偏左。近年来发行量在大报中排名第三，达33万多份。

4．The Daily Telegraph

The Daily Telegraph《每日电讯报》，创刊于1855年，原为一家"通俗类(popular)报纸，20世纪70年代后期成为"高质量的严肃性"大报，常反映右翼政治观点。在英国有"读《每日电讯报》，情牵帝国当年"一说。总部设在 Fleet Street，发行量约87万份。

5．The Independent

The Independent《独立报》，1986年创办，是英国资历最浅、较严肃的一份日报，属于 Tony O'Reilly 的 Independent News & Media 集团。支持自由民主

党的政治主张,反对保守党和工党。The Independent on Sunday 与其类似,逢周日发行。平均日发行量约 20 多万份。

6. The Sun

The Sun《太阳报》,一家全国性报纸。前身为《每日先驱报》,1964 年改为现名。1969 年被澳大利亚报业大王鲁伯特·默多克的新闻有限公司收购。原本支持保守党和民族主义观点。现摇摆在保守党和工党之间。

《太阳报》是一份不入流的低俗小报,靠着刊登耸人听闻的花边新闻和低俗淫秽的美女裸图赚钱,发行量约 300 万份。因该报还造出了两个词:Page three girl(《太阳报》上年轻迷人、胸脯丰满的第三版美女)和 Sun reader(指文化程度不高、持右翼观点的典型《太阳报》读者,带侮辱性)。

7. The Daily Mirror

Daily Mirror《每日镜报》,是一家支持保守党的全国性日报,属通俗类报纸。创刊于 1903 年,由英国里德国际公司镜报集团出版。是英国销量最大的日报之一,也最受英国人追捧,发行量为 149 万份。登缠绵悱恻、人情味(human interest)十足的新闻,爆料桃色艳事和头面人物私生活尤感兴趣,但比《太阳报》要严肃些。

四、英国新闻期刊

1. The Economist

The Economist《经济学家》,创刊于 1843 年,是英国供世界上层人士阅读的大型综合性周刊,与《金融时报》同属皮尔逊父子公司,是《金融时报》报业集团的台柱,名气响亮。约有 45 位编辑,12 名驻外记者撰稿。偏偏一律不署名,不搞"文责自负",刊物为每篇文章负责。每期约以一半篇幅刊载国际政治及时事文章,其社论深受重视,另一半专刊工商、金融、科学类稿件及书评。从历史上看,通常支持保守党的观点,只是偶尔支持工党。

160 年来,《经济学家》周刊始终忠实于创始人确定下的编辑方针:立场鲜明,避免客观报道。不仅报道国际事务和经济新闻,还刊登一篇篇观点犀利的分析文章,穿插辛辣争论,以粗俗的妙语等来吸引读者。在一个广泛刊登照片、利用色彩鲜明图解来引诱人的时代,《经济学家》独树一帜,继续强调不搞花哨版面,以精彩的文章及准确的统计数字和图表取胜。虽然外表平淡无奇,成就却光彩夺目。这家新闻周刊,畅销欧美,有口皆碑。之所以国际声誉卓著,是因为它的编辑质量高,提供了"所有值得阅读的新闻"。

《经济学家》是一份真正的全球性杂志,读者遍布 200 多个国家。自 1993 年以来,销量大增,每期发行量已超过 100 万份,销量最多的是在美国。这种供高级知识分子阅读的杂志能在英国十大重要而畅销的杂志中排名第八,实属罕见。

2. The Spectator

The Spectator《旁观者》,1828年创刊,全国性周刊中历史最悠久,面向高级知识分子。公开支持保守党,反对工党的政策,对英国亲美疏欧的外交政策,常提出批评。每期发行量达76万多份。

3. New Statesman

New Statesman《新政治家》周刊,为工党摇旗呐喊,最能反映工党的政策和主张。发行量约10万份。2008年其所有人Geoffrey Robinson将50%的股份卖给了Mike Danson。

五、美英通讯社

西方报纸、电台和电视上的新闻,大多由通讯社等媒体提供。下面简要介绍几家主要美英通讯社。

1. AP

AP(The Associated Press)(美国)美联社,成立于1848年,总部设在纽约市。2005年就已有1,700家美国日报和约5,000家广播电台和电视台靠该社提供新闻服务,现已成为世界最大通讯社。

2. UPI

UPI(The United Press International)(美国)合众国际社,成立于1907年,总社设在华盛顿,曾是美第二大通讯社,开创了一些重要的新闻报道业务。由于经营不善,曾两度申请破产,1992年6月被设在伦敦的中东广播中心公司买下。2007年8月后,该社又江河日下。

3. Bloomberg News

Bloomberg News(美国)布隆伯格新闻社,(港台译)彭博新闻社,1981年建立,集Bloomberg电视台、电台和一系列金融杂志于一体,是世界上最大、最知名的专门提供财经数据的公司。创建人迈克尔·布隆伯格(Michael Bloomberg)被誉为"金融信息大王",是世界百名富豪之一。2002年当选纽约市长。

4. Dow-Jones Newswires

Dow-Jones Newswires道-琼斯通讯社属道-琼斯公司所有,成立于1882年,是世界一流的商业财经信息提供商,同时也是重要的新闻媒体出版集团,总部在美国纽约,旗下拥有报纸、杂志、通讯社、电台、电视台和互联网服务,在全球拥有超过1500名记者。该社旗下拥有由近1,000名记者和编辑组成的实时新闻采编队伍,其母公司新闻从业人员更是多达1,800人。此外,该社还与美联社及日本经济新闻社等多家媒体建立了合作关系,进一步丰富了自己的新闻来源。

5. Reuters

Reuters (The Reuter's News Agency)（英国）路透社，1851年由路透(Paul Julius Reuter)创建，总部设在伦敦。2007年被加拿大（媒体大王 Kenneth) Thomson公司收购。是一家商业性通讯社。20世纪60年代以来，它播发经其压缩改编各国新闻报道后播发，美国也有几十家报纸订购该社新闻。业务遍及全球94个国家中的400个城市。该社拥有4.9万名职员，1,800名记者，138个分社。用19种语言报道新闻。但由于 Bloomberg News 和 Dow-Jones Newswires 的崛起和竞争，逐渐丧失了主导地位。

6. PA

PA (The Press Association)（英国）报纸联合社，成立于1868年，所属新闻(PA News)、体育(PA Sport)和数据设计(PA Data Design)三家公司组成英国全国新闻社，为报纸、广播电台和电视台提供全方位的新闻和信息服务。

应该说明，美国日报90%以上从通讯社（电讯社）获取本地区以外的世界新闻，美联社(The Associated Press)是主要来源，既有分布全国的工作人员，也有海外工作人员。这些报社包括《纽约时报》、《华尔街日报》、《华盛顿邮报》、《芝加哥论坛报》(The Chicago Tribune)、《洛杉矶时报》、《巴尔的摩太阳报》(The Baltimore Sun)和《波士顿环球报》(The Boston Globe)等少数大报相继自办通讯社后，其他报纸有了更多选择。美联社、合众国际社等通讯社等失去垄断地位。

7. 其他通讯社

除以上六家大通讯社外，英美还有其他几家规模较小的通讯社：BUP(British United Press, Ltd)英国合众社、IRN(Independent Radio News)（英）独立广播新闻社、ITN(Independent Television News Ltd)（英）独立电视新闻社、LPA(Labor Press Association)（美）劳工新闻联合通讯社、PA(Press Association Ltd)（英）报纸联合社、TANA(Trans-Asia News Agency)（美）全亚通讯社。

其他西方国家较有名的通讯社有：DPA（德新社）、AFP（法新社）和 ANSA（意大利的安莎社）。此外，俄罗斯的 Itar-Tass（俄塔社）也有一定影响。

第二节 新闻、电头及导语

一、何谓 News

对新闻的定义众说纷纭,连英英词典的词源意义也只是用 probably 这样不确定词:"Middle English *newes*, probably plural of *newe* (literally) that which is new, noun use of adjective; perhaps patterned on French *nouvelles*."(*World Book Dictionary*)这就是说,news 是 new 的复数。《现代汉语词典》的定义是:"报社、通讯社、广播电台、电视台等报道的消息。"事实上无论是报刊报道的新人、新事、新思想和新情况都突出一个"新"字,这是 news 的关键。否则,就不是新闻了。

一般而言,新闻(news)的定义有广义和狭义两种。广义的新闻泛指在媒体上出现的所有文章。狭义的新闻即"消息",单指对最新发生的事件的客观报道,而不表达报道者的意见。世界各国对广义新闻的功能的解释各异,不存在被全球媒体普遍接受的定义或规定。在我国,政府要求新闻界起宣传、教育和激励群众的作用。在西方国家,没有任何机构或个人指定它应担任哪种角色。尽管如此,其特性是共同的,即都是向公众报道新的事实,传递各种消息。这样,美英等国媒体就自我选择担任起提供信息、教育、改革、娱乐、激励等部分或所有角色。

西方媒体普遍认为具有新闻价值的消息包括:达官贵人和知名人士的活动;任何类型的政府活动;新的稀奇古怪的事件(例如罪行和灾害);披露令人兴奋或令人震惊的真相(涉及性和丑闻);新的社会潮流。具体而言,美英报刊常见的新闻报道中有以下这几个方面读者感兴趣的内容:(1)政治与政府(politics and government);(2)战争和恐怖主义活动(war and terrorism);(3)经济(business);(4)环境(environment);(5)犯罪与诉讼(crime and courts);(6)灾难(disasters);(7)罢工、示威游行及纠纷(strikes, demonstrations and disputes);(8)名人(famous people);(9)体育(sports);(10)娱乐(entertainments)。

众所周知,重要性、时效性、新鲜感、趣味性等是构成新闻的要素(见"二、新闻的价值")。舍此则不成为新闻。有人根据时效性的强弱及表现手法运用的不同而将新闻分为硬性、软性、中间层三个层次。硬新闻不但新鲜,而且题材较严肃,事实报道客观;软新闻则为轻松的社会新闻,具人情味;中间层新闻则介于前两者之间。

美国报刊新闻尤其强调猎奇,将之奉为天条,正如俗话所说:"狗咬人不是新闻,人咬狗才是新闻"(It is not news when a dog bites a man, but absolutely news when you find a man bites a dog)。为什么?说此话的 New York Sun editor John B. Bogart(1848—1921)解释道:"When a dog bites a man, that is not news, because it happens so often. But if a man bites dog, that is news." It describes a phenomenon in journalism in which an unusual, infrequent event is more likely to be reported as news than an ordinary, everyday occurrence (such as dog bites man) The news media generally consider an event more newsworthy if there is something unusual about it; a commonplace event is unlikely to be taken as newsworthy. The result is that rare events often appear in headlines while common events rarely do, making the rare events seem more common than they are. 为了加深对这句话的理解，不妨看看下面这幅美国政治讽刺漫画：

瞧，媒体是如何剧烈争抢这种庸俗的猎奇式"人咬狗"新闻的。

图中英文为"LOCAL NEWS"（当地新闻）

2009年4月美国《基督教科学箴言报》又刊载了一幅漫画，讽刺美国著名大电视台偏爱白宫奥巴马家宠物狗（White House Dog），胜过"全球经济危机"（Global Crisis）：

左边路标上字：白宫之狗　右边路标上字：全球危机

摄像机上分别为：ABC（美国广播公司）、CNN（美国有线电视新闻国际公司）、NBC（美国全国广播公司）、FOX（福克斯电视台）

事实上,不仅西方报刊如此,中国的也出现了这股猎奇歪风。如2003年11月25日,河北唐山市滦县发生了人咬狗的事,而且咬狗者邵某还与狗主人甲某产生了流血冲突。《燕赵都市报》《北京晨报》《北京晚报》等就此事都竞相报道。再如,即将谢世的人在遗嘱中把财产给了儿孙不是新闻,赠与宠物却是热门新闻。2000年3月,成都一位96岁法学博士去世,遗嘱写明财产全归相伴9年的狮子狗,成了全国各报追逐的奇闻。

从西方新闻理论来看,表扬好人好事的正面新闻不是新闻,只有"坏"消息才是"好"新闻,是"乌鸦嘴"。如天灾人祸、社会丑恶现象、突发的悲剧性事件等,其中尤其是战争,是最典型的"坏"新闻。这样,我们在看西方媒体的报道,总是看到"好"的新闻少,"坏"的新闻多,包括对中国的报道也是负面内容多,正面内容少。所以,No news is good news.(没有消息就是好消息)。新闻学的一个原则是:"好事不出门,坏事传千里。"每天在媒体上所见所闻尽是"坏事",不管是杀人放火,天灾人祸,无不即刻传播遐迩。在这种情况下,得不到什么消息才是最好的消息。这与西方新闻的理念是分不开的,可这与我国新闻界要求报道正面消息为主、负面消息为辅的原则是不同的。所以我国的媒体在西方有"报喜鸟"之称。

还有人认为,所谓新闻,无非是天南海北之事,你看NEWS不就是north,east,west和south的首字母缩略词吗!此说是否有道理,也只能"见仁见智"了。

二、新闻的价值

构成新闻的重要因素有六:及时性(Timeliness)、重要性(importance)、显著性(prominence)、相关性(proximity)、奇异性(unusualness)和趣味性(interest)。新闻内容应该做到三性:可信性、真实性和客观性。新闻的六要素和三性相结合才真正有价值。可有的却走猎奇的邪路。

三、电头(Dateline)

标题和作者署名行(byline)后,就是电头。如《精选本》第四版"Libby Defense Portrays Client as a Scapegoat"课里,"电头"(Dateline)——"Washington, Jan. 23",即1月23日发自华盛顿的消息。由于发稿地点和时间与消息的背景密切相关。有的电头还要注明通讯社,从而构成通讯社电头的三要素,如MOSCOW, Oct. 10 (AP)(美联社莫斯科10月10日电)。因《纽约时报》有自己的通讯社,不必注明。如果消息来源于莫斯科,也即现场报道(field report),或许更加准确可靠;如果来源于他地,而记者却在莫斯科报道,其消息的准确性和可靠性就要打折扣。

四、消息导语（Lead）种种

1. 重要性

消息报道中的导语十分重要，一般是第一个自然段，有时也由前两个自然段组成。迅速点出新闻的主题，这是消息这种新闻体裁区别于其他新闻体裁的一个重要特征。导语用三言两语写出消息中最主要的、最新鲜的事实，使读者先获得一个总的概念，并吸引读者继续看下去。可以说，导语是消息的概括，而标题又是导语的概括。

2. 作用

导语的作用是什么？美国新闻学家威廉·梅茨在《怎样写新闻》一书中认为有三点：① 告诉读者这条消息的内容是什么；② 使读者愿意读下去；③ 必要时制造适当的气氛。还有人认为导语的作用可以概括为：① 可以用简洁的文字反映出消息的要点，让读者大体了解消息的主要事实和主题思想；② 引出主题以及阐述、解释这个主题的新闻主体；③ 唤起读者注意，吸引读者看下去。

3. 形式多样

一百多年来，导语产生了"两代"。什么是第一代新闻导语？如前所述，在导语里必须具备 5 个 W 和一个 H 要素（When? Where? Who? What? Why? 和 How?），即何时？何地？何人？何事？何故？如何？具体地讲，就是在什么时候发生的？在什么地方发生的？事情牵涉到什么人？发生了什么事？事情为什么会发生？事情是怎样发生和发展的？西方新闻学鼻祖之一戴纳提出，新闻导语必须回答五个 W 和一个 H。这个观点，曾经在相当长的时间里被认为是导语写作的金科玉律。这样的导语具有具体、完整的长处，看了导语，对消息的主要内容大体上都知道了。短处是内容太多，主次不清，重点不突出；再则，文字和重点易重复，难以顺畅展开，这种报道缺乏悬念感，不适用于特写这样的软新闻体裁，于是一些新闻工作者对导语进行改革。1954 年，《纽约时报》总编辑在采访部里贴出这样一个布告："我们认为把传统五个 W 写在一个句子或一个段落里没有必要了，也许永远没有必要。"这里顺便提醒一下读者，所谓五个 W 和一个 H，凡是教过和学过"托福"（TOEFL）者无不知道，托福中的问答题往往都是这类问题。

通过改革，许多消息导语里只突出一两个新闻要素，其余新闻要素放在后面的主体或结尾，这样就可以更突出重点。这种出现在上世纪 50 年代至 70 年代的新闻导语，称为第二代导语。从导语的形式来分，有叙述式、设问式、评论式、结论式、描写式和对比式等等。有的新闻专家列出 10 多种导语，不管林林总总有多少种,都可归纳为 direct lead 和 indirect lead 两种。

在诸多导语中以倒金字塔式结构导语最为典型。五个 W 和一个 H 是构成一则完整的消息不可缺少的要素。以往直接的消息报道或纯消息一般采取"倒金字塔形式",其特点是将新闻报道最重要的五个 W 和一个 H 按重要性的顺序来用倒叙式头重脚轻地安排,把新闻的高潮和结论放在最前面的导语里,然后按事实的重要性递减的顺序来安排(in the order of descending importance),由此突出最重要、最新的事实。为帮助读者了解这种倒金字塔式结构,见下列西方新闻学著作中的图表说明:

The Inverted Pyramid Form
倒金字塔式

应该说明,现在新闻报道仍以倒金字塔式结构为主,但导语里不一定全部都包括五个 W 和一个 H,或许只有三个或四个 W,另一个或两个 W 出现在下面段落里。由于改革的结果,间接式导语 indirect lead 或延缓式导语 delayed lead 多了起来,但不是主流。

4. 报道手法翻新

导语形式变得多样,新闻报道手法也跟着出现了诸如"时间顺序式"Chronological Order Form、"悬念式"Suspended Interest Form 和"阐释性报道式"Interpretative Reporting Form。时间顺序式,有如香肠,一根接一根,所以又称为"香肠式"Wiener Form。这种按时间顺序的形式多用于体育比赛,作案过程,厂家发展或名人讣告之类的消息报道。"悬念式"多用于特写。"解释性报道式"与纯新闻的客观报道不同,着重探讨理念,事情成败原因,寻求答案等。这种形式尤其在刊物中居多。

第三节 文体与体裁

一、文体

根据《现代汉语词典》的定义,文体是文章的体裁;体裁指的是文学作品的表现形式。中外对 style 历来争议不断,如文体即形式或修辞、解说技巧等,约有二三十个定义,真是众说纷纭,莫衷一是。报刊文体大致有如下几种定义或说法:

1. 新闻体

journalese(新闻体),尤指 type of news reporting,是最常见的含有贬义的定义,即指报道性文章多陈词滥调,行文仓促,思想性或说理性肤浅,还不时夹着口语(*Webster's Dictionary*)。这个定论是以往受传统偏见的约束,瞧不起报刊英语,把它跟粗俗低级划等号。现在报刊质量早已大大提高,语言简明实用,富有创意,这是不争的事实。所谓行文仓促是不得已而为之,日报得天天出,与期刊有别。但现在罕见 Alan Warner 写的 *Short Guide to English Style* 一书中举例文章"Zoo Mountain Goat Leaps Lions' Enclose Rescued by Keepers"那样,充斥着如 lions and elephants 比作"monarches of the wilds"(与"King of beast"一样)、"brute creation"(无理性之动物)、"sawdust Caesar"(喻马戏团训狮员)等夸张或陈腐之词。至于夹着口语,这与为了表明"客观公正",记者以第三者口气论述有关(见"报刊语言主要特点""常用套语")。只要读了本节"体裁"所举三篇文章,便知一二。

改革开放后,由于以前众所周知的原因,国内不少人因跟不上时代和语言的发展,一时看不懂外国报刊,又视之为当代必读之物,才逐渐认识到其重要性。

2. 综合体

报刊是由消息、特写、社评、采访、杂文、传记等多种体裁组成的,甚至还有散文、日记、游记和小说连载等等,无所不包,集多种体裁与题材英语之大成,所以说它是综合体。还有人无奈地称之为特殊文体。

3. 实用文体

报刊题材多样,语言紧贴当今现实而又简明,学了就能用。

4. 文学文体

四川大学曹明伦教授在《中国翻译》一文里,根据 19 世纪英国诗人、社会评论家马修·阿诺德(Matthew Arnold)所说的"Journalism is literature in a hurry"(报刊新闻是匆匆写出的文学作品)这句话,将报刊新闻定义为文学作品。还有的学者也将新闻急就章归类为文学,既然是文学,那又是何种文学文体?值得探讨。

以上说明，要给报刊文体下一个众所接受的定义并非易事，这与人们从不同角度审视报刊和文体有关。

二、新闻体裁

新闻体裁（types/forms of news writing）指报道形式。如何划分与文体一样，也众说纷纭，莫衷一是。体裁的划分不但中外不同，中国也不统一。例如中国有的主张分为五类：① 消息，包括动态、综合、经验、述评等消息四类；② 通讯，可分为人物、事件、概貌和工作等通讯及小故事五类；③ 新闻特写，有人物、事件、旅行等特写及速写；④ 调查报告；⑤ 报告文学，一种介于新闻与文学之间的边缘体裁。有的主张分消息、特写、通讯、专访和述评五类。美英等国有人认为除消息报道体裁外，专稿、述评、采访、杂文、传记等等都是特写（feature）体裁。然而，人们较多倾向于将它分为消息、特写和社评三类。

1. 消息（News）

消息报道分两类：一类是通讯社的电讯或有的报道，短小精悍，内容最真实，被称之为"纯硬性新闻"（pure hard news），有的报纸为之专辟"Briefly"（简明新闻）栏；另一类报刊的报道比通讯社的要详细得多，但有的由于夹杂着记者的推测和描绘，往往能看出倾向，因而不如前者真实和经得起推敲。请见下面所选一篇报道文章（见《精选本》课文）的几段：

Libby Defense Portrays Client as a Scapegoat

Says White House Goal Was to Protect Rove

By NEIL A. LEWIS

1   WASHINGTON, Jan. 23 — I. Lewis Libby Jr., the vice president's former chief of staff, was made a scapegoat by White House officials to protect the president's longtime political adviser, Karl Rove, Mr. Libby's lawyer asserted in his opening statement on Tuesday.

2   The unexpected assertion may foreshadow an effort to put distance between Mr. Libby and the administration.

3   The statement by the lawyer, Theodore V. Wells Jr., was the first indication that Mr. Libby, who is facing five felony counts of lying to investigators, would seek to deflect some of the blame onto his former White

House colleagues.

4 Mr. Wells did not, however, fully explain the connection between an effort to protect Mr. Rove and the actions that led to Mr. Libby's indictment. It was also the first sign that there had been fighting within the Bush administration over the C. I. A. leak investigation.

5 Until Tuesday, Mr. Libby's defense on perjury and obstruction of justice charges was that he might simply have remembered incorrectly events he had described to a grand jury and to F. B. I agents. But Mr. Wells told the jury that White House officials, whom he did not name, wanted to protect Mr. Rove because they believed his survival as President Bush's chief political adviser was crucial to the health of the Republican Party.

6 Mr. Wells said that his client was innocent and that a decision was made that "Scooter Libby was to be sacrificed," referring to Mr. Libby by his nickname. It was important to keep Mr. Rove out of trouble, Mr. Wells said, because he was Mr. Bush's right-hand man and "was most responsible for seeing the Republican Party stayed in office."

7 "He had to be protected," Mr. Wells said.

8 Mr. Rove, who has not been charged, has acknowledged having been a source for a July 14, 2003, column by Robert D. Novak that first disclosed the identity of Valerie Wilson, who was known by her maiden name, Valerie Plame, as a Central Intelligence Agency officer. The disclosure led to the investigation resulting in Mr. Libby's indictment.

... (2007/1/24 *The New York Times*)

因此文已作为文选课文，所以不再说明课文的内容。以下只对报道性文章的特点加以分析说明。

该文的标题和副标题首先点出了文章的主题：其被告是舍卒保车的牺牲品。虽然记者引用的是第三者口气——被告律师的话论述，事实上也代表了他的观点或看法。第一段律师在开场白说得比标题更详细，使读者更明白了 What 和 Who（即两名涉案高官）。对此案已大致明白。第 2 段是首段的补充。第 3 段才点出律师姓名（Who），并说明其当事人（client）面临五项重罪的指控，其上述言论是 Libby 企图嫁祸于他人。记者作了似乎不完全站在律师一边的说明，以免有人指责报道不客观。第 4 段记者对律师的语焉不详加以说明而引出了第 5 段和第 6 段，说明为什么（Why）小布什总统要舍 Libby 保 Karl Rore 的原因。第 8 段说明何时（When）及案子的起因（How）。此篇报道共 29 段，以下段均为较详细地说明 How 这个过程、案发的详情和细节,是较典型的倒金字塔式的报道。

看报道文章应结合前面的文体、电头、导语及报道形式加以分析。本文语言简明扼要,并没有故意卖弄时髦语。如第 1 和 5 段都用 political "adviser"来表明 Rove 的身份,并未用时髦词"mentor"和"guru"便是一例。文字尽量"简约"的特点从标题便可见一斑(见"**报刊语言主要特点**")。

2. 特写(Feature)

新闻特写常指再现新闻事件、人物或场景的形象化报道,吸取了一般新闻报道和文艺作品的长处,结构则取两者之长。消息在导语部分往往把最重要、最新鲜、最吸引人的内容放在最前面,特写虽然也是一种新闻报道,但常采取引人入胜的悬念式(suspended interest form)写作手法,逐渐娓娓道来。见下文所选 6 段:

Hard Target

The hunt for Africa's last warlord

By Scott Johnson

1 Shortly after dawn last Dec. 14, four Ugandan Mi-24 helicopters banked low over the thick forest canopy of Congo's Garamba National Park. A dense fog had rolled in overnight, and the weather had turned nasty. Earlier that morning at a forward staging area in Uganda, a team of American military advisers equipped with large-scale U. S. government maps and Google Earth technology had shown the helicopter pilots what to look for—four distinct "fishhook shape" camps spread out in cleared areas of the park. In one of these camps, they believed, was Joseph Kony, the professed mystic who leads Africa's longest-lived insurgent group, the Lord's Resistance Army. Find Kony, the pilots' commander had said, and kill him.

2 Descending through the fog bank and hovering just above the tree line, the pilots spotted what looked like a rebel council meeting in the largest cluster of shelters, code-named Camp K. The gunships immediately unleashed a barrage of rockets and chain-gun fire. Reports from the helicopter crews later stated that several dozen people, including women and children, had been caught in the open. "I saw the helicopters come—they were black, and they were bombing us," recalls George Komagun, 16, one of the hundreds of child

soldiers in the Lord's Resistance Army. "I ran. We tried to fight the helicopters, but could not."

3   Two days after Operation Lightning Thunder began, Ugandan commandos finally reached Camp K. They found bloody trails heading into the jungle in all directions. Hastily dug graves dotted the site's periphery. Kony had been on the run for more than two decades, but this place had the look of a settled homestead. Acres had been cultivated with sorghum, cassava and maize. Stashes of sugar, rice and water in large plastic containers were buried all around.

4   Washington would love to get a look at the trove of evidence, which Ugandan investigators are still studying, including Thuraya satellite and cell phones, walkie-talkies and three Acer laptops. Soldiers even found a printer, a CD-ROM drive and an English-language dictionary. What they didn't find was Joseph Kony. "We have some hints where he might be now, but nothing like we had before the strike," says a senior U.S. military-intelligence official who was intimately involved with the operation's planning and execution, but is not authorized to speak on the record about it. "Kony has virtually disappeared from the face of the earth."

5   Kony is arguably the most-wanted man in Africa. Uganda's government has been chasing him for 23 years, ever since he donned a woman's dress, claimed to be channeling the spirit world and vowed to topple the country's president, Yoweri Museveni. Kony is a law unto himself. He claims to run the LRA according to the Ten Commandments, but he and the hundreds of forcibly conscripted children who serve as his killing squads are feared throughout the region for their horrific levels of brutality and the butchery of tens of thousands of defenseless civilians. Their swath of destruction has displaced well over 2 million people. Kony has forced new male recruits to rape their mothers and kill their parents. Former LRA members say the rebels sometimes cook and eat their victims.

6   Years of peace talks have consistently failed to deliver Kony. Dictators have fallen in many countries, and war criminals in Sierra Leone, Liberia and Ivory Coast have been brought to justice. Even Kony's longtime patron, Sudanese dictator Omar al-Bashir, has been charged with crimes against humanity by the International Criminal Court for his policy of ethnic cleansing

in Darfur. But Kony remains free to raid, plunder and kidnap. The ICC issued arrest warrants for Kony and three of his top commanders in 2005, but the papers sit untouched in a dusty office in Kampala, useless until Kony is captured. "Normally these kinds of conflicts in Africa are various shades of gray," says Julia Spiegel, a California native who documents the LRA's atrocities for the Enough Project, an independent group formed to stop crimes against humanity in Africa. "But this is very clear-cut. Going after Kony is just not disputable."

...(2009/5/16 *Newsweek*)

这篇特写的正副标题是:"追捕非洲最后一个军阀难上难"。第一段与报道性文章不同,不是开头就和盘托出难在何处,与标题的中心思想相互印证,让读者了解梗概。具体讲,Joseph Kony 是何人? 为什么乌干达政府和美国都要缉拿他? 为什么这么长时间都抓不到? 而第一段犹如写小说似的先描绘一番周围环境,如 dense fog, weather nasty,再徐徐托出直升机要搜寻的军阀,并未交代要缉拿 Joseph Kony 的缘由,以便吊足读者胃口。第2段写发现一个类似该军阀的营地后,武装直升机(gunships)便开火攻击,结果并未发现 Joseph Kony 被炸身亡。第3和4段说明挨炸营地四通八达,生活必需品一应俱全。尽管追踪人员武器精良,但 Kony 已消失得无影无踪。一直等到第5段而不是在第1和2段才揭露其罪行,阐明要将他绳之以法的理由。与报道相比,交代得笼统,留有悬念。如抓到的娃娃兵、遭强奸的母亲和遇害的父母及叛军吃人肉等并未点明 Where, When, Who 和 Whom 等。若是报道文章,就有制造假新闻之嫌。这也是两者写法的一大区别。第6段说明数年和谈也不中用。尽管许多非洲国家的独裁者均已受司法审判,国际刑事法院的追捕令(papers 指 arrest warrants)无人理睬。再则,尽管 Kony 罪证确凿,非洲这类冲突并非黑白分明,一目了然(various shades of gray)。再下面就谈到小布什自宣誓就任总统后就想将 Kony 捉拿归案等一系列过程和分析。此文最后引用 Kony 抵抗军一位逃脱魔掌的16岁孩子的话"People should eat Kony. He killed so many people"作为结尾。

纵观这6段,有较多背景和伴随性描绘,使读者如身临其境,新闻报道文章里少见,这在第5段尤为明显。其次,文笔较细腻。此文所写的内容不像报道性文章那样要求及时,所以看不出《韦氏词典》所说的"evidence of haste in composition"(仓促构思的痕迹)。此文对 Côte d'Ivoire(科特迪瓦)国名仍用旧称 Ivory Coast(象牙海岸),说明报刊语言有使用陈词和随意性的一面。

3. 社论和评论(Editorial & Commentary)

社论是一家报纸或杂志编辑部发表的权威性评论,代表编辑部的观点,是一家报纸的灵魂,要了解报纸对某事的倾向,需要从社论看起。常以第三者口吻说话,或对人对事直接发表意见,表明立场、观点和倾向,或提出问题,或号召人们采取行动。评论是署名文章,往往在报道文章后就报道中提及的人和事发表评述,启示读者。这是社论和评论所不同的。社评类文章也报道事实,但以评论表明立场为最终目的,这与新闻报道只叙事而不评论大有区别。在文字上,报道类文章一般较简明,社论则较严肃正规,评论文章则较活泼。评论可以嬉笑怒骂、讽刺影射,尤其常用借古喻今的手法。因此后两类文章较难读懂。读社论要了解有关人和事的背景,而读评论则还要有较深的语言功底和较广博的知识,因为专栏作家在文章中常引经据典。

众所周知,美英各大报刊都招揽资深新闻界人士,在专门栏目或版面如《纽约时报》的社论对面版(Op-Ed)和期刊的言论版[Opinion 或 World View (Page)]等发表权威性评论。

社论和评论往往都开门见山,在第一段点出论题,类似引子,引导读者往下读。接着就逐段逐点展开分析评说。末段则为结论。当然,有的写法并非如此,如将事实和结论都置于首段或前两段。这与特写采用的倒叙手法等有别。

Making the Punishment Fit the Crime

1   When illegal immigrants apply for jobs, they sometimes present made-up Social Security numbers. Too often prosecutors charge them with felony identity theft — which outrageously overstates the crime. The Supreme Court has called a halt to the practice, ruling 9 to 0 that federal identity-theft law does not apply.

2   Ignacio Flores-Figueroa, a Mexican citizen, gave his employer counterfeit papers that contained his real name and another person's Social Security number. When caught, he was charged not only with improperly entering the United States and misusing immigration documents, but also with aggravated identity theft, which carries a mandatory two-year prison sentence.

3   Justice Stephen Breyer, writing for the court, relied on a straightforward reading of the identity-theft statute, which requires that the defendant "knowingly" use another person's identification. The government, Justice Breyer said, failed to meet that test in this case.

4   The ruling is faithful to the statute's text and to Congress's intent in passing it. The law was aimed at criminals who steal the identity of a particular individual and do not just use random numbers. Mr. Flores-Figueroa, who

used his own name on his counterfeit card, was not trying to steal anyone's identity. He was trying to work in the United States without proper documentation — a crime, but a far less serious one.

5   The federal aggravated-identity-theft law has become a favorite of overzealous prosecutors. Last year, after a raid at a slaughterhouse in Postville, Iowa, nearly 300 immigrants were charged with identity theft. Prosecutors used the threat of long sentences and unwarranted charges to coerce the workers into forgoing a trial and pleading guilty to lesser charges.

6   A guiding principle of American law is that the punishment must fit the crime. The Supreme Court upheld this principle by insisting that undocumented immigrants who use false papers to get work be punished only for what they did.

(2009/5/6, *The New York Times*)

此社论标题是"要使罪与罚相当"。接着在第 1 段就以法院不当罪作出一致的裁决：将事实"illegal immigrants present made-up Social Security numbers"（虚假的社会保障号，即身份证号），而检察官常以"felony identity theft"（偷窃身份证这样的重罪）来指控他们。它以 immigrants, prosecutor 和 court 这样第三者的行事来表明本报的立场。以下几段只是具体举例说明三方案例，可说是第 1 段之补充。第 4 段说明为什么不是"theft"，所以第 1 段法院才作出"identity-theft law does not apply"的理由。原因是被告只冒用任何一个人的身份号而已，并未冒名顶替。

社论文字正规严肃，没有模棱两可的语言。其中只用了一个委婉语"undocumented immigrants"来指"illegal immigrants"。这与报道性文章具有随意省略、造词等特点更是不同。

第四节 报刊的政治倾向性

美英等国报刊均非公办，不代表政府，一贯标榜"客观"、"公正"，"独立"于政府和政党，"不受约束"，完全"自由办报"，置身"意识形态之外"。是政府的监督员(watch dog)，可批评政府各项政策，有乌鸦嘴之称，记者更戴上了无冕之王(uncrowned King)的桂冠，其实并非如此。

下面分别从立场、党派属性、惯用套路和用词四方面来看西方报刊的政治倾向性。

一、立场

事实上新闻业是有政治倾向的。例如1999年的科索沃战争，享有"舆论泰斗"美誉的《纽约时报》便渲染南斯拉夫在该省屠杀阿尔巴尼亚族，搞"种族灭绝"，鼓动对南动武。《时代》周刊发表"Why He Blinked"(他为何顶不下去了)一文颠倒事实，对南领导人挖苦。70多天狂轰滥炸后，南总统米洛舍维奇接受了北约要求时，竟说是"他引发了这场空中打击战"(he [Milosevic] set off the air war)。只有《华盛顿邮报》对战争的合法性质疑。

1998年美国诬蔑美籍华裔科学家李文和(Wen Ho Lee)窃密。《纽约时报》曾发表长篇耸人听闻的报道，主张搞逼供，引用官员的话："敲打头次数越多，他说的真话就越多。"后来只是轻描淡写承认报道失实。

纵观美英报刊和通讯社等媒体，应该说客观、公正的文章也是有的，但多数跟着本国利益或所支持的党派或政府的立场转。《纽约时报》的口号是"刊登一切适合刊登的新闻"(All the News That's Fit to Print)，路透社的格言是"以维护新闻报道独立正直为己任"(to safeguard the independence and integrity of news service)，其他报纸以此类推，全是鬼话。苏联解体后，一批知识分子移居美国，《纽约时报》为首的美国各大报竞相以头版头条大登特登这方面的消息。几个月后，他们中一些人发表声明，表示不习惯美国的就业和生活方式，决定返回俄罗斯。同样是这些报纸，有的不登，有的只在极不显眼的位置上刊登一则小消息，背后也是本国利益。这一点有的报刊说得很清楚，1997年11月《时代》周刊谈到中国由于经济的发展与影响不断提高、美国无力阻止，建议政府竭力把中国往有利于美国利益的方向拉(We cannot prevent enhancement of Chinese influence arising from its economic growth... though we should strive to channel it into directions that serve our national interest and peace of Asia)，一语道破天机。

二、党派属性

美英报刊有的支持这个党或利益集团,有的支持那个党或利益集团,有的支持自由派,有的支持保守派。如《纽约时报》与美国东部自由派权势集团关系密切,2004年公开表态支持民主党总统候选人,对国际问题的报道和评论基本上反映了政府的外交政策和动向。《洛杉矶时报》代表西部利益集团的观点,支持西部政客入主白宫。《华盛顿邮报》在政治上较多支持民主党,在2000年美国大选中就公开支持民主党总统候选人。《读者文摘》反映中产阶级的观点,政治上代表保守派。《美国新闻与世界报道》在政治上支持共和党右翼。应该说,这些大报和著名的新闻周刊大多代表富人的利益。

美国民间一直流传着这样一种说法,即《纽约时报》是那些自认为应该统治美国的人看的报纸,《华尔街日报》是实际统治美国人看的报纸。无独有偶,据戴维斯(Ross Davis)所著《英国新闻界内幕》(Inside Fleet Street)一书说,英国报界也流传着这样的一首打油诗:

The Times is read by the people who run the country.

The Guardian is read by the people who like to run the country.

The Financial Times is read by the people who own the country.

The Daily Telegraphy is read by the people who remember the country as it used to be. (缅怀念大英帝国者读《每日电讯报》。)

从这首诗里可以看出这些报纸的读者群体及其所代表的政治观点。

英国年鉴(*Britain* 1996)在介绍报纸(The Press)的政治倾向性时这样写道:

The press caters for a range of political views, interests and levels of education. Newspapers are almost always financially independent of any political party. Where they express pronounced views and show obvious political leanings in their editorial comments, these derive from proprietorial and other non-party influences.

Nevertheless, during General Election campaigns many newspapers recommend their readers to vote for a particular political party. Even newspapers which adopt strong political views in their editorial columns include feature and other types of articles by authors of different political persuasions.

(报纸迎合具有各种政治看法、兴趣和教育水平的读者,在经济上几乎与政党没有瓜葛。社评表达明确看法,具有明显政治倾向。可是,受到的影响只是他本身的,即使有外来影响,也与其他政党毫无牵连。话虽如此,大选期间,许多报纸都劝告读者将票投给某个特定政党。但这些报纸即使在社评栏中采取这种明显的政治观点,仍然刊登不同政治派别作者发表的包括特写和其他体裁的文章。)

年鉴在介绍期刊(The Periodical Press)时写道:

The leading journals of opinion include The *Economist*, an independent conservative publication covering a wide range of topics. *New Statesman and Society* reviews social issues, politics, literature and the arts from an independent socialist point of view, and the *Spectator* covers similar subjects from an independent conservative standpoint.

根据编者的研究,英国多数报刊如《泰晤士报》、《经济学家》和《旁观者》支持保守党的政策或主张,而《卫报》和《新政治家》则支持工党。

三、惯用套路

中国发展经济叫"经济威胁",发展军力,又叫"军事扩张"、"意图不透明"、"威胁全球安全",误导舆论。中国在海外没有一兵一卒,却是威胁;美国四处驻军,经常动武,为何没有"美国威胁论"呢?美英媒体高喊"正义、自由、民主",花样翻新,骗了不少世人。

1. 直接灌输,巧妙暗示

顺应和利用受众的心理定势,根深蒂固的看法和观念,用大量信息进行直接灌输、辅以巧妙的背景和心理暗示,是西方媒体惯用套路。

2. 预定角色,刻意误导

2003 年美国入侵伊拉克,借口摧毁核武器。美国媒体集体失声,无人责问布什政府证据是否确凿。记者在开战期间还与美军同吃同住(embedded reporters),成了掩饰真相、误导公众的"报喜鸟"了。对待闹西藏"独立",先设定达赖喇嘛是"西藏宗教领袖"、"人权卫士"和"人道传播者"。谁批他分裂国家,就扣上"不人道"、"不维护人权"、"破坏宗教自由"等帽子。这就是西方媒体先划框框,定调子,按非黑即白的思维模式,把事件描绘成好莱坞电影式的善恶之争,引导受众得出一个结论:"中国不想让西藏人民享有宗教自由。"难道民主改革前的奴隶生活就是自由吗?

3. 媒体政府,高度默契

报道同事件,出自西方媒体叫新闻,否则做叫宣传;同样是表达观点,西方媒体就一贯客观公正,别人讲出来就叫洗脑(brainwashing);别人采取同样行动,叫钳制新闻自由,发出不同声音,就不符合"普世价值"。2008 年在达赖煽动下,藏独分子闹事行凶,西方政府和媒体密切配合,污蔑中国政府侵犯宗教自由,杀害教徒。德国一家报纸还用别国的照片栽赃中国军警镇压藏民。

4. 利用媒体,颠倒黑白

美国是世界上最强大的国家,军费开销最多,海外基地也最多,在世界各地逞狂。然而,在国际媒体中却没有构成"威胁",反而经常以"威胁受害者"的形象出现,大讲美国可能受到的各种威胁,如恐怖活动、生化袭击、来自伊朗的威胁等等。这与美国政府利用媒体梳妆打扮,息息相关。

美国主要借助媒体,控制全球话语权。据统计,全世界互联网网页的内容80%是用英文书写的。可见,在全球化时代,世界决非平坦(flat),而是向讲英语的国家倾斜。美国"受害者"和"正义"形象就是这么来的。应该说,在争取受众意识、铺垫全球舆论方面确实达到了很高的专业水准,为他们在政治和外交空间争取到了相当大的回旋余地。之所以美国能成超级大国,媒体也功不可没。在美国,媒体对决策影响力除行政、立法和司法外处于第四位(fourth estate),所以舆论力量不可小觑。

四、用词

美国记者貌似用词十分考究,国内媒体常常在不知不觉上当。外交部翻译室老翻译家程镇球先生指出:"美国媒体把表示支持本国或本国政府的热情叫做'patriotism'(爱国主义),把别人表示反对美国霸权主义的愤慨叫做'nationalism'(民族主义)。好像中国人没有'爱国主义',只有'民族主义',而'民族主义'离'排外主义'(anti-foreignism)和'仇外主义'(xenophobia)也就不远了。"此外,他们视中国发展为"威胁"(threat),本身则叫"研发"(development)。

不仅如此,美国媒体对不支持政府对外政策的民众也如此这般。例如2003年美国侵伊前夕,《今日美国报》说:"美国媒体一直不重视报道反战情绪。""一些媒体的工作就是使民众为即将到来的战争做好准备,以推销战争为己任。谁提出疑问就骂谁不爱国。"

对政治制度不同于西方的外国政府常用"Communist regime"(共产党政权),"totalitarian state"(极权国家),"rogue state"(流氓国家)等字眼。"regime","totalitarian"和"rogue"均为贬义词,对有的记者来说,"Communist"也是贬义词。媒体对民众一贯进行这样的洗脑。

西方记者和政客对苏联解体和东欧剧变欣喜若狂,渲染"共产主义垮台或崩溃了",请看下面的报道:

Once an important buffer between pro-Western Pakistan and the Soviet Union, the country has lost much of its strategic importance since the **collapse of communism.** (*The Washington Post*)

美英报刊大力兜售西方价值观,还以"导师"自居,如《时代》周刊是这么写:
Even before the official summit began, Clinton **tutored** China's President Jiang **on American values.**

这里把克林顿向江泽民介绍美国价值观说成是"tutor"(上课)了。

五、对我国媒体的影响

西方大国在很大程度上操纵着国际舆论的话语权。国内媒体有时很难摆脱影响。北约绕开安理会,轰炸南斯拉夫进行78天之久,明明是侵略(aggression),却称为"打击"(strike against Yugoslavia,不少美国报纸当时天天用来充当专栏标题),遗憾的是,国内报章杂志包括有的英语学习杂志也跟着这么说。人家把北约一方美化成"国际社会"或"世界各国人民"(international community),把迫降条件美化成"和平方案"(peace proposal),而我们有的英文报纸却照登无误。

六、擦亮眼睛,提高警惕

一般而言,美英报刊对内政常持怀疑和批评态度,与政府唱反调,但在外交上则坚决维护本国利益,或与政府立场一致,或小骂大帮忙。作为新闻媒体的重要组成部分,报刊想完全独立于政府也是不可能的。虽然它常标榜"新闻自由",自诩"什么话都敢说","什么事都可报道",其实自由是有限的,国家安全总是高于新闻自由。如2003年3月,美国以反恐的名义和伊拉克拥有对美国构成威胁的大规模杀伤性武器为借口,发动伊拉克战争以来,这种"新闻自由"一下子变得黯然失色,因为政府要求媒体在这个问题上都必须与其立场和观点保持一致。凡不听话者,轻则警告,重则勒令暂停营业甚至吊销执照。记者Peter Arnett还为此丢掉饭碗,不得不到英国去谋生。何况文章是人写的,西方记者的世界观和价值观与我们不同,当然看问题的方法和立场就与我们大相径庭,多数文章的观点是我们不能接受的。如《纽约时报》等主要报刊,一提到中国就在"人权、贸易逆差、军事威胁"等问题上大做文章。读书看报,我们不但要能读进去,还要能跳出来。阅历不深、常看这类报刊的年轻人要擦亮眼睛,提高警惕,千万别让他们潜移默化了。我们对他们的文章一定要持分析、批判的态度,并使之为我所用。

了解以上情况,除有利于增强政治辨别能力外,也有助于读者加深对文章内容的理解。(见"**附录**""报刊从业人员常用术语")

第二章　语　　言

　　报刊内容涵盖美英国内外大事及各行各业,真是上至天文下至地理,无所不包,是一部活的百科全书,其词汇量和词义面也必然广阔无边。此章不可能像综合词典一样,对上百万个词汇一一讲解。读报要入门,必须掌握一定数量当今报刊常用的政治、社会、经济、法律、科技、宗教和间谍等基本词汇和新词语,编者尽可能重点讲解,针对学生初读报的困惑,指出词义从泛指到特指、从抽象到具体发生的词义变化。人们对时政文章最感兴趣,报刊上这方面的报道和评论文章也最多,不言而喻是详解重点。为使读者进一步了解报刊语言的多变及语法的变化,专门写了一章"跟踪语言的变化和发展"。为掌握报刊语言的一些规则,编者还尝试总结"报刊语言主要特点",帮助读者看报时,对报刊语言的特点更敏锐,从而易吃透文章内容。

　　"语言"与"读报知识"不能分开,读报知识介绍也不能面面俱到,所以在语言解说中尽可能两者结合。

　　学习任何知识都必须打好基础,读外刊也不例外。我们认为,学生在中学和大学低年级的阶段首先要夯实语言基础。到了大学高年级阶段,读报必须在报刊语言及其特点和读报知识这两项基本功上下工夫。编者采取的不是一开头就解说那些学生较陌生的词语,而是有针对性地从扩大他们所熟悉的常用词的词义面着手,增强读外刊的信心,消除"恐惧"感。

　　如一开始就领初入门者看下面这段短文,或许会吓退他们。此文是 2004 年美国大选期间共和和民主两党候选人 George W. Bush 和 John Kerry 竞选团队,相互诋毁,针对读者来函谈专题报道读后感,*Newsweek* 作出回复,文字很短,初入门者不熟悉的词语和背景知识却不少。

MAIL CALL[1]
Mudslinging[2] and the Race for the White House

Readers responding to our **cover story**[3] on the viciousness of the presidential campaign urged the candidates to tone it down. One said John Kerry and George W. Bush should "learn to behave with a little more pride, dignity and honor." But some said equating the attacks on Bush with those on Kerry is unfair. "Severely criticizing Bush's policies is not the same as **lying about Kerry's record in Vietnam**[4]," said one reader. Others thought we were wrong in proclaiming all **527 organizations**[5] suspect. "Legitimate 527s **level the playing field**[6], providing a way for regular folks like me to **put our wallets where our mouths are**[7], just like the big contributors," a reader wrote. Others think the mudslinging only obscures the bigger picture: "I want to know how we are going to deal with the health-care crisis, educating our children and creating and keeping American jobs. It's not what happened in Vietnam, **stupid**[8]."

(2004/10/4, *Newsweek*)

1. reply to mail
2. slime slinging or negative campaigning
3. 见第一节"扩大若干常见词的词义面""story"
4. 见"读报知识""总统选举"
5. ditto(同上)
6. be equal or fair
7. take action to support our statement or opinion(即不能光说而不做)如不知 wallet 即 money 会抓瞎。put one's money where one's mouth is 本来就是 informal phrase,改为 wallet 则更是俗用了。
8. 见"跟踪语言的变化和发展"

与其如此,不妨有针对性引导他们先见一篇文章中的两段,有的是熟词新义,想当然便会出错。

Carter, himself a critic of Bush, was 78 when he won **the prize**[1]. But Gore is just 59 and an active **presence**[2] in American politics, if only as a large thorn in Bush's side—and in the side of Democrats worried that he might **challenge**[3] them for the 2008 Democratic presidential nomination. Gore, who lost the 2000 election to Bush after a bitter electoral dispute that had to be resolved by the Supreme Court, has regularly said that he will not run for president again. But Friday's announcement touched off renewed interest in his plans...

"We would encourage all countries, including the big countries, and **challenge**[4] them to think again and to say what they can do to conquer global warming," Mjoes said in a news conference in Oslo. "The bigger the powers, the better that they come in front of this."(2007/10/12 *International Herald Tribune*)

1. Former US president Jimmy Carter won the Nobel Peace prize at 78 in 2002, and former Vice President Al Gore and the UN climate panel shared the peace Prize for climate work in 2007.
2. here referring to prominent political figure
3. compete against
4. encourage

这两段中,"presence"是个抽象指具体意义的词,西方长于抽象思维,中国人擅长形象思维,对这种用法不太习惯。两个 challenge 义不同,不能见到此字就认为只有"挑战"一义。

下面再举五例:

1. a high-profile military **presence**.
2. Sir Keith himself would agree that industrial policy now begins and ends with the treasury: an economic policy designed to foster the "**enterprise culture**".(*The Economist*)
3. Terrorists might hit American **interests** abroad. (VOA)

4. At the root of the problem is money. As a poor nation, China has few **resources** left over for cultural conservation after struggling to overhaul its command economy, dampen rising unemployment, take care of an aging population, put in infrastructure and modernize its massive military. (*Los Angeles Times*)

5. Even as Harper was carrying out his espionage tasks, America's Polish mole was discussing the case with Harper's own Polish case officer. Later, he passed on the entire **story** to U. S. agents, including word that the Poles had received congratulations from Yuri Andropov, the late Soviet President and former KGB chief. (*U. S. News & World Report*)

以上这五例是否都能将多义词对号入座,译为"存在"、"企业文化"、"利益"、"资源"、"故事"呢?显然不妥,那样会显得生硬,不合乎汉语的习惯表达法,甚至会闹笑话。

第一节 扩大若干常见词的词义面

不少常见常用词本来就是多义词,因书报读得少,词义面就窄。所谓多义词是指某个词本来就不止一个意思,还有的词的基本意思在不同的上下文有着不同的含义。另一个重要问题是词语的搭配不同,词义也不同。如 a hidden **agenda** 就与 trade **agenda** 意思不同,再如动宾结构宾语不同,词义也异。如 **challenge** your interest 与 **challenge** the judge's ruling 中这两个"challenge"意思迥异,在下面所举的大量例子中都说明了这种异同。这里的重点不是探讨一词多义及词义与词义之间的区别,而是说明它们是读报理解中的一大拦路虎,因为实践中常犯的一个错误是忽视某些词的多义性,越是常用词,引申义越多,有时连本国人也弄糊涂了。此外,interest 能有"组织、机构"和"企业、公司"的意思,抽象名词 presence 指具体能引申出那么多词义也是他们所料想不到的。

《泰晤士报》曾载文称,在现代报纸上,一个词有五六个意思是很平常的(见"Ironically")。这就增加了读报难度。为了引起读者重视和消除一些读报的难点,特在下面列出一些读者熟悉、报刊中常见而又往往难以把握的词语意义。编者相信,下列实例的解说定会开拓他们的视野。应当说明两点:第一、这里并未列举出词典中的全部词义。第二、例句解读并非正式翻译;省略部分以节省版面为目的,讲解重点是词典上查不到或语焉不详的词义。

一、Agenda

"agenda"的本意为"things to be done"。后来常作议会用语,指"议事日程"和"待议事项"。近年来,此字常见诸报端,词义也扩展引申了。我们原来可能只知:1. a hidden **agenda** 不可告人的动机;2. his private **agenda** 他个人的小九九;3. My **agenda** for today starts with cleaning out the cellar. 我今天的事(或任务)从打扫地下室开始。2008年美国驻华使馆教育交流中心一份 ALERT 的英文小册子列着几十篇美国出版的多种杂志文章的标题和提要,其中有好几个标题里都用 agenda 而弃用 program, plan 或 policy,似乎大有作为时髦词之趋势。下面举例说明这个词的上述词义和一些其他词义:

1. Mr Ma emphasises that links with China are just one dimension of his economic policy **agenda**. (2008/3/27 *financial Times*)

马先生强调说,与中国(大陆)的联系只是经济政策**议题/计划**的一个方面。

2. The Republican Party has lost its mind. To win elections, a party needs votes, obviously, and constituencies. First, however, it needs ideas. In

1994—1995, the Republican Party had after long struggle advanced a coherent, compelling set of political ideas expressed in a specific **legislative agenda**. (*Time*)

共和党已经失去了理智。要取胜,任何政党都要选票。还要支持者和赞助者。然而,党首先要有理念。经过长期的斗争,该党曾在 1994 年至 1995 年(民主党人克林顿任总统)期间提出了体现在具体**立法项目**上的一套有条有理、令人信服的政治理念,现在却提不出什么来了。

3. Democrats will use their new legislative muscle(注意此处用 muscle 这一形象词而不用抽象的 power) to advance an economic and foreign policy **agenda** that Bush has largely blocked for eight years. Even when the party seized control of Congress two years ago, its razor-thin margin in the Senate had allowed Republicans to hinder its efforts. (2008/11/5 *The Washington Post*)

2008 年大选后,民主党不仅成了"the party in the White House",在国会参众两院都成了"the majority party",而且在 2009 年又推荐了一位中意的大法官。成了真正意义上的执政党。今后,立法和施政都会推出符合该党理念的法案。此例的意思是:民主党议员将会利用立法增实力,提出经济和外交**解决的议题**(a list or program of things or problems to be addressed)。……

4. a. Over the next two years, U. S. congressional and administration efforts to move forward a **trade agenda** are likely to end up in stalemate, says Faux, a distinguished fellow with the Economic Policy Institute(研究所). Faux says that at least seven new Senate seats and 30 new House seats once occupied by supporters of free trade and investment are now occupied by critics of the Bush administration's trade policies... With the administration occupied with Iraq and the war on terror, Faux doesn't see how the administration will be able to muster the will to modify its **trade agenda** to deal with Democratic concerns. (*International Economy*)

在未来两年的时间里,美国国会和行政部门推动一项贸易**政策**的努力可能会陷于僵局……Faux 看不出小布什政府将如何能集中精力应对民主党的担忧而修改贸易**政策**。

b. Former presidential hopeful Elizabeth Dole, also addressing the gathering of more than 800 women from around the country, urged them to use their clout(用 clout 而不用 influence 是典型的新闻爱用短字、时髦词的特点) to advance **the agenda of women**, who she said comprise 53 percent of the

American electorate and 23 percent of donors to political campaigns. (*Campaign Spotlight*)

曾经有望入主白宫的 Elizabeth Dole（曾参与党内初选角逐中途退出）也对来自全国 800 多名妇女发表讲话，催促她们利用自己的影响力而提出妇女**计划**……

5. Some of Olmert's best choices for coalition partners are dovish parties with expensive **social agendas**. Amir Peretz's Labor Party, which won the second largest bloc of seats, campaigned on a platform of better pay for workers.

可供 Olmert 选择作为组建联合政府最佳伙伴的都是些主张在社会**计划**上大把花钱的鸽派政党。……

二、Challenge

美国有的政界人士如肯尼迪、克林顿很会用字。可不像小布什这位牛仔式总统却口无遮拦，常闹笑话，叫做"Bushisms"。克称政府部门的开支不用"spending"而用"investment"，困难、难题不用"difficulty"和"problem"而用"challenge"。也就是说，在他面前没有困难，只有挑战。但"challenge"不只"挑战"一义。请看：

1. He put forward some ideas to **challenge** the interest of all concerned.

他提出了一些新见解，**引起**了有关人士的注意。

2. Mr. Howard didn't **challenge** the Chairman's ruling.

霍华德不曾对主席的裁决**表示异议**。

3. Aggression **unchallenged** is aggression unleashed.

不反对侵略就是纵容侵略（美国前总统 L. 约翰逊宣传，出兵越南制止"侵略"。）

4. The attorney for the defense **challenged** the evidence as hearsay.

被告辩护律师**驳斥**该证据为道听途说。

5. The sentinel **challenged** us with "Who comes there?"

哨兵**喝问**我们："谁？"

以上这些 challenge 的词义，好一点的词典上都可查到，拙著《当代英汉报刊词典》还列举了"质问，指责"、"抗衡"、"经得住"、"攻击"、"抗议"、"否认"、"触犯"、"对付"等等词义，一般词典没有收录。

下面再举几个作 noun 用的例句：

1. "Unless we take some measures, we may be in danger of loving our heritage to death," Engelhardt told a conference on cultural conservation in Beijing last month.

Although the Communist regime recognizes the **challenge**, tackling it has turned out to be a relatively slow and haphazard business.

……共产党政权虽然认识到文化保护工作是项**艰巨任务**,但抓得不力,时紧时松。

2. FDR's second inaugural, delivered on January 20, 1937, radiated confidence, **challenge**, and reformist zeal.

在1937年1月20日,富兰克林·罗斯福连任总统,就职演说洋溢着信心、**干劲**和改革激情。

3. Pippen said, "This series could have been over a week ago if we read everything that was being said against us, that we weren't going to challenge them, and the Sacramento Kings were the biggest **challenge** the Lakers were going to face."

(原NBA芝加哥公牛队后开拓者队队员)皮蓬说:"……萨克拉门托国王队是(洛杉矶)湖人队(在西部争霸中)将要面对的最厉害的**竞争对手**。"

此外,challenged 作 *adjective* 委婉地表示"某方面有缺陷的"(used euphemistically to indicate that sb suffers impairment or disability in a specified respect)和"某方面缺乏的"(used to indicate that sb or sth is lacking or deficient in a specified respect),如:

1. my experience of being **physically challenged**

我有着**身体残疾**的感受。(见**"常见委婉语"**)

2. today's **attention-challenged** teens

当今**心不在焉**的青少年。

三、Community

community 的基本意义可概括为"a group of people"或"a group of nations",但是在不同的上下文或与不同的词搭配意思也异。如用于"the international community",一般指"国际社会";用于"the Atlantic Community""大西洋集团";"the European Community""欧洲共同体"。还有的学者认为:一般而言,大写为"共同体",小写为"大家庭"。但记者并不一定遵守大小写规则,在报刊上该大写的字却小写的现象相当普遍,尤其在英国报刊中居多。细究起来,此字比上述定义要广得多。在下面例句中尤其要注意其与不同词搭配而词义之不同。

1. Next week Thatcher travels to the United States, where she is expected to issue a spirited defense of British national sovereignty within **the European Community.** (*Newsweek*)

……撒切尔夫人预计会为英国在**欧洲共同体**内享有国家主权作出有力辩护(指不听任共同体摆布)。

2. The reports of a respected foreign correspondent were a different matter. Snow's stories in the foreign press(and the English-language *China Weekly Review*,published in the International Settlement in Shanghai)quickly filtered through **the Chinese intellectual community.**(*The China Quarterly*)

……斯诺在外刊上发表的报道文章很快就传遍了**中国知识界**。

3. the Shiite **community**(伊斯兰教派中的)什叶**派**

4. the indigenous **community** 土著**居民**,原居民

5. a large foreign **community** 大量外国**侨民**

6. a large Mexico **community** in the U. S. 在美国的大量墨西哥**移民**

7. a gay **community** 同性恋**群落**

8. community charge(英国)**地方劳务税**,(俗称)人头税

9. a. By 1968,however,Robert Kennedy had moved so far away from his assassinated brother's position that he was now competing with Eugene McCarthy in the Democratic presidential primaries for the favour of the antiwar movement and was also becoming a hero to **the black community.**(*The Times*)

然而到 1968 年,Robert Kennedy(也被暗杀)已跟遇刺的哥哥 John Kennedy 拉开距离,竟然与 Engene Mclarthy 在民主党内总统候选人预选竞争中相互讨好反战运动者(肯尼迪总统出兵越南)。这样,Robert 也成为**黑人大众**眼里一位英雄。

b. The resolution calls upon "**the communities** in Cyprus and their leaders to act with the most restrain."

联合国决议呼吁塞浦路斯**民众**及其领袖们要保持最大限度克制。(因塞国内曾遭到希腊和土耳其两国干扰。1974 年希腊曾策动希族军人政变,企图吞并塞岛。岛内土耳其族也曾先后闹独立,险些酿成内战。)

10. a. Most of those volunteering were doing so for the first time, for example, and many said they were eager to do more **community work** in the future. Says Jiang:"It's a major leap forward in the formation of China's civil society, which is vital for China's future democratization process."(2008/5/22 *Time*)

多数志愿者首次抗震救灾,热望今后做更多**社会工作**。……

b. "We are prepared to build a more cooperative relationship with China and wish to work with China as an active member of **the international community**," Mr. Clinton said at the signing ceremony. (*International Herald Tribune*)

克林顿先生在签字仪式上说:"我们准备与中国建立更好的合作关系,希望与中国这一**国际社会活跃**成员一道工作。"

c. The courage and success of the RAF pilots—of the Kuwaiti, Saudi, French, the Canadians, Italians, the pilots of Qatar and Bahrain—all are proof that for the first time since World War Ⅱ, **the international community** is united. (*The New York Times*)

……这一切都证明,自二次大战以来,**世界大家庭**第一次这么团结。(这里其实只指第一次伊拉克战争参战国:美英、西欧和若干阿拉伯国家。)

d. The occupation continues, in spite of the condemnation by **the international community**, a condemnation which was also voiced on various occasions in our organization [UN].

尽管遭到**举世**谴责,联合国内也在不同场合挞伐,伊拉克仍赖在科威特。

如果将以上三例都理解为"国际社会"就不太贴切。c. 例指为"国际大家庭"考虑到西方的想法;而 d. 例指"举世"则照顾到中国政治因素。国际社会有时指联合国组织,有时包括该组织成员国及其人民,不宜跟联合国画等号;有时只指西方国家。如出于美英领导人之口,甚至只指美国或美英两国,但仍盗用"国际社会"之名。the global/world community 或 the community of nations 也指国际社会。以前中国和苏联、东欧等社会主义国家也常称"社会主义大家庭"(the socialist community)。

11. Some **ethnic communities** may make a point of survival, but only those who are proud of their cultural roots. (*Cambridge Alumni Magazine*)

一些**民族**/(美)**少数民族**会强调要保留他们古老的风俗习惯,但只有那些对文化渊源引以为豪的民族才会这样做。

四、Dimension

dimension 的本义是"extent"和"measure out",下面举例或本义或引申义。

1. a. What is a nation's health-care system for? Obviously, to care for the sick and protect the health. Well, sure, but there is an additional **dimension.** (The *New York Times*)

国家建立医疗保健制度目的何在。虽然是为了保健治病。这么说当然没错,但还有另一**方面**的目的。

b. Most Americans apparently found the campaign boring, in part because a Clinton victory was widely assumed. Televised debates between Clinton and Dole, on Oct. 6 and Oct. 16, attracted media attention but low audience ratings. (Some said that Perot, who was excluded from the debates, could have added a **new dimension** to them.) (The *World Almanac*)

许多美国人显然对总统竞选感到厌倦,部分原因是普遍认为克林顿会胜出,所以克与 Robert Dole 在 1996 年 10 月 6 日和 16 日的两次电视辩论虽然引起媒体的兴趣,但收视率并不高。[有人说,被排除在总统候选人辩论之外的 Ross Perot(1992 年和 1996 年以独立候选人和改革党候选人参与总统竞选)要是能参与辩论,或许能别开**生面**,增加收视率]。

2. Thomas Murphy protested some of the President's Washington-oriented advisers, far more than Carter "are influenced by their own life-styles and they do not understand the **dimension** of the American public." (*Time*)

T. Murphy 声称,卡特总统身边一些顾问,高高在上,官僚习气重,架子远比卡特大,不了解**民情**(卡特原为花生农场主,较接近普通民众,顾问做官当老爷,不了解**下情**)。

3. But the mid-January outbreak of the Gulf war created a new and menacing **dimension** to dispel the general euphoria born of the NATO-Warsaw Pact declaration in November, which officially ended the cold war.

但是一月中旬海湾战争爆发(指伊拉克侵占科威特触发的第一次伊拉克战争)**风云突变**,使去年 11 月北大西的公约和华沙条约联合声明冷战正式结束,普天同庆的狂喜心情一扫而光。

4. President Carter therefore returns to Washington having done more than merely escaped the frustration and disarray of his domestic policies. He has confirmed and enhanced the foreign **dimension** of his presidency. (*The Times*)

所以卡特总统出国访问后返回华盛顿,不只是逃避了内政受挫乱局,还确立和提高了总统职位在对外政策方面的**分量**。

5. China with its massive military strength and daunting **dimension** can fight a protracted war.

中国人多势众,**国土面积辽阔**,能够打一场持久战。

6. Most of us were Catholics, and this added an extra **dimension** to the tension... There are international **dimensions** to our problems in Britain.

我们许多人都是天主教徒,这就增加了造成紧张局势的特别**因素**……对解决我们英国问题来说,还有种种国际**因素**。

7. The Macedonian argument has a Greek **dimension** too. (见"**学习方法**""**词义之确定及辨析**")

8. This does not mean that America needs to keep an armed presence of

cold-war **dimensions** in either place. (The *Economist*)

这并不意味着美国在这里或那里都需要保持冷战时期**水平/规模**的兵力。

9. Nothing in the Constitution mandates a dramatic denouement to the election-night drama—though as recently as 1980 the polls failed to predict the Republican takeover of the Senate and the **dimensions** of the Reagan landslide. (*Newsweek*)

宪法并未强求这场选举收场之夜要来一个出人意料的大结局。要知道,近在 1980 年,民意测验还没有预测到共和党会在参议院占多数,也没有预见到里根会以如此悬殊的**比例**赢得一面倒的胜利。

10. Her [China's] presence is felt, more than ever, all over the world, assuming historic **dimensions** in the world political situation.

中国影响空前,遍及全球。在世界政坛起着具有历史意义的**重大作用**。

11. They received no sudden revelation of Watergate's wider **dimensions**, used no James Bond wiles to score their scoops. (*Time*)

水门事件涉及的**面很广**,记者并非一下子就掌握全部内情,因而没有像王牌间谍詹姆斯·庞德那样耍弄花招,抢先报道独家新闻。

五、Establishment

"establish"常作"建立"讲,词源义是"make firm",作形容词为"stable"。现在"establishment"/"Establishment"的词义很广,常用于政治题材文章,可指建立起来的单位(机构)、权势集团、当权派等,但均从"建立"或"建立的机构"这一基本意义引申扩展而来。见例句:

1. **Intelligence establishment** became intelligence community because establishment became pejorative. (*The New York Times Magazine*)

情报界的"界"字已由英文字"establishment"改为"community",因为前者已成为贬义词。但英国报纸仍用"America's intelligence establishment",见《精选本》四版第 11 课第 2 段。

2. The Pentagon argues for a leaner military **establishment**, even though the gulf conflict has stretched its resources to the limit. (*Time*)

五角大楼力争缩小军事**建制**,即使海湾战争(指第一次伊拉克战争)已使其投入的兵力达到了极限。

3. Indeed the West German **establishment**, like the Polish and East German governments, seems to be cordially displeased with Judge Stern's judgment. (*Newsweek*)

确实,**西德当局**与波兰和东德政府一样,似乎都对 Stern 法官的判决打心底老大不痛快。(此处的 establishment 与 government 义同,这样理解带有当时的政治背景。)

4. Khomeini's curious blend of mysticism and activism still made him slightly suspect in the eyes of **the Islamic Establishment**—as a holy man who tried to run around with the Mob, one might say—but his following was growing steadily. (*Time*)

(前伊朗宗教领袖)阿亚图拉(Ayatollah)·霍梅尼把宗教上祈祷默念,悟道与神交往这一套与积极参政,活跃异常奇怪地融合在一起,在**伊斯兰世界当权派**看来,有点离经叛道……

5. a. *The Times* takes a middle-of-the-road view, claiming to represent the views of **the establishment** and is especially well-known for its correspondence column. (*Meet the Press*)

《泰晤士报》所持的是中庸看法,声称代表的是**现存体制**的观点。该报的读者通讯栏尤其闻名遐迩。

b. The Church of England is the official (established) church of the United Kingdom, created in the 16th century as a protestant church by the Act of Supremacy. ... It is one of the main forces of **the Establishment** in Britain. (Adrian Room)

英国国教会/圣公会是联合王国官方定为国教的教会,在 16 世纪由君主作为牧首(而非教皇)而作为新教会建立的。……英国国教会是英国**权势集团/社会既成权力结构**的一股重要力量。(见"读报知识""宗教")

c. Several senior strategists recommended that the White House adopt an anti-**Establishment** strategy, taking on organized labor, civil-rights groups, feminists and other GOP foils. (*U. S. News & World Report*)

几个资深谋士建议白宫采取反对**实力集团**的策略,准备同工会、民权团体、女权主义者和其他老大党(即共和党)内的不忠诚分子较量。

6. a. But Dole had the near-unanimous support of the GOP **establishment** and wrapped up the nomination after a shaky start. (*The World Almanac*)

但是(Robert)多尔在老大党(即共和党)**当权派**几乎一致的支持下而终于获得总统候选人提名,展开角逐,尽管起步不顺。

b. Despite his contribution in the field of social progress President Johnson "was never accepted by **the liberal Eastern Establishment**," Carter said. "I don't know why." (*Washington Star News*)

美国前总统卡特说,尽管 L. 约翰逊总统推动社会进步有功(他曾将"Great Society"作为主要施政纲领),却"从未被**自由派东部权势集团**所接受。我真不知道个中原因"。(根据 American Government & Politics 的释义: 1. 所谓权势集团是指社会掌握实权的那帮人,主要指保守的和秘密的统治阶级,并举例 an "Eastern Establishment"和 a Protestant Establishment 为例 。2. 社会某一方面(如政治、军事、社会、学术或宗教等某一界的)集体掌权者。(Eastern Establishment 在新中国成立之前和之后很长一段时间,我国一直译为"东部财团"。美国来访者说,洛克菲勒和摩根等财团概念在美国已过时,现在改称"利益集团"。)

c. Some **establishment** figures remain wary of Byrne because she defeated their candidate, but the new mayor has moved to patch up differences. (*Time*)

一些**当权派**人士仍在防范 Byrne,因为她击败了代表他们利益的候选人,然而这位新市长已开始弥合双方分歧。

d. I have been accused of being an **Establishment** hack, part of the capitalist conspiracy. Such charges can be easily laughed off... (*Newsweek*)

我曾被指责为某一**财阀**的笔杆子,是富豪在捣乱。……

7. a. The hotel is a well-run **establishment** (*Los Angles Times*)

这家旅馆是管理得好的服务**单位/机构**。

b. "It is truly regrettable. It is deplorable that a diplomatic **establishment** that is supposed to have extraterritorial has been mistakenly hit," Keizo Obuchi was quoted as saying by Kyodo News Agency. (AP)

真遗憾,也可悲,一家理所享有治外法权的外交**机构**居然遭到误炸。……

六、Interest

本书第一版在"常见的多义词"一章中就"interest"的词义试举了下列三例:

1. special **interests**

特殊**利益集团**(=an interest group)

2. human **interest**

人情味

3. Terrorists might hit American **interests** abroad. (VOA)

恐怖分子或许会袭击在国外的美国**机构**/美国驻外**机构**。

4. "The focus ought to be: Does big money in politics buy something?" she says. "And the answer is yes. Does it matter whether it comes from **overseas interests** or domestic ones? What's the difference?" (*The Washington Post*)

她说:"问题的焦点应该是:重金投资竞选能否获得一些回报? 这当然是

肯定的。资金来自海外**公司**/**企业**和国内**公司**/**企业**事关重大吗？有何区别？"

关于**此字**，The New Oxford Dictionary of English 的第 5 义是：(usu. interests) a group or organization having a specified common interest, esp. in politics or business: food interests in Scotland must continue to invest. 尤指在政治或企业方面有着共同利害关系的（即同业或同行）集团或组织：在苏格兰的食品企业必须继续投资。

看了上述释义，人们或许要问："为什么第(3)例是"驻外机构"而第(4)例则作"海外公司"讲呢？"根据美国情况和国际形势，恐怖分子常常袭击美国驻外的使领馆和军事基地，所以第(3)例定义为"机构"。第(4)例考虑到美国的文化背景而理解为"公司"，因为美国法律禁止外国任何个人或机构给美国候选人竞选捐款，以前的韩国商人因收买国会议员震惊美国而被称之为"Koreagate"。所以通常的做法是，外国为收买总统或其他高官，一般通过公司与竞选活动委员(PAC)或 lobby firm(游说公司)等联系，或直接或间接秘密地给其竞选捐款。若驻美使馆直接捐款，曝光后定会引起外交风波。

《英汉大词典》（第二版）第 5 义是：(常作～s)利益集团；同业，同行；利益相关者：(其中有一例是)the business ～ s 公司同业。网上的 the free dictionary. com 无这两本词典的第 5 义。

这就是说，两本词典释义有所不同，《英汉大词典》有"利益集团"而无 Oxford 的"政治机构"或"企业、公司"的词义，而以上(3)(4)两例正好符合 Oxford 的第 5 义。

七、Ironically

1977 年 8 月 15 日《泰晤士报》刊载一篇"Continuing our series of new words and new meaning"的文章，对 ironically 这个字作了如下说明：

IRONICALLY is one of the most popular introductory words... There is no shred of IRONY in its popularity, only haziness, IRONICALLY is evidently used to have several meanings：

 1. by a tragic coincidence；（万万没有料到）
 2. by an exceptional coincidence；（真是难以想到）
 3. by a curious coincidence；（出奇地巧合，出奇地没有想到或料到）
 4. by a coincidence of no importance；（无关紧要的巧合）
 5. oddly enough, or it's rum thing that；（说来也怪，你看怪不怪，真邪门）
 6. oh hell; I have run out of words for starting a sentence with.（真该死）

Study of modern newspapers suggests that meanings five and six are becoming by far the most common. This is a shame, because it devalues a useful word.

这种滥用和歪曲 ironically 词义的现象,现在可以跟 gategate 和 nikgate(-gate 和-nik 作构词成分不断造词,泛滥成灾到了滥用的地步)一样。为了说明 ironically 之滥用,见例句:

1. IRONICALLY is a powerful and explicit word. It is being weakened by use as an all-purpose introductory word to draw attention to every trivial oddity, and often to no oddity at all, *Ironically* those who use the word in this way are its worst enemies.

ironically 是一个用于有力和词义明确的字,但是现在其词义正常被削弱。原因是它被用作了各种意思开场白的字眼,旨在吸引人们注意每一个无足轻重的奇事怪事,而且常常根本一点都不怪,因为**万万没有料到**(相当于"by a tragic coincidence")的是,那些这样用的人倒成这个字死对头。

2. According to Deputy Assistant Secretary of State Robert Oakley, a key U. S. policy-maker for Southeast Asia, the Vietnamese are so eager to establish diplomatic relations that they have dropped their long standing demand for American aid as a quid pro quo(报酬;交换物)。

Ironically, Hanoi could have exchanged ambassadors with Washington two years ago if it had not raised the aid issue.

……**你说怪不怪**(相当于"oddly enough"),要是河内当初不向美国提出补偿援助要求的问题,河内和华盛顿可能在两年前就建交交换大使了。

b. Communists are finding more and more receptive ears to their propaganda that the revolution was a petit bourgeois change and merely amounted to replacement of Savak—the shah's hated secret police—with the SHEIKHIS (those of the clergy). The appearance of plethora(大堆;过多) of communist literature on the pavements of Iran's major towns and its easy sale are attributable to this.

Ironically all this is happening to a people with a high standard of living...

……**真是怪了**,碰巧这一切就出现在生活水平很高的民族身边……

一句话,ironically 当嘲讽讲主要指言语,用在其他场合则有事与愿违等意,不能机械地一律理解为"具有讽刺意味的是"。

八、Presence

presence 是词义面很广的词,cultural presence 指学校、教堂等教育、宗教等文化设施，financial presence 指银行、货币资金组织等金融机构。作外交用字，意为"显示军事力量"(showing the flag)。原来特指为避免或防止战争布署在所在地区的联合国维和部队。这种用法始于1958年，当时的联合国秘书长哈马舍尔德(Dag Hammarskjöld 1905—1961)派遣了一个30人的使团出访约旦，称为"U. N. presence in Amman, Jordan"。后来这种用法不再限于U. N. 机构，美国在中东的第六舰队也称为"the U. S. presence"(美军力量)。

现在不但词义广，用得有点滥，几乎成了一个万用词(a word of all work)。其次，有时含糊不清，不了解情况者很难定义，已超过任何一本词典和网上的释义。然而 presence 这个抽象词可用来表示具体意义，就会扩大产生新义。有时含糊、艰涩。出于政治策略，有些政客如哈马舍尔德就喜欢用这样的字。他曾说："There is **a UN presence** wherever the UN is present." 此处"a UN presence"指什么？"维和部队"、"外交官"、"外交使团"或"军事观察团"都可以。此语妙在可作种种理解，使对手或政敌抓不住话柄。

事实上，"a presence"还可指"出访的外交官"、在海外的"航空母舰"、"永久性军事基地"、"军队"或"警察"。下面所列第(2)至第(6)的例句基本上是显示力量或由此扩展引申而来的词义。后面几例谈及的"投资"、"开店设厂"等由该词的第一义或本义"the state or fact of existing, occurring, or being present in a place"或"being at hand"引申而来。

刚入门者往往一见此字就认为只有"存在"而似乎无他义。那么，下面就从该词作"存在"的意思起逐一举例说明从抽象到具体而引申扩展出多种意义：

1. A team of FBI and ATF investigators came to town, and a specially trained black Labrador named Iris, who sniffed out the **presence** of accelerants in the ruin of First Missionary Baptist, confirmed that the fire in fact was arson. (*Newsweek*)

一队联邦调查局和烟酒枪支专卖局调查人员来到镇上，一条受过特殊训练名叫 Iris 的黑色拉布拉多犬在第一传教士浸信会堂(此处省去了"church"。在美国南方的，我国称"浸信会"北方的称"浸礼会")的废墟里嗅出了催化剂气味("存在"二字可省去)。从而证实，这次教堂火灾实为纵火造成的。

2. a high-profile **military presence** 炫耀**军事实力**

3. maintain a strong **air presence** in Asia 在亚洲留驻一支强大的**空军**/在亚洲保持一支强大的**空中力量**。

4. His price for a coalition arrangement would have been political autonomy for Scotland and Wales, with which Labour agreed, as well as electoral reform to make proportional representation the basis for future

elections, which would give the Liberal Democrats a larger **presence** in Parliament. (*Time*)

联盟安排的代价是让苏格兰和威尔士实行政治自治,这一点工党倒是赞同的。还有选举改革,使比例代表制代替简单多数选举制作为未来大选的基础,这就使自由民主党因**席位的增加**而加强了在议会的**力量**。(见"**读报知识**"英国"议会选举")

5. a. Though President Bill Clinton's administration says it will maintain current force levels in the region, it's no longer just the extreme left wing that's calling for a rethink of **the U. S. presence**. (*Far Eastern Economic Review*)

……虽然克林顿总统的政府说,它们要在该地区(in Asia)保持现在的军力水平,但是要求重新考虑**驻亚美军的问题/美国在亚洲的驻军问题**不仅仅是极左翼人士。

b. The key decisions must still be made by and with Israel. The problem is how to give the Palestinians a homeland that would not pose a threat to Israeli security. Mr. Begin seems to think that this can be achieved only if Israel retains responsibility for security in the West Bank. This is not necessarily the case. An Israeli **presence** might exacerbate tension and provoke insecurity, whereas the Palestinians living on the spot, who have as great an interest in peace as the Israelis, might be able to police themselves more effectively. (*The Times*)

……关键问题是既给巴勒斯坦人一个家园而它又不对以色列的安全构造威胁。以色列总理贝京先生似乎认为,要能达到这两个目的唯有以色列继续负责约旦河两岸的安全。形势没有必要这样做。一支以色列的**驻军**或许会加剧紧张形势,搅得巴勒斯坦人心神不安……

c. Despite the problems with civilian reconstruction and pressures from European governments to consider leaving a force behind after IFOR leaves, the White House—with an eye on the presidential election campaign—will not even discuss for now any possibility of an American troop **presence** in Bosnia past President Clinton's December deadline. (*U. S. News & World Report*)

波黑战后百废待举,欧洲政府也要求考虑在北大西洋公约组组派驻该国执行《代顿和平协议》的执行部队撤离后留下一支部队。然而,白宫只盯着总统竞选,顾不过来,眼下根本不会讨论克林顿总统规定的年底撤军期限过后,美军是否**留驻**波黑问题。(这里的 presence 既有"force"也有"station"之义)

d. The Pentagon confirmed the **presence** of American troops in northern Afghanistan for the first time Tuesday and credited them with improving the effectiveness of U. S. bombing raids. (AP)

五角大楼在星期二首次证实美军**驻扎**在阿富汗北部,认为他们在那里有助于提高美国空袭效率。

6. Indonesians opposed to the **UN presence** in East Timor protesting Friday outside UN offices in Jakarta. The UN said 20 more people died at the hands of militias in West Timor, but Indonesia denied the claim. (*International Herald Tribune*)

印度尼亚尼人反对(UN mission 也可指)**联合国维和部队**驻扎在东帝汶,他们星期五在驻雅加达联合国办事处外举行抗议活动。

7. Britain is committed to maintaining a worldwide **diplomatic presence.** Diplomatic or consular relations are maintained with 183 countries and there are missions at nine international organisations or conferences. (*Britain*)

英国尽力保留驻世界各国的**外交使团/机构**。

8. Even those who did not question the President's motives found it difficult to defend his particular reshuffling of federal and state roles. Academic theoreticians and practical politicians alike see a need for a federal hand in helping the poor, since their problems are often created by national economic conditions. Only a federal **presence** can apply pressure to hold down the inequities stemming from a state's relative inability or unwillingness to deal fairly with the problem. (*Time*)

即使不怀疑(里根)总统意图者也发现很难为其提出的调整联邦和州政府的作用(的新联邦主张)进行辩护。……只有联邦政府**插手/干预**。(见上句中的"a federal hand")才能向州政府施压,迫使其减少对穷人的不公。因为这个问题是由于州政府的无能和无心公平解决造成的。

9. The **presence** in China of Coca-Cola, Pepsi, McDonald's, and Kentucky Fried Chicken has certainly helped spur the development of the domestic soft-drink and fast-food industries. (*Far Eastern Economic Review*)

可口可乐、百事可乐、麦当劳和肯德基家乡鸡在中国**投资/(经营)/开店设厂**肯定有助于促进美国国内软性饮料和快餐业的发展。

10. Also, confirm that a school truly offers the full range of courses you'll need to complete your degree at a distance. "Some institutions grossly exaggerate their online **presence**," warns Robert Tucker, president of InterEd,

a Phoenix-based educational research firm. (*U. S. News & World News*)

……一些学校明显夸大它们的网上**课程**……(见《精选本》四版第一课"语言解说",根据上下文,cultural presence 还可指"文文历史"或"文明史"。)

九、Story

作为学生见到"story"就认为只有"故事"一义并不奇怪,奇怪的是有一家大学出版社将一本 *News Reporting & Writing* 的原文书目里约 11 个"story"不分语言场合,一律译为"故事"。其实其中有的意思是"新闻",有的是"报道",有的是"新闻报道",还有的可能"稿子"、"文章"或"小说"等。

另一个值得探讨的词语是"cover story",Oxford 词典的第一义是:a magazine article that ia illustrated or advertized on the front cover。我们出版的双语词典基本都译为"封面故事",并加上类似"指杂志中与封面图片有关的主要文章"。美国出版的词典也有指"由杂志封面图片引出的专题报道"。但无论如何,译为"封面故事"与新闻的原则相悖。报刊所报道的尽管是已经发生、正常发生或今后要发生之事,但都视为"新闻",不可能去报道旧事。而"故事"有一义为"旧事"(见《现代汉语词典》),所以报刊标题都少用过去而尽可能用现在时态就是这个道理。当然,这是为了吸引读者。所以,如果要译得简明,与其译为封面故事还不如译为"封面新闻报道"当然,此语还有"掩盖每人身份或所做之事的托词或借口"、"掩人耳目的说词"等意思。此外,在 *USA Today*(2009/5/12)报头的一篇题为"Rising at Ground Zero("9·11"事件被炸平的世界贸易中心大楼遗址),a symbol of resilience"的短文里有一幅插图,文字说明下有 Cover Story,右边有 see Cover Story page▶,可见其词义扩大了,也指报纸头版(front page)(相当于杂志的封面)图片引起的专题报道。当然,"story"是个词义面很广泛的多义词。见例句:

1. a. "During the past six months, the world's **top story** has been Iraq. If we play our cards wrong, North Korea could become the **lead story**." (*Reuters*)

在过去六个月里,伊拉克一直是世界关注的**头条新闻**。若我们政策出错,朝鲜或许将代之成为**头号新闻**(=news)。

b. I think you'll do anything for a "gotcha" **story**. (*The New York Times*)

我看你们这些记者只要得到一条抓住你错误把柄的**消息**,什么手段都使得出来。(这是曾参与过美国总统竞选的 Ross Perot 骂记者的话)

c. Some reporters who were not included in the session broke the **story**.

吃了闭门羹的记者捅出了会议的**消息**。

2. Last December, the Post first reported that probes were being made in

each of those cities, but officials refused to confirm the **story**.

去年12月,《华盛顿邮报》率先报道,每一个那样的城市都进行调查,但是有关人员/官员却拒不证实这则**报道**(联系 reported 确定词义)。

3. The reporter beat out a **story** in time for the morning edition.

这位记者为晨报版及时赶出了一篇**稿子**。

4. The magazine has a different editorial approach: personality **stories** about well-known financial figures.

该杂志的编辑方针与众不同,把重点放在财经界名人的**报道**上。

5. The Mediterranean may lose its wild bluefin tuna. High-tech harvesting and wasteful management have brought world fish stocks to dangerous lows. This **story** explores the fish crisis—as well as the hope for a new relationship between man and the sea. (*National Geographic*)

地中海或许不再有其野生金枪鱼,高科技的捕捞活动和挥霍性的管理方式已使全世界的鱼类资源减少到了濒危程度。这篇**文章/论文**探讨的是渔业危机以及建立人类与海洋之间新型关系的愿景。

6. Even as Harper was carrying out his espionage tasks, America's Polish mole was discussing the case with Harper's own Polish case officer. Later, he passed on the entire **story** to U. S. agents, including word that the Poles had received congratulations from Yuri Andropov, the late Soviet President and former KGB chief. (*U. S. News & World Report*)

即使在苏联特工 James Durward Harper 在执行间谍任务时,美国安插的波兰人卧底还在与 Harper 自己的波兰控制特工的情报官员讨论 Harper 执行任务的情况。后来,这位卧底把这事的全部**机密**都传递给了美国特工,其中还包括波兰情报官员曾经获得已故苏联总统和前克格勃首脑安德罗波夫的贺词。

7. Curiously, in the committee report the phrase plausible denial was listed but not defined: it is a **cover story** which enables high government officials to disclaim knowledge of an intelligence activity. (William Safire)

奇怪的是,在委员会的报告里,这个"plausible denial"的词语(否认知情的说法似乎蛮有理或跟真的一样)是有的,但未下定义:这是一个为掩盖丑闻而**遮人耳目的托辞**,为使政府高官能对某一情报活动推说不知情而了之。

8. John told his **story**.

约翰把他的经历/身世都说了出来。

9. The teacher told him off for telling **stories**.

教师责备他谎话连篇。

10. It is quite another **story** now.

早已时过境迁啦,或那是老皇历啦。

11. This war is becoming the most important **story** of this generation.

这场(越南)战争是这 25 年来头等大事。

12. The old mountaineer also wanted custody of the children. The judge asked for his side of the **story** and, after a long moment of silence, the mountaineer slowly rose from his chair and replied, "Judge, when I put a dollar in a candy machine and a candy bar comes out, does it belong to me or the machine?"

这位年迈的登山运动员也要求获得孩子的监护权,法官要求呈诉**理由/道理**。他沉默了好长一阵子后慢慢从椅子上站起来说道:"法官先生,我把一元钱投进糖果机,吐出一根棒糖,归我还是归糖果机?"(言下之意,他妻子只生不养,像糖果机一样,无权监护孩子。)

13. As he points out, India feeds 17% of world's people on less than 5% of the world's water and 3% of its farmland—and, along with China, is seeing its cereal crop rise this year. Similar **success stories** are cropping up, in patches. (*The Economist*)

正如你所指出的,印度占世界水资源不到 5%,农田 3%,却要养活世界人口的 17%。与中国一样,今年粮食作物要增产。类似的**成功事例**其他地区也在不断涌现,尽管只是东一块,西一块,未连成片。

14. Since I had said good-bye to him on Thursday, we had gone through greater emotions than any mystery **story** could provide.

我俩在星期四分手后,相思相恋,酸甜苦辣,一言难尽,超过了任何一部侦探推理**小说**的描绘渲染。

十、Technical/Technically

用于外交,这个"technical(ly)"可因其意思含糊而能将政治上或外交上有些不便明言的事搪塞过去而免生事端。如说由于"技术原因"(for technical reasons),这次会议暂时不开或取消了,是常用的外交辞令。从两国关系来看,很可能是由于政治原因。还有的国家领导人因来访者与其对等职位的官员会谈因口出狂言或预计根本问题就是接见了也谈不拢,就借口因"健康原因"(for health reasons/for reason of health)而拒绝接见,其实患的是政治病,这是以前的苏联常用的外交辞令,现在有的国家还在用。

不少学生见到此字时往往脑子里就认为只有"技术的/地"这个意义,只要好

好查查学生词典或网上浏览一下,还有下列一些意思:

1. Technical

(1) "Precipitation" is a **technical** term used by weather scientists for "rain".

"降水"是气象学家用来指"雨"的一个**专门术语**。

(2) The university admits its Asian-American acceptance rate dipped three years ago, after some **technical** changes in admission procedures, but denies discrimination and says the rate is going back up. (*Time*)

这所大学承认,在招生手续作了一些**规则/规章/章程**改革后,亚裔美国学生接收入校的比例三年前就下降了。尽管如此,但该校却不承认有歧视现象,还说,亚裔入校的比例正在回升。[technical——according to a strict application or interpretation of the law or rules (Oxford)]

(3) a. Then Anderson realized that he'd forgotten **the Miranda warning**. He didn't want to blow an arrest like this by making a **technical** mistake. (*The Blue Nowhere*)

那时,Anderson 认识到他已经忘了对嫌疑人宣读米兰达预告(见"**法律用语**")。可他不想就这样由于犯了一个**法规程序**上错误而把这桩逮捕的大事搞砸了。

b. The result was a **technical defeat** for the government, but otherwise of limited importance.

对政府而言,该结果只是**法律上的一次败输**,在其他方面却无足轻重。

c. The arrest was a **technical** violation of the treaty.

这种逮捕在**法律**上是违反条约的。

(4) a **technical** fault 机械故障[technical——resulting from mechanical failure (Oxford)]

2. Technically

(1) The method of electing the President is peculiar to the American system. Although the names of the candidates appear on the ballot, **technically** the people of each state do not actually vote directly for the President (and Vice President). (*An Outline of American Government*)

选举总统的方法是美国制度特有的。虽然总统候选人的名字都列在选票上,但**确切地说**,各州选民事实并非将票直接投给总统和前总统而是投给了选举人。(见《当代英汉美英报刊词典》**electoral college**)

(2) In the U.S., the words college and university are often used

interchangeably. **Technically**, there is a difference.

在美国，college 和 university 作"大学"讲常不加区分，交替使用。**严格地**说，这两个字还是有区别的。（"确切"和"严格"都是从"技术"这个本义引申而来的意义，因为技术要求"精确"。）

（3）More substantively, Aldrich claims to have been told directly by former White House Associate Counsel William Kennedy that it was Mrs. Clinton who got Livingstone his White House job. Kennedy last week denied that. After some backing and filling, Livingstone said that while Kennedy **technically** hired him, the person he consulted about a White House job was Christine Varney, a former senior White House aide and currently a Federal Trade Commissioner. (*Time*)

阿尔德里奇更是往细里说道，里文斯通到白宫工作一事是前白宫助理顾问肯尼迪曾经直接跟他说，是克林顿夫人给了他这份工作。但肯上周予以否认。经过一阵磋商更正后，里文斯通改口说，虽然肯尼迪**事实上**/**按规定**说是雇了他，但里文斯通关于在白宫谋份差事的事所资讯的人却是瓦内，……

（4）Of course, the economy is in a worse place than it was when Hillary Clinton's husband was on the campaign trail. Today, the nation is perilously close to sliding into a recession; in '92, the economy had already started growing, though a jobless recovery doomed George H. W. Bush's re-election bid anyway. The lesson? Voters' perceptions matter more than whether the economy is **technically** expanding or contracting. (2008/1/21 *Newsweek*)

……但那时失业未见好转，结果老布什竞选连任泡汤。1992年虽说经济已经开始复苏。教训何在？说明选民切身感受比经济**事实上**是增是缩更加重要。

（5）**Technically**, you could be prosecuted for this, but I don't suppose you will be.

按法规办事，你为此会受到起诉，但我认为不会。

第二节　改朝换代产生和流行的词语

改朝换代是产生新词语和使一些旧语词流行的沃土,新政策、新理念、新思维就要用新语来表达。美国新总统组成的政府(Administration)和英国新首相组成的内阁(government),即使与其前任是同党,也力图开创一个新局面或一个新开端(A New/Fresh Start)。也就是说,新官讲新话,媒体凑热闹。总统、首相任期越长,产生和流行的词语越多。除了表达新政策、新思想等外,或鼓舞士气,或官腔官调,攻击对骂,或模棱两可,或兜大圈子(circumlocution),不一而足。新造、旧词新义有之,如 CREEP;私房话有之。有的连英英词典都定错词义,俚语、行话、党派之争的用语也处处可见。政治词语居多,但也不乏社会、经济、科技等用语。有的易懂,不少难解,要求深厚的国际知识和扎实的语言功底。编者将这些词语视为报刊基础语言。下面先举三例,考考我们不查词典或上网是怎么理解这些词语的:

(1) 2008 年 3 月 19 日 USA Today 以"A New Political Breed:Obamacans"为题发表的文章第一段是:

A new genus of flower(喻奥巴马) has been introduced into the 2008 presidential race. It's a cross-pollination of disenchanted, moderate-to-liberal Republicans and the movement that is Barack Obama's campaign.

Obamacans is what some people call them.

(2) 小布什政府高官二次伊战前回答伊是否有 weapons of mass destruction 时说:"It's a **slam dunk** case."

以上两例的 Obamacan 和 slam dunk 是何义? Obamacon 与 Obamacan 有何区别。

一、美国

为了使读者一下就接触到时代的脉搏,本节采取部分倒叙的手法,将执政才数月的奥巴马政府(Obama Administration)创造和流行的词语先行解说,然而再按时间顺序的先后从二次大战前执政的 F.罗斯福任总统至小布什政权产生的词语一一道来。并采取薄古厚今的原则,近几任杜撰的词语多讲详讲。应该说明,即使以前政府(Administration)的用语,有的也常见诸报端。

1. 从奥巴马狂看新词

从 2007 年起,2008 年的美国总统竞选就非正式地拉开了序幕,与"Office seeks the man"不同的是,不少自视是"presidential timber(材料)"的人都纷纷跃跃欲试,登场亮相,犹如一场 beauty contest。一些熟词有了新义。当时就提出过"Buy one, give one free"的口号,原指买一送一,此处意为"你投我票选上了,还白得一个能力很强的配偶"。如:希拉里(Hillary),其丈夫是前总统克林顿。奥巴马的夫人 Michelle 是芝加哥大学医院院长。民主党还提出过"common good"的口号,本来指公益,这里引申出机会平等,尤其是经济公平的概念,来对抗共和党人的口号优势。许多民主党人埋怨近十年共和党用诸如"遗产税"和"业主社会"等动听的言辞美化共党的重商主义自由市场观点。而民主党人如 Al Gore 和 John Kerry 在最近两届总统选举中对大企业(the big corporations)的攻击却给许多选民以陈词滥调的印象。"共善"的提法来源于古代哲学和罗马天主教教义,一度成为民主党人的口头禅。虽然希拉里、奥巴马等总统候选人在巡回演说常用,但作为竞选口号能否叫得响还是心中无数,结果令人生疑,所以后来未被采用。最后还是奥巴马用了 1944 年、1948 年和 1952 年共和党总统候选人都屡试不爽的"Time for a change"口号而笑到了最后,在党内,希拉里强调候选人之 experience,攻击奥是新手却吃了败仗。这个口号可攻击对手"fear of change",内含选民希望看到一张新面孔(a new face),并"represent a sharper break from the immediate past"(代表与即将成为历史的

贝拉克·奥巴马
(Barack Obama)
民主党(2009—)

布什那种独断专行、单边主义的做法决裂)。小布什不但在党内存在"Bush Fatigue"in the GOP,因为其支持率只有 20%,党内对他极其厌烦。为党建功立业过的共和党人(established GOP figures)如前国会众议院议长、极端保守派 Newt Gingrich 都对他严厉抨击(lashed out against Bush),其他有政绩的人士对他更不买账了。连欧洲人也创造一个缩略词"ABB"(anybody but Bush),即只要不是布什,任何候选人当总统欧洲都能接受。在美国,ABB 指的却是 (anything but Bush)要抛弃布什的政策,ABC 则是(anything but Clinton)不搞克林顿那一套。所以,连原本是共和党的部分支持者也投了奥巴马的票,新词用的是由 Obama 和 Republican 拼缀词"Obamacan",即投票给民主党总统候选人奥巴马的原共和党的选民或支持者。原来是两个字分开的。如:Clinton Republican,Reagan Democrat。保守派指责投奥氏票的选民是 robots,而造出了"Obamabot"这样的新词。照他们这派的意愿,选民投票应该发扬传统价值观,这就是他们 2006 年新造的"values voter"的意思。

奥巴马靠什么起家?为何能冲破种族藩篱,石破惊天地成为第一个入主白

宫的黑人？有人说是"It's the Economy, Stupid！"（见"**政治名言的理解与翻译**"）；有人干脆把 Obama 讲成"on-line Obama"，O 字母重读指靠互联网发迹的奥巴马。也指他年轻有为，对 IT 熟悉，用 wholesale fund-raising 之法代替只靠传统的 retail fund-raising dinner/party 等而集腋成裘，即靠网上的小额筹款而财大气粗，先在党内击败了实力不可小觑的 Hillary Clinton，然而再叫共和党人 John McCain 总统梦落空。竞选要拉票，拉票靠钞票。所以"Money counts"。尽管不少研究人员认为百年不遇的金融和经济危机帮了奥巴马大忙，其实看来，奥本人的 character, personality 及 eloquence 也是他成功之道。因为美国的政治名言是："All politics is personal."（千选，万选，全是本人在竞选。）正因为他个人有政治家天赋：组织才能出色、举止沉着镇定、口若悬河。竞选势头"Obamatum"大不可挡，这里 momentum 截了最后一节作派生词，big **mo**（大势头，却截了其头节作缩略词。）

用 Obama 之姓造词不止 Obamican 和 Obamacon（从狭义讲，Obamacan 指共和党过去和现在的官员，Obamacon 指原本支持共和党候选人、在社会问题上持保守观点选民的选民。从广义讲，两词义无区别，因共和党人中保守派是主流），还有：Obamacize 所谓"奥巴马化"或"像其那样行事"，无非是宣传他不但当为年轻的黑人参议员，四年后还居然问鼎白宫，是一个 self-made man, a success story（成功的范例）；"Obamafy"在某种意义上有与"Obamacize"相同的意思；"Obamania"这种复合词常见，所谓"奥巴马狂"只是一时现象，随着时间的推移，这个 mania 也会随之退潮。

在经济领域，这个新造的 Obamanomics，在竞选中指其振兴美国经济的笼统的经济主张。2009 年 1 月上任后，指其经济政策，有人称之为"New Deal"（F. 罗斯福"新政"）之翻版或 New New Deal。注资救助 Chrysler, General Motors 和 Ford 三大汽车巨头后被贬为"big government"或"traditional tax-and-spend president"（典型的推行大政府政策的总统），比罗斯福当年的"creeping socialism"（即社会主义的一套原则，如政府干预经济等悄悄成为施政纲领）还更露骨的社会主义，从而使这些词语消退近 10 年后又流行了起来。在众议院通过的经济对策法案中还加进了在公共事业建设中使用美国钢铁的保护主义条款，即"buy American"条款。不少人怀念 20 世纪中期不冷不热的称心如意的经济（Goldilocks economy）。于是这些词又都热火了起来。

为了走出经济衰退，有的学者建议只有世界经济最发达的美国和新兴的经济强国中国联合起来共同合作应对，于是创造了一个"中美组合"的新词"Chimerica"。还有的美国学者建设成立这两国的"Group of Two(G2)"全面解决气候变化、环境污染、政治冲突和危机等全球性问题。在外交上，Smart power

(巧实力)在其上台不久即成为时髦词。(见"**外交用语**")副总统拜登(John Biden)反对增兵阿富汗,媒体称 Joe makes no joke(约翰讲实话。Joe 与 joke 谐音)。

总之,每位总统任内,或多或少总会出些新词,有的人去茶凉,没有叫开,有的却流传下来,管中窥豹可见一斑,以下各举数例看看。

2. F. 罗斯福任期

民主党人 F. 罗斯福任总统近 13 年,其间至少有 7 个新词语红极一时。罗斯福上台,正值其前任共和党总统胡佛无法应付的 "Great Depression"(经济大萧条)。为克服力挽狂澜,他鼓励人们 "nothing to fear but fear itself"(胆子大,全不怕),认为他是 "rendezvous with destiny"(注定要肩负克服大萧条的历史使命,亦即天降大任),于是提出了新政策 "New Deal"(新政),使人民享有 "four freedoms" 即 freedom of speech and expression/every person to worship God in his own way/from want/from fear(言论自由、宗教自由、免于匮乏的自由和免于恐惧的自由),并与民众拉家常式谈话 "fireside chat"(炉边谈话),从而为克服 Depression 增强了信心。在外交上提出 "good neighbor policy"(睦邻政策),将 1941 年 12 月 7 日日本袭击珍珠之日定为 "day of infamy"(国耻日),并承诺 "We must be the arsenal of democracy"。当然也遭

富兰克林·罗斯福
(Franklin Roosevelt)
民主党(1933—1945)

到一些讽刺和批评。例如:推行 "New Deal" 时,摊子铺得太宽,用首字母缩略字,被称为 "alphabet agencies",连本党人士也说湮没在一碗字母汤里了(submerged in a bowl of alphabet soup)。为保就业,动用政府资金上马一批凑数工程,被批为 boondoggle。实行凯恩斯学派经济政策,后来艾森豪威尔总统批评为大搞社会主义一套 "creeping socialism"。

3. 杜鲁门任期

F. 罗斯福病故任内,副总统杜鲁门接班,仿 New Deal 提出了 "Fair Deal",造出了 "give 'em hell, Harry"(哈里,骂得好!如无 Harry,现指候选人在竞选中极力贬毁对手。)如无逗号则为其外号。还批评

哈里·杜鲁门
(Harry S. Truman)
民主党(1945—1953)

对手搞"red herring"（转移公众视线），抨击共和党控制的国会吃闲饭"do-nothing Congress"。为了与苏联对抗，提出了"Marshall Plan"，帮助西欧国家恢复经济，和"Truman Doctrine"，打着"防共"和旗号，援助希腊和土耳其，实际上是排挤英法势力，搞新殖民主义。

4. 艾森豪威尔任期

艾森豪威尔将军执政正值人们盼望结束朝鲜战争(1950—1953)之时，创造和流行词语有：他承诺："I shall go to Korea"（我要结束朝鲜战争），反对"engage in personalities"（人身攻击）。主张核扩军而非常规武器的 new look（新面貌），使国防面貌一新，"bigger bang for a buck"（要"花钱办大事"），对"苏联侵略"要进行"massive retaliation"，不然盟国会像多米诺骨牌（domino theory）那样一个个倒下。国务卿杜勒斯还鼓吹冒险的"brinkmanship"（战争边缘政策）。为防"赤化"，艾本人提出了向中东国家提供军事、经济援助的"Eisenhower Doctrine"。

德怀特·艾森豪威尔
(Dwight Eisenhower)
共和党(1953—1961)

5. 肯尼迪任期

肯尼迪于1961年开始执政，善耍嘴皮，行文讲究对仗，替代法国，一步步陷入越南战争。在就职演说里呼吁"ask not what your country can do for you, ask what you can do for your country"。"ask not...ask..."这一句型多次有人模仿。另一名言是"rising tide lifts all the boats"（水涨船高，国强皆受益）。他仿"New Deal"提出了"New Frontier"，要用拓荒精神来处理国内外大事，并与苏联展开太空竞赛。入侵古巴猪湾（Bay of Pigs)惨败遭抨击，又仿谚语"Success has many fathers, but failure is an orphan."而造出了"Victory has a hundred fathers, but defeat ia an orphan."（胜利争功劳，失败人人逃）。为遏制共产主义，发誓"We shall pay any price, bear any burden, meet any hardship, support any friend, oppose any foe, in order to assure the survival and the success of liberty."拼凑"Alliance for Progress"（争取进步联盟），拉拢拉美右派扼杀拉美左派政府。尤为严重扩大了越战（1957—1975），留下了"the Vietnam War syndrome"越战后遗症，原来医学术语，有了政治引申义，后来又引申为典型表现，意义更多了。他两次竞选出了个"Bailey Memoradum"事

约翰·肯尼迪
(John Kennedy)
民主党(1961—1963)

件,John Bailey 是一个州民主党主席,他写这个"内部文件"要天主教选民支持教友肯尼迪在 1956 年获得党代会副总统候选人的提名。1960 年肯在竞选总统时反而成了共和党离间他与新教选民关系的楔子。肯遇刺身亡至今仍是无头公案,有人怀疑是其天主教背景惹祸。近一两年,美国一直谣传要暗杀奥巴马,叫他成为肯尼迪第二。他的政府曾被理想化比作英国阿瑟王(King Arthur)宫廷所在地 "Camelot",现在指肯尼迪政府遗风,喻总统盛世王朝或白宫。肯当年是美国历史上最年轻的总统(46 岁),手下也年轻有为,吹成了"whiz kids"(神童)。其实肯政绩平平。Camelot 与 Whiz kids 后来都带有嘲讽意味。例如 Camelot 指他好色癖,不光彩的一面:Further Revelations from "the Dark Side of **Camelot**"。

林登·约翰逊
(Lyndon Johnson)
民主党(1963—1969)

6. L. 约翰逊任期

肯遇刺,手下 L. 约翰逊接班,名言是施政纲领 Great Society,标榜社会福利,打民权牌,吹"War on Poverty"。骂尼克松是个"chronic campaigner"(竞选精),自己却带头跟选民拥抱握手,大搞"press the flesh"。关于越战,他自己却要侵越美军带着战利品回国(Come home with that "coonskin on the wall.")。有人攻击他实行"big daddyism"(家长式统治),实际上是软硬兼施、讨价还价的"Johnson Treatment"。这样的南方政客遭人厌,有人就借当地生长的 magnolia(木兰)又造出了新词"smell of magnolias"(南方味)。

7. 尼克松任期

尼克松执政正值名记者和文学评论家 Henry Mencken 说的"In days of stress, in times of war,..."是涌现新词和旧词新义时代。其政府在水门事件前创造或流行的词语多达 35 个,如 black capitalism,鼓励黑人当老板。"New Federalism",州政府接管福利、教育和公交运输。"the (great) silent majority"(of my fellow Americans),指默默支持政府,不挑头闹事。尼主张撤军,让越南人打越南人的"Vietnamization","Nixon Doctrine"就是避免再打越南式地面战争(*No More Vietnam*)。他还将其他用语引入政治,如"game plan"(战略,策略,对策)本是橄榄球用语。期间,美国还创造了"hack it",不管遇到什么困难险阻,都要能克服并取得成功,

理查德·尼克松
(Richard Nixon)
共和党(1969—1974)

"Middle American"(美国中产阶级),"women's lib"等。

执政期间发生了"Watergate"事件,时逢杜撰政治词语的黄金时代。plumber,建筑上的管子工成为获取民主党全国委员会设在 Watergate 旅馆竞选情报的窃密组"the plumbers",因而"firestorm"案发引起公愤。说尼克松讲话有事实依据的是"operative statement",要作废或更正的是"inoperative statement"。《纽约时报杂志》称为:"a lie that no longer works",不能自圆其说的谎言。于是,他非法阻碍司法调查,捂盖子(cover-up),销毁文件为"deep-six"。尼解除调查水门事件的特别检察官 Archibald Cox 的职位,事发星期六晚造出了个"Saturday Night Massacre"的用语,后被模仿造出"Sunday Night Massacre"(指福特总统在 1975 年解除强硬保守派国防部长 James Schlesinger 和 CIA 局长 William Colby 等人职务)。由于举报者不愿透露身份,"Deep Throat"成了代号。尼克松对人手法粗暴,绰号"hardball"。他还搞政敌名单"enemies list"。说话还兜大圈子,now/then 不用,偏说"at this/that point in time",其助手还造出了"big enchilada"(要人,主要目标)。更有意思的是其 1972 年的"Committee for the Re-Election of the President"的缩略词"CRR"或"CREP"被同党的全国委员会主席 Robert Dole 改为"CREEP"后本无贬义,Watergate 案发后,不免使人联想到他在水门旅馆命人干偷偷摸摸、鬼鬼祟祟的窃听勾当。尼克松认为水门事件小题大做,Edward Kennedy 议员故意淹死女友而照样在联邦政府做官,可是"nobody drowned at Watergate"呀,为什么国会非要 impeach(弹劾)他不可呢? 另一个尼克松助手 John Ehrlichman 创造的另一个用语是"twisting slowly, slowly in the wind",原指提名出任公职者,在参议院批准任命中受反对党攻击折磨。现引申到领导人或官员受下台的折磨,犹如一具悬在空中受到风吹雨打的死尸,总统仍不肯体面安葬。

8. 福特任期

尼克松被迫辞职后,副总统福特接替,此人平庸(mediocre),继续推行缓和东西方关系的外交政策(détente),附带流行的词语有"quiet diplomacy"(悄悄外交)、"shuttle diplomacy"(穿梭外交)、"step-by-step diplomacy"(谨慎外交)、"back channel"(秘密联络渠道)、"bargaining chip"(讨价还价的筹码)等。

杰拉尔德·福特
(Gerald Ford)
共和党(1974—1977)

9. 卡特任期

1977 年由民主党人卡特执政,因是从事过花生交易的南方 Georgia 州人,贬称"peanut President"。因无多大成绩,只是个 one-term

President。他被认为是个"run against Washington"者,因为他没有在那个铺张浪费、贪污腐败、尔虞我诈(waste,corruption,fraud)的官场做过联邦官员,是个局外人(outsider),非 Washington pol,更受选民青睐。他到华府做官后,对"inside-the-Beltway politics"(华盛顿官场政治)来说是个 newcomer。他反对扶贫助残医疗制度(Mediaid System)中的"Waste, fraud, and abuse"。"three-martini lunch"是前佛州州长 Reuben Askew 所造,卡特用来反对不公正的税收政策,为什么企业家吃牛排和喝价值昂贵的马提尼酒的午餐,可免所得税,而工人吃香肠、奶酪却不能。1977 年,他要人们用"moral equivalent of war"打一场精神或道义仗,在和平时期作出牺牲,迎接能源危机等的挑战。他上任后从佐治亚州带来一些年轻的亲信,被贬为"Magnolia Mafia"(南方邦或死党)。夫人 Rosalynn Carter 被贬称为"steel Magnolia"。弟弟 Billy Carter 惹出"Billygate"风波,被指接受利比亚贿赂,要美放弃以色列而与阿拉伯国家示好。

吉米·卡特
(Jimmy Carter)
民主党(1977—1981)

peanut 还衍生出"peanut politician",无足轻重的政客玩弄无聊政治伎俩的"peanut politics"。二战期间,美国史迪威(Joe Stilwell)将军在日记中也称蒋介石为 peanut。

10. 里根任期

里根是个从小物起家的大总统,号称演说高手、交流大师(Gipper 或 Great Communicator),执政 8 年,是个 two-term President。任内创造和推广的用语约 20

罗纳德·里根
(Ronald Reagan)
共和党(1981—1989)

个,有他在与卡特竞选对问选民的"Are you any better off"(过上好日子了吗)? 煽动选民更换领导人。总统候选人辩论中不时地提醒对方:"There you go again."(你又说错了。)为击败对手,竟用"October Surprise",以在大选前夕(美大选在 11 月初举行)用出奇制胜的行动或策略,使对手处于被动地位。在竞选连任中用"morning in America",制造愉悦的政治气氛取胜。吹嘘其政府是"city on a hill",是治理的典范。他在经济上实行"supply-side economics",也作"Reaganomics"。外交上称苏联是"evil empire"。他推出"star wars"(星球大战计划),支持全世界的反共叛乱活动,削弱苏在第三世界的影响,称为"Reagan Doctrine"。里根从加州带了不少亲信任职,多数违规犯法,"sleaze(腐败) factor"使他很尴尬。最为严重的是 Iran-Contra affair/

scandal 伊朗—尼加拉瓜反政府组织丑闻始于 1985 年,里根政府背着国会与伊朗搞秘密武器交易,以"赎回"在黎巴嫩被绑架的美国人质,还把所得部分款项非法地秘密转交给反对尼加拉瓜政府的叛乱组织(contras)。此事使总统的两位助手被判刑。但他却是个"teflon(-coated) President",丑闻"不沾边",亲信又都一口咬定总统不知情。再则,他又以推脱术(plausible deniability)著称。其他词语如"Reagan Democrats"(投里根票是 older working-class voters,原民主党人或自由派候选人支持者)、"amen corner"(自动附和政党方针路线)、"amiable dunce"(和蔼可亲但无竞争力的领导人,滑稽可笑、无能耐的跟屁虫)、"stay the course"(坚持到底)、"level playing field"(平等或公平竞争),等等。

11. 老布什任期

老布什 1988 年当选总统,任内流行的词语有:党内保守派认为小布什虽属保守派,但"wimp factor"(懦弱)。与里根竞争党内总统候选人提名时,老布什曾将 Reaganomics 的保守的经济政策贬为"voodoo economics"。为改善国内外形象,布声称要领导一个更加有同情心的国家提出了"kinder and gentler nation"的口号,他认为领导人要有全球大视野,高瞻远瞩,创造了"the vision thing"。1988 年他倡导志愿服务,说要有"thousand points of light,"行善组织遍及全国。他与里根一样,曾誓言:"Read my lips. No new taxes." 要民主党人好好听着或看我嘴唇,决不增税。提倡以美国为世界警察的"new world order"。他与里根不同,既是个错误缠身"Velcro President"(维可牢,商标名),又因经济政策治标不治本而被贬称为"Revlon President"(一化妆品商标名)。1991 年第一次伊拉克战争前,要伊从科威特撤军的"line in the sand"(最后期限)。其他词语如:"move the goalposts"(取巧,中途改变游戏规则)、"inside the Beltway"(又称 Washington Beltway,美国统治阶级或政界等)、并衍生出"inside the Beltwayer"(美国领导人、政界人士、特权分子)、"inside the Beltway stuff"(政界或政府内部的小道消息)和"Beltway bandit"(专靠吃政府合同饭的中间商,犹如土匪路霸)、"out of the loop"(不在核心圈子里而不知情)等。

乔治·布什
(George Bush)
共和党(1989—1993)

12. 克林顿任期

1992 年民主党人克林顿击败老布什入主白宫,是位典型的演员式总统。尽管绯闻缠身,但经济搞得好,改革得力,是个 two-term President。任内仿 open covenants(意为公开外交)而创造的"New Covenant"作为施政纲领,但语义不明未用开。他重视南方白人保守派在大选中的影响力,造出了"bubba factor"、"bubba vote",及"bubba ticket"(与南方白人搭档竞选或正副总统候选人都是南方白人的竞选名单),叫竞选策划室(campaign office)"war room"。其夫人提出的扶老医疗保健计划,媒体不用 Medicare,造出了"Hillarycare",赞希拉里呼吁改革。克林顿砍 Social Security 社会福利开支,与共和党理念一致时,宣告 New Deal 政策不再作为民主党施政方针后说:"The era of big government is over."(即民主党自 F. 罗斯福社会保障的时代结束了。big government 在共和党人看来,主要指政府对经济和个人自由干涉过多,社会福利开支过大,所以以前称民主党政客是 tax-and-spend Democrats。)他指责南斯拉夫在波黑和科索沃实行"ethnic cleansing"(民族、种族和宗教清洗),力倡 Clinton Doctrine(克林顿主义)。声称:"需要用科索沃方式干预全球的"人道主义危机。"实际上公开借口对外干涉。1999 年的 Kosovo War(科索沃战争)就是具体体现。任内发生了涉嫌经济舞弊的"Whitewater"事件和性丑闻的"Monicagate"或"zip(per)gate"。与竞选主题(campaign message)一致或按党纲或候选人的方针路线行事的是"on-message",相反的是"off-message"。

威廉·克林顿
(William Clinton)
民主党(1993—2001)

13. 小布什任期

2000 年共和党人老布什总统的儿子小布什击败民主党候选人 John Kerry 后担任总统,在位 8 年(2001—2009),因经历"9·11"恐怖事件,发动阿富汗和第二次伊拉克战争及新保守派(neocon)的兴衰,新词语不少。例如为改变牛仔式保守派形象打扮成"compassionate conservative",打捆零星捐款"bundling"凑数。"chad"原本是"孔屑"转义为"(用手工)重新计票"。政府要员都是新保守派的干将,利用"9·11"事件,除发动反基地(Al Qaeda)的阿富汗战争外,为推行大中东计划,包括"freedom agenda"(自由计划)在内,制造舆论,时任 CIA 局长 George Tenet 坚称伊拉克拥有 WMD(大规模杀伤性武器"weapons of mass destruction")时说:"It's a slam dunk case"和"It's slam dunk.""slam dunk"由篮球的"灌篮"转义为 n. "a sure thing" or "a great success", adj. "decisive, without doubt"。于是 2003 年发动了第

乔治·W·布什
(George W. Bush)
共和党(2001—2009)

二次伊拉克战争。伊战时采取国防部长"Rumsfeld's strategy",用高科技武器破敌,靠"shock and awe"震慑。当伊军被打垮,萨达姆政权被推翻,他不说 overthrow/topple the government 或 replace the government 而用"regime change"(政权更替)。之后,小布什宣布"mission accomplished",军队作战任务完成了吗?事实上伊国内恐怖活动不断,他又宣布三字经战"war on terror"。因"terror fatigue",媒体用"insurgent"代替 terrorist。terrorist 更多指宗教意识形态驱使搞恐怖活动,insurgent 建立政权的意愿更强烈一些,两词略有细微区别。jihardist 也因观点不同而理解各异,既可作"holy warrior"(圣战战士),也可作"unholy terrorist"讲。由于国内党斗,面对伊战发生龃龉,布什政府要"stay the course"(顶住),决不"cut and run"(原〈航海〉弃锚开航;〈俚语〉逃跑,溜号,引申到政治上作仓促撤退),攻击民主党人是"cut-and-run Democrats"。将嫌疑人送到国外刑讯逼供,婉称特别引渡"rendition"不用"shipping the captives out for torture",还施用"waterboarding"(水刑)。他称伊朗、朝鲜等国结成邪恶轴心"axis of evil"。借口为不让敌人抢先发动袭击而主张采取 preemptive strike/military action,即先发制人的打击或军事行动(实为战争或侵略的委婉语)的"Bush Doctrine"。策划以街头政治开路搞颠覆的"Color/Flower Revolution"。他还常犯语法错误,挖苦为"Bushisms",常犯 blooper(愚蠢错误,洋相)或 redundancy 的错误。如:"**mis**understimate"和"**em**better"及 **Is** our children learning? Our priorities **is** our faith 等。其父老布什也犯 Bushisms。小布什仿"revolution of rising expectations"(兑现不了的承诺就会引发社会动乱)而造出了"soft bigotry of low expectations"(期望低而产生的不明显的歧视或偏见)。期间出现的其他政治词语还有"values voters"具有社会保守派价值观的选民,"bunker mentality"领导人犯错即将丢官或面对高涨批评而产生的孤注一掷的辩解或自卫心卫,"bridge to nowhere"耗费大量公款而未给多数人带来便利或利益的工程,chicken hawks 鸡奸男童的男性色魔,"faith-based"基于信仰的,宗教的,"culture of corruption"腐败之风,"benchmarks"共和党人犹如 God 不离嘴似将此字作为判断表现的试金石、尺度、标准或基准。此外,有人还将 netroots(由 Internet 和 grassroots 拼缀而成)由"普通网民"转义为"发展迅速的自由派博客世界"(blogosphere),而发展较慢的"rightroots"则意为"保守派博客世界"。

二、英国

二战前后有两位首相值得一提。一位是反面人物张伯伦(Nevil Chamberlain),1937—1940 年任首相期间,他这位有"黑伞男儿"(black umbrella boy)之称的首相对德、意、日采取姑息政策(policy of appeasement),纵容了法西斯发动二战。另一位是二战英雄丘吉尔首相(1940—1945;1951—1955),战后他是美苏冷战 iron curtain(铁幕)的鼓吹者,从他 1946 年鼓吹至 1989 年柏林墙的拆除或 1991 年苏联解体,双方进行长达 40 多年冷战,这有他的"功劳"。iron curtain 是西方政客和新闻界指责前苏联及前东欧国家二次大战后为阻止同欧美各国进行政治、军事、文化意识形态交流而设置的一道无形屏障。1946 年丘吉尔在美国密苏里州富尔顿(Fulton)市演讲时说,苏联设置了一道铁幕,隔断了欧洲大陆。此字并非 Winston Churchill 所造,而是由纳粹德国宣传部长弋培尔(Joseph Goebbels)1944 年在日记中首先使用,但由丘吉尔带头用开的。此后,类比构词出现。如:bamboo curtain 竹幕是西方政客和新闻界称中国为阻止同西方资本主义国家进行政治、军事、文化和意识形态的交流而设置的一道无形屏障,sand curtain 沙幕指为将以色列和阿拉伯国家分割开而设置的一道无形的犹如沙漠将他们隔开一样的屏障,paper curtain 纸幕,指旧南非白人政权宣布紧急状态后对各方面交流设置的阻碍或障碍,Jim Crow curtain 美国对黑人实行种族歧视和隔离而设置的一道无形屏障,lace curtain 网眼屏障指为阻止前苏联人到美国新英格兰地区旅行而设置的一道无形屏障,等等。此后还有其他一些首相,但未造出多少新字。从下列首相开始后,因欧盟问题的新词语增多。

1. 从希思到卡拉汉首相任期(1970—1979)

英国首相自保守党领袖希思任首相(1970—1974)期间,积极促进欧洲统一,1973 年倡导英国加入欧盟成立前欧洲共同体(European Community)。他被普通议员造反(backbench revolution)倒台后,由工党领袖威尔逊第二次出任首相(1964—1970;1974—1976),再次就英国加入共同体的条款进行谈判,并于1975 年经全民公决通过而最终使英成为其成员国。英国围绕着反对赞成加入前欧洲共同市场和欧洲共同体及现欧洲联盟造出了一些新词,流行一时。如:anti-European 反欧洲(统一)派,指反对西欧在社会、文化或经济上的统一或一体化派(的),或指反对加入欧盟的;早先指英国反对加入欧洲共同市场或欧洲共同体派。anti-Maastrichtian 反欧洲联盟条约的,反对欧盟的、反对欧洲一体化的。Euroskeptic/Eurosceptic/Eurodoubt(指反对欧盟扩大权限的)欧洲怀疑论者,(尤指英国)对前欧洲共同市场、欧洲共同体或现欧洲联盟的怀疑派。此外,也指对欧洲统一的怀疑派。英国是欧共体中三心二意的成员国,有着深刻的历史原因,二次大战后,它追随美国,与美保持一种特殊关系(special relationship),有的重要政治家如撒切尔夫人,宁当美国的小伙伴,也不当欧洲的头头。当初欧盟的前身共同市场和欧洲共同体成立时,英国就拒不参加,后来怕孤立而要求参加时又两次遭到法国总统戴高乐将军的否决,怕它成为美国的特洛伊木马。德国和法国历史上都曾是英国死敌,如欧盟实行政治、经济一体化,英国怕主权交给这两个欧共体发起国,所以疑虑重重,走在其他大国的后面。Europhile(尤指英国)亲前欧洲共同市场、欧洲共同体或现欧洲联盟者(由 Euro 和-phile 组合而成)。Europhilia(尤指英国)对前欧洲共同市场、欧洲共同体或现欧盟的亲善态度(由 Euro-和-philia 组合而成)。Europhobe(尤指英国)恐前欧洲共同市场、欧洲共同市场或现欧洲联盟者,恨前欧洲共同市场、欧洲共同市场或现欧洲联盟者(由 Euro-和-phobe 组合而成)。Europhobia(尤指英国)对前欧洲共同市场、欧洲共同体或现欧洲联盟的恐怖或憎恨(由 Euro-和-phobia 组合而成)。Europhoria 对欧洲统一的兴奋(症)(由 Euro 和 euphoria 组合而成)。Eurofanatic 尤指英国狂热支持前欧洲共同体或欧盟派。Pro-European 亲欧派的,支持西欧社会、文化或经济联合的;以前赞成英国加入欧洲共同体或共同市场的;现赞成或支持与欧洲联盟保持更紧密关系的。eurocrat 原欧洲共同市场、欧洲经济共同体、欧洲共同体、现欧洲联盟官员或官老爷;尤指英国不满其决策、早先加入这个组织国家派出的高级官员。

1976 年威尔逊因经济衰退等问题宣布辞职,由同党的卡拉汉(James Callaghan)接任首相职位(1976—1979),此人平庸,无建树。

2. 从撒切尔夫人到梅杰首相任期(1979—1997)

保守党人撒切尔夫人(Margaret Thatcher)在与希思争夺党权中获胜,接着在大选中击败工党出任首相(1979—1990),在位近 13 年,以强硬著称而获"Iron Lady"的外号,还因推行不分财富和收入的多寡,一律按比例交税的"poll tax"(人头税),不得人心下台。后来的政府将之改为 council tax(家庭房地产税)。这些政策和主张在政府内部分成三派:"dry/dries"坚定支持其强硬政策派;"wet/wets"对其这种政策持反对立场的反对派。[据 Oxford,"wet"作政治用语,一般指对有争议问题持自由派或中间派观点的政界人士;而 Safire's Political Dictionary 指抨击自由派和相信和解的政界人士用语;英国英语指鸽派(doves)];"dampish persuasion"指不坚定支持其这种政策的中间派。任内其他词语还有:Single European Act《欧洲单一文件》:经欧盟理事会(Council of the European Union)批准,于 1987 年生效,旨在消除欧洲联盟各国内存在的贸易壁垒,建立单一的欧洲共同市场,给予欧洲议会(European Parliament)更大的权力。"subsidiarity",Oxford 的定义是 the principle that a central authority should have a subsidiary function, performing only those tasks which cannot be performed effectively at a more immediate or local level,此处的"a central authority"令人难以理解。英国自加入欧洲共同体和欧盟后,一直若即若离,反对者大有人在,尤其是反对欧盟一体化(integration),反对成立欧洲中央政府。

subsidiarity 这个字的意思就是英国尤其在撒任首相时,一再提出的反对欧盟中央集权,干涉成员国的主权,这就是"中央权力机构只干中下层机构不得力的事,"才是此字的真正意思。《经济学家》周刊认为,此词在英国成了"限制欧盟干涉(英国事务)"的代名词。见例句:

There might be more opt-outs along the lines Britain demanded at Maastricht. '**Subsidiarity**'—code for limiting interference from Brussels—could be more strictly defined. (*The Economist*)

Falklands venture 福克兰群岛战争,指 1982 年英国和阿根廷之间因福克兰群岛(也称"马尔维纳斯群岛")的主权归属之争而发生的战争。虽然阿根廷战败,但并非放弃对该岛的主权要求。用 venture 而不用 war 表明胜负难定而具有风险。Falklands factor 福克兰群岛战争的影响:1982 年,英国和阿根廷因福克兰群岛主权归属之争发生战争,本来颇不得人心的撒切尔保守党政府自打赢这场战争后,经济情况并未改善,可是抖了一下殖民帝国昔日的威风,欺负弱国,于是又一次使该党取得大选的胜利。这说明外交对内政的影响。

因党倾轧、纷争不断,而撒又刚愎自用,被讽刺为"Style War"(一标题)(美国里根提出的"Star War"的谐音)。她最后让位给梅杰(John Major)(1990—1997),仍对梅较温和政策处处掣肘,于是梅杰的身边人抱怨说,"You can't win"(你怎么讨好她都不领情)。他执政时流年不利,闹上"mad-cow disease"(疯牛病),使英国人什么都可以吃但牛肉除外([we can eat]anything but beef),欧洲各国抵制英国任何牛制食品。在外交政策上也跟欧盟产生重大分歧。虽然经济情况好,但 1997 年大选还是败北。梅杰自创的词语只有一个"back to basics",针对道德水准下滑提出"回归传统道德准则"的政治口号,强调个人的责任感,但公众解读为恢复传统观念。此外,关于欧盟和其他事件的词语还有:"opt-out"不参与,脱离:为英语中固有的词语。20 世纪 80 年代后期特指英国的学校或医院脱离地方政府控制,如这类机构可被称为 opt-out schools 和 opt-out hospitals。到了 90 年代初,词义进一步扩大,指英国在签署 1991 年马斯特里赫特条约时,梅杰坚持对其中某些条款(opt-out clauses)如货币联盟采取的不参与政策,以免欧盟干涉内政。"single European currency" 单一欧洲货币。统一发行欧元(euro)是走向统一的一大步。这是《马斯特里赫特条约》(Maastricht Treaty)规定的,但英国和丹麦暂不参与,因国内对此问题尚存在较大分歧。

weighted votes 加权票,人口多增加的票数。此处"权"指秤砣,亦即加重份。One Nation 一国论。指英国不能因社会不平等而分裂成两个国家。1950年,英国的一些保守党议员发表了名为 *One Nation* 的小册子,提出了保守党应为国家社会公益事业作出更大贡献,防止国家分裂。这种观点对次年保守党执政后的政策产生了很大的影响。在 20 世纪 90 年代,保守党左翼和右翼就此问题展开辩论,使该论调又活跃起来。"Spycatcher affair"《抓间谍者》丑事,*Spycatcher* 一书由原任英国军情五处(MI5)特工 Peter Wright 1987 年所写,不但披露了军情五处的非法行为,而且谴责安全部门耍阴谋,反对 1974—1976 年任工党首相威尔逊。英国最高法院借故禁止出版,但在美国和加拿大等国立即成为畅销书,使当时的保守党政府极为难堪。Spycatcher affair 泛指限制新闻言论自由。"Stone of Scone" 斯科恩石,命运之石,1296 年英格兰国王爱德华一世从苏格兰把此石劫走,置于英王加冕的威斯敏斯特教堂(Westminster Abbey)。1996 年伊丽莎白女王决定物归原主,还给苏格兰。该石象征苏格兰被英格兰征服,苏格兰和英格兰国王都曾在加冕时用过此石,亦可称为"加冕石"或"登基石"。"the West Lothian question" 难以回答的问题,难题。1997 年英国议会在辩论是否向苏格兰放权时,工党议员 Jam Dalyell 一再提出这个问题:如果英国同意放权,苏格兰成立了议会,英国议会不再对苏格兰地方政府负责,英格兰议员将随之丧失对苏格兰内部事务的发言权,仍留在英国议会里的苏格兰议员仍享有对英格兰事务的发言权,而这是迄今英国拟向地方放权中的主要问题,因西洛锡安选区的议员首先提出而得名。

3. 从布莱尔到布朗首相任期(1997—2010)

1997 年工党领袖布莱尔(Tony Blair)开始长期担任首相直至 2007 年。他 1997 年大选成功改变了工党在野 18 年的地位,也使他成为 1812 年利夫普尔之后最年轻的英国首相。工党在 1997 年、2001 年和 2005 年举行的大选中三次击败保守党。他执政后积极倡议解决北爱尔兰问题,取得了重大成果,爱尔兰共和军(IRA)的 Troubles(暴力活动)已基本停止。在对外政策上,追随美国,在 1999 年科索沃战争(Kosovo War)和 2003 年的伊拉克战争中表现得尤为明显。他标榜 the third way,其实与美克林顿总统一样,即将左派和右派的理念相结合而形成的新中间路线。美英两国都不希望在政策上大起大落。(见**人物的重要性**)

他执政时创造了一些新词语并使有的词语流行起来。如:"New Labour"。"Old Labour" 指坚持公有制和以所谓的社会主义为基础、不放弃党章第四条(Clause Four)的工党。他还与小布什合谋侵伊,闹出 "intelligencegate",声称伊 45 分钟之内就能部署生化武器,用假情报误导国内外公众。这一假情报导致联合国前伊拉克武器核查人员、英国国防部武器专家凯利(David Kelly)自杀身亡和军情六处负责人提前退休。这一情报丑闻也称"伊拉克丑闻"(Iraqgate)。

此外,布还于 2006 年闹出 "campaign-finance scandal"/"cash-for peerage affair"(竞选资金或金钱换爵位丑闻),几个富翁捐款给工党竞选,布就建议女王授予爵位并获得上议院席位。此事使他本人和工党都受到很大打击。见例句:

If anything, his growing isolation seems to be fueling something of a martyr complex. Blair and his innermost circle have been dragged into a nasty **campaign-finance scandal—the cash-for-peerages affair** in which donors allegedly gave big loans to the Labour Party(and indeed the Conservative opposition)in exchange for seats in the House of Lords. Blair has been questioned twice, though not as a suspect. (*Newsweek*)

其他方面的一些词语还有:"Clause Four"第四条款:指工党1918年制定的关于该党致力于工业和服务业公有制的党章第四条条款,即"国有化条款"。拥护者为工党左派,反对者为右派。"committology"授权执行,指欧盟机构之一的欧盟委员会(European Commission)做出的决定,授权成员国委员会加以实行。"convergence"经济融合论(=economic convergence);(在前欧洲共同体和现欧洲联盟内为反对某一成员国的不合作态度或离心倾向,各成员国实现的)联合;(结成的)同盟;(不同政治制度国家间的)趋同共存论。"convergence thesis"融合论,中间派理论认为,资本主义和社会主义的极端性都已经消失,正逐渐消除分歧,趋于一致。"democracy deficit"民主赤字,指政府出台的某项政策向群众解释不够而遭唾弃,如欧盟宪法2005年在法国、荷兰遭公投否决便是一例。英国未举行公决。

2007年布莱尔无奈去职,财政大臣布朗(Gordon Brown)接班。布朗任期内,经济不振,丑闻不断。如expensegate不但执政的工党,其他两党领袖也都陷入骗取报销的丑闻中。另一个丑闻是"Whitehall employs dozens of union officials at taxpayers' expense"(2009/9/14 *The Times* 的标题),这是花钱"养人"。《泰晤士报》报道说,英国政府10个部门花纳税人的钱雇佣46名全职、87名兼职员工专为工会服务,每个部门支付给这些人的薪金总额在25万美元至748万美元之间,每年总计可达1662万美元。最后还闹出lobby scandal,指有大臣受贿,为个人或企业在法律的兴废上为其服务。

英国工党历来与工会(Trade Union)组织关系密切。来自英国选举委员会的数据显示,工会组织今年前6个月为工党提供约897万美元资金支持,占工党同期全部筹款金额的69%。这种情况犹如美国的Labor Union是民主党的竞选基地或票仓(political base)一样。

4. 保守党和自由民主党组成联合政府(2010年5月—　)

2010年5月的大选结果出人意料,两个大党——保守党和工党竟没有一个获得过半数议会席位,尽管保守党得票多于工党,于是该党不得不与理念不同的第三党自由民主党组成二战后第一个联合内阁(coalition government),由保守党领袖戴维·卡梅伦(David Cameron)出任首相,自民党党魁克莱格(Nick Clegg)出任副首相,不过,两党能联合多久是个大问题。由于两人长相酷似而有人创造个新词"Cleggeron"来称呼他俩。卡梅伦年仅43岁,是英200年来最年轻的首相。

第三节 党语和党争用语初探

在西方,党争激烈,相互攻讦是党派本性,party politics 无时无地不在,党争用语应运而生,阅读外刊时稍不小心,就会出错。要学得活,懂得透,须常读外刊,跟踪语言最新发展,拓展有关政治文化背景知识,因为党争用语随着美英国内形势的发展而不断产生。研究它有助于丰富报刊语言知识和提高外刊阅读能力。

新闻用言应是简明易懂的语言,如 *Newsweek* 的专栏作家 Fareed Zakaria 所写评论,均是开门见山,句子简短,用词大众化,堪称新闻语言的典范。*The New York Times* 的报道文章也是如此。然而,报刊因自造或援引的一些词语里,难免出现 euphemism,gobbledegook(官样文章,冗长而令人费解的话语),bafflegab(在政府报告或官方谈话中用一些易混淆和糊模不清的词悟,令人费解糊涂官场行话),officialese,Pantagonese(五角大楼行话)。CIAese 等等 weasel words(故意含糊其辞的词语),这犹如 George Orwell 所写的《1984》这本书里创造的 newspeak,弃 bad 而用 ungood 等一大堆弯弯绕、令人费解的俚语行话。因为除各党政要外,它们还雇用 wordsmith(词语专家,忠实地将主要的想法写成朗朗上口稿子的笔杆子或捉刀人),phrasemaker(在已写好的初稿上以警句点缀者,以增加稿子的分量),ghost 或 ghostwriter(捉刀人)和 speechwriter 等杜撰词语的高手,他们所说所写,媒体为求新而很感兴趣,所以常见诸报端,不过只有总统一级的撰稿人,身份才公开。他们有的是著名历史学家或专栏作家。

一、党语与党争用语之异同

党语与党争用语有所不同。党语往往指政党的行话或切口(cant),有时非党人士不懂。有的词同义异。如:

In 1932 Smith and Roosevelt competed for the Democratic nomination and bitterness developed between the two. Smith **"took a walk"** during the first term of the New Deal, and attacked Roosevelt in the 1936 campaign. (Willian Safire)

"take a walk"字面上因与党内领导意见不合,斗嘴后外出散步,实指脱党。其后,或跳槽,或另组新党。再如"go fishing"或"sit it out"也是早有的党语,指"身在曹营心在汉"。这种人 bolt(脱党)后,党魁就将他 read out of the party(宣布为不受欢迎的党员;原为宗教用语,逐出教门之义)。英国工党的"New Labour","Clause Four"(见**英国政党**介绍)和没有冠词的"conference"(工党发表的年会声明)也是典型的党语。党语不但美英政党有,中国也有,在反映解放战争的电影里,国民党将领总是"为党国效劳"不离口,共产党人则念念不忘

"为人民服务"。应该说明,有的党语与党争用语意思交叉,说是党语,又是党争用语。党争用语是带有党派色彩的语言"partisanspeak",而本节重点所论是共和民主两党用语,有些是党争用语,有的是普通意义或用法的词语。有的仅是理念不同用词各异。《华盛顿邮报》专栏作家 Roger Rosenblatt 早在 1978 年 7 月撰文说,因两党的政治文化背景不同,表达同一意思,却用词迥异,并举出了下列义同词异的党语:

Democrats	**Republicans**	**Democrats**	**Republicans**
total	corporate	disturbed	sloshed
influence	clout	innovations	software
truth	bottom line		

二、党争用语产生的原因

政党不同,理念各异。一上台总要刮新风,走新路,创新词。即使同一执政党,新人接班,也要讲话,令听者耳目一新。如若在野,更要唱反调,出奇招。竞选期间,各色政党与候选人纷纷登场吆喝,争取选民支持,新党语便满天飞,旧词屡翻新意也不足为奇。

党争用语是政党斗争专用语,有其独特性。如美国的"pro-life"、"pro-choice"、"rendition"、"quatoes"等就是典型的例子;有的如 climate change,尽管美国共和党和联合国召开的 United Nations Climate Change Conference 等都在用,但用意不同,各有解释。再如 *swift-boat*,共和党用作"揭穿(John Kerry 战功的谎言)等"讲,民主党认为是"攻击和诽谤(该党候选人)";还有的为社会所接受,便成了大众语言。

美国共和党人嫌"right wingers"难听,自称"conservatives"。此字有褒义,指维护传统;民主党人以"progressives"自诩,共和党人却爱叫他们"liberals",在此有影射放任过头、随心所欲的贬义。

党同伐异或政党相互攻讦是党争用语产生的一个最重要原因。共和党恨民主党人是"the blame-America-first crowd"(事事先责怪美国的那帮家伙)。民主党形容保守、顽固的共和党人犹如"floo-floo birds"(总在原地盘旋的恋窝鸟)、"Neanderthal wing"(停留在石器时代的死脑筋)和"dinosaur wing"(犹如恐龙般的顽固派)等。2004 年大选中,民主党总统候选人克里(John Kerry)挑战共和党时任总统小布什,双方进行电视辩论,共和党称克里辩论是"John Kerry's weaseling"(油腔滑调,像个黄鼠狼),而民主党则捧他是"John Kerry's nuanced approach"(明察秋毫)。因两党在竞选,这类口水仗司空见惯,各方都要雇佣媒体或舆论导向顾问"spin doctor/master"来捧场助阵。两党争斗尤其追求用语

的新奇,或故意含糊其辞,于是党腔党调层出不穷,令读报者一时难以理解。例如:

Considering Bush's astonishingly ambitious domestic agenda—don't forget **tort reform** and expanding No Child Left Behind to encompass accountability in secondary education—it was surprising that his second Inaugural Address was so focused abroad.（2005/1/31 *Newsweek*）

"tort reform"是民主党故意含糊其辞的用语,连"Double Trouble Speak"一文的作者对此用法也感到纳闷。

从克林顿掌权至小布上台以来,两党竞争更加激烈,各自招募类似中国师爷或幕僚的大师、顾问"guru"、民意测验专家或语言大师,新造的党争用语更多,尤其是当时的共和党更为"出众"。《美国新闻与世界报道》在2005年7月4日的一篇题为"Double Trouble Speak"文章中说:

In politics, Republicans and Democrats seem to be evolving separate language or, at least long lists of different nouns. Democrats warn of "global warming"; Republicans talk calmly about "climate change."… Other Republican/Democratic partisan pairs include quotas/goals and timetables, campus race preferences/race sensitive admissions… school choice/school vouchers.（在政治上,共和党和民主党似乎都在逐渐形成各自的语言,或者说他们至少还有一大堆义同词异的名词。民主党告诫人们要注意全球变暖,共和党则平静谈论气候变化。……两党其他的一对对党派用语还有……）

三、党争用语种种

1. 竞选口号和人身攻击

自1853年以来,美国都是民主党和共和党轮流执政。为争取选民,竞选人能否哗众取宠、笼络人心是关键。他们往往以经济、战争与和平和家庭价值观等作为竞选主题"campaign theme/message",其中经济往往是最大热门,打经济牌也最吃香。如1952年执政的民主党仍想以经济政绩吸引选民,于是打出的口号是:"You Never had It So Good."现常被反对党用来抨击政府的弊病。1980年共和党总统候选人里根的口号是:"Are You better off than You Were Four Years Ago?""你们的生活是否比四年前过得好?"暗示民主党执政四年不如四年前在共和党领领导下富裕。1992年民主党候选人克林顿的口号是:"It's the Economy, Stupid!"这次竞选的关键是经济! 他抓住了老布什执政四年经济不振的软肋。经济低迷时,打经济牌管用,如2008年的大选,奥巴马大胜,有人认为是1992年克林顿竞选时的翻版。经济繁荣时,候选人就更多地关注其他问题。如1952年大选时,民主党虽然克服了经济大恐慌"Great Depression",取得了反法西斯战争胜利,但朝鲜战争困扰着选民。共和党就打和平牌,其竞选口号是:"I Like Ike."艾克是候选人艾森豪威尔(Dwight Eisenhower)之昵称,二战功臣。选民一听,倍感亲切,相信这位叱咤风云的将军定能摆脱朝鲜战争,使美国重新走上和平安定的道路。Ike承诺:"I shall go to Korea."(我定要结束朝鲜战争。后来,go to Korea已引申为亲自抓难题。2000年大选时,克林顿执政八年,经济情况良好,但性丑闻闹得沸沸扬扬,国内面临宪法危机"constitutional crisis"和政界大分裂,选民渴望回归传统道德观,于是小布什靠"Compassionate Conservatism"和"A Uniter","Not A Divider"这两个审时度势的口号击败了Al Gore。还有的年轻候选人抓住对手年老守旧弱点。如1996年年轻的克林顿竞选连任的口号是:"Building a Bridge to the Twenty-first Century",即承诺要架设一座通往21世纪的桥梁,使选民联想到共和党对手多尔(Bob Dole)及前任总统老布什都属于旧世纪的人物,这一来就占了上风。

在竞选中,党争除口号外,两党候选人还相互攻讦,人身攻击"character assassination",抹黑对手"mudslinging"或"negative campaigning"。如1994年大选,民主党政府的内政部长Harold Ickes侮辱共和党总统候选人杜威(Thomas Dewey)是"man on the wedding cake",来影射他身材矮小。御用文人还攻击他是:"He is the only man able to walk under a bed without hitting his head."再如1940年大选,共和党总统候选人威基(Wendell Wilkie)被民主党政府的内政部长Harold Ickes嘲讽为"a barefoot boy from Wall Street"或"a simple, barefoot Wall Street lawyer",即别看他那温让恭谦让的样子,他是经济上发了迹的大富翁。1992年总统竞选期间,老布什骂克林顿及其竞选搭档戈尔"these two bozos"(这两个笨蛋)。2008年大选中,共和党副总统候选人佩林(Sarah Palin)诽谤奥巴马,说他与恐怖分子为伴(Our opponent is someone who sees America, it seems, as being so imperfect that he's palling around with terrorists.)(*Financial Times*)。

党争不但表现在两党,党内各派在初选中争取总统候选人提名战中攻讦也相当激烈。例如2000年小布什在与John McCain角逐提名时,就影射McCain领养的黑人小女孩是私生子。希拉里在与奥巴马选战中,克林顿就暗中散布说,现在还不是黑人当总统的时候。

2. 社会政策和主张

从社会政策和主张上看,共和和民主两党理念对立:前者是保守派,既得利益集团"vested interests"主张恢复固有道德价值观,强调法制,反对堕胎和同性恋,较少关心少数民族的处境和贫苦民众;后者是自由派,争民权,争少数民主权利,反对种族歧视,对堕胎、同性恋、吸毒等社会问题较宽容。双方在措辞上更是挖空心思,造出一批新词语。反对堕胎用"anti-abortion"就达意了,共和党杜撰出了"pro-life",令人想到其珍爱生命,民主党主张堕胎就是扼杀生命;民主党则造出"pro-choice",意为堕胎与否,妇女有权选择,不是共和党说了算。此外,共和党称胎儿是"fetus",而民主党则委婉地称之为"uterine contents",暗示子宫之物并非生命,"pro-life"是错误的。

由于两党对待种族歧视和民权运动的立场有别,故在对待浸礼会牧师、民权运动积极分子 All Sharpton 的评价迥异。共和党称 "racial charlatan Al Sharpton",即种族蛊惑分子阿尔·沙普顿,民主党则捧为 "civil rights activist Al Sharpton",民权运动斗士。

在宗教信仰用词上,民主党用 religious,2001 年小布什领导的共和党政府则用 "faith-based",意为宗教可以不信,但信仰则不是可有可无,事实上在他们的心里都明白,不过是义同词异、换换说法而已。不过,从词源上讲,faith-based 与 religion-based 还是有区别的,前者用于非宗教信仰的场合,且有贬义,后者则相反。共和党反对达尔文的进化论,2005 年秋天提出了 "intelligence design" 的谬论,实际是变相的上帝造人说。在这场争论中,共和党领袖小布什总统公开支持智慧设计论(见《精选本》四版 "The Evolution Wars")。里根任总统时,共和党提倡公立学校的中学生举行 "school prayer",集体祈祷。里根任总统后,共和党保守势力东山再起,被称之为 "Reagan Revolution",许多宗教名人如已故道德多数派领导人、电视传教的福音派牧师 Jerry Falwell 等福音派教士大力支持共和党,还企图将其改造成宗教性质的保守党,而共和党则将宗教作为拉选票的一张王牌。当时宗教势力膨胀,这是个全球性趋势,"fundamentalists"(原教旨主义者)大行其道,美报有篇文章题为 "Why God Always Wins?" 作了详析。

在对待黑人中学生择校问题上,民主党用 "school choice"。共和党原来用 "school vouchers",即所谓择校,就是发给黑人穷学生助学金或采用抵税等办法。后来其造词专家 Frank Luntz 又把前两个词语改为 "parent choice 和 equal opportunity in education" 及 "opportunity scholarship",这种玩弄文字游戏,旨在离间民主党与黑人选民之间的关系。

对待就业、入学等受到种族歧视的黑人和性别歧视的妇女予以补偿照顾的计划 "affirmative action program",两党也互不相让。民主党要求共和党总统老布什订出 "goals and timetables",而共和党则斥之为 "quotas"。意为民主党要求在增加黑人、妇女就业和入学人数等问题上订出分阶段的目标和时间表,而共和党则认为这是"配额制",决不答应。这个计划遭到 "white backlash"(白人的强烈抵制)。民主党要求在入学问题要有 "race-sensitive admissions",即要考虑种族因素,受过歧视的黑人不能与白人的考生一视同仁,应予以照顾,另加 50 分。共和党斥之为"campus race preferences",即大学入学的种族偏向,是变相的种族主义。在 1978 年的"Bakke case"(白人考生贝克状告加州大学,因照顾黑人考生而使他未被录取)中,校方败诉,该计划受挫。

对待其他社会问题如保障制度(Social Security)和医疗保健的改革,两党主张相同,但用词不同。民主党用"privatization"和"private health care",而共和党用的是"personalization"和"free market health care"。专替共和党抠字眼的 Frank Luntz 在 Word That Work 一书中认为,private 含有负面意义,private schools/health care 等都有一定程度的排他性和垄断性,这与"equal opportunity"不搭界。不患寡而患收入机会不均,private 则意含某些人获得有利条件,因而不是 fair advantage。此外,prevatize Social Security 也跟私营公司一样,具有获利的动机,因而与"capitalism"一样,分胜负又会产生成功者和失败者。"personalize Social Security"则意味着对退休金储蓄归个人控制,是"personal accounts",而不是掌握在公司手里的"private accounts",民众较能接受。实际上就是词异义同,欺骗民众。

3. 经济政策和主张等

在经济问题上两党斗的很凶。关于遗产继承税,民主党和媒体都用"inheritance tax"(遗产税)或"estate tax"(不动产税),共和党则用"death tax",意为人死了还要上税,真是税多得不近人情。这给支持该税的民主党以沉重的打击。美国人上遗产税有一定的标准,例如到了价值达 50 万美元的不动产才上税。我们知道,民主党标榜为农场主、小商人、手工业者等中下层民众利益代言。而共和党代表的是大企业家和中上层民众的利益。要上遗产税的都是富人,共和党当然就反对了。共和党主张家庭价值观,民主党则赞成信仰自由。结果结了婚的 couple 反而要多上税,称为"marriage tax",而共和党人斥之为"marriage penalty"对结婚的惩罚:按照美国联邦税法,所得税是按照家庭收取的。因此,一对夫妇合并收入报税时,税金会要超出婚前分别报税,一些人认为这是对结婚的惩罚。对待税改,民主党用"tax reform",而共和党则用"tax simplification"。为什么?民众一听税收或价格改革等字眼就本能地意味着要加税或提价,这与我国老百姓的想法一样。所以,"reform"被"simplification"所代替似乎是理所当然。再如:"tax cuts",共和党用"tax relief",意为税收减免,"relief"这个字不免使人感到税负过重而要缓解或减轻,显然更中听。

共和党为维护企业家的利益,不喜欢雇员与业主打官司,更痛恨滥诉风。克林顿 1996 年争取竞选连任总统时,共和党不断攻击"trial lawyers"大量资助他竞选,指责他不关心经济发展,使出庭律师成为主要捐款集团。他们靠打官司赚钱，妨碍了工商业的发展。这是民主党用语。共和党用"personal injury lawyers"，也被贬称为"ambulance chasers"或简称"chasers"，指鼓动事故受害者起诉的律师，他们犹如随着救护车警报声赶到急救室的人。为煞滥诉风，共和党用"lawsuit abuse reform"，民主党用的"tort reform"，语意含混。再如：共和党用"climate change"而不用"global warming"也是这个原因，认为全球气候变化是正常现象，不必大惊小怪，用不着签订关于减排二氧化碳的《气候协议》，妨碍美国工商业发展，小布什政府直到 2007 年 12 月在印尼巴厘召开的联合国气候变化会议上才被迫同意该协议。

克林顿执政八年，一再提到"fast track trade authority"[贸易快速审批权(法)]。因"fast track"使许多共和党人联想到克林顿掌权的时代，以小布什为总统的共和党政府决定将之改为"trade promotion authority（TPA）"。人们很难认为促进贸易(法)就更好，倒是前者更贴切，因为总统不受国会干涉，有权与外国进行贸易谈判，一旦达成协定，国会必须在 60 天内议决。

对待非法来美打工的外国人，共和党直接用"illegal immigrants"。而民主党则委婉地称其为"undocumented immigrants/workers/aliens"，意为没有正式合法文件的移民、工人或外国人。

4. 战争、战俘和窃听政策等

2003 年美国发动了第二次伊拉克战争（the second Gulf/Iraq war），至 2009 年 8 月，已有四千多美国士兵阵亡，仍看不到结束的曙光。对战事的评价两党对立，共和党轻描淡写地说成是 military difficulties。民主党则毫不客气地用了"military quagmire"，使人联想美国已陷入越战那样的泥淖。民主党人要求撤军，就被称之"the cut-and-run Democrats"（仓促逃跑的民主党）或失败主义的民主党。见例句：

Democrats as well as a few Republicans will renew their calls for Rumsfeld's head, but it is doubtful that Bush will dump his Defense secretary before the elections. That might be seen as a concession to **the "Defeatocrats,"** as the GOP likes to call the opposition. (*Newsweek*)

在对待战争带来的平民死亡问题上，共和党用了委婉语"collateral damage"，而民主党则直接用"civilian death"，意思是说因轰炸等造成平民死亡就说死亡了，何必遮遮掩掩，说成是战争的"附带损伤"呢？至于战俘（POWs），小布什政府称之为从阿富汗战争抓到美国的恐怖分子，送到欧洲、非洲等地建立黑狱，刑讯逼供，因为美国法律禁止使用酷刑，拷打犯人。共和党用的是"rendition"这个字，即非常规引渡。而民主党则揭露真相，干脆用"shipping captives out for torture"。

小布什政府打着反恐的幌子,侵犯人权,大肆窃听,闹出了个"eavesdropping affair"。民主党直接用词义清晰的"wiretapping"或"eavesdropping"这两个字。共和党自知理亏,用了令人含糊不清的"electronic intercepts",似乎是说,为了反恐,只是电子拦截(窃听)而已。

四、党争用语的目的和用词特点

党争用语是为政治目的、政党利益服务的。目的不同,对象不同,用语也有所区别。语言的力量不在于你说什么,而在于听者的反应或感受。口号式用语和人身攻击是为了竞选获胜,对象是选民,口号必须一语中的,有的还要具有亲和力。例如:"It's the Economy, Stupid!"和"I Like Ike!"等就是很好的例证。再如"Contract with America"(在克林顿总统任期共和党提出的为平衡预算、增加国防开支、减税等10条议案的总称)使共和党在与民主党斗争和国会选举中赢得了"all-Republican Congress",并使当时的共和党保守派代表人物金里奇(Newt Gingrich)当选了众议院议长(House speaker),被称为"Gingrich revolution"或"the 1994 Republican revolution"。诋毁对手必须抓住对方的真正弱点加以攻讦,否则不但难以奏效,反受其害。例如2008年大选中共和党攻击奥巴马与恐怖分子为伍就是一例。社会、经济等方面利益,打的是文字仗。有的措辞尖刻,狠击对方,如:"pro-life","death tax"等。再如"tax simplification"与"tax reform"一字之差,前者似乎更中听些。如:"software"本是电脑用语,"clout"属常用词,作为党语则分别用来指"innovations"和"influence"。有的如"personalize health care"看似很好的例证,其实是玩弄文字游戏,用来公关,以说服民众。再如"guidelines",肯尼迪和约翰逊的民主党政府曾用来指衡量工资和物价水平是否有利于国民经济发展。共和党人尼克松上台后,代之以"yardsticks",意思是一样的,并无新意。有的想换换概念,未必达意。如共和党以"trade promotion authority"代替"fast track trade authority"和以"equal opportunity in education"代替"school choice"等就是如此。应该说明的是,其中有些词语还会随着政府(Administration)的更迭而变化,今后还会再造出更多的新词语。

George Orwell 在其1946年出版的"Politics and the English Language"一书中说:"Political Language has to consist largely of euphemism, question-begging and sheer cloudy vagueness."也就是说,为掩盖其目的,政客所用语言必然充满着委婉语、晦涩难懂和含糊其辞的语言。这是对政治用语特点的概括。

应该说明,民主党人卡特和克林顿总统都曾发布过政府使用简明语言的文件,旨在建立亲民形象,但被保守派共和党总统否决了。在美国,大凡保守派、且又有丑闻缠身的总统就反对使用一目了然的语言,如小布什总统就是典型。任内党争用语里委婉词多便说明了这一大特点。有的是为避免刺激受众。有的是为了掩盖真实意图故意含糊不清或故弄玄虚。这正如专栏作家 E. J. Dionne 发表的一篇题为"Catching Up on Catchwords"(1996/4/22—28 *The Washington Post National Weekend Edition*)(紧追紧赶时髦词)的评论中所说,许多竞选用时髦词和政治术语都"hide real meanings behind a load of cant"。如阿富汗和伊拉克战争,美英在人员、经济、政治等诸多方面付出了惨痛代价,单就金钱而言,美国从 2001 年至 2008 年 9 月,已花掉纳税人高达 8,580 亿美元。又如战争使伊拉克生灵涂炭,文明遭殃,基础设施损毁,逼迫共和党政府用"euphemism"。如弃用"civilian casualties and deaths"而用"collateral damage"就很典型。若用"civilian deaths"会刺激已死亡十万的伊拉克人起来造反。再如:小布什政府用"rendition"而不敢用"shipping captives out for torture",也是怕国内外对它口诛笔伐。又如:民主党怕刺激在美国的拉美移民,对待非法移民故意说"undocumented immigrants"。要维护黑人利益,不便直说,所以杜撰出了"race-sensitive admissions"(大学接收新学生的种族敏感性,究竟是同意还是反对照顾黑人学生入学?令人不解)和"sensitivity training"(心理疗法用语,所谓敏感训练,指一种集体提高能力的训练方法,通过无题或议程的集体自由讨论,增强参与者对人际关系的重视程度,从而提高人际交往能力)。金融危机,大手花钱的美国人又变成"budget-sensitive"(斤斤计较;抠门了),跟 conscious, friendly(environment-conscious/friendly)(关注环保的/环保的)一样成为时髦后缀了,有助于语言简练,用滥了反而费解。还有的用词晦涩难懂,如民主党要维护人民和工会的利益,常支持他们与资方对簿公堂,对待"滥诉"持消极态度,便故意用

连美国人也不明白的"tort abuse"。有的是操纵语言,混淆词义,蒙骗民众,难道"privatize Social Security"就产生成功和失败者,而 personalize 就不会吗?两者有何区别?

这些党争用语政府机关盛行,现又扩散到报刊,有时令外国甚至国内读者莫名其妙。

这些"partisanspeak"或"partyspeak"正如"Double Trouble Speak"这篇文章里的漫画讽刺性说明:"Why say something clearly when you can use a jaw-breaking euphemism?"(能用拗口的委婉语,为什么要直说呢?)这大概是两党应了前总统杜鲁门的那句名言:"If you can't convince them, confuse them."(说服不了就蒙。)

习　题

阅读理解文章

"Double Trouble Speak"(2005 7/4　*U. S. News & World Report*)

第四节 外交用语

英语系和新闻系及涉外专业的毕业生,有部分人要从事外事工作,外事无小事,是一件有关一个国家荣辱的大事。何况时下,我国门大开,有大外交之说,商务、文化、旅游,对外开放城市都涉及外事,攸关国家对外形象。因此,必须知己知彼,方能立于不败之地。外事工作要求知识面广,2001 年在西安召开的外事翻译研讨会上,一位年轻翻译大吐苦水,谈到她陪外交部领导人出访柬埔寨,谈到朗诺(越战时曾在美国支持下发动政变,出任首相),压根儿不知他是何人。美国一位懂得多国外文为几任总统作过翻译的 Vernon A. Walters 在回忆录 *Silent Missions* 一书里说,有的语句卡壳,感到世上没有比这更难受的事了。翻译得小心谨慎。记得周总理谈及外援时,翻译一不小心,加一个零,结果只有照白纸黑字上的数字援助。此外,我们应关注报刊上的外交文章,尤其要从中悟出西方外交上常用不实的 overstatement 和 understatement(见"**常见委婉语**")。

一、外交分类用语

1. 官方外交

外交分官方外交(official diplomacy)和非官方外交(unofficial diplomacy)。官方外交俗称"Track One diplomacy"(第一轨道外交),其形式多样,因外交是内政的延伸,都是为本国利益服务的。所以西方大国有实行恃强凌弱的。如:

"gunboat diplomacy"炮舰外交是美国在 1890 年至一次大战期间在加勒比海和中美洲国家就采取这种列强外交。英国更是如此,鸦片战争就是典型的例子,当时的"Trade follows the flag."(军旗插到哪里,生意就做到哪里)就是这一政策的具体体现。这充分说明那"弱国无外交"的时代。再如"Bush Doctrine"或"Bush's Doctrine of pre-emption"(见"**改朝换代产生和流行的词语**"),见例句:

In backing Bush, voters rejected Kerry's argument that **Bush's doctrine of pre-emption** had led America into a quagmire in Iraq, and that the terrorists could be vanquished only by the shrewd deployment of diplomacy and international institutions. (*Newsweek*)

有收买拉拢的。如小布什 2001 年上台不按老规矩首访加拿大,访问了墨西哥,称"amigo diplomacy(朋友外交)"。再如:"dollar diplomacy"金元外交,1912 年,美国总统塔夫脱提出了所谓"以金元代替枪弹"的外交政策而得名。见例句:

In foreign affairs his [Taft's] efforts at international peace-keeping failed through poor management, and his **"dollar diplomacy"** poisoned relations with

Latin America. (*The New American Desk Encyclopedia*)

有大加宣传争取公众的 public diplomacy,也有以调解为目的,如：shuttle diplomacy 穿梭外交,来回奔波于两国或多国首都,原先尤指美国前国务卿、有 Super K 之称的基辛格(Henry Kissinger)对阿拉伯和以色列冲突进行斡旋。还有的怕公开施加压力反而会把事办砸,就采取 quiet diplomacy 悄悄外交或秘密外交,也是 Kissinger 首倡。

His [Reagan's] visit to China last spring finally restored a semblance of order to a jittery Sino-American relationship. And his aides claim America's **quiet diplomacy** is making progress in obtaining independence for Namibia. (*Newsweek*)

批评者认为官方外交呆板,缺乏活力和创造性。但官方外交有权威,也较严肃。

2. 非官方外交

非官方外交又称"semiofficial diplomacy"(半官方外交)或 semi-diplomacy 民间外交,俗称"Track Two diplomacy"(第二轨道外交),通常由前政府要员、退休外交官、著名学者和国际知名人士来担当,弹性大,既有官方背景,又不受约束,既可达到目的,又不必承担义务和风险。例如我国就曾通过知名记者斯诺向美国传话,以缓和两国关系。2009 年 8 月,美国还通过前总统 Bill Clinton 访问朝鲜,促使两名被朝关押的美记者获释。据报道,双方还讨论了两国未来关系,尤其是如何化解朝核问题。

半官方外交包括 people-to-people diplomacy(民间外交),在诸多非官方外交活动中,民间外交堪称独领风骚,领域宽阔,方式灵活,交往深入,三教九流皆可来往,既不受礼宾规格限制,也不受有无外交关系约束。以民促官,中日建交前走的就是这条路子。personal diplomacy 个人外交,实为"巨头外交"。而 national diplomacy 国民外交也是一种民间外交。民间外交形式多样,如中美的"乒乓外交",中日的"围棋外交",印度对中国展开过"体育外交",土耳其的"儿童外交",中国和沙特及美国和伊朗的"足球外交",巴基斯坦和印度的"板球外交",美国对古巴的"棒球外交"和对伊朗的"摔跤外交"等等。此外,当两国间关系到了 nadir(恶化到最低点或极点)时,还有 second channel 可逐渐打开局面,第二渠道主要指学术会议,可以弥补政府间谈判之不足,在打开僵局上起的作用愈来愈大。

二、美国对外政策及用语

自第 5 任总统门罗在 1823 年致国会的咨文中提出了"Monroe Doctrine"

(反对欧洲神圣同盟国家干涉拉美内政,并提出"美洲是美洲人的美洲"的政策主张)和第 28 任总统 Woodrow Wilson Doctrine(指其对民主在全球传播和普及的信念)以来,直到 1947 年起才有杜鲁门、艾森豪威尔、索南菲尔德(Helmut Sonnenfeldt)副国务卿、尼克松、里根、克林顿及其参谋长联席会议主席鲍威尔(Colin Powell)、小布什及其国防部长拉姆斯菲德(Donald Rumsfeld)等相互提出了 Truman/Eisenhower/Sonnenfeldt/Nixon/Reagan/Clinton/Powell/Bush/Rumsfeld Doctrine 等(见**"改朝换代产生和流行的词语"**、**"军事用语"**和《**当代英汉美英报刊词典**》,下简称《**报刊词典**》)。这些外交和军事政策往往人走茶凉,换了人就有对外政策的新思维来代替旧的政策。有趣的是艾森豪威尔总统还杜撰了 wage peace 一词,指既无战争,也无真正和平,那就展开意识形态竞赛,强调搞软的一手。

美国的外交政策一向在自由主义和现实主义之间交替进行。自由主义倾向于用多边主义和经济外交等方式,在全世界推行自由民主,侧重软力量。现实主义则比较侧重于实力政治,以军事对抗军事的硬实力。近几十年来不变的是,打着人道主义(humanitarianism)旗号如 human-rights policy, human-rights abuse(对人权的侵犯)、humanitarian crisis/relief(人道主义危机/解救,救济)等对外进行所谓的 humanitarian intervention(人道主义干预),新保守主义(neoconservatism)干脆以武力推广民主,入侵伊拉克就是典型。有的人往往被西方人道主义方行所迷惑,看不出背后的仇恨、傲慢和帝国主义侵略本性和意图。西方大国就是打着这样的旗号活生生将南斯拉夫肢解的,现在又对苏丹采取这一政策,而且 2002 年成立的国际刑事法院(the International Criminal Court)也对这种政策配合得惟妙惟肖。如前南斯拉夫领导人和波黑的塞族领导人都被关押,指控他们犯了人道主义罪行。现在又对苏丹总统下达逮捕令,但遭到非洲联盟和许多发展中国家领导人的反对。民主党强调 human rights and international cooperation 的对外政策,但出兵朝鲜、越南和南斯拉夫都是民主党领袖任总统时干的。另一个旗号是自由民主。小布什主张 unilateral action(单打独斗)。称其在国外扩大民主为"the freedom agenda"(自由计划),以战逼伊拉克"regime change"。自从捷克 1969 年以 Velvet Revolution(不流血革命)改制后,小布什在全球煽动 color/flower revolution,奥巴马搞 Arab spring。

奥巴马接手小布什政府留下的烂摊子,内外交困,实力开始衰落,执政不到半年便无奈地宣布正式放弃前任奉行的 unilateralism,强调与新兴国家的 cooperation,扩大国际上的 partnership。

三、对华外交政策及用语

美国对华采取的是 congagement(由 containment 和 engagement 拼缀而成)

遏制加接触和 comperation(由 competition 和 cooperation 拼缀而成)竞争与合作并存的政策。常在人权、民主、自由上做文章,对华友好人士称为"panda hugger"(亲华派),而不是 pro-china/chinese。2005 年,美国副国务卿、现任世界银行银长的佐利克(Robert Zoellick)提出,中国应在国际社会中超越当前"只是成员"的角色,扮演 responsible stakeholder,所谓负责任的利益攸关方。stakeholder 原意为赌金代管人。

2008 年又出现 G2(Group of Two)和 Chimerica(共同主导世界经济的中美经济结合体,由 China+America 拼缀而成),实为中国高增长,美国高消费。自哈佛大学一位教授杜撰出"Chimerica"一词后,人们还未来得及"消化"其含义,G2(两国集团)提法已在西方甚嚣尘上。衍生出"中美共治",说穿了无非是忽悠中国多掏钱买美国债,在外交上为美解困。

说是"合作",美方却不断对人民币汇率、中国产品发难,借口倾销等增收高额关税。商家打出 China-free(非中国制品)口号,表示可安全使用。同时又抓中国输美玩具等产品大作文章。尤其在政治上,美国在台湾和西藏等问题上不断干涉中国内政,并时常用 deterrent force 威慑我国,所以两国关系不可能充分互补性发展,只能在曲折中有所改善。

四、其他外交用语

transformational diplomacy(转型外交)实为和平演变。小布什在任时的 troop "surge"(兵力"急增"),换成了奥巴马政府的 smart power(巧实力)。2009 年,获奥巴马提名出任国务卿的希拉里(Hillary Clinton)在国会意见听取会上说,要用巧实力开创美国外交新局面,一夜就成了一个 buzzword。2004 年哈佛大学教授 Joseph Nye 在其出版的《软实力:世界政治的成功之道》就提出了硬实力(hard power)和软实力(soft power)结合,"硬实力"是支配性实力,如基本资源、军事力量、经济力量、科技力量等,"软实力"是指精神力量,如国家凝聚力、文化和意识形态方的受认同程度等。《纽约时报》发表了"How 'Sqft Power' Got 'Smart'"(怎么奥氏原来提出的"软实力外交"一夜之间变成"巧实力"了?)(见《精选本》第四版)文章,其中对 smart power 能否使美在外交上变聪明表示质疑。美国多年来对外政策不正常,一直是"军事上的巨人,外交上的侏儒。"这大概与任何国家视国家安全是 high foreign policy 有关。

另一个引起世人关注的就是在援助发展中国家的"Beijing Consensus vs Washington Consensus"有一外刊文章说,在外交上"北京共识"和过去南北对话(North-South dialogue)中的"华盛顿共识"截然不同,中国在与发展中国家交往时,承诺不像美国那样以干涉内政、强迫非洲国家改善人权等作为援助的先决条件,更不会像西方国家建议非洲大陆采行新自由主义或经济改革计划。一般而言,北京共识指"Chinese/China model"或"Chinese development mode/model",中国发展模式,华盛顿共识指"neoliberalism"。至于何谓北京共识或中国模式,外刊对此还有其他更多的含意。如 a form of a socialist market economy。对此,有评论称:"The Chinese model is quickly gaining appeal within the developing world and influencing a reassessment of Washington's antiquated(过去时)policies. In short, the Beijing Consensus uses China as an alternative model for development in the Third World, and serves a bellwether(领头羊)to the future of Western dominated development priorities."

在对外援助上,西方造出了 aid/compassion fatigue,日本右翼仿造出 apology fatigue(谢罪疲劳)。在谈判中要是从原有的主场退让了是 walk back the cat。双方直接对抗怒目相视 eyeball to eyeball,You blinked 就是顶不住退让了的意思。在谈判中常打这牌那牌的,如中国和苏联交恶时,美国就 played the China card。在双边或国际会议中 a position paper 等于是 an aide-mémoire=memo(randum),备忘录是掐头去尾的普通照会(verbal note),无实质性约束力。用途广泛,形式灵活,说帖[(美)talking points]、非文件(non-paper)和工作文件都属备忘记录。不要不顾上下文将 memo 都理解为备忘录,还有文件、内部密件的意义。position/white paper 不同的是:In diplomacy, a *white paper* is formal report issued by government to define its policy, while a *position paper* is a private guide to its diplomats. 外交交涉"representations",有"诉说、抗议"的意思。他方可能把球踢到你方"The ball is in sb's/the other court",为冷待来访高官,还可借口 for health reasons 或 for the reason of health,不能接见你了。technical(ly)也是含糊的借口字眼。有的用语难以把握其确切意思,如 yes-but formula, double track(例句见"**学习方法**""读报经验教训谈")等。

畅销书《大趋势》(*Megatrends*)作者 John Naisbitt 最近与夫人一道出版了一部新书,叫做《中国大趋势》(*China's Megatrends*),说中国实行的是 vertical(垂直民主),比西方议会民主、党派纷争强,中国集中力量反贪倡廉,成效较显著。其实,在民主自由方面,东西方都有值得相互借鉴的地方。(见"**附录**""外事人员常用语")

习 题

阅读理解文章

"How 'Soft Power' Got 'Smart'"(2009/1/14 *The New York Times*)(见《精选本》四版)

第五节 军事用语

一、美国军队的建制及预算

美军的建制及预算:现在美军共设立十大作战司令部([list of]current combantant commands)。其中依照地区原则或职责(regional responsibilities)划分为六个司令部:1. Africa Command(AFRICOM) 2. Central Command (CENTCOM) 3. European Command(EUCOM) 4. Pacific Command(PACOM) 5. Northern Command(NORTHCOM) 6. Southern Command(SOUTHCOM)。此外,还设立了四个职能司令部(functional responsibilities):1. Joint Forces Command (JFCOM) 2. Special Operations Command(SOCOM) 3. Strategic Command(STRATCOM) 4. Transportation Command(TRANSCOM)。

美国确实是军事上的巨人,海军竟然有11个航空母舰战斗群,空军的各种各样的战斗机更是数不胜数。陆军的坦克和其他战车不计其数。导弹多样先进。

2008年和2009年的军费分别高达8,000多亿美元,约占全球military expenditure 的一半。接近GDP的5%。这么高额的预算,奥巴马政府能扛得住吗? 见2009年4月的一幅"Defense Spending"漫画:

由于小布什政府穷兵黩武,使美国"入不敷出",天文数字的债务压得新政府喘不过气来。奥巴马上台不到半年,便在新的National Security Strategy里决定放弃preemptive strike 和 unilateralism,把军事行动作为last resort(最后手段)。其实,这也是奥巴马政府的无奈之举。下面在解说军语前先见一个有军语的例句:

Instead, at a time when Russia's defence budget is a fraction of what it was in the cold war, they prefer to resurrect Russia's ageing bomber-fleet to fly **ineffectual sorties** against the West—just as Mr Putin has lately resorted to verbal offence as a form of defence. (2007/11/15 *The Economist*)

鉴于俄罗斯的防卫预算只是冷战时期的一小部分,为了回应美国要在波兰和捷克建立导弹防卸系统,普京并扩充军备,而是重新启用俄罗斯老化不堪的战斗机群,进行针对西方的 fly ineffective sorties 的飞行。这不过虚晃一枪,跟他近日口头上反击如出一辙。上面"ineffective sorties"有两义:① 无效出动飞行架次 ② 战机未携弹(出击)飞行。不携弹飞行当然也就是无效出动飞行架次,从上下文看,第②义更合适。第①义使人不明白。又,when 在此处表示对比,有"既然"或"鉴于"等意思,instead 也是一样。

二、二战和越战产生和流行的词语

战争是产生语言的土埌。二战时创造了 shellshock(战争或战斗疲劳症,现已被 combat fatigue 所替代)、foxhole(散兵坑)、blitzkrieg(闪电战)等词语。越战期间因政界分歧,给各派人物贴上了"hawks"(鹰派)、"doves"(鸽派)、"dawks"(中间派)的标签,并喊出了赢越战先得赢"hearts and minds"(民心)的口号,使这个 1906 年由美国前总统 T. 罗斯福的用语一时很流行。不过现在仍常用,如:"A lot of us feel like we have our hands tied behind our back... They say we are here to win the **hearts and minds** of the Iraqi people, but I just don't see that happening."(*Christian Science Monitor*)此外,还有"coonskin on the wall","Vietnamization","Vietnam syndrome"等新造词语。

三、第一次伊拉克战争

1990 年萨达姆(Saddam Hussein)侵占科威特,次年爆发了第一次海湾战争,一些新词也应运而生。如"desert cat"(指驻海湾地区的加拿大空军)、"desert cherry"(参加海湾作战的士兵)、"Desert Saber"(沙漠军刀作战计划,地面战争的代号)、"Desert Shield"(防止伊侵占科威特后企图继续进攻沙特的沙漠的作战计划)、"Desert Storm"(发动对伊进攻的沙漠风暴作战计划)、"Desert Sweep"(发动最后的扫荡作战计划)、"SchwarzKopf boot"(沙漠军靴。Norman SchwarzKopf 是此战中的多国部队总司令,美军中央司令部司令。)等等,不过这些新词语都不如"the mother of all battles"时髦,且至今模仿其所造词语仍不断见诸报端。此语源自第一次伊战前夕,1990 年,萨达姆称:"Let everyone understand that this battle is going to become the mother of all battles."接着,"the mother of all..."媒体模仿,造出了指规模、效果都是最大、最好的,如

mother of all parades/parties 等等许多新语。但也用于戏言,前总统老布什戏谑地称其夫人 Barbara Bush 是"the mother of all Bushes"。值得注意的是"the mother of all battles"被 *Salon* 这家在线杂志(on-line magazine)移作标题而语义扩展为"protests against the second Iraq war"。尽管有的人视为 the mother of all clichés(最令厌烦的陈词滥调),其实不然,如美国空军 2003 年 3 月 13 日试爆的最大常规炸弹——重 9450 公斤的高威力空中爆炸弹就没有用 the largest 或 heaviest bomb 而用的是"the mother of all bombs"。

四、阿富汗战争和第二次伊战

阿富汗反恐战代号是 Operation Enduring Freedom(持久自由作战计划)。从此"war on terror"流行至今。

二次伊战贯彻"Bush's Doctrine of pre-emption"(先发制人军事政策),代号是"Operation Iraqi Freedom"[伊拉克自由(作战)计划]。新词频生并激活一些词语。如仿"window of opportunity"(不可坐失的良机),要对伊采取"window of Vulnerability"(攻敌要害的良机。原指冷战时美国陆基导弹易成为苏联第一次打击的目标。)(这两个词语均仿科技用语"launch window"。)。小布什要"regime change",选择萨所在地作为"target of opportunity"(机不可失的打击目标),实施"decapitation strike"(斩首打击),对伊狂轰滥炸"shock and awe"(震慑轰炸或行动),指所有参与美英联军攻伊的国家都是"coalition of the willing"(志同道合的联盟),时任国防部长的 Donald Rumsfeld 指随军记者为"embedded reporters"。阿富汗和伊战每年花掉的 the sinews of war(战争的支柱,喻"军费")高达 2 千亿美元。

五、新战略产生的词语

一些战略新思维催生新词语。如美国在朝鲜战争失败后,承认打不赢地面战争(land wad),于是出台了"massive retaliation"(大规模报复战略或政策),把赌注押在 nuclear deterrence(核威慑)力量上。"new look"新面貌政策以核武器为主。后来苏联也有了核武器,于是有了"flexible response strategy"。苏联首先发射卫星(sputnik)后两霸又在太空竞赛,里根提出"Strategic Defense Initiative"(战略防御倡议),俗称"Star Wars",即星球大战计划,旨在使对方只能挨打,不能还手。

老布什认为难度太大,Star Wars 缩小,改为"Ballistic Missile Defense"(弹道导弹防御计划),重点发展"Theater and National Defense system"(战区导弹和国家导弹防御系统)。小布什宣布退出 Anti-Ballistic Missile Treaty,2004 年

在阿拉斯州部署"antimissile defense system"的一部分的"interceptor missiles"（拦截导弹），还计划在波捷部署防御导弹。这样一来，美苏 Strategic Arms Reduction Treaty（削减进攻性战略武器条约）如同废纸。2009 年 1 月奥巴马上台，美俄重开新约谈判，各削减三分之一战略核武器谈判于 4 月达成共识。

美国制定在欧洲与苏联打一场大战的同时，还能在其他地区打一场小战的所谓 One and a half war 或 1 1/2-war strategy（一个半战争战略）。2005 年国内发生了卡特里娜飓风（Katrina），兵力已捉襟见肘，无力多派兵救灾，国内怨声载道。在克林顿打"Kosovo War"（1999）和小布什打二次伊战，先后出台的战略思维讲速战速决，辅之以出兵前就想好退路的（Colin）Powell Doctrine/principle（曾任小布什政府国务卿），第一次伊战是此论范例，只将伊赶出科威特，而并未穷追（hot pursuit）占领伊。二次伊战改为 Rumsfeld Doctrine，国防部长拉姆斯菲尔德作战方案，依靠技术优势，利用空中攻击、情报信息、特种部队、多军种合成战及地面部队快速出击等特点迅速取胜。也叫 Rumsfeld war/strategy。此外，弱方攻美要害的 asymmetric(al) warfare（不对称战争），如"9·11"恐怖袭击。这一军事用语还用来形容囚禁在古巴关塔那摩美军基地监狱的三名嫌疑人上吊自杀进行的抗争。

美军还征召同性恋充数，1993 年制定了"don't ask, don't tell"（不问/不说）的法律。2010 年废除，他们可公开服役。见 Newsweek 的报道：

Not to everyone, it turns out, Gen Peter Pace, another Marine who heads the Joint Chiefs of Staff, caused a storm last week when he called homosexual acts "immoral" in response to a question from *the Chicago Tribune*. He explained later he was expressing a personal view, but NEWSWEEK has learned it wasn't the first time he'd done so. At 2005 Wharton School leadership seminar, Pace told grad students also in response to a question: "The U.S. military mission fundamentally rests on the trust, confidence and cooperation amongst its members. And the homosexual lifestyle does not comport with that kind of trust and confidence." In both instances, Pace was arguing the merits of **"don't ask, don't tell"**—a 1993 law that says gays and lesbians can serve in the closet.

六、对华和俄罗斯的政策

1991 年苏联解体后，美对中国继续实行军事、外交上的 containment（遏制围堵）和 engagement（接触）政策，即 congagement。奥巴马上台继续向台湾出售武器，希望两岸永远处于不战不和的分裂状态，反对 G1，即大陆与"台湾"是一个国家集团。Warsaw Pact（华沙条约）解散后，NATO 不但不解散，反而 eastward enlargement/extension（东扩），拉东欧国家入约，挤压俄罗斯战略空间。

七、行话和委婉语

美国国防部还常用一些行话，称为 Pentagonese。例如用 options 代替 choices，tradeoffs 代替 trades，maximize 等于 strengthen，software 等于 thinking，escalate 替代 raise，the state of art 意为 what can be done now，situational awareness 为 know what's going on，spasm 为 reflexive response 等等令人不解的词语。军事上的委婉语打仗时也常见诸报端（见"常见委婉语"）。

八、其他

有人仿 cold/hot war 造出了 cold/dry/hot peace。cold peace 指敌对势力间脆弱和平局面，hot peace 西方报刊称当前为"热和平"时期。说"和平"，指世界整体，特别是大国间关系；话"热"，指局部冲突，恐怖主义；dry peace 指即使阿以媾和，巴勒斯坦立国，以色列却控制着这一干旱地区的水源，对巴只是令人干渴的和平。

此外，Old soldiers never die 这句名言是老兵精神永存或老兵永不死（只是暂离去）(They just fade away)。1951 年被杜鲁门解职的五星上将麦克阿瑟 (Douglas MacArthur) 在国会讲话时援引一首民歌歌词。媒体又仿造出 Real stars never die or retire 和 a general's never-die optimism 等。见例句：

And Wesley Clark, who went into the primaries late and poorly organized but still nurses a **general's never-die optimism**.（*Newsweek*）

阅读理解文章

"A Plan Under Attack"（2003/4/7 *Newsweek*）(《上下册》三版课文)。

第六节　社会用语

美国名记者、文学评论家 Henry Menken(1880—1956)说,"in times of change..."社会变革节奏快,影响大。种族歧视、男尊女卑等传统道德观、主流文化等都无一不受到冲击,运动一浪接一浪,新词不断催生,旧词不时衍生新义。

一、争民权,反越战,新词生

20世纪60年代,反越战(Vietnam War,1957—1975)争民权席卷美国,新词随之涌现。"Black Power"(黑人权力)运动爆发后,又有"Brown Power"(美籍墨西哥人褐色人权力)、"Flower Power"(hippies 主张通过爱情和非暴力实现社会改革,使用的口号是花儿派权力),"student power"、"Red Power"(印第安人权力)、"Gay Power"(同性恋权力),有人还造出了"green power"(金钱魔力)。

反越战运动也带来不少新词。1937年首创的 sit-in 在1960年由民权运动静尘示威后时髦了起来,仿此造出了许多新词,举《纽约时报》在1965年报道中的一个例句便可见一斑:"There have been sit-ins, lie-ins(卧地抗议示威), stand-ins(黑人插队以示对种族隔离的抗议), eat-ins(聚餐会), sleep-ins(静卧示威), swim-ins(游泳活动或抗议), and sing-ins(听众参加合唱的群唱节目。)从此例句可以看出,"-in"作后缀不但具有 sit-in 中作"有组织的抗议示威活动",还具有"eat-in"和"prance-in"(歌舞聚会)等公开的集体活动的意思。

二、女权运动

60年代中期,妇女也不甘落后,爆发了女权运动,产生了像"Women's Lib"、"feminism"、"feminist"、"chairperson"、"consciousness-raising"(觉悟提高,源于中国共产党用语)、"male chauvinist"(大男子主义者)、"sexism"(性别歧视)、"sexual harassment"(性骚扰)、"girlcott"(仿 boycott 抵制)等新语。随之又仿 Women's Lib 诞生了旨在使男性摆脱传统社会形象和角色的"Men's Lib"。90年代初那些最激进好斗的女权主义者被一保守派电台论战者抨击为"feminazi"(主张男女等的纳粹分子)。不过,这个女权运动不但要求男女平等等积极一面,也有要求性自由等消极面,所以最后不被社会所接受。

三、反正统文化运动

从20世纪50至70年代初,美国青年中出现的"counterculture"("反主流或传统文化而形成的群体文化",此字用counter而不用anti,内含替代),当时的这部分美国青年如hippies和yuppies(嬉皮士和雅皮士)、反对越战者、辍学人士等所持的一种与正统文化对着干,试图用drug culture,sexual freedom,do your own thing等在婚姻、事业、爱国主义等方面搞自由放纵,由此产生了一些反主流文化的词语,又被称为"hippie language"(嬉皮派或游戏人生族语言):如:bummer(不愉快的经历),bust(逮捕),cosmic(巨大的),down(情绪低落的经历),far out(最高级的),gig(职业),goof on(取笑),groove on(欣赏),heavy(有力的,强大的),into(有兴趣的),off(杀死),organic(重大的),outasight(顶呱呱的,了不起的),pig(警察),put down(侮辱),put on(戏弄),rap(话题广泛的交谈,闲聊),rip off(偷),shuck(诡计,骗局),spaced(昏昏沉沉的),speed(安非他明,毒品中的兴奋剂),stoned(服毒品后麻醉了的),strung out(吸毒成瘾的),together(调整得好的,情绪稳定下来了),trip(经历),up(情绪振奋的经历),vibrations(印象,感想)。

在这些词语中,绝大多数原是美国俚语,报刊在铺天盖地报道这一运动时一度成了新闻词语(journalistic words),因为它们具有新、奇、短小等新闻用语简约的特点。其中只有一小部分仍用作俚语或普通词语保留下来外,大部分早已被媒体所淘汰。

四、多元文化运动

70年代,美国掀起了PC运动,此PC非彼个人电脑,personal computer,而是political correctness或politically correct。

political correctness 政治上的正确运动或政治上正确的观点是全世界左派力量兴起的一部分,美国左派则是反越基础上跟上来,反映少数民族、妇女等弱势群体要平等、争自由的愿望,略似中国那时的政治挂帅,站稳政治立场,具有一定的进步性。在美国大学校院掀起,由主张多元民族文化的自由派或左派中的黑人中产阶级的政治代表打头阵,反对以欧洲为中心的主流文化,认为是"白人至上"的种族和性别歧视、文化帝国主义思想,根源是西方文化。要求实行双语、多民族文化史并重的教育,主张回归非洲文化,向源于欧洲的美国文化叫板。目标包括争取妇女堕胎的选择权,反对性骚扰,强化艾滋病防治,提高黑人和其他少数民族的政治、经济地位,政府保障穷人生活,争取黑人和妇女就业和入学配额;改革课程和师资;创立一套新的替代语言文字,如:

PC Word	NonPC Word
illegitimate child	child of single mother
gay husband or wife	domestic partner
fireman	firefighter

	续表
humanity	mankind
Hispanic	Latino
ballot-box stuffing	nontraditional voting
adult day-care center	nursing home for aged or disabled people
man	oppressor
policeman or lawman	police officer
mailman	postal worker
prostitute	sex worker
lover	significant other

PC运动有极端的一面,"物不平则鸣"完全可以理解。顺便提一句,the other person 指第三者,不是什么 the third person。后来保守派反击(backlash),诬蔑其为校院里的"新麦卡锡主义"(a new McCarthyism)。虽然已陷入低潮,但余波荡漾,随处可见,具有"政治上正统的观点"、"政府认可的政治观点"、"说得恰切些"、"说得不得罪人"等意思。现在常用作戏言、幽默或讽刺。如 environmental correctness, morally/patriotically/nutritionally correct 和 sartorially(男装的,衣着的) incorrect。上列有的 PC language 已流行开来,如媒体更多用 Latino, police officer 和 firefighter 等, sex worker 作为委婉语也保留了下来。

五、社会问题出新词

美保守派和自由派在这几大问题上斗争:school prayer, abortion, gay/same-sex marriage, crime 和 drug,并由此产生不少委婉语和党争用语(见"**美式保守派和自由派**")。

六、造词能力

近几十年,美英等国家时新跟社会风气,给年轻人贴上不同"标签"。诸如 hippies, Generation X, beatniks, peaceniks 等称号。1953年 hippie 出现后,不断模仿造出新字来。如 yeepies(逸皮士,指精力充沛的老人或"雅皮士"的父母。由 youthful energetic elderly people 缩略而成)和 yippies(易比士,出现于20世纪60年代,是政治上活跃的嬉皮士。成员来自国际青年党,组织者是鲁宾和霍夫曼。易比派厌恶战争,愤世嫉俗,不愿受社会条规约束。由 Youth International Party 的首字母缩写与 Hippies 拼缀而成)等。

Generation 似乎一直是报刊中的时髦词,肥仔多了,也称为一代。社会学家在总结和描写历史时,往往将有共性、出生同时代的某一特定群体称为"代"

(generation)。如美国根据时间先后顺序就可从南北战争到现在分为诸如 Missionary/Lost/G. I./Silent/Babyboom/Beat/Thirteenth/Millennial Generation 等这几代人。这里的所谓"代"是特指某一群体,并非一代。因此有的学者认为用词不当。2001 年《美国新闻与世界报道》曾发表文章指出,"代"这个词经常把某个小群体的经历和人生态度强加给同时期出生的整整一代人,无视其地区、种族、阶层等重大差异。美国马萨诸塞大学的一位教授主张摒弃这种不科学的提法。再则,即使这样划分,有的也含糊不清。社会学家这么用,记者纷纷效仿,出现了诸如 Generation XXL 等滥用和赶时髦的现象。

Obama 等人 2009 年年初刚组成政府就产生了 Generation O(bama),有人称之愚蠢或昔日惹是生非的一代,如今却领导着美国,奥巴马和财政部长蒂莫西·盖特纳有何共同点?《华盛顿邮报》说,他们都是受歧视的"琼斯一代"(Generation Jones,1954 年至 1965 年出生的人)。"Jones"在美国俗语中有"染上毒瘾"的意思。"琼斯一代"介于"婴儿潮一代"和"X 一代"之间,因学历评估考试平均成绩最低,被称为"愚蠢的一代"或"被遗忘的一代"。随着电视在 20 世纪 70 年代迅速推广,这一代成了电视迷(couch potato,整天呆在沙发上看电视,更多指退休老人),且青年吸毒者较多。奥巴马在自传中称:"曾吸过毒,且小时候不爱学习。"奥巴马周围有不少"琼斯一代"。国土安全部长珍妮特·纳波利塔诺、白宫办公厅主任伊曼纽尔和常驻联合国代表苏珊·赖斯都属于这一代人。在白宫官员中,三分之二属于这一代或比这一代更年轻。具有讽刺意味的是,"问题时代的人"反而当了大官,"管理"考试拔尖的"婴儿潮一代"。"琼斯一代"出生时,离婚家庭、吸毒者猛增,反越战示威弄得社会乱哄哄。不过,《华盛顿邮报》分析说:"'琼斯一代'并非混混,书本知识少点,但在克服困境过程中锻炼了实用性思维,具有不依靠专家解决危机的能力。"类似现象在日本也有,不过叫做"族",这"族"那"族"也不少,这是题外话了。

习 题

阅读理解文章

"Yawns: A Generation of the Young, Rich and Frugal" (2008/5/4 *The Associated Press*)(《精选本》四版课文)

第七节 经济用语

众所周知,美国是全球首屈一指的经济大国。据《泰晤士报》网站2008年"中国梦已取代美国梦"一文章称,2007年美国的GDP 13.8万美元,中国是3.2万亿美元,人均4.6万美元对5,300美元。另一说中国的GDP相当于美国的三分之二。虽然夸大了(overblown),GDP包括外国投资在内,GNP(国内生产总值)较可靠性。然而,天有不测风云,2008年爆发了subprime mortgage crisis(次级贷款危机),引起美国乃至全球震动的financial crisis/meltdown/storm/tsunami(海啸)金融危机。尽管小布什政府有两次earmarks(专项拨款)用来bailouts(救市),还接管了两家最大住房抵押贷款机构"Fannie Mae"(房利美)和"Freddie Mac"(房地美),常指责民主党人实行大政府的共和党,这次轮到挨批在搞国有化和社会主义,跟艾森豪威尔批评F.罗斯福的"New Deal"和杜鲁门的"Fair Deal"为creeping socialism一样的理念,说明市场(invisible hand)与政府(visible hand)缺一不可。美联储(Federal Reserve Board)主席伯克南(Benjamin Bernanke)说,刺激经济复苏最好的办法是"从直升机往下撒钱。"于是人们送给一个雅号"Helicopter Ben"。据2009年5月《纽约时报》网站称,由于奥巴马上台后为振兴经济,扩大救市等开支,美国今年的财政赤字预计将占国内生产总值的12.9%。据美联社2009年10月统计,债务总额达11.42万亿美元的天文数字,相当于经济规模的65%。平均分摊到每个美国人身上是4,700美元以上。

一、从次贷危机到经济衰退或危机

次级贷款指向给信用评级低和收入不高的人贷款。这些人往往没有资格获得要求借款人有优良信用纪录的优惠贷款。放贷机构愿贷,是利率远高于优惠贷款利率,1996年至2006年房价飞涨了85%。购房者受到低利率(后被调高)贷款诱惑纷纷购房。

但是,高利率和低信贷、低收入也使得次贷的拖欠还贷比例高于优惠贷款。因此,次贷也是风险高业务。从2007年开始,利率不断调高,房地产(real estate)泡沫破灭,房价猛跌,借款人付不出逐步上升按揭月份钱,拖欠还贷和丧失房产抵押品赎回权(foreclosure)比例急剧上升,100多家次级住房抵押贷款放贷机构除Fannie Mae和Freddie Mac外,许多大银行或关门或申请破产,证券市场崩溃,投资者蒙受重大损失,不得不重新评估自己正在承担的风险,从而引起金融市场剧烈动荡。这就是次贷危机及其引发的遍及全球的金融危机,其后果又必然导致实业危机。这样,一场全球性的经济衰退或危机便迅猛袭来。

2008年12月下旬,*The Salt Lake Tribune* 有一幅漫画描绘当初低收入者纷纷购豪宅,上面不但有电视卫星天线,还有直升机的停机坪(属夸张手法)。然而,次贷危机爆发,房产泡沫破灭后,他们又返璞归真,真是一画寓万言。

房子上写:Excess(过度消费)

左下方牌子上写:For sale

牵着狗的人问:"Where Are You Going?"背包者答:"Back To Reality."车上写着:the New Frugal(回归现实,由奢入俭)

二、金融和经济危机的祸根

与其说次贷危机是这次金融危机、经济衰退或危机的始作俑者,还不如说经济上极端保守主义是祸根。早在1928年,美国前总统胡佛在竞选总统时提出的与家长式管理和国家社会主义相对立的一套经济政策主张时说:

We are challenged with a peacetime choice between the American system of rugged individualism and a European philosophy of diametrically opposed doctrines — doctrines of paternalism and state socialism.

这就是所谓的"Government is best which governs least"[要想管得好,(政府对企业)就得插手少]。rugged individual 具有强烈个性的人,也指住在未开发边疆者。rugged individualism 不受拘束、自由放任认为是美国民族特点。此处 rugged individualism 意近 laissez-faire,即要政府放手不管。《金融时报》等称之为经济新自由主义、经济自由主义、经济极端保守主义、撒切尔主义或撒切尔-里根执政时期的保守主义。原美国联邦储备委员会主席格林斯潘(Alan Greenspan)也与他们两人一样过分鼓吹私有化(英国在撒执政时买房者确实多了,里根甚至要把一些政府机构如气象局都私有化)、输出民主和市场自我调节,不用监管,格还在写的一本书中斥责呼吁加强监管的人愚蠢,感赞金融市场的魔力。2008年10月8日《金融时报》网站发表了一篇"The Rise and Fall of Conservatism"的文章指出,起源于撒切尔夫人和里根时期的保守主义,过分鼓吹自由竞争私有化、反对征税、输出民主和市场自我调节,结果为引发一场席卷全球的金融灾难埋下了祸根。其实以前就有过类似危机,不过规模不如这次大而已。例如 1987 年的股市崩盘、1994 年的墨西哥金融危机、1997 年的亚洲金融危机和 2000 年的互联网泡沫破裂等。在盛行了近 30 年后,正走向衰落,思想的钟摆将朝相反方向摆动,并配以漫画说明。

钟摆效应　被甩出地球的三个人从左至右分别为:里根、撒切尔夫人和格林斯潘。

三、出招应对,G20 开会

为了紧急应对金融危机,20 国集团(G20)于 2008 年 11 月在华盛顿召开。中国和印度一跃成为 geopolitical powers(地缘政治大国)或新兴经济大国或经济体(emerging economies),会加速 Eastphalian(伊斯特伐利亚)秩序的形成,它是仿"Westphalia"造的新字。源于 1648 年建立了现代国家体系的《威斯特伐利亚和约》(the Treaty of Wesphalian)。西方国家通过推行的殖民主义,将美洲、非洲和亚洲人民纳入该体系之中。只要其他地区的国家在社会制度上与欧洲和北美不同,就会被贴上"不开化"的标签。

四、金融危机催生新词

有人说,金融危机是 Pax Dollarium(美元主宰下的和平)闹的,要跟美元脱钩(decoupling),就像反对 Pax America(美国主宰下的和平)一样。欧洲还有人主张搞欧美元 Doro(Dollar + Euro)或 Eullar(Euro + Dollar)。我国在 G20 伦敦峰会(2009 年 4 月)前夕提出了改革国际货币体系的新设想,即用超越主权、并能保持货币值长期稳定的国际储备货币取代美元,这就是"a super-sovereign currency"(超主权国际储备货币),得 BRIC(金砖四国)(由 Brazil,Russia,India 与 China 四国首字母组成,与 brick 谐音)的支持。俄也提出类似中国的货币设想,称之为"a supernational reserve currency"。经济危机后,欧盟内又出现了两个新词 PIGS 和 PIIGS。这两个字始于希腊的债务危机蔓延至西班牙、葡萄牙和爱尔兰等欧元区成员国。四国英语国名首字母缩合成 PIGS(猪),一些媒体不客气地称为"笨猪四国"。另一种说法就是再加上意大利,成为 PIIGS,称为"欧猪五国"。为应付危机,各国都要实行"严格节约措施""siege economics"。"保守的经济政策""old time religion"又会吃香。自由派也推出"量入宽松政策""quantitative easing money policy"。

金融危机还带来"recession chic",经济衰退时尚,这个销售用语指大堆高价品牌商品打折降价成时髦。另一个是仿 fashionista[时尚达人(粤语:时髦之人)]的"recessionista",找老牌知名公司(established company)打折的名牌货,就是经济衰退时购物迷的特点(recession+-ista)。经济出现萧条,那么"depressionista"就会取代"recessionista"成为时髦。还有的国家提议将G8(西方七国加俄罗斯的八国集团)改为G20。G2(中美两强)也随着 Chimerica 或 Chindia(由 Cina+India)(中印大同)走俏起来。有的词语不解释不好理解。再如:China+India+ME(Middle East)+Africa 等于投资市场+石油+非洲原料与市场。

奥巴马拨款救市(bailouts)还加进"buy American"(买国货)条款。美国各大银行及有的公司都"向政府财政求助""go to the well",不可能"一毛不拔""zero out",是否"愿意发放信贷""nation's credit window"或"将黄金兑换美元""nation's gold window"。美国常挥舞的贸易大棒 301(the 301st provision of the U.S. Trade Act)(301条款)或 Special/Super 301(对歧视其产品的国家采取带有破坏性的一般和特别的报复)更会频繁了。

商业和企业领域随着全球化和高新技术不断创新,人才便成了具有决定意义的时代。金融危机带来大批裁员,也引起趁机高薪征求人才。head hunters 猎头公司造出了诸如"golden handcuffs/cuffs"(金手铐,指高薪留人)、"golden hello"(高薪)、"golden parachute"(黄金降落伞,人去薪留,直到合同期满)和"golden handshake"(补偿金)等词语,随之出现了"gold collar"金领阶级和"new collar"(新领阶级,指比其父辈更富裕和受过更高深教育的白领工人),对中老年人的"ageism"(年龄歧视)。公司要"brand extension"(品牌延伸或扩展),suitor 也由"求婚者"引申为"企图收购竞争者",feeding frenzy 由"拼命争食"引申为"疯狂的竞争"。仿 blackmail 造出了"greenmail"(以套购股票作兼并威胁)。还出现了诱人用信用卡疯狂购物的"merchants of debt"(债商)[仿 merchant of death(军火商)]。

企业丑闻与政治丑闻如 Watergate 一样,引申出新义。加之媒体跟风造词能力强。例如2002年是美国大公司会计丑闻频发年,Enron(安然)、World Com(世通)和 Xerox(施乐)等大公司为虚报利润而做假账(cook the books),股民损失惨重,证券业和公司诚信扫地。Enron 曾在美国500强大企业中名列第七,"massive accounting scandal"破产后,Enron 转化成普通名词或动词,成为"cheat"的同义词,《纽约时报杂志》举例称:

a. The verb is simply the name, as in "He got **enroned** last Thursday."

b. "I don't want to **Enron** the American people," said the Democrat Tom

Daschle, defining the new verb in his next sentence, "I don't want to see them holding the bag at the end of the day just like Enron employees have held the bag."

不但如此，enron 还衍生出 enronesque（做假账的）、enronish（靠不住的）、enronism（造假风）、enronista（安然式破产责任人，大骗子）、enronite（冤大头）、enronitis（造假症，指其他大公司也有此或大或小的问题）、enronlike（像安然公司那样的）等新字。这些词语，除 enron 外，只能风靡一时，但是熟悉这些字，抓住 cheat 核心义便会举一反三，见一知十，根据这些后缀，增强猜词（义）能力，加深阅读理解，就不那么困难了。

上面以 enron 为例，举出一批后缀造词，这里再举几个加前缀造词的例子。outsourcing/offshore outsoucing（外包），又类比造出 crowdsourcing（群包）和 insourcing（内包）。加拿大还提出与其 offshoring 还不如 nearshoring（让邻国如加拿大和墨西哥等国干的近包）等等不同想法的新词。

世贸组织（WTO）组织的一些缩略词和用缩略造词也大行其道，令人目眩。为"BIT"（bilateral investment treaties）（双边投资条约）、"BTA"（border tax adjustments）（边境税调整）、"NAMA"（nonagricultural market access）（非农业市场准入）、"NTB"（nontariff barriers）（非关税壁垒）、"TRAIPS"（trade related aspects of intellectual property）（有关智力产权方面的贸易）以及"Everything but arms"（允许最贫穷国家除武器外的所有产品进入欧盟市场）等等。内地与香港实现 CEPA（Closer Economic Partnership Arrangement），与台湾也达成 ECFA（Economic Cooperation Framework Agreement），同时还创造了个"Chiwan"新词。

此外，以前还发生过 dotcom crash 或 bursting of the (high) tech bubble（高科技股尤其网络经济股市泡沫的破灭）。

早有人料到这次金融危机会演变成经济危机。如英国记者 Larry Elliot 在 2007 年就以 "Three bears that ate Goldilocks economy"（2007/9/24 *The Guardian*）为题发表警世文章。"Goldilocks economy"这里"金发姑娘经济"是 20 世纪 90 年代中期新词，指美国既不冷也不过热的"称心如意的经济"。文章借用《格林童话》里 Goldilocks and the Three Bears 的故事。

2009 年 10 月，美国出了一本分析这次危机的新书，与主流经济学派不同的是，*Animal Spirit* 的作者认为，经济既有规律，也动荡不安，反复无常，犹如动物。

习　题

阅读理解文章

"The Captain of the Street"（2008/9/29 *Newsweek*）。

第八节 法律用语

在美国,法律和医学专业难学。本节所论多数为常见的法律用语(legal words),外行望文生义,随时会闹笑话,如 action 指"诉讼(权)",词义变窄了,class action 为"集体诉讼"。律师业赚大钱,一直很火,一场官司有时闹得沸沸扬扬,如橄榄明星 O. J. Simpson 杀妻及其男友悬案闹了几年。20 世纪 80 年代末,纽约一黑手党头目 John Gorty 也一审再审。我们有必要学些法律术语,但要说得在行、译得地道,绝非一般英语、新闻专业师生所能胜任。

一、一般法律用语

编者在纽约目睹美国审判制度之开放与新奇。进入法庭,首先映入眼帘的是正面墙上的"In God We Trust"(吾信吾主)几个大字,令人怀疑美国是"法治"还是"神治"。可随意旁听,法官前面有一排陪审团席(jury box),还有被告席和公诉人或/和原告团席。由陪审团作出有罪无罪的裁决(verdict of guilty or not guilty)。

逮捕疑犯(suspect)首先要出示 arrest warrant(逮捕证,拘留状),当然对现行犯 arrest without a warrant of flagrante delicto 例外。根据 Miranda rule(米兰达规则),在讯问在押的嫌疑人之前,警察必须告知对方有权保持缄默和聘请律师等权利。这些权利叫 Miranda rights,这种预告或提醒叫 Miranda warning。1996 年因犯罪嫌疑人 Ernesto Miranda 曾自证有罪而定罪后,被最高法院裁定违宪,反而无罪开释。对嫌疑人审讯,美国宪法第 5 条修正作出了不得在刑事诉讼中强制自证其罪(self-incrimination)的规定。如果某人"invoke/take the Fifth (Amendment)",即根据该条保护,拒绝提供证词(refuse to testify)。

出席民事法庭只有原告 plaintiff/complainant,被告 defendant,被告方 defense 的辩护人 defense lawyer/attorney/counsel 或 defendant's agent。刑事案,原告则是检察机关,检察官有 U.S. (district) attorney(倾向译为俗称"联邦检察官"federal prosecutor), state's attorney(州检察官)、district attorney(各州地方检察官或公诉人,华人译"地保管")或 public prosecutor(检察官,公诉人)、chief procurator(检察长)等,由他们诉讼(lawsuit)、公诉(indictment),被告律师和被告本人答辩(defense in lawsuit),当然也可提出反诉(counterclaim),这就听当事人或委托人(client)的意见。当然,所有被告都有抗辩权,All the accused pleaded guilty or not guilty 绝大多数均表态服罪与否。原告、控方或讼诉方也有律师。被告律师可挑选 grand/petty jury(大/小陪审团)的 jurors(陪审员)(每

次都有多余几位到场供选)。会钻法律条文空子的滑头律师称 Philadelphia lawyer;有用同种相亲、同类相惜打赢官司。被告是黑人,尽可能多选黑人陪审员。菲律宾前总统马科斯(Ferdinand Marcos)夫人伊梅尔达在美国遭起诉,辩护律师大名鼎鼎,挑的陪审员女性占多数。公诉人或原告、被告及其律师对簿公堂时,听起诉、抗辩的虽是法官 judge/magistrate(民事法官)/chairman 或 presiding judge(审判长)/federal judge(审理犯联邦法的联邦法官)/(associate) justice(最高法院法官)/chief justice(最高法院院长)或 local justice(地方治安法官),但做审判的主要是 the jury。伊梅尔达的辩护律师对 jury 说,假设你们的丈夫生前犯法,请问你们该不该背黑锅。结果,jury deliberation(经审议)后,The jury acquitted her。如果她是个 detainee,法官得当庭宣布解除羁押,恢复其人身自由。若 The jury declared her guilty,法官才能根据法典 condemn 或 sentence 她,如:She was sentenced to three years in prison/life imprisonment 等。这就是说,jury 和 judge 各司其职。如果说:"The jury is still out."陪审团还没有取得一致意见,还未回到法庭来宣告被告是否有罪;还可喻对某事尚无定论,见例句:Kim Young Sam has decisively demonstrated his will to undertake the task of political and social reform. But in economic field, **the jury is still out.** (*Far Eastern Economic Review*)

法庭还要下达 witness order(传证人令),在 box/chair(证人席)上就座,under oath(宣誓)testimony(证言)全部属实(truth)。否则,就犯了 perjury(伪证罪)。如前副总统 Dick Cheney 办公室主任利比(Lewis Libby)判刑罪状就是 perjury,另一条罪状(count)是 obstruction of justice(妨碍司法执行)。罪行有轻有重(misdemeanor/felony),有的只要 reprimand(训诫),有的军法只罚 internment(禁闭),有的只要 house arrest(软禁或就地监禁)。刑期(term of imprisonment)有长有短,不过美国有的州已废除 capital punishment 或 death sentence(极刑),有的还可 reprieve(缓期执行)。当然也有 wrong detention(冤狱)和 conviction(不法关押和判罪),例如 2000 年美籍华人科学家李文和在美核武和核能研究中心工作,曾下载一些资料。当时美反华浪潮高涨,众议院、能源部、媒体联合炮制一起所谓中国窃取美核弹头的间谍案,判处 solitary confinement(单独监禁),最终在一位秉公执法的联邦法官审理下翻案,法官还谴责了政治干预司法(politics was involved in the process)。为了早日解禁,李或其律师与控方之间达成 plea bargain/bargaining 或 plea bargaining agreement (有条件认罪协议):经法庭批准,被告为了避免受到较重的处罚与控诉人达成承认一条较轻罪状的协议,从而使控诉人不再对其他罪状提起诉讼。简言之,即关于被告如何认罪与司法机关如何处理的法制。见李案的例句:

The case began disintegrating last month at a bail hearing(保释审理或受理申诉). An FBI agent whose testimony was key in denying Mr. Lee bail in December said he had repeatedly erred in that testimony. In accepting the **plea bargain**, U. S. District Judge (= federal judge) James Parker said that the government's actions had "embarrassed our entire nation." (*The Associated Press*)

从上例可以看出,在刑事诉讼案如间谍或毒品走私贩卖案中,没有原告,控方是国家检察机关,作证的是 FBI agent。被告如对地方法院的 verdict(判决)或 sentence 不服,可 appeal(上诉或申请复议)到更高一级法院。

二、新词和一度流行的时髦词

调查克林顿总统绯闻扯出了两个新词:Paula Jones disease 波拉·琼斯症,滥诉风:琼斯是克林顿任阿肯色州长时的低级女雇员,貌不出众,但在总统的政敌怂恿下,事隔数年控告克林顿性骚扰,此案虽经法院驳回,但媒体炒作,她名利双收。《华盛顿邮报》专栏作家 Steven Brill 鉴于滥诉风严重,虚耗大量人力和物力,造出该词。Paula Jones affidavit 波拉·琼斯式宣誓(声明书):即否认控诉属实的声明。

小布什上台后因 9/11 事件而发动了阿富汗战争也造出了一些新语。弃 terrorist 而代之用 insurgent,令人迷惑。把战争抓来的 POWs 称为 captives,关在关塔那摩基地的 detainees 既不作战俘(POW)也不作犯罪嫌疑人审理,违反 Geneva Convention on the Treatment of Prisoners of War(关于战俘待遇的日内瓦公约),一些词流行起来。如:(special) rendition,waterboarding(水刑,水牢)做法是"呛水",还建立黑狱 black hole, secret CIA prison camps 或 illegal prisons 刑讯逼供,委婉地称之 physical persuasion(身体说服)。调查水门事件的独立特别检察官(independent special prosecutor)始于 1973 年,独立于司法部,1994 年调查克林顿绯闻时变为 independent counsel 委婉用法了。

三、易误解词语

有的法律用语易使外行误解。如:lodge/file/submit a complaint 投诉;起诉,控告,class action,one-self action 自诉,take action against sb 起诉某人。U. S. attorney 与 U. S. district attorney 同一官职,他们分在各区而不在首都华盛顿司法部工作,与 district attorney 不同。trial attorney 与 trial lawyer 都是出庭律师,前者诉讼,后者辩护。brief 诉讼双方向法院提出的"诉讼文书",hearing 在美国国会指调查听证会,意见听取会;法律上还可指审讯、审理、开庭等。与不同字搭配意思不同,如 hearing officer 组织意见听取会的政府特派调查员。听证、审讯、作证不是道听途说。Hearsay is no evidence. 传闻不是证据是法律界的名言。organized crime 我国等一些国家指带有黑社会性质的犯罪团伙或集团,美国指黑手党家族(mafia family)。

四、其他

民主党对最高法院(the Supreme Court,俗称 high/highest court)法官颇有微词,原来顽固或保守派占多数,称为 nine old men(终身职,有的直至寿终),cult of the robe,意为律师一旦成为法官,披上法袍,似乎就比一般官员(ordinary mortals)高出一头,最高法院的法官(justices)更是不可一世,犹如黄袍加身或《圣经》里的 holier than thou(比你神圣、圣洁或献身)。

盗贼等作案前还常 case the joint(踩点),当然现也作正当的"实地勘察"的戏言。有的采取 wolf-pack robbery(狼群式抢劫),指流窜作案,如狼群出没。语言基本上是比喻,只是时间一长,人们不经意忘了。法律术语虽严谨,但这一点也不例外。例如借用棒球术语 strike three(棒球比赛的第三击,击球手的第三击如果不中,就要被罚出局。喻"成功的最后机会")就有:(1) three-strikes law 三次重刑事案犯判无期徒刑的法律。(2) Three strikes and you're in—for life without parole. 犯下三次重大刑事案就给关,判无期徒刑,不准假释。(3) three-strikes-and-you-are-out law 三击出局,终身不得假释的法律。

习 题

阅读理解文章

1. "Libby Defense Portrays Client as a Scapegoat"(2007/1/24 *The New York Times*)(《精选本》四版课文)

2. "Judge Sees Politics in Los Alamos Case"(2000/9/15 *International Herald Tribune*)

第九节 科技用语

本节从三方面说明常见诸报端的科技用语：科技新语不断、造词能力出众和旧词不断扩展引申出新义。为了说明科技用语与一般用语之异同，不妨先见《精选本》(四版)一课文"Nanospheres leave cancer no place to hide"有如下一段文字：

The team then applied a higher-power infrared laser to each tumour site for 3 minutes to heat the tissue. After a few weeks, they found the tumours had been almost completely destroyed. Eighty per cent of the mice treated survived for more than seven weeks, while all the **control mice**, who did not receive the nanoshells, died after three weeks. (2007/6/21 *New Scientist*)

此例中的"control mice"理解为"控制鼠"逻辑不通。此处词义变窄，成为"用作检查调查、实验等比较标准的集群或个体"，即"对照实验物或实验调查等对照物"。"control mice"意为"与实验鼠作对比鼠"，以检查结果。最后一整句的意思是："80%经过纳米弹治疗的患癌老鼠，存活了七个多星期，未经治疗的三星期后就死了。"

一、科技新语不断

科技发展催生新词，多旧词新义。有些只有内行懂，有些外行也喜闻乐见，或看了只要多查词典或上网就能理解，中文译词，多新词新义，大致可以猜懂，这是汉语灵活的一大长处。

1957年，苏联发射了第一颗人造卫星，不用 artificial satellite 而用俄语"sputnik"。此后美苏太空争霸拉开了序幕。1969年 Apollo 号宇宙飞船登月，带出 moonman、moonfall(登月)、moonwalk、lunar module(登月舱)、Lunar rover(月球车)、space suit(宇航服)、pulsar(脉冲星)、neutron star(中子星)、black hole(黑洞)、recovery(本义为"恢复"、"复得"，空间技术表示"溅落宇航员的载回"或"舰战机的返航降落")等等新词。2001年神舟号飞天，西方媒体造了由 taikon 和 astronaut 拼缀而成的 taikonaut(中国太空人)。发射期间人们不断听到说发射窗很短，这个20世纪60年代造出的词语"launch window"，其实专指航天器、导弹等为达到预期会合等而择定的"最佳发射时段或时机"。有人又仿造出"window of opportunity/vulnerability 及 gold/credit window"等(见"**军事/经济用语**")。这在语法上称为类比(analogy)构词。

医学界革命也出新词。如 CT，MRI（核磁共振成像），genetic code（遗传密码）、DNA、human genome（人类基因图谱）、human embryos（人类基因胚胎），clone，test-tube baby（试管婴儿）、transexual operation（变性手术）等，而 viagra（伟哥）、morning-after pill（一种房事后吃的新避孕药）、botax（肉毒素）、prozac（百忧解）等新药也应运而生。

nano(technology)（纳米技术）发展令人惊奇，因其应用前景极其广泛，因而用"nano-"作前缀造出了许多新词（见"Nanospheres leave cancer no place to hide"这一课后的"语言解说"）。

交通工具的发展也令人瞩目，如 maglev train（磁浮列车）、support magnet（悬浮磁铁）等。

武器也日新月异，发明出了 ABM（反弹道导弹）、MIRV（多弹头分导重复大气层运载工具）、stealth auto bra（汽车隐形罩）、night-vision goggles（夜视镜）、depleted uranium shell（贫铀弹）、E-bomb（电磁炸弹）、thermobaric/graphite/smart bomb（温压、石墨、精确制导炸弹）、acoustic/volumetric weapon（声学、声爆武器）等。

"IT"新词之多，令人咋舌。构成网络亚文化浪潮的这"客"那"客"就有 blog（博客，另译"博录格，部落格"）、blogging（写博客者或博主，另译"博格，布格"）和 blogger（另译"部落客"），hecker，flasher（闪客），witkey（威客），geek（极客）、podcast（播客）和 twitter（推特）上的 tweet（微型博客）等等。有的令外行目眩，如 browse 浏览（网页），browser（浏览器），solid-state drive（固态硬盘，这个 drive 竟成"硬盘"了）和 flash memory（闪存记忆），stuxnet（网震。一种电脑病毒），Moore's Law（以莫特尔公司共同创办人 Gordon Moore 姓氏命名的莫尔定律，即计算机芯片每 18 个月更新一次）等。此外，网络和形形色色的网站数不胜数，如 Internet，WWW，Google，Yahoo，Sina，YouTube，Wikipedia，Myspace，Facebook，Skype，Second Life，527 groups，等等。

二、造词能力出众

本节所谈科技词语的造词能力包括三方面：一是某个字有了新义，就跟风造出许多新词；二是截某词的一半作词缀而新造出许多派生词和拼缀词；三是复合词和仿造词。例如：因 launch window 有了新义，接着类比造出了 window of opportunity/vulnerability 及 credit/gold window 等；而 sputnik 发射后，"-nik"作后缀造出许多诸如"beatniks"（垮掉的一代），"Vietnik"（反对越南战争者），"peacenik"（反战者），refusenik（抗命者），computernik（电脑专家），follknik（民歌迷）等。nanotechnology 出现后"nano-"作前缀造出了 nanoshell（纳米弹）、

nanoparticle(纳米粒子)、nanosphere(纳米球)等派生法构成的新词。这种造词能力很强。拼缀法利用科技英语造词在报刊中常用，例如：Internet 与 entrepreneur 组成"netpreneur"(网络精英)，与 grassroots 拼缀成"netroots"，与 right 结合，组成"rightroots"；Web 与 economics 拼缀成"webonomics"，与 magazine 成"webzine"。wiki 与 economics 拼缀成"wikinomics"，与 reality 成"wikiality"(由多数人决定的现实)。wiki 还构成"wikinovel"、"wikiproject"、"wikiworld"等等复合词。(欲了解更多的 IT 用语，可读《上下册》四版里的"Yesterday's Newspaper"这一课)

三、旧词引申出新义

尤为值得注意的是，科技用语转用后，不断扩展引申出新义。如：作为域名的"dotcom"引申为"因特网和其他信息技术"；"上网公司"；"网络公司"；"高科技公司"等，"dotcom crash"就指这类高科技公司的泡沫或神话的破灭。soft landing 指人造卫星、飞船等软着陆，后来引申到经济体制改变而未引起较大震荡或破坏。hardware 原指计算机硬件，扩展引申为"军事武器和装备"，泛指设施，现又喻"法"；software 指计算机软件，扩展引申为"武器研发、计划和使用说明"，泛指服务，战争中的人类的"思想"，作"thinking"是美军界行话，还喻"创新"，现又引申为与"法"相配合的"德"和"宗教"。chemistry 喻"(人际)关系，人缘"，"electricity"喻"热情"。"ground zero"原指核爆炸"损失最大的中心点"，现喻 9·11 事件后"原世界贸易中心大楼的遗址"。chad 喻手工重新计票，brain cell 喻"智力"，brain dead"极其愚蠢的"。rocket science 火箭科学，现喻"复杂、高深难懂之事"。countdown 本来指发射卫星飞船的"倒计时"，现喻在竞选或其他重大事件中"最后的紧张令人生畏、激动人心的时刻"、"行将出现的摊牌局势"。firestorm 指核弹等爆炸引起的"大火暴"，现可喻"强烈的反响"或"不满"、"愤怒"或"竞选前最后几天"等。"hemorrhage"本义为"大出血"引申为"人才等流失"。创世大爆炸的"Big Bang"喻"影响深远的举措"。"lightening rod"喻"替罪羊"。defuse 为去掉引爆信管，现可指"缓和"或"解除"易引危险或不利之事。fulcrum 是杠杆的"支点"，喻"支柱"、"支持物"。The rubber meets the road. 指"汽车轮胎在高速公路面临安全性能的考验"，引申为"紧要关头或真材实料的考验"。fault lines"断层线"，现喻"党派"等分界线。political fault-line 政治断层带，指政治的关键地区、重要地方或国家等，如同地球上的大陆板块断层带。有时喻地方虽小，却极其重要，因为其变动(地震)会带来极大震荡。见下列两例句：

(1) Traditionally, American party politics has had **fault lines**—blacks vote

differently from whites and southerners from northerners. (*The Atlantic*)

从传统上看,美国的党派政治一直线界分明:黑人与白人、南方人与北方人投票趋向不同。(即黑人和南方人往往将票投给自由派的民主党候选人,而白人和北方人则投给保守派的共和党人。)

(2) Palestine, a tiny place, straddles one of **the world's political fault-line**. The crack from the small point threatens the peace of larger nations, the economy of every oil importer. (*Time*)

巴勒斯坦地方虽小,却横跨一条世界政治地震断层带上。一丝风吹草动,就叫一些更大国家不得安宁,殃及每个石油出口国经济。

另一种语义是,专有名词转化成普通名词或动词,语义也引申扩展了。如网名"Google"作 *v*. 意为用谷歌搜索或传播信息。"YouthTube"(从视频传到网上)。一个网上的 527 group 名叫"Swift Boat Veterans for Truth"(寻求越战真相快艇老兵)。"swift boat spot"是 2004 年大选中用来攻击民主党总统候选人 John Kerry 越战经历的电视广告,作动名词 swift-boating,*v*. swift-boat,意为"声讨候选人弄虚作假","揭露(官员、候选人的谎言、欺骗、造假或扩大其军旅经历等)";从反对派或政敌来说也有"诽谤"之意思。

阅读理解文章

"Nanospheres Leave Cancer No Place to Hide" (2007/6/21 *New Scientist*)(《精选本》四版课文。)

第十节 跟踪语言的变化和发展

有人说,"莎翁再世变个文盲"。笔者耳听一位北大英语老先生说:"看不懂报刊了,生词太多。"另一位北大教文学的博导说:"拿不准报刊上词确切意思。"还有一位退休前在南师大任教、毕业于北大的老先生说:"教了一辈子文学,觉得不行。用你的书教报刊文选后,受益匪浅。"这里无意贬低文学。本书第一版前言里已经阐明,没有文学基础,连基本的报刊语言都看不懂,里面充满着西方文学典故和圣经故事。再则,文学是一切语言的基础,这是不言自明的道理。本节旨在说明,教文学的也得与时俱进,读读现代语言的报刊,紧跟语言的变化和发展(keep up with the language),拓展有关文化背景知识。报刊涉及的面广,内容不断翻新,堪称活的百科全书。只有在这两方面"紧跟",才不会由于国内开放前几乎与外界隔绝,而使一些满腹经纶的老先生落伍。"三天不摸手生",活到老,学到老,对我本人也是如此,半点也松懈不得。

本节从四个方面说明语言的变化。至于各领域引申义的词语除个别外,重点置于政治、外交、军事、经济、宗教、科技、法律等语言解说里。

一、词义变化多奇妙

词义变化的例子首推"**It's the Economy,Stupid!**"里的"**stupid**"(见"**政治名言的理解与翻译**")。再如:

1. Defining Moment

1994 年在编注《美英报刊文章阅读》(精选本)(第一版)一课"Big Crime,Small Cities"里读到了"defining moment"时不得其解。见例句:

(1) Crime has come of age here as well. For many it hit home after a football game at Myers Park High School last Aug. 24. Two youths exchanged words in the school parking lot. One of them, a 16-year-old, pulled a semiautomatic pistol and shot the other in the leg. A 17-year-old nearby who heard the shots pulled a rifle from a car and opened fire. Several hundred terrified students fled for cover, including 15-year-old Marcus Grier. He died minutes after a rifle shot hit him in the head.

Grier's death was a **defining moment** in the city's most violent year. He was one of 93 homicide victims in 1990, more than double the toll for 1988. (1991/6/10 *Newsweek*)

当时网络尚未如此发达,唯有查词典是唯一可以解答的工具。*The Random*

House Dictionary of the English Language 和《英汉大词典》(第一版)的释义都是"决定性或关键的时刻"。可从上下文看显然不符合此例的意思。后来,又查阅了1998年出版 The New Oxford Dictionary of English,词义是:an event which typifies or determines all subsequent related occurrences("为其后发生之事树立典型的事件,开先河之事件"简言之,"典型事件")。这样,"Grier's death...the city's most violent year"就好理解一些了。

后来又在1999年出版的《英汉大词典》补编本里见到了此语的例句及译文:

(2) Indeed, the 1990s have been filled with **defining moments**. Think about it: The Gulf war, the Rodney King beating, the O. J. Simpson case, the Oklahoma City bombing, Magic Johnson's HIV announcement, the 1994 Republican congressional victory, even the North American Free Trade Agreement. Each has been called a **defining moment** by somebody—often by a lot of people. (1997/9/19 The *Wall Street Journal*)

上世纪90年代确实经历了太多的**决定性时刻**。想一想吧:海湾战争,罗德尼·金挨打,辛普森案,俄城爆炸案,魔术师约翰逊宣布染上艾滋病毒,1994年共和党在国会赢得胜利,甚至还有北美自由贸易协定。每一桩都曾被某些人,常常是被许多人,称作**决定性时刻**。

上述英语例句里的"defining moment"的译文令人不解,用 Oxford Dictionary 的词义去解读也不完全合适。译文里把海湾战争、辛普森案等作为决定性时刻的说明,语言逻辑不通。于是决定在网上和参考书里寻找解疑的答案。有家网站的解释跟 Random House Dictionary 一样。接着查 American Government & Politics,第二义:The pivotal event of a new era(新时代的关键或重大事件),举例说明:The German invasion of Poland in 1930 was certainly a *defining moment* because it started World War II. 最后查 *Safire's New Political Dictionary*,定义:significant action or event that illustrates character(说明性质特点的意义重大的行动或事件)。这两本书上的词义一下令人顿开茅塞:伊战、黑人金被白人警察暴打致伤……一系列事件正好说明了这个时代发生的在美国国内外有着影响深远的重大事件。1990年,时任国务卿的 James Baker 将此语的范围用得更宽:

The Iraqi invasion of Kuwait is one of the **defining moments** of a new era.... If we are to build a stable and more comprehensive peace, we must respond to the **defining moments** of this new era (指的是20世纪中叶)。

从此例可以看出,*American Government & Politics* 的释义出于 Mr. Baker 的这次讲话。不过"moment"确有作"时刻"讲的意思,但 defining 的词义变化

了,有一篇报道汶川大地震文章有此例句:

If the crisis had a **defining moment**, it came on May 19 at 2:28 p.m., exactly a week after the quake. That was when the entire country paused for three minutes. Traffic came to a halt, flags were lowered to halfmast ... (2008/5/22 *Time*)

如果将第一句理解为:如果说这场灾难有一个**决定性时刻**的话,那就是正好地震一周后的5月19日下午2点28分。如将"决定性时刻"根据上下文改为"具有纪念意义的重大时刻"则符合原文的意思。之所以这么改还因为20世纪90年代后,"defining"这个分词已成了意为"significant"的形容词。现在"defining event/achievement/hour"等也常见诸报端。早在1991年1月29日老布什总统作国情咨文报告时开头就言简字明地说:

"I come to this House of the people to speak to you and all Americans, certain that we stand at a **defining hour.**"

当然也可理解为"转折性时刻"。"文革"期间,要是给某人的问题"定性"、"戴帽子"可是要命的事。上下文是理解的关键。可以大体猜出define(界定,下定义)引申轨迹来。

2. Launch Window

"launch window"这个宇航术语是个20世纪60年代创造的,window当时指美国和苏联在一个很短暂的时间(brief periods of time)发射飞向金星的宇宙飞船,以期会合或连接在一起。这个"brief period of time"当时指"during one of the periodic 'windows' for such shots"。通过对接,人们想象中似乎在天空中定有一个洞或窗(an imaginary hole or window)才能使火箭将飞船发射升空。现在,"launch window"也可用于导弹和反导弹(anti-missile missile)两者遭遇的"最佳或最有利的发射时机或时段"。根据此义,又仿此造出"window of opportunity"(采取行动或进行攻击不可错失的良机)。

这些"windows"均意为"small space or short period to get sth accomplished"。20世纪70年代,又仿造出"window of vulnerability",英文释义是"a time just ahead when improved Soviet missiles forces, in theory, be able to destroy most of America's silo-based Minuteman ICBM in a literal bolt from the blue"(苏联导弹力量提高后,在理论上就能突袭美国部署在发射井里的民兵洲际弹道导弹,或苏方第一次打击就攻击美方易被攻击的陆基导弹)。里根在1981年刚任总统选择此语为其庞大的国防预算辩护时说:

"I'll confess, I was reluctant about this, because of the long way we have to go before the dangerous **window of vulnerability** confronting us will be appreciably narrowed."

这里"window"的意思发生了变化,成为"目标"的意思。以上是window引申出的新义。后来 window 或 open the window 又在经济用语上引申出 be willing 和 close the window 为 be unwilling 的新义。见例句：

"No big deal—I'm supposed to write a speech closing the gold window."
（William Safire）

此系时任负责货币政策的财政部助理部长 Paul Volcker 在 1971 年 8 月 13 日与尼克松去戴维营的直升机上好奇引起的。他问尼克松撰稿人 William Safire 与经济学家 Herbert Stein 为啥咬耳朵，回答"the gold window"或"the nation's gold window"，意思是"It named the Treasury's willingness to covert gold into dollars."即指定财政部同意将黄金折合成美元。"the nation's credit window" referred to the Federal Reserve's willingness to offer credit.（联邦储备委员会同意信贷。）这两个"windows"的意思均说明银行出纳曾一度不愿意信贷(at one time behind barred windows)。这样一解释，上面整个句子的意思是："没有什么大事，我拟为总统写一篇他不同意将黄金折合成美元的讲话稿。"我的老天，不了解背景，连美国人也看不懂，难怪北外英国教授 David Crook "文革"后去美国恍如隔世，成了桃源中人了。由此可见报刊英语的重要性。

这样的扩展引申犹如"-in"一样，当时 sit-in 刚造出时，"-in"作复合词用时只有"有组织的抗议或示威"；后又扩展为"公开的集体活动"。

3. Orwellian 添新义

大凡见到"Orwellian"这个字，不少人几乎都一律诠释或译为"奥威尔式的"。但何谓奥威尔式的？先见下列三部词典的释义：

朗文词典称，奥威尔（George Orwell）（1903—1950）写了 *Animal Farm* 和 *1984* 这两部小说而负盛名。……这两部小说使大众对政治的看法和描述受到很大影响，书中所描绘的政治制度有时被称作 Orwellian（奥威尔式的）(Both novels have had a great influence on the way people think and write about politics, and political systems like those described in the books sometimes called Orwellian.)

The New Oxford Dictionary of English 在奥威尔词条下的简介是：... his work is characterised by his concern about social injustice. His most famous works are *Animal Farm* (1945), a satire on Communism as it developed under Stalin, and *Nineteen Eighty-four* (1949), a dystopian account of（描写反乌托邦的）a future state in which every aspect of life is controlled by Big Brother，在 Orwellian 只注 *adjective*，并无释义。

《英汉大词典》（第二版）的释义是：(英国小说家、新闻记者)奥威尔的；奥威尔风格的；受严酷统治而失去人性的社会的；作 *noun* 用的词义是：奥威尔崇拜者;奥威尔研究者。

《当代英汉美英报刊词典》只有 Orwell 的介绍,而在 newspeak(新话):指极权主义国家流行的政治套话,是歪曲、含糊不清的宣传性语言。英国作家 George Orwell 的政治讽刺小说《1984 年》中创造的一个词,-speak 成为构词成分后不断造出新词,表示行话、术语、专门用语。如 budgetspeak(预算行话)、Haigspeak(美国前国务卿黑格用的政治或外交行话)等。未收录 Orwellian 词条。

以上这些词典对"Orwellian"的诠释使读者难以得出关于此字较明确的意思,朗文讲有时指政治制度。牛津索性不注释。《英汉大词典》注释较具体,有可取之处。

弗朗克·伦茨(Frank Luntz)博士曾是美国共和党抠字专家,被《纽约时报》捧为"语言奇才"。*Words That Work* 一书第Ⅲ章"Old Words, New Meaning"中写道:

Most people use the term **Orwellian** to mean someone who engages in *doublespeak*, the official language of the totalitarian government in George Orwell's 1949 novel 1984. Doublespeak twists and inverts the definitions of words and eliminates terminology the oppressive regime considers politically incorrect in an effort to thereby also eliminate the subversive concepts associated with them.

Because I counsel corporate and political clients on what words work and which expressions to avoid, some have predictably caricatured what I do as **Orwellian**, painting my message memos as sinister dictionaries of doublespeak. I coach people in euphemism and spin, they charge, clouding the debate rather than clarifying it. But I am not **Orwellian** in the sense that these critics mean, or in the way Orwellian has been defined by today's popular culture. My explicit aim is to get people to use simple, straightforward language, and if these critics had actually read Orwell's short but powerful essay "*Politics and the English Language*," they would realize that **calling someone Orwellian is not an insult. The term is actually a badge of honor.**

第一段意思是:许多人用 Orwellian 这个字的意思是指某人说话不开门见山,故意用弯弯绕,这就是奥威尔的小说《1984 年》里描写独裁政府用的官话套话。……

第二段意为:他给公司和政界人士做语言顾问,有些顾客讽刺他说的那一套——哪些词语对受众有效果,哪些应该避免使用是奥威尔所用的

doublespeak,……但我不是那些批评者们所说的那种意义上的 Orwellian,也不是今天普遍已将之定义为 doublespeak 的 Orwellian。我要大家都使用简明易懂的语言。这些人要是真正读过奥氏简短而影响很大的这篇文章——"政治与英语语言",称某人是 Orwellian 不但不是侮辱,显然是在恭维奉承。

此外,Luntz 博士在第三章的开头援引了奥氏此文一段:

"A man may take to drink because he feels himself to be a failure, and then fail all the more completely because he drinks. It is rather the same thing that is happening to the English language. It becomes ugly and inaccurate because our thoughts are foolish, but the slovenliness of our language makes it easier for us to have foolish thoughts."

上述说明,Orwellian 这个词有贬有褒,既有"doublespeak 或 doubletalk"之贬义:deliberately euphemistic, ambiguous, or obscure language. 这一说明比上述词典的定义都明确,但也有"语言大师"之褒义。不过,这一新义是 Luntz 博士的一家之见。

4. Cowboy 新解

cowboy 虽非报刊常用词,但里根及小布什都叫 cowboy 和 Crawford cowboy 总统。2008 年前纽约市长 Rudy Giuliani 在共和党初选中也有人说他是 "an urban cowboy"。1980 年,欧洲新闻界称美国选了一位 cowboy 做总统可以理解,里根在演艺生涯中曾演过牛仔片。为什么说小布什和朱氏也是牛仔呢?

何谓 cowboy? 多数人只是从电影中看到牛仔一副趾高气扬、放荡不羁、敢于冒险的模样。*Longman Dictionary of English Language and Culture* 的注释是:"美国依然认为牛仔是诚实、独立、强壮的男子。这种带有浪漫色彩的观点源自电影和书本而非来自现实生活。在人们的心目中,牛仔穿蓝色牛仔裤、牛仔靴,戴牛仔帽。在美国,人们有时度假时去干牛仔所干的活。"

威基百科(Wikipedia)释义:1. A hired man, especially in the western United States, who tends cattle and performs many of his duties on horseback. 2. An adventurous hero. 3. *Slang* A reckless person, such as a driver, pilot, or manager, who ignores potential risks.

Safire's Political Dictionary 定义为 a political rebel; usually one flamboyantly (炫耀而自负地) opposed to party discipline. its synonyms: maverick and mugwump. 还说:"The word was reapplied to the George W. Bush style because of his Texas background(指他在得州有牧场)as well as his willingness to take unilateral action."小布什初任总统时共和党在国会也占优势。当时,不但他本人,共和党高官们如议员也都趾高气扬,得意忘形,有人因此犯法丢官。

单凭上述定义似乎都与 2007 年 3 月 12 日 *Newweek* 发表的题为"Wrong Time for an Urban Cowboy?"的文章中关于小布什的"a Crawford cowboy"和 Giuliani 先生的"an urban cowboy"的对比式诠释不恰合。见例句：

But from a different angle, Giuliani's leadership style seems out of sync with history's pendulum. Why would voters want to replace a my-way-or-the-highway Texan with a shut-up-and-listen New Yorker? Exchange **a Crawford cowboy for an urban cowboy**? A woman, African-American, Hispanic, Mormon or Vietnam POW would represent a sharper break from the immediate past.

这是否说南部牛仔和城市牛仔与西部牛仔含义不同。事实不是这样。应该说，那些词典和威基百科定义是对的，主要是作者在前面对小布什和朱氏的领导作风，已作了生动简洁描绘，具有单打独斗性，符合萨氏政治词典的解释。把朱氏说成是牛仔，除其领导作风与小布什相似外，作者给他戴上一顶"城市牛仔"帽子，具有嘲讽意味。怕朱氏一旦当上总统，又会重复小布什发动伊战等那样独断专行、单打独斗的误国施政方针。

该刊认为，尽管朱里安尼任纽约市长时治安有功，在 9·11 反恐战中表现出色。但从另一个角度来看，朱氏的领导作风似乎跟历史的钟摆不合拍，为什么要选一位不能容忍异见、独断专行的纽约人当总统，来换一位为所欲为、无法无天的得州人呢？为什么要用一位克劳福德（小布什在得州家的）农场牛仔来换一位几乎一模一样的城市牛仔呢？选一位女人、非裔美国人、拉丁裔美国人、摩门教徒或越战战俘（分别指有意参加 2008 年总统竞选的希拉里、奥巴马及麦凯恩等人）当总统都能代表跟过眼云烟一刀两断。

总之，所谓这两位"南部牛仔"和"城市牛仔"的意思是"独断专行，单打独斗；为所欲为，独裁式的领导作风"。这与电影里的西部牛仔形象不同。今后如果再有一位领导人像布什那样行事，或许会被称之"another Crawford cowboy"或"a Bush style cowboy"，那么这番释义就不是多此一举了。

二、词义变化溯根源

词义的扩展引申是报刊语言不断变化发展的一个主要因素，有多种形式，如从抽象到具体、从泛指到特指、从专有名词到普通名词等，反之亦然，其中有的是转喻产生的词义变化，如从泛指到特指、从某一领域转用于另一领域等就是如此。各类用语项下已列举多例，这里不再重复。

1. 从具体到抽象和从抽象到具体

从舍具体用抽象和舍抽象用具体来看，各有各的难处。不过从编者以往教书和现在媒体译文来看，虚实对转，虚转实意义含混、艰涩而似乎更难把握。这跟汉语的基础是象形文字，国人善形象思维，西人长于抽象思维有很大关系。例如 presence 用于外交、军事作具体意义讲时，指"showing the flag"（显示军力或炫耀武力），引申出至少有七八个意思，还可引申出非外交意义，词义较难把握而易误读，这在"扩大若干常见词的词义面"里已作了详细的举例说明。至于 democracy, economy, power, 作具体意义加上不定冠词意义变化后，有人往往仍错误地作抽象意义理解。还有一种不可数的抽象名词变为复数形式也易产生误解。如：combat fatigue（战斗疲劳症）变为 combat fatigues 语义变化了，作"作战服"讲，至于 hostility 变为 hostilities（战争）、hospitality（友好款待）变为 hospitalities（招待礼节）。entitlement 变为 entitlements（社会保障计划）曾是 20 世纪 80 年代初的时髦词。liquidity 流动性，指拥有流动资产状况，资产变现能力等，平素不接触金融词汇会感到陌生。对 nudity 当裸体图片、镜头或场景讲也不习惯。modernity（现代事物，新式东西）更不会用，觉得别扭。

2. 从泛指到特指

从泛指到特指，在"科技用语"里已举例说明 control 用在 control mice 一语里而发生的词义变化。

3. 名词的变化

从专有名词到普通名词词义生变的例句已在其他用语里举了数例。最新的就数 Swift Boat Veterans for Truth 这个 527 组织中一个为政党竞选攻讦的组织，现在 swift-boat 不论作动名词、动词或形容词都有"揭老底"或"诋毁"之义。例如：

a. Democrats vowed again yesterday not to get '**swift-boated.**' (*The Hill*)

昨天国会民主党议员再次发誓不能再受到克里那样的攻击诽谤。

b. Ms. Sheehan could no longer be ignored, **the Swift Boating** began. Character assassination is the [White House political strategist] Karl Rove tactic of choice, eagerly mimicked by media surrogates. (*The New York Times*)

一旦 Sheehan 女士不再能置之不理后，揭老底/人身攻击的战斗就打响了。……

4. 词性的变化

词性的变化也产生新义。如 multinational 成名词为"跨国公司"，given 成 *prep.* 作"considering"讲，变为 *n.* 后词义为"a known or established fact or situation"。

5. 从某一领域转用于另一领域

某一领域的词语转用于另一领域引起词义的变化。如：股票用语的 initial public offer 指"首次公开募股"，用于竞选则转义为候选人"首次获得的筹款"。

宗教用语 true believer 原指"虔诚的信徒",后在集团中作"铁杆分子"或"同志"讲;反对党指这类人为"狂热分子";在美国指"保守派"或"极端保守派";西方或社会主义国家指死扣教条、原则的"教条主义者"或"保守派"。再见"101"这个很时髦的学校用语。101(读 one-0-one)原为大学本科生选课时目录上的代号,现扩展引申为"基础课"、"基本功";"基本战略战术";"含有介绍材料的广告"等。如《上下册》四版就有一课"Holy War 101",还用作 adj. 。go-to 也不是原来"go to"的意思,而又有了"能搞定的"、"得力的"的新义;logistics 原为军语"后勤",现引申为"物流"。至于"wheels within wheels"作"鸡毛蒜皮的小事"讲,只是一人用过,词典、网络尚未接受,不足为训。

6. 时代变化

在研究现代报刊用语时,尤其要注意随着形势的变化跟风的词语。如:2002 年美国竞选资金法改革出台后,以前给政党捐款的 soft money 如再这样筹款即变为"非法的竞选捐款",Solid South 原指美国南部为民主党的可靠票仓,现在铁杆南部不再,已成为 fluid South 了。Super Tuesday 的词义也发生了变化,不再专指南部诸州,可指任何区域在任何星期二举行有诸州参与的初选。Katrina 飓风一词成"自然灾害能摧毁一座城市"的代名词。Deep Throat《低音嗓门》原为美一电影名;1973 年 Watergate 事发时期作"提供消息的神秘人物的代号"讲;2005 年后指时任 FBI 副局长 W. Mark Felt,等。

再如:冷战结束后"cold war"为"过时或无用的政策"。因在荷兰的"Maastricht"市签订的欧盟条约,美国将该词作"扩大了的国家主权"讲。another Yalta 告诫西方国家与苏联这样的共产党领导人打交道时切莫上当受骗。源于雅尔塔会议(Yalta Conference),二次大战行将结束前夕,美、英、苏三国政府首脑于 1945 年 2 月在苏联克里米亚的雅尔塔举行会议,为彻底打败德、日做出了一系列重大决定,同时会议却为在欧亚两洲重新划分势力范围而秘密签订了《雅尔塔协定》和发表了《克里米亚声明》。美国有些领导人如小布什等至今仍对 Yalta Agreement《雅尔塔协定》持批评态度,认为该协定将波罗的海三国如立陶宛和东欧国家划给苏联是错误的。用在国际关系上,指二战后美苏划分范围的雅尔塔体制。Finlandization 芬兰化是 20 世纪 70 年代常用的国际政治行话,所谓"芬兰化",因为芬兰之于苏联,虽未被并入苏联版图,但在其压力下,一切都为它所左右,形成一种"不战而降的局面"。常用来指非共产党掌权的某些欧洲国家像芬兰一样,屈从于苏联的压力而采取与其保持友好关系或亲苏的外交政策。后来东欧社会主义国家使用该词的意思是,保证政治上拥有主权,经济上享有自由,但同时必须与前苏联保持睦邻友好关系。苏联在戈尔巴乔夫掌权后,实行"改革和开放"政策,东欧人将芬兰化看做是同超级大国合作的样板。

苏联解体后,该词即成了弃之不用的外交用语。color/flower revolution 颜色或花儿革命倒是流行开来,一度成为西方搞政权更迭(regime change)的惯用手法。ayatollah 阿亚图拉是对伊斯兰教什叶派领袖的尊称,如伊朗已故宗教领袖 Ayatollah R. Khomeini(霍梅尼),转喻搞一言堂、独断专行的当权派或权威人士。

三、语言的弃旧换新

　　凡事推陈出新,语言也不例外。有人认为,政治语言变化最快,这跟每隔几年领导人就更换、班子就改组不无关系。再则,媒体对政治语言的变化和发展也比其他领域敏感,也是一个原因。9·11 事件后以及奥巴马上台前后至 2009 年 3 月这一短暂时期,涌现大量新词可见一斑。有的新词必定要挤掉一些旧词。

　　常读外刊者确实可以发现一些弃旧换新的例子。如(white)backlash(指白人对民权强烈抵制、集体反对)之所以在此词义上能取代 backfire 或 reaction,是因为带有奴隶主鞭子色彩。再如 gay marriage 在 *Newsweek* 上就比 same-sex marriage 使用的次数少得不成比例,尽管"gay"比"same-sex"字短或更具报刊用词的特点,大概由于其有"快乐的"意义,遭到保守派选民的抵制吧。媒体的目的是为了扩大销量赚钱,最好是谁都不得罪,财源滚滚,用词得全面考量。sanitation services 替代 garbage removal 就是很好的一个例子。恐怕这也是委婉语逐渐增多的一个重要原因。不妨再举一例 phrase 弃旧换新的例子,如"between the devil and the deep blue sea"(进退两难)或"between Scylla and Charybdis"(处于锡拉岩礁和卡律布狄斯大旋涡之间;腹背受敌,进退两难。指 Homer 史诗 *Odyssey* 中的典故)可能已不时尚,尼克松总统国内事务顾问 John Ehrlichman 在水门事件作证时的用语"between a rock and a hard place",牛津词典定义为 *informal* 用法。再看 *Safire's Political Dictionary* 说明:"The phrase is a colloquial updating of the classic between Scylla and Charybdis."这本是西部方言,因尼克松是西部人,到华盛顿做官时带了一帮西部亲信,因白宫常用,也就在全国用开了。原来 Ehrlichman 用时意思较含糊,意为处于左右为难的困境中;现在指在道德上处境两难。20 世纪 70 年代,《华盛顿邮报》还仿此 phrase 发表社论"Between Iraq and a Hard Place"。90 年代后当人们注意到此双关语后就成了美国流行的用语。看来正式书面文体就一直能将之排斥在门外。当然,所谓新的词语的更换是一个渐进的过程:有的已经流行开来;有的正在进行;还有的只是美国潮流或一家之见,尚处于见仁见智中。不过,下面所列

This word replaces that word,大多数取自美国专家著作①。

Was	Is Now
backfire/reaction	backlash
barnacle 难以摆脱的追随者	hanger-on（追随者）
big bug	big shot/wheel（要人，大亨）
blue dog Dems 南方民主党保守派	boll weevils 棉铃象甲②
candie-box returns	phony votes
caretaker 房屋看管人	estate manager 房产管理者
come-outer	bolter（脱党者）
fugleman 组织者，发言人	henchman（贬）重要的助手
floater 尚在观望的选民	swing voter 摇摆不定的选民
garbage removal 垃圾搬运	sanitation services 卫生服务工作
gay marriage	same-sex marriage
housewife	stay-at-home mom
hunker 20 世纪 40 年代纽约州以 Hunker 为首的民主党内保守派	conservative Democrat, Demopublican③
impotence 阳痿	E. D. /erectile dysfunction 勃起功能障碍
organ grinder	partisan newspaperman
persimmon 柿子；肥缺	plum 李子；肥缺
roorback 中伤候选人或政敌的诽谤性谣言	gutter flyer 恶毒下流的竞选传单、小册子等
secretary	administrative assistant
stewardess	flight attendant
Sunday School	civil service reformers
swing around the circle	tour the country
trimmer 骑墙者，见风使舵者，趋炎附势者	opportunist
used car	pre-owned car
waiter/waitress	server
wire worker	small-time political manager
young scratcher	antimachine Republican
Young Turks 党内的反对派、反抗派	angry young men 对现存体制不满的少壮派，"愤青"

应该指出的是，事情不是一成不变的。现在的新词说不定成了明日之黄花。而昨日之黄花可能成为香饽饽。即有些被摒弃或消亡（die）的词或许还

---

① *Words That Work* p. 70；*Safire Political Dictionary's* Prolegomenon xii.
②③ 编者所加。

会重生(born again)。例如 snollygoster(无原则性的政客)和 mossback(反动派,拼命反对任何进步或改革者)就因杜鲁门总统喜欢而又获得新生。Philippic(抨击性演说;痛斥)在艾森豪威尔任总统时又重新出现。不过,这毕竟是少数。

四、语言语法创新

1. 语言的发展

报刊是造词工厂,新语在文字上首先见诸报端,已在本书政治、外交、军事、科技、经济等用语里举例,此处不再赘述。语言形式发展变化不如新词产生的速度那么快。记得笔者在 50 年代上大学时,"One has difficulty **in** doing sth"中的"in"不能省,后来"in"通常省略。2004 年出版的英国 *Longman Dictionary of English Language & Culture* 在 difficulty 条目举例仍未省略:"She had great difficulty **in** understanding him"。可美国有份杂志的例句却省了(见"**读报知识**"九、国会是"Bureaucratic Empire"第 3 段),这或许只有美语变了。再如:

The two men will attempt to **prevent** the party's local election campaign launch in Leeds **being overshadowed** by questions about Mr Blair's future and renewed speculation about a handover deal between them.(2004/5/4 *The Times*)

此句里的"prevent...(from) being overshadowed"是省略、新创,还是记者或编辑的疏忽大意?*The Times* 可是英国第一块金字招牌的 quality paper。不过在"It's the Economy, Stupid!"里的"名词+Stupid"成了被模仿的惯用语,尤其常被报刊用作政治标题。(见"**政治名言的理解与翻译**"),不但如此,stupid 这个词义的变化似乎与引申扩展不搭界。见例句:

(1) The Foreword Was "The Mideast, **Stupid**!" (David Twersky)

(2) Others think the mudslinging only obscures the bigger picture: "I want to know how we are going to deal with the healthcare crisis, educating our children and creating and keeping American jobs. It's not what happened in Vietnam, **stupid**." (2004/10/4 *Newsweek*)

(3) Not since James Carville helped Bill Clinton take the White House 16 years ago by reminding him "**it's the economy, stupid**," has the nation's economic state played such a key role in a presidential campaign. CNN's New Hampshire exit poll found that 97 percent of Democrats and 80 percent of Republicans expressed anxiety about the economy. (2008/1/21 *Newsweek*)

(1)(2)例中的"stupid"是否"lacking intelligence or common sense"意思呢?

(1) 中东以往是首要问题,真愚蠢! 或愚蠢的是以前把中东作为首要问题。

(2)……现在不是越南战争发生的问题,真愚蠢。

如果说第(1)例没有上下文不好断定 stupid 词义的话,第(2)例可说得很清楚。医疗保健、教育子女、创造工作机会和使企业不外包是现在人们要在 1994 年大选中候选人要拿出对策加以解决的民生之事,至于发生在越战中民主党总统候选人 John Kerry 是否背叛战友等问题与现在的实际问题相比已是过去、无关紧要的事了。

如果此字作"Reader is merely being urged to keep the central issue in focus"或如第(3)例所报道的是 Carville reminded Clinton 而后来成为克氏的竞选口号而获胜,所以意为"remind sb of central goal"。这样,(1)(2)例的意思是:

(1) 中东:以往可是首要解决之题!

(2) 不要忘了,现在所面临的可不是以往越战中所发生的那些陈芝麻烂谷子的事。

从这两例并结合"It's the Economy,Stupid!"说明 stupid 不过是词义扩大了,但"(It's +)名词+stupid"这种句型该是个创新发展。有点类似北京口语"傻帽儿"也引申出新义来。

此外,在"报刊语言主要特点"一节"简约"里,状语从句省掉连词、主语和助动词等成分,而将形容和过去分词等用作句法应该是句法或语法上的创新发展。这是英语从"形合"为主向汉语"意合"为主靠拢的"中化"趋势,英国文化协会(the British Council)2009 年甚至大胆预测,汉语会超过英语成为世界第一语言,这样讲是故意耸人听闻。但西方年轻人当中的汉语热却是不争的事实。"北漂"来找饭吃的也越来越多,expat(移居国外)也流行开来。(见"An American in Beijing",2008/April/4 *Time*,已作《精选本》四版课文。)

2. 语法的变化和发展

在谈语法的变化发展前,读者拟先读"新闻语言主要特点"中"简约"和"时尚"这两方面中语法和句式上的变化和发展,其中有些值得探讨。

谈到现代英美报刊文章,不妨听听一位政治幽默家的忠告:

"When we disregard the rules altogether we get anarchy or, worse yet, Enron."—political humorist Bill Maher[①]

Maher 的忠告,犹如中国人常说的"没有规矩,不成方圆"。我本人搜集了两个这样的例句:

(1) Paris **announced** that the General **will** visit Brazil as the guest of President Gonlart during the latter part of this year. (*AP*)

---

① Robert Luntz: Word That work, Hyperion, 2007, p1

(2) Meanwhile, never forget the state of the opposition parties. Quite the most important question there is the Fulham by-election, probably in April. It **is** a Tory marginal, with Labour second and the Alliance third **at the last general election**. The Tories can afford to lose it in midterm. The battle that matters is between Labour and the Alliance. (1986/1/31 *Financial Times*)

如果说第(1)例符合现代语法学家的规则,第(2)例中的"is"在说明是 at the last general election 里不用"was",可见现代新闻人员写报道,写评论,都要求迅速,这是优点,可是文字有时并不那么考究。

下面是王宗炎老先生在谈到这种语法上的所谓变化时比喻说:"有的句子前后脱节,好像前进中的列车突然分为两截,使人为之愕然。"例如:

Sir Arthur **argued** that industrial revolution **is** impossible without an agrarian revolution first. (1979/10/24 *Newsweek*)

Gingrich **believed** that an editor **edits** best who **edits** least. (1979/8/13 *Time*)(仿"Government is best which governs least.")

Randolph Quirk 指出,要是所追述的话在作者执笔时仍然适用,可以免除时态的呼应。他所举的例子是 Socrates *said* that nothing *can harm* a good man. 在现代书刊中,这种例子比比皆是:

Mondale **was telling** his hosts that Washington **wants** the U.S. Chinese honeymoon to continue. (1979/9/10 *Time*)

Her colleagues **hinted** that she **may try** to talk to the Pope again next month. (1979/10/22 *Newsweek*)

在现代书报中,从句的时态与主句不相呼应的往往有之。

In Hongkong, the local office of the United Nations High Commissioner for Refugees **found** itself so short of funds that it **decided** to cut off the $1.20 daily food allowance provided for 17.000 Vietnamese refugees in the colony who **are unemployed** but capable of working. (1979/8/13 *Time*)

are unemployed 分明与 found, decided 在时态上没有一致关系。本来可用 were unemployed,因为在做出决定的那个时候,那些难民是失业的。

His comments **left** observers in no doubt that the Shah **had been swayed** by the counsels of those who **urge** him to resist the opinion of a hardline military-run government. (1978/10/21 *The Economist*)

left 和 had been swayed 互相配合,urge 可不然。要是改为 urged,谁也不能说错。

Among his critics... there **remained** a wide-spread belief that Carter

himself had not provided the leadership the nation **needs.** (1979/8/6 *Time*)

remained 和 had not provided 合拍，needs 则并非如此。

有的既有呼应，又无呼应。有时一个句子有两个宾语从句，一个与引述动词的时态互相呼应，一个则不呼应。这是另一种复杂情况，不妨注意。

President Park's government **had shown** once again that it **was** more than capable of coming down hard on its opponents—but not that it **can break** South Korea's seemingly endless cycle of repression, protest, repression. (1979/10/29 *Newsweek*)

was 与 had shown 配合，can break 并不。

至于在同一段文章中，上句保持时态呼应，下句不守常规，更非少见：

It（指 the separate statement issued by South Africa's prime minister）**said** that there **would be** no reduction of South Africa's military presence in Namibia until there **was** a "complete and comprehensive cessation of hostilities." It **went** on to say that South Africa **insists** that a firm date **must be fixed** and **kept** to, whether or not the violence **continues**——and South Africa's troops **are** still there. (1978/10/21 *The Economist*)

would be 与 said 有同一时间基准，insists 与 went on 各走各的路。

从以上各例可以看见，在现代文章中，不讲时态呼应的句子是很多的，情况也很复杂，这是耐人寻味的语法现象。*

习　　题

阅读理解文章

"Wrong Time for an Urban Cowboy"（2007/3/12 *Newsweek*）

---

* 王宗炎：《汉英语文研究纵横谈》北京大学出版社，1997，第 255—258 页。

第三章 广告与漫画

第一节 广告(Advertisement)

一、广告内容和语言特色

广告在美英报刊尤其是报纸中,约占篇幅的一半以上。西方广告内容广泛,千奇百怪。除了新产品、新技术、求职、招聘、娱乐、旅行、烟酒、购车置业等外,甚至还有色情和出租丈夫的广告。有些广告有助于我们了解这些国家的社会生活,甚至政治、经济、科技等动态。广告使用的照片和文字必须要有针对性,能打动和招徕顾客,激起购物欲望。因此文字必须简明、生动、形象,经常运用比喻、双关、夸张、对仗、拟人化等修辞手段。

二、广告的分类

1. 竞选广告

竞选广告得付款,不过宣传推销的不是商品。美国共和党的抠字眼迷、民意调查专家 Frank Luntz 也说:

"The key to emotional language is its simplicity and clarity", says Republican pollster Frank Luntz. "It has to be immediately believable and authentic. If it requires you to think it's less powerful; if it requires you to explain, it's less powerful." (2007/12/24 *Newsweek*)

他这里讲的竞选广告(political ad),要煽情必须简明。常抓竞选对手竞选主题或纲领的弱点。自"9·11"恐怖袭击事件后,通常使用恐惧策略最管用。正如《新闻周刊》总结小布什的竞选策略讽刺道:"The only thing we have to use is fear itself"。再看以上同期的一篇"The Roots of Fear"的报道文章中奥巴马是如何看待这一问题的:

So when the student asked America's climate of fear, Obama pounced. "We have been operating under a politics of fear: fear of terrorists, fear of immigrants, fear of people of different religious beliefs, fears of gays that they might get married and that somehow that would affect us," he declared. "We have to break that fever of fear... Unfortunately what I've been seeing from the Republican debates is that they are going to perpetuate this fearmongering..."

也就是说美国的所谓的竞选成了"a politics of fear"。那么事实是否如此呢？见下列几幅广告：

（1）一幅 2007 年就展开 2008 年大选前哨战的图示广告（display ad）（此图不清楚而作无图处理）词是："Pushing Voters' Button：The threat of immigration."移民潮威胁美国人的工作，饭碗涉及普通选民的切身利益。若一方候选人主张采取宽容政策，另一方就以此做广告：抓敏感问题：以移民潮的威胁来吓唬他们，抛弃对方。

（2）下幅是 2004 年大选时，小布什和切尼针对民主党候选人 John Kerry 作的广告，用奔袭的狼群作比喻：

狼群下面的文字说明此广告是：PAD FOR BY BUSH-CHENEY 04 AND THE REPUBLICAN NATIONAL COMMITTEE AND APPROVED BY PRESIDENT BUSH

主题是：Primal Fear：Bush said Kerry's weakness would draw predators.

首要恐惧：布什说克里的软弱会招来食肉动物，"软弱招人欺"。他鼓吹"弱肉强食"的森林法则，美国这么强大，谁敢侵犯？显然是玩弄竞选伎俩。

（3）其父亲老布什在 1988 年大选中也利用与民主党候选人 Michael Dukakis 在两人辩论和竞选中发现对手较理性，就利用 the "Willie Hortorn ad" 而赢得大选的胜利。见广告：

1988 年美国大选时民主党总统候选人迈克尔·杜卡克斯（Michael Dukakis）给定罪的黑人杀人强奸犯 Horton 发放周末休假证（weekend pass），该犯在休假期间又犯了暴力罪。于是，这就成了竞选中的一个大问题。共和党总统候选人老布什抓住此事做文章，攻击对手处理罪犯过于软弱。在冷战时期的美国，强硬派占上风，杜卡克斯犯的这个错误是他落选的一个主因。画面只用了 Kidnapping，Stabbing，Raping 三个字就将选民从 Dukakis 那里吓跑了。

2. 商业类

在报刊中,商业广告居多。如丰田汽车公司在《新闻周刊》刊登广告,推销一款名叫"陆地巡洋舰"(Land Cruiser)的越野车,广告词说道:

> You don't close your eyes when you drive a car...
> so why should you when you buy one?
> TOYOTA LAND CRUISER.
> When there's no road, it makes its own.

翻译广告不宜全文照译,只要将精神译出即可,试译为:"开车得睁眼,买车得瞪眼。"言下之意,"你应睁大眼睛,比比看看,定会选购这款车。""前面若无路,此车当先锋。"这句话说明这款车越野性能极好。丰田公司在中国的广告词是:"车到山前必有路,有路必有丰田车。"这类具有画龙点睛的广告词,使人难以忘怀。

(1) 2008年开始美国三大汽车厂通用(GM)、克莱斯勒(Chrysler)和福特纷纷向联邦政府申请注资救助。2009年6月通用已申请破产保护。于是出现了下面一幅关于废旧汽车的广告:

底特律的一个废旧汽车处理厂墙上写着:Detroit Auto Capital?(底特律,汽车之都?) Bring it Back(还我英名来)。Buy American(快买美国车)。(Reuters)

(2) 乍一看左边这张《新闻周刊》上的图片，就知道此人正在为某事揪心。这就吸引读者要问个究竟。再看上面的标题："FRUSTRATED WITH CORPORATE TRAVEL COSTS?"立即就知道这位老总正在为公司出差费用的上升而烦恼。怎么办？有办法。这家澳大利亚最大的旅行理财集团 UTAG 的广告词说："Call now to make an appointment with a UTAG Corporate Travel Manager and find out how to cut your travel expenses up to 35%."

"只要当面向 UTAG 公司分管旅行业务的经理咨询，贵公司的出差开支就会下降35%。"

广告词寥寥数语，便诱人得出结论：值得向这家咨询公司花钱请教。

(3) 右图是《美国新闻与世界报道》上刊登的一则德国"汉莎航空公司"（Lufthansa）的广告，为招徕乘客，广告词只有一句话："There's more to Lufthansa than just nice smiles.""汉莎（航空公司）的服务远不只是甜蜜的微笑，还有更多的关爱。"原图下面还有一行未能印出的小字"This is an authentic passenger statement"说明："此话非本公司自夸，而是乘客所说的一句实话。"借用乘客的赞美词做广告，可谓用心良苦。

(4) 右图是美国杜邦(Du Pont)公司在《时代》杂志上登载的一幅广告,它说"The feet of a six foot tall, two hundred pound runner will absorb roughly 352,000 pounds of stress per mile. Unless Du Pont Hytrel helps absorb it first."意为"一位6英尺高、200磅重的赛跑者,每跑一英里,他的脚要承受约352,000磅的压力。别担心,穿上杜邦公司生产的(Hytrel)热塑性高弹体的鞋,就能帮您减压。"也就是说,只有顾客穿了这种Hytrel的运动鞋,才能减轻脚所承受的压力,轻松参加竞赛。可编译为:"穿上Hytrel鞋,脚下轻松跑如飞。"

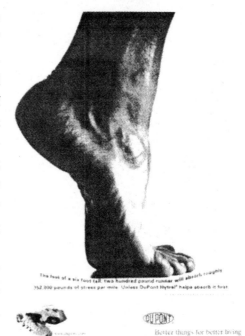

(5) 分类广告,有的配有小图,有的没有。下面是《哈泼斯》杂志刊登的分类广告,有Personals(征婚交友类),Artwork, Publications, Library Services, Business Opportunities, Gourmet(美食家), Professional Services, Gifts, Travel, Real Estate(房地产), Education 等类。若对有些分类广告乍一看不太懂,细看内容就明白要推销什么和提供什么样的服务了。如Library Services说明图书馆能给读者提供出书、编辑书稿和代笔等项服务。

3. 公益类

2009年5月,起初被称为猪流感(swine flu)的甲流在美流行。见下面一幅公益广告:

5月26日,美国首都华盛顿一名女子从预防甲型 HINI 流感的宣传海报前走过。(法新社)

英文以 A(HINI)(甲型 HINI 流感)为题,下面的说明是:

Cover your sneezes; Wash your hands! Use soap and water; If you are sick, stay home. (打喷嚏,要掩鼻;搓肥皂,勤洗手;患了病,勿出门。)

第二节 漫　　画

　　漫画有别广告,画家从新闻取材,通过夸张、比喻、象征、寓意等手法,借幽默、诙谐的画面,针砭时弊。漫画犹如社论,立场鲜明,内行一看,就知奥妙。有些漫画十分含蓄,缺乏背景知识和想象力,一头雾水。有时一画或一言寓两事。语言简洁,常用时髦词、委婉语和名言。如:"The Bug Stop here."稍不注意,易欣赏或理解有误。

一、种族歧视

　　丑化奥巴马:2008年7月21日,《纽约客》杂志刊登了一幅丑化民主党总统候选人奥巴马的封面漫画。这幅"恐惧的竞选"漫画中,身穿穆斯林长袍的奥巴马和打扮成恐怖分子的妻子在白宫的总统办公室,相互击拳致意。墙上挂着拉丹的画像,壁炉里焚烧着美国国旗。

二、财经类

1. 被骗贷款酿危机:

　　(从左至右)Fed(美国联邦储备委员会)和 Banks(银行):I'll Let You Borrow Some more...(再多借些吧……)

　　Consumer(消费者):Isn't That How We Got Into This Mess?(还嫌糟得不够吗?)

2. 开放信贷又遭讽:

代表美国者：Finally! Credit Markets Are Thawing!("信贷市场终于解冻了!")救生圈上字：The Economy(经济)

北极熊代表失业者：Yipee(哎呀!)(对 Thawing 表示惊恐) Thawing 是双关语,冰融化了,北极熊也像房贷者一样被淹死了。
(2009/4/2 *Time*)

3. 多少年来美元币值全靠中国、日本、沙特等国借债输氧支撑。画讽刺说:

画上端写着：Federal Reserve Note(联邦储备委员会钞票);

美元上方写：United States of America(美利坚合众国);正在吸氧者身上写：Value(币值);氧气罐上写：Foreign Life Support(外国救命罐);最下方写着：The Dollar;植物根部问号,问还能硬撑多时不贬值?
(2008/1/23 *The Tampa Tribune*)

三、阿富汗和伊拉克战争

1. 失败

黑板上字：OPERATION LOST CAUSE(军事行动代号：败局已定的事业);最底下一行字是："IT'S A COMPROMISE. THE WHITE HOUSE MAKES THE PLAN AND THE CONGRESS GETS TO NAME IT"(两不吃亏：白宫订计划,代号国会定。仿"总统出主意,国会做决定"。

(2007/4 *The Observer*)

2. 虐囚丑闻

为虐囚丑闻辩解：有施刑者还有为之辩护者。于是 2008 年中旬美国《自由

记者报》讽刺时任国务卿赖斯(Condoleeza Rice)既施刑还狡辩。见画和说明:

TORTURE AND TRUTH(酷刑和实情)

赖斯语:WE DON'T CONDONE TORTURE AND WE DON'T STRETCH THE TRUTH[我们不容忍酷刑,也歪曲实情。图中赖斯正使用刑具拉伸"事实真相"(此处的"The Truth"采用拟人化的手法)的手脚,施用酷刑。]condone 还仿 Condoleeza 容忍酷刑。

四、社会百态

1. 失业:因经济衰退,描绘平民生活的讽刺画更多。因限于篇幅,只举一画。

乞丐身边牌子上写着:LIFE COACH(谋生活有道。生活能力强,配当教练了。)(2009/4/1 *The Columbus Telegraph*)

2. 枪支、毒品等泛滥:枪支管制一直是美国争论不休的问题,个人可自由拥有枪支,造成社会和校园不断发生枪击事件。见画:

(1)(左图)母亲:HOW WAS SCHOOL TODAY?(今天学校情况怎样?)

孩子:YOU KNOW, SAME OLD BORING STUFF...(你知道的,还是老一套那些令人生烦恼的老玩意儿——没劲……)

(右图)母亲笑颜开:MUSIC TO MY EARS...(这话我可最爱听……)

桌上报纸上字:SCHOOL SHOOTING(校园枪击)

第三章 广告与漫画　　133

（2）菲尔普斯：北京奥运会 8 块游泳金牌得主 Michael Phleps（吃毒事曝光）在换气还是吸毒？（2009/2/10 *Los Angeles News*）

3. 戏谑胖人

2006 年 12 月登载在《新闻周刊》上一幅漫画，女子对还在抹嘴的胖子说："YOU ATE THE FOOD PYRAMID."意为："吃一座食物金字塔啦，还减什么肥？"此画妙在"food pyramid"，一语双关，又极尽夸张之能事，说明能吃的全吃了。食物金字塔表示生物群中食物关系的生态金字塔，主要捕食者排在最顶层，每层皆以下一层为食，植物类通常排在最底层。

4. 通信方式如此进化：人类可能连书不会读、字不会写了。见画：

THE EVOLUTION OF COMMUNICATION 通信的进化：从左至右分别代表：FIRST WRITTEN WORD（最初书面语，手写文字），MOVABLE TYPE（活字印刷），MASS PUBLICATION（大批量出版物），EMAIL（电子邮件），第五个人用 TWITTER（推特），说："140 CHARACTERS. WHAT MORE IS TO SAY?"（140 个字符。还有什么可说的?）（利用 TWITTER（微型博客）用户可以发送最多 140 个字母的"TWEET"，TWEET 是一条短信的俗称。）（2009/3/31 *The Denver Post*）

5. 上帝造人说与进化论

2005年9月12日刊登在《新闻周刊》上的一画一言寓两事漫画,只要结合课文"The Evolution Wars"(2005/8/15 *Time*)(《精选本》四版课文)和"Floods Ravages New Orleans"(2005/8/31 *The Washington Post*)(三版课文)两篇文章读一读,我们就不难看懂此画的含义。左边电视画面显示的"KATRINA"(卡特里娜飓风),右边坐在沙发上的是一男一女,那位男士说:"SO THIS IS INTELLIGENT DESIGN."〔原来这(卡特里娜飓风)就是"智能设计"。〕此处还暗讽智能设计竟能造人。intelligent 智能(能通过内置显微处理器)处理信息。

五、国际

1. 美式民主:下列两画讽刺美国的所谓民主:

这是2006年1月28日和2月28日分别发表在美国政治卡通网上的两幅漫画,讽刺小布什政府到处散布民主自由而到头来自吞恶果的尴尬处境。左边的一幅中的两个人分别是小布什和哈马斯(Hamas),英文字为"DEMOCRACY IS ON THE MARCH!!!"(民主在大踏步前进!)哈马斯被美视为巴勒斯坦的恐怖组织,美国和以色列的死敌。然而它在美国支持的于1月26日举行的立法选举中却击败温和的主流派法塔赫获胜而执政,使美感到震惊,于是急忙表态拒绝给予援助和在外交上打交道。

这幅伊拉克两大教派 Sunnis(逊尼派)和 Shiites(什叶派)武斗场面的漫画，画中美国的坦克兵却不无讽刺地说："NOW THAT WE'VE BROUGHT DEMOCRATIC DEBATE TO IRAQ. LET'S QUIETLY PULL OUT."(既然我们把民主辩论已带到了伊拉克，那我们就悄悄地撤走吧。)看来美国到处宣扬的民主就是让那些国家武斗不断，内战不止，国无宁日，民不聊生。这真是对美式民主的莫大讽刺！

如能将上面两幅画结合现在巴勒斯坦和伊拉克的形势，就能理解得更深。关于哈马斯上台执政的情况可结合"Sobbing Settlers' Resistance Fades As Troops Clear Homes"(2005/8/18 *The Times*)这篇文章来看。

2. 自造的阿富汗战争

随着"9·11"恐怖袭击事件发生、美国对阿富汗塔利班政权动武后刊载在《国际先驱论坛报》上的这幅漫画。当初为抗击苏联入侵阿富汗，美国及其盟国悄悄地武装阿游击队。苏联为巩固其入侵不断武装阿傀儡政权。具有讽刺意味的是，过去那些"Made in France, Made in USA, Made in Russia, Made in Belgium, Made in Italy, Made in Great Britain, Made in Israel"的武器，现在却反过来都被塔利班用来迎战美国2001年对它发动的攻击了。漫画说明，塔利班是美国和前苏联在冷战时期争夺势力范围和资源的产物。

习 题

错误改正

1. 看对下页四幅画理解有错否？"one-o-one"究竟是何义？(见"**常见委婉**

语")"Exit"是"出口"还是相当于"way out"("出路")何在?

黑板上写着：ASKING FOR BAILOUTS 101(救市101种策略)
老师：We pride ourself on being a business school that keeps curriculum with the times(我们自己的商学院课程能够与时俱进而感到自豪。)
门上方写：Exit(出口)

2. 下画中的"It's the Economy, Stupid!"究竟该作何理解。(见"**政治名言的理解与翻译**")

"牛"代表牛市,华尔街房贷证券热炒,股价暴价。牛身上字：华尔街。身穿胸前有"06"字样的驴(民主党)手举牌子上的字：It's the Economy, Stupid(蠢货,是经济!)(提醒注意重要的还是经济问题)2006年中期选举时,民主党抓股市泡沫做文章,赢得国会多数议席。

3. 下画中的"Insurgents"(见"**常见委婉语**")和"U.S. Arms"是何义?

左右两个人分别代表：INSURGENTS(反叛分子)和U.S. ARMS(美国军火,美式武器)双方交火,使用的都是美式武器。(见五、"国际"2.**自造的阿富汗战争**)

4. 下画中的"Torture Memos"中的 memo 此处是何义？（见"**外交用语**"）。

　　自由女神脚下台子上字：JUSTICE 司法（公正）　自由女神手持 TORTURE MEMOS《逼供备忘录》哭泣

第四章 读懂标题和报刊用语主要特点

第一节 读懂标题

报刊标题(Headline)常用的有主题、副题、插题、引题、提要题等几种形式，不过现在趋向于只采用主标题。一般说来，英美报刊标题，突出"点"，一语中的；中文报刊标题照顾"面"，面面俱到。两者各有千秋，区别较大。标题是新闻也是报刊的"眼睛"。应该生动、炯炯有神、引人入胜；反之，索然无味，无人愿看。它是新闻内容的高度概括，用字简约，画龙点睛。

报纸报道性文章标题是编辑加的。期刊有的标 Contents 或 Top of The Week(本周要闻)，有的不标。有趣的是，刊首标题与文本标题不尽相同，如 *Newsweek* 2007/12/31—2008/1/7 的这期的 Top of the Week 所列的一个标题是"Competition：'China Isn't a Threat But an Opportunity'"，而 text 内作者标题却是"A Race We can All Win"。这是为了照顾编辑与作者视角不同采取的折中办法。

读懂标题，要先看副标题或提要。如有一篇文章，主标题是"The Greening of America"(1996/2/12 *U. S. News & World Report*)。乍一看，greening 费解，subheadline 是"This year, Candidates will spend more money than ever buying your votes"。这样就明白了，"greening"此处指"dollar or money"。同时必须掌握其主要特点；了解背景情况与有关文化知识；具有文学功底。

一、标题特点

1. 缩略词

标题要简短，而不得不使用缩略词(Abbreviations and Acronyms)，汉语标题也有此特点。

(1) 机构。报刊中常用政治、军事、经济、文化、教育等重要机构的简称，如：

a. **EU'S** Future：The Vision and the Slog

　　EU = European Union(欧洲联盟)

b. Splintered **PLO** Struggles to Stay Alive

　　PLO = Palestine Liberation Organization(巴勒斯坦解放组织)

c. The Great Superpower Spy War　**KGB** vs **CIA**

KGB = Komitet Gosudarstvennoi Bezopastnosti(克格勃,前苏联国家安全委员会);vs = versus;CIA = Central Intelligence Agency

 d. **NATO**: Who, What, Why?

  NATO = North Atlantic Treaty Organization

 e. **OPEC** to Raise Production

  OPEC = Organization of the Petroleum Exporting Countries

 f. World Bank, **IMF** — Do They Help Or Hurt Third World

  IMF = International Monetary Fund

 g. **MIT**'s Leader Shape Program

  MIT = Massachusetts Institute of Technology(麻省理工学院)

为了快速读懂新闻标题,有必要熟悉一些"重要国际组织(Important International organizations)名称缩写"如 G8,ASEAN(东盟)等。

(2) 除机构的首字母缩略词外,标题也常用其他形式的缩短词(shortening word)如:

 a. No Hope for 118 Crew of Russian **Sub**

  Sub = submarine

 b. University Entry Hard for Would-be **Vets**

  Vet = Veteran(退伍老兵)

 c. Put the **Sci** Back in **Sci-fi**

  Sci = science;fi = fiction

 d. America's **Exam** Anxiety

 e. The Economy Sucks. But Is It '**92** Redux?

必须注意,缩短词的拼法是固定的,不能随意乱造。

2. 短字

不妨先看英国前首相和诺贝尔文学奖得主丘吉尔(Winston Churchill)是怎么说的:

"*Broadly speaking, the short words are the best, and the old words best of all.*"

报刊爱用常见的短字(short word)是报刊用语的一个特点,这一特点体现在标题上尤为明显。如:

 a. The **Gems** of War

  用"gems"不用"jewels"

 b. Dayton **Accord**, Reached

  用"accord"不用"agreements"

c. Case Probed
用"probed"不用"investigated"
d. Carter Man in China
用"man"不用"representative"

读者一定见过这些词汇,但用在标题上时,或许不一定知道其中如 man 和 accord 的意思。编者建议。初学者应该读记 Terry Fredrickson & Paul Wedel 合写的 *English by Newspaper* 和 Janice Abbott 写的 *Meet the Press* 这两本书里的 The Vocabulary of Headlines(报刊标题词汇一览)里的标题词汇,这对看懂标题和正文大有裨益。

Vocabulary of Headlines

Headline Word	Common Headline Meaning	Example
air	to make known, broadcast	TV **Airs** "Facts" on Arms Delivery
assail	to criticize strongly	Soviets **Assail** US on A-tests
balk	to refuse to accept	Union **Balks** at Court Order
bid	attempt, offer	New Peace **Bid** in Rhodesia Union Rejects Latest **Bid**
bilk	to cheat	Clerk **Bilks** City of $1 m.
blast *n.* 　　 *v.*	explosion; strong criticism to criticize strongly; strike with explosives	Tanker **Blast** near Manila Reagan **Blasts** Democrats
blow	injury/disappointment suffered	Carter Poll **Blow**
boost	help, incentive	Industry Gets **Boost**
cite	to mention	Management **Cites** Labor Unrest for Shutdown
claim	to declare to be true	Man **Claims** Ghost sighting
claim (claim the life of)	to kill	Bombs **Claim** 40
coup	revolution, change in government	Generals Ousted in **Coup**
deal	agreement	Pay Pits **Deal** Hope
drive	campaign, effort	Peace **Drive** Succeeds
due	expected	Greek FM **Due** Today
envoy	diplomat	American **Envoy** Taken Hostage
eye	to watch with interest	Women's Groups **Eye** Court Vote

第四章 读懂标题和报刊用语主要特点

feud	dispute; strong disagreement	Border **Feud** Danger to Regional Peace
flay	to accuse; criticize strongly	US **Flays** Soviet Block
foe	opponent; enemy	Reagan Talks with Congressional **Foes**
foil	to prevent from succeeding	FBI **Foils** Bid to Hijack Plane to Iran
gut	to destroy completely by fire	Year's Biggest Fire **Guts** 178 Homes
haul	large quantity which has been stolen and later discovered	Cannabis **Haul**
ink	to sign	Thailand, Malaysia **Ink** Sea Treaty
jet	aeroplane	Three Killed in **Jet** Plunge
lash out	to criticize strongly; accuse	Warsaw Pact **Lashes out** at Nato Missile Plan
laud	to praise	PM **Lauds** Community Spirit
launch	to begin	Police **Launch** Anti-crime Drive
line	position; demand	Israel Softens **Line**
loom	expected in the near future	Treaty Dispute **Looming**
nab	to capture	Gang Leader **Nabbed**
net	to total	Drug Raid **Nets** £1 M
	to capture	Patrol **Nets** 2 Prisoners
ordeal	painful experience, drama	Jail **Ordeal** Ends
office	an important government position	Minister Quits: Tired of **Office**
opt	choose; decide	Swiss **Opt** to Back Tax for Churches
pact	agreement, treaty	Warsaw **Pact** Ends
pit	coal mine	**Pit** Talks End
plunge	steep fall	Dollar **Plunges**
poised	ready for action	Bolivian Workers **Poised** to Strike
poll	election, public opinion survey voting station	Swedish **Poll** Shows Swing to Right Voters Go to the **Polls** in Japan
rap *n.*	accusation; charge	Corruption **Rap** Unfair Says Senator
v.	to criticize	Safety Commission **Raps** Auto Companies.
rock	to shock; to surprise	Gov't. Report **Rocks** Stock market
rout	to defeat completely	Rebels **Routed**, Leave 70 Dead
row	a quarrel, argument, dispute	Oil Price **Row** May Bring Down Gov't.
sack	dismiss from a job	Jail Chief **Sacked**
sack (from "ransack")	to search thoroughly and rob	14 Held for US Embassy **Sacking**

snag	problem; difficulty	Last Minute **Snag** Hits Arms Talks
snub	to pay no attention to	Protestants **Snub** Ulster Peace Bid
solon	legislator	5 **Solons** Killed
squeeze	shortage, scarcity	Petrol **Squeeze** Ahead
stance	attitude; way of thinking	New **Stance** Toward Power Cuts
strife	conflict	Inter-Union **Strife** Threatens Peace Deal
sway	to influence or persuade	President Fails to **Sway** Union Strike
swoop	sudden attack or raid	Drug **Swoop** in Mayfair
vie	to compete	Irish Top Ranks **Vie** for Office
void	to determine to be invalid	Voting Law **Voided** by Court

3. 省略

(1) 标题往往只标实义词,略去虚词。省略最多的是冠词和动词"to be",其次是介词、连词、助动词和代词,有时连实义词甚至主句也省略掉。这是因为新闻多节省版面,但以不影响理解为前提。例如:

  a. Italian Ex-Mayor Murdered
   ＝(An)Italian Ex-mayor (Is) Murdered
  b. Married Women to Get Care Allowance
   ＝Married Women (Are) to Get Care Allowance
  c. Rail Chaos Getting Worse
   ＝(The) Rail Chaos (Is) Getting Worse
  d. No Survivors in Gulf Air Crash
   ＝(There Are) No Survivors in (the) Gulf Air Crash
  e. Alaskan Oil for Japan?
   ＝(Will There Be) Alaskan Oil for Japan?
  f. Have Dollars, Will Sell
   ＝(If You) Have Dollars, (They)Will Sell
  g. Ballots, Not Bullets
   ＝(The Algerians Want) Ballots, (Do) Not (Want) Bullets
  h. When America Itself Is the Target
   ＝When America Itself Is the Target, (the Reaction in America Has Been Much Greater Than That in Britain to the Bombs in Docklands and Manchester)

(2) 并非所有的冠词都能省略。如:

  a. West Point Makes a Comeback

"西点军校东山再起"。"make a comeback"是成语,"a"不能省。

b. How America Sees the World

"美国怎样看待世界?""the World"冠词不能省,如省了,词义不同。

c. Killing in the Name of God

"邪教教主以上帝之名大开杀戒。""of God"作定语修饰"Name",所以这个"the"也不宜省去。当然也有因排行需要或从美观原则出发而保留冠词的。

(3)"and"常被逗号所取代。如：

a. Thailand, Malaysia Ink Sea Treaty

＝Thailand (and) Malaysia Ink (a) Sea Treaty

b. Woman Kills Husband, Self

＝(A) Woman Kills (Her) Husband (and) (Her)self

c. Volunteer, Terrorist Killed in an Ambush

＝(A) Volunteer (and) (a) Terrorist (Are) Killed in an Ambush

(4)动词"to be"有时由冒号取代,如：

a. Chinese Cooks: Masters at Turning a Turnip into a Flower

＝Chinese Cooks (Are) Masters at Turning a Turnip into a Flower

b. Kaka: Brazil's Mr. Perfect

＝Kaka(Is) Brazil's Mr. Perfect

(5)动词"say, said"用冒号或引号代替。如：

Mao: We Should Support Third World Countries

＝Mao (Says) (That) We Should Support (the) Third World Countries

(6)以名词作定语替代形容词组成的标题,常常既无动词也无连词,具有双重节省效果,但不宜效仿。如：

a. Channel Tunnel Halt

([英吉利海峡]隧道工程[暂]停[施]工)

b. Shotgun Death Riddle Drama

(枪杀事件,扑朔迷离)

c. Zoo Escape Drama

(动物园猛兽出逃,虚惊一场)

4. 时态

动词时态用法大大简化。如：

(1)几乎都用一般现在时,这是标题的另一个重要特点。新闻所述的事件多半是刚刚发生、正在发生或将会发生,按英语语法规则应用动词的相应时态。但为了使读者感到是"新闻"而不是"旧闻",常用一般现在时来表示：

A. 过去发生的事,如:

    a. 13 **Die** as crowded Van Crosses M4

    b. Jeweler **Is** Slain

B. 正在发生之事,如:

Schools **Ask** Parents for Money Toward Books

(2) 用动词不定式表示将来时态,如:

    a. Peking **to Fire** Test Rocket to South Pacific

    b. At Least 4 **to Leave** Cabinet as Clinton Begins New Transition

(3) 过去分词表示:

A. 现在状态,如:

    a. U. S. Car Makers **Viewed** as Threat by Europeans

    b. Case **Probed**

B. 过去状态,如:

Colombian **Sent** to U. S. for Drug Trial

C. 正在进行状态,如:

Brazil Elite **Forced** to Make Loans

D. 现在完成状态,如:

Petrol Bomb **Found** outside Cardiff Conservative Club

这些标题中用动词不定式和过去分词所表示的时态与日常英语并无不同,只要语言基础打好了,一看就明白。动词现在式、不定式及过去分词在标题中所表示上述时态如何确定呢?一是主要看导语(lead)。二是根据常识。如:

Schools **Ask** Parents for Money Towards Books

这个"Ask"究竟是表示过去正在进行还是将来进行时态呢?若不看下面的导语是难以确定的。

Dozens of schools throughout Britain **are asking** parents to help to pay for textbooks...

再如:

Brazil Elite **Forced** to Make Loans

RIO DE JANEIRO, May 6 (AP) — The economic elite of Brazil **is being forced** to lend money to the Treasury at 6-percent annual interest over two years...

(4) 应该说明,引语和设问式标题中,除现在时外,还可能有其他时态,如:

a. "I **Was** Not His Mistress"

b. Jones **Planned** to Kill Carter?

c. How 'Soft Power' Got 'Smart'

d. "We **Won't** Quit"

这些时态的应用,主要是为了强调动作的时间性,否则会产生误解。

二、情况与知识

但对初学者来说,要读懂标题,还必须要有各种文化知识,了解全球政经、文化、体育、人物等等动态,否则,若不看消息体的导语和特写体的全文,单凭标题就望文生义,肯定会闹出许多笑话。见例句:

1. Bush's Monica Problem

乍一看还以为小布什总统也出现了克林顿与 Monica Lewinsky 那样的绯闻(Monicagate)。此标题是在揭发布什逼几个司法部联邦检察官(U. S. Attorney)辞职,任用亲信。**Monica Goodling** 从而才揭开布借反恐大搞窃听的内幕。

2. **Cook's** View of Humanitarian Intervention

乍一看,不知道(Robin)Cook 曾任英国外交大臣(1997 — 2001),还可能认为是"厨师"。

3. **Venus** Rising

不了解 Venus(Williams)是网坛美国黑人女明星,还可能认为是"金星"。

4. **WHO** Ranks France First in Providing Health Care

不了解 WHO 为 World Health Organization(世界卫生组织)缩写,还可能认为是"谁"呢。

5. **A Bosnian** Sort of Peace

"Bosnia"(波黑)为"Bosnia and Herzegovina"(波斯尼亚和黑塞哥维亚)的简称,有媒体常将它误译为"波斯尼亚(地区)的"。须知这是脱离南斯拉夫独立,为此打了多年内战的一个国家。例子中的"Bosnian"指"波黑的",而不是指"波斯尼亚(地区)的"。再如 Georgian conflict,指 2008 年俄格(鲁吉亚)冲突。

三、具有文学功底

标题体现编者和记者语言素养和文字技巧等综合水平,有的标题一字、二字或寥寥数字,有的拖沓冗长,有的平铺直叙,有的引经据典,有的极具艺术技巧,讲究修辞手段。日报天天出,不能过夜。期刊编者有时间推敲,标题比报纸精炼优美。据观察,美国报刊又不如英国报刊那样讲究修辞,标题大多易懂些。(见"**报刊用语主要特点**"四、引经据典,修辞色彩浓)

第二节　报刊语言主要特点

报刊语言的主要特点是简约、时尚、创新、引经据典、修辞色彩浓、(插)图文(章)并茂和程式化。这些特点与报刊体裁有关,报道性文章语言是非正式的,与公文体不同,也与高雅的文学语言有别,介于雅俗之间。本节所谈简约、创新等例子,是从语言运用的角度而言的,不是严格的语言学分析。省略、用缩略词、短字、句法上等的"简约",突出一个"短"字,其中有的用法与汉语很相似,尤其是名词代替形容词作定语用,这早在上世纪30年代就曾有学者指出过。所谓"时尚",主要指语言时尚,时髦词大量涌现,与创新有关。"创新"指报刊语言新、奇、活的特点,体现在新言新语层出不穷,旧词不断引申出新义,推陈出新,标新立异。语句、语法也在发展创新,只要读了"跟踪语言的变化和发展"这一节,就一目了然。"修辞色彩浓",主要指报刊常运用各种修辞手段,引经据典,成语典故多,用语新颖别致、形象生动。与文学语言相比,报刊语言在这些方面紧贴现实,更突出些。"图文并茂",主要指插图等与文章配合,交相辉映。文章里所插图表、漫画等加上简练的语言,形象生动、幽默等特点得到充分体现。程式化指读者能谅解和明白的常用套语及新闻报道中固定的几种形式。应该说明的是,简约、时尚、创新和修辞色彩浓这四方面相互关联,创新是动力,而这些特点则正在推动当代英语向前发展。

一、简约

报刊文体在 type of news reporting 里,非正式书面语言居多,为节省版面,语言简短,在不影响理解的基础上能省即省,这跟全球化,信息化时代,生活节奏更快有很大关系。

一般语法书上说,省略大多指英语口语句子里可省去各种句子成分;句子结构的省略;句子成分的省略。我们不妨先翻到前面"新闻体裁"里那篇 "Libby Defense Portrays Client as a Scapegoat" 的文章,看小标题及正文里的三段,分析一下有哪些省略形式:

首先标题就省略了 Libby('s) Defense(lawyer) Portray(his) Client as a Scapegoat。其次,小标题中 the administration 指的是第二段里的 the Bush administration。还有缩略词如 Op-Ed = Opposite Editorial(page)时论专栏版。最后,第三段中的 *The Times* 指的是第二段里提到的 *The New York Times*。

上面有四种节省的形式:省去了所有格;节省了名词作修饰语后的名词;简称;缩略词。用缩略词、简称、短字、名词修饰名词、省略"to be"和"and"等简称

第四章 读懂标题和报刊用语主要特点　　　　　　　147

形式已在标题特点里点明,此章不再重复。有的在其他文体里也常省掉的如逗号等,此处不多浪费笔墨。以下拟集中谈谈具有报刊特点的简约。

1. 修辞手段

修辞手段指报刊语言常用的借喻、提喻法及比喻等手法,力求简约。如尼克松回忆录题为 *No More Vietnam*,这里 Vietnam 指代 the Vietnam War。再如:Ronald Reagan's 49-state **landslide** on November 6 put him in commanding position to kick off the nation's third two-term Presidency in 28 years. (1984/11/19 U.S. *News & World Report*)"landslide"比喻一面倒的胜利,后面也不加 win 或 victory。

2. 词性转化

转换词性这种言简意赅的手段在英语报刊上蔚然成风,是英语"一词多性"的体现。如 multinational 由形容词转化成名词,省掉了 corporation;名词修饰名词,或省去前者,或省去后者。在前面已有一例是省略前者的,再举一例省去后者的:Once an important **buffer** between pro-Western Pakistan and the Soviet Union, the country has lost much of its strategic importance since the collapse of communism. (*The Washington Post*),此处 buffer 指冷战时夹于东西方两大阵营或大国之间的缓冲国。此字后省去 state 或 zone;有的将专有名词转化成动词,如"**Tom** sb"作例子,举一个当今最时髦的词:When John Kerry was nominated in 2004 because of his Vietnam combat experience, the Republicans **Swift-Boated** him. (2006/7/3—7/10 *Newsweek*)。若不用"Swift-Boated",则要用一大段文字说明共和党怎么利用 527 组织中一个名叫 Swift Boat Veterans for Truth 网站在 2004 年大选期间对民主党总统候选人 John Kerry 这个越南战争的英雄进行诋毁攻讦一大段文字。

3. 构词手法

构词手段:现代语言尤其报刊语言里拼缀词和派生词尤其多。当然从某种意义上说,任何构词手段都能达到省略的目的。举一个最新的例词,以往里根获取原本是民主党候选人选票和克林顿获得共和党支持者的选票用的还是 Reagan Democrat 和 Clinton Republican,到了奥巴马竞选和当选,就拼缀成 Obamacan/Obamacon。例如《经济学家》在 2008 年 10 月 23 日就以"The rise of the **Obamacons**"为题发表文章,副标题是"A striking number of conservatives are planning to vote for Obama"。此例说明,英语字在向简化发展。再如 **governator** 州长终结者,指美国演员、加州州长阿诺德·施瓦辛格(Arnold Schwarzeneger),他曾在 1984 年和 1991 年分别主演过 *The Terminator* 和 *The Terminator II:Judgment Day*(《终结者》和《终结者 2:世界末日》),故有此称。

这种拼缀例子之多,不胜枚举。

派生词:此处尤其要谈谈这种用"国名+-ization[化]或-fication[化]"构成的词,可将一国某方面的特点或形势勾画出来,是美英报刊常用的一种构词手法,具有高度概括的特点,与"another+国名或地名"一样节省。例如:Albanianization 阿尔巴尼亚化指一个国家甘于政治孤立,结果随之而来的则是经济贫困化。Colombianización=columbianization 哥伦比亚化即某国出现的像哥伦比亚那样贩毒集团用毒资收买政界人士和资助政客竞选等腐败现象。Iraqification 伊拉克化指美国向伊拉克交权,以便仓皇脱身(cut and run)。美国在 2003 年发动伊拉克战争并占领伊拉克后,发现其想使它变成一个西方式国家并非易事。占领军到处受到打击而疲于应付,国际上受孤立,国内遭抨击。因此,美想早日撤军,让伊拉克人自己去收拾这个烂摊子,犹如越南化计划。

另一种是"领导人+-ism"。如 Thatcherism 撒切尔主义,指 1979—1990 年间任英国保守党首相 Margaret Thatcher 所推行的一套强硬的右翼政治、经济政策。再如 Reaganism 指里根任加州州长和总统期间提出的如减税、小政府、自由企业、控制货币供应等的经济政策,也叫 Reaganomics(里根经济政策)的。

以上这种派生词如 Reagan Doctrine 这样的"领导人+Doctrine"一样,是报刊最喜欢给领导人施政方略得出结论,总结其内外政策的用词。类似这些词语,《报刊词典》里大多有例句。

4. 句法上的简约

为适应信息化社会快节奏的需要,报道文章常使用简单句尤其是扩展简单句(expanded simple sentence),其方法有:

(1) 多用介词引导的名词短语(noun phrase),少用从句(subordinate clause)。如:

No longer are the swarming peoples of Asia and Africa sunken, as for centuries past, **in a passive acceptance of their lot.** (*The New York Times*)

例句中用"(in a passive) acceptance of their lot"而不用从句"who accepted their lot"。

(2) 句法结构前移:如以简洁方法表现人物的性格特点,不用关系从句,而只是将职业、头衔或人名前加用的某些形容词或起修饰作用的同位语前置,使修饰语变长,类似中文。如:

A quiet, tubercular physicist named Robert Goddard appeared before a board of military-weapons experts. (*Newsweek*)

通常写法为 A quiet physicist named Goddard who was tubercular 或 a physicist, a quiet and tubercular man named Goddard,此例将 named 省去报刊

中也常见,那就成了起修饰作用的同位语。

(3) 用一个主谓结构或句子直接置于被修饰语前作定语。如:

Changes in social mores, especially in the counterculture years of the 1960s, resulted in an **"anything goes" philosophy** that contributed directly to the rise in violence, drug abuse, divorce and out-of-wedlock births. (1996/8/5 *Financial Times*)。

通常的语序应该是:philosophy that anything goes(＝anything is alright)。

(4) 用引号省去"that"作同位语结构。如:

The attitude "time is money" has more influence on business communication in US than it does anywhere else.

通常是:The attitude that time is money...

(5) 时间状语从句省掉连词、主语和助动词等成分,而将形容词和过去分词等用作起句法。见下面一段文字:

(a) So consider these scenes from March 2004, described by two former top Justice officials who, like other ex-officials interviewed by *Newsweek*, did not wish to be identified discussing sensitive internal matters. (b) Attorney General John Ashcroft is really sick. (c) **About to give a press conference in Virginia**, he is stricken with pain so severe he has to lie down on the floor. (d) **Taken to the hospital for an emergency gallbladder operation**, he hallucinates under medication as he lies, near death, in intensive care. (2007/6/4 *Newsweek*)

在这段文字里,共有四个句子。a. 正常句;b. 简单句。关键在 c. d. 句,没有分别用时间状语从句"When he is about..."和"When he is taken...",而只是将形容词和过去分词引起的状语前置而省略了"When he is"。据王宗炎老先生在《向张道真同志进一言》文章"三、英语习惯和修辞问题"里认为,"**about to return** to the hall"不能放在主语前头,只能说"When he was about to return..."[1]。可现在这种用法在报刊上较多,可能是一个省略的新趋势或与报刊文体有关。另一本语法书说,像这样的结构可省去主语和助动词。[2]

(6) 常用连字符号(hyphen)"-"而组成形容词性的自由连缀词组,带有一定的感情色彩,具有临时性和诙谐性特点。这也是一种定语前置,而且有增多趋势。如:

His only "non-political" gesture was to delete some pointedly wry reference to

---

[1] 王宗炎:汉英语文研究纵横谈,北京大学出版社,1997,第 245 页。

[2] 薄冰:英语语法,开明出版社,1998,第 585 页。

"total victory"and a **"pick-up-our-marble-and-go-home** philosophy. "(*Newsweek*)

不过,前置定词太多,相互关系反而不清,弄巧成拙,近年又有回摆趋势。这跟中文里,一些前置修饰语改为后置,相映成趣。

二、时尚

1. 语言上的时尚

所谓时尚,即报刊语言一直引领当代语言潮流。报刊如落俗套,则无人问津,也不会有现在成千上万份报章杂志。这一点在**"跟踪语言的变化和发展"**节里作了说明。编者看了2008年一年的*Newsweek*,发现一些报刊用语在变,弃旧换新现象明显。如作恩师、顾问、师爷讲常用 guru,少用 mentor,用 adviser 的则更少。再如:same-sex marriage 比 gay marriage 要用得多。African Americans(blacks)和 stay-at-home moms(housewives)等也逐渐用得多起来了。这一点在那节的语言"弃旧换新"里作了说明。不妨看一例句:"You give'em hell! You stand those bullies down!"Retha Justice, a **stay-at-home mom** from Jeffersonville, Ind., told [John] Edwards after hearing him speak at the airport in Louisville on Thursday night.

为了说明语言的时尚,接着再看现代美国青年的用语:

CONTEMPORARY YOUTH LANGUAGE AND DEFINITIONS[①]	
WORD	**DEFINITION**
Bro	Friend
Bling	Bright, flashy jewelry
Bootylicious	Very sexually attractive
Diss	To disrespect someone
Fo'shizzle	An affirmation of a comment or action
Ghetto	A description of urban and/or poor culture
Got game	Ability that earns the respect of others
Hella	Word used to give emphasis to something. Ex:That pizza was hella-good.
Holla	A greeting to get one's attention
Jonesing	An intense, overwhelming craving(渴望)
Mac Daddy	A man who gets everything he wants
Phat	Cool, good-looking
Player/playa	Someone who has many relationships

---

① Frank Luntz: Words That work, Hyperion, 2007, pp. 54—55.

Screen shopping	Window shopping on the Internet
Shout out	Hello to
Tight	Excellent/Outstanding
Trippin'	Description of overexuberant(精力等过分充沛的) behavior
Wacked/Whack	Something very abnormal

当然,报刊中"常见时髦词"是其用语的一个重要特点。(见本章第四节)

2. 语法的时尚

语法的变化发展也是明显的,许多原来语法书上要求的时态一致,有的已有逐渐被打破之势,这在前面章节和下面的"语言语法创新"里举例为证,尽管语法学家不一定都同意这种用法。时尚与创新密不可分,本章中的"简约"、"创新"出现了许多用字。句式上的变化发展,这也是一种时尚。(见**跟踪语言的变化发展**""语法的变化发展"。)

三、创新

当人们发现新事物、遇到新问题、新思潮、爆发出新思维火花时,报刊作为新闻平面媒体的先锋,就要与时俱进,用鲜活词语紧跟形势,老一套吃不开。另一方面,由于全球化,英语作为第二语言更加遍及世界各国,中国学英语的人数已经超过了美国人口,有了三亿多,各地风土人情、生活习惯和社会环境不尽相同,这就必然会使报刊在报道和评论中出现不同的表达形式和词语,现在就有人说有 Chinese English, India English 等。据美国名记者,文学评论家门肯(Henry Mencken)(1880—1956)估计,每年大概会出现 5 千个以上的新词语。伊利诺伊大学英语系主任丹尼斯·巴伦也说:"英语非常灵活。这是它得以生存并且蓬勃发展的原因。"并且英语的词汇还在继续地快速增长。他说,每年有 3000 到 5000 个新词加入英语,"其中有数百个成为通用语"。

报刊语言的创新不仅表现创造新词或旧词新义,还在句型、句法、语法等方面打破常规,标新立异。

1. 新词新义如潮涌

新闻用语准则与丘吉尔说的"... the old words best of all"相反,为了炒作新闻,吸引读者,报刊成了造词工厂。新词多是新闻用语的一个重要特点。例如 2008 年 3 月 19 日 *USA Today* 以就"A New Political Breed: Obamacans"为题发表文章。再如:pandahugger 是最新造的词,意为"亲华派"。2009 年 6 月 11 日《泰晤士报》网站报道,英语词汇已突破百万大关,其中新入选的词汇有:"Jai

Ho!"意为"取得一项重大成就","slumdog"随着《贫民窟的百万富翁》的电影而走红,用来形容"贫民窟生活的孩子",Web 2.0 即"很快来到你身边的新一代产品和服务",globalization3.0,指中印等一大批新兴国家引领时代潮流,等等许多新语。这在"**语言**"尤其是在"跟踪语言的变化和发展"的章节里,已举例详讲,此处不赘。

2. 语法、句法结构的变化发展

打破常规,时态不一致,句法结构的变化已在"简约"和"跟踪语言的变化和发展"及本节"报刊用语主要特点"之一的"简约"里作了说明。现在打破语法和词法常规在报刊中也偶见。例如《经济学家》在一篇文章中将"prevent sb from doing sth"中的"from"是省略掉呢还是疏忽而打字漏掉了。(见"**跟踪语言的变化和发展**"四、语言语法创新)

四、修辞色彩浓,常引经据典;用语新颖别致,形象生动

如前面所言,报刊语言修辞色彩浓,常引经据典,成语典故尤其在标题里居多。如:

1. 引经据典,成语典故多。如:

(1) West Point Makes a Comeback

(2) Thatcher Hits the Road.

此两例中的"makes a comeback"和"hit the road"均为成语。

(3) Liberty Is the True Mother of Invention

套用谚语"Necessity is the mother of invention"(需要是发明之母)。

(4) Pride and Prejudice — Film Location

Pride and Prejudice(《傲慢与偏见》)是英国作家 Jane Austin 所写的一本小说的书名。文章谈的是电影选景中出现的类似问题。

(5) A Farewell to Arms

文章谈前苏联共产党总书记戈尔巴乔夫向前美国总统里根建议彻底销毁核武器的事。引用了海明威所著小说的书名。

(6) A Tale of Two Hearts

文章谈的是一个心脏病人换了人造心脏的事,套用了狄更斯写的名著 *A Tale of Two Cities*(《双城记》)的书名。

(7) 文学典故和圣经故事不但在标题里,在正文中也很多。在第一版"前言"里曾举数例,事实上 the ides of March, the writing on the wall, the Achilles' heel, Pandora's box, *The Adventures of Tom Sawyer* 中 Tom Sawyer 骗小朋友一同刷围栏的小伎俩也见诸报端:

So to be effective, Bush's successor must be a tough-minded but flexible and humble chief executive with a talent for building bridges, not burning them. For instance, preventing terrorism is less a matter of war than a subtle diplomatic challenge involving international coordination and a convincing projection of Western values. It's a group activity, which means that the next commander in chief will need a **Tom Sawyer-like skill in getting other kids in the global neighborhood to paint the fence**. This requires charm and leadership. (2007/3/12 *Newsweek*)

此外,古典及现代作品名及人物常见诸报端,这在"标题特点"和"人名背后文章多"里已举例说明。

2. 标题常运用各种修辞手段。 如比喻、音韵、反语、夸张、双关语等手段以求得生动、形象、幽默、讽刺等效果。例如:

(1) 音韵(见第一版"前言""世界知识"第 3 例):

a. Ballots, Not Bullets

此标题表达了阿尔及利亚人民要自由选举,而不要动刀动枪。记者用"Ballots"和"Bullets"这两个发音近似的词来达到某种语言上的效果。

b. Responsibility Reaps Rich Rewards

押头韵(alliteration),指中国农村联产承包责任制带来大丰收。

c. Bovver Boy's Hover Ploy

当时任英国国防大臣的 Michael Heseltine 因在 Westland 直升机公司卖给美国还是欧洲国际财团的问题上与撒切尔夫人意见相左而辞职。这个标题的四个字为间隔押(尾)韵(alternate rhyme)。应该指出,这并不是最佳运用音韵的手段。

d. Thatcher's Style Wars

指撒切尔夫人任英国首相时凌驾于内阁之上,刚愎自用和独断专行的作风。美国总统里根在任时大搞星球大战计划(Reagan's star wars)。因此可以看出,style wars 是 star wars 的谐音,为讽刺性俏皮语。

e. 在正文里也用。见**"学习方法""**一、词义之确定举例 5."

(2) 双关:

a. 在本书漫画财经类第 2 例中的"thawing"即双关语。

b. On a Slippery Slope

此文有一张图片说明在老布什政府任白宫办公厅主任的 John Sununu 在向下滑雪,意含他因丑闻而正在走下坡路。

c. African Statesman Still Sowing Seeds for Future

坦桑尼亚总统尼雷尔(Julius Nyerere)退休后,在远离大城市的家乡的一个村子里播种收割,以农为乐。然而非洲局势动荡,许多国际领导人都千里迢迢去向他求教治国之道。所以,这位政界元老仍在为非洲的未来而播种。因此标题中的"Sowing Seeds"是个双关语。在正文和图片里也常用双关语。如民主党曾想撮合希拉里和奥巴马两人组成总统竞选正副候选人搭档,奥说了一句双关语:"You don't run for second."(我竞选不是为了当副手;我跑步不是为了得第二。)2009 年 6 月里根总统夫人 Nancy 在纪念里根诞辰 100 周年委员会上看到奥巴马用左手签字时也来了一句双关语:"Oh, you're a lefty."(lefty 有"左撇子"或"左派"之义。)

(3) 矛盾修辞法(oxymoron):

a. A Heroic Failure

前众议院议长 Newt Gingrich 因党内招怨被迫辞职,*Time* 此文哀叹他"虽败犹勇",代鸣不平。

b. A Big Small Company

大而灵活的公司。此外,在正文里也有 benign neglect, lean federation, splendid misery 等此修辞法(例句见《报刊词典》)。

至于借喻法、提喻法和委婉语均在本章分节单讲。

(4) 比喻,尤其常用隐语(metaphor)

A. 标题用比喻举例:

a. A Dove Taking Wing

撰稿者将联合国比作一只展翅起飞的"和平鸽"。

b. Whitewater May Drown Democrats

克林顿竞选连任时,政敌抓住他在阿肯色州州长任内白水开发公司的关系大做文章,民主党怕"白水事件"牵连,遭到"水淹(drown)"。

B. 正文也常用隐语,在军事、政治、外交领域如:

a. Soon after the **opening gun of the campaign**, the **standard-bearer** was denounced as a **hatchetman**. (William Safire)

以上以黑体词,均可视为军事、政治隐语。意为"竞选一开始,这名旗手就背上了职业诽谤鬼的骂名"。

b. The single most striking change has been the official recognition that the **flagship** of the third term, the poll tax, was an error. (The *Times*)

"flagship"旗舰,此处喻头等大事。

c. We must be the **great arsenal of democracy.** (Franklin Roosevelt)(见"**政治名言的理解与翻译**")

政治领域的人或事常以动物作比喻,简直成了 political zoo。例如:elephant(象;美国共和党党徽,代表共和党),donkey(驴;美国民主党党徽,代表民主党），hawk（鹰派），dove（鸽派），bald eagle（白头鹫或秃鹰；秃头政治领导人），lame duck（跛鸭，指任期将满、连任无望或任期将满而依法无法再连任的官员），eat crow（吃乌鸦，被迫认错或收回前言），rubber-chicken circuit（为筹款竞选奔波的巡回鸡宴），floo-floo bird，dark horse，wheel horse（驾辕马；忠实可靠的党员），war horse（战马；老练的政客），stalking horse（掩护马；为分化对方力量或掩护己方而推出的候选人），fat cat（肥猫；竞选运动主要资助人），gerrymander[Albridge Gerry 为前马州州长。原用 salamander（蝾螈）；两词拼缀而成后，意为本党利益而对议员选区的重新划分，喻不公正划分选区]，gypsy moth（舞毒蛾；东北部共和党温和派），boll weevils（棉铃象甲虫；南方民主党保守派），blue dog Dems 与 boll weevils 喻义同，Tammany Tiger（塔慕尼协会的老虎堂；腐败的纽约民主党组织的别名；腐败统治和党棍政治），paper tiger，(British) Lion[（不列颠之）狮；英国]及最新杜撰的 pandahugger，等等。

宗教领域：西方绝大多数人信教，宗教用语引申到政治等方面的隐语不少。如 all things to all men, bleeding hearts, born again, bully pulpit, crusade, church elders, nobody shoots at Santa Claus, Bible belt, holier than thou 等（见"**宗教**"及"**附录**""宗教词语"）。见例句：

a. He[Harry Truman]seemed **all things to all men** and all men including New Dealers and anti-New Dealers, Roosevelt friends and Roosevelt enemies, old friends and new ones...(Jonathan Daniels)

all thing to all men 比喻为人人满意，八面玲珑：批评政客们为私利讨好各方。

b. Even so, if money were the only issue, he could have made millions as a lobbyist. Allen's former White House colleagues were surprised by the pettiness of the alleged crimes, especially since Allen was regarded in the ranks as being a bit stuffy and **holier-than-thou.**(Newsweek)

holier-than-thou 比你圣洁或献身的：形容持一本正经的伪君子状的表现。

c. There are only two groups that are beating the drums for war in the Middle East—the Israel Defense Ministry and its **amen corner** in the United States.(Patrick Buchanan)

amen corner 自动支持的中心，阿门角是教堂内教徒坐席，教士布道时，频频用"阿门"（诚心所愿）附和，喻"跟屁虫"。

因美英国家生活水平高，人们普遍酷爱运动，于是将许多运动语言用于政治等各方面例子或许是最多的。如拳击的 hat in the ring, arena；赛马的 dark horse；美式足球 political football, game plan；垒球 hardball；篮球 full-court press, slam dunk 等等。下面再举数例：

a. He (George Shultz) has been not only a **blocking back**, but a **relief pitcher** for Mr. Reagan, and he must be tired of running interference for him and getting him out of trouble. (*The New York Times*)

"blocking back"阻截能力很强的后卫，橄榄球用语。在政治上指对批评、攻击等左拦右挡，企图使他人摆脱困境者。"relief pitcher"替补投手，棒球用语。在政治上指由他人代替自己出面对政敌进行攻击。

b. Former Secretary of Defense, Dick Cheney, long considered a potential presidential candidate, may **toss his hat in the ring** for the Senate in 1994 as a **warm-up**. (*Time*)

"toss/throw one's hat in the ring"公开宣布参选，单棍对打(single-stick)和拳击用语，拳手抛帽进场，表示他愿参赛。1912年，T.罗斯福用此语示意参选总统。warm-up指Dick此举或为参选总统作准备。

c. At a heated NCAA convention in Dallas, university presidents overcame a dogged **goal-line stand** by money-minded athletic directors and trimmed the number of days and allotted to organized basketball and football activities. (*Time*)

"goal-line stand"背水一战，橄榄球用语。goal-line是球门线，按照橄榄球比赛规则，达阵(touchdown)指抱球冲过对方球门线触地就算得分。在计分中，达阵得分最多，此比赛没有真正的"球门"。当对方逼近球门线时，防守队员会奋力围堵。所以"mount a goal-line stand"就是"孤注一掷，背水一战，守住最后关口"的意思。

d. Clinton adviser Mandy Grunwald, one of two women who is a full partner in a major media firm, is a master of **jujitsu politics** — turning an attack into a counter-attack.

"jujitsu politics"柔道式政治或竞选战术，指以攻对攻或针锋相对的竞选策略。

科技用语作隐语的也很多，这一点已在"**科技用语**"一节里作了讲解。此处不再举例。

其他各行各业的隐语都见诸报端，这与报刊载文涉及的面广有关。下面不妨再举数例有关经济、法律、黑社会、赌博及动物如 hog、dog 等方面数例隐语。

a. blue chip 指热门股票，a blue-chip team 则指一流的班子或团队。

b. The jury is (still) out. (见"**法律用语**")

c. The President summoned his top political advisers—essentially **the Georgia**

Mafia—eight Governors and assorted energy experts, environmentalists, labor bosses, businessmen and congressional leaders. (*Newsweek*)

　　Mafia 指黑手党。此处的 Georgia Mafia 所谓佐治亚帮,指来自卡特家乡、在其政府任要职的 Joseph Power, Hamilton Jordan 和 Griffin Bell 等佐治亚州的死党或亲信。中国四人帮(Gang of Four),外刊有译 Shanghai Mafia 的。

　　d. 赌博用语。如 put one's cards on the table 喻"摊牌"。再如:

With millions or even billions of dollars on the line in bills before Congress, **the stakes run high.** (*U.S. News & World Report*)

　　"The stakes run high"赌注大,风险高。

　　e. 动物如猪、狗均可用作隐语。如 eat/live on high hog 猪臀尖上等肉,喻"过着富裕的生活"。至于 dog 被视为人的朋友或爱物,ankle-biters, attack dog, bird dog, Kennel dog 等均为隐喻。如 1954 年艾森豪威尔执政时因失业率高,国防部长 Charles E. Wilson 在记者招待会上打比喻说:"I've always liked **bird dogs** rather than **kennel dogs.**"

　　此处 Wilson 将愿意搬到就业机会多的地方居住的失业者比作 bird dogs,就地等靠要的比作呆在窝里汪汪叫的狗(kennel dogs)。

　　(5) 类比

　　类比(analogy)构词的特点仿照原有的同类词造出其对应或近似词。如仿 cold war 造出 hot war,并又杜撰出 cold/hot/dry peace;仿 T. 罗斯福总统的 Square Deal 造出 New Deal, Fair Deal, New New Deal 等等。有的已在政治、经济、科技等用语里对这种跟风式造词法作了举例说明。

　　3. 用语新颖别致,形象生动活泼

　　用语新颖别致、形象生动活泼是报刊语言一个吸引读者的重要特点。如"减少"不用 decrease,如不是刀砍 cut, trim,就是斧劈 ax;力量不用 power, strength,而用 muscle,"会议"或"讨论会"不用 conference, meeting 而用 powwow 等。不妨再举数例:

　　(1) The president may be correct to think he can defuse the controversy merely by revising the policy. But he is wrong to suggest that the policy—rather than Sununu—caused "the perception problem." Over the weekend, the former Governor began to experience the **drip-drip-drip** of damaging details that in the past has been part of the ritual undoing of other controversial government figures. (1991/7/8 *Time*)

　　drip-drip-drip 因对某事坚持不懈或不断的批评、报道和宣传而产生犹如"滴水穿石"一样的影响或效应。该词尤其常用于揭批犯错官员,直到其罢官为止。

(再见《精选本》四版第 12 课"Path of the Storm"第 9 段例句)。

(2) Gonzales, the president's lawyer and Texas buddy, went on to replace Ashcroft as attorney general. Today he is **twisting slowly in the wind** — a phrase from Watergate — facing a vote of no confidence from the U. S. Senate. Only the president's still unflagging support has kept him in office. Gonzales has been accused of politicizing the Justice Department by presiding over the firing of U. S. attorneys — apparently so they could be replaced by more dependably loyal partisans. (2007/6/4 *Newsweek*)

常作 twist slowly, slowly in the wind (见"**改朝换代产生和流行的词语**")。

(3) We were **eyeball to eyeball**, and I think that other fellow blinked. 见"**政治名言的理解与翻译**"。

(4) 报刊里的漫画,语言更是形象生动活泼。

五、图文配合,交相辉映

报道文章里插有图片、照片,甚至还有漫画,使文章生色。好处是:
1. 吸引读者。如:

Is America's new declinism for real?

By Gideon Rachman

首先映入人们眼帘的是署名行(by-line)后这幅画:头带星条旗帽、拄着拐杖、步履蹒跚的秃鹰(bald eagle),然后再是对此画寓意提出疑问的标题。这幅无文字说明的画,不但代替了副标题或提要,而且更形象生动,说明美国已老态龙钟,垂垂老矣!可标题却对美国衰落论提出疑问,这就使文章更引人入胜。(已作《精选本》第12课课文)(见"编书谈""一、选材与课文 6.")

(2008/11/24 *Financial Times*)

2. 真实又节省篇幅

"眼见为实",人们看到报道文章,又见插有图照时更加可信。一图千言(A/One Picture is worth a thousand word),凡照片、图表文字说明过的,一目了然,无需赘言,节省了篇幅。先见"Star Wars: The Next Version"(2004/5/4 *The*

第四章 读懂标题和报刊用语主要特点　　　　159

New York Times)文章里的照片及文字说明:

Clamshell doors cover 70-foot-deep missile silos at Fort Greeley in Delta Junction, Alaska, where a missile defense system is under construction. Ralph Scott, a fort spokesman, is shown on the site.

这幅照片说明美国在阿拉斯加建设反导弹防御体系,发射井深达70英尺。

再见另文"China's Growth Poses Opportunity and Risk"(2004/3/3 *The New York Times*)图表:

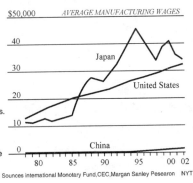

Distinct advantages
Chinese wages remain far below American and Japanese wages, despite rapid economic growth. Figures for China and Japan may include some items counted as benefits in the United States. Large annual variations in Japanese wages mostly reflect fluctuations in the exchange rate between the dollar and the yen.

此图表说明中、日、美三国制造业平均工资对比,说明日美高于中国,而中国和日本每年工资的变动反映了与美元挂钩汇率浮动有关。

这两图省去文章一大段文字,即使加上,也不能说明得如此清楚。

3. 释疑解惑

(1) 有助理解难点。有的时候文字表达远不如图示直观明白。1987年我编文选一版时见到下列评论:

In order to succeed, Reagan and his advisers must first come to some agreement about their goals—and then try to rebuild the consensus about American foreign policy that has yet to recover from **the debacle that ended a decade ago on the roof of the U. S. Embassy in Saigon.** Despite its successes so far, the Reagan administration has done little to unite Americans around a coherent approach to the rest of the world. (1985/1/7 *Newsweek*)

何谓"the debacle that ended... on the roof of the U. S. Embassy in Saigon"? 我百思不得其解。突然想起了美国从南越撤退时，见到有一幅直升机从使馆屋顶将人吊走的图片，于是作了下列注释：

here refers to the fact that North Vietnamese troops and the National Liberation Front entered Saigon only hours after the U. S. completed an emergency airlift of embassy personnel (and thousands of South Vietnamese) standing on the roof of the embassy building.

记得 2008 年或 2009 年在对比美国今后怎样从伊拉克撤退与越战溃败逃离对比时，该刊又一次刊载了这幅照片，可惜未收集起来。

(2)《精选本》四版有篇"Nanospheres leave cancer no place to hide"文章(2007/6/21 *New Scientist*)，怕人们对这个治癌新法了解不透，特加上三幅图加以辅助说明，下面是其中的一幅：

Nanospectra developing AuroLase™ therapy, a medical device which incorporates a new class of particles to selectively destroy solid tumors.

说明纳米光谱研发的商标为 AuroLase 疗法，是一种包含一组新的粒子，能分清癌细胞和未受扩散波及的细胞，摧毁顽固癌肿的一种治疗装置。

(3) *Newsweek* 在论及"family man"重要性时，于 2007 年 2 月 26 日一期同时发表两篇文章，其中有一幅前马州州长罗姆尼与孩子嬉戏，家庭生活其乐融融的插图（见"**读报知识**""**价值观**"），使读者深刻理解何谓"family man"，对保守派候选人有何重要作用。

4. 图表漫画语言简练、形象生动、幽默等特点得到体现

漫画本身就形象幽默，常用多种表现手段，配合文章，相互辉映。当然也有图文均丑陋的，如奥巴马执政不久，有家地方报纸将奥比作订计划的猴子，该报还加以说明给毙了。在"（**广告与**）**漫画**"里已举数例说明，此处不再赘言。

此外，它们还可以使读者看起文章来轻松些。

六、程式化

程式化不同于陈词滥调（cliché），而是公众体谅和明白的套数。

1. 常用套语（conventional phrases）

除见本章第六节"**常用套语**"外，另外一种套语是：

(1) ...two former top Justice officials who...interviewed by *Newsweek*, **did not wish to be identified**...

(2) A Gonzales aide at the time (who **asked not to be ID'd**(=**identified**) talking about internal matters) said there was a "miscommunication" and "genuine confusion" over who was in charge. (2007/5/25 *Newsweek*)

从两例中"did not wish to be identified"和"asked not to be ID'd"及"declined to be named"等即提供消息者不愿公开自己的身份或姓名，免受牵连。有时记者故意卖关子，吊读者胃口。

2. 报道程式

导语里离不开5个W和1个H，尽管现在不一定要置于第一段。

新闻报道基本上是时间顺序式、悬念式、解说式和调查式等几种形式，尤其倒金字塔结构最常见。其他新闻体裁另当别论。

七、其他特点

报刊语言表达法还有以下次要特点，但只是与以上六大特点相比相对次要。

1. 外来语多

随着全球化兴起，国际交流日益频繁，英语成了出口大户，进口大家。这是门肯当年谈论新词根源，始料未及。记者用外来语，想卖弄学识，二来也想使外国读者有亲近感，三来英语找不到对应词来表达得贴切，如北京奥运会吉祥物"福娃"，最终还是定译为汉语拼音，针灸几十个穴位一律音译更是明证。外来语多从"**其他方面的读报知识**""**议会名称林林总总**"里也可见一斑。再如：

(1) Two weeks ago she was in Moscow, and her private meeting with President Gorbachev, whom she warned about backsliding on **perestroika**, topped the main Soviet TV evening news broadcast. (*Newsweek*)

"perestroika"为俄语，意为"改革"，词义相当于英文"reform"。

(2) To San Francisco **fengshui** guru Steven Post, who has seen interest grow from a "trickle to a torrent," the assumption that people are affected by their surroundings is common sense. (*Newsweek*)

"fengshui"汉语里的风水近年西方建筑界赞不绝口，认为合乎环保精神。

2. 被动语态较多

华中科技大学外语学院的黄勤教授 2007 年在《上海翻译》杂志第三期发表的"我国的新闻翻译研究：现状与展望"一文，在引用尤江华老师的话说："……新闻英语文体中被动语态出现频率在各类文体中最高……"这或许与本书讲的"**常用套语**"多有关。当然较多的还是科技文体，以示客观论述。

3. 俚语、行话多

美国新闻语言里俚语、俗语、行话多，这与报道、采访文章中引用各界、各地被访问者有关。行话切口在"**党语和党争用语**"已论及，这里不妨举两例：

And finally, Capitol Hill may simply reject most of the proposed cuts, one by one. The spring swarm of "**Boll Weevils**," Southern conservative Democrats willing to support Reagan's first round of spending curbs, may be replaced by an autumn flight of "**Gypsy Moths**," moderate Republicans from the Northeast who are reluctant to reduce social spending further. (*Time*)

4. 即兴造词

这里只举两例：

(1) abstentionist party 逍遥派，指一批投弃权票选民

(2) ... Khomeini thus established himself as leader of the revolution by calling upon the armed forces to overthrow the Shah. Hundreds of thousands of copies of the letter were distributed in Iran. As a Tehran University professor put it: "We were struggling against autocracy, for democracy, by means of **Xerocracy**." (*Time*)

"xerocracy"为新闻语言即兴造出来的俏皮字。Xerox 是日本有名的施乐复印机的商标名。因下面例句中的词语 autocracy 和 democracy 中有-cracy，而即兴将-cracy 加在 xerox 上，这样就造出了 xerocracy，意为"通过复印反伊朗国王的文件，催生民主"。

习　题

阅读理解文章

Is America's new declinism for real? (2008/11/24 *Financial Times*) (见《上下册》或《精选本》四版)

第三节 报刊语言弊病

新闻语言有短、新、奇、活等优点，也存在着如下弊病。

一、用词出格多

a **bimonthly** publication 通常理解为"双月刊"，可有的作"半月刊"讲。尽管有的词典建议如作半月刊时最好用 semimonthly，参议院议长用 President，有时却用 Chairman 替代，jail 与 prison 也不分。再如：

The Maoist insurgency lasted from 1996—2006, during which time 13,000 people died. (2008/4/15 *The Christian Science Monitor*)

from 1996 to 2006 才是合适的，这只能说其随意性太大。似乎只要读者看懂了就行。

二、陈词多

如：1. candle-box returns；2. forty thieves；3. ring

例 1 指"假票"(phony votes)；例 2 指过时的"掌管着钱袋的政客"(politicians in control of finance)；例(3)作"政治组织"(political organization)讲因贬义而弃用。这都是陈旧用词。此外，不用新国名，仍用 Burma 指 Myanmar(缅甸)，Ivory Coast 指 Côte d'Ivoire(科特迪瓦)。这同时也说明其非正式或随意性的一面。

三、不看对象行话多

如：1. resource center；2. learning experience

例 1 指"图书馆"；例 2 指"教室"。

四、加缀构词滥

这方面的例句已在"语言知识"里提到过，例如用-nik,-in,-nik,-gate, generation 造出的新词，多如牛毛，难怪出现 fed-up 的现象，而滥造出了如 gatenik, nikgate, 和 gategate 等词。

五、求新弄巧成拙多

报刊常舍通俗求时髦，如小布什时期的 surge："Obama: bracing for a last minute **surge**—even if it doesn't come."(2008/11/3 *Newsweek*)(见"**常见时髦词**")

此句中的"surge"就不如"bounce"词义准确。例如党代会后民意对候选人的支持率会一度升高,就用"convention bounce/rebounce"。现在各行业增加、升高等有都用 surge 的倾向。

六、任意扩大词义

在这方面的例子 ironically 比较典型,它可作任何意思的语句开头词,已无任何"具有讽刺意味"的意思,成了含糊不清或模棱两可的字。其次,presence 已几乎成了一个万能词,因含混、艰涩,不易理解。事实上,stupid 连许多美国人也不知道其扩大了的意义。

七、赘词多

这里不妨先见一本权威书的举例批评:

A crisis is, of course, a serious turning point by definition. But the habit of automatic-modifying leads to many other redundancies, among them:

absolutely conclusive	future plan	organic life
agricultural crops	general public	original founder
awkward dilemma	grateful thanks	patently obvious
close proximity	hired mercenary	personal friend
complete monopoly	irreducible minimum	personal opinion
completely full	lonely hermit	present incumbent
divisive quarrel	meaningless gibberish	true facts
end result	mutual cooperation	ultimate outcome
entirely absent	new record	violent explosion
exact counterpart	old adage	vitally necessary

To test the logic of such knee-jerk(不经思考而自动用上的) modifiers, turn them around. Are there gentle explosions? Pleasant dilemmas? False facts? Impersonal friends? Treat adverbial intensifiers with the same reserve as adjectives. *Very urgent*, *highly unusual*, *extremely serious* — the adverbs add only shrillness.

Definitely is generally expendable. *The ambassador will definitely leave tomorrow* says nothing more than that he'll leave. *Undue* can be particularly fatuous:

The government cautioned against *undue* alarm over Skylab.

They didn't mean that there was reason for due alarm. They meant there was no cause for alarm.

The conservative group complained that the court was taking *undue* liberties with the Constitution.

Strike *undue*. Adverbs like *relatively* and *comparatively* are usually mere padding:
Relatively few senators answered the quorum call.

The number of football injuries is *comparatively* high this year. Relative or compared with what?*

这类赘词读报时往往习以为常,见怪不惊罢了,稍加思索并不难发现,比如:

1. Adapting to the India effect will be traumatic, but there's no sign Corporate America is turning back. Yet the India challenge also presents an enormous opportunity for the U.S. If America can handle the transition right, the **end result** could be a brain gain that accelerates productivity and innovation. India and the U.S., nations that barely interacted 15 years ago, could turn out to be the ideal economic partners for the new century. (2003/12/8 *Business Week*)

2. House Banking Committee Chairman Jim Leach (R., Iowa) and Sen. Alfonse D'Amato, chairman of the Senate Whitewater and Banking Committees, reportedly are ready to proceed with reports and hearings on matters as diverse as the **Travelgate scandal** (in which White House Travel Office employees were fired and then smeared)... (The *Wall Street Journal*)

Travelgate scandal"出差办公室人事丑闻"将-gate 和 scandal 两个意思相同的词和词缀用于同一个词语,类似汉语"破天荒第一次"的说法。-gate 源出 Watergate,本来就是"丑闻"的意思,再加上 scandal,显得画蛇添足。

八、省略过度

过分节省"of"等字而将许多名词堆积在一起。在"标题特点"中谈到有些标题既无动词也无连词,如"Shotgun Death Riddle Drama"就是一例。这使得有的英语词句更接近汉语语序堆词,搞得英语不像英语或无视语法规则,令人费解,弄巧成拙。如:

1. A paper published by **the UN Development Programme Poverty Alleviation and Social Development project** based in Quito argues that worsening

---

* Rene J. Cappon: *The Word: An Associated Press Guide to Good News Writing*, The Associated Press, 1982, p26.

income distribution has accompanied market-oriented economic reforms in nearly all Latin American countries.（*Financial Times*）

2. **The Lakers' evolution into play off favorites under coach Phil Jackson** is testimony to the way they're accommodated themselves to him.

3. Mr. Cheney supported that view...."not going to protect one staffer ＋ sacrifice the guy...."（2007/1/24 *The New York Times*）

例 1 应加"of"而成为"the Poverty Alleviation and Social Development project of the UN Development Programme";例 2 为省略定语从句而使主语变得那么长,这与有的"句法的简约"的例句一样,不足为训。例 3 用"＋"号来替"and"更是省过头。

九、避免重复用词过头,反而用词不当

为了避免用词的重复,有的词语用得很牵强附会,词义不够准确。如《美英报刊文章阅读》(精选本)(第二版)(下称《精选本》)第 13 课"Lobbyists Out Of Shadows Into The Spotlight"（1985/2/25 *U. S. News & World Report*）为例,作者在文章中竟用 outfit 和 hitters 指 lobby(ing) firms。

十、标题编排令人生疑

标题应简短且用字简约,但有时在一篇报道中分别有两部分不同的内容而分成两行的。如:

It Isn't the Cow That Are Mad

It's the People That Are Going Mad

这种排行是可以的,可有的只有一个内容却排成三行甚至四行。有人誉为艺术性编排;本人认为有正文不够标题来凑之嫌。还有人说成出于无奈,这正表明编辑功力差。

十一、体例不统一

标新立异,随意性大,是弊病,还是创新? 只能见仁见智? 如:

1. 专有名词第一个字母该用大写的用小写,有时在一篇文章中体例也不统一。如"Beijing Dreams of 2008"（2000/9/7 *International Herald Tribune*）一文中的 the Bid Committee(申奥委员会)是对的,但有时写成 the bid committee。再如"Why the Monarch Must Stay"（1996/3/11 *Newsweek*）一文将组织机构(the) commonwealth (英联邦)的第一个字母小写。又如第 15 课"Decision:It's Bush"（2000/12/14 *International Herald Tribune*）一文中的职称"the new vice

president, Mr. Cheney"也小写。在正式文件中有的字大写和小写意思不一样，如 community, 如大写，则表明为一个正式组织，小写则不然。

2. 标题的大小写，英美也不统一。孰是孰非，很难说清，还是大体有个框框好，现在这样搞法好像有些出格。英国报刊和美国的一些刊物的标题除了第一个字母和专有名词（即使专有名词的缩略词，英国报刊也只是第一个字母大写，如 NATO 就写成 Nato）外，其余一律小写。如在引语中不注明标题会被误解为正文中的一个句子。如：

    a. The poverty challenge for Ecuador's populist (*Financial Times*)

    b. African Statesman Still Sowing Seeds for Future (The *New York Times*)

3. 拼写不统一，有的甚至在同一篇文章也有此现象。如：

    hard liner   hardliner

    life style   lifestyle

十二、语言尤其是背景知识错误屡见不鲜

搞错领导人职务十分常见，例如苏联或中国领导人是党主席还是总书记就说不清。有的自称中国问题专家，竟把八一帽徽说成是天安门图像，真是丢人。（见"报刊、网络和词典亦有错"）

习　　题

阅读理解文章

"Beijing Dream of 2008"(2000/9/7 *International Herald Tribune*)读后举例说明体例不统一之处。

第四节　常见时髦语

创新是报刊语言的一个特点。时髦语自然常见诸报端，英文谓之 buzzword，兼指重要但又难懂的专门术语，有时带贬义。《纽约时报》专栏作家 William Safire 在政治词典里给的词义是："小部分行话或含糊其辞的时髦词(a snipet of jargon; or a vague vogue word)..."1974 年出版的 *Buzzwords* 一书作者 Robert Mueller 将此字界定为小集团内切口或行话、俚语、头面人物爱用的词语等。时髦词语里有新词，但绝大部分是旧词新义，不常看报者望文生义，往往出错，连本国人也难免。较之而言，汉字灵活，造词方便，新义新词虽然居多，但一般不上网或不查词典大体就可以猜出词义，字难词易，的确如此。

一、政治领域

1. Smart Power：奥巴马执政之初想用 soft power 作外交政策，后改用 smart power。

政治时髦语最多，有的昙花一现，有的风行多年不衰。

2009 年最热门当属 1 月 13 日 Hillary Clinton 所说的"smart power"(见"外交用语")，次日，《纽约时报》在"How 'Soft Power' Got 'Smart'"一文中第一段就报道称：

In her confirmation hearing yesterday, Hillary Clinton used the phrase **"smart power"** four times in her opening statement and nine times during her testimony. Cue the headline writers: "Clinton Vows to Lead Using **'Smart Power'** Strategy"; "Clinton seeks a **'smart power'** Middle East strategy," "Hillary Clinton says **'smart power'** will restore American leadership."

2. surge：Safire 的政治词典解释得很清楚"sharp increase in troop strength"，即"兵力激增"。首见于小布什 2004 年 8 月的讲话：

(1) ...so they [U.S. troops] can **surge** quickly to deal with unexpected threat.

(2) President Bush did the unexpected: To quell the sectarian and terrorist warfare, he ordered a **surge** of an additional 30,000 to the crucial area of Baghdad and its environs...

据 2007 年 3 月 5 日 *Newsweek* 在一篇文章中报道，布什怕英国撤军伊拉克局势更加混乱，决定增兵：

(3) Several officials on both sides of the Atlantic (who all declined to be named

when discussing the internal debate on security issues) say there was real consternation among Bush's aides about the prospect of a British withdrawal at a time when the president was planning to make the case for a **surge** of troops.

从这三例可以看出,白宫人员故意避免使用越南战争逐步升级 escalation 而用 surge 一词,吸取了当年缓慢少量多次增兵的教训,妄想快刀斩乱麻,一次猛增兵力,正好符合报刊语言求新求变的特点。

3. stay the course:这个时髦语原为赛马术语,course 作"跑道"讲。里根总统论经济和 L. 约翰逊总统谈越战都用过,指"call for unwavering resolve and persistence in policy",小布什说:"'Stay the course' means keep doing what you are doing. 'Stay the course' also means don't leave before the job is done."可理解为"按既定方针办,不完成任务,决不收兵",或"坚持到底,决不半途而废"。从下列例(1)看,与"cut and run"(不体面地仓促退却或撤军)的意思相反。

(1) 2006 年 10 月两党伊拉克调研组两主席之一的 James Baker 接受采访时说:

Our commission believes that there are alternatives between the stated alternatives... of **"stay the course"** and "cut and run".

又如:

(2) And he'll tout the new Medicare prescription-drug-benefits, urging seniors to **stay the course** despite early bureaucratic snafus that have left some without coverage.

4. blue/red/purple state or America:众所周知,red 原来只是代表共产党的颜色,如 Red China;*Better Dead Than Red*(一反共书名);而 blue 代表忧伤。现在其词义扩展了,"red"用来表示支持共和党的州或美国,而"blue"则代表民主党。此外,还可根据本书"读报知识"(共和党内保守派是主流,民主党里自由派占多数)引申为"保守派"(占优势的)或"自由派"(占优势的)州或美国。

在 2008 年和 2004 年的大选中,在计票晚上,美国全国广播公司专门在纽约民主广场上画了一张大地图,用颜料喷涂红蓝两色。把美国版图相当完整地切割出了两大板块:西部、东北部沿海和五大湖区沿岸是支持民主党的蓝色美国,而从广阔的中西部腹地直到南方沿海的州都是共和党的红色美国。见例句。

(1) Kerry looked down on Bush and saw the worst of **Red State America**, a know-nothing who blustered and swaggered, even though his head was stuck in the sand.

(2) Then, as now, a party establishment — based in Congress,

governors' mansions and Georgetown salons — viewed him as a loud-mouthed lefty whose visibility would ruin the Democratic brand in **Red States**.

(3) It's smaller than you'd think. Coming off a clockwork convention, Bush last week shook Kerry's support in crucial **Blue States** and gained ground in the Southwest. But W still doesn't stand for "wrapped up".

此外,还有两党势均力敌选情不明的州,原本称为 battleground states,即两党要争夺选票的战场州。此词是尼克松竞选主管在1968年反对共和党极右派头目 Barry Goldwater 的南部竞选策略(southern strategy)(争取南部诸州民主党势占绝对优势的白人选票之计)而推广用开的,后来该语又与"swing states"连用,但现在由于有了 red 和 blue,两色相混便出现"purple states"这是最时髦的说法,指举足轻重的州。但如是"purple America",则指两党势均力敌、平分秋色的美国。见例句:

(4) Pundits and academics who see a non-partisan "**Purple**" **America**, rather than one divided between Red and Blue, are searching for an excuse, McConnell says. "They're looking for a way to explain away what happened last fall. Look at the map: the fact is, the country is overwhelmingly Red."

5. guru:原本为印度教锡克教圣人或教师,现在已取代"mentor"作"谋士、顾问、大师、恩师"讲。见2007年美联社在中央情报局特工 Valerie Plame 身份被泄露而追查到小布什的军师 Rove 等高官时的报道:

Democrats, armed with subpoenas for President Bush's **guru** Karl Rove and other top aides, are pressing the White House...

rabbi 与 guru 意近,在政治用语上是同义词。在政界内部或核心圈子里用 rabbi,对外用 guru。两字都用来替已过时的 mentor。pundit 也从印度传来,指学者跟 gura 相近。

6. fatigue:近年来在政治外交方面的时髦词。如"aid/apology/compassion fatigue"等。美国国内对小布什竞选班子一再对选民用 terror fear 这一招(见"**政治名言的理解与翻译**""The only thing we have to use is fear itself")感到反感,加上政府连续进行反恐战而使民众一时感到越反越恐,且看不到战争结束的尽头,"9·11"事件后美国并未再受到反恐袭击。这两方面使民众深感受到蒙骗而产生厌恶,于是又出现了"terror fatigue",反恐疲劳症(援助、道歉等同此)。2008年大选又仿造了个 Bush fatigue。见例句:

Instead, Clinton and Obama have tried to differentiate themselves by making the race about something else: which one of them can *win*. For Democrats still frustrated by presidential losses in 2000 and 2004, that's no small thing. Many party activists fear that an unpopular war, worries about the economy and **Bush fatigue** alone won't be enough for Democrats to regain the White House, especially if, like John Kerry, their candidate turns out to be no match for the GOP's disciplined attack machine. (2007/12/10 *Newsweek*)

二、经济和其他领域

1. outsourcing：既是经济也是 2004 年大选的一个时髦语，不仅指 (offshore)outsourcing 还衍生出"nearshoring"（见"经济用语"）。近十多年来，美国许多的公司为降低成本，开始把软件开发等"外包"给印度、俄罗斯和中国等国家。2004 年大选，争取提名为民主党总统候选人的 John Edwards 和 John Kerry 就"就业机会的外流"令国人担心的问题向共和党总统 G. W. 布什发难。因此，外包不仅成了使白领担心的社会问题，还成政府决策的难题。见例句：

(1) And Edwards did it by focusing on a phenomenon that seems destined to occupy center stage in November against George W. Bush: the travail engendered by global trade, which brings cheap goods and services here, but which also exports American blue-collar and white-collar jobs to countries that do the work more cheaply and without the labor and environmental laws Americans must follow. The new buzzword of dread on the trail is **"outsourcing"**.

(2) Undecided voters don't dislike Bush or what he has done. They just want to know if Kerry can do better for them on job loss and at least as well as Bush on security. That requires fresh, positive ideas about **outsourcing**.

2. 101：本是美国大学课程在学校目录上大一学科的代号，后引申为"基础（课）"，并常作标题，如：Holy War 101, Bailouts 101, Religious Literacy one-o-one, Consumer Protection 101 for Visitors from China, 等等。作 *adj.*, 词义扩展到"初步的"，"具有介绍材料的"。

此外, It's the Economy, Stupid! 除句型仍然时髦, stupid 亦然。

阅读理解文章

1. "Word of the Year" (2009/1/3 *Los Angeles Times*)

2. "Catching Up on Catchwords" (1996/4/22—28 *The Washington Post National Weekly Edition*)

第五节 常见借喻词和提喻词

报刊中多借喻词和提喻词,与委婉语、竞选用语和法律语言等相比较易理解,不过得具有较广泛的文化背景知识。不妨先举一例:

Beijing's deal with **Brussels** clears a WTO hurdle — but quick entry is unlikely.(*Far Eastern Economic Review*)

此例中的 Beijing 和"Brussels"是何义?

凡世界各国首都均可指代所在国及其政府,凡战争地、协议签订地和重要机构的总部所在地也均可用来喻指此战争、协议和该机构。地名是这两种修辞格里用得较多的。

一、常用借喻法

1. 常见借喻法

借一事物的名称指代另一事物,称为借喻或借代法(metonymy),如以 the Crown 喻指"皇室事务",Pentagon 指代"美国防部",the blue helmets 喻"联合国维和部队"等。英语中往往用一个词代表整个事件或背景。在现代英美报刊语言中常见到以地名或国名代表整个事件。* 如 Vietnam/Viet Nam 指"越南战争",Bosnia 是"波黑"的简称,喻"波黑战争",Hungary 指"匈牙利事件",the Gulf"海湾战争",Dayton"代顿协议"或代顿和平协议,Post-Soviet 苏联解体后,等等。见例句:

(1) Yet in the years since **Viet Nam**, critics in and out of uniform have repeatedly charged that too many officers have become cautious bureaucrats, adept at Pentagon politics perhaps, but interested more in advancing their careers than in preparing for the brutal exigencies of combat.(*Time*)

然而,自从**越南战争**开始以来的年代中,军内外批评家一再指责道……

(2) Once the political chaff is dusted away, the minidebate over **Bosnia** is instructive. Both Bush and Clinton were saying the same thing.(*Time*)

这是《时代》周刊报道 1992 年美国大选时,老布什代表共和党总统候选人与民主党候选人克林顿进行电视总统候选人的辩论,此例中的 Bosnia 指的就是借喻"波黑战争"。political chaff 指的是"竞选废话"。

(3) Washington concluded after **Dayton**, when NATO bombers seemed to bring him [Milosevic] to the negotiating table...(*Time*)

Dayton 为美国俄亥俄一城市,是波黑和平协议签订地。此例不能说"代顿

---

* 陆国强:现代英语词汇学,上海外语教育出版社,1983,第 66 页。

后美国断定……"。这里的 Dayton 是指 1995 年关于结束波黑内战和版图划分等而达成的协议,称 the Dayton (Peace) accords[代顿(和平)协议]。这样就好理解了。其正式名称应是"Bosnia and Herzegovina Peace Agreements"。

2. 另类借喻法

陆国强先生在论及借代曾举 November 等词语为例说明:"在涉及美国初选或大选时,报刊常以词代事的方式进行报道。"*

现在用年份缩略词既可指代选举及经济情况,如"The Economy Sucks. But Is It '**92** Redux?"(2008/1/21 *Newsweek*)(经济不振,是否这是 1992 年大选时经济情况和大选形势的翻版? 当时因老布什执政时经济衰退,竞选连任败给了克林顿)。此外,还可借喻战争。如:

The decisive step toward victory in Iraq, say military officials, will be to crush Saddam's elite Republican Guard. At least three Guard divisions are massed outside Baghdad, facing the American invaders. In '**91**, the Americans used air power and their superior armor to badly maul some of these same Republican Guard divisions. But it is often overlooked that several of the Guard battalions stood and fought and then made an orderly retreat, living to fight again another day. (2003/4/7 *Newsweek*)

此例中的"'91"指 1991 年以美国为首的联军发动的第一次伊拉克战争。这种以年份或日期指代战争或事件如英文里用 9/11 指 2001 年 9·11 恐怖袭击事件,也是报刊中常用的一种形式,正如 since 1949 指代新中国成立。

二、提喻法

以局部代表全体,或以全体喻指部分,称为提喻或举隅法(synecdoche),报刊中较普遍,例如:Bosnia 代表"波黑",London 代表英国,Kremlin(克里姆林宫)代表前苏联,(现)俄罗斯,Kremlinology(苏联/俄罗斯学),Washington 代表美国,还可代表东部,如 Washington mafia,喻指东部权势集团,cutthroat 代表 assassin(暗杀)或 murder。

三、一词数义

为避免用词重复、使读者产生联想等原因,作者常使用这两种修辞手段。在报刊文章中,为简约、换词等目的,这两种喻词用得尤其多。如 Foggy Bottom(雾谷),是美国首都华盛顿一地名,国务院所在地,喻"国务院",在修辞格里称借代法。又因其外交政策像雾蒙蒙的深山低谷一样模糊不清,令人难以捉摸,颇像"'雾'底洞",因此又用做隐喻(metaphor)来比喻"国务院的政策"。再如

---

* 陆国强:现代英语词汇学,上海外语教育出版社,1983,第 67 页。

Washington 做借喻指"美国或联邦政府",做提喻指"美国",做隐语可比喻为"贪污腐败(corruption)、尔虞我诈(fraud)和铺张浪费(waste)的官场"。

四、常见借喻和提喻词一览

以下是编者经年累月在读报和编书过程中积累的上述两种喻词,这对初读报者扩大知识和词汇面是极其有益的。

Word	Meaning	Metonymical/Synecdochical Meaning
Broadway	百老汇大街(纽约一街名)	纽约戏剧业,美国戏剧业
The capitol	美国州议会或政府大厦	(美国)州议会,州政府
The Capitol	(美国)国会大厦,州议会大厦	美国国会,州议会
Capitol Hill	国会山(国会大厦所在地)	美国国会
Donkey	驴	美国民主党
Elephant	象	美国共和党
ends of Pennsyl-vania Street	宾夕法尼亚大街(首都华盛顿一街名)两端	美国国会和行政当局,白宫和国会大厦,美国行政和立法部门
green berets	绿色贝雷帽	(美国)特种部队
The Hill	= Capitol Hill	美国国会
Hollywood	好莱坞(洛杉矶一地名)	美国电影业、电影界或娱乐业
John	约翰(美国人一常用名)	美国人
J Street	华盛顿一街名	美国特工处
K Street	华盛顿一街名	美国游说界
Langley	兰利(弗吉尼亚州一地名)	中央情报局
Madison Avenue	麦迪逊大街(纽约一街名)	美国广告业
Oval Office	椭圆形办公室	美国总统办公室,总统(职务)
Pentagon	五角大楼	美国国防部
Silicon Valley	硅谷(美国加州一地名)	美国高科技集中地
1600 Pennsylvania Street	宾夕法尼亚大街(华盛顿一街名)1600号	(美国)白宫,总统府
Uncle Sam	山姆大叔	美国政府;美国人
Wall Street	华尔街(纽约一街名)	美国金融界
White House	白宫	总统府,行政部门
Buckingham Palace	(英国)白金汉宫	英国王宫
The City (of London)	伦敦城	英国金融界;英国商业界
Downing Street	唐宁街(伦敦一街名)	英国首相府或首相;英国政府或内阁
Fleet Street	舰队街(伦敦一街名)	英国新闻界或报业

Lion	狮	英国
London	伦敦	英国或政府
Scotland Yard	苏格兰场（伦敦一地名）	伦敦警察局，该局刑事调查（侦缉）处
Ulster	阿尔斯特（在爱尔岛北部）	北爱尔兰
Westminster	威斯敏斯特（伦敦西部一住宅区）	英国议会或政府
Windsor	温莎（英格兰东南部一城市）	英国王室
Whitehall	白厅（伦敦一街名）	英国政府
Brussels	布鲁塞尔（比利时首都）	欧洲联盟；北大西洋公约组织
blue helmet	蓝盔	联合国维和人员
blue helmets	蓝盔帽	蓝盔部队，联合国维和部队
Horn of Africa	非洲之角	索马里和埃塞俄比亚
Elysée Palace	爱丽舍宫	法国总统府，法国总统职位
Quai d'Orsay	凯道赛（巴黎一码头名）	法国外交部
Kremlin	克里姆林宫	前苏联；前苏联政府；俄罗斯；俄罗斯政府
Moscow	莫斯科	前苏联；俄罗斯；俄罗斯政府
Gulag	古拉格群岛	（前苏联）劳改营，劳动改造管理总局
Evan	伊凡（前苏联和俄罗斯人常用名）	前苏联人；俄罗斯人
Beijing	北京	中国；中国政府

习 题

阅读与理解文章

"A Plan Under Attack"（2003/4/7 *Newsweek*）读后指出文中的喻词。

第六节　常见委婉语

委婉语多是报刊语言的一个特点,也是读报者理解上的一大难题。委婉语(euphemism)修辞格原本用来谈论生理及病、死、卖淫、同性恋等令人尴尬、不快或禁忌的话题。有的较文雅礼貌,有的含糊其辞,以使听者顺耳,读者舒服。应该说明,有的词既时髦也是委婉用法。如 commissioning 就是一例。(见"**学习方法词义之确定及辨析**")

一、社会领域委婉语

2007年10月2日至11月,上海举办了一届智残者奥林匹克夏季运动会,2007年10月1日出版的 Newsweek 上一篇题为"Shanghai Soften up"的文章,报道里用的"The Special Olympics World Summer Games"。"the special Olympics"就是委婉语。在这篇文章中的其他委婉语还有: the less fortunate, special-needs pupils,以及 Four years ago the city began setting up a network of "Sunshine Home" to provide activities and vocational training for **mentally challenged students** ages 16 to 35.

上海在四年前就开始为16岁至35岁的智残学生提供活动和职业训练而建立了一系列充满温暖的智残人场所。

对于残疾人,报刊为不得罪任何一方读者,一般不会或不应用 the retarded/disabled/deaf/crippled/deformed/disabled/handicapped 等,但可以用 people with mental retardation/disabilities 等。不过最受青睐的委婉用法是: physically/mentally/visually/vertically challenged(身体、智力、视力、有缺陷及个子不高的)。

此外,还有 physically inconvenienced(身体不便的), partially sighted(只有部分视力的), visually impaired(视力受损的)和 the otherly abled(其他方面有能力或残疾的人)等等。

社会领域的委婉语很多,如1971年美国政府想举行一个全国性会议,讨论老年人问题,对老年人用哪个词呢? 最后决定用 aging: the White House Conference on the Aging. 用得好,只说他们正在上年纪,而不是已经老了。其他的词如 elderly 太明显, sunset years 太悲观, senior citizen 已过时,2007年又造出了个 junior citizen,这大概也是为了"与时俱进"吧。此外,还有: the graying Army(灰军、银发大军), the senior citizens(高级/年长公民), the gray hair(银发族), the aged(上了年纪的人), the golden-agers(黄金时代的人), the seasoned men（经验丰富的人，老手），the veterans（经验丰富的人），the well-preserved persons（保养有方的人），the mature men（成熟的人），the longer living（长寿者），the second childhood（返老还童），getting on in years（渐上年纪的），past one's prime（过了风华正茂年纪的），feeling one's age（觉得上了年纪的），stricken in years（年迈的）等。未婚同居（nonmarital cohabitation）称为 covenanted relationship。鳏寡或空巢家庭被迪斯尼公司称为 post-family customers。弃 anti-abortion 而用 pro-life，赞成 abortion 者为反驳 pro-life 而杜撰了 pro-choice。prostitute 不用，而委婉地称之为 sex worker, street walker, call/escort/sing-song girl 以及 lady of pleasure the night/evening 供玩弄的妇人，一夜情之人等。

2008 年将纽约州州长和一些高官拉下马的一家名叫帝王俱乐部（Emperor Club）的妓院自称是"club"、"adult fantasy service"或"escort service"而不用 brothel 或以前的委婉语 house of ill repute 及 call-girl ring 等。同性恋不用 homo sexuality 而用 gay partner/companion, the crime against nature（鸡奸）。社会上一些不愿将自己的工作告诉问者的说自己是 consultant。再如解职不用 dismiss/sack/fire 而用 agreed departure（协议离开/职），derecruit（减招），downsize[使（规模、尺寸）缩小，缩编，精减]，ease out（悄悄离开），get the walking ticket/papers（接到走人通知书），ICE（involuntry career event）（非自愿的履历改变），INA（involuntary normal attrition）（非自愿的自然减员），manage down=lay off[放在一旁（下岗）]，outplace（调职，助谋新职），rif（劳力减少），rightsize（使规模、尺寸合适或缩小，优化人员配置），be selected out（遴选出局），slim（减肥）等等，不一而足。

美国农业部 2006 年 11 月中旬发表的报告指出，美国共 3,400 多万人贫困挨饿，竟弃用 hunger 而用 very low food security（极低食物安全程度），真亏想得出来，政客为掩盖真相，确实成了杜撰和操弄语言的魔术师了。

二、政治领域

一位评论家曾经说，美国务院待一年，胜读大学几年书。外交上很讲究修辞，三分说成十分，小题大做，修辞上称 overstatement；有的十分只说三分，大事化小，小事化了，修辞上称 understatement。越战时，美国为攻打越南北方（当时称北越）而侵入了柬埔寨，美国官方不用 invasion，而用 incursion。大败不用 rout, heavy defeat 或 retreat，而用 strategic withdrawal, phased withdrawal（分阶段撤退），retrograde maneuver（向后机动，转进），retrograde maneuver（向后机动，转进），redeployment（重新部署），adjust the front（调整前线）等。

bombing 用 pacification（平定）。这样，委婉语就成了政客歪曲事实、掩盖丑行、欺世盗名、愚弄他人，奸商蒙骗消费者，记者追求语言新奇的手段，因而泛滥成灾，语言遭到污染，该直说偏要弯弯绕，受众不知所云。例如美国决定从越南撤军，尼克松 1969 年就用了 Vietnamization。老布什出尔反尔，承诺不增税，后来不明说 tax increase，改用遭人嘲讽的 revenue enhancement（岁入增加），人称 Bushisms。战争、侵略不明用 war 字而用 future unpleasantness, preemptive action（先发制人的行动），preventive strike/war（预防性打击/战争），police action（以联合国名义进行的治安，如朝鲜战争/维和行动），protective reaction, unwelcome visit 等。平民死伤或遭屠杀，不明言 civilian casualties/death，而称 target process error，或言战争或空袭时的"附带性损伤"：In the air war against Saddam, targets are picked to minimize what is euphemistically called collateral damage. 调查克林顿绯闻和小布什泄露特工身份案的独立特别检察官，不用 (independent) special prosecutor，而用模糊的 independent counsel。"9·11"事件后，小布什将 POWs 称为 captives，媒体将 terrorists 称之为 insurgents。此外，还有：Bush terror/fatigue, regime change，称酷刑或严刑拷打为 physical persuasion（大约是仿花钱打揝的 currency persuasion）和 in-depth interrogation，战俘异国刑讯逼供是（extraordinary）rendition，所以黑狱叫 CIA camps 和 black hole，煽动骚乱称 uprising（起义），用 self-sacrifice bomber 指自杀性炸弹袭击者等。

前几年在波黑和卢旺达等国西方指责的 ethnic cleansing（民族、种类、宗教清洗），实际是种族灭绝（genocide）。与希特勒的 final solution（最后的解决方案）大规模屠杀（mass murder）就类似。

以上有些是说话兜圈子（circumlocution syndrome）。难怪 U. S. News & World Report 在一篇文章的漫画里讽刺说："能用拗口的委婉语，何必直说呢？"这与现在简明英语运动（plain English campaign）和写作指南背道而驰。此外，还应说明，这些委婉语与例词并不完全对应，在上下文、色彩和分量上有一定区别，不可简单套用，要体会使用中的种种区别。

习 题

阅读理解文章

"Double Trouble Speak"（2005/7/4 日 U. S. News & World Report）（见"党争用语"）从中找出哪些是委婉语。

第七节 常用套语

一、报道、评析常用套语

为了表明"客观公正",美英报刊记者以不肯定的第三者口气论述,如用"有人"、"人们"等;有的用"据称"、"据闻"、"据估计"等不确定的字眼及"事实不可容否认"、"可以认为","根据"等较确定的套语。有的为省时,常用固定写法用语(set expressions);还有以不确定的口气或审慎的态度报道,是怕事主找上门来纠缠。例如 2003 年美国女特工身份泄露案 Valerie Plame Leak case 就涉及退休记者 Robert Novok,《纽约时报》记者 Judith Miller 和《时代》周刊记者 Matt cooper,特别检察官以国家安全及保密法为由逼迫他们出庭作证。前面章节提到的这篇文章"Libby Defense Portrays Client as a scapegoat",报道的就是如此内容。有的用"事实不容否认"、"可以认为"等,以证明所言非虚假新闻,有事实依据或目击证人等。这也是报刊常用被动语态的一个重要原因。我们不如读读安徽大学马祖毅先生写的《英译汉技巧浅谈》一书中关于这类常见写法。如:

It affords no small surprise to find that... 对于……令人惊讶不已
It can be safely said that... 我们有把握讲……
It cannot be denied that... 无可否认……
It has been calculated that... 据估计……
It has been illustrated that... 据说明……,据图示……
It has recently been brought home to us that... 我们最近痛切感到……
It is alleged that... 据称……
It is arranged that... 已经商定……,……已做准备
It is asserted that... 有人主张……
It is claimed that... 据称……,有人宣称……
It is demonstrated that.. 据证实……,已经证明……
It is enumerated that... 列举出……
It is established that... 可以认定……
It is generally agreed that... 人们通常认为……
It is generally recognized that... 一般认为……,普遍认为……
It is hypothesized that... 假设……
It is incontestable that... 无可置辩的是……
It is learned that... 据闻……,据说……,已经查明……

It is mentioned that... 据说……

It is noted that... 人们注意到……,有人指出……

It is noticed that... 人们注意到……,有人指出……

It is outlined that... 概括地说……

It is preferred that... 有人建议……

It is quite contrary to our expectation. 与我们的期望恰巧相反。

It is reputed that... 人们认为……,可以认为……

It is striking to note that... 特别令人注意的是……

It is taken that... 人们认为……,有人以为……

It is undeniable that... 事实不容否认……

It is universally accepted that... 普遍认为……,……是普遍接受的

It is usually considered that... 通常认为……

It is weighed that... 权衡了……,考虑了……

It may be argued that... 也许有人主张……

It was described that... 据介绍……,有人介绍说……

It was first intended that... 最初就有这样的想法……

It was noted above that... 前面已经指出……,等等。

不过,据本人纵览近几年报道性文章,上述这类套语用得越来越少。

二、消息来源常用套语

西方新闻除标明是何报刊或新闻社外,都要说明消息来源(news source),以示信而有据。如:

Japan's Surplus Shrinks as Oil Prices Rise

Tokyo Also Buys More From the U. S. as
Its Exports to Rest of Asia Expand

Compiled by Our Staff from Dispatches

TOKYO — Japan's trade surplus with the world dropped 19.3 percent in July from a year earlier, largely because of surging oil prices, **the government said Thursday.**

(上述为)政府所言,官方所言。其他常用的有:The police said, according to U. S. officials and experts/a new study 等等。

在消息来源中,以有单位、姓名最具体,事前会要求"所谈情况可以发表,披露来源,但不得指名道姓,说出是谁提供的消息",新闻用语是"background";而 deep background 则要求绝对不能泄露姓名。

下面再来看一下 sources 对 reporters 所提的要求或条件用语:除

backgrounder（对某事或某项政策进行的背景情况介绍会，新闻吹风会，情况通报会）和 deep background（深层背景）外，还有 not for attribution 不供引证的，不公布新闻来源或消息提供者姓名的：往往用据政府消息灵通人士称等含糊其辞，一笔带过，万一捅了娄子，记者决不牵累他人。off the record 不供发表的，仅供参考。on the record 可供发表的，宜公开报道的。on lobby terms（英）以在议会休会室提供消息为条件的，指大臣或下院议员要求，不得说明来源。这样记者不必去挖掘消息，就了解情况，与 not for attribution 同。Lindley Rule 林德利规则指记者与高官谈话后不得直接援引、甚至不得报道以此官员发表的关于时局的谈话。此规则以 Ernest K. Lindley 的名字命名。

此外，还有如前面提到的"not to be ID'd"消息提供者不愿公开自己的身份等的用语。由于"要求"、"条件"或"约定"的限制，报道文章就只能用如下一些较含蓄的套语：

according to analysts（据分析家称）/AP reports（据美联社报道）/authoritative sources（据权威人士称）/commercial quarters（据商界称）/the data made available（据此间获得的资料表明/证明…）/diplomatic sources（据外交界人士称）/financial quarters（据金融界称）/industrial quarters（据产业界称）/informative sources（据消息灵通人士称）/military sources（据军方人士称）/neutral sources（据中立人士称）/observers（据观察家称）/official sources（据官方人士称）/reliable sources（据可靠人士称）/semi-official sources（据半官方人士称）/the spokesman/spokeswoman（据发言人称）/the sources close to the White House（据接近白宫人士称）/usually reliable sources（据通常可靠人士称）/well-informed sources（据消息灵通人士称）/witnesses/eyewitnesses（据目击者称），等等。

当然，以上不一定都用"according to"，还可以用"said"、"revealed"、"announced"和"quoted"等。例如：a witness said（目击者称）；a source close to the Pentagon revealed（一位接近五角大楼的人士披露）；foreign radios announced（外电播报）；foreign wire services were quoted as saying（援引外国通讯社的报道称），等。

习 题

阅读理解文章

"Big Maoist wins could reshape Nepal's politics"（2008/4/15）读后找出本节举例的套语。

第五章 读报知识

读报知识的重要性,"前言"作了说明。报刊上至天文,下至地理,几乎无所不包。本书不可能面面俱到,只能作重点介绍。编者几十年自学、教外刊和编书的经验和教训,可以得出这样的结论:若不了解本章介绍的读报核心知识,如美英政府的组成、体制、党派、宗教、价值观及其内外政策等等,就会望文生义,似懂非懂,甚至味同嚼蜡,完全失去读报的兴趣,影响当代语言的学习。反之,就会读得透,理解得深,学习兴趣陡增。难怪授课教员普遍认为,英美等国家的各种文化背景知识是学生读报的主要障碍。这是因为有的知识上下文里是找不到的,单凭词典也查不出,甚至连专门介绍美英文化的教材也忽略掉,必须具备文外知识。不妨举两例看看:

1. Yet even while they frustrate Clinton, the newly elected Republicans may push him to spend more time on external affairs. **Traditionally Presidents who find their domestic programs thwarted by midterm elections seek solace overseas**. Scarcely had health-care reform been shredded when Clinton aides reported that their boss, who had almost completely ignored diplomacy for most of the previous 21 months, was spending much more time on Haiti, North Korea, Syria and Northern Ireland—with mostly salutary results, it should be recorded. (*Time*)

此段有两个问题:一是为什么1994年中期选举共和党大败民主党,控制了国会,就会一面使民主党总统克林顿受挫,一面兴许促使他在对外事务上花更多的时间;二是为什么说:"总统发现其国内施政方案在中期选举中受阻,通常会在国外事务上求得慰藉。"换言之,中期选举对总统而言有何弦外之音?国内施政计划受阻,总统与国外签订的协议难道就不会受到国会的干扰?他有何妙招或特权?

再如已作《精选本》四版课文"He's just like you and me, except for the £31bn fortune"里有这么一个句子:

2. He [Warren Buffett] was born in 1930 in a house in Omaha on the banks of the Missouri River, the son of Leila and Howard, a Republican

stockbroker elected to Congress **on a platform described as "to the right of God"**.（2008/3/9 *The Sunday Times*）

何谓其"platform"（党纲，政纲）是"to the right of God"？哪个党 God 不离口，并称为"party of God"？在该党之右，是自由派还是保守派？（见"政党"等）

在知识介绍中，编者力图摒弃那种空洞条文，尽可能根据本人读报感受、教学经验和编书体会，将读报知识跟难句揉在一起，既可使学生懂得透彻，又提高了可读性，免于枯燥。兴趣是最好的老师，"上瘾"就能在知识和语言方面获得双丰收。

第一节 美 国

一、国名

美国是美利坚合众国简称，the United State of American，简称 America（也有美洲之意），the States（如 Are you from the States?），U.S.A. 或 the U.S.。这些都较浅显，至于美国国玺、硬币上的拉丁文国训 E Pluribus Unum，为"合众为一"，由各族各州联合组成"合众为一"的合众国，此外，还有 the nation of nations 和 the city on/upon a hill 等。前者指美国是一个移民的国度，全世界各民族、各种文化都融入美国，合众为一。后者的"山巅之城"典出《圣经·马太福音》（Matthew 5：14）。1630 年马萨诸塞湾殖民地总督温思罗普（John Winthrop）在一次演说中说："We shall be as **a city upon a hill**, the eyes of all people are upon us."可用来喻政府理想或光辉的榜样；美德或成功的典范。例如前总统里根夫人说［She（Nancy Reagan）evoked one of her husband's most memorable phrases, saying］："I can tell you with certainty he still sees **the shining city on the hill**."（*The New York Times*）（此处加了"shining"，并将"a"改为"the"指里根政府，突出政府取得的辉煌成就而成为光辉的榜样；也曾被 1984 年民主党总统候选蒙代尔（Walter Mondale）等人用来喻指美国，看下列例句：

Mondale has frequently said that he would rather lose a campaign for decency than win one predicated solely on self-interest. In his final days, he made that a constant refrain, ending his speeches with a reference to 17th-century cleric John Winthrop's **"city on a hill"** a metaphor for America much favored by the president.（*Newsweek*）

喻美国大概与美国独立前漂洋过海来到美国的清教徒当时的看法有关，他们在欧洲受政府和宗教束缚和迫害而来,视之为庇护所,他们的向往之地,他们的 the city on the hill。

二、简况

　　美国在 17 世纪和 18 世纪前半期为英国殖民地。1775 年波士顿爆发独立战争,反抗英国人的控制。1776 年 7 月 4 日,在费城召开了第二次大陆会议,通过了 Declaration of Independence《独立宣言》,正式宣布建立美利坚合众国。1783 年独立战争结束。1787 年制定了联邦宪法。1789 年华盛顿当选为第一任总统。1812 年,英国以加拿大为根据地入侵美国,再次爆发抗英独立战争。战后,美国完全摆脱了英国的统治。后来又爆发了 American Civil War(1861—1865)南北战争。1862 年 9 月,林肯颁布了 Emancipation Proclamation《解放黑奴宣言》。南北战争后,美国工业化发展迅速。此后的两百多年间,经过一再领土扩张,发展成现在拥有 50 个州的国家。

　　美国是联邦(制)共和国,有成文宪法(written Constitution)。宪法规定,除国防、外交、外贸、高等司法、保安和州际商业调节由联邦政府负责,其他所有权力由各州政府行使。美国的政体是总统制,国会由参众两院组成,主要的政党是共和党和民主党。

　　美国最主要的特点是高度多样化:自然面貌千差万别,民族和文化类型多种多样,经济生活五光十色。

三、联邦政府

1. 组织机构

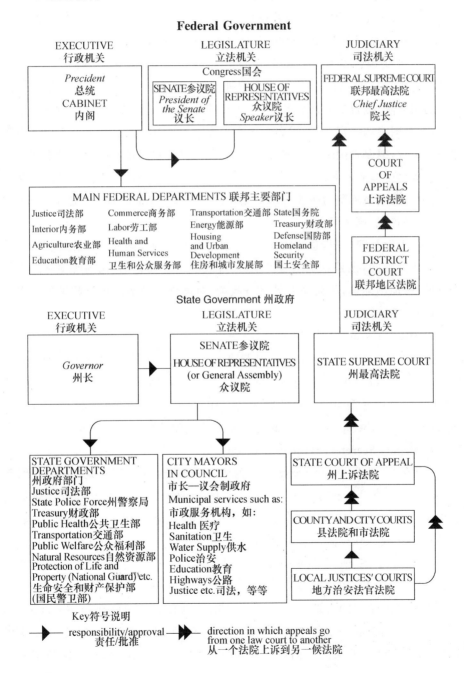

看了上图，人们可能会问：

2. 国务院＝中国国务院或外交部吗

大家常在报上看到美国"国务院"(the Department of State，报刊上常用 the State Department)，那么，它与我国的 State Council 或我国及其他国家的外交部(the Ministry of Foreign Affairs)的职能是否相同呢？

1781 年美国曾设有外交部(the Department of Foreign Affairs)。1789 年联邦政府成立，7 月，首届国会通过重建外交部的议案。9 月外交部改名国务院。当时的国务院，除负责对外事务外，还兼管部分内政，包括管理领地，与联邦法院联系，保管国玺和档案，以及发布总统文告等。后来有关内政的部分工作转由其他部门负责，但保管国玺和档案、发布总统文告以及联邦政府同州政府之间的联系等事务仍由国务院兼管。这种兼有内政职能的国务院是与其他国家的外交部不同，更与我国国务院的职能有别。此外，不但 Department 译为"院"，Secretary of State 还译成"国务卿"了。

美国不设总理一职，总统代表国家，掌握内外全局。国务院(通过国务卿)既是主要政策顾问，也是总统主要助手，还代表美国在联合国、北约等国际组织发表意见，参加国际会议，协调对外经济政策，对国外文教活动进行政策指导以及颁发护照、签证等。

3. Dept of War＝Dept of Defense 吗

美国国防部(the Department of Defense)最初称陆军部[the Department of War (1789—1798)]，并管辖海军。后又改称 the National Military Establishment，直至 1947 年才用现名，the War Department 也改组为 the Department of the Army(陆军部)，与海军、空军组成国防部的三军。

4. Deputy Secretary＝Under Secretary 吗

美国有的部设 Deputy Secretary 与 Under Secretary，有人笼统译为"副部长"或"副国务卿"。事实上，凡设有这两个官职的，Deputy Secretary 一职低于部长而高于 Under Secretary，应译为"常务或第一副部长或副国务卿"。如果不设 Under Secretary 副部长或副国务卿，由 Deputy Secretary 直接负责某方面事务，如 Deputy Secretary of State for Political Affairs 就是"负责政治事务的副国务卿"。港台有译"次国务卿"的，国防部副部长译为"国防部次长"。此外，还有两个常被译错的官职：一个是将国防部的 Deputy Assistant Secretary for Acquisition Management 译成"负责探测管理的副部长帮办"，acquisition 这里的意思应该是"武器采购"；而英国的 defence procurement 则译为"国防军需"。

另一个将邮政局(Postal Service)的 Chairman of the Board of Governors 译成"管理委员会主席",Board of Governors 应改译为"理事会"。

国务院的高官分下列五个等级:

Secretary of State 国务卿

Deputy Secretary of State 常务副国务卿

Under Secretary (of State for Political Affairs) (负责政治事务的)副国务卿

Assistant Secretary (of State for East Asian and Pacific Affairs) (负责东亚和太平洋事务的) 助理国务卿

Deputy Assistant Secretary 助理国务卿帮办

四、三权分立,各自为政

1. 何谓三权分立

美国宪法(the Constitution of the United States)规定,联邦政府由三个主要部门——行政、立法和司法(即总统和内阁、国会和最高法院)组成,但各自分立,各不从属。这就是所谓的三权分立[scparation of the three (constitutional) powers],各自为政,故又称"三头政治或政权"(triumvirate/troika)和"三头怪物"(three-headed monster)。三个部门既互相独立又相互联系和制衡。也就是说,美国政治制度是建立在各种力量相互制衡的基础上,这就是美国人所谓的"民主"。同时也是了解美国政府和政治的基础性知识。

2. 制衡制的理论基础

对美国人而言,要获得自由,就应严防政府。为此,开国元勋提出了分权说。三权分立的制衡制度的理论基础源于英国历史学家约翰·阿克顿[Sir Lord (John) Acton,1834—1902]爵士的名言:"Power tends to corrupt; absolute power corrupts absolutely."他断言:"权力产生腐败,绝对的权力产生绝对的腐败。"根本原因在于,公共权力一旦为个人、某个团体或政党所掌握,常常会异化为牟取私利的工具。

如何相互制衡? 下图标明了各自的权限,越权即是违宪。

A SYSTEM OF CHECKS AND BALANCES

The Constitution provides for three equal and separate branches of government, but each is to some extent dependent on the other two and there is a partial interweaving of their functions.

相互制衡制

联邦宪法规定政府有三个平等独立的部门，但每一部门在一定程度上要依赖其他两个部门，同时它们的职能有一部分是互相交织的。

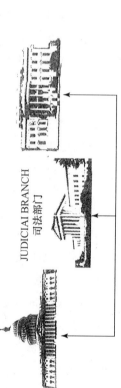

EXECUTIVE BRANCH 行政部门

President suggests legislation to Congress
Issues executive orders, rules and regulations with the force of legislation
May veto legislation passed by Congress

总统向国会建议立法
发出有立法效力的行政命令和规章
可以否决国会通过的法案

President appoints federal judges
May grant pardons from punishment for offenses against the United States

总统委任联邦法官
可以对冒犯美国的罪行赦免惩罚

LEGISLATIVE BRANCH 立法部门

Appropriates funds for Executive Departments
May create or abolish Executive Branch
May impeach and try members of the Executive Branch
May override a Presidential veto
The Senate must approve Presidential appointments and treaties

为行政部门拨款
可以设立或取消行政部局
可以弹劾及审讯行政部门人员
可以推翻总统的否决
参议院批准总统的任命及条约

Appropriates funds for the Judiciary
May create or abolish lower federal courts
May impeach and try members of the Judiciary
Decides how many justices may sit on the Supreme Court
Determines the appellate jurisdiction of the Supreme Court

拨款给司法部门
可以设立或取消较低级的联邦法院
可以弹劾及审讯司法部门人员
决定最高法院的法官人数
决定最高法院的受理上诉权

JUDICIAL BRANCH 司法部门

May declare Congressional legislation unconstitutional

可以宣布国会的立法违宪

May declare any Presidential or Executive action unconstitutional

可以宣布任何总统或政府行动违宪

五、总统

1. 继任顺序(order of succession)

总统是一国的首脑,事关国家命运,继任顺序由宪法规定。一旦死亡、遭到弹劾(impeachment)、辞职或丧失履行职务能力,由副总统(Vice President, Veep)继任。尽管许多副手都像小媳妇似的,做事慎小慎微,形象卑微,如卡特任内的蒙代尔(Walter Mondale)和老布什任身边的奎尔(Dan Quayle)都被讽刺为 Throttlebottom(无用的讲话不敢大声直说而是结结巴巴的副总统)。只有艾森豪威尔和小布什左右的尼克松和切尼(Dick cheney)例外,有职有权,说话有分量,深得总统信任,副职成为荣升踏脚石(stepping-stone),总统宝座可望可即(only a heartbeat away),毕竟接班者不多,仕途算是船到码头车到站了(political dead end)。凭副职经历竞选总统成功倒是有的,如杜鲁门、尼克松和老布什。正副总统出缺时,由众议院议长(House Speaker)继任,接着依次是参议院临时议长(President Pro Tempore of the Senate),然后是依任命次序排列的内阁阁员。

2. 何谓总统制(Presidential System)

总统制(presidential system)或总统制形式政体[presidential (form of) government],是共和制或联邦国家政权组织形式,美国是联邦共和国,以总统为政府首脑,主要特点是总统及其领导的行政部门与立法部门[即国会(Congress)]各自分立;总统民选,不由立法部门产生;各部部长由总统任命,对总统负责或报告工作(report to the president);总统领导的政府(如 the Obama Administration)或由各部部长及总统指定的官员组成的内阁独立于国会,由总统直接控制,是总统内阁制,阁员不对国会负责或报告工作,但应邀出席国会主持的听证会,是二元制政体国家。这是区别于议会制的最重要特点。总统向国会报告工作,但无权像国王一样解散国会。世界上实行总统制的国家很多,美国是最具代表性的国家之一。

3. 帝王总统(imperial president/presidency)

美国宪法第二条(the second article)规定,行政权力赋予总统这一最高行政长官。"互相制衡的制度"表列出了总统与国会和法院各拥有的权力,此外,美国总统还是国家元首、政府首脑和武装部队总司令;有权召开国会紧急会议。总统的行政命令与法律具有同等效力。内阁由各部部长和总统指定的其他官员组成,实际上只起总统助手和顾问团的作用。可见其权力之大。

"帝王总统"原指前总统尼克松,表面嘲笑白宫卫队服装为"imperial uniform",实指其权力过分膨胀,超越宪法赋予的总统权限,俨如帝王。他否决的法案国会往往不能获得三分之二多数,再次通过而成为法律。他越权时常以行政特权(executive privilege)作挡箭牌。白宫办公厅主任等人就像亲王,与国会议员打交道时颇像太监,以行政特权为由,拒绝国会监督而使制衡(checks and balances)失效。imperial presidency 一词源出美国著名历史学家斯莱辛格(Arthur M. Schlesinger, Jr.)的同名著作。为了理解得更确切,请看一美国历史书的说明:

Impoundment created a furor on Capitol Hill, and when Congress failed to override his vetoes of bills challenging his policy, it appeared that Nixon was in total command. The White House staff, headed by H. R. Haldeman ("the Prussian") and John Ehrlichman, dominated the Washington bureaucracy like princes of the blood or oriental viziers and dealt with legislators as though they were lackeys or eunuchs. When asked to account for their actions, they took refuge behind the shield of "executive privilege", the doctrine, never before applied so broadly, that discussions and communications within the executive branch were confidential and therefore immune from congressional scrutiny. Critics began to grumble about a new **"imperial presidency"**. No one seemed capable of checking Nixon at any point. (*The American Nation*)

Jimmy Carter's informality was the perfect emblem of a post-Watergate reaction against **the "imperial presidency."** (*The American Nation*)

现在该词也指前总统小布什(George. W. Bush)。他专权独断,大搞单边主义(unilateralism),在新保守势力(neocons)支持下,在全球扩张谋霸,还借反恐,违反人权,对国内外所有组织和人员大肆窃听,尽管当时民意测验支持率直线下降,民主党人在国会里实力不够强大,制衡不了他。

4. 总统梦

(1) 工作重,不自由:美国不设总理,总统双肩挑,内政外交亲自抓,繁忙可想而知。此外,他不但常要与国会较量,还要处理(总统)府(内)阁争权,犹如黑帮抢地盘(turf fight)。过了总统瘾者常抱怨是无人肯干的苦差事,白宫(即总统府)好似"the big white jail"(杜鲁门总统语)和关鸟兽的 cage。见尼克松助手霍尔德曼如是:

You could have put the President's life in jeopardy.... Just tell him he can't go, that's all. He **rattles his cage** all the time. You can't let him out.

此处 rattle his cage,指尼克松企图跳出樊笼。此语常指政治领袖等企图摆脱周围人物施加的种种束缚和限制,如保卫人员不准总统任意接触群众或外出等。

(2) 趋之若鹜：尽管如此，美国高官，上至联邦官员，下至州长、市长，都想过总统瘾，心痒(itch to run for the White House/presidency)，手痒(presidential/palm itching)，患上相思病(presidential/Potomac fever)，犹如虫叮(bitten by the presidential bug)，大有"壮志"(fire in the belly)未酬死不休的决心。例如第20任美国总统加斐尔德，当选前曾自叹：

I long ago made the resolution that I would never permit the **Presidential fever** to get lodgment in my brain. I think it is the one office a man should not set his heart upon.

年过古稀，还要最后一搏(last hurrah)，里根70岁高龄圆了总统梦，且73岁还竞选连任获胜，成为 a two-term president。下面的英文例句讲的就是他：

Although even staunch Reaganites believe he is too old for anything other than a kingmaker's role in 1980, he has by no means ruled out a **last hurrah**. (*The New York Times*)

富兰克林·罗斯福虽因患脊髓灰质炎而行走不便，连任三届以上，共和党人称之为 third termites。在第四届任内病故。1951年，国会终于通过第22条修正，限制总统任期不超过两届。克林顿过了八年的总统瘾，夫人希拉里(Hilary)2008年仍参与民主党总统候选人的提名争夺战。共和党候选人麦开恩72岁还跟小伙子奥巴马(34岁)角逐。

下面这幅登在2008年5月5日《新闻周刊》漫画极具讽刺意义：

争取共和党总统候选人提名的 John McCain(左)、民主党的 Barack Obama 和 Hillary Clinton 还在初选就已在宣誓就职(inauguration)，尤具讽刺的是希拉

里竟坐在其丈夫 Clinton 的肩上(意为踏着他的肩膀想爬上总统职位)正式宣誓:"I, Hillary Clinton, Swear to Uphold..."

(3) 瘾大者的种种贬称:chronic campaigner, chronic 这个字使人不免联想到慢性病,不好治,L. 约翰逊就暗指尼克松。屡战屡败叫 perennial/perpetual candidate,曾指史塔生(Harold Stassen)、克里夫兰(Grover Cleveland)和三度竞选、三度落选的布兰恩(William Bryan)等人。

(4) 拼身心的游戏:总统竞选是玩命,付出代价。据美国一家网站的研究报告,奥巴马竞选紧张过度,老了两岁半。1984 年里根竞选连任成功时,《美国新闻与世界报道》"Four More Years"一文说:Most voters, however, agreed with Nancy Reagan's(里根总统夫人) comment on the end of the long 1984 campaign:"I'm glad it's over."

该文又说,乐此不疲的大有人在,1984 年大选投票站和竞选办公室刚关张就有人为 1988 年大选跃跃欲试了:Even while candidates and their weary aides were closing campaign offices around the country, speculation began percolating(透漏出) about presidential candidates for 1988. Ahead on Republican charts: Vice President George Bush, Representative Jack Kemp of New York and Senator Bob Dole of Kansas. Leading among Democrats: Senator Hart of Colorado, Governor Mario Cuomo of New York and Senator Edward Kennedy of Massachusetts.

以上种种事例说明总统是众所瞩目的职位,要是能如我们中国人讲能天时、地利、人和,美国人说"... who seek the Presidency... Circumstances rather than a man's ambition determine the result. If he is the right man for the right time, he will be chosen."(Richard Nixon,见"**政治名言的理解与翻译**")和 presidential timber(总统材料,指其 background, personality and voter appeal)有门。过了总统瘾,死也瞑目了。

六、总统选举

总统选举(presidential election)也称大选或普选(general elections)。选举除进行总统和国会联邦一级选举外,还举行州议会、州长和其他地方如市镇议会等的选举,也就是说,还有成千上万名地方民选官员都要选举。美国宪法规定,总统选举每隔四年举行一次,日期是可以用四除净的那个年份的 11 月的第一个星期一后的第一个星期二举行。候选人获胜后称为当选总统(President-elect)(港台译"候任总统"),在上届总统届满之年的 1 月 20 日午时宣誓就职。一届任期四年,因任期限制(term limits),不得超过两届。

1. 两党制

所谓选举,自 19 世纪中叶以来,美国政治制度是竞争性的共和党和民主党的两党制,无非是你方唱罢我登台,容不得第三党染指,因为简单多数(plurality)选举制有利于两党,不利第三党或小党。在目前的美国体制中,即使实行比例代表制(proportional representation),第三党或独立候选人获得第三名也无法胜出。

2. 两个阶段

总统选举分两个阶段:党内的提名阶段(nomination stage)和全国性投票决出总统的最后阶段。

第一阶段是共和和民主两党先进行政党预选(presidential primary),然后各自召开全国党代会(Democratic/Republican national convention),最终敲定各党正式总统候选人和副总统候选人[常称作"竞选伙伴或搭档"(running mate)],组成如 2008 年民主党正副总统候选人竞选名单:Obama-Biden ticket(奥巴马-拜登名单)。第二阶段进行普选,由全国各州选民在两党候选人中推选总统。

(1) 预选:预选,也称初选或党内选举。多数州举行预选[primary (election)];少数州举行预选会议,即"地方政党骨干会议"(caucus),逐级选出代表州出席全国党代会的代表。

primary election 遴选参加某一公职竞选的政党候选人。政府各级选举都有预选,从市长、选区内国会众议员、州长或参议员,直至总统。在"不公开的"(closed primary)预选选举中,只有本党的注册党员可以投票,是党内关门预选。在"公开预选"(open primary)中,某党登记党员可以参加另一政党预选投票,称为 crossover voters,"跨党"投票人。总统预选在州一级举行,按照各州法律,有些州直接投票,有些州则把票投给"保证"在党的提名代表大会上支持某一候选人的代表。州预选有时会爆出冷门。与 primary 一样,caucus 也分 closed/open caucus。

(2) 普选:第二阶段便是普选(general election),即总统选举而不是总统候选人提名的选举。普选(popular election),选民投的是普选票或民选票(popular vote)。

3. 选举团的作用

根据美国宪法规定,总统经各州选出的总统选举人(presidential electors)选举产生,叫"选举团"(Electoral College)制度。虽属间接选举,但选举团成员是选民选出的,所以也具有直选因素。

选举团诞生于 1787 年美国宪法会议期间。制宪原意是远见卓识的人组成选举团,聚到一起代表全民来选总统。但实际上,由于全国性党派很快控制了选举,选举团徒有虚名,实际上代表后台党在该州的势力,投谁的票,事先就安排好了。

选民在大选日选出的是"选举人"[(presidential) electors],而不是总统和副总统。哪个总统候选人在某州得到票最多,就会囊括该州选举人票(electoral vote),他有权指定选举人。这种"赢家通吃"(winner-take-all)的制度只有缅因州和内布拉斯加州例外。在这两个州,只有两张选举人票经全州普选产生,其余(九分之五)选举人票按州国会议员选区投票结果分配。各州在国会里有多少国会议员,就有几个选举人。尽管每个州参议员都是两个,但众议员的数量则取决于各州在10年一度的人口普查中的人口数量。据2008年统计,7个人口最少的州每州只有一个席位,而加州却有55个选举人,纽约州和得克萨斯州分别有31个和34个。在50个州中,阿拉斯加和特拉华等7个州和哥伦比亚特区只有3个。因此,加州、得州和纽约州是总统候选人"必须取胜的州"(must-win states)。但2000年大选例外,尽管戈尔在纽约州和加州都赢了小布什,还是落选。当时民主党怀疑小布什弟弟任州长的佛罗里达州在计票上捣鬼,要求在几个县重新手工计票,chad一词转义一度成了时髦词。最后最高法院拍扳定案。

选举人于12月中旬在各州首府进行选举总统和副总统的投票,但最后的选举结果要到第二年1月初由国会正式公布。全美50个州加上哥伦比亚特区共有538张选举人票,要当选总统必须赢得半数以上,至少270张以上的选举人票。在12月选举人投票时,如果所有的总统候选人都未能获得过半数的选举人票,总统将由国会众议院选出。

4. 选举人票与普选票不一致咋办

候选人普选票再多,选举人票少一票,也得把总统宝座拱手让给对手。2000年小布什最终赢得了佛罗里达州的25张选举人票,戈尔眼见煮熟的鸭子飞了。这种情况在美国历史上先前已发生过两次,分别在1876年与1888年。

5. 参选总统资格

美国宪法规定,参选总统者必须年满35岁,是本土出生的美国公民,这就排除了能耐大的外来户如基辛格(Henry Kissinger)和施瓦辛格(Arnold Schwarzenger)。基辛格出生在德国,曾任尼克松和福特政府总统特别安全助理和国务卿,誉为超人(Super K.)。施瓦辛格出生在奥地利,曾任加州州长,在1984年和1991年分别主演过 *The Terminator* 和 *The Terminator II: Judgment Day*(《终结者》和《终结者2:世界末日》)等影片。为此还创造一个"州长终结者"的词"governator"(由 governor 和 terminator 拼缀而成)。演技大大超过二流演员里根。为此,两人都竭力要求修宪,让能者出头。以往的总统候选人的潜规定有三条:信教、白人、家庭观。东部几乎没有候选人能胜出,因为美国人不喜欢 Washington,Washington Belt 权势集团圈,名声不佳,联邦资深议员也当不上总统，投票记录表明是 flip-floppers，反复无常。奥巴马只任了两年议员，一直投票反对出兵伊拉克，占了便宜。希拉里参议员投过一次赞成票，就揪过没完没了。John Kerry 等败北就是因为他们的立场、观点等突然转变而使选民在政治上对其失信有关。

奥巴马当选后又有人认为，WASP(= White Anglo Saxon Protestant 英裔上层或中产阶级的白人新教徒）在必须让出政权的情形下，他们也是"不予外人，宁予家奴"。不管怎么说，黑人是家人，总胜过外人。奥巴马和希拉里争夺总统候选人提名能最后胜选，多少沾了这方面的光，尽管奥巴马不是美国传统上的黑人。他是黑白混合体，也就是英文所说的 biracial，这使他与一般的黑人不同，加上他在白人家庭和社会成长的经验与受到良好的教育，成就了他是一非常独特的非裔美国人。能说会道，善纳忠言，成为年轻人、中下层选民和少数民族眼里的改革旗手，一炮走红。不过种族歧视阴魂不散，不时暗杀谣传，会不会落得林肯与肯尼迪遇刺下场，还很难讲。

自由派的白人对黑人有种与生俱来的原罪感，所以肯尼迪等参议员力挺奥巴马，非把他送进白宫不可。加上年轻世代白人对小布什的强烈不满，为奥巴马进军白宫带来空前动力，终于实现了曾在肯尼迪政府任司法部长的罗伯特·肯尼迪早在 1961 年的预言："40 年后美国会出现一位黑人总统。"

"不予外人，宁予家奴"的说法毕竟是用中国古语来比喻与我们不同制度国家的政治。再则，当今尚非"大同世界"，罕见有国家让一个生于他国的人来担任国家的最高领导人。

6. 选举：金钱政治，富人游戏

如果说上述条件是硬件的话，参选者还得要有跟得上的软件——钱，"这是通往白宫的钥匙"。(英国《独立报》)。竞选靠选票，选票靠钞票。1996 年大选克林顿对阵共和党候选人 Robert Dole。*U. S. News & World Report* 一文标题是 "The Greening of America"，副题为 "This year, candidates will spend more money than ever buying your vote"。说明入主白宫得金钱铺垫。小布什 2004 年花了 3 亿多美元，对手克里(John Kerry)，只少花几千万。据负责竞选中心(Center for Responsible Politics)估算，竞选经费总数(gross political product)高达 39 亿美元。2008 年竟创 53 亿记录，总统选举本身就花掉 24 亿美元，比 2004 年的 6 亿行情翻了好几番。

候选人一方面依仗政府的公共资金所得，公民直接捐款，候选人所属政党和利益集团(如 PAC)筹款，尤其要依仗现在可以无限制地"投资"于选战的大企业。另一方面，就得靠本人及家人的资产。家底不厚者是玩不转的。总统候选人大多是百万或亿万富翁。据 2007 年《华盛顿邮报》报道，打算在 2008 年竞选总统的约20位人士中,"至少有10位民主党和共和党的总统候选人是百万富翁。"奥巴马是百万富翁,共和党总统候选人麦凯恩(John McCain)是"与钱攀亲,妻子是亚利桑那州啤酒大亨的女儿,罗姆尼(Mitt Romney)是竞选人首富,资产在1.9亿至2.5亿美元之间"。希拉里中途退出,与奥巴马和好的一个重要原因是欠债太多,奥答应给她还清,许愿封官。可见西方式选举是富人游戏,金钱政治。为此,有不少人铤而走险,因slush fund(秘密资金;行贿资金)受审、下台或自杀。

所谓"民主多样性",穷人富人一样可以参选公职,甚至还有谚语说:"If working hard,even a cowboy can be president."这全是鬼话。

当然,仅凭金钱还不够,大财阀Nelson Rockefeller和罗姆尼都未能获胜,还要看是否是那块料(presidential timber)。

7. 527组织兴起

大选中给政党捐款(soft money)被麦凯恩—范戈尔德竞选资金改革法(McCain-Fingold campaign-reform law)2002年取消后,便出现为竞选助阵的527 organizations/groups (527组织)。自称无党派偏见,拉一派,打一派,有的报刊称之为秘密捐款战(Secret Money War)。名字源于界定他们的税法条款(Section 527 of the U. S. Tax code)。他们是非营利性组织,捐款不受限制,超过了soft money(给政党的无限制捐款)。竞选资金改革法才出台几年,被取缔的soft money等于又卷土重来,因为最高法院在2010年初裁决,允许企业可以无限额限制地捐款于选战。

527组织所获捐款大多来自亿万富翁如George Soros等人,少数来自对选战感兴趣的普通选民,旨在影响选情。

在2004年大选中首次在电视和网络上替小布什呐喊攻讦的527组织有:Swift Boat Veterans for Truth(报刊常用the Swifties,为在越战中"寻求真相的快艇老战士")、America Coming Together(美国团结在一起)和Progress for America(Voter Fund)[美国前进(选民基金)];支持民主党候选人克里(John Kerry)的527组织有:Move On Org. (Voter Fund)[前进组织(选民基金)]、Texans for Truth(寻求真相的得克萨斯人)和Media Fund(媒体基金)等。the Swifties最臭,由此引申出新义。现在"swift boat"除含攻击和诽谤外,有一网站已定义为"揭穿战功谎言和欺蒙拐骗行为"(expose the lies, deceit and fraud of self-glorifying public officials or candidates for office who exaggerate their military service by lying about their feats of heroism and combat wounds)。它攻击克里并非越战英雄,而是个胆小鬼。见例句:

'**Swift-Boating** Obama'

Can the presidential candidate repel the sort of attacks that did in Kerry?

2008 年大选，这类组织也很活跃，为 John McCain 和 Barack Obama 攻讦。为省略，报刊常用"527"或复数用 527s 而略去 organization 或 group。见例句：

This year the game has been defined, and dominated, by three numbers: **527**. Run by political pros and accountable largely to themselves, the groups are loud, mean and devastatingly effective. they are also loaded, in part from lavish donations from billionaires like George Soros and T. Boone Pickens, who are blunt about their desire to influence the vote. So far this campaign, Democratic and Republican **527**s like Move On and America Coming Together on the left, and the Swift Boat Veterans and Progress for America on the right, have raised upwards of $300 million. they could bring in tens of millions more before Election Day. (*Newsweek*)

Involved are only those groups organized under Section **527** of the U. S. Tax Code. Originally reserved for political parties and political action committees—which do report their contributions and spending to the Federal Election Commission—Section **527** has been used in recent years by groups that claim to be engaged in "issue" and not in electioneering.

The legislation requires the "**527-groups**" to register with the Internal Revenue Service and report on a quarterly basis all contributions of $200 or more and spending of $500 or more. Otherwise, they have to either reorganize or disband. (*Campaign Spotlight*)

8. 奥巴马算是第几位总统

2008 年当选、2009 年就职的 Barack Obama 到底是第 43 任还是第 44 任美国总统，第 22 位总统克利夫兰当了不连续的两任。2002 年《世界年鉴》(The *World Almanac* 2002)在介绍 Grover Cleveland (1885—89;1893—87)时是这么说的：

"According to a ruling of the State Dept., Grover Cleveland Should be counted as both the 22th and 24th president, because his two terms were not consecutive."

上述这段引文说明，克利夫兰分别担任了第 22 任和第 24 任美国总统，而不能说第 22 位和第 24 位美国总统。因此，应该说奥巴马是第 44 任而不是第 44 位总统。美国立国以来只能说共有 43 位总统。上述两个概念，不能混为一谈。

还有人说奥巴马是第 44 届美国总统，显然也是错误的。因为有的总统，如艾森豪威尔、里根、克林顿和小布什都连续担任过两届总统，F. 罗斯福在位后期正值二次大战，由于情况特殊，他曾连续担任过三届以上总统。从华盛顿到 2009 年奥巴马共 56 届，因此只能说他是第 56 届总统。two-term president 指一任连任两届(共八年)的总统。克利夫兰分别担任过第 22 任和第 24 任不连续的总统,但表达不同,是 twenty-second and Twenty-forth (22nd and 24th) president。(见"**附录**""美国选举常用语")

Obama Makes History(2008/11/5 *The Washington Post*)

七、国会

1. Bicameral Congress

美国参照了英国议会,组成了两院制国会(a bicameral/two-house/two-chamber Congress),较小的院 the Senate(参议院),也非正式地称为 the upper house/chamber;大的 the House of Representatives(众议院),也非正式地称为 the lower house/chamber。不管州的大小或人口的多寡,每州享有两名参议员名额,全国共有 100 名参议员。众议员名额则由人口多寡决定。据 2008 年统计,美国 7 个人口少的州每州只有一名众议员,而加州一州就有 53 个席位。2005 年,全国共有 435 名众议员。国会现有议员共 535 名。参议员任期 6 年,每隔两年改选三分之一。众议员任期两年,因此国会每两年为一届。议员与总统不同,无任期限制,可连选连任。

2. Divided Government

在美国政体中,总统职位和国会不会一直由同一政党掌控,美国选民也不希望出现这种局面。否则权力分散就无意义。美国的政府分权不仅体现在政府行政和立法机构的成员不可身兼两职,即议员不可同时在行政部门任职,反之亦然。而且,这些民选官员则由分别举行的选举产生,尽管选举日是同一天。再则,选民可以故意挑选不同政党背景的总统候选人和议员候选人。这就是所谓的两个机构和两党分治或分掌政府(divided government)。

3. 与总统较量的权力

美国宪法规定,国会为最高立法机构。首届国会于 1789 年组成,主要职权为立法权;行政监督权;条约及官员任命的审批权(参议院);宪法修改权;对总统、副总统的复选权等。尽管国会可通过无须总统签署的决议案,但无法律作用,仅表示国会对某些问题的态度。

此外,两院还享有某些特权,参议院可以相对多数票批准或否决总统任命的高级官员,以三分之二的多数票批准总统与外国缔结的条约;众议院可提出各项财政法案(参议院只有修正、变更、补充之权)。国会对总统、副总统及官员有弹劾权,提出弹劾权属众议院,裁决弹劾权属参议院。简言之,众议院控制着拨款权;参议院控制条约和政府人事任命的批准权。

4. 两院议员的身价

虽然参众两院权力相等,但参议员席位分量更重,更具威望,因为参议员(Senator)代表的选民范围更广,数量更多(七个小州例外),任期更长。而且由于其人数少,因而受到全国更大的关注。众议员(representative),顾名思义,是最接近民众的代表,因选区范围较小,且任期短,每两年就得改选一次,更需要代表民众的利益说话。事实上,不管参议员还是众议员,均从州选到国会任职,都需要为州的利益代言,否则就有丢官之虞。所以与其说他们为国家利益、政党利益进行立法斗争,不如说为地方利益效劳,以保官帽。这句名言"All politics is local"真实地反映了他们的州本位思想。

5. 副总统有投票权吗

众议院的主持人由选举产生,称为议长(the Speaker of the House, the House Speaker)或简称 the Speaker;美国副总统是参议院当然议长(the President of the Senate),缺席时便选出一位临时议长[President Pro Tempore (of the Senate)]主持会议。至于参议院议长,报刊上既用 President,也用 Chairman,并不规范。临时议长和议长一样,通常都是由国会多数党(majority party)议员担任。宪法规定,除了在表决时出现票数相等而相持不下(tie)的情况,参议院议长才有投票权,以便打破这一平局(The U. S. Constitution provides that Vice President can vote only in the event of a tie.),出现对执政党和该党政府有利的局面。(例句见"**学习方法**""词义之确定及辨析")

6. 何谓 Majority or Minority Party

同一政党在参众两院都占多数议席,那该党就是多数党(majority party)或清一色的某党控制的国会(all-Democratic/all-Republican Congress),少数者为少数党(minority party)。有时一个党在参议院的席位占多数,就被称为参议院多数党,而在众议院只占少数就被称为众议院少数党。即使是多数党,也并不一定是执政党,总统就是该党领袖担任。相反,在多数情况下,往往国会的少数党才是某种意义的执政党。这与部门和政党分治(divided government)有关,也表明制衡制深入民心,选民故意分别投票给两党任两个部门职务的候选人。

7. 有哪些重要官职

国会除了 President of the Senate, Speaker of the House 和 President Pro Tempore 等外,国会中的两党领袖,尤其多数党领袖及常设委员会主席都是实权人物,对法律的兴废举足轻重,由两院各党核心小组选举产生。

下面列出他们的部分英汉对照官职:

floor leaders 国会政党领袖,指参议院和众议院中的多数党领袖和督导(或副领袖)、少数党领袖和督导(或副领袖),他们由本党议员选举产生,主要任务是控制本党党员在国会的活动。Whip 或 Party Whip 亦作 Assistant Floor Leader,早先译为"党鞭",源于 whipper-in(在猎狐中帮猎人赶猎狗者),与其本身的职务相符。他要游说本党议员支持本党议案,敦促他们出席重要议案的表决会议。与英国不同的是,美国 Whip 无权实行党纪。现在此职译为"督导",也译得很好。不过有个别词典将其译为"组织秘书"似乎太笼统,词不达意。

  Senate/House Majority Leader 参议院/众议院多数党领袖
  Senate/House Minority Leader 参议院/众议院少数党领袖
  Senate/House Majority Whip 参议院/众议院多数党督导
  Senate/House Minority Whip 参议院/众议院少数党督导
  Senate/House Assistant Majority Leader 参议院/众议院多数党副领袖
  Senate/House Assistant Minority Leader 参议院/众议院少数党副领袖

以上的多数党/少数党副领袖即多数党/少数党督导。编者读报发现,报刊上常用后者,前者只用于共和党人。例如下例中的 Rober Dole 是当时的共和党参议院多数领袖,而副领袖则为 Alan Simpson:

  Says **Senate Assistant Majority Leader** Alan Simpson of Wyoming: "Here we are making a suggestion that we limit the cost-of-living allowance to 2 percent and, Lord, you would think that the earth had crashed." (*U. S. News & World Report*)

  此外,在报刊上常看到 Senate/House Republican Leader; Senate/House Democratic Leader,这里只是加上个政党,Leader 即 floor leader,指的是多数党领袖,见例句:

  Like scores of other farm-state lawmakers, including **Senate Republican Leader** Bob Dole of Kansas and **House Majority Leader** Richard Gephardt of Missouri, the Democratic congressman from Indiana wanted to protect the profits of local farmers who sold grain to Iraq. (*Newsweek*)

  Chairman of the Standing Committee of appropriations/Armed Forces/Banking, Housing (Finance) and Urban Affair... 拨款/军事/银行/住房(或财政)和城市常设委员会主席,等等。

八、国会选举

1. 何谓 Congressional Election

  美国国会每两年一届,至 2008 年 11 月 4 日大选后,国会已是第 110 届(the

110th Congress)。在四年一次的总统选举中,选民不仅要选出新总统,而且同时要选出 435 位众议员和三分之一参议员。在大选中人们往往更多地关注总统选举,事实上国会选举同样重要。既然国会是每两年一届,那么,除总统选举中举行国会选举外,还有另一次选举,称为中期选举。

2. 何谓 Midterm Election

中期选举[midterm (elections)],顾名思义是指美国总统四年任期中间(即接近第二年结束时)进行的国会参议院和众议院选举。其结果经常被视为是对总统前两年政绩的全民公决。在美国政治中,重要性仅次于大选。因为中期选举改选参议院部分席位和众议院全部席位,同时也改选州和地方政府的许多官员。总统的党能否在此选举中取得国会多数或与反对党相当的议席,对总统能否顺利施政关系重大。而州和地方选举也攸关他能否两年后竞选连任,或其为党的下任总统候选人能否顺利接班,所以共和和民主两党展开激烈的斗争。

3. off-year/off-off year/special election(s)

midterm election 常略作 midterm,见例句:

Losses of even two or three seats in the Senate and 20 or so in the House, regarded as normal for the President's party at **midterm**, would shave the Democrats' margins so thin as to perhaps bring back legislative gridlock. (*Time*)

作中期国会选举,还有另一个词,那就是 off-year election。比较而言 midterm 比 off-year 用得更多,但早先报刊也常用,如:

A CNN/*USA Today*/Gallup poll in late March showed Clinton trailing "the Republican Party's candidate for president" by 50 to 43 percent. And Republicans stand to make gains—possibly big gains—in the 1994 **off-year election.** (*U. S. News & World Report*)

《纽约时报》专栏作家 William Safire 说:"In recent years, however, **midterm** is increasingly taken to mean 'halfway through a president term'(比前面的英文释义说得更简明), while **off-year** is sometimes, but no longer usually, taken to be a synonym for that."也就是说,off year 的词义有所变化。国会每两年举行一次选举,而有些州长和地方一级的公职选举在国会选举之间的奇数年份进行,可是现在在英语中尚未有任何专门词语来表达这种选举,因此也用 off-year。这样,"中期选举"就有两个不同的意思:midterm 指非大选年在双数年份举行的国会选举(不少州长和地方官员选举也在双数年份举行),而 off-year 既非指大选年,也非指国会选举年,而指某些地方在单数年份举行是选举年,称为小选年。

可是,在上世纪 80 年代又出现了一个用来指小选年的新词"**off-off year**",

这大概与 off-year 词义变化才创造的。其实,说得简单一点,off-year election 可指除总统选举年以外的任何年份举行的选举。

special election 是美国用语,所谓特别选举是指总统以下的所有民选官员。如议员等任期未满,但因突然去世或辞职等原因出现职位空缺而举行的补缺选举,译为"补缺选举"更能达意。英国的 by-election 只指下院议员的补缺选举,比美国的 special election 所指的范围要窄些。下例解释清楚:

There are three basic types—primary, general and local. In addition, **"special elections"** can be called which are limited to one specific purpose, e. g., filling a vacancy. (*Guide to Election*)(见"**附录**""美国选举常用语")

九、国会是 Bureaucratic Empire 吗

这是美国新闻界的看法。见 *Reader's Digest* 1990 年 7 月号上有一篇题为 "Why Congress Doesn't Work"的文章,摘抄如下几段:

1   **Bureaucratic empire.** In 1946, the last time the Hill(喻"国会")underwent sweeping reorganization, 34 House and Senate committees were run by powerful senior members. Today Congress has 47 committees and 232 subcommittees, each with its own staff and territorial imperatives(范围内必办之事).

2   Congress's bureaucratic empire is maintained by an army of invisible aides—about 32,000 in all. As lawmakers focus more on raising re-election money, their subordinates have been ceded wide latitude to draft legislation, plot strategy, handle lobbyists and even decide how to vote. Top salary for a Senate committee staff director is now $95,715. "Too much is being done by anonymous people," says former Senate Majority Leader Howard H. Baker, Jr. "Congress needs to return to its role as a policy-making agency. It must stop acting like an aggregation of (一群,一帮) bureaucrats, pseudo(伪,假,冒牌的)-Presidents and pseudo-Secretaries of State."

3   What's puzzling to many is that Capitol Hill has become steadily less responsive to national needs even as legislators have become more qualified. "Congress has a spectacular amount of individual talent," laments former House Rules Committee Chairman Richard Bolling (D., Mo.) "But institutionally it has great difficulty performing."

再看《世界年鉴》"How a Bill Becomes a Law"(立法过程)的介绍:

1   A senator or representative introduces a bill in Congress by sending it to the clerk of the House or the Senate, who assigns it a number and title. This

procedure is termed **the first reading**. The clerk then refers the bill to the appropriate committee of the Senate or House.

2 If the committee opposes the bill, it will table（搁置）, or kill, it. Otherwise, the committee holds hearings to listen to opinions and facts offered by members and other interested people（有关人员）. The committee then debates the bill and possibly offers amendments. A vote is taken, and if favorable, the bill is sent back to the clerk of the House or Senate.

3 The clerk reads the bill to the house—**the second reading**. Members may then debate the bill and suggest amendments.

4 After debate and possibly amendment, the bill is given **a third reading**, simply of the title, and put to a voice or roll-call vote（呼声或唱名表决）.

5 If passed, the bill goes to the other house, where it may be defeated or passed, with or without amendments. If defeated, the bill dies. If passed with amendments, a conference committee（协商委员会）made up of members of both house works out the differences and arrives at a compromise.

6 After passage of the final version（法案文本）by both house, the bill is sent to the president. If the president signs it, the bill becomes a law. The president may, however, veto the bill by refusing to sign it and sending it back to the house where it originated, with reasons for the veto.

7 The president's objections are then read and debated, and a roll-call vote is taken. If the bill receives less than a two-thirds majority, it is defeated. If it receives at least two-thirds, it is sent to the other house. If that house also passes it by at least a two-thirds majority, the veto is overridden（被推翻）, and the bill becomes a law.

8 If the president neither signs nor vetoes the bill within 10 days—not including Sundays—it automatically becomes a law even without the president's signature. However, if Congress has adjourned（休会）within those 10 days, the bill is automatically killed; this indirect rejection is termed a pocket veto（搁置否决权）.

  Note: Under the Line Item Veto Act［在整个法案中删除个别项目的《单项否决权》］, effective Jan. 1, 1997, the president was authorized, under certain circumstances, to veto a bill in part, but the legislation was found unconstitutional by the Supreme Court, June 25, 1998. (*The World Almanac* 2007)

上述所引文章和资料说明，国会叫做"官僚帝国"并非凭空捏造，被总统杜鲁门骂为"do-nothing Congress"和媒体贬称"can't-do Congress"，"don't-work Congress"也有事实根据。究其原因有四。

1. 第 1 段：机构臃肿重叠。凡行政部门有的机构，为制衡，国会也要设立相对应的部门，所以其委员会多达几百个。

2. 第 2 段：各种高薪助手和其他名目的人员多如牛毛，犹如大军，达几万人之众。议员虽有五百多位，但不干立法实事，因任期无限制，成天忙于竞选连任筹款，陷入竞选活动委员会（Political Action Committee）人员或游说人员（lobbyist）包围圈，因而授予其下属权力的自由度太大（their subordinates have been ceded wide latitude...），他们可以起草立法，竟然能操纵议员做出议案修正、立法兴废的投票决定。2006 年 11 月 20 日《新闻周刊》在"Decline and Fall"一文中也评论称："[Tom] Delay brought a new brazenness to the game. Now lobbyists were in the room, writing legislation."再则，三十多年来 95% 以上的众议员都能竞选连任，参议员的连任也常如此，所以每届国会都是旧面孔占绝大多数，议员职位几乎成了终身制。例如瑟蒙德（Strom Thurmond）在国会一口气度过了 48 个春秋，他最后一次竞选连任参议员是在 1996 年，当时已 94 岁高龄。2002 年 12 月 5 日在参议院大楼，为他举行了百岁生日庆祝会。还有今年 92 岁才病逝的伯德（Robert Byrd）竟然担任过 51 年参议员和 6 年众议员。这些老油条办事缺干劲，改革无动力，国会成了一潭死水。所以前参院多数党领袖贝克呼吁："Congress needs to return to its role as a policy-making agency."

3. 第 3 段：不是议员无能，而是制度（institutions）使然。立法机构不愿意改革立法，当然使人难以施展才华，发挥议员应有的作用。这都是当官迷思想在作怪。

4. 立法程序（bill-into-law process）复杂。法案经 first/second/third reading 的过程，充满修修补补，两党、两派和各种利益集团争斗和妥协。如果不一审就否决，议案只能一看二慢三通过。因而政府政策在很多问题上只能起微小变化，这就是权力分散、严格制衡的结果。总的来说，有好的一面，但也有因党争或派性作怪，有些紧急议案如预算等拖不起，闹不好政府工作就要停摆，1981 年至 1995 年这 14 年间，政府就有五次 shutdown。first/second/third reading（一审、二审和三审），table 作动词，英美词同义异，pocket veto, Line Item Veto Act 等都是议会用语。

十、国会是"Rich Man's Club"

1985 年 11 月 24 日，《纽约时报》发表了"The Rich Get Richer and Elected"

一文,揭露众议院已不是人民的议院,而成了富翁俱乐部。难道参议院能例外吗?所谓"民主多样化"和"民众参政议政"(political participation)等都不过空话而已。可是坐在国会中的那些既得利益者集团(vested interests)不愿修改现行竞选法规。读了下面的这篇文章的几段便不言自明。

1　　WASHINGTON, Sept. 23 — The House of Representatives, which prides itself on being "the people's House," has been turning into **a rich man's club**.

2　　The representatives newly elected in 1984 were almost four times as wealthy as the first-term lawmakers elected only six years before,...

3　　... As a result, it is increasingly difficult for candidates of modest means, particularly women, to mount successful challenges to entrenched office holders.

4　　One solution, the authors contend, is a system of public financing for campaigns, but Congress seems in no mood to change the political rules any time soon.

5　　"The lower chamber is going upper class," said Mark Green, the president of The Democracy Project, a public policy institute (研究机构) based in New York. "But this evolution from a House of Representatives to a House of Lords (贵族院) denies the diversity of our democracy. It establishes a de facto (事实上的) property qualification for office that increasingly say: low and middle income need not apply." (1985/11/24 *The New York Times*)

十一、总统与国会

1. 总统与国会是何关系

美国总统是国家元首,政府首脑,也是武装部队总司令。要说明总统与国会的关系,得先了解各自的权限。美国宪法规定,联邦政府一切行政权属于总统。总统是军队统帅,可召集各州国民警卫队。有权宣布紧急状态。宣战权虽属国会,但经国会授权,总统可调动军队参战。总统负责对外关系,有权缔约,但需经参议院批准。总统有权与外国谈判和签订行政协议(executive agreements),无须经批准。总统批准或否决国会通过的法案。每年1月份提出国情咨文,文内主张构成立法议程,但制定内外政策需国会支持,有权否决国会法案,两院各以三分之二的多数可推翻否决。如国会通过南非种族隔离制度(apartheid)制裁法案,遭里根否决,国会又以2/3多数通过此项立律。总统须服从国会的否决、弹劾,有权任命内阁部长、驻外使节、最高法院法官,但须经参院批准。

上述关系可概括为:"总统出主意,国会做决定。"总统任何提案建议必须形成法案(bill),并经国会提出,批准立法,否则总统无权行事。然而,国会的绝大部分法案又都是根据行政部门的建议而提出的。

2. 府会倾轧为哪般

总统和国会往往不是由同个政党控制，民主党人担任总统，往往共和党人就占国会两院或一院的多数议席。反之亦然。这就是两党分掌政府或分治（divided government）。总统为了竞选连任须政绩斐然，虽受宪法限制不能连任三届，但为了留名青史或本党下次大选，也要出政绩。在野党要执政，就得处处与总统较劲。正如英国一位政治家所说："反对党的职责就是什么都反对"（The duty of an Opposition is to oppose.）。总统某些施政方案，国会难以采纳。政府（Administration）与国会争斗常作报刊题材。先看杜鲁门骂 do-nothing Congress 的：

Promising to "give them hell（臭骂他们，诋毁对手），" Truman launched an aggressive "whistle-stop"（竞选途中在小火车站作短暂停留）campaign. Traveling by rail, he made several hundred informal but hard-hitting speeches. He excoriated（痛斥）**the "do-nothing" Republican Congress**, which had rejected his program and passed the Taft-Hartley Act, and he warned labor, farmers, and consumers that if Dewey won, Republican "glutton of privilege" would do away with all the gains of the New Deal Years. (*The American Nation*)

杜鲁门是 F. 罗斯福任内去世于1945年接任的民主党总统。1948年竞选连任，对手是杜威（Thomas Dewey）。杜鲁门是新政的忠实追随者。为求新，提出了套用"New Deal"的"Fair Deal"（公平施政），即管制经济、鼓励私有企业等一套施政方案，绝大部分被共和党控制的国会否决。不但如此，国会反而对着干，通过杜反对的反劳工法"the Taft-Hartley Bill"。因此，他痛骂国会不干正事，共和党是"贪得无厌的特权分子"（gluttons of privilege）。

再看《新闻周刊》"Four More Years"文章中反映总统里根刚连任就发誓与国会较量：

1　　Ronald Reagan's 49-state landslide on November 6 puts him in commanding position to kick off the nation's third two-term Presidency in 28 years.

2　　The clear verdict of some 92 million Americans taking part in the nation's 50th presidential election: An overwhelming stamp of approval on Reagan's brand of leadership over the last four years—although that support was not extended to enough other Republicans to avert collisions with a divided Congress.

3　　The Reagan avalanche that buried Democratic challenger Walter Mondale fell short of gathering the strength needed in Congress to carry out the

President's hopes of staging a "second revolution" in Washington.

4   Even so, Reagan vowed to turn up the heat on balky legislators by "taking our case to the people" if his programs are blocked.

5   "The people made it very plain that they approved of what we're doing," was how the President summed up the results. His chief rival in Congress, Democratic House Speaker Thomas "Tip" O'Neill, disagreed and hinted at an early collision with Reagan and a stalemate in government by declaring, "There is no mandate out there. (1984/11/19 *U. S. New & World Report*)".

这篇"再任四年"的文章的第1段：里根在1984年竞选连任中对阵民主党候选人蒙达尔时，取得了一边倒胜利。第2—3段：虽然选民对他大力支持，并未让共和党在国会占多数席位，或成为 all-Republican Congress。

这样，他的财政和税务改革计划（以减税为重点），即所谓的第二次革命，就难以避免与国会发生冲突。第4段：他发誓要拼一场，放风要举行全民公决（referendum）(take our case to the people)。第5段：反对党众议院议长奥尼尔顶嘴，示意奉陪："（咱们）那儿还没有授权哩。"(There is no mandate out there)。"里根尚未发表国情咨文，公布施政计划，好戏就开场了。

第二篇是《时代》周刊以"Determined to Do What Is Right"为题的访谈录中，看看老布什又怎样痛恨民主党控制的国会，副标题就说：The President says that in domestic policy, unlike foreign affairs, little can be achieved without first beating down the Democrats。

1   **Q. We are struck by your ability to lead an international coalition for a common purpose in the gulf and your inability to lead in the same way on domestic issues. Do you have an explanation for this**?

2   **A.** There is a very simple one. We don't control either house of Congress. Having said that, and in anticipation of the question, I asked [my staff] if we'd summarize whether we've made any accomplishments at home or not. I think they're rather impressive on a wide array of issues.

3   But the simplest answer to your question is that in domestic affairs, to pass legislation, to accomplish your ends, you've got to go to a Congress that has a different philosophical approach to many issues — most issues. In terms of achieving objectives, certainly there's an unfulfilled agenda, but there are some steps that have been taken that I think are very, very important on the domestic side. Very important.

4   ... He said, "So much have I done, and so much have I left to do," as he

looked at the ceiling. Well, it is true. We have made remarkable progress given the fact that we have to fight back a Congress that is committed to a different philosophical course. But to accomplish things, you have first got to beat down the Democrats. And that is not true in foreign affairs. (1991/1/7 *Time*)

此文的副标题与第 4 段最后一句话"And that is not true in foreign affairs."意思一样。为什么总统外强内弱呢？因为"The President also negotiate 'executive agreements' with foreign powers which are not subject to Senate confirmation",总统有行政特权,与外国所签的一些条约、协定,不必送参议院审议批准即可生效,而内政则不然。所以,总统通常由于内政计划在中期选举受挫时,就出国去寻求慰藉或浇愁(Traditionally, Presidents who find their domestic programs thwarted by midterm elections seek solace overseas.)。

本文是记者采访,记者问,老布什答。第 1 段：记者问布什在海湾准备与伊拉克作战能组成国际联盟,而在国内问题上却不能呢？第 2 段：布什说在内政上也做出了令人印象深刻的成就。第 3 段布什说因国会受民主党控制,遇事都得经国会批准立法,民主党议员与他理念不同,有些计划尚未完成。第 4 段：他吹嘘在内政上做出不少成绩,但还有不少工作尚待去做。实际上他在内政上乏善可陈。不过,他把话锋一转,要做出成绩先要战胜不同理念民主党控制的国会。在对外事务上就不一样了。

这里,老布什对民主党及其控制的国会不满言于溢表。例如：全文中的"a hostile Congress","(you have first got to) beat down the Democrats",等等。

《时代》周刊还有一篇文章,描写克林顿与共和党控制的国会就预算问题进行党争,很有代表性。1995 年法定的预算花光了,可是控制着钱袋(hold the congressional purse strings)的国会不同意追加预算,结果政府就不得不关闭(shutdown)一些政府机构,连驻外使馆签证处、博物馆、社会保障署等都得关门。奥巴马也曾为此发愁过。这是自诩为世界唯一超级大国的耻辱。

3. 谁占上风

话说回来,总统在与国会的斗争中往往占上风。看老布什在上述同一篇文章中就"宣战权"答问：

Q. You've described yourself as a strict constructionist（对宪法咬文嚼字的解释者） where the Constitution is concerned. How do you construct the words "Congress shall have the power to declare war"?

A. They have got it right now. I have the powers of the Commander in Chief. There are a lot of historical precedents involved in all of this. You have the War Powers Resolution, you have the fact of some 200 applications of force (使用武力), five of which were solemnified by a declaration of war. So we look at history, and we talk to lawyers. We consult [with Congress].

布什这番话的意思是：宣战权在国会，可是从历史上看，美国动用武力约二百次，只有五次正式宣战。也就是说，总统是武装部队总司令，可以进行不宣而战的战争，像朝鲜战争和越南战争这样的大战美国都未正式宣战。当然，他领导打的第一次伊拉克战争即海湾战争是得到了国会的授权而获得"宣战权"的。

总统与国会斗争中具有的另一件重要武器是"行政特权"。所以当他在国内的施政方案遭到国会拒挠或否决时，就把注意力集中在外交，以取得成果。西方不亮东方亮，使他不至于国内外都无政绩可言。这就较全面地回答了本章开头第一例中提出的部分问题。

此外，有威望的总统在与国会的抗争中能利用手中权力，对本党议员采取笼络、封官许愿等手段，并动用舆论，向国会施压，最终达到目的。但共和党总统老布什是个失败者，原誓言不增税，后来不兑现诺言，不但违背本党原则，还被民主党揪住出尔反尔、反复无常的把柄。

当然，双方都得作必要的妥协，因为西方流行的理念是："政治是妥协的艺术或产物。"如果说各种独立势力之间的相互制衡就是"民主"的话，那么他们之间的对话、妥协和平衡就是"政治"。所以双方都应该是："In politics a man must learn to rise above principle."

值得注意的是，凡总统职位和国会多数议席分属两党的，这种行政与立法部门的争斗就会常见诸报端。

4. 谁播下斗争的种子

美国号称是世界上最健全的民主制国家，可为何总统与国会争斗不断呢？凡事都有两面，正是这种美国宪法规定的民主制度埋下了两虎相争的种子。具体讲，缘由大致有五：

（1）政治制度使然：美国宪法规定政府由行政、立法和司法三个部门组成，各自独立。这种公权制而造成的制衡制为内斗埋下了祸根。

（2）多党制：严复先生早就注意到多党制的弊端，"但幸政门繁多，不致使一党得以专权。"但不专权就得争权。争权为了各自利益，方法是通过选举控制政府，这就因 party politics 形成的争斗。

（3）政党理念不同：两党理念不同引发斗争。共和党是所谓的富人党，民主党则自称是穷人的代表，处处较劲，导致受其控制的机构矛盾不断。

（4）利益不同：联邦与地方利益集团之间矛盾引发冲突。总统为全国计代表国家利益;国会中党中有派,议员为保官而维护选区的地方利益,这就难免发生利益分配抵触。有人认为,政治的定义是"对价值的有权威的分配"。可在美国,却哪一方不具备这种权威。

(5) 选民投票倾向和意图也是引发斗争的一个原因。制衡制深入民心,老百姓不是怕他们斗,而是希望他们斗。《华盛顿邮报》曾针对这种情况道出的缘由是:

"Americans dislike handling too much power to either party, so they tend to entrust each with Congress or the White House but not both."

这就是说,选民对共和和民主两党都不太信任,常常不愿意一党独霸行政和立法机构,免使(政)府(国)会勾结,失去制衡(checks and balances),这种制度被认为是防止滥用权力的万全机制。

5. State of the Union message 与国会的关系

总统咨文(message of the President)是美国总统向国会提出施政报告和法案建议等统称,主要是国情咨文(State of the Union message)(the Union此处作 the United States of America 讲)和预算咨文(Budget message)。报刊常用国情演说或报告(State of the Union address/speech/report)。根据议事程序法,总统无权提出法案,只能由参众两院的执政党议员就总统咨文的内容整理为议案(bill)提出。至于总统提出的经济报告或外交政策报告(Economic/Foreign Policy Report)不是提出议案建议,所以不称 message,而是 report。国情咨文有时也用 report, address 或 speech,是报刊随意用字所致,不足为训。

国情咨文最具代表性,每年年初国会开幕时,总统报告国内外情况,提出应当采取的政策措施,实际上就是施政纲领,即要国会通过的议案清单。草拟国情咨文的过程中,总统也要征询国会领袖的意见。因此,国情咨文在形式上虽无法律效力,但随着行政权日益扩大,变成总统领导国家的有力方式。实际上逐渐具有国会工作纲领的意义,变成总统操纵或进行立法活动的工具。

国情咨文起源于美国开国总统乔治·华盛顿。1790年第一个国情咨文言简意赅,全文只有850字。但是随着美国疆土的不断膨胀和扩展,国情咨文的篇幅越来越冗长,1995年克林顿发表的国情咨文是美国有史以来最长的,宣读时间花了80分钟。另外,关于其他一些国家,如俄罗斯、墨西哥、巴西等,总统也向国会提出国情咨文,类似我国总理每年在人大做的"政府工作报告"。

习 题

阅读理解文章

1. "Out of the Gloom, A Silver Lining"(2006/11/20 *Newsweek*)

2. "Shutdown"(1995/11/27 *Time*)(曾做《精选本》二版课文)

十二、司法机构

1. 司法机关为何不如总统和国会"出风头"

美国司法机构(U. S. Judiciary)设 1 个联邦最高法院,12 个联邦上诉法院,90 个地区法院和若干特别法院。最高法院拥有最高司法权。由 1 名院长(Chief Justice,首席大法官即美国联邦和州最高法院院长;而 Chief Judge 则是首席法官,亦即下级法院院长)和 8 名大法官组成,大都顽固守旧,叫做 9 个老朽(nine old men)。他们由总统提名经参议院批准任命,并规定如无失职行为,将终身任职。法官席位出缺时,任命方可补充新法官。大法官不是民选官员,无须筹款、竞选、与老百姓接触。此外,最高法院也很少与总统或国会发生正面直接冲突。他们不是新闻人物,罕见接受采访,新闻界的报道也很少。再则他们常常只是做出"违反宪法"的权威裁决,几乎无人包括总统在内再敢说三道四。

2. 高法裁决震动大

最高法院有权宣布联邦和各州的任何法律为无效。为此,共和党和民主党或保守派和自由派都争夺对法官的任命,争斗相当激烈。民主党总统想任命自由派法官,共和党总统则反之。例如:Robert H. Bork 原是耶鲁大学法学教授,1973 年被共和党总统尼克松任命为司法部副部长。水门事件期间,总统命令开除调查水门事件的特别检察官 Archibald Cox,尽管上司宁可辞职拒绝服从,Bork 却照办无误。1982 年里根任命此人为上诉法院法官,1987 年又任命他为最高法院大法官,但遭到民主党控制的参议院拒绝,尽管参议院借口他的"司法约束"(judicial restraint)等观点不合司法主流,实际上是指他的极端保守派观点难被民主党自由派接受。结果 Bork 没有当上大法官。此后,"bork"还成了一个动词:

To **bork** is to wage a political campaign against a nominee, using all the modern tools of electoral politics, including paid and free media. (*American Speech*)

意为"竭力阻止(任命)",进而引申为利用媒体"诋毁(某人)"。最高法院的裁决对这两派或两党关系重大,如 2000 年美国大选在佛罗里达州的计票问题上两党候选人申请对簿公堂时,最高法院的 9 位法官中共和党比民主党总统任命的法官多一票,结果 5:4 做出了有利于小布什裁决,使他入主白宫。看 2002 *World Almanac*(《2002 年世界年鉴》):

2000 Presidential Election:Rehnquist and O'Connor joined a conservative majority in 2000's *Bush v. Gore*, Which settled that year's presidential election by blocking, 5—4, a recount of votes in the hotly contested state of Florida and effectively confirming victory for George W. Bush. The court found that differing recount procedures in various jurisdictions violated the Equal Protection Clause. (Rehnquist 和 O'Connor 都是共和党总统任命的保守派大法官,并先后担任过院长。以公平保护条款为名,阻止佛州法院做出在几个县以不同方式重新计票的裁决)

再如:1876 年的美国大选与 2000 年美国总统选举十分相似。1876 年 11 月 7 日,总统选举结束后,美国内战时期的志愿军少将、共和党人、俄亥俄州州长卢瑟福·海斯(Rutherford Hayes)认为大势已去,上床睡觉了。但第二天发现总统选举远未结束。那一年对选举结果的争议持续了 4 个月。由于争论不断,国会不得不推迟总统就职日期。在第二年 3 月 4 日,总统就职最后期限前两天,国会建立了一个两党联合的特别选举委员会(Special Election Commission)。该会包括 8 名共和党人,7 名民主党人。最后将所有有争议的选举人票都判给了海斯,结果他以 185 张比蒂尔登 184 张选举团票当选为美国第 19 任总统,仅比对手多一张,外号"一票总统"。

3. 裁决有利于普通百姓吗

掌权者富人占绝大多数,因而多数裁决维护富人和强势或既得团体的利益,不利于穷人和弱势群体。例如 1976 年最高法院裁定,国会关于个人出资竞选数量的限制违宪(unconstitutional)。这样,穷人就难以从政。再如:2010 年 1 月,最高法院允许企业可限额限制投资(invest 用得妙,投资求回报)于选战(华盛顿邮报)。政客当选后当然得投桃报李,站在大企业或大富翁立场上行事。2003 年在 Grutter 诉 Bollinger 一案中裁定,在就业和入学方面照顾黑人和妇女的政策计划(affirmative action)违宪。这样,黑人和妇女只有继续吃亏下去。

最高法院有时违反民意,做出有利于政商勾结的裁决。例如:近几年美国枪击案尤其是校院枪击案频仍,枪支泛滥是重要原因。据 2008 年统计,个人持枪达 2 亿支。为此民间要求限制或禁止个人持枪的呼声不断高涨。但美国步枪协会(National Rifle Association)势力强大,是总统和国会议员尤其是共和党人的竞选捐款大户,与政界有着千丝万缕的关系,以该会为代表的一部分人士认为,个人持枪是宪法权利,并主张放宽枪支管制。由于美国宪法修正第二条语言模糊,这场争论长久,一拖再拖。2008 年 6 月 26 日,美国最高法院以 5 比 4 做出了裁决,明确个人有权持有和使用枪支,同时推翻了华盛顿特区实行了 32 年的禁枪令。显然,这项裁决未能顺应民意,却偏向了商人的生意和政界人士的官瘾,听从富人和当权者意旨。

4. The Supreme Court Follows the Election Results

高法在内政问题上的裁决,要看两党或两派势力消长和顺应富人意旨,在外交上,也是新当权派的工具。为侵略扩张政策辩护,下面这句名言概括了这一特点。

The Supreme Court follows the election returns.

也就是说,最高法院总是跟着政治行情跑。美国19世纪末20世纪初不断向外侵略扩张,最高法院的法官不分是非,频频为侵略扩张合法化张目,美国记者和幽默作家Finley Dunne(1867—1936)为此创造了一个嘲讽时政的杜利先生(Mr. Dooley)的形象,杜利先生讽刺说:"不管宪法能否使美国的军事占领合法化,最高法院总是按照新当权者的意旨行事。"(No matter whether th' Constitution follow th' flag or not, the Supreme Court follows the election returns.)即法官能使不合法的也能说成是合法的。(flag指军旗,意为军旗插到哪里,法院就跟到那里)

2005年3月,*International Herald Tribune*配合文章刊载的下面这幅漫画,形象生动地说明了"The supreme court follows the election results."新闻界大声责问为什么法官不开审虐待战俘(POW)这一违反日内瓦公约的大事,却专注植物人Terri Schiavo是否安乐死这样的小事,显然在帮小布什捂盖子。

拿着棍子追打的戴头套人挂的牌子上写着:"P.O.W."(战俘);左侧法官说:Don't You See We Are Busy?!(难道没看见我们正忙着吗?)中间法官手中文件:Terri Schiavo Case(泰里・夏佛案是关于植物人与安乐死之争案)。

美国多数案件的审判由州法官主持。州法官由选举产生或由州长和州议院司法委员会协同任命,任期长短不一。

5. 法院和高院法官

Supreme Court of the United States	美国最高法院
Chief Justice	首席大法官,在美国指院长
Associate Justice	陪审大法官(报刊常用"justice")
Lower Court	低级法院

United States Court of Appeals	美国上诉法院
United States District Court	美国地方法院
Judicial Panel on Multi-district Litigation	联区诉讼陪审团
Special Court	特别法院
United States Claims Court	美国索赔法院
United States Temporary Emergency Court of Appeals	美国临时紧急上诉法院
United States Court of Appeals for the Federal Circuit	美国联邦巡回上诉法院

(见"附录""美英司法系统一览")

十三、州政府(State Government)

1. 组成与联邦政府相似吗

没有两个州是一模一样的。有些州面积较小；有的面积比世界上许多国家还要大。各州都有人口组成带来的社会问题。因此，州政府的形式在许多重要细节方面各有不同，不过，也有几乎共同的特点。

在美国，联邦和州一级政府实行三权分立，州政府都有三个部门：立法、行政和司法，而地方政府，政权架构则由本地人民自行决定。

除内布拉斯加州只有单一的州立法机关参议院外，所有州都有两院制的州立法机关，上院(the upper house/chamber)通常称为州参议院，下院(the lower house/chamber)称为州众议院、州众院或州议会。后者往往较大。在大部分州里，州参议员任期比国会参议员任期短，只有四年，州众议员任期两年。

州长(Governor)是一州行政首长，由民众投票选举，多数州任期为四年，少数州为两年。

州长的权力在州宪法里有列明，一般来说与美国总统的权力类似。以州而论，相当于副总统的职位是副州长(Lieutenant Governor)，他是由全州的民众投票选举的。他主持州参议院的会议。若州长逝世、退休或被罢免，则由他继任。

如果说美国人恨联邦政府是由于其官僚主义、腐败、尔虞我诈、阴谋诡计、脱离人民，高高在上，不办实事的话，对州以下的地方政府还是比较满意的，因为他们贴近人民，为百姓办事。记得多年前一位知名专栏作家在 The New York Times 发表了一篇题为"Why Americans Hate Government"的文章就谈及此事。

2. 州议会英文名称种种

美国的州议会(state legislature)除 Nebraska 州为一院制(unicameral/one-chamber legislature)外,其余均为两院制议会(bicameral/two-chamber legislature)。the Capitol 或 capitol(非 capital)作为州政府大厦可喻各州"州议会"和"州政府"。然而州与州的议会英文名称不尽相同。根据《2007 年世界年鉴》所载的 State Government 栏列出的州议会英文名称是:Legislature 既是通称,也是多数州如 Alabama, California, New York 等 26 州的正式名称。其次,有 Arkansas, Georgia, virginia 等 19 个州用 General Assembly(这里的 General Assembly 与"联合国大会"字同义异,应根据上下文加以区分,切勿混淆);最后,还有 Montana, North Dakota 和 Oregon 3 州用 Legislative Assembly 及 Massachusetts 和 New Hampshire 两州用 General Court。至于报刊和其他非官方出版物混用的现象很普遍,如加州议会为 California State Assembly 就是一例。由于,有的报刊用法随时生变,所以不作为训。

美国 Nebraska 州议会称为 Legislature,议员为 Senators(参议员)。除 Senate(参议院)各州相同外,众议院英文名称除 56 个州都与国会(Congress)组成的名称一样,称为 House(of Representatives),也有 Nevada, New York, New Jersey 和 Wisconsin 4 个州称为 Assembly。不过各州这些名称有时也变。

十四、市政府(City Government)

市政府的组织结构类型在全国差别极大。不过,几乎所有市政府都有某类选举产生的地方中央议会(central council),并有一位由各部门首长协助的行政官员处理市务。

市政府有三种普遍类型,但徒具虚名,许多城市已把二、三种类型结合成一种混合形式。

1. 何谓 Mayor-Council form/system

市长—议会型/制政府,是美国最古老的市政府形式。直到本世纪开始之前,这种形式在差不多所有美国城市通行。结构类似州政府和全国政府,有民选市长担任行政部门首长,有民选的、只有一院的市议会。市长有权任命各部门首长及其他官员,有时要经市议会批准,有权否决议会通过的城市法令,负责制定城市的预算,这被视为强市长制(strong mayor system)。弱市长制(weak mayor system),市长由议会选任,一切听命于议会而无强市长制赋予的权力。

2. 何谓 Commission form/system

委员会制/型是立法行政合二为一,由一组官员负责,通常有三个或三个以上,由全市选举。每位委员监督一个或一个以上城市部门的工作,其中一名任主席,常称市长;但其权力与同僚一样。在密苏里州哥伦比亚市由七人组长,均兼职志愿者,按规定不拿工资。

3. 何谓 City-Manager form/system

城市行政长官制/型：manager 意为"an appointed chief executive",不能做"经理"讲。此型是 council-manager system,由 commission-manger system 演变而来。由于城市问题日益复杂,需要有专门管理知识,但被推选的政府官员往往不合格。于是便是把大部分行政权力包括执行法律和提供服务授予训练有素的人士处理,但此人由议会任命,必须听命于民选官员组成的市议会。

十五、其他地方政府(Other Local Governments)

1. 各州是否都设县

联邦政府、州政府及市政府,都不能概括美国政府的全部。据美国人口调查局调查,美国的地方政府有 78,000 多个县、自治区(municipality)、镇、校区及特区。

县通常是州以下的行政区,包含两个或两个以上的镇及数个村。但康涅狄格州和罗德岛州却没有县或相当于县的单位。有的市如纽约市因为太大,所以划分为五个独立的行政区(borough),如曼哈顿区和布鲁克林区,区下设县。此外,弗吉尼亚州的阿林顿县(Arlington County)是市区,也是郊区,由单一制的县政府管理(a unitary county administration)。

县政府由选举产生的县委员会、专员委员会或监督委员会(county board, board of commissioners or supervisors)管理,但现在普遍主张由县政府或行政长官(executive)取而代之。

2. Parish 和 Borough＝County 吗

县的英文是"county",路易斯安那州却有相当于县的政府单位,称为"parish",有译"教区"或"堂区"的,既然相当于县(correspondent to a county),为免引起误解或歧义,还是译为"县"为宜。阿拉斯加州的情况也是如此,用的是"borough",既然"similar to a county",也译为"县"好。

3. Commissioner 是 Dogcatcher 吗

正如州政府和市政府一样,有若干选任官员执行县委员会决定,官员名称各州不尽相同：加州的县政府官员是 supervisors,德州为 judges,路易斯安那州为 jurors,新泽西州为 freeholders,纽约州为 county legislators,佛罗里达州如 Dade 县为 commissioners,等等。正因为如此,人们有时难以确定这些官职的词义,混淆时有发生。如果在 New York 州说："I'm a commissioner."人们会误认为你是一个捕狗员(dogcatcher)。美国的一句俗话是："他连捕狗员都选不上"(He is not even qualified to be elected a dogcatcher.)。意为他根本无资格当选,因为 dogcatcher 由选任官员任命,不是民选。

4. Mayor 是"镇长"吗

县以下是镇和村政府(Town and Village Government)他们通常委托民选的委员会或议会(elected board or council)处理事务,委员会名称各异:镇或村议会、镇行政管理成员委员会(board of selectmen or selectwomen)、监督委员会、专员委员会。委员会可能有一个主席或会长负责行政首长的职务,或可能有一个民选镇长(elected mayor)。

十六、政党

1. 民主党和共和党

不了解美国民主党和共和党(the Democratic Party and the Republican Party)的背景,很难回答为什么共和党人恨民主党人赞成的遗产税(estate tax),将它称之为人死了还要上税的"死亡税"(death tax)。2008 年共和党总统候选人麦凯恩(John McCain)愿意与一个具有不断征税、不断花钱、不断当选(tax and spend)的大政府(big government)理念的民主党候选人较量,而不愿挑战一个求变的奥巴马(Barrack Obama)。若读了 2005 年 7 月 4 日 U. S. New & World Report 发表的"Double Trouble Speak"文章,不知情者会发现更多读不懂的词语和句子。所以,编者将政党知识也视为读报知识中的一个重点。

2. 政党起何作用

政党是美国政治制度的基础。奇怪的是宪法没有关于政党的规定。政党是担任竞选工具的,有了这个工具,就可以把竞选公职的候选人向选民推荐,但宪法也没有关于政党这个角色的规定。

3. 两党演变轨迹

一般而言,美国采用两党制度(two-Party system)。就是说,有两大政党即现在的民主党和共和党支配了联邦、州及地方的政治。不过,其他党也十分活跃,特别在州和地方选举中,这些党会成功地选出它们的候选人担任职位,并且对政府施政发挥相当大的影响。例如在 20 世纪的最初 30 余年,社会党(the Socialist Party)便选出两位众议员以及 50 位以上市镇和城市的市长。进步党(the Progressive Party)曾多年占有威斯康星州的州长职位。1974 年有一位无党派(independent)候选人击败共和党人和民主党人,当选为缅因州州长。

在早年全国范围的竞选中,小政党只有一次选出一位候选人竞选总统。那是 1860 年,当时的共和党是一个新党,提名亚伯拉罕·林肯(Abraham Lincoln)竞选总统。即使在那个时期,两党制度已根深蒂固,但这竟使得另一庞大政治组织即辉格党(the Whig Party or the Whigs)在数年内分崩离析,留下共和党和民主党成为称雄政坛的政党。

美国建国初期就出现了两个党,即赞成联邦制的联邦党(the Federalist Party)和反联邦制的反联邦党(the Anti-Federalist Party)。18世纪末,联邦党处于统治地位,第一和第二任总统都是联邦党人。19世纪初叶,该党政治上开始失势。反联邦党势力却不断上升,该党建党时称为共和党(非现在的共和党),后来改称民主共和党(the Democratic Republican Party)。自1800年托马斯·杰斐逊(Thomas Jefferson)当选总统至1828年均是该党执政。第三任至第六任总统都是该党党员。此后,党内发生分裂,一派以安德鲁·杰克逊(Andrew Jackson)为首,于1828年当选总统后改称为今天的民主党。19世纪30—50年代时期,先后出现了反民主党的辉格党(the Whig Party,报刊上常用 the Whigs)、主张黑奴自由的自由党(the Liberty Party)和号召西部禁奴制的自由土壤党(the Free-Soil Party)。他们后因蓄奴制问题发生分裂,1854年反蓄奴制一派合并组建了今天的共和党。此后,便开始了民主和共和两党相争、轮流执政的两党统治制度或特权。为省略,报刊常用 the Democrats(Dems)和 the Republicans(Repubs)(民主党/共和党)和 GOP(共和党)。

4. 各自代表哪些阶层

19世纪中叶,两党成立初期,民主党势力主要在南方,代表农场主、手工业主和小商人利益;共和党势力主要在东北部,代表北方资产阶级利益。南北战争期间,民主党代表南方奴隶主的利益,共和党则主张维护国家统一,反对南方奴隶主叛乱。19世纪末美国进入帝国主义阶段后,两党在国内外重大政治主张方面已无原则区别。但由于历史传统关系,民主党标榜它是中下层人民即弱势集团代表,故求平等和机会均等,并自诩为全民党(the party of the people);共和党代表中上层阶级,并素有大企业党(party of big business)和富人党(party of the rich/haves)之称,并被民主党称之为特权党和私有垄断党(the party of privilege and private monpoly),所以维护工商业主的利益。例如小布什就反对减少温室气体排放的国际公约。它是既得利益集团,故求自由,反对政府的干涉。所以共和党人主张"The government is best which governs least",就是这个道理。换言之,共和党主张"小政府大市场",反对政府干预市场经济和增税。在选举中前者获得蓝领工人、黑人等少数民族以及穷人的选票较多,而后者则获得资本家、大农场主、自由职业者、高薪阶层的多数选票。但是,有的人由此认为民主党正在变为"穷人党"(party of the poor/havenots)显然是错误的。民主党的政治立场是中间偏左,又叫自由派。共和党是中间偏右,主张维持现状,即使非改不可,也反对剧烈的变革,主张渐进式,一步步慢慢来,故称保守派。在推行国内外政策的具体做法上,两党有所差异。例如对待国内问题,一般来说民主党似乎更重视民生、福利和教育等事业,其极左派是学院派(academics);共和党则往往更强调安全、国防,其极右派是宗教界的福音派(evangelicals)。这也与一个较重视穷人利益和一个要维护大企业财源有关。

南北战争后民主党一蹶不振,在野24年。1933年富兰克林·罗斯福执政后,该党连续执政20年,是最兴旺的时期。1861年亚伯拉罕·林肯就任总统,共和党首次执政。此后,一直至1933年这70多年中,除16年外,均由共和党执政。

5. 理念不同的代表人物

在美国近代史上,最典型的代表两党不同理念的人物非民主党总统F.罗斯福和共和党总统里根莫属。

(1) 凯恩斯学说——民主党政策核心:1932年罗斯福当选总统,次年1月上台执政,正值19世纪30年代"经济大萧条"(Great Depression)。他倡导"新政"(New Deal),采用英国经济学家凯恩斯(John Keynes)学说,扩大政府开支,实行财政赤字,刺激经济,增加就业,走出了大萧条。他主张增税,首创社会保障制度(Social Security)。此后几十年,这是民主党大体奉行的政策,也是区别于共和党政策的一大特点。新政使他深得选民的好感。他1940年打破不准一任连任三届(no 3rd term)的传统,1944年又连续当选四届任期的总统。次年,正值二次大战胜利前夕,罗斯福病故。

然而,这些政策也暴露出一些弊端,并遭到共和党的强烈抨击。据说新政干将Harry Hopkins认为,只要扩大政府开支,刺激经济,多花钱来支持联邦政府的工程项目上马,减少失业大军,改善民生,就可以获得选票而连选连任(spend and spend, tax and tax, elect and elect),加之因新政而成立许多机构其中多数为缩略字母名,政府被讽喻为湮没在一碗字母汤里了(submerged in a bowl of alphabet soup),官僚主义盛行。这些使民主党此后被打上了the "tax-and-spend Democrats"或"大政府"(big government)的标签,意味着"赤字财政"、"增税"、"福利社会"和"扩大政府职能"等成了该党的代名词。共和党一贯反对罗斯福的"新政",反对"大政府",反对政府干涉,主张恢复"自由经济"。"低税收"、"平衡预算"、"减少政府开支"、"小政府"(small government)是该党的同义词。可是,此后的几任总统都不得不执行凯恩斯学说经济政策,连最保守的共和党总统尼克松也曾说:"We're all Keynesians now."尽管民主党人对罗斯福大加赞扬,称他是"the Gallant Leader"和"the Gideon(英雄) of Democracy"。共和人则抨击他是"the New Deal Caesar"、"the Raw Democrat"、"The American Dictator"、"the Franklin Deficit(赤字) Roosevelt"和"that Man in the White

House"(最常用的代称,因对他们太愤怒而不愿提及其名字),等等。

(2) 自然受惠论(trickle-down theory)——共和党的一贯主张:1981年共和党人里根上台标志着凯恩斯学说——"新政"理论的统治基础的结束,极端保守派要求取消政府监管和大力推行私有化"自由企业"或"市场万能论"的主张得势,实质上就是后来 Washington consensus 的雏形,向国外普遍推广,就埋下了 2008 年经济危机的种子;民主党人仍将罗斯福奉为神明,直至 1984 年里根竞选连任获胜后,这时的它才觉得恪守"新政"和提倡政府干涉而"劫富济贫"的传统政策和主张行不通了,必须政策更张。美刊是这么报道的:

The voters also issued warnings to both major political parties. Democrats already are scrambling to take the hint to forget nostalgia over the New Deal and exercise some control over the fragmented special-interest groups(支离破碎的特殊利益团体,指色情、同性恋、吸毒等群体) vying for(竞争) national attention under their banner. Senator Gary Hart of Colorado, who had fought Mondale(民主党总统候选人) to the bitter end for the Democratic nomination and then worked for Mondale's election, observed: "We can no longer simply propose redistribution of wealth. We must also create opportunity for everyone, including the middle class." (1984/11/19 U.S. News & World Report)

里根实行的低税率的供应学派经济政策(supply-side economics),被称为"Reaganomics"。这套经济政策由减税、小政府、自由企业和控制货币发行量四部分计划组成。其实就是供应学派经济政策,其核心为一方面大幅减税与减少政府管制,以刺激消费与投资,另一方面则大幅扩增军事支出。《纽约时报》专档作家 James Reston 曾套用上述民主党的话来讽刺其政策:"... hope and pray, borrow and borrow and spend and spend for more weapons"(不断祝愿,不断借钱,不断花钱买武器)事实证明,在里根任内,该政策虽达到振兴经济增长的目标,预算赤字亦随之暴增。难怪里根的这一系列政策在预选中曾被其同党候选人,后成为其副总统的老布什视为"巫术经济政策"(voodoo economics)。民主党人则认为,里根的减税政策主要惠及有钱人,对穷人而言,不过是杯水车薪。

这套政策理论基础仍是"滴漏经济论"、"自然受惠论"或"利益扩散论"(trickle-down theory),此乃共和党人所长期信奉的一种经济理论,认为政府与其将财政补助直接用于社会福利事业和建设,不如将补贴用于促使大企业的发展,大企业生意兴隆了,中小企业也繁荣了,消费者也富裕了,这样就能促使整个经济的发展。民主党则认为这是为大资本家服务的经济理论。1932 年共和党总统胡佛在竞选中就反对民主党的大众救济法,提倡此说。

到了上世纪 20 年代后期,里根任期结束,1989 年老布什接班后,经济开始停滞,并随即转入衰退,市场经济的一些缺陷需要政府来补救,似乎凯恩斯学说又会复活。

(3) 民主党的新政策——中间道路：民主党人克林顿于1993年上台执政,尽管抨击里根的经济政策是"急功近利、瞻前不顾后",反对共和党总统的减税政策。但这并非标志着"里根经济政策"的结束,主张国家干预经济的新凯恩斯主义的重新抬头。相反,克林顿1996年签署了重大的福利计划改革法案,政府大大削减了这方面的开支,实行以预算盈余为优先目标的经济政策。这就表明民主党从此告别了罗斯福的新政,在一些重大的政策问题上向共和党靠拢,并在经济上取得骄人的成绩,此后不但能平衡年预算,而且还有盈余,比里根和老布什时代好。

2001年共和党人小布什执政后,由于"9·11"事件,他以反恐等名义发动阿富汗和伊拉克战争至2008年9月9日,反恐战支出总额达8580亿美元,其中大部用于这两场战争,达8100亿元。他竭力扩军备战,耗资庞大,年国防预算达到创纪录的5000亿美元。这样,每年的国家预算又失去平衡而再次负债累累。使国债增加了近一倍,达10万亿美元,每年要付的利息达2000亿元。2007年又发生次贷危机,使经济走入不景气时期,危及全球经济。

综上所述,难怪前总统艾森豪威尔的撰稿人Emmet Hughes在1952年大选时就两党的政策作出这样结论性评论："民主党怕民众不信任其外交政策犹如共和党怕他们不信任其内政一样。"这是因为民主党被描绘成"the Party of War"(因朝鲜战争和越南战争均由其总统发动),而共和党则是"the Party of Depression"有关。其实Hughes的评论说民主党是"战争党",从现在来看不全对。共和党在老小布什执政时不也打了两场伊拉克和一场阿富汗共三场战争。说共和党是"萧条党"还真有些道理。例如20世纪30年代的Great Depression,正值Hubert Hoover执政,老布什执政时又恰逢经济不振(The economy sucks)。民主党人克林顿收拾残局,不但年预算不负账,还有盈余。接着小布什上台,同党前高官指责他穷兵黩武,导致美国"破产"。美国两党之争,也可给我们一些启示,效率与社会公正,生产与分配,两者必须兼顾,偏向任何一头都会出问题。

6. 松散的组织

两党从中央到地方均有各自的党组织,主要负责竞选事务。两党均无固定党章、党纲,也无固定党员,凡投票或捐款支持某党候选人者即视为该党党员。按照惯例,两党均以本届总统候选人为本党临时领袖,由他推荐党的全国委员会主席,主持竞选事宜,直到下届大选。总统在任期内即为该党领袖。而反对党则无领袖,其在国会的领袖能发挥一定的与执政党总统对抗的作用。

7. 两党党徽——Donkey & Elephant

民主党党徽是"驴"(Donkey),又被称为驴党。共和党党徽是"象"

(Elephant)，又被称为象党。大选中常有"驴象之争"的说法和漫画，指双方争夺总统职位，寓意第三党不能入围，"驴"踢"象"踩，不死即伤。

8. 理念不同，用词各异（见"党语和党争用语"）

9. 第三党及其运动

（1）形形色色的第三党：关于第三党，《美国选举》的小册子里英文表达得很清楚。

Third party：In the parlance of American politics（美国政治用语），"third party" refers to political parties outside the two-party system which are perceived to have a significant base of support. In the 20th century, that has come to mean a party that is not the Republican Party or the Democratic Party and can play some role in influencing the outcome of an election.

也就是说，第三党在美国指除共和党和民主党这两个主导美国政治的政党以外的任何其他政党；英国指除工党和保守党以外的任何其他政党，他们对影响竞选结果起不了重要作用，但2010年的大选却打破了这一格局，为此大党均未获得过半数席位而不得不与小党组成联合内阁。根据这个定义，美国可说是无第三党，至于美国得克萨斯州一家计算机公司总裁、约有20亿美元的亿万富翁罗斯·佩罗（Ross Perot, 1930— ），他曾在1992年自己出资以无党派候选人的身份竞选总统，1995年创建改革党（the Reform Party），次年以改革党候选人的身份再次角逐此职，但均告落选。2000年，原是极右派的共和党人布坎南（Patrick Buchanan）控制了改革党，竞选失败后，该党便消亡了。

另一个国际政党叫自然法则党（the Natural Law Party），在美国建于1992年，是一个持自由派立场的政党，领袖是一名大夫，叫John Hagelin，曾在1992年、1996年和2000年参与总统选举，但只获得不到0.1%的选票。2004年它支持一位民主党总统候选人，此后便宣布解散。

现在唯一还存在的第三党是美国绿党，正式英文名是the Green Party of the United State，而不是早先的the Greens/Green Party USA，与世界上其他国家的绿党类似。自2001年起，该党活动积极，提倡环保，社会公正，尊重多样化，提倡和平和非暴力，主张人不分等级高低，均可参政议政。在1996年和2000年大选中，党魁纳德（Ralph Nader）参选总统尤其令人注目。迄今为止，在地方选举中，该党人员获得最高官职只是在缅因州和加州众议院选举中当选过众议员，且都不是以绿党而是以无党派人士（Independent）的身份竞选获胜的。现有党员约305,000人。2008年7月12日，美国绿党推举来自佐治亚州的原民主党国会黑人女众议员辛西娅·麦金尼（Cynthia McKinney）为本党总统候选人，说唱乐手罗莎·克莱门特为副总统候选人，参与11月的美国总统选举。绿党的黑人女性参选总统拉走了奥巴马的部分选票,只赢得0.1%选票,在所有参选党派中得票居第六位。此外,美国还有宪法党(the Constitution Party)和古典自由派党(the Libertarian Party)等小党。总之,美国第三党在现行选举制度的制约下和两大党的夹击中,难以生存坐大,或自生自灭,或在竞选失望中解体。

(2) 何谓第三党运动:所谓第三党运动(third-party movement),是指退党者(boiler)发起组建新党的运动,对两党掌权体制似乎是一个威胁,但在美国现行政治体制下成不了气候。

十七、美式自由派和保守派

美国的自由派和保守派有何特点?他们之间有何区别?与民主和共和两党有何关系?若不了解这类党派知识,会对许多政治、经济和社会等方面的文章读不太懂,理解不透。所以,本人也视之为读报知识中的重点之一。为了表达透彻,学以致用,从三方面着手:先看英文解释,再举例进行汉语解说,最后的阅读分析一篇文章作结尾。不过下面先问四个词语,看看能否解答得了。

Demopublican, Repubocrat, true-blue conservative, true-red liberal 何意?

1. 何谓 Liberals & Conservatives

Liberal: In American politics, "liberals" tend to be people who are somewhat ideologically left-of-center. They tend to favor more power at the federal level and federal intervention to regulate economic issues and certain social issues, particularly social issues involving rights of minority groups. Traditionally, the bases of liberal support have been in minorities, urban voters, labor unions and academia, though that is evolving as U.S. politics change.

Conservative: In American politics, someone who is right-of-center politically. Of the two major parties, the Republicans are generally considered more conservative. In the United States, conservatives usually emphasize free-market economic principles and often prefer state and local government power to federal power. Traditionally, conservative support has come from business leaders. (*United States Elections*)

Liberal: Currently one who believes in more government action to meet individual needs; originally one who resisted government encroachment(侵犯) on individual liberties. (William Safire)

2. 两派区别何在

美国的自由派和保守派有何区别?不了解美国国情者误认为自由派主张自由放任、绝少干预的市场经济,插手越少越好的"小政府"政策;而保守派主张联邦政府集权，对经济多加干预的"大政府"政策。事实上正好相反，这种误解是由于望文生义产生的。按照美国政治用语，自由派与保守派，主要根据个人在经济与社会问题两个层次上的立场来划分。在经济层次上，自由派主张累进税以平均财富，重视社会福利，重视医疗保险和救助，主张政府多制订计划以调整及解决经济问题。他们的主张也就是要政府多干预、多为小市民谋福利的"大政府"政策；保守派则主张自由放任、绝少干预的市场经济，主张插手得越少越好的"小政府"做法。这两种主张与其字面上的含义正相反。

在社会层次上，自由派争民权，争少数民族权利，反种族歧视，同情同性恋权利，反对死刑，对色情、堕胎、吸毒等这类问题采取较宽容的态度，实际上，这就是采取放任的自由主义态度。保守派则极力主张恢复传统道德观与价值标准，强调法律与秩序，主张恢复死刑，反对色情、堕胎和同性恋，较少关心少数民族的处境和贫苦民众，批评自由派是"bleeding heart"（心肠过软的假善人）或"do-gooders"（不切实际的慈善家）。经济层次上的自由派与保守派，可能和社会层次上的自由派与保守派相一致，即在经济方面采取自由派立场的人，在社会问题上也常常采取自由派的立场；反之亦然。但这种关联性并不是绝对的，有的人是经济上的自由派，社会上的保守派；或者是经济上的保守派，却是社会问题上的自由派。如2008年竞选总统的共和党候选人麦凯恩（John McCain）在政治经济上都是保守派，但在社会层面上却持自由派观点（socially liberal）。在经济和社会层面上均属保守派的占少数，他们是极端保守派，如以往的国会议员Barry Goldwater和Jesse Helms就属此类，他们在政治上更是floo-floo birds，被称为the Old Guards（极端保守的共和党人）。所以，仅用自由派与保守派很难对美国政界人物做出适当的分类。

3. 两党与两派有何关系

从美国政党来看，民主党的政治立场是中间偏左，又叫做自由派。共和党的政治立场是中间偏右，又叫做保守派。左、右之间的区分到底在哪里？一个简单的区分方式是：左派追求平等，右派追求自由。传统上，左派是弱势团体势力的集结，故求平等。而右派则是既得利益者的集合，故求自由。要求自由者反对政府集权，不希望受到政府权力的干涉，所以右派多主张"小政府"。要求平等者要依赖政府权力来调节贫富差距，所以左派多主张"大政府"。

若不了解两派的区别，有的读者就难以明了《时代》1996年8月12日发表的题为"Bye-Bye, American Pie"一文中为什么自由派和保守派、民主党和共和党在社会福利问题上斗得如此激烈，自由派为什么支持F.罗斯福实行新政，推行社会福利制度，反对1996年进行的福利救济计划的改革。更难明白为什么在民主党总统克林顿签署了福利改革法案后自由派斥之为"背叛"(betrayal)(见第一版**前言**)。若不了解在美国民主党内自由派占多数,在共和党保守派是主流,有些文章和词语往往就难以理解,如 Repubocrat 指共和党自由派,Demopublican 民主党内的保守派,true-blue conservative 和 true-red liberal 分别指货真价实民主党内的保守派/共和党内的自由派等。

4. 党内有派

毛泽东曾说:"党外有党,党内有派。党外无党,帝王思想;党内无派,千奇百怪。"这句话,用来形容美国的民主、共和两党,最恰当不过。不但两党各自都有实力相当的对立党,而且,由于此处无暇涉及的种种历史原因,两党内部都有着形形色色的派别。某些派别的思想倾向,甚至与对立党的主流同流。有的选民,价值观和登记的是共和党,却把票投给民主党,媒体分别造出"克林顿或奥巴马共和党人"(Clinton Republican 或 Obamacan)新词。或者,派别主张与对立党的政策无异。例如,共和党内,有一群传统的地缘政治派,他们与民主党的主流一样,也对出兵伊拉克颇为反感。所以共和党才有 Repubocrat, true-blue Republican;民主党内有 Demopublican, true-red Democrat。

然而美国新闻界和政界喜欢对外国政界人士也打上这种党派分类的烙印。例如 wet 这个字指"温和派",指不赞同撒切尔夫人任英国首相时推行强硬的货币经济政策的英国保守党政界人士或有自由倾向的保守党人,他们认为这种政策造成了大批工人失业和社会的苦难,有的新闻媒介称他们为"温和派"(moderate),也有称鸽派(dove)的;美国报刊根据美国政见分类法将之划分为"自由派";撒切尔夫人称之为"wets",指他们为一批"没有骨气的人"或"幼稚的软骨头"。下面请看美刊或许怕美国人不懂而故意在"wet"后加注"liberal":

But the rhetoric couldn't disguise the many substantive differences among the Tories over the handling of the strike, some of the government's economic programs and its efforts to reduce unemployment, which last month reached nearly 3.3 million. Said Ian Gilmour, a leading Tory "**wet**"(**liberal**). (*Newsweek*)

5. 何谓 Neocon

neocon 是英文 neoconservatism 或 neoconservative 之简称。新保守主义是"鹰派"(right wing, conservative or hawk)同义词。出现于 20 世纪 70 年代,代表人物是美国前国会参议员和驻联合国大使 Patrick Moynihan 等民主党自由派。与传统的保守主义相同,也重视资本主义式的自由经济,反对国家干预,但既不赞成空想社会主义的改良方案和政治、经济人人平等的平等主义,也不赞同传统的保守主义,认为民众资本主义是理想之道,为了福利国家,政府对经济可进行一定程度的干预,对穷人实施补贴和医疗扶贫计划。可以说,新保守主义比较温和,愿意接受有限政府干涉。撒切尔和里根式的新保守主义则更极端。

2001年小布什(G. W. Bush)任总统后,同年的"9·11"事件导致美国新保守主义更大崛起。新保守主义综合自由主义和现实主义,对外强制推行美国民主自由,具有原教旨主义(fundamentalism,喻极端保守或右翼的政策或主张)色彩的理想现实主义,以伊拉克为"大中东计划"实验场,编造谎言,发动第二次伊战。推行中连连受挫,而推行者除副总统切尼外,都纷纷下台。他们根子很深,跟美国近代出现的 Barry Goldwater, Jesse Helms 和 Newt Gingrich 等极端保守派如出一辙,异曲同工。他们只是暂时蛰伏,且不乏接班人。一旦形势有利,就会东山再起。

与上面提到的 liberal 标签一样,记者也给新闻人物乱贴。例如奥巴马反对伊战便成了"鸽派"(liberal dove),可是当他说:"If we have actionable intelligence about high-value terrorist targets and President Musharraf(巴基斯坦总统) will not act, we will."《华尔街日报》就此发表了"Barack Obama, Neocon"的社论。

6. 两派之分说端详

这篇谈 2006 年美国国会中期选举的短文,描写一位共和党白人和一位民主党黑人候选人在保守的田纳西州角逐参议员议席,竞相在社会问题上装成坚定的保守派。语言不难,但要有扎实的上述党派知识,才能真正看懂。下面结合所学讲解。

A GOP Balancing Act

Bob Corker's strategy: Run away from Bush,
but not so far that he loses the conservative base.

BY RICHARD WOLFFE

1   Bob Corker needed to add some flair to his flagging campaign. The GOP candidate should have been running a simple Senate race in **conservative Tennessee**[1]. But he was trailing by several points last month, so the White House and party leaders stepped in. Their solution: **a new campaign manager in the form of a rumpled, martini-drinking,**

1. background

cigar-chewing veteran of Tennessee politics[2]. Back in 1978, Tom Ingram helped transform a lackluster candidate for governor—Lamar Alexander—by dressing him in a folksy **red plaid shirt**[3]. And it was Ingram who put Fred Thompson in a **red pickup truck**[3] in his 1994 Senate race, turning the Hollywood actor and lawyer into a **good ole boy**[4].

What could Ingram change about Corker, the starchy former mayor of Chattanooga? Everything but his clothes, apparently. Speaking to a group of sheriffs last week, Corker was buttoned up in a charcoal pin-striped suit. ("We need to change that," Ingram later grumbled in a Nashville bar.) Still, Ingram has helped turn the Corker campaign around with new ads and a new message—that Corker is a self-made businessman from Tennessee, while **his opponent, Harold Ford Jr., has never held a real job outside Washington politics. Ingram dropped ads attacking Ford as a liberal**[5], replacing them with references to **the Ford family machine—and by extension, the African-American politics of Memphis**[6]. "I'm the candidate of change," Corker told NEWSWEEK over a bowl of chili in a Jackson diner. "My opponent certainly hasn't shown much independence. He votes with his party 80 percent of the time."

2. the image of a wealth GOP politician; rumpled, martini-drinking, cigar-chewing: (fig.) rich people, upper class

3. red plaid shirt, red pickup truck: farmers' clothes, (fig.) ordinary people or Republicans; Generally, Republicans are richer than Democrats. In order to win the election, Republican candidates try to dress and act like an ordinary person. Here red is the color for Republican or conservative.

4. (*complimentary*) conservative (*cf. derog.* redneck)

5. suggests Ford is a carpetbagger (or parachute candidate) and Washington insider; Ford is a social conservative and political liberal, so he is not a party-line Democrat.

6. a. Ford succeeded his dad in the House at 26. A scion(名门后裔) of one of black America's great political dynasties. But family is a two-edged sword: the Republicans are making much of the Ford clan's legal woes. (His uncle is awaiting trial on extortion charges and aunt was ejected from the state Senate after allegations of vote fraud.) Running attack ad after attack ad on "The Ford Family Political Machine," Corker and the Republicans have hinted that Ford would engage in similar shenanigans (诡计).

b. tackics: use racial discrimination against black candidates

3   Stuck with an unpopular president and an even less appealing party, **Corker is distancing himself from the White House and the GOP-led Congress. Yet he also needs the conservative base to turn out to vote—and they are unsettled by his divided loyalties.** [7] When Corker stopped by conservative talk radio in Nashville, the questions were unusually hostile. "I know I'm not going to vote for Harold Ford," said one caller after Corker left the studio. "But **it's like the lesser of two evils.**" [8]

4   Many social conservatives have been wary of Corker since the primaries, when his rivals portrayed him as a **pro-choice Democrat.** [9] (Tennessee **Right to Life** has not endorsed Corker because **he once opposed limits on state funding for abortion.** [10]) More recently, Corker has moved to heal the rift with his primary foes. Former congressman Ed Bryant, who once campaigned as "the **real conservative**"[11] against Corker, is stumping for him in rural west Tennessee. "Bob may not be as intense as I am," Bryant told NEWSWEEK, "but he's a solid conservative."

5   Solid may be the best Corker can do, and he's trying to make it his virtue. "I know I'm not the best-looking candidate in this race," he told the group of stony-faced sheriffs. "I know **I'm not the most articulate.**[12]" But he is still the most conservative, and that might just be enough.

(2006/10/30 *Newsweek*)

7. a. Cork is in a predicament. He doesn't know how he can appeal to the conservative voters (base).

   b. The record indicates he is not a real conservative.

8. Voters don't like the two candidates but they have to make a choice.

9. pro-choice: in favor of for abortion right to life: against abortion

10. here indicates Corker is a social liberal.

11. Republicans try to paint Corker as a real/solid/the most conservative.

12. Corker can't clearly express himself about his stand on social issues, esp. on abortion: a social conservative or liberal, a solid conservative or a centrist. Thus he is in a predicament.

ON THE STUMP: Corker blasts Ford as a party-line Democrat

13. In his campaign speech, Corker attacks Ford as a typical liberal.

　　此文有两点费解：为什么候选人要共和党派人包装？标题 A GOP Balancing Act 下的副标题作了诠释：参议员候选人 Bob Corker 与因伊战不得人心（unpopular）的小布什总统和无吸引力（less appealing）的共和党距离拉得太大，不保持共和党人的保守派本色，票仓（conservative base）就丢了。不拉开距离，就成了国会众议员、民主党候选人 Harold Ford Jr. 的靶了，说他是"小布什第二"，他肯定也是落选。因此，只好走钢丝。

　　第二点怪在共和党是保守派，又在田纳西这个保守州与民主党竞争，理所当然稳操胜券，可是候选人偏偏在堕胎这个区别自由派和保守派的重大问题上让对手抓住了把柄，使保守派选民对 Corker 起了疑心，所以，campaign 缺热情（flagging），民意测验落后（trailing）几个百分点。

　　共和党能否在参议院占多数议席，涉及小布什能否在最后两年顺利施政，不能置之不理。于是插手帮忙，给 Corker 找了好竞选主管，改变其形象，弥合党内分歧，改变竞选策略。因无证据而不说 Ford 是自由派，先攻他是外来户（carpetbagger），是贪污腐败、尔虞我诈、铺张浪费的华盛顿圈子里的人（Washington insider）。再诽谤他家族是竞选机器（Ford family [political] machine），祖父是一个"extremely powerful man"，父亲担任过国会众议员，aunt 曾是州参议员，而他 26 岁当选为众议员。uncle 涉嫌敲诈勒索（extortion charges）待审，aunt 因选票舞弊被逐出州参议院，由此暗示，Ford 也会使用同样的竞选诡计等。最后又利用种族歧视，离间白人选民，说 Memphis（田纳西州一城市）是黑人政治的天下（African-American politics of Memphis），Ford 当上众议员不足为奇，可让他担任代表全州的参议员就另当别论了。

　　文章最后说，尽管共和党人将 Corker 描绘成这样那样的保守派，可连他自己都说不清楚究竟是何派,还承认他不是个 best-looking candidate。

此文谈竞选关键是选民看两位候选人是自由派或是保守派,那么,图片中的"On the stump: Corker blasts Ford as a **party-line Democrat**"该如何理解和翻译呢? 编者认为,诠释为"typical liberal"是正确的。再则,按照党的方针路线行事(Corker 主要指 Ford 在众议院的 80%的投票记录)的民主党人也就是"典型的自由派"。

结果 Corker 居然以 51%比 48%的微弱多数胜出。Ford 的败选不是对手攻击他 the Ford family political machine 和 family scandals 及 Washington insider,主要是该州黑人只占 17%。白人在民意调查时往往支持黑人候选人,正式投票时变卦。这就是前洛杉矶市长 Tom Bradley 1982 竞选加州州长时的遭遇被新闻界称之为"布拉德利效应"(the "Bradley effect"): White voters often tell pollsters they support black candidates, but they don't always follow through. 在 Ford 身上也应验了。尽管奥巴马于 2008 年创造了历史、入主白宫,美国要彻底消除种族歧视,仍非易事。

十八、骷髅会

1. Order of Skull and Bones 是何组织

The Order of Skull and Bones 骷髅会,常简称"Skull and Bones"口语称"the Bones",又名"死亡兄弟会"(the Brotherhood of Death),是美国权势集团最大的秘密帮会,成立于 1832 年,标志是上面为一个骷髅,由一个人的头盖骨和两节交叉的肢骨,下面写着"322"的数字和 Founded 1832。关于这个数字,有两种说法:一说是该组织由耶鲁大学一个叫威廉·亨廷顿·拉塞尔(William H. Russel)的学生创建,他 1832 年在德国求学时受到一个传说的启发:希腊雄辩家狄摩西尼公元前 322 年去世之时,正是雄辩女神升天之日。据传说,女神后来又回到了骷髅会成员中间。322 成为神圣数字,美国前驻苏联大使哈里曼(Averell Harriman)手提公文箱密码锁的密码。2004 年民主党总统候选人克里还视 322 为某种准则或密码。另一种说法是"32"表示成立于 1832 年,后面的"2"表示是德国"光明会"的第二个分会,1832 年拉塞尔在德国进修时入会,回国后仿建,为美国历史上最保密的组织,入会犹如跻身精英社会。

2. 在政界有何势力

此会始建于耶鲁大学,名字命名为拉塞尔信托会(the Russel Trust Association),已为美国输送了第 27 任、41 任和 43 任三位总统及副总统、上百位部长、议员,培植了几十个大家族财团,会员称为 Bonesmen 或 Bonies(骨人)。2004 年两党总统候选人 George W. Bush 和 John Kerry 都毕业于耶鲁大学,是该会成员。

该会极为秘密,不允许 Bonesmen 泄密,盛传是情报界孵化器,才有这样的报道：When asked what it meant that he and Bush were both Bonesmen, former presidential candidate, John Kerry said, "Not much because it's a secret."老布什总统在自传中也说："My senior year I joined Skull and Bones, a secret society, so secret, I can't say anything more."报刊常用"Bones"或"Skull and Bones",省略了"Order"。见例句：

Yale, which Kerry entered in September 1962, was a better fit. Kerry loved Yale from the first weekend he spent showing his roommate and fellow St. Paul's grad, Barbiero, the campus shrines, most importantly the dark mausoleum of Yale's most prestigious secret society, **Skull and Bones.**（*Newsweek*）

It is not clear when George W. Bush and John Kerry first met. Kerry once recalled Bush, none too fondly, to writer Julia Reed of Vogue magazine: "He was two years behind me at Yale, and I knew him, and he's still the same guy." Bush says he has no recollection of meeting Kerry at Yale. Both presidential candidates were members of the same college secret society, **Skull and Bones**, but brothers they were not. The two men had disliked each other before they knew each other.（*Time*）

十九、院外游说群体

在美英等国,活跃着一个引人注目的院外说客群体或集团(lobbying group),受雇于公司、企业、工会、社会团体或外国政府及民间组织,专门在国内的立法和行政机构间游说,为政策的变化和立法的兴废向这些权力部门施加压力和影响,为客户谋求各种政治与经济利益。他们能言善辩,深谙政治,以极大能量搭建起复杂的"权力走廊"(power corridor),形成政治舞台一道独特风景。院外活动在大多数民主国家是允许的,奉为民主重要原则之一。人们视之为牙医或律师：不喜欢,又离不开。话虽如此,lobby groups 常被贬称为"压力集团"(pressure groups)。声名狼藉,又叫"Beltway bandits"。

Lobbying groups & PACs 在美国等国举足轻重,了解美国等国国情不可不知。

1. 何谓"Lobby"

lobby 院外是意译,指议会和旅馆的大厅、休息室、接待室或客厅,英国议院里的分组投票室。游说客多在议会讨论某项立法前和政府讨论某项政策期间在

这些场所游说议员和政府官员,故称院外活动。为了对这个字认识得更清楚,见美刊文章中的一段释义:

Lobbying, a practice as old as the nation's government, got its name from the cozy relationship struck up in lobbies of the Capitol (美国国会大厦) and nearby hotels between members of Congress and those seeking favor. (1985/2/25 *U.S. News & World Report*)

2. 谁开创了 Lobbying

各老牌民主国家至今仍在争论,院外活动作为政府和公众之间互相影响的一种形式,发明权究竟属于谁。

英国人认为,"院外活动"和"院外活动人士"两个术语是他们发明的,最初用来称呼普通请愿者。那时政府部门没有专门接待机构,又不允许请愿者进入官员和议员的办公室,他们只好聚集在过道或走廊里活动。

美国人则认为,拥有院外活动的发明权。院外活动集团最先在这里依法行事。1789年通过头条宪法修正,保证了"向政府递交请求"的权利。美国也最先出现职业说客,提出申诉,或给官员们进言献策,无所不能。美国最先制定院外活动集团的行为规范,《院外活动法》1876年通过,规定应在国会正式登记。1946年又通过《院外活动调节法》,强化登记制度。院外人士不仅要申报本身情况,还要表明为谁工作,多少报酬与活动经费。随后许多国家群起效仿。

3. Lobbyists 何其多

美国某院外活动集团人士说:"如果我没说错的话,在您的印象中,说客不太受人欢迎,只会向政府官员或国会议员行贿送礼,请他们吃喝嫖赌(booze and broads)","也许,两百年前是这样。但今天这些手段吃不开了"。

最风行的说客是不计其数的行业联合会。比如棉花理事会迫使议员通过法案,促进美棉出口,同时阻挠通过限制棉花出口的法案,活动经费由所有棉商提供。

除了全国性的大型院外活动集团,还有私人院外活动集团。尽管说客披着各种伪装,但基本上以律师、贸易协会代表和公关顾问面目出现。实际上则由律师、前议员助手和离任政治家组成。一家以 Robert Gray 为首的华盛顿著名的院外活动集团 Gray & Company 竟然有 100 名说客,与共和党有着千丝万缕的关系。而 Akin, Grump, Strauss, Haner & Field 法律公司则因斯特劳斯 (Robert Strauss) 入伙成为最强大的院外活动集团之一。斯特劳斯与好几任总统私人关系密切,曾任美国驻苏联、俄罗斯大使。还有一些公司的老板也是如此。如 Nancy Reynolds 是里根总统夫妇的朋友。Anne Wexler 曾是卡特在白宫的重要助手。他们公司生意兴隆。据报道,他们受高额报酬诱惑,在政府和游说公司之间任意跳槽,犹如出入高楼大厦的旋转门一样,易如反掌,又叫"旋转门或走马灯似的院外说客"(revolving-door lobbyists)。据 2005 年的资料,国会注册的说客多达 3.5 万。现在只会比以前更多。

美国最大的腐败就是贿赂公行,腐败合法化。后面所谈的游说丑闻是如此,2008 年自金融危机爆发以来,逐一曝光的华尔街高管欺诈案都与政府部门有着千丝万缕的联系,也是如此。2009 年还暴出向中国 26 家国企高管行贿丑闻,实属可恨之至。

4. 为谁帮腔　为谁忙

院外活动集团在西方国家普遍存在,在美国尤盛,华盛顿游说集团名目繁多,人员多如牛毛,他们以华盛顿为总部、联邦一级官员为游说目标。其中多数或是游说法律公司雇员,或为外来顾客聘用。其余则为工会、公司、州政府和其他地方政府效力。也就是说,在美国不但有为国内利益团体游说的公司[lobby(ing) firms],还有为国外利益效劳的游说集团。这就是所谓的外国代理人。其任务及行动计划公开,在司法部有关外国代理人的年度报告中可以查到。有一家公司的客户就包括乌兹别克斯坦驻美国大使馆。再如 Arab Lobby(阿拉伯国家院外游说集团,援阿游说集团)和 Israel Lobby(以色列院外游说集团,援以游说集团,院外以色列帮)等。此外,一些游说集团还与外国政府签有合作合同。

这些外国代理人收费高昂,工作效率也很高。据说,菲利普·史密斯公司为阿富汗北方联盟进行了相当成功的游说,它仅仅由于促进北方联盟代表参加阿新政府就获得 10 万美元。俄罗斯人也曾利用过华盛顿的说客。美国不少议员接受台湾贿赂,为"台独"撑腰壮胆,"藏独"、"疆独"也是如此。

5. 为何叫"Third House"

众所周知,美国国会由两院组成,哪来的"the Third House"? 称那些 the lobbyists 或 lobby groups 为 the Third House 无非是因为他们游说参众两院议员,有时能左右法律的兴废,故有此谑称。见例句:

The Third House—America's democratic process not only expects that citizens will participate in political activities such as voting and running for public office, it has given rise to a part of the political process that may be unique to the United States and that has come to play an integral role in how the government operates. They are the lobbyists, and their existence and increasingly important role is rooted in a concept that can be traced back to the founding of the nation: the First Amendment right "to petition the Government for a redress of grievances." (*The Third House*: *Lobbyists and Lobbying in the States*)

6. 何谓"K Street"

K Street 即 K 街,喻游说公司、华盛顿或美国游说界。因为美国许多顶尖游说公司都设在首都华盛顿 K 街,此街名就作代称。看例句:

Elected majority whip in '94, Delay soon teamed up with Grover Norquist for the **K Street** Project (named for the home of the top D. C. lobby shops)(一游说公司名). The plan: invite lobbyists into his kitchen cabinet to craft legislation, push shops to hire only GOP (and especially Delay) staffers and get corporate clients to fund only GOP campaigns, Has it worked? With the number of lobbyists doubling since 2000, 29 Delay alumni have scored major spots on **K Street** (Hastert's tally: six); the GOP regularly beats Dems 2-1 in congressional campaign fund-raising efforts, and its majority in the House has grown by nine seats since 1999. (*Newsweek*)

7. 政坛丑闻何其多

高官贪财,议员受贿,院外集团欲达目的,投其所好,"各取所需"。只要看幅漫画便一目了然。

题为:Things of Value to a Member of Congress(议员所好)

图中文字依次为:Travel, Golf, Dinner, No Recorded Any Contact With Jack Abramoff(没有与杰克·阿布拉莫夫的接触记录)(2005/12/28 *The New York Observer*)

阿布拉莫夫是 2005 年年底引爆美国共和党丑闻的火药桶,美国印第安部落通过他向国会议员提供了数百万美元全部来自赌场收入的非法竞选资金。

2005 年 Jack Abramoff 案发,包括共和党众院多数党领袖 Tom Daley 在内 20 多位两党议员及助理涉嫌辞职。Delay 参与中饱德州竞选资金,触犯了法律。

2006 年,随着案情发展,多个重量级议员和白宫高官与这名超级说客的联系相继浮出水面,其中包括白宫资深顾问卡尔·罗夫(Carl Rove)、三名共和党众议员,一直被认为和阿布拉莫夫丑闻绝缘的民主党也牵扯进来。

罗夫穿针引线。据美联社 2005 年 14 日报道,曾与阿布拉莫夫共事的 3 位匿名人士称,阿经常炫耀与白宫高级顾问罗夫关系密切。2002 年由阿牵线,马来西亚一名前领导人得以在白宫会见布什总统。阿也因此捞到一大笔酬劳,替他搭线正是罗夫。《纽约时报》、《时代》周刊等媒体还登出了布什和阿合影的照片。

8. 第五产业

2008 年处共和党在参众两院都失去了多数党地位,成了 all-democratic Congress,院外团已在大显身手。难怪有人将"游说业"说成是继美国媒体后的第五大产业。《纽约时报》为此登了一幅漫画:

女秘书说:(Mr. Smith, there are 35,000 lobbyists here to see you...)(史密斯先生,有 35,000 个说客想要见您……)
桌上的牌子为:(New Congress)新国会。

习 题

阅读理解文章

"Path of Storm"(2006/4/17 Newsweek)(《精选本》四版课文)

二十、竞选活动委员会(PAC)

1. 为谁服务

PAC 是 Political Action Committee 缩写,所谓"竞选活动委员会",实际上也是 lobby group,指任何候选人或政党正式的竞选委员会之外的竞选机构,此类机构隶属于公司、工会或其他组织。议员本人也组织 PAC。它们尤其向位内国会议员候选人捐款,并从事其他与竞选有关的活动,难怪现任议员绝大多数都能竞选连任。

2. 创建目的

PAC 于 1944 年由美国的大工会组织产业工会联合会(the Congress of Industrial Organization [CIO])首创,资助拥护工会主张的候选人。上世纪 60—70 年代,企业为对抗工会也成立了 PACs。80 年代有些国会议员(现有几百人)开始建立 Leadership PACs,向党内议员捐款竞选,扩大他们在党内的势力。

有的 PACs 被视为党派集团,不是共和党就属民主党,不是保守派就是自由派。但多数是无党派。他们的重点不在乎所属党派,而在于候选人对 issues 所持看法。

PACs 有三类:major business PACs；major labor PACs；ideological PACs。

3. PAC 与议员的关系

参众两院共有议员 535 名,差不多人人周围都有几个乃至几十个经常打交道的"说客"。他们大力资助竞选,议员们当选后得投桃报李,为他们效力。连共和党前总统老布什都主张取缔这种组织,因共和党执政时往往民主党人在国会占多数议席。可是为议员连任埋单的 PACs,国会能通过立法加以取缔吗？我们来看布什是如何冠冕堂皇地说:

It's time to give people more choice in government, by reviving the ideal of the citizen politician who comes not to stay, but to serve. One of the reasons there is so much support for term limitations is that the American people are increasingly concerned about big-money influence in politics. We must look beyond the next election, to the next generation. The time has come to put the national interest above the special interest—and totally eliminate **Political Action Committees.** (George Bush)

二十一、宗教

1. 政治影响大

说到美国国情,人们首先想到自由民主的政治制度,强大的军事经济实力,发达的科技,先进的教育体系,等等,很少人会想到宗教,更不会有与上面提到的美国政治、经济、文化等联系起来,也想不到美国竟有一半以上的人认为,上帝是美国民主的道德支柱。美国大约 90% 人信教,它不仅是世界上世俗(secular)大国,也是宗教大国。法规制约行为,宗教控制内心。也就是说,宗教是他们的灵魂。

现在的中国，无神论者（atheist）占绝大多数，对西方国家的宗教及其语言相当陌生，可是对我们这些学习英语和新闻的学生而言，要理解词语、解读文章，离不开宗教知识。不懂圣经故事和希腊神话，就等于不了解我国的儒家文化一样。也就是说，只了解表面上的美国，而非真正的美国。要了解美国的宗教，必须知道现代基督教和犹太教。

2. 教会与国家

美国许多开国元勋认为，同一伦理道德必然基于同一宗教。但是，由于美国奉行政教分离，尊重宪法赋予的宗教自由，从严格意义上来说，美国从未有过同一宗教。不过，建国期间，大部分美国人为新教徒，因此尽管新教派别繁多，但至少都赞同宗教改革运动的思想。

美国历史上爆发过不同信仰者之间严重冲突，波士顿等城市本土出生的新教徒与来自爱尔兰等国家的天主教移民之间爆发了一场真正意义的宗教战争，酿成巨大的生命财产损失，其暴力倾向和分裂性远远超过今日的文化冲突。有人认为现在美国进行的反恐斗争也是一场宗教战争。英国的北爱尔兰，几十年来主张爱尔兰统一的天主教徒与反对者新教徒一直在斗来斗去。尽管不同教派的基督徒从未体现出大一统，但到20世纪中叶，美国开始自称为"犹太基督两教合一"（Judeo-Christian）的社会，美国的三种信仰至少信奉同一经书，即希伯来人的《圣经》。这一事实说明美国是统一整体。

"犹太基督两教合一"概念，最初含有"兼容性"，但如今似乎已具有"排他性"，并不涵盖穆斯林、印度教徒、佛教以及其他许多1965年后涌入美国的各类宗教信徒。美国社会今日如此多元复杂，很难一言自我定位。或许有史以来从未出现过像今日美国这样在宗教上百花齐放的社会，从某种意义来说，这可溯源到美国的开国元勋们当年做出的提倡宗教自由的决策。*

3. 宗教题材常见诸报端

报刊中宗教题材的文章很多，如 *Newsweek* 几乎每期都有这方面的报道和评论和布道广告，每当重要宗教节日，这类文章更多，有时还出特刊。一些文章还夹杂宗教知识的小测试。如 2007/3/12 *Newsweek* 在一篇题为"The Gospel of Prothero"的文章（Steve Prothero 是 Boston University 的教授）中就有这么一个测试：标题是："Religious Literacy 101"（宗教知识基础），说明是："Take this quiz, a modified version of the one Prothero gives to his Boston University students, to see how you fare."

---

* 参考了美国驻华文化处出版的 2007 冬季刊《新交流》

有的文章标题就是正误题。如 True or False：The Major Religions Are Essentially Alike（2007/7/2-9 *Newsweek*），报刊登载这么多的文章，占如此多的篇幅和版面，估计是要付钱的，因为有的问答题等于在传教。

4. 基督教的三大教派

经历几次的分化和改革，现代基督教（Christianity）有三大派别。它们是天主教（Catholicism or Catholic Church）、新教（Protestantism or Protestant Church）和东正教（Eastern Orthodox/Orthodox Church，或无 Eastern，译为正教）。犹如政党党中有党、派中有派一样，新教因政治和社会原因分化成不同的宗派（denominations），如公理宗（Congregationalism）、路德宗（Lutheranism）英国圣公会（Anglicanism）、循道宗（Methodism）、长老会（Presbyterianism）和浸礼会（Baptism）等。

（1）天主教：天主教与罗马教廷关系紧密，所以有些人仍称 Roman Catholic Church（罗马天主教），是世界上最大的统一基督教派别和宗教团体。天主教实行教皇至上论（Ultramontanism），教皇享有至高无上的权力。高级神职人员除教皇（Pope）外，依次为 cardinal（红衣主教）、archbishop（天主教）、bishop（主教）和 father（神父）。教皇对所在国的红衣主教等有任命权（这一点是我国与罗马教廷建交谈不拢的主要原因）。在美国，天主教徒占 20%，仅次于新教，有神父约 8 万，连同其他神职人员共约 20 万人，美国天主教在海外十分活跃，有近万人从事传教活动。但在美国政界，天主教不如新教徒活跃，担任过总统的只有肯尼迪（John Kennedy）一人，所以有人认为其在 1963 年被刺有教派背景。因该教禁止教神职人员结婚，闹出许多性丑闻，令教廷震惊和蒙羞。现代主义的兴起也给传统的天主教教义带来了威胁。

（2）东正教：东正教也称正教，希腊、俄罗斯、塞尔维亚、阿尔巴尼亚、保加利亚和乌克兰是主要信正教的国家，在美国信徒极少。

（3）基督教：a. 美国新教：新教曾被译为"更正教"、"抗罗教"、"耶稣教"等教名，是美国最大的基督教教派，人们普遍把美国看做一个重要的基督教国家，教徒占 50%，在美国社会，具有举足轻重地位。Protestant 或 Protestanism 源出德文 Protestanten（抗议者）。新教诸侯和城市代表强烈抗议天主教会等级森严的僧侣制、僵硬的教条、腐败堕落的行为。其后 protestant 衍生为新教各宗派的共同称谓。新教主张教会制度多样化，不赞成强求一律，强调直接与上帝相通，无须神父（father）中介。主要教派有：the Bapist Church（浸礼会，最大，尤其在南方信徒众多）、the Anglican Church（英国圣公会）、the Methodist Church（卫理公会，也译为循道会、美以美会）、the Lutheran Church（路德会、信义会）、the

Congregationalist Church（公理会）、the Presbyterian Church（长老会），等等。新教教士 minster/clergyman/pastor/ecclesiastic（牧师）等与天主教神职人员不同，可以结婚。

b. 英国国教：the Established Church 指 the Church of English 或 the Anglican Church（英国国教会或圣公会）。最高牧首（the Supreme Governor）和基督教的保护者（defender of the Faith）或世俗领袖（Secular head）是现任英国女王。宗教领袖是坎特伯雷大主教（the Archbishop of Canterbury 或 the Primate of All England 全英首主教），其他高级神职人员依次为大主教（Archbishops）、主教（Bishops）和教长（Deans），根据首相提名，由君主任命，均为贵族院议员。其他一般神职人员（ecclesiastic）有 rector/vicar（牧师）、curate（助理牧师）、deacon（执事）等。

5. 犹太教

犹太教（Judaism）历史上最悠久，基督教和伊斯兰教（Islam）也发源于此，是美国第三大宗教，犹太教徒（Jewish）虽然仅占人口总数 1%，只有六百多万人，美国却是世界上犹太教徒最多、影响力很大的国家，有五千多所会堂（synagogue）。他们在外交上积极支持以色列，成立了 Israeli lobby（以色列游说集团或以色列帮），政治能量可观，如 2000 年曾推出民主党内保守派人物（Demopublican）Joseph Lieberman 为该党副总统候选人。在新闻界和财界也颇具影响。

6. 势力无孔不入

美国有三十多万座教堂寺庙，美国人每年给宗教的捐款比花在体育上的费用多 10 倍，达 500 亿美元。美国国歌里有"上帝保佑美国"的歌词，在国情咨文里也常用"God bless you, and God bless America."（见 1986/2/5 *The Washington Post* 刊载里根作的 The State of the Union message）。1991 年 1 月 30 日 *The New York Times* 转载老布什所作国情咨文报告的结尾也有"May God bless the United States of America."总统就职进行宣誓要把手放在《圣经》上。每一届国会都由国会牧师主持祈祷开幕。军队里有随军教士（chaplain），在医院、监狱、机场等机构和公共场所也有神职人员提供宗教服务。美国有 85% 以上私立中小学学生就读于教会学校，哈佛、耶鲁、普林斯顿等许多名牌大学全由教会创办。现有宗教广播电台 1200 多家，电视台 12 家，报刊 5000 多种，《圣经·新约》印刷量上亿册。硬币和法庭墙上也刻着"In God We Trust"。正如前最高法院大法官 William O. Douglas（1939—1975）在 1952 年所说："We are a religious people, whose institutions presuppose a Supreme Being."（我们是个虔诚民族，社会习俗以上苍为前提）。也就是说，从各方面看，美国是一个宗教性很强的国家,至今,宗教力量在诸多困扰美国社会的棘手问题上,如 abortion, gay, drug, crime, school prayer and Bible reading at public schools 等,仍然扮演着十分重要的角色。宗教在国内维系道德秩序、缓解社会矛盾、推动社会进步及配合政府外交政策,对第三世界进行"传教"渗透活动等方面都发挥着相当大的作用。美国虽不是神权国家,但宗教作用与媒体一样,离开了宗教,就没有今天这么强大的美国。

7. 政教"貌离神合"

(1) 与政界保守派一唱一和:美国宪法第一条修正规定政教分离(separation of church and state),即联邦政府平等对待各类教派,也不干涉其活动;宗教也不得干预政府事务。应该说,两者基本上是分离的。但事实上又很难截然分离,宗教在社会问题如人工流产、同性恋、性自由、吸毒、犯罪、公立学校祷告和政治如选举和外交等方面,都扮演着重要角色,宗教界往往与政界保守派一唱一和,施加影响。

美国政界的保守派和宗教保守派或极端保守派(指福音派 the evangelicals or Evangelicalism 是跨宗教的,天主教、新教、犹太教、伊斯兰教等都可加入)或 fundamentalists(原教旨主义者)都认为,传统道德观的沦丧是万恶之源。美国自越南战争出现反正统文化(counterculture)后,世风日下,离婚率陡升,同性恋大行其道、神职人员绯闻不断,自由化泛滥成灾。这些使美国社会陷入道德价值观和安全危机的深渊。在他们看来,解决之法就是要恢复基督教传统文化,强调道德和价值观及社会的责任感对每个人的召唤。于是,宗教界就出面来填补真空。2006 年 11 月 13 日 *Newsweek* 上有一篇"An Evangelical Identity Crisis"的文章,配上:"Evangelicals: Their Long Path to Political Power"图表详解:1976 年卡特当选总统,福音派传教人士进入政坛,发动了历时 30 年成长壮大的运动,在这些重大问题上的立场是:60.3% 赞成伊战,75.3% 反对堕胎,79.8% 赞成死刑,85.4% 赞成 school prayer。该派教主中 liberal 极个别,moderate 和 conservative 少数,多数是 ultraconservative。

(2) 与小布什总统的关系:2004 年总统选举,共和党人就是打宗教牌,宣传小布什信仰虔诚、敢于负责和富有正义感,抓住了宗教保守派,成功化解了国内外的强烈不满,赢得了大选。这表明宗教影响不容低估。

小布什连任成功后不忘回报,2005 年美国宗教界对达尔文的进化论发起了第二回合挑战,他们宣扬所谓智慧设计论(intelligent design),实际上是变种的上帝造人说。一些基督徒宣扬,动植物的结构如此复杂精妙,不可能是自然演进的结果,达尔文的自然选择论无法回答生命如何起源的问题,必定有外界智慧起了引导作用。虽然他们解释不了这个智慧力量从何而来。卷入这场争论的除了

第五章　读报知识

实力强大的宗教界人士外,还有美国共和党保守派总统小布什。后来最高法院做出裁决,宣布在课堂上教授"智慧设计论"违法,才算平息了这场争论。读者不妨读读《精选本》四版课文"The Evolution War"(2005/8/15 *Time*)。

(3) 与里根总统的关系:1980年里根竞选成功,次年上台执政后,有人用Reagan Revolution来指里根时代共和党保守派的东山再起。靠的就是里根与福音派或原教旨主义派(即基督教保守派或极端保守派)密切合作,共和党God不离口,有"party of God"之称,它利用宗教界人士宣传造势、捐款和投票,2006年中期选举时造出values voter这个新词(意指以道德价值为准则的选民,凡不同意其价值观的选民,不但票投错了,在道德上也低人一等);基督教保守派企图将共和党改造成带宗教性质的政党。不妨看几段谈里根与基督教右翼关系美英书刊,便会看清美国政教分离的真相及宗教在政治生活中所起的作用,对美国国情了解得更透和更全面。请看一部美国历史书两段文字:

1　　Reagan began the campaign with several important advantages. He was especially popular among religious **fundamentalists**[1] and other social conservatives and these groups were increasingly **vocal**[2]. President Nixon had spoken of them as a "**silent majority.**"[3] By 1980 the kind of people he was referring to were no longer silent. Fundamentalist TV preachers were almost all fervent Reaganites and the most successful of them were collecting tens of millions of dollars annually in contributions from viewers. One of these, the Reverend Jerry Falwell, founded **Moral Majority**[4] in 1979 and set out to create a new political movement. "Americans are sick and tired of the way the amoral liberals are trying to corrupt our nation," Falwell announced in 1979.

1. 原教旨主义指对教义教规等要不折不扣遵守,喻"极右派或极端保守派(ultraconservative)"

2. uttered or produced by voice

3. 前总统尼克松用此词指支持政府,在越战期间不参加反战示威的沉默多数派

4. 1979年由浸信会Falwell牧师建立,全美各州都有支部,会员400万人以上,总部设在弗吉尼亚州Lynchburg。实为游说集团(political lobby),是an ultraconservative "Christian New Right"。因其立场遭众多反对而被迫于1986年改为"自由联合会"(the Liberty Federation)。支持前南非白人政权种族隔离制度(apartheid),有人称之为"amoral majority"缺德多数派。

2　　During the first Reagan administration Moral Majority had become a powerful political force. Falwell was against drugs, the **"coddling"**[5] of criminals, homosexuality, Communism, and abortion, all things that Reagan also disliked. While not openly anti-black, he disapproved of **forced busing**[6] and a number of other government policies designed to help blacks and other minorities. Of course, **Walter Mondale**[7] was also against many of the things that Falwell and his followers denounced, but Reagan was against them all. In addition, Reagan was in favor of government aid to private schools run by church groups, something dear to the hearts of Moral Majority types despite the constitutional principle of separation of church and state. (*The American Nation*)

5. treat in an indulgent or protective way（溺爱，宠坏）

6. 为取消种族隔政策，美国地方教育委员会强制用校车送中小学生到区外的学校就读，使黑人和白人学生合校。后来保守派又发起反对强制黑白学生合校的运动(anti-busing movement)。

7. 1984年民主党总统候选人，被里根击败

　　以上第一段：里根在总统竞选中有几大优势：一是得人心。在宗教界极端保守派和其他各界保守派人士中人气高。二是能获得大量竞选捐款。原教旨主义的电视传道士几乎都是里根的"信徒"（Reaganites），捞到受众的大量捐款。三、舆论占上风。Falwell 牧师（Reverend）在布道时不断攻击民主党自由派败坏社会道德、腐化堕落。

　　第二段：在里根第一届任期的默契配合下，Moral Majority 已成为一股强大的政治力量，凡其反对的，里根也不喜欢，就连种族歧视，双方也都立场一致。此外，里根还不顾宪法政教分离的原则，用公款支持教会团体办的私立学校，取悦于 Moral Majority 这样的团体。

8．接受和物色总统候选人

　　先看一段英国杂志关于里根总统选接班人的报道：

　　As the Republicans look beyond Mr Reagan, the campaigning for the 1988 presidential nominee is already upon them. At this stage, two candidates are way ahead of the field. Representative Jack Kemp from Buffalo is the conservatives' choice, considered by them to be the true heir of Reaganite orthodoxy. But in front, at this point, is Vice-President George Bush, Mr Reagan's designated heir, blessed, at least informally, with the laying on of presidential hands (plus the even holier hands of the Moral Majority's leader, the Rev. Jerry Falwell). (1985/3/30 *The Economist*)

这段文字说明，连里根选接班人，Falwell 牧师也要插一手，深怕选个不称心的总统。虽然国会众议员 Jack Kemp 是保守派人选，但当时 George Bush（老布什）是副总统，理所当然的既定接班人（designated heir）。这里作者用了宗教语言"blessed, with the laying on of presidential hands"对老布什的授职行了按手礼的祝福。里根不是神职人员，所以 Falwell 牧师的手是 holier hands（圣手）。

读者可查看：2007 年 6 月 4 日 *Newsweek* 上一篇题为"In Search of a Political Savior"的文章，副标题 Evangelicals aren't flocking to the GOP front runners, and don't know where to turn. 报道福音派在为 2008 年大选物色中意的总统候选人。

除宗教题材外，报刊还引申宗教用语到其他话题的文章。如：

Come now, and let us reason together. （耶和华说）来吧，我们彼此辩论：引自《圣经·从赛亚书》，系美国前总统 L. 约翰逊为了在政治上能与党内外人士取得共识最喜欢的一句引语。

come-to-Jesus meeting 皈依基督，改邪归正

"If you think there's some **come-to-Jesus meeting** Willie Brown had, you're dreaming," says Mary Adams of the American Heart Association, a leading anti-tobacco lobbyist. (*The Economist*)

kiss-of-death 似益实害的，帮忙会带来毁灭性或灾难性后果的，帮大倒忙的；源自《圣经》，指犹大以接吻为暗号出卖耶稣，喻某党利用某些不得人心的团体支持候选人，反倒害他落选。例如 1984 年美国大选中，同性恋和女权主义者等组织支持民主党总统候选人 Walter Mondale，实际上是帮倒忙。

Claibourne Darden, a pollster in Atlanta, said Democrats in the region were attached to a coalition of "feminists, labor unions, blacks and homosexuals. Talk about a **kiss-of-death** crowd among Southern politicians." (*U. S. News & World Report*)（见"附录""宗教词语"）

> 习　　题

阅读理解文章

Jerry Falwell, Moral Majority Founder, Dies at 73 (2007/5/16 *The New York Times*)

二十二、价值观

1. 何谓 values

世界各民族都有各自的理想和追求的目标。这两方面组成了价值观。价值观规范人们行为,提供精神指南。

2. 各行各业都有价值观

美利坚民族的价值观受英国文明影响最深,包括英国在内的西方文明则源于古代宗教意识和古希腊、古罗马的世俗意识。价值观表现在各个领域,政治、法律、宗教、教育、社会、经济等方方面面都有各自崇尚的价值观。

如在政治层面,英国议会制和英国哲学家洛克(John Locke,1632—1704)的建国论和天赋人权说,对美国政治思想产生重大影响。所以才有言论自由、不得侵犯个人的隐私,文官决策、武官执行的特征。

再如在人生方面,有生活价值观或我们以前常讲的人生观。如:认真工作、勤奋努力、乐观豁达、珍惜时间、金钱至上、追求独立、崇尚竞争、崇拜物质、崇尚平等、乐善好施等。*

3. 共和党不离口的道德和家庭价值观

1981 年编者去美国念书,次年正赶上中期选举,有的候选人在电视台竞选演说里常说:"I'm a family man."类似中国古代人所说的:"谁言治国先齐家。"美国社会价值观也讲"尊重和关心家庭的健康发展"。美国发展到今天,经历 counterculture 运动后,正统或传统文化已发生了巨变,尽管如此,保守派和自由派在 school prayer, abortion 和 same-sex marriage 等社会重大问题上仍在争得不可开交。保守派(包括宗教界人士在内)认为,传统道德观的沦丧是当今社会的万恶之源。而传统道德观又以 family values 为核心,当然也是反对支持堕胎和同性恋权利者的代名词。

family values 首先出现在 1966 年由 Andrew Greeley 牧师和 Peter Rossi 合

---

* 以上参考了王恩铭:《当代美国社会与文化》,上海外语教育出版社,1997,第 188—191 页和第 202—206 页。

写的 The Education of Catholic Americans 书里，十年后共和党才在竞选党纲里宣称：

"Divorce rates, threatened neighborhoods and schools and public scandal all create a hostile atmosphere that erodes family structures and **family values.**"

此后，family values 成了共和党人口头禅，不断攻击民主党候选人持自由派观点，就是放纵性自由，听任家庭解体、同性恋盛行，惊呼美进入了 permissive era（放任自流的时代）。

4. 两党候选人同打一张牌

民主党候选人在社会问题上一般持自由派观点，不突出家庭价值观这一竞选策略，以免被动。克林顿夫妇为吸引老年人和保守派的选票，在突出经济主题的同时也提出道德和家庭价值观的口号，两者相结合，赢得了大选。见例句：

They swung heavily to Clinton in 1996, when he married [moral] values and economics by making things like the Gingrich-proposed curbs in Medicare spending a test of values. If Gore too can and combine values and economics, he'll pull these latter-day Erin Brockoviches（坚贞不渝者）into his camp. (time)

对此，宗教界极端保守及与 Jerry Falwell 牧师齐名的 Pat Robertson 这个利用广播传教的牧师（在 1988 年还竞选过总统），曾在 1996 年大选中对克林顿夫妇谈论家庭价值观表示强烈不满：

"When Bill and Hillary Clinton talk about family values, they are not talking about either families or values. They are talking about a radical plan to destroy the traditional family and transfer its functions to the Federal Government."

此处 Pat 指责 Clinton 夫妇是自由派的家庭价值观，破坏传统的家庭，把家庭应起的作用转给联邦政府去承担，由政府去干涉人们的自由。

再如：在 2008 年大选中，奥巴马夫人也破例打出家庭价值观这张牌。见例句：

"He is incredibly smart, and he is able to deal with a strong woman, which is one of the reasons why he can be President." (Michelle Obama)

米歇尔当时为什么说其夫能管好家里的女强人妻子（原芝加哥大学医学院副院长，为全力协助夫君竞选而辞职）就会成为一个能（胜）任总统（工作）的理由呢？显然，她用不同的话语在打"齐家有方，治国有道"的"family values"牌。

对共和党总统、议员等候选人而言，"family man"成为口头禅，是这个形象关系到能否赢得保守派选民的选票进而赢得大选的关键。所以不但在两党之间，在共和党内初选也打这张牌。如 2008 年的总统竞选前哨战比以往历次大选都提前打响,在共和党表态参选而名列前茅者(front runners)中,这个牌打得最积极的要数前马萨诸塞州州长罗姆尼(Mitt Romney),他信奉实际一夫多妻制的摩门教(Mormonism),但至今仍守着原配妻子,他在这篇文章的插图里展现与孩子们一起嬉戏,家庭生活其乐融融的情景。

文字说明:Pitch Perfect? Romney's image as a family man may woo the GOP base and change party fortunes post-Bush. (2007/2/26 Newsweek)意为罗氏以 family man 的形象出现,说明他重视家庭价值观,或许这可以安抚共和党的基本选民,从而改变小布什后共和党的厄运。即小布什是自有民意调查以来支持率最低的总统,会连累本党,打 family values 牌或许能帮助共和党赢得大选。

再看该刊同期的另一篇题为"We're a Happy Family"文章的第一段:

Most jokes that politicians tell don't make you laugh because they're too carefully calculated to be funny. Mitt Romney tells one that's carefully calculated and funny. "I believe marriage should be between a man and a woman," he recently told an audience of conservative Republicans. "And a woman, and a woman and a woman."

这段文字里"marriage...between a man and a woman"和"A woman, and a woman and a woman"值得玩味。根据语法规则,Romney 把可以不用的前两个"a"都用上,接着又用了三个"a woman"。明白人一眼就可以看出,他是在含沙射影同党竞争者中有过两次离婚史、在社会问题上持自由派观点的前纽约市市长朱里亚尼(Rudy Giuliani)和一次离婚史的国会参议员麦凯恩(John McCain)。这对像 Giuliani 这样的候选人伤害很大。例如已故大财阀、前副总统 N. 洛克菲勒,数度竞选,数度落选,原因就在于此,选民们反对他的口号是:"We elect a leader, not a lover"。

在美国区别共和党和民主党的一个特点是,凡大谈特谈这个"values"或那个"values"者准是共和党人(2006年,他们还杜撰了一个新词"values voter"),所以民主党人有此一说:"If we wanted our elected officials to talk about values, we wouldn't be Democrats. We're Republicans." *

共和党与民主党及共和党内不断在 family values 这个问题上打嘴战，多数候选人都想证明自己是 a real/solid/true/compassionate conservative 或 moderate/middle/more/most conservative，只有少数如 Barry Goldwater 和 Jesse Helms 这样共和党人的言行才是 a fundamentalist 或 ultraconservative，而非仅仅是 a true-red conservative。

二十三、电影分级制

1. 影片为何分级

一些好莱坞制片商用满是脏话、暴力和性等镜头的电影来诱惑分辨力和自制力不强的青少年，给美国带来了无数的社会问题，引起家长、宗教界和政界保守派人士的激烈抨击。1968 年美国电影协会（Motion Pictures Association of America）决定由其下属单位电影审查和分级管理处（CARA—Classification and Rating Administration）实行电影分级制（Motion Picture Ratings System），即按类（category）分为"普通级"和"限制级"等制度，说明影片适合哪一类观众观看，旨在事先打招呼，让观众，特别是父母了解影片是否有不适合青少年观看的情节。该管理机构的评判标准包括影片的主题、语言和情节是否粗俗下流，有无暴力、裸体、性、吸毒、酗酒等诲淫诲盗，不堪入目的镜头。他们按照这类情节的有无和轻重程度给影片定级，供家长们决定是否允许子女观看。在给影片定级时，还邀请家长一同观看，一起讨论决定影片的级别。机构的人员相信，这样评定出来的级别最能代表普通父母的想法。但是这种定级并无法律的强制效力。为了更加明白这种分级，我们不妨看下面一段英文文字较浅显易懂的说明：

Under the leadership of Jack Valenti, who left the White House to become President of the Motion Pictures Association of America（美国电影协会）, Hollywood accepted a rating system for films in 1968. Those in **G category** would be family movies; the others would be **M** (suggested for mature audiences), **R** (restricted to persons 16 or older unless accompanied by a parent or guardian), or **X** (no one under 16 admitted under any circumstances). (William Manchester)

2. 共分几级

1990 年后，美国电影协会的电影审查和分级管理处将所有电影按内容分为五类，实行下列新的分级制：

---

* Frank Luntz: Word That Work, Hyperion, New York, 2007, p. 218.

① G category　G 类：G 类的 G-rated films　G 级影片，即大众级，适合各种年龄段观众（general audience）观看的影片，也可以说是家庭影片（family films/movies）。该级别的电影内容父母可以接受，影片里没有裸体、性爱镜头，吸毒和暴力场面非常少。对话也是日常生活中可以经常接触到的；

② PG category　PG 类：即宜在家长指导下（parent guidance）观看的影片，一些内容儿童不宜观看。该级别的电影基本上没有出格镜头，即使有，也是一闪而过，此外，恐怖和暴力场面不会超出适度的范围；

③ PG-13 category　PG-13 类：即 13 岁以下儿童宜在家长指导下（parent guidance suggested under 13）观看的影片。该级别的电影没有粗野的持续暴力镜头，一般没有裸体镜头，有时会有吸毒镜头和脏话；

④ R category　R 类：即限制级，限制（restricted）观看的影片，意为如无家长陪看，16 岁或 17 岁以下青少年不得观看。该级别的影片包含成人内容，里面有较多的性爱、暴力、吸毒等场面和脏话；

⑤ NC-17 category　NC-17 类：17 岁以下儿童禁看（no children under 17 admitted）影片。影片中有清楚的性爱场面，大量的吸毒或暴力镜头以及脏话等。原来为 X category（X 类），X 级影片只宜成人，16 岁以下青少年禁看的影片（not for children; restricted to adults）。1990 年改为 NC-17。

此外，还有 XXX category　XXX 类：所谓 XXX 类级影片并非电影协会定出，而是电影院或色情影片商用此说明某些电影具有强烈的性爱曝光镜头，招徕看客。

如果不了解美国电影分级制，而一般英文词典又不列出上述有些词条，那么就不知道下面例子中的 PG-13 等讲些什么：

The study found the highest incidence of smoking in **R-rated films.** But there was no difference in the amount of smoking between **PG** and **PG-13 films.** (The *Christian Science Monitor*)

英国的 Board of Film Censors（电影审查委员会）与美国一样，也根据电影中描写的色情、凶杀、抢劫等内容分成几级，允许或限制不同年龄段的儿童观看。

二十四、电视节目

1. D. L. S. V. 指何内容

1996 年 12 月，美国电视业代表宣布建立一种电视在家长指导下儿童宜看的电视节目按类分级制（TV Parental Guidelines），旨在使家长事先了解节目的内容。1997 年 10 月 1 日正式实施。这是在修改和发展电影分级制的基础上对广播和有线电视节目再加上 D, L, S 和 V 的标记（注意：这四个标记在不同的

guideline 条中内容稍有不同）。为了解得更详细和清楚，结合上面电影分级制的说明，读者只要阅读以下段落，便一目了然。

On Dec. 19, 1996, representatives of the television industry announced the creation of TV Parental Guidelines, a rating system intended to give parents advance information about the content of programs. The guidelines, modeled after the Motion Picture Ratings System and developed by a broad spectrum of industry representatives, began to appear on broadcast and cable television programs in Jan. 1997. On July 10, 1997, most of the television industry, after negotiations with advocacy groups, agreed to add the labels DLS and V to the existing ratings. The added labels, which went into effect by Oct. 1, provide more specific information about the degree of violence, coarse language, and sexually suggestive content. Some of the networks that did not add the labels Oct. 1 began to add their own parental advisories to shows.

2. 节目分几类几档

分级节目有两类：一类为儿童类。另一类所有观众类，即老少皆宜类。

儿童类节目分档如下：

（1）TV-Y　All Children（适合所有儿童观看的节目）　This program is designed to be appropriate for all children.

（2）TV-Y7　Directed to Older Children（只宜七岁以上儿童观看的节目）This program is designed for children age 7 and above.

所有观众类节目分类如下：

（1）TV-G　General Audience（适宜各种年龄段观众观看的节目）　Most parents would find this program suitable for all ages.

（2）TV-PG　Parental Guidance Suggested（宜在家长指导下观看的节目）This program contains material that parents may find unsuitable for younger children. Many parents may want to watch it with their younger children. The theme itself may call for parental guidance and/or the program contains one or more of the following: moderate violence (V), some sexual situations (S), infrequent coarse language (L), or some suggestive dialogue (D).

（3）TV-14　Parents Strongly Cautioned（只宜14岁以上儿童观看的节目）This program contains some material that many parents would find unsuitable for children under 14 years of age. Parents are strongly urged to exercise greater care in monitoring this program and are cautioned against letting children under the age of 14 watch unattended. This program contains one or more of the following: intense violence (V), intense sexual situations (S), strong coarse language (L), or intensely suggestive dialogue (D).

(4) TV-MA   Mature Audience Only(只宜成人观看的节目)   This program is specifically designed to be viewed by adults and therefore may be unsuitable for children under 17. This program contains one or more of the following: graphic violence (V), explicit sexual activity (S), or crude, indecent language (L).

第二节 英　国

一、国名

英国是大不列颠和北爱尔联合王国的简称,英文的正式名称是 the United Kingdom of Great Britain and Northern Ireland,简称 The United Kingdom 或 (the)U. K。Great Britain,Britain 和 the British Isles 都只能作为非正式用法。此外,还有一个要值得小心的简称是 England,如果你说一个 Scotsman(苏格兰人)或 Welshman(威尔士人)是 Englishman(英格兰人),他会认为你伤了他的民族感情而感到不快甚至愤怒,因为虽然英伦三岛中 England 最大,各方面实力最强,但对 1707 年的《联合条约》(the Act of Union),那两部分尤其苏格兰也是迫于无奈,所以至今其分离倾向也是时高时低,从未中断。

二、简况

1640 年英国爆发资产阶级革命,1649 年 5 月曾宣布为共和国。18 世纪下半叶发生工业革命。1801 年,爱尔兰并入版图。19 世纪,进入大英国帝国(the British Empire)的全盛时期,是比现在的美国还强盛的超级帝国。人口占世界 25%,陆地占 1/4,即其殖民地遍布五大洲,自称"日不落帝国"。第一次世界大战后,殖民地人民开始觉醒,独立运动高涨,这个老牌帝国走向衰落。1921 年允许爱尔兰南部 26 个郡脱离其统治,国名也从"大不列颠及爱尔兰联合王国"(the United Kingdom of Great Britain and Ireland)改为现名。不仅如此,1931 年英国被迫承认自治领在内政、外交上独立自主,殖民体系开始动摇。第二次世界大战后殖民体系解体,沦为现在的二流国家。由不可一世的 the British Empire,一次大战后改为 the British Commonwealth(of Nations),最后又被迫将 British 删掉而成了 the Commonwealth(of Nations)(在英译汉中,为区别其他的 commonwealth 仍加上"英"字而译为"英联邦")。名称的更改是这一巨变的很好例证。不过英国毕竟是老牌帝国,经济文化发达,创新能力强。

三、体制与宪法

英国既实行议会民主制,又保留君主立宪制(a constitutional monarchy)。与以色列一样,宪法是一部不成文法(unwritten constitution),基本表现有三:议会通过的法案或立法条令,称为制定法或成文法(statue law);法院积累历来判决而形成的法令,称为判例法或普通法(the common law);虽无明文规定,却对政府运作起着重要作用的规则和习惯(rules and practices)的习惯法(conventions)。有关政府结构、机构、职权和运行原则,主要散见于各种宪法性法律之中。

提到君主及其权限,议会、中央和地方政府机构、官职及其运行等,容易引起混淆和误解,只要细看下页的联合王国政府组织机构图解,便可一目了然。

四、联合王国政府组织机构

Government in the UK

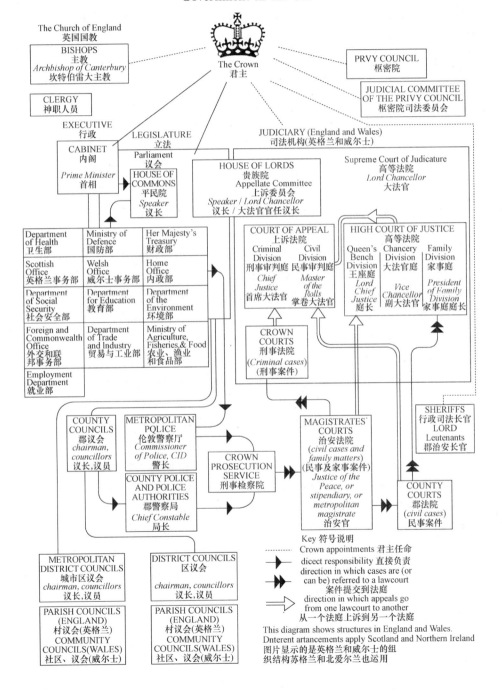

五、权力的分配

从上图可以看出,联合王国政府由行政、立法和司法三个部分组成,君主处于国家权力顶端,是正式的国家元首,最高统治者(supreme ruler)。但与沙特阿拉伯王国君主握有绝对实权不同,权力受宪法限制。立法权属于议会,行政权归内阁。主要政党是保守党和工党,由于实行政党制(party government),政党在政治、经济、社会等方方面面扮演着不可或缺的角色。本章将介绍这方面的知识。

六、国王

1. 权力和影响

国王(King)或女王(Queen)是世袭的国家元首,议会的重要成员,司法的首领,全国武装部队的总司令和英国国教的世俗领袖。现英国女王的全称为:"托上帝宏恩,大不列颠及北爱尔兰联合王国和她的其他领土及领地的女王、英联邦元首、基督教的保护者伊丽莎白二世"。在法律上,英王的职权有:任免内阁首相、大臣、高级法官和各属地的总督;召集、终止议会的会议和解散议会;加封贵族和颁授荣誉称号;批准和公布法律;统帅军队;对外宣战和媾和等等。赋予国王的这些权力(powers)大多是虚的,国王统而不治(The monarch reigns but does not rule.),只是摆设(figurehead),活动多数属礼仪性质。根据君主立宪制(constitutional monarchy),实权已让给内阁和议会。每年报上看到 Queen's Speech(女王敕语),即施政演说,在每年议会开会(在当年的10月份或11月份至第二年的10月份或11月时宣读,有效期一年。新一届议会的开幕日期则视何时举行大选而定),宣读的施政方针,类似美国的国情咨文(State of the Union message),由内阁拟定,女王只是照本宣科而已。

国王的影响在于是臣民的偶像,要靠本身的人格魅力、知识和经验。他/她定期与内阁阁员会晤,对内阁决策,有权要求首相通报和商议。君主连续在位,而执政党则像是来来往往的过客。例如伊丽莎白二世1952年登基,至今已与从丘吉尔到卡梅伦等共12位首相和无数政治家议政,积累了丰富经验,像世袭常务政治顾问,起点咨询作用。现在,在维护国家统一、保持大国地位和促进经贸等方面也起着不可替代的作用。这就是世界不少国家废除了君主制而英国的君主立宪制能历久不衰的奥妙所在。

2. 产生方式

英国王位为世袭制。1701年颁布的王位继承法规定,英王去世后由长子或长女及其后嗣继承,依次排序,男性优先女性。长子死亡,子女继承。若无子女,则由次子或后嗣继承。英王如无子女，才由其弟继承，并禁止天主教徒继承王位。1952年继位的现任女王伊丽莎白二世(Elizabeth Ⅱ)是英国汉诺威王朝的第十一代君王。

3. 王位继承酝酿改革

据2008年9月25日《泰晤士报》网站的报道：英国政府计划修宪，已草拟提案，其中包括废除禁止天主教徒继承王位的规定，并将允许长女先于次子继承王位。自1688年后制定的继承法都禁止天主教徒继承王位。按照法律规定，国王继位时要向议会宣称自己反对天主教教义。现在提案已成法律。

七、行政机构——内阁

从狭义讲，government一词在英国可指组织机构图表上executive(行政)，即内阁或首相和内阁，responsible government 为责任"内阁"制，The Prime Minister has formed a government(首相已组阁)。从广义讲，government是全体大臣和副大臣的总称，也包括各部的政务次官和其他高级官员，可说相当于美国"总统＋Administration"，可与议会的关系又不相同。

八、政府行政部门及官职

1. 政府部门和大臣名称多不同

英国政府主要部门已在政府组织机构图表中列出，各部名称和主管大臣官衔英文原名并不一致，绝大多数沿袭成习。各部有叫Ministry, Office或Department的，主管大臣或称Secretary，或称President，或称Chancellor。从字面上看，似乎差别很大，其实不过是因袭旧名而已。如外交和联邦事务部、内政部、苏格兰事务部等都是由英王的秘书处扩大成部的，主管人本来都是英王秘书(King's Secretary of State)，所以现在的部长沿用了旧的官衔，称为Secretary of State。枢密大臣、掌玺大臣和大法官等职也是设立时间较长，一般由贵族担任，故称Lord，如Lord Chief Justice(高等法院王座庭庭长)。英王爱德华三世封其子为兰开夏郡的兰开斯特公爵，后来亨利四世将该郡财产和司法权收归王室，并设立Chancellor of the Duchy of Lancaster(兰开斯特公爵郡大臣)一职，至今未变。贸易工业部现用Department，先前称委员会(Board)，现在的报刊有时仍用Board。至于农业、渔业和粮食部、国防部、卫生和社会保险部等，则迟至20世纪才成立，故改用Ministry。

在报刊中一般用非正式的简称，如"the Foreign and Commonwealth Office"(外交和联邦事务部)(报刊中也常随意用Ministry of...不足为训)，一般简称"the Foreign Office"(外交部)，而大臣也由全称"Secretary of State for Foreign and Commonwealth Affairs"(外交和联邦事务大臣)简化为"Foreign Secretary"(外交大臣)。

2. 大臣分几类几等　各司何责

政府各部门的官员分两类：大臣、副大臣和政务次官是政务官员，一般由议员充任并与内阁共进退；其他为文官，不受内阁更迭的影响。政府内部的领导核心——内阁，由首相、枢密院长和重要大臣组成，统称"内阁大臣"，其他大臣则是"非内阁大臣"。内阁大臣必须是上议院或下议院议员，一般在 20 人左右。

大臣大致分为四个等级(four tiers of ministers)：the ministers in the Cabinet; the ministers of Cabinet rank(这类大臣有时是内阁大臣，有时又不是); the ministers of state(常用 state minister 国务大臣，也称副大臣); the parliamentary secretaries(政务次官，也称 junior ministers 或 miniministers。他们是国务大臣在下院和各部办事的骨干)。这些政务官员与各部首席文官称为常务次官或内阁次官(Permanent Undersecretaries/Secretaries, Cabinet Secretaries)不同。他们是内阁大臣主要的常务顾问，职位比政务次官高一级。文官指常务次官及其下属政府官员，又称职业官员，实行常任制。

在四个等级之外还有一级官员，称之为 Parliamentary private secretary，议会的私人秘书，由后座议员(backbencher)即普通议员担任，表面上是为减轻大臣的工作担子，实际上协助大臣与后座议员联络。后座议员造反，曾使希斯(Edward Heath)、撒切尔夫人和布莱尔等下台让贤。所以这一级官员也不可小觑，统计数字表明，60%以上担任此职者都晋升为大臣。

3. 易混淆的官职

英国与美国的体制不同，官职繁杂，如财政部就有 First Lord of the Treasury(首席财政大臣)、Chancellor of Exchequer(财政大臣)和 Chief Secretary to the Treasury，后者有工具书译为"财政部首席大臣"，那么此职与首相兼任的"首席财政大臣"有何区别？是否高于财政大臣？事实上，他是财政大臣副手，但如译为常务副大臣也不合适，因为副大臣由政务次官担任，不如试译为"财政部常务大臣"。再如 Permanent Secretary，有译"常务大臣"的，则将"Permanent Under Secretary 译为"常务次官"。实际上两者是同一官职，居各部文官之首，应统一译为"常务次官"。再如 Parliamentary Secretary 和 Parliamentary Undersecretary 也是同一官职，宜一律译为"政务次官"。又如 First Sea Lord 或 Sea Lord，有译"海务大臣"的，与 First Lord of the Admiralty (海军大臣)看成两个部门的官职了。事实上 First/Second/Third/Fourth Sea Lord 都是海军部"副大臣"。如前首相丘吉尔在下面的介绍中说他曾任海军大臣：

He[Winston Churchill] was home secretary(1910—11), a dynamic **first lord of the admiralty**(1911—15)…(The *New American Desk Encyclopedia*)

九、内阁种种

这里谈的都是议会制责任内阁、影子内阁和看守内阁,而美国实行的却是总统负责的内阁(president's cabinet),这将在"英美政治比较"中再来探讨。

1. 何谓"Responsible Government"

内阁制(cabinet system[of government]/government)是"责任内阁制"(responsible government)的简称。内阁不但指首相,还包括阁员,组成一个集体的行政部门,由议会产生、对议会集体负责(collective responsibility)的权力组织形式。美国总统也想将内阁组成一个工作集体,但这种团队精神很少能超过新总统上台后的短暂蜜月期(honeymoon period)。内阁制最先在英国实行,到18世纪末,已逐渐形成一套较完备的制度,基本内容为:内阁由议会中占多数席位的一个政党或由几个政党联合组成。对议会负责,受议会监督;议会通过对内阁"不信任案"(vote of nonconfidence/no-confidence)时,内阁应总辞职,或提请国家元首下令解散议会,重新选举,以决定内阁去留。内阁首脑称"首相"或"总理",阁员称"大臣"或"部长"。

2. 何谓"Shadow Cabinet"

影子内阁亦称"预备内阁"、"在野内阁"。英国大选虽名为每隔5年举行一次,但执政党可在这5年中任何有利时机举行选举,这就迫使在野党随时做好准备。一旦赢得选举,便能及时让国家机器运转起来。一些西方国家的在野党为争夺政权,在议会党团内部按照内阁的形式,组成一个准备上台执政的班子。

1907年英国保守党首先使用"影子内阁"一词。从19世纪到20世纪初,英国由保守党和自由党轮流组阁,以后又演变为保守党和工党轮流执政。在此情况下,通常由取得议会多数的一个大党组织内阁,而获得次多数席位的另一大党则在议会下院中挑选该党有影响的成员组成影子内阁。议会进行政策辩论时,影子内阁的各部"大臣"或"某方面事务发言人"就各有关问题作主要发言。其后,如果组织影子内阁的政党在大选中取得议会多数议席,影子内阁就转化为执政内阁。

3. 何谓"Caretaker Government"

看守内阁也有译"看守政府"或称"过渡内阁"(transitional government)。"看守内阁"是指议会通过对政府不信任案后,新内阁还没有组成,或新国会没有产生前,仍暂时负责维持日常工作的内阁。"看守内阁"一般由原政府或原政府中的其他大臣组成。主要任务是负责继续处理日常政务或筹备下一届大选。新内阁组成后,看守内阁即行解散。

4. 何谓"Coalition Government"

所以组成"联合内阁"是因为在大选中没有一个政党获得过半数的议席,如不与它党组成联合内阁在议会占多数席位,那么一党组成的内阁随时有倒台的危险。

十、立法机构——议会

1. 议会制是何种政体

议会制也称"国会制"、"代议制"。议会为国家最高权力机关,首相和内阁成员都由议会产生,government,指"内阁"或"首相和内阁"对议会而不是对首相负责,并向议会报告工作,是一种立法和行政一体的政治制度。此外,议会还可对首相、各大臣进行口头质询(Parliamentary question)。在采取议会制的国家中,议会既有立法权又有对政府的某种监督权。议会对政府在形式上有制约作用,即政府须由议会授权由多数党组成,在议会对政府的主要施政方针不支持,或通过对政府的不信任案时,除非解散议会,政府必须总辞职。事实上还是在议会占多数席位的执政党说了算,除非党内内讧或联合政府中的小党退出。议会制与内阁制相适应,政府实行内阁制的都属于议会制国家。18 世纪以来的英国是议会制君主国的典型,第二次世界大战前后的法兰西第三、第四共和国是议会制共和国的典型。反之,政府(不论是否叫内阁)如由君主或总统直接控制而非对议会负责的则是二元制国家。议会制和二元制都是政权组织形式。

2. 议会制的英文种种表达

议会制(政体)或代议制(政体)在英文里有种种表达法,最常见的是 parliamentary system (of government)。此外,还有 parliamentary government, parliamentarianism, representative/representational government/(political) system [代议制(政体)]等。

3. 为何政府的中心是议会

议会(Parliament)是英国最高立法机关,由英王、贵族院和平民院组成。英国政府的中心是议会,不仅拥有立法权,还有行政决策权。首相和内阁成员都由议会执政党产生,且都是议员。他们均可提出议案,一旦提出,大体都能顺利通过。不像美国那样,因党派之争而把议案修改得支离破碎,或是双方处于僵持状态,议案无法通过。这与行政和立法不像美国那样独立分权,议会的多数党就是执政党,首相又是多数党党魁,普通议员必须接受党的领导和纪律,支持法案通过,否则要受党纪处分。因而,英国议会被视为一个高效的立法办事机构,能 get work done,不像美国的 don't-work Congress。但有批评者说,这是牺牲议员的自由意志为代价的。难怪 The Economist 评论说：[British] politics is based on the iron disciplines of the British party machine.

4. 议会分几院　各司何职

议会仿古罗马的两院制组成下列两院：

贵族院(House of Lords, the Lords)，又称上院(the Upper House)，形式上是英国最高立法机关，有最高司法权但立法权已被削弱，只能提出动议，对下院通过的法案表示赞同、反对或提出修改意见，并无决定立法的实权。现在主要由新封终生贵族(635名)、世袭贵族(92名)、上诉法院法官和教会首要人物(26名)组成，共有753名。原来的成员中世袭贵族占多数，他们不是经选举产生，也无杰出成就或贡献，不过顶着贵族头衔罢了。1999年，上院改革，除92名贵族留下，仍享有投票权外，656名世袭贵族已失去了议员资格。议长由大法官(Lord Chancellor)兼任。

平民院(House of Commons, the Commons)，又称下院(the Lower House)，有议员646名，与上院不同，经选举产生，任期5年，主要职能为立法、监督财政和政府。与上院不同，握有实权。

值得注意的是，报刊上常用缩略词 MP(member of Parliament)，仅指平民院议员。

十一、议会选举——大选

1. 议会选举是全体议员的选举吗

英国的议会选举(parliamentary election)，也称立法选举(legislative election)，实际上就是下院即平民院选举。

按宪法规定，平民院议员由直接选举产生，每5年举行一次。不过执政党可以通过内阁选择对自己有利的时机要求女王解散议会，提前选举。

2. 采用何种选举制

英国的议会选举实行的是简单或相对多数制(plurality 或 simple majority system of voting)，而不是非要获得的选票过半数的多数(majority)，即议会不按各政党候选人获票比例分配席位，而是看谁在多少个选区获票占第一位。简言之，是得票多者当选的选举制度(first-past-the-post electoral system)。

在这种赢家独占制度下，一个政党只要选票集中的选区多，如大城市，就可以多得议席，有时会产生看来奇怪的结果。例如1951年大选，丘吉尔领导下的保守党获票48.0%，少于工党的48.8%，但议席反而比工党多26个，因而得胜。工党1974年2月取代保守党，情形亦与此类似。而小党由于选票分散，所得议席寥寥无几。这与美国普选票多而选举人少丢掉总统职位一样。

这样的选举制度不利于新党、小党,他们认为既不公平又不民主,让少数选民支持的政党霸占多数议席,主张改革为西欧其他国家普遍采用的"比例代表制"(proportional representation),而不是选举独裁制(election dictatorship)。还主张废除首相可以选择有利时机确定大选日期的特权,要求改革为议员固定任期制,遭到享有既得利益的保守党和工党的反对。除非改革派有朝一日上台或者在多党联合政府中享有很大发言权,这样的改革难有实行之日。2010年大选后组成联合政府,大党迫于无奈,今后有可能放行比例代表制。

英国下议院选举的原则是每一个选区都有数目相等的选民,每一个选民都有平等的选举权,即"一人,一票,一价"(one man/person, one vote, one value)。大家都是平等的,一人不能投两票(plural vote),每一个选民只能投一票给一个候选人,在这个选区内获得最多票者当选为本区的下院议员。整个英国被分为646个选区(parliamentary constituency),所以,下议院一共由646名成员组成。

3. 为何议会选举即大选

议会选举结束后,国王或女王召见多数党领袖,请他出任首相并着手组阁,议会表决通过后,新政府即告成立。最大的在野党依法成为正式的反对党,组成"影子内阁"。

从以上可以看出,英国的议会选举是议会选举和行政选举不分的大选(general election)。

十二、议会有哪些重要官职 (Party)Whip 有何职责

1. 贵族院

Speaker 上院议长兼任 Lord (High) Chancellor (大法官,集立法、司法和行政大权于一身的一个首脑人物);Deputy Speaker 副议长:上院的副议长兼任上院委员会主席,主席是任命的;Party Leaders 政党领袖。

2. 平民院

Speaker 议长;Deputy Speaker 副议长:下院的副议长由筹款委员会主席和两名副主席兼任,主席由选举产生;Party Leaders 政党领袖。

上述两院中的政党领袖指相当于美国国会 Majority/Minority Leaders, Whips 等职务的官员,任务是约束本党党员在议会中的活动。

Chief Whip 总督导;督导长是议会的政党领袖,相当于美国国会参众两院多数党或少数党领袖(Majority/Minority Leaders),负责执行党规党纪,鼓励议员积极支持党及其制定的政策,尤其要督促本党议员出席议会的重要辩论和表决,并将普通议员的意见反映给党的领袖。见下面《英国年鉴》(Britain)的说明:

Outside Parliament, party control is exercised by the national and local organisations. Inside, it is exercised by the **Chief Whips** and their assistants, who are chosen within the party. Their duties include keeping members informed of forthcoming parliamentary business, maintaining the party's voting strength by ensuring members attend important debates, and passing on to the party leadership the opinions of backbench members. Party discipline tends to be less strong in the Lords than in the Commons, since Lords have less hope of high office and no need of party support in elections.

Deputy Chief Whip(政党在议会中的)副总督导,副督导长

Government Chief Whip/Chief Whip of the majority party (议会)执政党或多数党总督导或督导长：即英国下院执政党总督导,正式头衔为"财政部政务次官"(Parliamentary Secretary to the Treasury),有时贬称为"patronage Secretary"(恩赐或授予的次官)。其他的执政党督导(Government Whips)(其中有一名为副总督导)中有三名是英国王室官员,有五位名义上担任"财政部委员会委员"(Lords Commissioners of the Treasury),还有五位是助理督导(Assistant Whips)。上院的执政党督导均在王室担任官职,同时也是政府发言人。在议会两院均设有反对党总督导(Opposition Chief Whips)和助理督导。见下面《英国年鉴》的说明：

The detailed arrangements of government business are settled, under the direction of the Prime Minister and the Leaders of the two Houses, by the Government Chief Whip in consultation with the Opposition Chief Whip. The Chief Whips together constitute the 'usual channels' often referred to when the question of finding time for a particular item of business is discussed. The Leaders of the two Houses are responsible for enabling the Houses to debate matters about which they are concerned. The formal title of the Government Chief Whip in the Commons is Parliamentary Secretary to the Treasury. Of the other Government Whips, three are officers of the Royal Household (one of these is Deputy Chief Whip), five hold titular posts as Lords Commissioners of the Treasury and five are Assistant Whips. The Opposition Chief Whips in both Houses and two of the Opposition Assistant Whips in the Commons receive salaries. The Government Whips in the Lords hold offices in the Royal Household; they also act as government spokesmen.

Opposition Chief Whip/Chief whip of the minority party (英国议会)反对党总督导或督导长,在英国议会两院均设有反对党总督导和助理督导(Opposition Assistant Whips)(见上英文说明)

(Party) Whip 党鞭，督导（见美国国会"重要官职"）分：Government Whip 执政党督导和 Opposition Whip 反对党督导：

The Prime Minister receives £82,003 and the Lord Chancellor £126,138. (The Leader of the Opposition receives £64,257 a year; two **Opposition whips** in the Commons and the Opposition Leader and Chief Whip in the Lords also receive salaries.)(*Britain*)

Assistant Whip 助理督导

3. 何谓 One-/Two-/Three-/Four-line Whip

Whip 这个字还指英国议会通知，上面列着议会一周议事安排是政党督导或党鞭向本党议员发出要求的书面通知，因在通知下面划多少线来表示会议或议事的紧急与否，如通知下面不画线，说明议事不重要，议员可以自由出席会议；如果只划了一道线（one-line whip），说明不紧急；二道线（two-line whip），说明要议的事之重要；three-line whip，以示紧急，是议员非出席的表决（voting）会议；four-line whip 则为"若缺席，自担风险"。见例句：

The sustained condemnation came after peers voted overwhelmingly, by 250 to 75, to reject a total ban on smacking. Both the government and the opposition Conservatives imposed a **three-line whip** on peers forbidding them from supporting an outright prohibition.(*Reuters*)

十三、司法机构

英国司法机构（British Judiciary）已在王国政府的图表里列得很清楚。法院分民事法院和刑事法院两个系统。民法系统按级分为郡法院，高等法院，上诉法院民事庭，上议院；刑法系统按级分为地方法院，刑事法院，上诉法院刑事庭，上议院。高等法院又分设王座庭，大法官庭和家事庭。上议院是最高司法机构，是民事和刑事案件的终审机关。高等法院的大法官由上院议长兼任。（见"联合王国政府"组织机构）

十四、地方政府（Local Government）

英国分英格兰、苏格兰、威尔士和北爱尔兰四部分行政区划。英格兰划分为43个郡。苏格兰下设32个区。威尔士下设22个区。

英国分设三个层次的政府：中央政府；地方政府；苏格兰、威尔士和北爱尔兰的地区性政府。英格兰由中央政府直接治理。

英国在伦敦威斯特敏斯特（Westminster）设有议会，在伦敦还有其他政府机构。在威尔士、苏格兰等地区,现在也有了自己的地区性议会和执行机关。但是它们并不独立于英国政府,两者不是一种联邦的关系。有学者认为,英国既非单一制也非联邦制,而是地区制国家。但这要看从那方面讲。下面就英格兰、威尔士、苏格兰和北爱尔兰地方政府结构作一个简介:

1. 英格兰分哪三类政府机构

在英格兰,有伦敦自治区32个,伦敦城议会(Corporation of the City of London)1个,都市区议会(metropolitan district council)36个,单一地方议会(unitary council)46个,区议会(district council)238个,郡议会(county council)34个。地方政府可以分为三类:

(1) 非单一制权力机构(non-unitary authorities):即具有"二级制地方政府"结构的行政郡(county),包括一个郡议会(council)和若干个区议会。两级政府各有不同的职责范围,如郡级负责教育,区级负责城镇规划。

(2) 单一制权力机构(unitary authorities):即同时具有郡和区议会职能的"一级制地方政府",是英格兰一级制地方政府的一种。另外,还有都市区议会、伦敦自治区和伦敦城议会也是一级制地方政府。

(3) 伦敦自治区(或行政区)(London boroughs):共有32个,其中12个在内伦敦,20个在外伦敦。

2. 威尔士、苏格兰和北爱尔兰议会独立于英国政府吗

(1) 威尔士:威尔士在1998年产生了最高的威尔士国民议会(National Assembly for Wales),其他基层共有22个单一制权力机构(unitary council),其中包括:9个单一郡议会(unitary county council)、10个单一郡自治区议会(unitary county borough council)、3个市议会(即具有城市地位的一级制政府),由单一地方政府提供主要的地方服务。

(2) 苏格兰:苏格兰的最高议会是1999年成立的议会(Scottish Parliament),其他基层议会都称council共有一级别议会32个,其中29个在本土,3个议会在岛区(奥克尼、设得兰和西部群岛)。

(3) 北爱尔兰:1998年成立了最高的地方议会——北爱尔兰议会(Northern Ireland Assembly),其他还有基层的区议会26个,是单一的地方政府,直接提供有限的地方服务。

除上述主要的地方政府单位外,在英格兰还有农村的最小的行政单位村和镇议会(parish/town council),在苏格兰和威尔士,有社区议会(community council),主要起咨询作用,只具有限的法定职能。

从上面可以看出,地方的地区最高议会也有用Parliament或Assembly的,但都加以上Scottish、Northern Ireland等地方限定词,以区别于设在伦敦

Westminster 区的国家议会"Parliament"。

这三个地区的议会当然也都可以以用 Parliament 或 Assembly：Scottish/Welsh/Northern Ireland Parliament/Assembly。只能处理教育、环保等地方事务，外交、国防等则由国家议会负责。这犹如美国州和联邦的分权。与美国一样，其他的地方议会则用 councils。

十五、政党

翻开英国近代史，人们可以看到，政府都由保守党和工党轮流执掌或联合执掌。两党制根深蒂固，第三党受到选举等限制难以壮大。

1. 工党和新工党（Labour & New Labour）

(1) 1979 年至 1994 年的大选为何屡败

工党（the Labour Party）成立于 1900 年，原名"劳工代表委员会"，1906 年改用现名。二次大战至 2008 年，工党已联合或单独组阁 7 次，是保守党的主要对手。它曾标榜"社会主义"，主张通过"议会斗争"和"议会民主"方式进行改革。虽然工党党员大部分是工人，但领导人的行动和政治策略代表也代表富裕资产阶级的利益。工党原先一贯主张扩大国有化，限制资本外流。对外政策强调英国的"民族利益"，曾一度主张退出欧洲共同市场，单方面进行核裁军，并反对美国在英国部署核导弹。后来内外政策均有较大变化。工党自 1979 年以来一直在野，已在 4 次大选中败给保守党。英报认为，该党政策正在向右转，与撒切尔夫人推行的一些做法相似。后来改革派领袖史密斯出任领袖。不幸的是，1994 年 5 月，正值保守党梅杰政权风雨飘摇，工党声望上升之时，史密斯猝然去世。这样，工党又陷入了内部权力斗争，保守党获得急需的喘息机会。

(2) 何谓布莱尔的"New Labour"

1995 年以改革家著称的布莱尔（Tony Blair）出任该党领袖，并在 1997 年的大选中击败保守党，改写了该党在野 18 年的历史。

工党的胜利靠的是布莱尔的"走第三条道路"（the third way）和改旧工党为"新工党"（New Labour）。就是走前保守党首相撒切尔夫人实施的市场经济和旧工党一贯提倡的社会主义传统之间的道路，新工党利用保守党的手段来达到自由派目标。与此同时，布莱尔推行大刀阔斧的革新，削弱工会对党的控制及左派的影响。改革党章，放弃了党章第四条国有化的条款（Clause Four），主张党应将传统的价值观与劳动人民现在的愿望相结合，使工党跟上英国社会的变化，成为一个中左的"新工党"。2001 年和 2005 年两次大选，工党又大获全胜，这是由于赢得了中间选民的支持，成了通吃型政党（catch-all party）。布莱尔也成为领导工党连续三次获得大选胜利的第一位首相。这跟战后英国社会结构变化，中间力量兴起有关。美国的克林顿也鼓吹第三条道路(the third way),奥巴马在大选中同样靠拉拢中间力量上台。

2007年布莱尔因在伊拉克开战等问题上跟美国总统小布什亦步亦趋,吃了大亏,声誉扫地,国内问题也不如意,被迫将首相一职交给财政大臣布朗(Gordon Brown)。因经济不振,在次年5月2日的地方议会(local councils)选举中遭遇黑色星期五(Black Friday),得票率仅24%,不但不如保守党(44%),连第三党自由党(25%)都不如,难怪该党在2010年大选中败北。为省略,报刊常用Labour(工党),如Labour's plan(工党计划)。

2. 保守党

(1) 曾长期执政

保守党(the Conservative Party)的前身为1679年成立的托利党(the Tory Party),1833年改称保守党。1912年国家统一党并入保守党,称保守统一党,简称保守党。为省略,报刊常用the Tories或the Conservatives(保守党)。在力量占优势的选区扎根深,自身又较能抑制内阁,屡次大选击败工党,从1951年至1964年和1979年至1997年曾长期执政。从不公布党员人数,据估计为180万左右,大多来自社会上层。保守党代表英国垄断资本家、大地主和贵族的利益。

(2) 撒切尔夫人有何政绩

1979年撒切尔夫人执政,大力推行"货币主义"经济政策(monetarist financial policies),通过严格控制货币供应量和减少公共开支等手段控制通货膨胀。她与美国共和党的主张不同,反对削减个人所得税,主张加强法律和社会治安,限制工会权力,加速私有化,将某些国有企业恢复为私营,有走极端市场经济倾向。对外主张加强防务,增加军费,加强欧盟前身欧洲共同体各国的合作,协调外交政策和欧美立场,加强大西洋联盟,尤其强调英美的"特殊关系"。

应该说,她在经济上取得很大成绩,使英国摆脱了"欧洲病夫"的尴尬。里根在美国也跟撒切尔唱和,主张市场至上,放松必要的政府监管,结果爆发次贷危机,现在西方又普遍强调政府作用,向凯恩斯主义一边摆。可见物极必反。撒也是如此。由于一意孤行,推行不分财富和收入多寡,一律按比例交税的人头税(poll tax)失去民心而被迫下台。

(3) 为何在大选中屡败于工党

1990年梅杰接班上台,内外政策均有所调整。但因爆发"疯牛病"(mad-cow disease)跟欧洲联盟的关系紧张,党内又纷争不断,不如当年一致对外,加之梅杰能力平庸,政绩乏善可陈。结果在1997年大选中被工党击败。此后,党内一直缺少强有力的领导人,在2001年和2005年两次大选中连遭败绩。2010年大选,该党在下院650个席位中获306席,稍多于工党的258席,未能过半,现任领袖卡梅伦（David Cameron）不得不与自民党组成联合内阁。

3. 自由民主党

（1）在近年来的选举中有何斩获

自由民主党（the Liberal Democrats 或 the Liberal Democrat Party）常简称为 Lib Dems（自民党），是自由派的政党，第三大党。1988年由自由党和社会民主党内多数派组成，正式名称为社会自由民主党（the Social and Liberal Democrats）。该党实力尚不如保守党和工党，但很有前途。Nick Clegg 是该党领袖，现在联合政府中任副首相。在2010年大选中仅在国家议会（Parliament）中占有57席，比以前的63席少了6席。其余政党获28席。

（2）内政外交主张

自民党提倡社会自由主义，减少政府对个人自由的干涉，反对成为 nanny state。不提倡经济过分自由的政策，而是提倡社会公正、福利国家和经济。主张减少中低收入群体的税收。在外交上，倡导多边外交政策，反对英国参与伊拉克战争，主张从伊撤军，以拥护欧盟著称。在选举中主张采用比例代表制（the ［system of］ proportional representation）来代替赢者全得的简单多数制（the first-past-the-post system）。

十六、英国君主制的废留之争

据1988年的民意调查，多数英国人认为，女王的首要任务是英国国家形象的代表，其次是公民和家庭生活的楷模。伊丽莎白二世确实是英国人生活的典范，然而王室（royal family）成员却不争气，离婚、偷情丑闻不断，不免使英国人闻之而怒不可遏，他们所缴的税款居然供他们过着伤风败俗的腐朽生活。因而，英国一度要求废除君主制的呼声高涨。据民意测验，竟有高达三分之一的人主张废除或对其进行彻底改革。

1997年戴安娜王妃在巴黎丧身车祸，2005年查尔斯王子与情人卡米拉低调成婚。于是，查尔斯、戴安娜、卡米拉之间的三角关系，戴安娜王妃的死因以及媒体盛传的她与一位马术教练、还有一位

Queen Elizabeth juggles a normal life at home with royal duties that take her around the would.

普通心脏外科医生之间的"真挚爱情故事",都成了人们茶余饭后的话题,并杜撰了一个不知何意的"Squidgy"。据说1989年除夕,有位男子打电话给Diana,称为"Squidgy",并一再说:"I love you."戴安娜则在电话中诉说其婚后所受折磨,并同意与其约会。小王子哈里对王室(royal family)来说更是一个"麻烦的制造者":2001年偷偷酗酒和吸毒,2004年考试作弊并与记者大打出手,2005年在一个化装舞会上把自己打扮成了带着十字记号袖标的纳粹军官,背着女友去偷欢等等。这些丑闻在一定程度上打破了人们将王室看成是道德模范的神话。于是在英国社会又引起了一轮是否有必要保留君主的争论。不论结果如何,这些都表明英国王室面临着生存挑战。

2008年5月,尼泊尔废除了君主制。可仅在欧洲,就有英国、西班牙、荷兰、瑞典、挪威、丹麦和比利时仍保留着君王;在非洲有摩洛哥、莱索托;在亚洲,有沙特阿拉伯、约旦、泰国、日本。这些也有着形形色色的君主,有的只是名义的君主,有的握有国家实权。英国是最古老的资本主义国家,民主制在人们的头脑中已深深扎根,君主制显然不符合历史潮流。可时至今日,英国仍未实行共和制。那么英国缘何要保留君主制呢? 总的来说,英国君主制的存在顺应了英国民族、宗教和政治特点,是历史传统的产物。具体讲,大致有以下列几个缘由:

1. 反对君主制会动摇民族意识的基础

君主制给人一种时代的错觉,但大多数英国人认为它很自然。要废除君主制就意味着对社会的打击,除非能创造一种使他们可以表达和弘扬其民族特点的新体制。

2. 君主制与英国历史密不可分

在英国人看来,以往大英帝国的辉煌和高度文明与君主制息息相关。看到现在的君主,就使他们回忆起往昔"日不落国"在世界上的地位。

3. 英国人不喜欢共和制

在英国历史上与其作战的都是共和制国家,如英法百年战争和拿破仑战争及美国的独立战争。此外,英国在17世纪也曾实行过共和制,并不成功。

4. 国王比总统更能代表国家形象

共和国选出的总统难免在有些问题上偏向一党利益,因为他/她是一个政党的领袖,执政时不能脱离政党政治;英国君主却能对政治持超然态度。君主不干预政治,并在政治辩论中不支持和反对任何一方而持中立态度,即使一方如工党曾提倡公有制的"社会主义"也罢。因此君主不可能用不体面的政治行动手段如Watergate那样来玷污自己的名誉。所以君主更能代表国家利益,平衡党斗。

当首相与其议事时,君主能抱着不偏不倚的公正态度,以其丰富的政治知识经验谈看法,提建议,真正从名义上担当起领导国家的政治责任(political accountability)。

5. 君主比总统更能凝聚人心

君主不仅类似总统,象征国家,还带有宗教性质,如英国君主为英国国教世俗领袖,是有独立倾向的威尔士和苏格兰与英格兰合在一起的凝合剂,这就使英国不会分裂。女王长子 Charles 于 1969 年册封为威尔士亲王(Prince of Wales)就是出于维护国家统一的考虑。英国君主还能起反对种族歧视、促进种族包容、宗教安抚人心的作用,还能超脱于党斗之上,当仲裁人,但实际权力不如泰国和沙特国王那样大,不能一锤定音。

6. 伊丽莎白二世已成为民族精神和道德价值观的代表

看来在英国君主制正在部分取代教会的职能,大多数人是透过神秘的面纱和宗教传统去看待王室的,这跟其他国家搞个人崇拜,神化政党领袖差不多。

7. "统而不治"成优点

人们不用担心王室滥用权力。因此,执政党和反对党都乐意效忠王室,这样做可以抑制握有实权的政治家飞扬跋扈。在首相和议会看来,君主被剥夺了政治实权,有这个摆设并不碍事,反倒可以充当润滑剂,缓和矛盾,起不可替代的作用。

8. 有助于维持大国地位和促进经济发展

英王是 53 个英联邦首脑成员国公认的象征性国家元首(head of state),有了英王才能维持英联邦的存在。女王能促进经贸的发展,她访问到哪里,生意就做到哪里(Trade follows Her Majesty's visit)。王室成员还常出国访问,担任促进贸易的使者(ambassadors of trade)。此外,英王也是世人争睹和崇拜的偶像,王宫和王室礼仪也是游人注目的中心,君主制的存在每年可使英国赚取大量的旅游观光收入。

9. 王室有严格的家规

王室面临的危机是有的成员胡作非为闹出的丑闻,但由于伊丽莎白二世女王威信较高,处事能力强。例如她能沉着应对 1996 年前后那场危机,在依法纳税和控制王宫的修缮规模等方面自我约束,严肃家规,吸取了战后君主专制政体垮台的教训,平息众怒,最终都能渡过难关。再则,女王和王室成员一直从事慈善事业,单女王为此在 1996 年就亲自露面 585 次,平民出身、车祸丧生的戴安娜王妃更是突出代表,赢得英国人的尊敬,这也有助于君主制在英国的延续。

10. 王权面临改革而非废止

虽然王室的生活方式遭到抨击,但大多数人更倾向于改革,而不是废除君主制。虽然戴安娜之死,群情激奋,但并无人袭击王宫,诉诸暴力。看来求稳怕乱,人心思定,在恐怖主义肆虐的今天,讲和谐、盼发展已成主流。

政界要人如英国前首相丘吉尔认为:"议会民主制和君主立宪制并非十全十美,但这是人类迄今所创造的最好的政治体制。"另一位英国前首相梅杰也道出了最有说服力的理由:"没有人能设想除君主立宪制外,英国还能实行其他别的什么体制。"看来这两位英国政治家所说的话,基本上概括了大多数英国人对君主制的看法。当然,对于上述10个理由和丘吉尔等政要的说法也只能见仁见智。

习　题

"Why the Monarchy Must Stay"(1996/3/11 *Newsweek*)(《精选本》四版课文)

十七、何谓英联邦(The Commonwealth)

1. 由哪些成员国组成　与英女王有何关系

英联邦(the Commonwealth[of Nations])这一联合体由英国和已经独立的前英国殖民地(colonies)或附属国(dependencies)及两个特殊的成员国(太平洋上的瑙鲁和图瓦卢两个小国)组成,原称"大英帝国"或"不列颠帝国"(the British Empire),第一次世界大战后改称联邦。

英联邦不设立议会和内阁等共同权力机构,但尊重共同的君主(common sovereign)。此外,联合王国的女王还是加拿大、新西兰、澳大利亚等旧英联邦国家和二战后的成员国如斯里兰卡、牙买加、斐济等国的女王。有的已实行共和制的成员国也承认女王象征英联邦元首(the symbolic head of the Commonwealth)。也就是说,联邦成员国得承认英国君主名义上为该国元首。各成员国政府首脑定期举行会议,但其结果对成员国没有约束力。这样,女王就有助于拉近这些成员国与英国的联系,促进相互间的经贸往来,从而保住共同体不散伙。

英国和联邦成员国互派高级专员(high commissioner,不称大使),以保持联系。英联邦成员国间的贸易关系较密切。但随着地区经济一体化的发展,情况也有所变化,如澳大利亚近年与东亚的关系就加深了许多。

2. 联邦是何组织　英能主宰吗

随着时间的推移,英国已不再是英联邦的主宰。英文的名称也由"the British Commonwealth"改为"the Commonwealth of Nations"或简称为"the Commonwealth"。英联邦内部的联系也越来越不稳定,成为一个松散的、相互进行政治、经济磋商和合作的组织。截至 2008 年,英联邦包括英国在内共有 53 个成员国(2002 年津巴布韦暂停成员国资格,2004 年巴基斯坦恢复了成员国资格,这么一减一加,现在成员国数目保持不变)。总部设在伦敦。组织机构有:英联邦政府首脑会议、亚太地区英联邦政府首脑会议、英联邦部长会议、英联邦秘书处和英联邦基金会等。

十八、英美特殊关系(Anglo-American Special Relationship)

1. 英国为何要维持这种关系

英国由 the British Empire 变为 the Commonwealth,是世界民族独立运动高涨和老牌帝国解体的写照。二战后,英国国力日衰,美国取代英国,成为资本主义世界霸主。在世人眼里,英国早已成为二流国家,但至今放不下架子,仍在死撑门面。为此,英企图借助与其同文同种的美国力量维持大国地位和对英联邦的控制,把同美国的联盟作为对外关系的基石,在政治、经济和军事上依赖美国,在许多重大的国际问题上追随美国的政策,坚定地站在美国一边,保持着一种"特殊关系"(special relationship),有时甚至不视本国为欧洲国家。

2. 谁首创这一关系

首创这种关系的是丘吉尔,他在 1945 年 11 月 7 日向平民院发表讲话时说, "We should not abandon our **special relationship** with the United States and Canada about the atomic bomb."

次年 3 月,他在美国密苏里州富尔顿市威斯敏斯特学院(Westminster College)煽动冷战,使铁幕(iron curtain)一词流行时,再强调道:"Neither the sure prevention of war nor the continuous rise or world organization will be gained without what I have called the fraternal association of the English-speaking peoples. This means a **special relationship between the British Commonwealth and Empire and the United States of America.**"

这两次讲话奠定了亲美疏欧外交政策的基础。其后的首相们大体沿袭这条路线,难怪法国的戴高乐(Charles de Gaulle)当年坚决反对英国加入欧洲共同体,怕英成为美国的 Trojan horse。

1979 年撒切尔夫人执政,认为美是英"最主要的盟国",北大西洋联盟是"英对外政策的基石",西欧防卫离不开美国。1997 年工党领袖布莱尔(Tony Blaire)上台后,对美国更是亦步亦趋,英当时是唯一跟随美国轰炸伊拉克"禁飞区"(no-fly zone)的国家,在轰炸南斯拉夫时与美国一样猖狂。在发动对南斯拉夫空袭和阿富汗战争以及伊拉克战争中,又前后为克林顿和小布什充当马前卒。

为此,布莱尔被媒体贬讽为小布什的"哈巴狗",他本人却自嘲是美国的"导盲犬"。

3. 美欧对英各有何期待

另一方面英国又逐步融入欧洲,想跟德、法一道,在欧洲一体化进程中发挥主导作用。美国需要英国这个重要的、特殊的欧洲伙伴帮忙架设它通往欧洲的桥梁,与欧洲对话沟通,协调与欧洲诸强之间的政策、立场和关系。惟其如此,英欧关系才显示出独特的价值和魅力;英美特殊关系对于欧洲来说也是如此。英国认识到自身优势,要发挥超出实力的影响并保持自身大国地位,就必须同时成为欧洲和美国独特的、中心的重要角色,两者不可偏废。布莱尔明确提出要在美欧之间发挥桥梁和枢纽作用。

4. 国内外政要有何评论

这种左右逢源,从中渔利的外交战略却受到了国内外的质疑和挑战。试图恢复大国地位的抱负与力不从心的现实之间形成巨大反差,关系到英国的外交政策定位和方向。正像一位工党议员所诘问的:"为什么英国不能保持一个独立于美国政府之外的外交政策?"2006 年 4 月,保守党领袖 David Cameron 说:"We should be solid but not slavish in our friendship with America."

英美特殊关系是应该建立双向道的基础上的,但美国有时对英国颐指气使,对英的要求置之不理引起国内外的种种评论。例如前西德总理施密特(Helmut Schmidt)曾辛辣地讽刺道:"The Anglo-American 'special relationship' is so special that only one side understand it."

再如:英国《独立报》也在 1992 年的一篇社论上不满地评论道:

"The special relationship between this country and the United States is at its worst when the American authorities demonstrate arrogance and insensitivity and their British counterparts are supine(苟安的)."

5. 英国无外交

《金融时报》在 2007 年 6 月 28 日一篇文章里报道了工党内部反对紧跟美国的呼声高涨。见 2006 年《新闻周刊》对英国首相布莱尔的评论:

Tony Blair, 49, is seen by some as President George Bush's **foreign minister, or even his pet dog.** Many of his critics do not believe that the British prime minister supports Bush's policy on Iraq as a mere subordinate, rather that he does it out of conviction.

有人说他是美国布什总统的 foreign minister,甚至是 pet dog。许多批评者认为他支持布什的伊战政策,不是出于本身的坚定信念,而是听话的下级。

后来 Blair 决定将职位交给 Gordon Brown(原财政大臣),美国的一幅漫画又讽刺道:

狗圈上写着 Bush(布什),左边离去的狗指布莱尔,10 号(首相府)门前的狗指布朗。

左边原来拴着的这只狗 Tony Blair 走了,Gordon Brown 正等待着套上狗项圈。事实上也是如此,美奥巴马政府主张增兵阿富汗,布朗随之附和并行动。这大概就是 Anglo-American special relationship 的核心内涵吧。

现在工党下台了,保守党与自民党组成联合内阁,卡梅伦的对美外交政策是否能如其上面在 2006 年所说的那样有改变呢?人们将拭目以待。

第三节　英美政治比较

英国是议会民主制和君主立宪制国家,美国是联邦共和国制国家。政体各不相同。英国是议会制;美国是总统制。因而从总统与首相、议会、政党、大选等等方面来看,既有相同点,也有不同之处。了解这两种政治制度的异同,对两国和世界其他许多国家的体制就不言自明。否则就会妨碍理解。例如,克林顿1993年上台,民主党却在1994年国会中期选举中失势,等于对总统头两年政绩的全民公决。《时代》周刊一文此段值得思考:

More important for Clinton, it was a pointed rejection of many of the themes of his two-year term. Indeed, **if the U.S. had a parliamentary democracy** like Britain or Japan, instead of a fixed four-year presidential term and a separation of executive and legislative powers, **he would be out of office.**

为什么说"If the U.S. had a parliamentary democracy,... he (Bill Clinton) would be out of office"呢？与"rejection of many of the themes of his two-year term"有何关系？要是在英国,会有何后果？

一、国家体制形式不同

两国体制的形式不同,英国是"君主国",美国是"合众国"或"联邦共和国"。换言之,以君主(King/Queen)为国家元首的政权组织形式的为君主国；国家元首或代表机关由选举产生的为共和国。"美利坚合众国"1776年成立合众国,是联邦制的一种形式。1787年通过宪法,成立"联邦共和国"(Federal Republic),是共和制的一种形式。

二、政体有别

国家体制形式不同,政权组织形式运作程序也有别。英国政体是议会制(parliamentary system of government),即议会是最高权力机关,政府(指内阁和首相)集体对议会负责的一种政治制度,因而也可以说是内阁制政体(cabinet government)。当今,世界上许多国家都是议会制政体。政府由议会多数党产生,议会既有立法权又有对政府的监督权和制约权。如议会对政府的主要施政方针不支持,或通过对政府的不信任案时,政府(指内阁)就得总辞或倒台。这说明,英国是单一权力政体(unitary government),是一元制政体国家。所以我们在报上看不到英国像美国总统与国会斗争的文章,所见的是执政党和在野党在议会的较量。

美国是合众国,联邦制的一种形式,实行的是总统制(Presidential system/government),总统既是国家又是政府首脑,掌握行政实权。总统由选举而非由议会产生。政府(指 Administration)内阁成员由总统任命并经参议院批准。内阁独立于国会,实行总统制内阁(President's cabinet)。政府由总统直接控制,不对国会负责,是二元制政体国家。所以我们在报上更多看到的是总统与国会间的斗争。

两种不同的政体主要区别在于:议会制政体一旦执政党成为少数党,就变为在野党,政府(指内阁)就要下台。美国则不同,反对党控制了议会,总统照样干下去,只是处处受其掣肘罢了。府会之间斗来斗去,叫做制衡;议会制,the legislative and the executive branches are one,行政(内阁)与立法(议会)是一码事,缺少相互制衡(checks and balances),首相代表行政和选民。唯一制约是执政党要在议会拥有多数席位。

三、国王与总统

英国国王(King/Queen)为世袭元首,美国总统则定期经选举产生。国王虽至高无上,然而王权受宪法限制,多数属礼仪性质,实权归内阁和议会;美国总统既是选举产生的国家元首,又是政府首脑,掌握行政实权;部长由总统任命,对总统负责;总统向国会报告工作,但无权解散国会,对国会通过的法案可行使否决权。因此美国的总统有职有权。

四、首相与总统

英国首相与总统所处的地位大相径庭。主要表现在:

1. 产生方式迥异

首相由议会多数党党魁出任;总统由全民选举,经选举团间接产生。

2. 与议会关系有别

首相提出的政策法案,往往原封不动地获议会批准,概率要大大高于总统,因为首相由执政党出任,在议会占有多数席位;美国总统掌执行政部门,而国会的多数席位往往受反对党控制,如里根、老布什和克林顿政府都处于通过一个法案都得与国会激烈较量一番的局面。再则,有的法案即使最终获国会批准,议会占多数议席的反对党总要加上了一些附加条款,有的多得犹如 christmas-tree bill。此外,首相对本党议员的控制力要大于总统。因为在美国,即使是本党议员也不一定支持根据总统建议提出的法案,在议员看来,"All politics is local."

3. 行政权分大小

英国政府的内阁是议会遴选首相为首的内阁,要对议会负责;美国政府的内阁由总统直接掌控,不对国会负责。因而总统的行政权要大于首相,国会在有些大事上如战争往往限制不了总统,且总统有着首相没有的行政特权。

4. 任期长短各别

总统任期是固定的;首相任期名为五年,却可因不信任案或因执政党提前大选等而随时或可能提前走人。

首相无任期限制,例如撒切尔夫人和布莱尔都曾连续三次担任首相。美国总统现在只限连任两届。

5. 助手顾问班子规模大小有别

总统的助手和顾问团班子庞大,除内阁外,总统有着人数可观、班底齐全的总统府人员和非正式的私人顾问团(kitchen cabinet)。单一政体下的首相则只需要小得可怜的内阁秘书处和若干私人助手。这是因为总统往往要应对一个对立政党占多数议席的国会对其施政方针的制衡而不得不有一个庞大齐全的助手和顾问班子;国会也成立了与行政部门相对应的几十个委员会(committee),还有几百个其他小组委员会(subcommittee)。庞大的政府机构表明,二元制政体有利也有弊。

五、议会(Parliament & Congress)

英国实行的是"议会制",而美国则为"总统制",两者有很大差异。

1. 两院制各有千秋

英美两国议会均效仿古罗马的两院制。英国贵族院(又称上院)主要由新封和世袭贵族、上诉法院法官和教会首要人物组成,不经选举产生,也无实权。法案绝大多数由首相和内阁直接提出,先在下院获得批准,再送上院通过,最后呈送女王御准后成为法律。上院和女王无否决权,只是走走形式而已。

美国参众两院议员均由直接选举产生,握有能与总统相抗衡的实权。法案由议员提出,总统只能提出立法建议,在参众两院获得批准后,才交总统签署后成为法律。但总统可行使否决权。在个别情况下,总统否决的法案,如国会仍以三分之二多数重新通过,无须经总统签署,自动成为法律。如里根任总统时,对前南非白人政权采取姑息政策,与其接触交往。国会贸易制裁法案就是这样通过的。

2. 议席多寡讲究各异

美国国会中有多数党和少数党,由共和党和民主党在参众两院所占的席位多寡而定,值得注意的是,多数党不一定是执政党,往往是在野党。这与英国情况不同,英国议会的多数党一定是执政党。

3. 官职名称不尽相同

UK	US
Speakers(上院和下院)议长	Speaker 众议院议长；President 参议院议长
Deputy Speakers 副议长	President Pro Tempore 参议院临时议长
(Government/Opposition)Chief Whips(执政党和反对党的)总督导或督导长	Majority Leaders (参众两院)多数党领袖
Deputy Chief Whips(执政党和反对党)副总督导	Minority Leaders (参众两院)少数党领袖
Whips 督导	Assistant Majority/Minority Leaders(参众两院)多数党或少数党副领袖即 Majority/Minority whip
Assistant Whips 助理督导	Deputy whips 副督导

4. 官职不能相互套用

需要注意的是，英美议会的官职有的不能相互套用，否则会引起歧义而产生误解。如果把美国的"Majority Leader/Whip"用于英国议会政党官职，人们会误解为"执政党首相/督导"，因为在英国议会的多数党即执政党；"Minority Leader/Whip"为"反对党领袖/督导"。反之亦然，如将英国的 Government (Chief)Whip 用于美国国会，也会产生误解。

议长的英文称谓美国参议院既用 President，报刊用 Chairman 是非正规用词。此外，参众两院都无正式的副议长和 Assistant Whip。从表上可以看出，英国的 Chief Whip = 美国的 Majority/Minority Leader；Deputy Chief Whip = Majority/Minority Whip。

5. 政党督导或领袖能否兼职有别

英国是议会制，立法行政是一体，所以执政党的 13 位督导均在王室和行政部门任职；美国的多数党和少数党领袖和督导及议员均不得担任行政职务。

6. 重大法案通过与否　政府和议会影响各异

在美国，法案遭否决，总统照干，国会也不用解散，重新大选；如果英国议会拒绝批准政府重要的施政方针或法案，说明执政党内有人造反或跳槽，丧失占多数议席的地位，因此法案不得人心。或政府总辞职，或解散议会，举行大选。议会通过对政府(指首相和内阁)不信任案，也是一样的后果。这是因为美国是行政和立法分治的二元制政治体制；英国是议会制，议会是最高权力机关，政府(指内阁)要对议会负责，是一元制体制。议会强烈不满，执政党就有下台危险。这就部分回答了本节开头提出的问题。

7. (Party) Whip 权力大小不等

正因为法案和不信任案通过与否对英美政府和议会影响不同,英国的党鞭责任重大,必须实行铁的纪律。党员如不按党的路线投票,执政党可能成为在野党;在野党也可能因此成为执政党或继续成为在野党。

美国的党鞭权力不如英国的大,控制不了本党议员,不能令其按本党方针路线投票,因为美国是二元制政治体制。请看:

Party Whips, a hallmark of parliamentary systems, are much less powerful in the U.S. political system and rarely can compel a particular lawmaker to vote a particular way. Votes in the U.S. Congress are not typically cast wholly along party lines, as is the case in many parliamentary systems. (*Campaign Spotlight*)

再看英国当时执政的保守党为追随美国的老布什总统 1991 年发动第一次伊拉克战争,而工党内部却存在着对伊拉克"制裁派"和"战争派"。下面的报道对比了两国的党纪和英国政党对不听话的党员软硬兼施的做法。

There has been no British equivalent of the ambitious young anti-war American congressmen—not so surprising in a country whose last experience of war was the successful Falklands venture(即英国和阿根廷之间发生于 1982 年的福克兰群岛战争), rather than Vietnam(越战), and whose politics is based on the iron disciplines of the British party machine.

Instead, dissent has been left to Labour left-wingers beyond the reach of party whips(这里指工党左翼政治家不怕党鞭纪律制裁,反对开战或提前开战), and two elder statesmen already sated with carrots and unimpressed by sticks. (而两位政界元老对两党的软硬兼施策略虽已厌烦,但已习以为常,无动于衷) Those old enemies, the former Tory prime minister Edward Heath(the only senior Tory to oppose an early war with Iraq), and Mr Healey, are now working in parallel; they met this week for discussions at the Centre for Global Energy Studies in London, set up by the former Saudi oil minister, Sheikh Yamani. (*The Economist*)

六、内阁(Cabinet)

1. 内阁组成、作用和成员背景有别

英国的内阁由首相、枢密院院长及外交、国防和财政等重要大臣组成,通称内阁大臣(cabinet ministers),必须是议会多数党或执政党上院或下院议员。检察总长、政务、经济和财务等部次官及国务大臣等则为非内阁大臣(non-cabinet ministers)。

英国内阁是行政决策的核心；美国是总统制，内阁无决策权，只起顾问作用，由各部部长(secretaries)和总统指定的其他官员如总统安全事务特别助理等组成，无非内阁部长。但一些直属局等单位的负责人，如中央情报局局长、美国贸易谈判代表等为非内阁成员(non-cabinet members)。此外，内阁成员不能是国会议员、行政和立法部门官员都不能相互兼职，总统还可任命个别在野党人士担任阁员。

2. 两码事的 Shadow Cabinet 和 Kitchen Cabinet

因选举制不同，英国有"影子内阁"；美国却没有，也无必要。总统却有个所谓的"厨房内阁"，是总统非正式的私人顾问团，作用大，有"核心内阁"之称。这两个"内阁"是两回事，后者是戏称，因他们常同总统在厨房聚会，商讨和决定施政大计。

七、大选(General Election)

1. 覆盖的面大小各别

英美大选各异，美国大选常称"总统选举"(presidential election)，包括联邦、州和地方官员的选举；英国大选只是选举下院议员的议会选举。

2. 总统首相选举大相径庭

总统与议员选举虽有联系，但却是同时分别举行的选举，由于选举同日举行，结果随出随报，举国关注，媒体随即评论，这点可以办到。当然最后结果可能是两回事。细心的读者会发现 general elections 用复数，指 Congressional/legislative election 加 presidential election。如大选只指总统选举或中期只指国会选举，用单数即可。如民主党两院席位均占多数，是多数党，但总统可能是共和党人。这种格局在美国政坛常现。甚至是选民有意为之，以便相互制衡，跟三权分立用意相同。民主党奥巴马政权府会均占多数，反映出人心思变的迫切性。

英国实行的是议会制民主，大选事实上是英国议会选举，哪个党在下院获得多数议席，就成为执政党，英王便任命执政党领袖(the Leader)为首相。也就是说，英国行政领导人的选定或选举与立法选举(executive/Parliamentary/legislative election)是一回事，议会中的多数党一定是执政党。日本、印度等国都是如此。

3. 政党作用有别

美国是总统制，实行的是以总统候选人而不是以政党为中心的选举；在英国，政党处于选举和其后政府治理的中心。在美国，尽管政党在选举中具有重要作用，总统候选人能否当选，关键靠他/她本人是否是 presidential timber。所以美国有套用的政治名言入木三分地说："All politics is personal."（千选，万选，全是本人在竞选）。("All politics is local"见"**政治名言的理解与翻译**")

4. 定期与否分得清

美国大选的日期是固定的,每 4 年一次,不能更改,又称"常规或定期选举"(regular election)。角逐者可以从容准备;英国每 5 年一次大选,但在位首相可趁有利时机随时要求女王解散议会(dissolve Parliament),提前举行大选(go to the country)。如 1983 年和 1987 年的两次大选,首相撒切尔夫人的任期还有一年才届满,但根据民意测验和地方选举的结果,她提前举行大选,结果保守党连胜两次。布莱尔也是如此,1997 年 5 月上台执政,本来在 2002 年 5 月举行的大选提前到 2001 年 6 月 7 日。2005 年举行的选举也是如此。这两次工党也获得了胜利。当然也有失算的。例如前首相希斯就在 1974 年的闪电式选举中败北。这种突然袭击式选举对执政党极为有利,迫使主要反对党随时应战,只好组成影子内阁或预备内阁(Shadow Cabinet),阁员称为影子内阁大臣(Shadow Minister)或某方面事务如外交事务发言人(Foreign Affairs Spokesman),以便熟悉情况,随时准备执政。现在一些小党主张废除陈规,改为固定任期制。这与五、议会 6. 重大法案通过与否……就全部回答了本节开头提出的问题。

八、政党

政党是美英两国政治制度的基础,两国又都是两大政党轮流执政。然而由于组织上和政体上的不同,政党间也存在差异。

1. 政党组织分松紧

美国的联邦制和总统制都有组织上分散的特点,政策权力分散在州和地方基层党组织,在竞选中的 primary 和 caucus 最后到 party national convention 便说明了这一特点。不在选举年,全国政党组织几乎不存在,而且各级党组织人士变动频繁;英国的议会民主制和君主制以集中为特点,立法行政一体,因党的组织和目标单一,各政党为迎接大选等活动必须常备不懈,弦绷得较紧,总是盯着决定议会席位多寡和行政首脑的选定的大选以及选后的政府治理。政党充分发挥作用。美国却不同,政党力量和作用较弱。

2. 领袖地位各高低

选举制度不同,政党领袖地位各异。英国政党领袖地位较稳固,即使大选失利,仍是党头头,除非改选落马。美国的总统候选人为该党当然领袖,大选失利,地位随之泡汤。这样,该党群龙无首,直到四年后下一次的党代会推选出总统候选人。英国的反对党一定要有领袖,而美国的在野党就难说。这跟英国随时可以提前大选有关。

3. 竞选策略有区别

英国国土面积小,人口组成相对单一。而美国是庞然大物,人口组成复杂。

有着各种对立派别、阶级、种族和社会利益团体，众口难调。在竞选中，政党必须投其所好。相形之下，英国两大党都支持社会福利计划，又没有那么多派别和利益对立团体，即便苏格兰、威尔士的要求和需要与众不同，也无伤大局。因而各党竞选策略比较单一，目标比较统一，"得伦敦者得天下。"London 是首都，英最大城市，占人口 1/7，是政治、文化、经济、金融中心，许多大企业总部，也是新闻宣传中心，力量辐射全国。

4. 党纪有无显异同

英国执政党提案获议会批准可以预料，党纪是紧箍咒，党员必须投赞成票；美国党中有党，派中有派。常因眼前利益同床异梦(strange bedfellows)。例如国会中共和党和民主党保守派(Republican and Democratic conservatives)可以临时携手反对两党自由派(liberals)的提案。更为奇怪的是，有些议员为了维护本州落后的如军工企业，使工人就率高，竟与其他具有同样情况州的议员结盟，反对此项法案，而不管这些议员是何党何派，以从联邦政府的 pork barrel（腌肉桶；喻联邦政府财政部，政治分肥）多捞几块肉吃，讨好本州选民。这犹如 logrolling，邻居们为劈林种地，抛开分歧和成见，相互合作，一起"滚木头"一样。对此，政党领袖只好干瞪眼。英国的议会候选人靠党吃饭，不是靠其个人奋斗，选举围着政党转，候选人腰杆子不硬，当选后得乖乖听党的话，否则竞选连任没戏；美国议员候选人正好相反，虽然有威望的总统和政党，可以帮助筹款，但在竞选期间，候选人的竞选班子代替了党组织，政党退居处于次要地位，当选后自然就目无党纪，所关注是竞选连任，投票着眼选区利益，唯恐落下把柄，秋后算账，而不是考虑整个国家福祉。美国名言"All politics is local."道破天机。

5. 属性强调见轻重

英国是议会制，政党与领袖密不可分。美国却不同，政党较弱，纪律松弛。领袖或总统候选人的政党标志不如英国那么突出，拉票，敲敲边鼓。政党可做出抛弃本党无望获胜的人士，选择政党倾向不明确者作候选人。说白一点，犹如赛马，不管张三李四，谁胜出希望最大，就挑选(recruit)当总统候选人。1952 年共和党抛弃 Robert Taft 而选择 David Eisenhower 就是明证。再如第 17 任总统 A. 约翰逊是民主党人，被共和党提名为林肯的竞选搭档(runningmate)。获胜后，任副总统。1865 年林肯被刺身亡后，他接任总统。奥巴马击败希拉里，当上总统候选人，靠的就是改革调子最高，胜出希望最大。

此外，候选人在竞选前可以出于有利竞选的目的而改变党派色彩或脱党。例如现任纽约市市长 Michael Bloomberg 就是"Democrat-turned-Republican mayor"。2008 年他又想以"third-party or independent candidate"身份竞选总统。这在英国少见。

6. 政策主张不尽同

英国的保守党与美国的共和党有相似之处,两党都属保守派,代表强势群体。然而,在税收上却各行其是。共和党倡"减税",以鼓励投资与生产;保守党则在国营企业私有化上下工夫。财政政策也有不同。例如共和党总统里根就不断举债,扩大军费开支,而保守党的撒切尔夫人则着眼平衡开支。但两者都强调自由竞争,市场经济至上,大砍社会福利。

工党与民主党较相似,都代表弱势群体,工会都是其坚定的支持者。然而,以前的工党宣传"国有化"和"社会主义",与民主党党纲截然相反。再则,2007年后的"新工党"对待工会势力与民主党一样,主张不断加强相互支持,2009年还闹出丑闻(见"**语言**""改朝换代产生和流行的词语"二、英国)。两党都倡导在资本主义与社会主义之间走"第三条道路"。此外,英美国内对立两党也并非水火完全不能相容,趋同地方也不少,出现了两党政治(bipartisan politics)的说法。

在西方国家中,两党轮流执政的格局以英美为代表,与此不同的是一党独大,或多党共存。日本的自民党,由于执政太久,下台以后,竟然没有一个政党可以举起大旗,导致组阁困难,组成以后也险象频生,直到2009年民主党上台执政才改变这一局面。意大利在过去,经常要靠组织联合政府才可组成一届政府,但组成以后,往往不能长寿。2010年大选后的英国说不定也会步前意大利和现以色列后尘。这样一比,两党政治有它的优点。

7. 在朝在野境遇异

由于美国实行的三权分立,若国会是民主党人占多数议席,则总统往往由共和党人担任。反之亦然。最高法院多年来一直是5比4,持共和党保守派观点的在法官多一票。所以,常常是 the party in/out of the white House。2008年 Barack Obama 当选总统后,国会也由民主党把持,有一名保守派法官要退休,Obama 趁机任命一位持自由派观点者,而使民主党就成了真正意义上的 the government party,共和党则成为 the opposition party。这样,施改纲领就较易获得国会通过。这在美国历史上是不多见的几次中的一次,不过一般只能持续两年。

英国是一元制国家,执政党必须在议会占过半数席位,否则就得下台,成了反对党。还有的国家,一个政党虽然议席占多数,但未过半,达不到组阁要求,所提法案不能保证获得批准的票数,就得与其他小党或大党组成联合内阁(coalition government)。否则,地位不保,政府(指首相和内阁)随时会倒台,像一度的日本和现在的以色列等国,首相频换就是这个道理。

8. 竞选:政党作用大小殊(见七、"大选")

9. 左派右派

左派和右派(the left and the right)指政策主张相对开明或保守。源出英国议会的座位安排,在传统的英国议会中,辉格党(the Whigs,工党的前身)一向坐在议事大厅的左边,而托利党(the Tories,保守党的前身)则坐在右边。这是左派、右派政治术语的由来。美国参众两院亦采用了这种安排:民主党员坐在国会会场左边,而共和党员则坐在右边。

  left wing"左翼"指持相当开明观点的政界人士;而 leftist"左派"一词,在西方人眼里,一般指共产主义者、马克思主义者或社会主义者。

第四节 其他方面的读报知识

一、各国体制形形色色

当今世界 190 多个国家中,国体(state system)名称的形式各种各样,标有国家称谓的有以下十种:

共和国(Republic)指国家代表机关和国家元首由选举产生。现今世界上有 125 个共和国,如法兰西共和国等。

王国(Kingdom)指国王为国家元首的君主立宪制国家,如英国国名为大不列颠及北爱尔兰联合王国。现今全球共有 16 个王国。

公国(Principality)是君主立宪制的一种形式,如安道尔公国、列支敦士登公国等。

大公国(Grand Duchy)君主称为"大公",由大公掌握国家权力的国家,如卢森堡大公国等。

联邦(Confederation)由若干成员国、邦、州或地区组成的统一国家,如瑞士联邦等,有的国家称之为"联盟"。

合众国(United States)是联邦制的一种形式,如美利坚合众国、墨西哥合众国等。

民众国(Mass-State)禁止一切政党活动,是没有政党的国家,如大阿拉伯利比亚人民社会主义民众国。

酋长国(Emirates)以部落酋长为国家元首的国家,如阿拉伯联合酋长国等。

教皇国(Papal States)以教皇为国家元首的国家,如以前的梵蒂冈,现改为梵蒂冈城国(Vatican City)。

苏丹国(State of the Sudan)一切执行权归苏丹的国家,如前阿曼苏丹国,现为苏丹共和国等。

世界上还有一部分国家,由于政体的特殊性,没有标明国家的属性。如日本、巴林国等。

二、议会名称林林总总

世界各国议会名称不尽相同,除英联邦国家叫 Parliament 以及美国和拉丁美洲一些国家用 Congress 外,法国和一些讲法语的非洲国家用 National Assembly(国民议会,下院),葡萄牙、土耳其、科威特、约旦等国也称国民议会。阿富汗是 Grand Assembly(大国民会议),阿文是 Loya Jirga(支尔格大会)。还有的国家如斯洛文尼亚议会只用 Assembly。此外,希伯来语 Knesset 为以色列议会,挪威议会用 Parliament 或挪威文 Storting,瑞典的 Parliament 也用瑞典文 Riksdag,丹麦的 Parliament 用 Diet 或丹麦文 Folketing,芬兰用芬兰文 Eduskunta,西班牙用西班牙文 Cortes,德国是 Federal Assembly(联邦议院),德语为 Bundestag,俄罗斯为 State Duma(国家杜马),中国是 National People's Congress(全国人民代表大会),日本的国会叫 Diet,摩纳哥公国叫 National Council(全国议会),现在这些议会名称已被收入英语词汇的远非全部,但也足以证明议会名称之多了。

记者在选择议会用词时,常用外来语,这在"**报刊语言主要特点**""七、其他特点"已经论及,此处不赘。不妨举个例句,小布什访问一些中东和阿拉伯国家时,有刊物就是这样用的:The Bush Administration... In a speech to Israel's **Knesset**, which was regarded as an attack on Barack Obama and other Democrats.(2008/5/26 *Newsweek*)

三、人名背后文章多

人名是读报知识不可或缺的组成部分。本节不讨论原是专用人名后来成了普通名词的词语,如 boycott(抵制)、guillotine(断头台)和 sandwich 等;也暂不谈文学作品中的一些人物的喻义,如 Babbit 喻"典型的市侩或实业家",Gatsby "暴发户",Micawber "幻想突然走运的乐天派",uncle Tom "听命(于白人)"或 "逆来顺受,讨好(别人)",等等;更不谈像 Bill Gates 喻"世界首富"这样人人皆知的人名。这里想探讨一些初学者不晓而又常见诸报端的公众人物,若我们熟悉西方当代名人(notable personalities)及其名代表何义及说明什么,就可理解得更透,乃至哑然失笑。

1. 绰号简称常成拦路虎

见了绰号或简称,莫名其妙。如:

(1) **Bubba** and **Dubya**:Warming Up(*Newsweek*)

(2) It's smaller than you'd think. Coming off a clockwork convention. Bush last week shook Kerry's support in crucial Blue States and gained ground in the Southwest. But **W** still doesn't stand for "wrapped up."(*Newsweek*)

这两例有两个问题:Bubba 指的是谁? Dubya 和 2 例中的 W 又指的是谁?

Bubba 乡巴佬,指美国前总统克林顿。一般以开玩笑的口吻对傻乎乎的美国南部乡巴佬或土包子的称呼。克林顿虽毕业于耶鲁大学,并游学牛津大学,但毕竟出生于阿肯色的穷乡僻壤,所以得此诨名。前总统 L. 约翰逊也曾被称为"Bubba"。

第(2)例"W"指是 George W(ashington) Bush（即 junior Bush 或 Bush junior）。如指 elder/senior Bush 则说 George Bush。因父子两人都曾任总统。"Dubya"是美国南方人对字母"W"的发音，为此有人故意将小布什写作 George Dubya Bush。

2. 政策思想藏人名

人名可代表某人的政策思想主张或党派标志。如提到经济学家 John Keynes 就知其主张扩大政府开支、实行财政赤字，刺激经济、维持繁荣的政策。西方当前应付金融与经济危机，采取的就是其做法。Joseph McCarthy 或 McCarthyism 等于"迫害狂"、"白色恐怖"或"反共歇斯底里"的代名词。《时代》周刊和《新闻周刊》1992 年 8 月各有一篇文章用人名喻指政策主张的例句：

(1) Americans by and large don't want great swings in the conduct of foreign affairs, which is why a **Barry Goldwater** or a **George McGovern** doesn't get elected; the art form rests in reinventing the center. (*Time*)

若不了解这两个人的背景就不知戈德华特和麦戈文都曾作为美国共和党和民主党总统候选人参选总统。由于前者持极右路线，是个疯狂反共、反华派参议员，曾鼓吹轰炸苏联，并由此而有人造出了一个"Goldwaterize"的字，意为"使选民认识到候选人或其政治主张对社会的危害而感到害怕"；后者持极左路线，曾提出激进的社会和政治改革方案，并许诺要不惜一切代价结束越南战争。所以他们都未能当选。现在这两个人的名字已分别成了"极右"或"极端保守派"和"极左"的代名词。据此，我们就知道此例意为："美国人基本上不喜欢在外事上左右摇摆太大。这就是戈德华特式或麦戈文式的候选人落选的原因。竞选的技巧在于不左不右，根据形势重新确立新的中间立场。"

(2) We should neither **McGovern** our foreign policy nor have **Jesse** at the helm. (*Newsweek*)

这里 McGovern 成了动词，不过在当初 *Who's Who in America* 或美国百科全书中都能查到此君。可是 Jesse 又是何许人也？若读者不知道此人的全名及其政策主张就很难从工具书和网络上查寻到。美国民权运动领袖也叫 Jesse (Jackson)，可是其政策主张与例句中的意思不符。知情者一看就知道，他就是曾红极一时，生前曾任国会参议院军事委员会主席的赫尔姆斯(Jesse Helms)。主张与 Goldwater 如出一辙，反共、反华，可以说是 Goldwater 的接班人。此人还提出了带有治外法权色彩的 Helms-Burton Act（赫尔姆斯—伯顿法），D'Amato Act（达马托法）及反对堕胎的 Helms-Hyde Bill（赫尔姆斯—海德法案）。这样，我们知道此例意为："我们既不应该让麦戈文那样的极左派掌管对外政策，也不应该让杰西这样的极右派在对外政策上掌舵。"

因此，要看美国国会自由派和保守派争斗的文章，非了解此人的身世不可。又如：英国《金融时报》在克林顿执政 1994 年底发表的一文中有两个带有人名的词语也含有党派特点：

（3）**The Gingrich Congress** also passed ambitious legislation to deregulate （取消管制）the telecommunications market and to begin what will be a long battle to eliminate farm subsidies.（*Financial Times*）

（4）In this year's state of the union address he [Clinton] sought voter approval by solemnly declaring "the era of big government is over" —a line that could have come straight out of **the Gingrich contract.**（*Financial Times*）

何谓"the Gingrich Congress"，"the Gingrich contract"及"The Gingrich revolution"？如不了解 Gingrich 其人其事和 Contract with America 就会一头雾水。

Newt Gingrich 纽特·金里奇曾一度是美国共和党保守派头面人物。1994 年中期选举，共和党人在国会的参众两院都成了多数党，金里奇当选为第 104 届国会众议院议长，这就意味着该院被极端保守派所控制。他当时踌躇满志，雄心勃勃，提出了许多如"与美国签订契约"（即向美国社会作出承诺，套用法国思想家卢梭的《社会契约论》The Social Contract，也译《民约论》）等主张，并处处与克林顿政府（the Clinton Administration）较劲，曾迫使政府 shutdown 等。因多数主张过于偏激，一年多他就从巅峰上掉了下来。后来还由于偷漏税受到国会的公开斥责（censure）。在 1998 年的国会中期选举中，共和党虽然仍保留了国会多数党的地位，但他过度渲染克林顿绯闻造势，反而导致共和党议席减少，引起党内不满。此事说明，在民主制度下，甚至政党也不能左右民意。他的失败实际上与 Goldwater 和 Helms 一样，是美国极端保守派失势。所谓 Gingrich contract 即 Contract with America。而 Gingrich revolution 也称 1994 Republican revolution，即共和党提出了 Contract with America 的 10 项保守派的改革计划。

3. 公司品牌人名见

人名可代表知名公司、品牌乃至方法或内容的创新。如 Wal-Mart, J. P. Morgan, Morgan Stanley, B & Q 等美英知名大公司都是以其创始人命名的。再如：Ford 既代表 Ford Motor Company，也代表其创造的生产流水作业法（assembly line method）。又如：美国著名黑人女节目主持人 Oprah Winfrey 创造了热门节目 Talk Show（脱口秀）。下面这些新词就是很好的例证：

（1）Oprahbate 奥普拉式辩论，即访谈式竞选辩论，不需要主持人做中间人，而直接由在场选民提问，美国总统候选人就此展开辩论，尤指 1992 年老布什和克林顿之间进行的第二次辩论（＝talk-show debate）。（由 Oprah 和 [de]bate 缩

合而成)

(2) Oprahfication 竞选奥普拉化,即访谈式竞选,指由选民参与、以个人提问题为重点的访谈式竞选(=talk-show campaign)(由 Oprah + -fication 组合而成)

这两个字在当时网络不发达时由两本英汉词典收录为条目,可都未说明 Oprah 是美国家喻户晓的"名人访谈节目"或"脱口秀"(Talk Show)主持人。她是黑人,全名为 Oprah Winfrey。如不了解她背景具有"访谈"的意思就出不来解释。

4. 性格抱负人心显

(1) **The Hillary Factor**, when the phrase was coined, referred to the question: Will Hillary Clinton help or hinder her husband's chances? But **the real Hillary Factor** is the double bind(进退两难) that affects all successful or accomplished women—indeed, all women who do not fit stereotypical images of femininity: women who are not clearly submissive are seen as dominating and are reviled for it.

Hillary Factor 希拉里因素,喻女强人倾向,对丈夫仕途的影响祸福参半。如希拉里对克林顿竞选是帮忙还是添乱? Hillary Clinton 毕业于耶鲁大学法学院,获博士学位,据传能力超克林顿,权力欲极强。克林顿卸任后,她旋即竞选成功纽约州国会参议员,2008 年争夺总统候选人提名失利,出任奥巴马政府的国务卿。新闻界认为,这种现象反而在政界会引起人们的忧虑,同时,这种缺乏柔顺气质,支配欲强的女人反而招惹男尊女卑偏见的责难。如 2008 年她在竞选时,有人喊:"A woman's place is in the home."就是典型的例子。

(2) Those who urge a last-ditch stand against Soviet influence everywhere, a sort of **Churchillian resistance** sometimes suggested by apocalyptic right-wingers, overestimate both our will and our resources. (*Foreign Affairs*)

若不了解二战时期的英国首相丘吉尔(Winston Churchill)是个反共、反苏(联)人物,就不了解为什么 1946 年他在美国密苏里州富尔顿市指责苏联设置了一道 iron curtain(铁幕),隔断了欧洲大陆,从而开始了美苏几十年 Cold War 的历史。若不知道在二战时德国狂轰滥炸,迫英屈服,而他性格坚强,领导英国"不屈不挠抵抗",就不理解 Churchillian resistance 是什么意思。

5. 名人经历蕴玄机

了解名人的生平尤其是重要履历就会知晓有的片言只语和外号指的是何人、何意及语言出处。如:

(1) The new world order is American, and it's being run by a **CIA President.** (*Newsweek*)

此处 CIA president 不是中央情报局局长,局长为 CIA Director。至 2008 年选出总统后共有 43 位,其中只有老布什(George Bush)在 1976 至 1977 年出任过 CIA 局长,那么这个 CIA President 就非他莫属。当初同党的共和党总统福特任命他任此职时,他任驻华联络处主任,竞选总统的兴致甚高。对此任命,他认为是有人想断送其仕途,因为 CIA 很臭,国内外都不得人心。无独有偶,俄罗斯的普京就曾被西方报刊称之为 "KGB President",因为他在克格勃工作过。再如:

(2) We have got to and will continue right down that path. And I [George Bush] hope it is the path that leads to peace. But you asked the toughest question of all. I had a Congressman in here today, and he said to me, "You know, my brother was killed in Vietnam. You've just got to wait." And I said, **"You are looking at a guy that had a squadron of** 15, **and nine of them were killed in one way or another.** I know exactly what you are talking about." ("Determined To Do What Is Right", *Time*, January 7, 1991)

这篇文章采访的是老布什,谈的是即将发动的第一次海湾(伊拉克)战争。这里,如果在注释中只是简单地介绍一下 George Bush 何年何月任美国总统和副总统,而不介绍他在二战时曾在海军航空兵中队中任过尉官的这段经历:After graduating from Phillips Academy in Andover, Massachusetts, Bush, at 18, became the youngest commissioned pilot in the U. S. Navy during World War Ⅱ, flying 58 combat missions in the Pacific. 那么就不知道布什所说的 "a guy" 就是指他本人。

(3) **The Great Communicator** was back from the nation's heartland, his spirits buoyed by the belief that he had made headway in the most difficult selling job so far in his presidency: convincing Americans, particularly skeptical Republicans, that they should accept his record 1983 budget—and its record $91.5 billion deficit. (*Time*)

(4) Seven years after he left office, we may have forgotten why Ronald Reagan was dubbed **the Great Communicator.** (*Newsweek*)

了解前总统里根的经历后就知道 "交流大师" 或 "沟通高手" 都是里根的美称。不少媒体认为,里根之所以能两次赢得大选的一个重要原因是他当过电台体育节目广播员和演员,表演和表达能力俱佳,能将自己的主张、纲领等如演戏般把好的一面表达出来而赢得选民的好感,因而与选民的关系和谐融洽

(comfort factor),请看一家杂志的分析报道:"How much of the President's popularity will rub off on other Republicans in the future is the big question. Most experts agreed that Reagan's triumph stemmed mainly from the '**comfort factor**'—his personal rapport with voters."(*U.S. News & World Report*)

关于里根,下面再举一例:

(5) Most of all, Ronald Reagan made us proud to be Americans again. We never felt better about our country and we never stood taller in the eyes of the world when **the Gipper** was at the helm. (*The New York Times*)

为什么说:"吉普尔掌舵"和"让我们为吉普尔胜一场/打胜这一场"? 吉普尔与里根有何关系? 美国圣母大学(University of Notre Dame)在20世纪20年代是全美常胜的橄榄球队, Gipper是该队最佳选手George Gipp的外号,25岁病故前嘱咐教练Knute Rockne: "Someday when things look real tough for Notre Dame, ask the boys to go out and win for me."一次比赛败局已定时,教练就用"为Gipper争光"的口号来激励士气,反败为胜。这段体坛佳话拍成电影,扮演Gipper者正是日后当总统的里根,他竞选时常用"Let's win this one for the Gipper"拉票。这样"the Gipper"就成绰号,连吉普车牌照也是吉普尔(jeep with the license plate GIPPER)。使用时省去"Let's",只用"Win one for the Gipper"。

不但如此,里根任总统期间,他在演说和国情咨文报告中有时还引用了影片中的台词,如"Go ahead—make my day"等。

我们知道里根从政前是演员,就可猜出在引用台词,除"Let's win this one for the Gipper"外,还有:

(6) I have my veto pen drawn and ready for any tax increase that Congress might even think of sending up. And I have only one thing to say to the tax increasers. **Go ahead—make my day.**(见"政治名言的理解与翻译")

(7) Where we are going, we don't need roads.

这是里根1986年2月4日在国会作国情咨文报告中所引用的"*Back to the Future*"的电影脚本中的台词。

综上所述,人物背景知识与对词语的理解,文字的分析有很大关系,建议读者应看一些有关美英两国自二战以来历任总统和首相的有关介绍文章或历史书籍,不但要记住他们的父姓和已名、简历,应尽可能记住他们在任职期间所推行的政策。美国总统提出了不少对外政策或主张,如 Eisenhower/Nixon/Reagan/Clinton/Bush Doctrine。英国首相也提出了不少对内政策或主张,如Thatherism, Blarism 等。

应该说明,上述名人的喻义决不全面,相信在报刊中一定还有更多其他喻义。

6. 作品人物寓意深

在当今的报刊中,古希腊和罗马政治家和学者、神话中的诸神和圣经人物及其他文学作品中的人物随处可见。除开头提到外,再如 Homer, Cleopatra, Noah's Ark, the Achilles' heel, King Arthur and his Camelot 等也常见报,文学尤其古典文学或西方文明,乃是报刊语言文化之渊源。

四、地名里头有名堂

1. 地名作喻词不少见

这在"常见借喻词和提喻词"里已举多例,下面只再举一例:

As a new school principal, Mr. Mitchell was checking over his school on the first day. Passing the stockroom, he was startled to see the door wide open and teachers bustling in and out, carrying off books and supplies in preparation for the arrival of students the next day. The school where he had been a Principal the previous year had used a check-out system only slightly less elaborate than that at **Fort Knox.**

第二段最后一句话的后半句为什么说"那个学校的出库制度(check-out system)之严仅次于诺克斯堡(Fort Knox)"呢?

Fort Knox location since 1936 of U. S. Gold Bullion Depository(自1936年后,它就是美国金库所在地或黄金的储存地),难怪其出库制度该严厉到何种程度了。所以 as safe as Fort Knox 或 like Fort Knox 比喻"非常安全保险"。

2. 地名暗喻贫富

在英文里有直接用地名来喻贫富。如以前在英国文学作品中描写伦敦的 the East end 和 the west end(东区和西区)就暗喻"穷人区"和"富人区"。下面再举一例:

"The U. S. is no longer a full ambulance service," Chan says. "It only goes to the rescue if **Beverly Hills** is on fire. It may turn a deaf ear to one in **Harlem or Bronx.** "(*Time*)

《时代》周刊为什么说 Beverly Hills 失火有人救,Harlem 和 Bronx 遭灾无人问呢?原来美国,穷富两重天啊!Beverly Hills 贝弗利山(庄)是洛杉矶富人区,在好莱坞附近,电影明星的豪华别墅成片,也喻"明星阶级"。Harlem and Bronx 哈莱姆和布朗克斯是纽约市穷人区(Borough)。在美国,去 Las Vegas 或 Disney World 所在地佛罗里达的 Orlando,就意味着吃喝玩乐。提到华盛顿的

Arlington 就意味着到 National Cemetery 去哀悼亡故者的悲哀。提 New York City 的 World Trade Center 就对恐怖主义咬牙切齿，又对死难者寄予绵绵哀思。

五、地名面前防陷阱

地名混淆，常闹笑话，如 Black Africa 指哪些国家或何地？与 sub-Saharan Africa/countries 有区别吗？其实是一码事。据 1999 年统计，包括南非、肯尼亚、津巴布韦、马拉维等国在内的 46 个国家。谈到非洲时这两个地名常交替见报。如：

The Third World is likely to produce new tests of the administration's diplomatic prowess. Pressure is mounting in the United States and in **Black Africa** for Washington to abandon its policy of "constructive engagement" with the racist regime in South Africa. (*Newsweek*)

一些国内和港台媒体甚至将作国名用的 Bosnia（波黑）都译错了，在外交上会捅大娄子。再如，叫苏丹的有几个国家？这也不能含糊。

1. 地域划分有讲究

除归属未定地区外，有的地域划法因国而异。例如英国等国将捷克、匈牙利、罗马尼亚等视为中欧国家，但我们和美国以前称之为东欧国家。The East 和 the West 指政治和经济概念，而不是地理概念。东方国家的日本和以色列、大洋洲的澳大利亚，新西兰也划入西方国家。俄罗斯和土耳其横跨欧亚大陆，俄自称是"欧亚国家"，土则愿被划入"欧洲国家"，力求加入欧盟捞好处。

2. 国名相似易混淆

据统计，到 2008 年 8 月，全世界已有 192 个国家（不包括科索沃 Kosovo）。有字同地异的，如 Georgia 在美国是佐治亚州，在中亚是格鲁吉亚国名；国名混淆也是常事：

1. Austria 与 Australia：Austria 奥地利；Australia 澳大利亚。

2. Congo 与 Congo Republic：Congo 的全称是 The Democratic Republic of the Congo，常作 Congo-Kinshasa（刚果［金］［沙萨］）；Congo Republic 的全称是：the Republic of the Congo，常作 Congo-Brazzarille［刚果（布）（拉柴维尔）］。

3. Liberia 与 Libya：Liberia 利比里亚，在非洲；Libya 利比亚，也在非洲。

4. Mauritius 与 Mauritania：Mauritius 毛里求斯，是岛国；Mauritania 毛里塔尼亚，同在非洲。

5. Morocco 与 Monaco：Morocco 摩洛哥，在非洲；Monaco 摩纳哥，在欧洲。

6. Niger 与 Nigeria：Niger 尼日尔；Nigeria 尼日利亚，均在非洲。

7. Republic of Serbia

塞尔维亚共和国有两个：一个指南斯拉夫、后为塞尔维亚共和国，是一个国家；波黑也有一个塞尔维亚共和国，但不是一个国家，是波黑的两个实体之一。常用塞尔维亚文书写"Republika Srpska"。

8. South Africa 与 southern Africa：South Africa 南非；southern Africa 南部非洲：常指赞比亚河以南的非洲国家和地区。见例句：

Yet the 1984 election did little to erase America's doubts about Reagan's ability in field of foreign policy. Opponents of the administration's military budget, its **southern Africa** policy...(*Newsweek*)

9. Switzerland 与 Swaziland：Switzerland 瑞士，在欧洲；Swaziland 斯威士兰，在非洲。

国名变更也使人产生误解，如 Côte d' Ivoire 以前的国名是 Ivory Coast(象牙海岸)，Sri LanKa 以前是 Ceylon(锡兰)，Congo 以前是 Zaire(扎伊尔)，Samoa 以前是 Western Samoa(西萨摩尔)等等；还有是英文的国名变更了，如缅甸，前用 Burma，现在是 Myanmar；Cambodia 一度用过 Kampuchea；还有的是国家消失了，原来的加盟或联邦共和国都纷纷脱离而独立成了主权国家，如苏联(the Soviet Union)和南斯拉夫(Yugoslavia)就是如此。不过在英美报刊中，像缅甸这样的情况，用 Burma 的多于 Myanmar；像上面的两个刚果的情况，更多地是一个用 the Congo，另一个用 Congo Republic，以示区分。而我国则分别用刚果(布)和刚果(金)。至于西方惯用的 North/South Korea 分别译为朝鲜和韩国，值得注意。

3. 首都多了区分难

学生常问："到底开普敦还是比勒陀利亚是南非首都？"可见学生往往用中国情况套用其他国家，认为一国只有一个首都。世界上有两个首都的国家现在共有四个(以色列除外)，他们是：

(1) Bolivia(玻利维亚)，首都(Capitals)：La Paz(administrative)(拉巴斯：行政首都，我国称"法定首都")，Sucre(Judicial)苏克雷：司法首都；(2) Côte d' Ivoire(科特迪瓦)，正式(official)首都是 Yamoussoukro(亚穆苏克罗)，事实(de falcto)首都 Abidjan(阿比让)，我国出版的《世界知识年鉴》称前者是政治首都，后者经济首都；(3) Montenegro(黑山)，行政首都 Podgorica(波德戈里察)，正式(official)首都 Cetinje(采蒂涅)；(4) The Netherlands(荷兰)，其正式首都 Amsterdam(阿斯特丹)，行政首都 The Hague(海牙)(我国称"政府所在地"首都)。

全球最多首都的国家数 South Africa，有立法、行政和司法三个首都：Pretoria(比勒陀利亚)，Cape Town(开普敦)和 Bloemfontein(布隆方丹)。

1948年以色列建国定都 Tel Aviv(特拉维夫)，次年迁往 Jerusalem，许多国家的大使馆仍设在 Tel Aviv。耶路撒冷是巴勒斯坦和以双方称首都，地位未定。缅甸首都原是 Yangon/Rangoon(仰光)，现定都 Naypyidaw(内比都)。韩国首都 Seoul 原称"汉城"，现改称"首尔"，个中原因，值得玩味。

与众不同的是，1996年出版的 The Oxford English Reference Dictionary (Second Edition)只列出上述国家一个首都，如 Bolivia 的首都是 La Paz，South Africa 是 Pretoria。大概认为立法首都即议会是最重要的，这涉及该国的政体是否与英国一致的问题。如系总统政体国家，行政首都就是最重要的。

六、时间弄清休马虎

1. 何谓"Chronology of World Events"

世界大事年表记载着各年代世界发生的重大事件，这也是读报知识的一部分。众所周知，历史知识是分析文学和语言作参考的重大文化背景知识。本章不谈新闻写作中的五个"W"里的"时间"，也不谈国家和宗教及习俗节日，翻开美国出版的 The World Almanac（《世界年鉴》），首先映入眼帘的是"Chronology of Events"(大事年表)，它按年月日分 National(美国内)，International 和 General 三部分。打开 The Oxford English Reference Dictionary 的附录(Appendices)，第一个便是"Chronology of World Events"，从远古一直记载到现在，所有全球大事历历在目，像是一部简明世界史，读来令人兴趣盎然。人们可以从中获得许多国际知识。附录二是"Chronology of Scientific Development"。1991年出版的《英汉大词典》第一版附录五是"Major Literary Events of the English-Speaking Nations"，虽是英语国家语言、文学纪事，但仍有不少世界其他大事的记载，如55—54BC 罗马统帅 Julius Caesar 再度帅军远征，自 Gaul 入侵不列颠；1337英法百年战争开始，等等。令人不解的是，第二版删了。

2. 时代背景知识对读报有何重要意义

时代背景在理解分析一部作品、一篇文章或一个片段或句子时有时起着关键作用。许多古典文学作品，如不了解时代背景，今天是很难读懂的。甚至现在报刊有时也同样如此。例如：*Time* 在1992年8月10日发表"One Degree of Separation"一文有这么一段：

On the other hand, the choice of President this time has rarely been more important; ***1992 is a year, like 1815 or 1945, when a great transformation of global politics is under way.*** The old verities (general law or truth) that shaped U.S. policy have vanished; for 45 years all candidates shared the basic belief that America's main job abroad was to contain communism, though some took a more confrontational line, some a more conciliatory(和解的) one. The next President faces an entirely different challenge, grappling with seismic(像地震那样巨大而突然的) changes in which the choices are confusing, the directions obscure.

这三个年份,说都是全球政治处于巨变年代。从 Oxford Dictionary 的附录一查悉:

1915　Napoleon returns; raise army; defeated at Waterloo; banished to St Helena 拿破仑战败于滑铁卢,放逐到非洲圣赫勒拿岛。这就是说,他发动的战争结束了,法帝国(French Empire)崩溃,皇帝被赶下了台,征服全球的野心毁灭。其他政治力量在一战(1914—1918)中又会重组。

1945　Yalta Conference. War ends in Europe(May), United Nations formed... Potsdam Conference. 重要的是二次大战结束,联合国成立,世界政治力量在发生巨变。

至于1992年,该附录主要记载着英国的政情。此外,还有:Bosnia(波黑) declares independence. Sarajevr besieged by Serbs(萨拉热窝被塞尔维亚军队围困)及 UN intervenes in Somalia,等。显然这些事件跟全球政治巨变沾不上边。这时,我们就应提前看看世界大事记,果然1991年记载着 USSR breaks up... Yugoslavia: Civil war... Warsaw Pact dissolved... 再查一下列国志(Nations of the world)中的 Russia,便知道苏联于1991年12月26日正式解体。其解体和华沙条约的解散标志着美苏两国冷战的结束,美国成为唯一超级大国,难怪《时代》周刊这么说:"The old verities that shaped U.S. policy have vanished... for 45 years... America's main job abroad was to contain communism..."从1946年丘吉尔提出铁幕论后便掀起冷战,至1991年正好45年。在此期间,遏制共产主义仍是美对外政策核心。1992年是老布什与克林顿角逐总统宝座的大选之年,以往的候选人总是拿苏联说事,现在对立面消失了。那么,他们在竞选中又拿什么问题做文章才能占上风呢?双方都感到方向不明,道路不清。这样一分析,此段的意思就清楚了。

此外,年代在报刊语言中还可作借喻法,用来指代战争和美国大选中期选举。(见"报刊语言主要特点")

3."October"和"November"在美国何年有何意义

我们再从实例看看时间的重要性。例如:1980年,当时的副总统候选人老布什发表竞选声明说:

(1) All I know is there's a concern, not just with us but I think generally

amongst the electorate. Well, this Carter's a politically tough fellow. He'll do anything to get reelected, and let's be prepared for some **October surprise**.

(2) Democrats jumped on the news, calling Bush a hypocrite. Republicans on Capitol Hill worried that the attacks on Bush's integrity would further sink his poll ratings and hurt the GOP in **November**(2006/4/17 *Newsweek*)

上面两例提到的两个月份 October 和 November 都与竞选有关。在前面的章节已经提到,美国大选和中期选举的举行都在 On the Tuesday following the first Monday of November。这里初学读报者要注意 Nov. 究竟指美国总统选举还是中期选举,凡能被 4 除净的年份的 Nov. 指的就是大选,否则则指中期选举。单数年份则指 Special election 或 local elections。当前大选也包括 Congressional/local elections 在内,从(2)例的年份来看,2006 年非大选年,是国会中期选举之年。(1)例的 Oct. 是 1980 年,大选年,11 月举行选举。10 月还出现 Surprise,在此何指？原是拿破仑名言:"战争的成败决定最后五分钟。"喻"无人可预测胜负属谁"。此处指为打败对手,在竞选前夕出奇,叫对方措手不及,无时间反应的出奇制胜之举。最初指 1980 年民主党卡特为在大选前最后一刻,策划空降突击队,想用武力解救出被伊朗扣押的大使馆人质,沙漠演习时出事曝光,计划泡汤。直到共和党人里根上台人质才获释。又据说,当时共和党竞选班子曾与伊朗密谋,故意推迟释放人质。后来此语引申为"选举前出奇招。"台湾陈水扁炮制假枪击案中两弹负伤,转败为胜,更是无耻之尤了。

4. "April 15"有啥蹊跷

1986 年,当时的里根总统作国情咨文报告中提到了这个日期。见例句:

(1) Your schedule now requires that the budget resolution be passed by **April 15**, the very day America's families have to foot the bill for the budgets that you produce(指国会议员提交的). (*The Washington Post*)

何谓"April 15 the very day America's families have to foot the bill for the budgets"呢？再见下列两例就清楚了。

(2) In a two-hour stop in Iowa, a state he lost in 2000 by little more than 4,000 votes, Mr. Bush used the occasion of the **April 15** tax-filing deadline to renew his call to make permanent the tax cuts he has championed over the last three years and to assert that the economy is recovering nicely because of them. (*The New York Times*)

(3) In Palfrey's telling, she was a model citizen. "I paid my taxes on time every April 15th," she writes, and says she filed tax forms for her employees

with the IRS. (*Newsweek*)

April 15 是填好税单交国税局(美国称 IRA, "国内收入署")的最后期限,如逢周六或周日,顺延至 4 月 16 日或 17 日。正如第(1)例所说,这种税款供联邦政府预算开支。4 月 19 日也是第一季度分期缴纳估算税款的日期。"April 15 is tax day." 逾期,犯了联邦法,会被判罚款,重者判刑。

5. 联邦财政年度预算始末于何时

The line was accompanied by some less public but even sharper whip cracking. Before the President spoke, his aides had begun passing a disconcerting message to the 22 Republican Senators who will be up for re-election in 1986. Its essence: how much help Reagan gives them now in raising campaign funds, and later by making speaking tours through their states, will depend heavily on how much they cooperate in shaping a **fiscal-1986 budget** to the President's liking. (*Time*, March 25, 1985)

在前面的章节中已读到,预算是美国总统与国会激斗的重大议案,往往时间紧迫,容不得总统慢慢来。总统要花钱,国会控制着钱袋。此例涉及的 1986 年度的预算为何从 1985 年 3 月就让总统揪心了呢?照常人想法,下年的财政年度该是从 1 月 1 日开始,12 月 31 日结束。事实并非如此。美国下一个财政年度从当年(即例句中 85 年)10 月 1 日开始到第二年的 9 月 30 日止。争论焦点是民主党要增税,共和党反而要减税,尤其要给(企业界)富人减税。双方理念不同是经常在预算上斗法的根本原因,(见美国"政党"等介绍)往往花上几个月的时间才能达成妥协,那时新的财政年度也就快开始了。可见弄清时间,马虎不得。

七、美英等国情治机构知多少

国家安全为头等大事,称为 high foreign policy,经济援助政策则为 low foreign policy。美英等国情报和治安机构常见诸报端,有的一般词典中查不到,行话更费解。如:

(1) Since 1978 **the Mossad** has run a top-secret spying operation in the United States. (*Newsweek*)

(2) To the British press, the director of **MI6** is usually referred to as "M"—as in the James Bond thrillers. (*Time*)

(3) Those talks appear to have gone nowhere. Saddam is almost surely alive; the spy, according to a knowledgeable source, has been **"compromised"**... (2003/4/7 *Newsweek*)

以上三例中的"Mossad"和"MI6",1991 年出版的《英汉大词典》竟然未将其列入词条,其他的小英汉词典就更查不到了。再则,这些机构常用简称,犹如一锅字母汤,还夹杂着一套行话,如(3)例里的"compromised" meaning that he/she is probably dead。再大的综合词典也顾不过来,连网络都无此义。具备这方面知识,能扫除阅读障碍今后留学进修和从事外事工作也会获益。这里将美国、前苏联、俄罗斯、英国、法国和以色列的主要情报和治安机构作一简介。

1. 美国

到 2008 年为止,美国共有 16 个情治机构,常见诸极端的如下:

FBI (Federal Bureau of Investigation)联邦调查局是负责国内治安和反间反颠覆活动的政府机构,成立于 1908 年,属司法部管辖,全国设有 58 个地区局。

CIA(Central Intelligence Agency)中央情报局是 1947 年根据国家安全法(the National Security Act)建立的独立机构,从事国外的情报与反情报活动,搜集有关国家安全情报,向总统和国家安全委员会(the National Security Council)汇报。也从事国内的反情报活动,须与 FBI 取得协调,并经司法部长批准,以防重演"水门事件"(the Watergate Affair),非法搞国内侦缉。20 世纪 80 年代获准在国内秘密搜集外国情报。它不受公众监督,别称 invisible government(无形政府)。语出 David Wise 和 Thomas Ross 合写的同名著作。也叫 shadow government(影子政府)(仿英国的"影子内阁"),指侵犯人身自由,如影随形。总部设在弗吉尼亚州兰利(Langley, Langley 可指代 CIA),雇员约 15,000 名。为保障公民自由权,该机构不具有国内治安职能。正副局长由总统提名,参议院批准。

中情局曾控制着先前的 10 多个情报机构,据称由于在"9·11"事件和伊拉克战争中情报工作失误,地位已大大削弱,原来控制的其他机构有向总统汇报工作的任务,已划归国家情报总监(National Intelligence Director)。

Defense Intelligence Agency (DIA)国防情报局是总局,听取国防部所属情报机构汇报。

National Security Agency/No such Agency(NSA)国家安全局是国防部情报机构,保护本国通信安全和通过截收、破译、窃听来搜集外国通信情报的密码机构,成立于 1952 年。又名 Central Security Service,属绝密单位,已有 50 多年历史,美国政府一直讳莫如深,总说"No Such Agency"(没有这个部门),缩写与国家安全局一样。媒体讽刺说,美国国家安全局的英文名字不是"National Security Agency",而是"No Such Agency"。直到 20 世纪 70 年代初,美国政府才肯认账。

National Geospatial-Intelligence Agency(NGIA)国家地理空间情报署的前身为国家显像和绘图署(National Imagery and Mapping Agency),是国防部的作

战支援机构,专事搜集地理和空间情报。

National Reconnaissance Organization/Office(NRO)国家侦察局,通过侦察卫星搜集外国通信情报,隶属国防部。

Counterintelligence Field Activity(CFA)反间作战活动署是国防部绝密反间机构。

National Counterterrorism Center (NCC)国家反恐中心,是为防止"9·11"事件重演于2005年成立。

Terrorist Threat Integration Center(TTIC)防止恐怖威胁综合中心,由国土安全部、国家反恐中心、国防部和其他有关机构的成员组成,旨在防止恐怖分子袭击美国机构。

National Intelligence Council(NIC)国家情报委员会是负责汇编CIA等情报机构材料而成的《国家情报评估报告》(National Intelligence Estimate),并对美面临的安全问题和挑战作出前瞻性评估。

National Security Council (NSC)国家安全委员会是白宫的总统顾问机构,为有关国家安全的内政、外交和军事政策等重大问题提出全面的建议。成员有总统、副总统、负责总统安全事务特别助理、国务卿、国务部长、参谋长联席会主席和中央情报局局长等7人。

United States Secret Service 特工处,常简称 Secret Service,原隶属美国财政部,2002年国土安全部(Department of Homeland Security)成立后,划归新部管辖。原从事查抄伪币等经济事务,现专司保卫总统和其他高官、来访领导人的人身安全。

2. 英国

英国主要有三大情报机构,因为GCHQ太机密,常见报的是MI5和MI6。

MI 5 (Military Intelligence, Section Five) 军(事)情(报)五处是沿用战时旧称,并非军方情报部门,事实上是英国两个情报局之一,正式名称为 the Intelligence Service(安全局),相当于美国FBI,负责国内安全及国内反间活动。据内线揭露,该处曾策划暗杀过外国领导人,还曾涉嫌策划搞垮1974年2月上台的威尔逊工党政府,秘密调查其是否窝藏苏联特务,从而闹出丑闻。

MI 6 (Military Intelligence, Section 6) 军(事)情(报)六处也是沿用战时旧称,正式名称为 the Secret Intelligence Service(SIS) (情报局),职能相当于美国CIA。

GCHQ (Government Communications Headquarters)政府电信总局是英国从事保障电信安全、搜集外国通讯情报、破译密码等任务的政府机构,职能相当于美国的NSA。据揭露,美英对伊战前夕,曾窃听联合国秘书长科菲·阿南

(Kofi Annan)的谈话。

Defense Intelligence Staff (DIS)国防情报局。

Joint Intelligence Committee 联合情报委员会,统筹管理所有情报部门,受议会监督。

SIS (Secret Intelligence Service)情报局(＝MI6)

Intelligence Service＝Secret Service 或 MI5

Circus＝British Secret Service (英国)情报局(＝MI5)

British Secret Service 情报局(＝MI5)：Secret Service 与美国特工处名同职异

Scotland Yard 苏格兰场是伦敦市警察局的旧称,已成为刑事调查处或侦缉处(The Criminal Investigation Department)的同义词。1829 年该局初建时设在该处,后已两次迁址,1890 年迁至泰晤士河岸新苏格兰场,1967 年再迁至威斯敏斯特区新苏格场。

3. 苏联

提到情报机构或斗争,下列这两个机构常映入读者的眼帘：KGB (Komitet Gosudarstvennoi Bezopastnosti) 克格勃(1954—1991)起美国 CIA 负责对外情报活动及 FBI 负责对内的反间和维持治安的双重作用的苏联政府机构(英译 Committee/Commission for/of State Security[国家安全委员会]);GRU 格鲁乌即苏联军队总参谋部情报总局(英译 Chief Directorate of Intelligence of the General Staff)

4. 俄罗斯

Federal Security Service/Federal Service of Security(FSS)联邦安全局系由联邦反间谍局改组而成,前身是 KGB。1995 年,叶利钦将原联邦反间局改组为联邦安全局,强化其内外职能,不仅反间,还刑侦恢复了因改组剥夺掉的一系列特权,拥有预审权、侦讯室及特种部队。

5. 法国

法国的主要对外情报机构：

DGSE(Direction Generale de la Securite Exterieure)对外安全总局

6. 以色列

以色列情报机构是 Mossad 和 Shin Bet：

Mossad 莫萨德,以色列情报和特务局(英译 the Institution for Intelligence and Special Duties),负责对外的情报机构,创建于 1951 年。Al 意为至高无上,是 Mossad 的化名(Al 为希伯来文,等于英文 above)。

Shin Bet/Beth 辛贝特：以色列"国家安全总局",负责对内的安全机构。

Malmab 马勒马卜,负责以色列国防安全的绝密机构,同时也派工业间谍在国外活动,捞军火工业所需第一手情报。20 世纪 80 年代中期,美国海军情报官员乔纳森·波拉德(Jonathan Pollard)败露,曾为类似该机构的"拉卡姆"间谍组织(因此案而被撤销)效力。(见"**附录**""间谍行话")

习 题

阅读理解文章

The Spy game (2005/3/19 *The Economist*)

八、重要"智库"(Think Tank)

1. 有些公司、基金会等是何机构　有何作用

读者看报,常会见到下列例句中的学会、基金会、研究所、公司等机构:

"The trade atmosphere is very difficult," said Lawrence B. Krause, international economist at **the Brookings Institution.** "Indeed, one could call it foul." (The *New York Times*)

According to Francis Fukuyama, a former member of the State Department policy-planning staff now at **the Rand Corp.**, there has been a "role reversal" between the superpowers. (*Newsweek*)

He told Reagan that the President was in the thrall of a cabal of archconservatives. He claimed that American think tanks, citing **the Heritage Foundation** in Washington and **the Hoover Institution** in California, were feeding Reagan plans "designed to break down the Soviet economy." (*Time*)

Michael Novak, specialist in religion and public policy at **the American Enterprise Institute**, contends that the problem dates back to the 1930s. "Many millions of American parents, born poor during the Depression, didn't know how to bring up their children during conditions of affluence." (*U. S. News & World Report*)

于是读者心中不免要问,这些究竟是什么机构? 起何作用? 上述机构都是为美国政府在研究政治、外交、军事、经济、社会、科技等方面出谋划策、拟订计划的政策研究或智囊机构。它们出"点子",影响总统和高官,造"主义",引导舆论。think tank 造于 1959 年。有人说是杜鲁门 1964 年庆祝他 80 岁生日讲话时带头用开。此后便在新闻用语中取代了 brain trust(智囊团),一度成为时髦词。

作为当今世界唯一的超级大国,美国的力量还体现在思想、价值观等"软件"方面。美国盛产"主义",各种思想、主张层出不穷。在这方面,智库发挥了独特

的作用,在美国决策方面的影响力具第五位(fifth estate)(见"报刊的政治倾向性")

2. 五花八门的智库

所谓思想库是指以公共政策为研究对象、影响政策选择为目标的非赢利机构。有两个重要特点:"独立性"和"现实性"。思想库不是在象牙塔内做学问,只从事经世致用的研究,而是以影响政府决策为使命。思想库具备的这两个特点实际是相互矛盾,标榜独立超脱。又与现实政治和各种势力搭上千丝万缕的联系。正是这种微妙的矛盾,使得思想库能够在美国政治和外交决策中呼风唤雨,独树一帜。

随着美国外交"民主化"程度的扩大,知识界在外交决策过程中的影响力也日益扩大,几乎垄断了美国外交思想的"话语权"。这些人汇聚在思想库里,以专家、学者的身份出现,凭借智力,成为剖析时政、指点迷津的权威。当代美国社会中的思想库可谓五花八门,数量惊人,仅在华盛顿特区就有大大小小 100 多个综合类或专业性的思想库。由此可见美国这类机构有成千上万,下面除个别英国和瑞典的研究所外,主要介绍有一定代表性、对美国政府起重要作用并常见诸报端的若干机构:

American Enterprise Institute 美国事业研究所系美国事业公共政策研究所(the American Enterprise Institute for Public Policy Research)的简称。1943 年由摩根财团创建,当初称"美国事业协会",1962 年改为现名。它是保守派的重要政策研究机构,为共和党权势集团出谋划策。它与布鲁金斯学会并称为华盛顿的两大思想库,有保守的布鲁金斯学会之称。一译"美国企业研究所"。

Brookings Institution 布鲁金斯学会是美国著名的综合性政策研究机构,创建于 1927 年,取名于学会成立时的理事会副主席、圣路易斯市企业家、华盛顿大学董事会主席 Robert Brookings。与民主党关系密切,以持自由派观点著称,常被称为"开明的思想库"。

Rand (Corp)兰德公司成立于 1948 年,总部设在加州圣莫尼卡(Santa Monica),是以军事为主的美国综合性战略研究机构,享誉首创世界智囊团。表面上是非营利的民间机构,实际上受军方和大公司集团控制(Rand 由 Research and Development 或 Research and No Development 缩合而成)。

Heritage Foundation 传统基金会,成立于 1973 年,创建人约瑟夫·库尔斯是美国极右组织约翰·伯奇协会创始人。另一创建人保罗·韦里奇也系右翼政客。代表着美西南部利益集团极端保守势力的利益,是极右翼分子的主要政策研究机构。经费主要由库尔斯本人、大企业、家族基金会和个人捐助。

Hoover Institution 胡佛研究所系胡佛战争、革命与和平研究所(the Hoover Institution on War, Revolution, and Peace)简称,美国重要的保守政策研究机构,有"共和党影子内阁"之称,素以研究共产主义和反共而著称,是前总统胡佛于 1919 年为其母校斯坦福大学创建的。

Cato Institute 加图研究所:以古罗马政治家 Marcus P. Cato 命名的美国自由派的思想库,主要为政府出谋划策,知名度远不如兰德公司、布鲁金斯学会等研究机构。

Pew Research Center 皮尤研究中心 2004 年建立,是非赢利的无党派美国新闻研究机构,通过民意测验和社会科学研究,自称向人们提供美国和世界重要事件、思想态度、发展趋向等方面的客观事实和信息,在政策方针问题上,保持中立,俗称"事实库"(fact tank)。

International Institute for Strategic Studies(英国)伦敦国际战略研究所创办于 1958 年,侧重研究军事思想和防务政策,研究对象包括世界各个热点地区。每年发表的《战略形势报告》,分地区和专题论述一年来国际形势的发展变化;每年还出版一本《军事力量对比》手册,以全新的数据介绍世界各国的军事力量。该所人员精干,来源广泛,流动性强,因对世界各国军力分析精辟,享有盛誉。

Stockholm International Peace Research Institute(瑞典)斯德哥尔摩国际和平研究所成立于 1966 年,在分析和搜集战略均衡、军备竞赛和裁军情报方面,举世公认的权威科研中心。《SIPRI 年度报告》,汇集了各国军备更新、世界军火贸易、裁军谈判方面的最新资料,常被广泛引用。

九、重要国际组织(Major International Organizations)

国家组织有时也令人混淆,如 the Human Right's Committee 是一个 UN body(机构),而 Commission on Human Rights 或 2006 年改现名的 the Human Rights Council(人权理事会)是一个政治论坛(forum)。重要国际组织如下:

African Union (AU)非洲联盟(见 Organization of African Unity)

Asia-Pacific Economic Cooperation (Group) (APEC)亚洲和太平洋经济合作组织,(简称)亚太经合组织。中国、中国台北和中国香港都是该组织成员。

Association of Southeast Asian Nations (ASEAN) 东南亚国家联盟,(简称)东盟:1967 年 8 月在曼谷成立,至 1999 年柬埔寨加入该组织后,已有 10 个成员国。

Caribbean Community and Common Market(CARICOM) 加勒比共同体和共同市场于 1973 年建立。总部设在圭亚那首都乔治敦。

European Union (EU)欧洲联盟,(简称)欧盟：成立于1993年11月。1997年6月,欧盟领导人在荷兰首都阿姆斯特丹达成了《阿姆斯特丹条约》(Amsterdam Treaty),1999年5月生效。欧盟条约设立的(主要)机构(European Treaty institutions)有：

(1) European Council 欧洲理事会：即首脑会议。下属 Council of the European Union 欧盟理事会,即部长理事会(Council of Ministers),是拥有绝大部分决策权和立法权的实权机构。

(2) European Commission 欧洲委员会：常设和执行机构

(3) European Parliament 欧洲议会：监督和咨询机构,有部分立法职能

(4) European Court of Justice 欧洲法院：仲裁机构。

(5) European Court of Auditors 欧洲审计院。

欧盟后来又达成相当于宪法的《里斯本条约》,2009年11月,根据此条约,选出欧盟理事会主席(即欧盟总统)和外交政策高级代表(即外长),似乎真成为联邦或合众国体制了。

Group of Eight (G8) 八国集团：也称"7+1集团",指西方7个工业国家,"1"指俄罗斯。现因中、印、俄、巴西等新兴国家的崛起,要求以G20代之的呼声高涨。

Group of Twenty(G20)二十国集团由20个国家集团财政部长和中央银行行长参加的会议,1999年12月16日在柏林召开首届会议,是一个国际经济合作论坛,属于布雷顿森林体系框架内非正式对话的一种机制。按照惯例,国际货币基金组织与世界银行列席该组织的会议。20国集团的GDP总量约占世界的85%,人口约40亿。

该集团的成员包括：八国集团成员国、作为一个实体的欧盟和澳大利亚、南非以及具有广泛代表的发展中的新兴经济国家；中国、阿根廷、巴西、印度、印度尼西亚、墨西哥、沙特阿拉伯、韩国和土耳其。这些国家的国民生产总值约占全世界的85%,人口则将近世界总人口的2/3。创立20国集团的建议是美国等西方7个工业化国家的财长们1999年6月在德国科隆提出的,目的是就有关国际经济、货币政策举行非正式对话,以利于国际金融和货币体系的稳定。20国集团旨在推动国际金融体制改革,为有关实质问题的讨论和协商奠定广泛基础,以寻求合作并促世界经济的稳定和持续增长。为克服近年金融和经济危机,曾召开过几次首脑会议。

International Criminal Police Organization (ICPO—Interpol) 国际刑事警察组织,(简称)国际刑警组织。

League of Arab States (Arab League) 阿拉伯国家联盟,(简称)阿盟：阿拉伯国

家组织。

North Atlantic Treaty Organization (NATO) 北大西洋公约组织,(简称)北约, 是由西方主要国家组成的军事集团,总部设在布鲁塞尔。1949年4月4日成立。近年来,为遏制俄罗斯,北约战略发生了变化。首先,它一心东扩 (eastward enlargement),企图将苏联、南斯拉夫除俄罗斯以外的所有加盟共和国都纳入NATO成员国的势力范围。北约从事侵略往往以人权为借口,实际上企图对凡是不符合西方价值观的国家都进行军事干预。

Organization of African Unity (OAU) 非洲统一组织,(简称)非统组织或非统是全非性组织,1963年在埃塞俄比亚首都亚的斯亚贝巴举行的非洲独立国家首脑会议上成立。有53个成员国。于2002年更名为"非洲联盟"。

Organization of American States (OAS) 美洲国家组织:1948年建立的政治组织,总部设在美国首都华盛顿。

Organization for Economic Cooperation and Development (OECD) 经济合作与发展组织,(简称)经合组织成立于1961年,现有20多个成员国,大多数为发达国家,总部设在巴黎。

Organization of Petroleum Exporting Countries (OPEC) 石油输出国组织,(简称)欧佩克,由13个主要石油生产国的联合组织,1960年成立,总部设在维也纳。成立后,即夺回了制定油价和控制石油的生产权。

Organization for Security and Cooperation in Europe (OSCE) 欧洲安全与合作组织,前身为欧洲安全与合作会议,1973年成立,1994年更名。

United Nations 联合国是继国际联盟 (the League of Nations) 后于1945年成立,总部设在纽约。现已包括世界上大多数主权国家,共有192个成员国(不包括Kosovo)。有6个主要机构:大会,安全理事会,经济及社会理事会,托管理事会,国际法院和秘书处。由联合国秘书处行使行政职责,秘书长为最高长官。联合国大会拥有主要的审议权,一国一票,但通过的建议对成员国并无约束力,影响主要体现在舆论上。安理会由5个常任理事国和10个非常任理事国组成,主要是维护国际和平及安全;有权调查任何国际争端,促使当事国和平解决争端,并可组织成员国采取经济、军事制裁行动。还设有其他机构或委员会,分别负责国际经济、社会、司法、文化、教育、健康等领域的事务和问题。联合国部队的主要任务是维和。

第六章 翻 译

第一节 政治名言的理解与翻译

一、对译论的看法

翻译理论与技巧,异彩纷呈,着实热闹非凡。然而毕竟仍有这样的共识:语言和文化知识是基础,理解是前提。否则译文定会读来拗口,看来别扭,听来刺耳。在学生大本阶段宜多讲一些"翻译十大技巧"(北大教授辜正坤语)。"信、达、雅"及"形神兼顾"等我国译论也可适当介绍或融合到十大技巧中去。反之亦然。至于国外译论,译界普遍认同北大已故语言学教授王力提出的英汉两种语言的区别。英语强调"形合"(hypotaxis),汉语强调"意合"(parataxis)。外国译论要结合汉语特点,不宣教条式照搬。有的如异化、同化跟中国早有的直译、意译差不太多,不必非跟风追捧,讲"法治"较"僵硬"、讲"人治"较"柔软""灵活"。其实,千论,万论,还是尤金·奈达讲的"译意"(Translating means translating the meaning)是高论。

二、常见诸报端

本节所译政治名言,既有谚语,也有格言。有的虽非名言,但却常有政界人士或记者引用或套用,见诸报端。有的时过境迁,但反映出美英国内政治的普遍真理,所以才一直流传下来。如:

a. "The Bug(窃听)Stops Here"(2006/1/9 *Newsweek* 上的一幅漫画说明)就是套用"The buck stops here."

b. "All Politics Is Personal"(2007/12/24 *Los Angeles Times* 标题)和"All Politics Isn't Local"(2008/9/6 *Newsweek* 标题)(政治乃全球化的政治)就是套用"All politics is local."

c. When the going gets tough, these cops get going. The other way. (前面情况一危急,这些警察就退缩开溜了)就是仿"when going gets tough, the tough gets going."

有的名言是近一二十年所造,由于报刊求新和时尚是其一大特点,它们更是成了常见的引语或套语,甚至成了时髦语似的。例如:"The Foreword Was the

Mideast, Stupid"就是套用克林顿总统的竞选师爷所写:"It's the Economy, Stupid";"Read Their Lips:No New Internet Tax"套用美国前总统老布什所言:"Read my lips. No new taxes"等等。

三、读报刊,紧跟语言的变化和发展

读报上有的语句,不知出处,教员或文选编者不一定讲解或讲而不透。此类例子所在多是。再则,有的名言,既无释义,也无译文可资参考。Safire 词典里的"proverbs and axioms",有的只说来源,并无释义。若不常读报刊,熟谙两国政治、历史、社会等文化知识,就会抓瞎。本人就摔过筋斗。当然,最怕的是望文生义,似懂非懂,笔者经常引以为戒。下列的英文名句,有的已有译文,但值得商榷;有的是编者试译,以便向方家请教。

1. A fish rots from the head first.

    1988年民主党总统候选人杜卡克斯(Michael Dukakis)在与时任副总统的老布什竞选时,用希腊谚语抨击共和党执政的里根政府道德水准低下。买卖鱼的人都知道:"鱼烂头先烂。"此语喻"上梁不正下梁歪"。

2. a war to end all wars 以战止战。见例句:

    In his postwar speech to Congress, Bush acknowledged that his plan was not perfect. Said the President, "The victory over Iraq was not waged as '**a war to end all wars.**' Even the new world order cannot guarantee an era of perpetual peace." (*Time*)

    1917年威尔逊总统决定放弃中立立场、参加第一次世界大战。他的这一警句成为参战国的口号。现常用作讽刺语,事实上以战止战只能为下次战争准备条件。源出英国作家 H. G. Wells 1914 年写的书名:*The War That Will End War*。后来"a... to end..."句型常被记者模仿。如 **Alphonse-and-Gaston routine to end all Alphonse-and-Gaston routines**。

3. A Woman's place is in the home.

    女人就该待在家里做家务。2008年美国总统初选时,前总统 Clinton 夫人 Hillary 在与 Barack Obama 争夺民主党总统候选人提名战中人群中喊出了这句男尊女卑谚语的口号。结果,她吃了大亏。

4. All politics is local.

    美国前众议院议长 Thomas("Tip")O'Neil(1912—1994)的解释是:"If you want to understand the political behavior of members of Congress, you must know what issues affect their home districts, what their constituents really care about."这就是说,美国国会议员并非以身许国,而是为选区效劳。

如多通过一些分肥立法(pork-barrel legislations),为举州或选区多拉些联邦政府出钱的工程和福利项目,就能连选连任,不愁丢官帽。据此,试译为:(1)国家,党派去他娘,地方政治记心上。(2)千政治,万政治,不如家门口/分肥政治。

此类名言无定译,得视上下文所谈何事再动笔,本人曾读到一篇谈全球某事文章,意为:千政治,万政治,都是本国利益/政治利益摆首位的政治。All politics isn't local 则为举国或全球政治之义。

5. Ask not what your country can do for you; ask what you can do for your country.

莫问国家能为你做什么,要问你能为国家做什么;莫向国家伸手,要为国家效力;一心只想奉献,莫向国家伸手。语出美国前总统肯尼迪1961年的就职演说。此后,"ask not...; ask..."就让记者捡来模仿造句并讽刺他的风流韵事。如:

And so, my fellow Americans, **ask not what your country can do for you; Ask what you can do for your country.**

My fellow citizens of the world: Ask not what America will do for you, but what together we can do for the freedom of man. (John Kennedy)

The Actual Quote: ... "Rather **ask what you can do for your concubine**"... (*Time*)

6. Defeat has a thousand fathers and victory is an orphan.

失败怨大家,胜利独自夸。[仿谚语 Success has many fathers, but failure is an orphan. (见 **Victory has a thousand fathers.**)]

7. Defeat is an orphan.

失败独自担。意近"吃不了兜着走。"(见 **Victory has a thousand fathers.**)

8. Don't change horses.

不要中途换马。指在位总统竞选连任时,要求选民在危机或战争时期不要更换政府,或在紧要关头不要改变领头人。林肯在1864年、F.罗斯福在1940年和1944年的竞选中都用过类似比喻:"**Don't swap horses in the middle of the stream.**"

9. Don't cross the bridge till you come to it.

船到桥头自然直。源出诗人朗费罗(Henry Longfellow)所写的 *The School of Salerno*(见 **Don't roll up your pants legs...**)

10. Don't get mad. Don't get even. Just get elected. Then get even.

此语出于克林顿竞选谋士James Carville。语言不难,一般词典里都有

"get even"的释义,试译为:

休上火,莫斗气/嘴,胜出算账不嫌迟。

11. Don't just do something, stand there!

老实呆着吧,别来添乱了。美国民主党总统候选人 Adlai Stevenson 在 1956 年大选时如此抨击共和党总统艾森豪威尔的国内政策。1970 年,共和党政府的劳工部长 George Shultz 用来反对政府对企业的干预。

12. Don't look past the next election or you might not get past the next election.

走马看花搞竞选,名落孙山必无疑;盯紧竞选,不怕落选;心不在焉搞竞选,要想过关难上难。语出 2005 年前总统克林顿接受 CNN 采访时的一次谈话。

13. Don't roll up your pants legs before you get to the stream.

不到溪边,不卷裤腿。意近中国成语:"船到桥头自然直。"(见 We'll double-cross that bridge... ; In politics a man must...)

14. Don't sell America short.

19 世纪 90 年代,根据股市行情分析,投资家认为股市将下跌衰退,美国金融家 John Pierpont Morgan 却说:"别低估美国的股市行情。"或"切莫小看美国的经济实力。"

15. Every Man a King.

大家都是王。美国前路易斯安那州州长 Huey P. Long 的口号,整句口号为:大家都是王,全是无冕王(Everyman a King, but No Man Wears a Crown)。他是贫民主义者,主张均贫富。这个口号的意思是,人人皆平等,财富该分享,70%的财富不该集中在10%的人手里。

I'm for the poor man—all poor men. Black and white, they all gotta have a chance.... **"Every Man a King"**—that's my slogan.

16. Every man has his price.

人各有价。语出英国 Robert Walpole 爵士 1734 年在平民院的发言"I know the price of every man in this House",意为"此间人人都可收买"。

17. Few die and none resign.

没有死人辞职,哪来空缺?语出反对党——联邦党 1801 年给新任美国民主共和党总统杰斐逊的一封信,反对赶走前任留下的官员。此信的片段是:"If a due participation of office is a matter of right, how are vacancies to be obtained? **Those by death are few; by resignation none.**"

既然人皆有权当官,哪来空缺可填?上届政府死人少,辞职卸任更莫谈。这种行政立法部门之争是宪法只规定:"总统任命官员要听取参议院建议并获得批准(advise and consent)。"辞退他们也如此这般,却只字未提,这就引起行政与立法部门之间在官员去留上的争吵。

18. forgive but never forget.

　　旧恶一笔勾,旧怨记心头。语出 1968 年美国前总统肯尼迪的一次电视演说(仿 forgive and forget)

19. Go ahead—make my day.

　　(把增税法案)送上来试试看!我不大笔一挥毙掉,这一天就算白过。里根为兑现不增税的诺言,在美国商会放话,国会将增税法案送来签署,他就大笔一挥否决掉,不信试试看。此语原是名演员 Clint Eastwood 在电影 *Sudden Impact* 里扮演恶汉哈利(Dirty Harry)对试图掏枪的嫌疑人说的一句台词,意为"你胆敢试试看!我不一枪毙了你,这一天就算白过。"

20. (go) fight City Hall

　　这里 City Hall 指衙门进难,因而意为:别跟官僚衙门斗啦,白费力气了!进门难上难,费力不合算。另一种说法是:"**You don't beat City Hall too often.**"(见 **You can't fight City Hall**)

21. Government is best which governs least.

　　要想经济好,政府插手少。一种极端市场经济或自由资本主义理论,里根等人就主张放任主义政策(lasséz-faire),让市场去自由调节。就是要政府放弃监管的报右派的经济理论。2008 年金融危机爆发后威信扫地。这里的 government 指政府干预经济和社会生活的程度。(见 **liberals and conservatives**)

22. government of money, by money, for money

　　钱有、钱治、钱享。一美国漫画家批评美国金钱万能,仿林肯名言"government of the people, by the people, for the people"于 1999 年所造。

23. government of the people, by the people, for the people

　　民有、民治、民享。语见美国前总统林肯 1863 年葛底斯堡演说(Gettysbury Address),举世传颂。

　　...a new birth of freedom... that **government of the people, by the people, for the people**, shall not perish from the earth.

24. How you stand depend on where you sit.

　　升官不升官,要看坐哪边。芝加哥大学教授 Arnold Weber 引自美国预算局前雇员 Rufus E. Miles 的一次讲话。

25. I don't care what the papers say about me as long as they spell my name right.

　　只要有福享,哪管人骂娘。语出腐败的前纽约民主党党棍"Big Tim"

Sullivan 的一次讲话。

26. I'd rather be right than be president.

   总统宁肯不当,正义也要伸张。语出美国参议员 Henry Clay 1839 年的一次演讲,意为"宁愿失去当总统的机会,也不愿停止抨击北方废奴制度"。他反对废奴,未能当上总统。此言带有酸葡萄味。

27. If it ain't broke, don't fix it.

   能够凑合使,干吗要修理;不要多此一举。语出在美国卡特政府任预算局局长的兰斯(Bert Lance)关于政府改组的一次讲话,意为不要轻易变动机构或政策。

28. If it walks like a duck, and quacks like a duck, then it just may be a duck.

   说话走路像赤佬,一抓就准跑不了。语出美国前工会反共头子 Walter Reuther 的一次演说。

29. If nominated, I will not run. If elected, I will not serve. 见 The office/job seeks the man.

30. If you can't beat/lick them, join them.

   赢不了,早入伙(以便从中获利);胜不了,成朋友;败下阵,快归顺。这是吹得天花乱坠的商战策略,美国人的阿 Q 精神,政界、商界时髦语,倒不失为保住面子的好办法。

   All too often, the attitude of the workers' representatives, heavily outnumbered, "has been **if you can't beat them, join them.**" They've had to dance to the bosses' tune. (John Garraty)

31. If you can't convince them, confuse them.

   说服不了,就把他们搞糊涂;说不服就蒙。美国前总统杜鲁门的格言。

32. If you can't stand the heat, get/stay out of the kitchen.

   怕烤别下厨。意为政治家要提得起,放得下,不要一遇压力,就打退堂鼓;担不起重任,趁早不要干。美国前总统杜鲁门的名言。他不善辞令,讲起话来乡土气很重,骂起人来也快言快语。他说这话时任参议员,后来任总统的 L. 约翰逊也用不同的比喻说出同样的道理:"My daddy told me that if I didn't want to get shot at, I should stay off the firing line. This is politics."(老爹说,怕当靶子别当头,搞政治就是这样。意为"搞政治犹如站在第一线,常常受到攻击,压力很大。承受不了,趁早别干"。)

   Those of us in language's artful dodge who make a living correcting others must learn to strike a noble pose and take the gaff when we goof. Nobody stands taller than those willing to stand corrected. As F. D. R.

said, "**If you can't stand the heat, get out of the kitchen.**"

Wait—no. That was Harry Truman. (*The New York Times Magazine*)

33. If you don't go to other people's funerals, they won't go to yours. 你不去烧香，他不来拜佛。政治谚语。

34. If you don't like the heat, get out of the kitchen 见 **If yon can't stand the heat...**

Not all U.S. presidents, who are remembered for their gift with words, were noted for their eloquence. Some were admired for their use of direct, nononsense language—none more so than Democratic President Harry Truman (1945 – 1953). Two of his most famous contributions are used in everyday language today—"the buck stops here" (a slogan he kept on his desk), and "**if you don't like the heat, get out of the kitchen.**" (*Campaign Spotlight*)

35. If you don't want to get shot at, you should stay off the firing line. 见 **If you can't stand the heat...**

36. If you have an elephant on a string, and the elephant starts to run—better let him run. 拴住大象腿，看他哪里逃。政治谚语。

37. If you want a friend in Washington, buy a dog.

华府交朋友，不如养条狗。指美国首都华盛顿尔虞我诈，人心巨测，人不如狗，西方以狗为人类忠实朋友。有人称为杜鲁门名言，但无实据。

38. ill-housed, ill-clad, ill-nourished.

[the ~]屋不避雨，衣不遮体，食不果腹者；(喻)穷人：美国前总统 F. 罗斯福用语。

Clinton's decision probably clinches his reelection. Americans today no longer wish to carry so much of the burden for those Roosevelt called **the "ill-housed, ill-clad, ill-nourished."** (*Time*)

39. In politics a man must learn to rise above principle.

本人曾自认为此语不难理解，就信手译为：(1) 玩政治，就顾不得原则。(《美英报刊导读》)。2007 年，在 *Newsweek* 的一篇文章中看到了如下似乎是对此语的诠释："A successful politician knows when to make compromises without appearing to abandon his or her dignity or moral compass." 颇有启发，于是感到(1)译过头了，似乎政治家都是不讲原则的无赖。于是就在《当代英汉美英词典》里将之改译为：(2) 搞政治，不能只讲原则。译文(2)之所以符合原文的意思，西方流行的理念是："政治是妥协的艺术或产物。"也就是说,政治家得该妥协的时候就妥协,不能死抠教条。例如美国前总统 L. 约翰逊曾被誉为具有妥协本领(art of the possible)的大师。当今美国,常用较含蓄的比喻替代,见 We'll double-cross that bridge...; Don't roll up your pants legs...

40. **In politics, as in sports, the name of the game is to have a winning team.**

    政坛如球场,胜败的关键全仗有常胜将军领军/带班出马。

41. **It's the Economy, Stupid!**

    这是1992年克林顿竞选总统期间,其谋士 James Carville 在竞选总部办公桌上放的一块牌子上写的字。2008年5月8日《南方周末》在一篇题为"英国工党失利:第三条道路的终结?"的文章是这么解读的:那么工党为什么这次失利呢?用克林顿当初竞选的名言来说:"注意经济,傻瓜!"《最新英语通俗词典》也译为:"蠢东西,要谈的是经济。"2004年美国大选和2006年中期选举期间,香港凤凰卫视中文台的首席政治评论员一再提到这句话,说:"是经济问题,傻瓜!"2008年《世界知识》第22期在一篇题为"助奥巴马者,经济也"的文章里更是错得离谱,说什么当年,民主党新秀克林顿赢了共和党老布什,克林顿对失利的布什说:"傻瓜,那是经济问题!"我的一位高翻朋友就此问题曾分别请教过几位英美人士,他们也都众说纷纭,莫衷一是。《英语词汇学教程》(1997:326)虽用作例句,但并未加以解释或翻译。这就是说,他们可能都给"Stupid"这个字将军住了。事实上不但我们有的国人,在去年5月28日一篇西班牙《起义报》题为"达尔富尔?是石油,笨蛋(estúpido)……"的文章中,西班牙报人和《参考消息》也都将此字理解错了。

    1992年美国大选选情是,在位总统老布什竞选连任。在他任内,外交上正逢令其和西方兴奋不已的时期:1989年柏林墙被拆除。1991年打败了伊拉克总统萨达姆。同年苏联解体;但在经济上却乏善可陈,被贬称为"治标不治本的总统"(Revlon President)。由此可以说明,卡氏当时是提醒克林顿要抓住对手政策上的弱点不放,而不可能有悖常理,骂自己的主子是"傻瓜"。根据《纽约时报》专栏作家、美国政治语言权威 William Safire 编的 *New Political Dictionary* 的解释:stupid 的这种用法首见于1964年由 Billy Wilder 执导的电影"*Kiss Me, Stupid*",并无贬义,只是"formulaic reminder of central issue or goal"。据此,可简单将其试译为:(这次竞选的)要害是经济!经济问题是(这次竞选的)关键!千万不要忘记打经济这张牌!(见**"跟踪语言的变化和发展"**)

42. **Money is the milk of politics.**

    金钱是抚育政治的乳汁;离了金钱,政治免谈。

43. Never hold discussions with the monkey when the organ grinder is in the room.

　　摇手风琴的主人在场,别跟猴儿瞎嚷嚷;头头在场,别找下属商量;要找墨索里尼本人,不找外交部长。引自英国前首相丘吉尔在英驻意大利大使请示他是找墨索里尼(Mussolini)还是外交部长 Count Ciano 谈问题时的答语。

44. Never murder a man who is committing suicide.

　　见人上吊,别再动刀;(在竞选中)别干落井下石那样缺德的事。前总统威尔逊曾说:

　　"I am inclined to follow the course suggested by a friend, who says that he has always followed the rule **never to murder a man who is committing suicide.**"(Woodrew Wilson)

45. Nice guys finish last.

　　好人总是倒数第一。意为好人做不得。语出20世纪40年代布鲁克林道奇棒球队一名队员。1988年美国大选老布什当选。评论者认为多少应归功谋士使出狠招(dirty tricks),对手杜卡克斯(Michael Dukakis)过于 nice 和 reasonable。足见"好人定输"这句话在美国这个社会不无人生哲理。有人认为,戈尔(Al Gore)2000年败选,也跟一本正经、道貌岸然、像个教授有关,能赢得知识分子选票,普通人却不买账。小布什为人随和,满嘴俚语,口无遮拦,反而吃香。(见 **Winning isn't everything, it's the only thing**)

46. No man ever went broke underestimating the intelligence of the American voter.

　　要想选得上,蒙骗样样讲;不靠蒙骗选不上。美国名记者、评论家 H. L. Mencken 的名言。

47. Nobody shoots at Santa Claus.

　　圣诞老头人人夸,抨击福利计划是傻瓜;存心跟贫穷选民过不去,势必落选。双党候选人都不敢碰,所以福利计划压得联邦政府不堪重负。

48. Old soldiers never die.

　　老兵精神永存;老兵永不死(只是暂离去)(They just fade away)。1951年朝鲜战争时期,杜鲁门撤换力主炸我东北的五星上将麦克阿瑟(Douglas MacArthur),麦在国会讲话时自找台阶下,援引兵营流行民歌歌词。此语常被仿用,如: **Generals never die.**

49. Please your boss, cover your ass and always, always be cautious.

　　巴结上司,掩盖丑事,时刻小心惹祸。这是在华盛顿官运亨通的诀窍。露出屁股(your ass 或 butt),指让人抓住把柄,就要挨批。报刊常引用部分,尤其"cover your ass"居多。

Barnet shows me the ropes, then leaned back and laid out his philosophy of how to succeed in his bureaucracy: **Please your boss, cover your ass and always, always be cautious.** (*Time*)

50. Politics ain't beanbag.

    政治是男人们的玩意儿;政治不是儿戏(小孩、女人和禁酒主义者最好还是不玩为好)。语出幽默作家邓恩(Finley Peter Dunne)(1867—1936)笔下塑造的杜利先生(Mr. Dooley)的一句名言。beanbag 作"小孩玩的豆子袋,做游戏"讲。

51. Public office is a public trust.

    公职肩众任。克利夫兰 1884 年竞选总统时,用时任新闻秘书 W. C. Hudson 讲的名言,体现官员廉洁,现常引用。

52. Read my lips, No new taxes 见"改朝换代产生和流行的词语"

53. root, hog, or die

    恪尽职守,要么走人。谚语。猪荒年掘地刨根寻食,不然就会饿死。此语由美国前总统杰克逊引入政治词汇而用开的。

    Root, hog, or die—work for your office, or leave it—support the party, right or wrong—are the terms of the agreement.

54. Show me a good loser, and I'll show you a loser.

    输得起,就服你。尼克松喜欢的名言。他连续两次竞选失败,并不气馁,a good loser,最终如愿。有时只引用前半部分。

55. Speak softly and (always) carry a big stick.

    说话要温和,大棒不离手;要软硬兼施。语出美国前总统 T. 罗斯福,他主张实行胡萝卜加大棒的外交政策(carrot and stick)。

    A later Republican President, Theodore Roosevelt (1901 - 1909), led the nation at a more tranquil time when the United States was emerging onto the world stage. His famous dictum, "**Speak softly and carry a big stick,**" entered the general, and not just the political, lexicon—one of a number of blunt admonitions from the former leader of the "Rough Riders" (the name of the cavalry unit he led during the Spanish-American War). (*Campaign Spotlight*)

56. (We will) spend and spend, (and) tax and tax, and elect and elect.

    据说语出民主党总统 F. 罗斯福亲信、新政(New Deal)干将 Harry Hopkins,意为只要舍得花钱,尤搞得民心的联邦工程,减少失业大军,就能不断当选。后来常被共和党用来攻击民主党的"大政府"政策,把联邦政府的钱袋当作议员分肥的"肉桶"(pork barrel)。此语有两个译例:(1) 不断花钱,不断征税,不断取得选票的政策。(《英汉美国社会知识小词典》);(2) 花钱多,征税多,选票多多多。(《当代美英报刊词典》)

应该说,译文都很达意,原文并不难,一些常被套用或仿造的名言,倒要参照背景知识才能译得到位。例如里根在就任总统后不久,针对批评,他说:

"Our current problems are not the product of the recovery program that is only just now getting under way, as some would have you believe; they are the inheritance of decades of **tax and tax, spend and spend.**"(我们面临的问题并不是像有人哄你们那样,是刚起步的经济恢复计划闹的,而是民主党人几十年滥增税、猛开支(的"大政府"政策)种下的祸根。

57. Supreme Court follows the election returns. 见"读报知识""司法机构"
58. The basic maxim of democracy should always be: Turn the rascal out.

民主格言要记牢,赶走流氓第一条。美国历史学家 Arthur Schlesinger, Jr. 认为是名记者 Charles A. Dana 1872 年讲的名言。美国作家德莱塞(Theodore Dreiser)在其 1914 年出版的政治小说 *The Titan* 里也写道:"There could be but one thing left—an appal to the voters of the city to **turn the rascals out.**"

59. The best politics is no politics.

不讲党派的政见,才是最好的政见;派性少,政见好,派性无,高招出。语出美国前国会参议员 Henry (Scoop) Jackson,意为两党要一致支持政府的国家安全政策。见里根一次国会讲话:

This year, I will be asking Congress for the means to do what must be done for the great and good cause. As Scoop Jackson, the inspiration for our Bipartisan Commission on Central America, once said, "In matters of national security, **the best politics is no politics.**"

60. The buck stops here.

这是杜鲁门办公桌上一块牌子上写的一句话,前总统肯尼迪对此言解释得很透彻:

President Truman used to have a sign on this desk which said: "**The buck stops here**"—those matters which involve national security and our national strength finally come to rest here.

换言之,下级都可以说,I don't know enough about it to decide, so I'll pass the buck to you. 这就应了中国和尚担水吃的故事。可杜氏是总统,事关

国家安全和实力,不能推诿责任(pass the buck),玩踢皮球的把戏。这句不难理解的名言,四本词典有四种不同的译文:(1)责任止于此。(意为勿再把责任往别处推,原系美国总统杜鲁门办公桌上的座右铭)(《英汉大词典》第二版)。(2)该责任不能再推诿了(英汉双解剑桥国际英语词典)。(3)责任到此不能再推(《朗文当代英语大词典》)。(4)责无旁贷(《英汉美英报刊词典》)

前三例的译文大同小异,(1)例只是把肯尼迪的诠释"those matters…finally come to rest here"译了出来,因而译文不像内容富有哲理的格言。(4)例虽用了成语,但何事使他"责无旁贷"呢?如前面加上"我来拍板,……"就表达得体了。当然,词典只是释义而非翻译,不能苛求。

61. The dogs may bark, but the caravan moves on forever.

大篷车赶路忙,哪管群狗叫汪汪;听蝲蝲蛄叫,还不种庄稼了。指我行我素,休管他人闲言碎语。美国出版商 Mortimer Zuckerman 引用的中东国家的谚语。

62. The duty of an Opposition is to oppose.

反对党的职责就是遇事唱反调;反对党就该唱反调,对执政党提案一概反对(自己却什么议案也不提)。语出英国前辉格党议员 Tierney。英国前首相 Derby 勋爵曾说:

"When I first came into Parliament, Mr Tierney, a great Whig authority, used always to say that **the duty of an Opposition was** very simple—it was, **oppose** everything, and propose nothing."

63. The first casualty of war is the truth.

意近孙子所言:"兵不厌诈。"也近美国二战悍将巴顿的名言:"战争离不开欺骗。"试译为:枪炮一响,真话光光;战争始于欺诈。

64. The first essential for a Prime Minister is to be a good butcher.

译前先看下面摘自《时代》周刊文章里的一段说明:

When Nixon implored his old friend and Secretary of State William Rogers to order the resignation of White House aides John Ehrlichman and H. R. Haldeman, caught up in the Watergate scandal, Rogers refused, telling Nixon he should do it himself. There followed one of the age's grand political soap operas, with teary meetings, prayers and arguments. But Nixon did it. Later he would recall the words of Britain's heroic Prime Minister William Gladstone: **"The first essential for a Prime Minister is to be a good butcher."**

从上可以看出,这句出自英国前首相 Willian Gladstone(1809—1898)

的话是多么沉重。古今中外,逼走部下伤人,是"六亲不认"。艾森豪威尔和老布什曾分别要办公厅主任 Sherman Adams 和 John Sununu 辞职犯难,惹祸的是多年的亲信。当然,凡事得从两方面看,领袖们如不将这种不得人心的人解职,视为不抛弃朋友的美德(virtue)或江湖义气;迫于压力不得已下手也是一种需要(necessity)。那么首相到底该如何行事呢?笔者试译为:做首相先要铁面无情或敢于辞退部下。当然,此处的 butcher 不一定只指辞退部下。

65. The office/job seeks the man.

这是以往美国总统竞选中常用的名言,笔者未见有译例,在两本书中分别试译为:(1)官职可遇不可求。(《美英报刊导读》第一版)(2)(与其)主动求官不如征召出山。(《当代英汉美英报刊词典》)(3)钻营不如应召。

上译是否妥切?孰优孰劣?要判断这类译文不能仅凭文字,还得了解美国总统竞选史。先看尼克松 1958 年未任总统时的看法:

"I have a theory, that in the United States those who seek the Presidency never win it. Circumstances rather than a man's ambition determine the result. If he is the right man for the right time, he will be chosen."

再看专栏作家 Claydton Fritchey 1967 年采访时任加州州长里根的一段报道:

When asked about White House aspirations, he [Ronald Reagan] declined to be drawn out because, as he reminded the reporters, in this country, "**The office seeks the man,**" not the other way around.... Ask Eisenhower. The General fled to Paris in 1952 and tried to hide out in NATO, but it didn't work.... It's time somebody seeks The Office instead of vice versa."

时势造英雄,这种人扭捏作态,不愿当候选人(reluctant candidate),非要"征召"(draft)才肯答应。历来比随时准备接受提名的(available)胜出率要高,如艾森豪威尔、尼克松和里根就持此种看法,先后当上了总统。事实上,他们都在幕后积极活动,采用的是如 2008 年大选中 *Newsweek* 评论前副总统 Al Gore Practices the Zen of "(the art of) running by not running" 或 "campaigning hard by staying out",大有无为而无所不为之势。现在的情况与先前的已截然相反,个个都提前显身手。

从美国总统竞选史来看,只有南北战争时期的将军 William Sherman (1820—1891)是真正的 reluctant candidate 和 draft 也不出山的人。他的名言是:"I will not accept if nominated and will not serve if elected."(提名不受,当选不干。)此语称为"Sherman statement",并被套用。如 2005 年副总

统切尼(Dick Cheney)说:"If nominated, I will not run. If elected, I will not serve."(提名不参选;当选不就任。)至于主张蓄奴主义的议员 Henry Clay 说的"I'd rather be right than be president."是假话。

综上所述,笔者认为,上述两例都译对了。(1)例直译,(2)(3)例意译,却比(1)译得传神。

66. The only thing we have to fear is fear itself.

语出 F. 罗斯福在 1933 年就任总统时发表的第一次就职演说的第三段:

So first of all let me assert my firm belief that **the only thing we have to fear is fear itself**—nameless, unreasoning, unjustified terror which paralyzes needed efforts to convert retreat into advance.

这是他为了鼓舞士气,战胜经济大恐慌(Great Depression)讲的,后来成了竞相引用的名句,文字做了改动,常用"nothing to fear but fear itself"。口语,前面常加上"We have..."。有种种译例:(1)我们唯一值得恐惧的就是恐惧本身(《英美报刊文选》)。(2)我们唯一要恐惧的就是恐惧本身(1932 年福兰克林。罗斯福总统在就职演说中说的一句话,现在其他场合也有引用)(《郎文当代英语大词典》,2004)。放不开手而译得不像地道汉语关键是译者给"itself"捆住了手脚。(此外,第(2)例还将年份搞错了,美国总统的就职典礼都在奇数年份举行。)编者曾译为:(3)我们什么都不怕,怕只怕自己害怕(《当代英汉报刊词典》)。(4)胆子大,全不怕。

(3)例译得直白和口语化,从内容和形式上看都是原文的翻版,只是把英文"itself"在汉语中变成了"ourselves"而已。第(4)例意译,从反面着手,文字简短达意。翻译时,正反虚实互换,改动词性,词序,增删,是常有的事,要得"意"忘"形"(即"译意"),跳出原文形式束缚,抓住实质才能译得透。

借"9·11"恐怖事件蹿红的小布什,每逢紧要关头,如 2003 年侵伊和 2004 年竞选连任,他都用"terror fear"这一招,屡试不爽。2006 年中期选举时,他故伎重演失灵,*Newsweek* 挖苦:The only thing we have to use is fear itself. 竞选策略全不用,单用闻之丧胆这一招。

67. The United States has never lost a war or won a peace.

美国从未输过战争,也未(通过谈判)赢得过和平。前国务卿 William Rogers 外交用语。意含"战则胜,和则败。"现常用来抨击在野党私下与敌人和谈,不支持政府主战。说明美国人"善战不善和"。

68. They loved him most for the enemies he made.

疾恶如仇,人人爱戴。纽约州州长 Grover Cleveland 1884 年争取民主党总统候选人提名时的竞选口号,其后更加简洁有力:"**Loved for the enemies he made.**"

69. They never go back to Pocatello. 见 **You can't go back to Pocatelo.**

70. To the victor belong the spoils of the enemy.

    选举胜利好当官。前国务卿 William Marcy 认为胜选出官,即典型的政治分赃制度(spoils system)。

71. too little and too late

    战备不足,供应太迟。原指 1885 年英军在苏丹被困 10 月直到统帅丧生两天后援军才到达。后引申至多种场合,再引申出 "enough and in time"。二战后期,盟军取得节节胜利,获得了 "enough and in time" 的表扬。此语常被引用,如 "Congress Doesn't work"(1990/July *Reader's Digest*)一文就以此作小标题。

72. too old to cry

    真想像孩子那样大哭一场。美国政界人物落选时伤心语。

73. too proud to fight

    不屑一战。指美国为中立太自豪了而不屑于参战。一战时,一艘英国客轮被德国潜艇炸沉,许多美国游客陪葬。威尔逊总统死抱住调解国地位不放,并说:"The example of America must be the example not merely of peace because it will not fight, but of peace because peace is the healing and elevating influence of the world and strife is not. There is such a thing as a man being **too proud to fight.** There is such a thing as a nation being so right that it does not need to convince others by force that it is right..." 威尔逊针对国内的反战派讲的,也为不参战辩解。后来反而用来对他嘲讽,直到对德宣战方休。

74. Trade follows the flag.

    军旗插到哪里,生意就做到哪里。指英国采取武力开路、掠夺弱国的炮舰政策,鸦片战争就是典型。现在已改为:"Trade follows Her Majesty's visit."(女王陛下访问到哪里,生意就做到哪里)。

75. United we stand, divided we fall.

    合则兴,分则败。源出 John Dickenson 1776 年发表的 *The Patriot's Appeal* 中的诗句:"By uniting we stand, by dividing we fall." 后来成为美内战时期的口号。

    The Civil War era slogan "**United We Stand, Divided We Fall**" may well apply to the Reform Party. This third party, which Texas multi-millionaire businessman Ross Perot created using the "United" part of the phrase, dissolved into the "Divided" portion at its August 11-13 presidential nominating convention in Long Beach, California. (*Campaign Spotlight*)

76. Victory has a thousand fathers.

胜利来居功。语出总统肯尼迪1961年讲的话,为入侵古巴的猪湾事件(Bay of Pigs)失败承担责任,下半截为 but defeat is an orphan(失败独自担)。(仿谚语"Success has many fathers, but failure is an orphan.")

77. Watch what we do, not what we say.

要看我们干得怎样,别听我们讲得漂亮。语出尼克松政府司法部长米切尔(John Mitchell)在水门事件听证会上的证词。

78. We'll double-cross that bridge when we come to it.

到了桥边,还愁过不了河。double-cross 美俚指背叛,此处指绕道,桥指代原则。不是过桥而是绕道。(见 **Don't roll up your pants legs...; In politics a man must....**)

79. We must all hang together, or we shall all hang separately.

大家必须团结,否则一个个绞死;不团结,死路一条。美国前总统F. 罗斯福有名双关语。

80. We must be the great arsenal of democracy.

我们必须是民主国家的伟大兵工厂。F. 罗斯福宣布援英抗德和其他轴心国广播演说("Our country... is the arsenal of democracy.")。此处的"democracy"在翻译时作可数名词讲。

We must be the great arsenal of democracy. For us this is an emergency as serious as war itself. We must apply ourselves to our task with the same resolution, the same sense of urgency, the same spirit of patriotism and sacrifice we would show if we were at war. (Franklin Roosevelt)

81. We were eyeball to eyeball, and I think that other fellow blinked.

我们原是眼珠瞪眼珠,后来对方眼睛眨了一下;起先双方怒目相视,后来对方挺不住了;双方一度势不两立/较劲,而今对方已认输/示弱。此语上半截或下半截常被记者套用,如:There the adversaries stood, eyeball to eyeball. (*Newsweek*)。语出美国前国务卿 Dean Rusk 关于与苏联谈判的一个报告。

82. What did he know, and when did he know it?

他知道哪些,啥时知道的? 语出 1973 年美参议院多数党领袖 Howard Baker 调查尼克松涉及水门事件(Watergate)时用语。现已成为调查高官,尤其是总统,是否牵涉不轨行为的关键用语,并常被引用。

83. What's good for General Motors (... is good for the country.)

对通用汽车公司有利或对大公司有利(对国家就有利)。故意误引美前国防部长、曾任通用汽车公司总裁的 Charles Wilson 的话来证明艾森豪威尔政府偏爱大企业。

Yes, Sir, I could. I cannot conceive of one because for years I thought **what was good for our country was good for General Motors**, and vice versa. The difference did not exist. Our country is too big. It goes with welfare of the country. Our contribution to the nation is considerable. (Charles Wilson)

84. What's good for the goose ought to be good for the gander.

要求一个人做到的事,人人应该都做到;善恶正邪,人所共知;人人心中有杆秤,善恶自分明。见例句:

[George] Bush laid down this code partly because he has long believed in it and partly because he was appalled by the lax ethics of the Reagan era. Sununu's disregard of this principle has many Bush allies very angry. Said one: "**What's good for the goose ought to be good for the gander**, but it isn't for Sununu." (*Time*)

85. When lawful's awful, treason's reason.

坏事合法,叛逆有理。

86. When the going gets tough, the tough get going.

情况越恶劣,好汉越卖力。语出尼克松政府司法部长米切尔(John Michell)在水门事件的证词。他卷入此事被判刑。第一个"going"可理解为"condition",第一"tough"理解为"difficult or hard";第二"tough" *n.* "a tough guy"(硬汉),"get going"为"start to work"。此言能否意译为"越是困难越向前,困难压不倒英雄汉"。类似"明知山有虎,偏向虎山行"或"疾风知劲草"。

87. When the water reaches the upper deck, follow the rats.

船沉鼠先逃;树倒猢狲散。语出 F. 罗斯福政府任海军部长 Claude Swanson 的讲话。

88. Whenever you have to start explaining—You're in trouble.

越讲越糊涂,越说越不清。语出英国前辉格党议员 Tierney 的讲话。

89. Win one for the Gipper. 见"其他方面的读报知识"人物背景的重要性

90. Winning isn't everything, it's the only thing. 不是一定要赢,是非赢不可。即球场如战场,不胜即败。(见 **Nice guys finish last**)

91. With friends like (these), who needs enemies?
    有这种朋友,还需要敌人吗?有反讽意味,说朋友帮倒忙。

92. (in the)wrong war, (at the)wrong place, (at the)wrong time (and with the)wrong enemy 是常被套用或仿用的标题,如《纽约时报》曾载文批评小布什反恐战用的是"Wrong Time, Wrong War"为标题。再如 Wrong Time for an Urban Cowboy (2007/3/12 *Newsweek*)。语出朝鲜战争(Korean War 1950—1953)的第二年,美军逼近中朝边境鸭绿江,美军司令麦克阿瑟(Douglas MacArthur)主张轰炸中国,杜鲁门不批准,参谋长联席会议主席 Omar Bradley 将军站在总统一边,他在国会说,朝鲜战争是"在错误的地点、错误的时间和与错误的敌人打了一场错误的战争"。

93. You can get a lot more done with a kind word and a gun, than with a kind word alone.
    软硬兼施比只软不硬更有效。美国黑社会头目 Al Capone 用语,经济学家 Walter Heller 用此来比喻工资和物价控制的关系。

94. You can't beat somebody with nobody.
    无名小卒不上阵。说此话是在野党发现执政党不得人心,但又感叹本党缺乏一个能与在职总统或首相抗衡强有力的领袖人物。

95. You can't fight City Hall.
    谁也斗不过官僚衙门;谁对那官僚衙门也没有办法。表明说此话者处于一种无助的处境。(见 **go fight City Hall**)
    For the smouldering diplomats, the encounter was a new lesson in international relations. Around the U. N. the word was being passed that you can say what you like about the United States but **you can't fight the City Hall.** (*Newsweek*)

96. You can't go back to Pocatello.
    回不了老家了;老乡不买我的账。叹息虽在华盛顿官运亨通,但失去了家乡的支持。源出一位爱达荷州 Pocatello 市国会参议员说的一句话,现常改为:"**They never go back to Pocatello.**"

97. You can't have your cake and cut it, too.
    既想要保留蛋糕,可又想要切开吃掉。套用成语:"You can't have

your cake and eat it too."例句中把"eat"改成"cut",意为你们既要保留 Social Security,可又想要削减它,这是矛盾的。这就是常说的:"You can't have it both ways."意近汉语成语"鱼和熊掌不可兼得"。下例的意思是,你们必须让步,不能随心所欲削减 Social Security,否则不要指望我们招待你们。

At one such ceremony, the targeted participants were Maryland Senators Charles Mathias, a Republican, and Paul Sarbanes, a Democrat. Neither showed up for the occasion at a seniors' center in Brentwood, Md., though both sent aides who listened warily as about 30 elderly citizens voiced their grievances before handing over the cake along with the advice: **You can't have your cake and cut it, too.** (*U. S. News & World Report*)

98. You can't make a soufflé rise twice.

蛋糕酥鼓不了两次。语出 Alice Roosevelt Longworth 对杜威(Thomas Dewey)第二次参加总统竞选的评论,意为他第二次不可能像第一次那样讨选民喜欢。他第一次惜败于杜鲁门,尽管民意测验预测他会获胜。

99. You can't win 'em all.

谁都不可能是常胜将军;胜败乃兵家常事。

100. You don't beat City Hall too often 见 **You can't fight City Hall.**

101. You don't hurt somebody by shooting yourself in the foot.

害己损人不明智。

102. You scratch my back, I'll scratch yours.

你帮我忙,我也帮你忙。语出在林肯政府任国防部长的 Simon Cameron 的讲话。

第二节　对号入座式单词转换翻译的弊病

英语常用词大都一词多义，引申义较宽较活，汉语靠双字词限制词义，意思较清楚。经验不足或不认真的译者往往见到"politics"和"culture"时都会对号入座地译为"政治"和"文化"。其实，这两个都是意义广泛的字。当然，culture 则更广，因为语言是文化的载体。我们理解和翻译时，要注意具体意义，不然会造成死译而不合乎汉语习惯表达法。当然，所谓具体意义，是指词义的缩小，万变不离其宗，都属于总的意义，犹如美国各州都有州法，但却不能超越联邦宪法一样。还有 resources 这个字，也有的译者不分汉英词义有别也犯类似的毛病，几乎全译为"资源"二字。

一、Politics/Political

所谓政治，美国政界人士或学者都作了种种解释。美国前总统 John Kennedy 对其新闻秘书 Pierre Salinger 深有感悟地说："政治就像美式足球，一攻一守，谁能突围得分就是胜利。明白这个道理，就经历过困境。"(Politics is like football If you see daylight, go through the hole.);还有人说："政治是翻跟头的真理"(Politics is the truth of somersault)。这两种说法对政治理解偏颇或玩世不恭，政治学者 David Easton 的定义："政治是对价值有权威的分配。"*这话有道理，不然美国总统常与国会就施政纲领斗得你死我活，最终又怎能出台法令，进行施政呢？他们是代表，也就是权威，能将各利益集团摆平，取得妥协。《现代汉语词典》的定义是"政府、政党、社会团体和个人在内政及国际关系方面的活动，"并解释了政治与经济的关系。所以我们在解读它与其他词联用时可以具体一些，不一定非要理解和译为"政治"，尽管那些缩小了的词义也归属政治范围。"常用借喻法"(3)political chaff 就是一例，下面不妨再举几例：

(1) Kennedy was an up-and-coming senator, a bachelor playboy whose **political campaign** was funded by his father's vast fortune. (*The Guardian*)

(2) Efforts have been made before to curb the influence of money on **political campaigns**, and this year will see another attempt. (*U.S. News & World Report*)

上面两例中的"political campaign"，*American Government & Politics* 的词典的释义是：A formal effort established by law to obtain effective office; the

---

* 宁骚：《美国政府与政治》，北京大学出版社，2005，第 4 页。

contest for popular support between candidates prior to an election. 即"竞选"或"竞选运动"或"活动"。网上的英文的释义是："In democracies, political campaigns often refer to electoral campaigns."此释义引出三个问题：言下之意，在一党制掌权国家里，领导因不进行公开竞选，那就只指"政治运动或战役"。在所谓的民主国家里，虽然现在常指"竞选活动或运动"，但并不是有时就不能指"政治运动"，或理解为"政治运动"就是误译。事实并非如此，例如美国在越南战争时有大规模"anti-war movement"（见 community 第9例）和黑人求民权、反歧视的"March on Washington"（见《报刊词典》）等政治运动。再如：美国支持蒋介石打内战，不断有人搞 blame game，提出"Who Lost China?"的责问，实际上为寻找美国对华政策失败的替罪羊。1950年2月。从麦卡锡（Joseph McCarthy）(1908—1957)参议员为首的共和党极右派及民主党保守派终于跳了出来，掀起了一场美国内的反共运动，叫 McCarthyism。他在国会指控国务院有共产党员或其同情者潜伏着。红帽子满天飞，搞得人人自危。为此，公务员要宣誓不是共产党才能保住饭碗。被迫害者如怀特（Theodore White）、斯诺（Edgar Snow）等国务院人员和记者都因此丢掉饭碗而生活陷入困境多年。他所攻击的对象甚至包括杜鲁门总统、国务卿马歇尔（在抗日战争期间曾来华调停过国共内战）等政界要人。1952年他赢得连任，又攻击新上任的艾森豪威尔政府官员。1954年麦卡锡在与军方对质（Army-Mccarthy hearing）中失去支持。他树敌过多，声名狼藉，终遭参议院同僚弹劾。McCarthyism 一词如不是指20世纪50年代"反共歇斯底里（运动）"，就是指"毫无凭据、乱扣帽子的迫害行为"，已成为"迫害狂"、"反共歇斯底里"或"白色恐怖"的代名词。见例句：

（1）**McCarthyism** breeds fear, suspicion and unrest. It turns neighbor against neighbor. (*The New York Times*)

此例所言颇像我国的文化大革命，只是规模较小。这场运动还创造一些词语，如"red baiting"指以莫须有扣上红帽子进行政治迫害。

（2）Stevenson was followed by Scott Lucas, a former majority leader of the United States Senate, who made a strident anti-Communist speech, probably to prove that Democrats were just as anti-Communist as Senator Joseph McCarthy, then the nation's foremost **red-baiting** demagogue(蛊惑人心的政客). (*America in Search of Itself*)

值得注意的是，"political"在各词典里并无"electoral"或"campaign"的释义，"politics"也无"campaign"或"election"的解说，为什么？"竞选"或"选举"等都是政党活动，无须赘言。下面再多看几例：

（3）The seven ruling and opposition politicians admitted to receiving as much as $57,000 from Hanbo, but claimed the money was a proper **political contribution**, Prosecutors charged the money was a bribe, punishable by as many as 10 years in prison. (*The Asian Wall Street Journal*)

(4) Seven politicians acknowledged in court that they received money from Hanbo Steel Industry Co., but said it was in the form of legitimate **political donations.** (*The Asian Wall Street Journal*)

以上两例报道的是同一件,有7名执政党和反对党政界人士承认从 Hanbo 钢铁公司收受了多达5.7万英镑的 political contribution/donations,自认为合法,但检察官可不这么看,指控他们是受贿,可判处多达10年的徒刑。这里,我们在理解或翻译时,在判决结果公布前就犯难了。如理解为 campaign contribution/donation(竞选捐款),且数目没有超过法律的限额,那就合法。但如果译为"政治献金",那就像陈水扁式受贿,或买官卖官。当然,检察官肯定是认为"政治献金"或 slush fund(政客为操纵选举等目的而非法设立的秘密资金;公司对政客的行贿资金),使这些官员能在立法的兴废、政策规章的制定为该公司谋利。

从上述可以看出,"竞选捐款"和"政治献金"是两个完全不同的定义,但都属于"政治"这个总的范畴。

(5) William Casey was not a small time **political manager.**

威廉·凯西不是一个无足轻重的竞选主管。

(6) The bulk of the money comes from only about 10 percent of the population and from **political action committees** of corporations and trade groups like the American Bar Association. Many individual givers often work for companies with PACs or belong to a profession likely to be affected by federal legislation.... The money matters. An example? Late last year, Congress committed $493 million to begin production of 20 B-2 stealth aircraft planes the Pentagon says it does not want or need. Pressure to build the planes came from contractors. From 1993 through late 1995, **political action committees** representing 32 B-2 subcontractors gave nearly $8 million to members of Congress, urging their support for the B-2. Norm Dicks, a Washington Democrat, led 67 other Democrats who crossed over and voted with Republicans to vote for the planes. Since 1993, Dicks has received $84,000 in B-2 subcontractor **PAC** money. (*U.S. News & World Report*)

此例中的 Political Action Committee 可参考读报知识对 PAC 的介绍而译为"竞选活动委员会"。至于"political advance man"则为"为竞选活动先吆喝"或

"助选人员"。

下面不妨再举例说明 politics 也有"竞选"之义。

(1) The Texas race probably marked a modern low in **attack politics**, with its unsupported charges of drug taking, pocket-lining and political corruption.

(2) This is at least a disarmingly honest attitude, perhaps best labeled **negative** new **politics**. In Texas, gubernatorial candidate Clayton Williams, who is lately calling his opponent a liar, ran an ad that began with the lament that "Ann Richards is running a negative campaign."

(3) It is cowardly for Bush to campaign around the country, looking like an unemployed airline pilot, alternately doling out goodies and practicing **slash-and-burn politics**.

以上3例都与(2)例最后一句中的最后两个字"negative campaign"同义,均为"攻讦性竞选"、"抹黑对手的竞选"、"贬毁对手的竞选"等意思。但此处的"negative politics/campaign"如照字面意思理解为"消极竞选",就正好将意思颠倒了。请看例句:

Negative campaigning got out of hand in several congressional races. Political scientist Norman Ornstein of the American Enterprise Institute said that too many campaigns were marred by attacks on "candidates' morality and integrity and by innuendo, falsehood and triviality." (*U.S. News & World Report*)

此例讲得很清楚,"negative campaigning"是这句句子最后指的"attacks on candidates' morality... and triviality"。

(4) In an era of **single-issue politics** and highly organized lobbing, it will be difficult for Congress to restrain itself to the degree necessary to meet Carter's goal. (*National Journal*)

Safire's Political Dictionary 的释义是: reduction of a campaign or election to a single issue(把竞选活动或选举缩小为一个如 abortion 或 tax 这样的问题。)这就是说,此例中的 politics 指的是"campaign"或"election",与 political campaign 义同。

通讯发达后又出现了"retail/wholsale politics"的词语,分别指"小打小闹的竞选"和"利用电视、网络等各种现代式工具大范围竞选造势"。

此外,politics 还有"技术、手腕、策略"等词义。见例句:

All this provides ammunition for those in both parties who want to **play politics** with the issue. (*The New York Times*)

"所有这些都给两党要在这个问题上耍手腕、搞攻击的那些人提供了炮弹。""play politics" Oxford 的定义是:act for political or personal gain rather than from principle.

2003 年第三届全国高校英语报刊教学研究会上,本人就"political campaign"作了上述发言,有的教师觉得顿开茅塞,说在翻译时常遇到这个问题而不得已死译为"政治"。

二、Culture/Cultural

"culture"或"cultural"与"politics"和"political"的情况类似。现在人们见到此字就不加思考、省时省力地译为"文化(的)",什么西瓜文化、企业文化、汽车文化、土鳖文化、水果文化、饮食文化、依赖文化,等等,不一而足。如果这样,大学里语言系、历史系、哲学系等一律改称为文化系岂不更好。其实,文化的范围比政治更广,政治也属文化范畴。《现代汉语词典》的定义是:"人类在社会历史发展过程中所创造的物质财富和精神财富的总和,特指精神财富"和"运用文字的能力及一般知识"。

1987 年,编者在编《美英报刊文章选读》(上下册)(第一版)时遇上了该词,觉得理解为文化不合适,有的虽然在上下文中已释义,但还是特请在北大任教的美国德州大学教授 John Rumrich 作了注解。有人撰文说,enterprise culture 只能译为"企业文化",我看未必。见下列例句和释义:

(1) Air Force whistle-blower Ompal Chauhan warned against **a type of cultural conditioning** in which a typical Pentagon manager "thinks more about his future employer than his current one. Loyalties become confused."(U. S. News & World Report)

"a type of cultural conditioning" — a kind of situation in the Pentagon which teaches the officials to act the way a typical Pentagon manager does.

(2) If the government sets the right climate, Thatcher believes, new businesses will flourish. But is modern-day Britain capable of creating the kind of **enterprise culture** Thatcher envisions? The plain truth is that British companies do not, for the most part, work as efficiently as their competitors. "Yes, we're creating new companies," says Stuart Slatter, director of the Institute of Small Business Management of the London Business School, "but there is very little evidence that they will be a major source of new jobs." Slatter cites what amounts to a **cultural handicap**: "People lack the get-up-and-go to go out and succeed."(Newsweek)

a. enterprise culture — a good business climate or environment.

b. a cultural handicap — lack of energetic business drive, force, etc.

(1)例指五角大楼出现的"一股习以为常、损公利己的歪风邪气",因为其管理军工企业的官员假公济私,不忠于职守,而满脑子想的是复员后去他所监管的企业去谋个肥缺,这就必须导致监管流于形式。(2)例在第一句已指明是"right climate",根据上下文"enterprise culture"当然指的是"良好的企业气候或环境",或"企业发展的良好氛围"。(2)例在最后一句冒号后作了注释:缺乏企业家的那种敢于冒险、奋斗创新取得业绩的开拓或进取精神。

综合上述三例中的"cultural"或"culture",分别可指"风气"、"气候"、"环境"或"氛围"、"进取精神"。根据(1)例,"dependent culture"可理解为"依赖陋习或歪风",这些都属于"文化"范畴,只不过具体化罢了,但意思上与全句或全段更贴切。而下例的"culture"与(2)例的意思相同,理解为"气氛":

(3) The "war on terror" has created a **culture** of fear in America. (*The Washington Post*)

再看下列两例:

(4) Many of us were given pause by the Republican convention in Houston, at which Pat Buchanan seriously proposed religious warfare, **cultural cleansing** and rooting out dissatisfied Americans who have infiltrated their own country block by block.

(5) The refugees are Nepali-speaking people of southern Bhutan. What started out in 1990 as a campaign to force all citizens to wear the traditional Bhutanese dress and speak the Dzongkha language has grown into a macabre "**cultural cleansing**" exercise.

(4)例中的人物 Pat Buchanan 是美国20世纪90年代活跃于政坛的极右翼的政界人士,两次参与共和党总统候选人提名,但均以失败而告终,后又参加改革党角逐总统职位也未果。他提倡"cultural cleaning"指"对共和党内异己的清除,尤其是对党内持不同政见即非保守派的清洗"。(5)例讲的是不丹对居住在该国的尼泊尔难民进行服饰和语言上的同化,怕这是"宗教、民族/种族清洗"的前奏。这两例中的不同"政见"、"宗教"、"民族特点"等也都可归纳进"文化"的范畴。最后再举几例:

(6) But I am not Orwellian in the sense that these critics mean, or in the way Orwellian has been defined by today's **popular culture.** (Frank Luntz)

此例中的 popular culture 如译为"大众文化"或"通俗文化"都不当,理解为义近 conventional wisdom(普遍看法)倒更贴切些。(见"跟踪语言的变化和发展""Orwellian 新解")

如到网上搜索或查较大的词典,还有其他与文化相比词义较窄而又包含在文化概念或范围之内的意义。如文明、人文、教育、教养、修养、熏陶及采取同样生活方式之群体等。见例句:

(7) **Physical culture** is important, but we must not neglect the **culture** of mind.

此例的第一个 culture 可理解教育,第二个也可理解与教育近义的熏陶、培养。整句的意思是:"**体育**固然重要,但不应忽视心灵**陶冶**。"

(8) the singles/drug culture

独身主义者阶层/瘾君子群体

作技术用语,culture 还有栽培、种植、养殖、培养等词义。例如:

(9) Indeed, in many regions, "forestry" is synonymous with plantation culture.

在许多地区,"林业"事实上就是**森林栽培**的同义词。

三、Resources

resources 与 politics 和 culture 不同,后者词的总义广,而前者原本在汉语里只指自然资源,现已扩展到指人工资源和其他许多人或事,词的总义比 politics 更广,或许是仅次于文化吧。这是由于有人常不顾上下文或词的搭配而一律译为有时意思含糊、有时是多余的"资源",即使在官方的公文里也存在这样的赘词。一方面或许是因为我们词义面窄。另一方面可能是不愿意上网或查词典费劲。更重要的是或许我们不愿意探讨表现的意思是否明确,语言是否符合汉语的习惯表达法。之所以说"资源"现在在汉语里词义广,不妨看两句对话:

A:听说你还没有女朋友,我给你介绍一个。

B:好呀!你手里的资源一定很多。此处"资源"指"女子"了。

资源有时意思含糊。举例来说,如果有人说:"你们学校资源很丰富。"人们很难知道他指的是人才多、设备好或校舍多,还是指资金充足,因为该词也可指钱,钱是财力的体现。记得几年前杨澜在香港阳光卫视台采访台湾亲民党主席宋楚瑜时对宋说:"听说你们党资源不多"。宋答道:"是啊,我们党钱不多"。这是一例,此外,resources 确实也有 money 的意义(见下第 6 例)。

为了说明问题,不妨先看英英词典的词义。*The New Oxford Dictionary of English* 的定义是:a. a stock or supply of money, materials, staff and other assets that can be drawn on by a person or organization in order to function effectively:local authorities complained that they lacked resources.

b. a country's collective means of supporting itself or becoming wealthier, as represented by its reserves of minerals, land, and other assets, c. *N. Amer.* available assets. 此外,还有其他词义。a. 义面较广,指可动用的所储备的钱、物资、人员和其他资源。b. 义指的是一国所蕴藏或储备的矿产、土地和其天然资源。这与汉语词典义同。c. 义指所有资财。

在汉语中,"资源"词义也扩展了。在汉语行文中,常见到"人力资源部"(有人理解为更多的指培养人才,可以前中外人事处、局或部也培养人才)、"浪费财力、物力资源"等字眼。这里有一个常识问题,也有一个对资源这个词词义的理解问题。"人力"、"财力"或"物力"是不是资源?如果是,那么,"人力部"、"浪费财力、物力"行不行?何必再画蛇添足,加上"资源"两字呢?

退一步说如果在汉语里义广或含糊或许可以的话,那么,在英文的具体句子里是否可漠视上下文和背景而一律理解或译为"资源"呢?见例句:

(1) Because of limited insurance coverage, many people will have to look to their own **resources—both emotional and financial**—to care for an infirm or recovering relative at home. (Steven Findlay)

由于投入的保险面窄,所以许多人为了照顾家里年迈体弱或正在康复的亲人而不得不考虑自己有多大的**精力和财力**。(此处是否要加上"资源"二字才放心?)

2009 年 4 月 2 日在伦敦召开的 20 集团会议前夕,鉴于国际货币资金组织(IMF)连续为冰岛、乌克兰、匈牙利等国借出资金,**资源**面临枯竭。因此,不少国家支持**增加财政资源**。这里所谈的"资源"不就是"资金"吗?增加财政资源不就是"增资"[increase its financial resources(资金)]吗?

(2) These people will tend to flood the cities, exacerbating already strained urban **resources**.

这些人往往会大批涌往城市,使市区本已负荷过重的**各种设施**会因此雪上加霜。(此处如改译为"资源",指什么?)

(3) The head of state treasured manpower and **resources**.

这位国家元首珍惜人力**物力**。(若改译为"资源",那么人力是否资源?)

(4) On top of his supposed rhetorical failures, Mr Clinton stands accused of starving the drugs war of **resources**. When he arrived in the White House, Mr Clinton cut the staff of the drug tsar's office by 83%. He also cut money devoted to interdicting cocaine at the border. In the last two years of the Bush administration, the interdiction budget came to around $2 billion a year; this year it stands at a mere $1.3 billion. (The *Economist*)

除了被认为所谓的宣传不力失误外,克林顿还被指责不向反毒战提供迫切需要的**人力和财力**……

　　这里的 resources 从上下文看显然指的是人力和财力,因为缉毒人员和预算都减少了。如改译为"资源",两者相比,何者更确切明白?

　　(5) The Pentagon argues for leaner military establishment, even though the gulf conflict has stretched its **resources** to the limit. (*Time*)

　　五角大楼力争缩小军事建制,即使海湾战争投入的**军力/兵力**达到了极限。如果此处,理解或译为"资源",即与 leaner military establishment 如何呼应?

　　(6) At the root of the problem is **money.** As a poor nation, China has few **resources** left over for cultural conservation after struggling to overhaul its command economy, dampen rising unemployment, take care of an aging population, put in infrastructure and modernize its massive military. (*Los Angeles Times*)

　　根本的问题是钱。中国是一个穷国,没有留下多少**钱**用作文物保护……

　　这段文字表明,"resources"在此处与上一句中的"money"同义。不妨再举一个义同的例句:

　　(7) "Where universities are heading now is toward becoming global universities. We'll have more and more universities competing internationally for **resources**, faculty and the best students." (*The New York Times*)

　　大学前进的方向是要争取成为全球性大学。越来越多的大学会参与对教育资金、教师和最优秀学生的国际竞争。这里西方世界第一大报《纽约时报》表达得很清楚,而不是以 resources 一字蔽之。

　　从以上几例可以看出,除了"resources"可译为"资源"外,还可译为"设施"、"人力"、"物力"、"财力"、"钱"、"资金"等。

　　据以上解说,我们平时在媒体上常耳闻目睹所谓"智力资源"、"跨国公司挖掘中国大学**资源**"。如是译文,宜改译为"**人才**";"大学**资源**库"改为"**人才**库";"制作**资源**"改译"**设施**",等等。

　　可能有人会说,以所以说"资源"是出于策略,有时谈事要含糊一点,以免被人抓住把柄闹笑话而丢脸。这种说法或许有在汉语里一定道理,但在理解、翻译或教员授课时,对 resources 一词的讲解或翻译决不能这样笼统含糊而使学生不知所云。不过话又得说回来,看来现在这股用"文化"、"资源"时髦风的 big mo,是谁也挡不住了。

　　从另一方面看,或许这跟西方与国人的思维不同有很大关系。虚词实译,实词虚译是很常见的事。这里还有个习惯的问题,如 pull, leverage,译为"拉扯","杠杆作用"就不如"影响"好。其他处已提到,此处不赘。

第七章　学习方法

第一节　网络和读报工具书

一、读报工具书重要性

在谈要"学会利用和使用网络和读报工具书"及"勤上网和勤查词典"之前，必须知道网络和工具书的用处及读报要有哪些必要或得心应手的工具书。

网络和工具书好比老师，又不同于一般意义的老师，老师不能老陪伴着教我们，它们却是人们自学、研究无处不在的"老师"；与老师相比，学问要更大更全面；没有脾气，是我们的良师益友，又比良师益友还要好，因为它们随时随地都毫无保留地专心为我们终生服务。这样的老师是任何人自学和做学问不可或缺的。

笔者能在网络尚不发达编出美英报刊文选的一个重要原因，当时具有各种各样的工具书多达几十本，除语言工具书和百科全书外，还有美国政府与政治、美国外交史、美国历史、宗教、文学、经贸、经济、年鉴、地理、人名、情报、核术语和气象等专门词典，简直像个读报的小图书馆。加上平时积累的资料，所以编起书来较顺手，有东西可写，尽管水平不高和我因病不能上网。

众所周知，网络比任何工具书都全面和得心应手，尤其是语料库可纠正错误和提高英文水平。相对而言，工具书落伍了。我珍惜它，自己靠它自学而成。此外，有的工具书并未入网，且仍有学者查词典解疑释难，可见词典尚有用武之地。

俗话说："工欲善其事，必先利其器。"我们在中学和大学低年级打英语基本功时用的如 Oxford Advanced Learner's Dictionary of Current English 是适用的，但到了大学高年级要读懂英文报刊，这本词典在词汇上不够多，知识面不够广。为了能学会看报，我们需要两方面的知识，即语言知识(knowledge of the language)和文化知识(knowledge of the culture)。根据笔者多年的读报经验，开始时应先用下列词典较合适。

1.《当代美英报刊词典》(2007年6月由北京大学出版社出版)是主编根据多年的读报和教学经验及在编注报刊文选系列课本的基础上，针对初学报刊者掌握新闻词语不多和国际知识贫乏而编写的，尽管里面有一些小儿科错误。尤其难能可贵的是,本书还列出同义词、近义词和反义词及参考词语。

2.《美英报刊导读》(第二版)是附有英文索引的词典式参考指导书。它与报刊文选读本相辅相成,相得益彰。二版还纠正了《当代美英报刊词典》里的若干错误。

3. Longman Dictionary of English Language & Culture(2004年由商务印书馆出版)是一本集语言与知识于一体的通用词典,缺点是收词少和没有列出词源。

4. The New Oxford Dictionary of English (Oxford University Press 出版)是一本定义准确的好词典。

5. Webster's New World Dictionary of the American Language 是韦氏美语词典系列中一本读报最好的工具书。

6. The American Heritage Dictionary 特点是收词量大,俚语、俗语均收入书内;释义明晰、准确,深入探索词源,为同类词典所不及。此外,附录中还有人物、地名、美国大学简介,对读报刊很重要。书中还有大量插图,有助理解。

7.《英汉大词典》(第二版)(上海译文出版社出版)它是国内英汉词典收录英语词条最多的一本综合性词典,与一版相比,在释义等方面进步很大。

二、学会利用工具书

一个人学问再大,记忆力再好,也不可能将网络和工具书的内容都装到脑子里。所以网络发达前人们常说,一个人的工具书再多,也没有图书馆的书多。还有人说:"坐三年图书馆就成了学问家。"如果不好好利用各地各单位的这座宝库,岂不可惜!北大已故赵诏熊教授曾对我说:"你知道吗?李(赋宁)先生没有事就坐在图书馆看词典玩。"可见李先生多么重视这座宝库啊!打开宝库,许多问题迎刃而解。遇到问题不找词典帮忙,就好比"放着河水不洗床"。难怪有人讲,好的词典就像聘请了几位高明的英语教师,要随时请教。

2003年1月,一位北京师范大学院士在中央电视台访谈节目中谈到他对指导研究生说:"你们可能从我这里什么也没学到,但是学会了如何查词典。"可见挑选几本好词典和学会查词典是多么重要。编者刚做研究,遇上问题向老先生请教时,他们总能从这样那样的工具书里找到答案,这对我启发很大。一个人仅知道要有工具书还不行,要知道什么问题查什么工具书,还要会熟练使用。同样一本工具书,某人可能找不到答案,另一个人能查找出来。这里面大有学问。现在网络只要打上几个关键词,详情就历历在目,不必以前那样费力,恍如隔世。尽管如此,在确定有的词义时,也往往要上几家网或查几本词典才行,以前老先生做学问一丝不苟的精神值得学习。

三、勤上网和查词典

为了说明勤上网和查词典的重要性，最好举例说明。

1. 职位不明

有的词典将 Shadow Chancellor 译为"影子内阁大臣"。其实是"影子内阁财政大臣"，影子内阁大臣是"Shadow Minister/Secretary"，有文章为证：

Now that the Baker-Aziz talks have failed, John Prescott, the shadow transport secretary, is pushing the possibility of a peace initiative by FranÇois Mitterrand. He wants the matter discussed during talks with French Socialists scheduled for next week which may include Mr Kaufman and *the shadow chancellor John Smith*. Mr Prescott thinks a Mitterrand initiative would be attractive: it would be European and socialist, and it would keep both sides talking beyond the deadline... The crude explanation is that Mr Kinnock and Mr Kaufman were threatened by a shadow-cabinet revolt this week. Those *shadow ministers* — Robin Cook, Mr Prescott and Bryan Gould are the most prominent — who would be opposed to an early, American-dominated war have not actually plotted; but Mr Kinnock is well aware of their views. (1991/1/12 *The Economist*)

影子内阁大臣全称是"Shadow Chancellor of the Exchequer"，这跟"foreign secretary"的全称是"Secretary of State For Foreign and Commonwealth Affairs"一样。当时的影子内阁名单上列着 John Smith 是影子内阁财政大臣。

英汉词典是从英英词典翻译编纂而成的。任何译者，文字水平和背景知识毕竟局限，难免出错，即使 Homer sometimes nods（大诗人荷马也有打盹时；智者千虑，必有一失嘛）。如自认为具有"里程碑"意义的词典就曾受到业内人士多方纠错，不当之处也非个别。因此，读者一定要在工作中多查英英工具书和上网，不能贪图省事，迷信权威。

2. 望文生义

阅读时要做到完全懂，不能只凭原来对某词的理解，望文生义，也不能不懂装懂或不求甚解。应该仔细阅读全部词义，然后根据上下文确定词义，才会少出错。在翻译时，尤其是政治和科技文献的词语要求准确，差一点就会闹出大问题。无数译例证明，越是常用语，引申义越多，越容易望文生义闹笑话，要语感强，做个有心人才成。

编者 1987 年编报刊文选时选了《新闻周刊》一文，遇到了"gunship"这个字时差点犯错。见原文：

The virtual absence of any opposing air cover turned the operation into a turkey shoot for the Iraqi warplanes, which were reportedly flying as many as 800 sorties a day. **Helicopter gunships** also joined the fray.

乍一看 helicopter gunship 是"载直升机的舰艇",可又一想,为了不犯"man-of-war"误解为"战士"的错误,就查 The *World Book Dictionary*,才知道应理解为"武装或攻击直升机"〔a helicopter carrying heavy machine guns and rockets for support of ground troops(为支援地面部队而携带着重机枪和火箭的直升机)〕。

再如:2002 年 2 月 6 日《参考消息》在翻译《南华早报》(*South China Morning Post*)发表的一篇文章中有这么一句译文:

他说:"在**后勤**和 IT 业领域,香港是联系大陆与世界的纽带。……"

这句话中的所谓"后勤(业)",英文为"logistical"或"logistics",在《英汉大词典》和《英汉经济综合词典》等工具书中都只有用作军语义。可例句译文与事实不符,香港怎么能作为大陆与世界联系的后勤呢?事实上在此处是"物流的"或"物流业"的意思,英文定义为"flow of goods and materials"。当然,这个词义对大多数读者来说现在已不新鲜,可当时网络尚未如此发达普及。

又如:《新民晚报》和《参考消息》分别就"interests"这个多义词在下面两句话中分别误译为"利益":

2001 年 7 月联邦调查局发出警告,称美国在海外的**利益**可能受到袭击。

澳大利亚官员 17 日说,他们得到的新情报表明,在印尼还会发生针对西方人和西方**利益**的恐怖活动。

从上下文和汉语词语搭配关系等方面来看,"interests"译为"利益"不通,"利益"不能"袭击",若理解为"organization"(组织,机构)就对了。(见"**语言**""扩大若干常见词的词义面")

又如:有人在翻译英国、爱尔兰和北爱尔兰各派就北爱问题达成的 Good Friday Agreement 时译为"美丽/美好星期五协议",更是望文生义。Good Friday 应是复活节后星期日前的那个星期五,这天是基督教会纪念耶稣被钉死在十字架上和传统的斋日和苦修日。由此可见,是"耶稣受难节"。协议是那天签订的。

需要勤上网和查词典的根本原因,在于中西文化知识不尽相同,人们的思维和对事物的认识有差异。对于有些词语、语法,英美人不会产生误解,中国人却极易理解出错。这里不举复杂的段落或句子,只列出若干初学者极易望文生义的词语:**button man** 非"穿有纽扣服装的人",而是黑手党"杀手";**battle/combat/military fatigues** 非"战斗疲劳(combat fatigue)",而是"战斗服或军服";**cooker**

非"厨师",而是"炊事用具";**corporate welfare** 非"公司福利",而是"国家给公司的补贴";**court reporter** 非"法庭记者",而是"法庭记录员/书记员";**general doctor** 非"多面手医生",而是级别较低的"通科医生";**industrial relations** 非"工业关系",而是"劳资关系";**knowledge worker** 非"有知识员工(**knowledgable worker**)",而是"处理信息和数据的技术人员";**knowledge management** 非"知识管理层",而是"知识和信息管理";**lazy Susan** 非"懒惰的苏珊",而是"餐桌上放菜的转盘";**nonperson** 非"不是人",而是"无足轻重或无权利之人","被遗忘或被漠视的人",至于 **unperson**,则指故意抹杀某名人,干脆连名字都不提;**press book** 非"新闻或报刊书",而是剪刀加糨糊贴成的"剪报册";**policy bank** 非"政策银行",而是"一种赌博彩票的庄家";**pour oil on trouble waters** 非"火上浇油",而是"排解纠纷";**sleeping policeman** 非"在睡眠中的警察",而是"减速杠";**student-driven car** 非"学生开的车",而是"教练车";**Sunday driver** 非"星期天开车者",而是"不常开车的新手";**state trooper**(美)非"国家军人",而是美国"州警察或交通巡警";**state trial** 非"国家审讯",而是"政治犯审判";**truth drug** 非"真药或毒品",而是"诱供药";**The phone is ringing off the hook** 非"电话从钩子上掉下来",而是"电话忙得不停";**Whistle blower** 非"吹哨子的人",而是"敢于揭露上司的谎言或丑闻者";**yellow press** 非"黄色报刊",而是"低级报刊",指故作耸人听闻报道、哗众取宠的报章杂志;**Yellow Pages** 非"色情专页",而是电话号码本中"厂商地址和广告专页",等等。

像上述这类易引起中国读者误解的词语很多,如有人能编出一本这样的词典来,定受国内广大英语学习者欢迎。

四、报刊、网络和词典也出错

1. 报刊背景知识不明

读者在看书读报过程中一定要带着问号,俗话说:"尽信书不如无书。"本人在看报和编书过程中,偶尔会发现除印刷错误外,美英报刊文章既有背景知识失当,也有用字遣词欠妥。例如:

The NATO-led Implementation Force (IFOR) has separated Bosnia's warring armies. Territory has been traded. **Bosnia-Herzegovina now consists of two awkward "entities" — Republika Srpska and the Federation of Bosnia and Herzegovina**; But ending the war is not the same as securing the peace. Unless Bosnia and the international community resolve the much more difficult problems of reconciliation and reconstruction, Agnesa Hadjic's moment of tranquility could evaporate like so many Balkan mirages. (1996/4/1 *U. S.*

News & World Report)

(……波黑是由两个别扭的实体组成：波黑塞尔维亚共和国和**波黑联邦**……)

此处记者搞错了，波黑联邦应改为"穆斯林和克罗地亚族联邦"(the Muslim-Croat federation)组成。

2. 报刊语言错误

(1) boll weevils 棉铃象甲，美国《时代》周刊用来喻"南方民主党保守派"，即以政治见解保守，常投票给共和党候选人而著称，因而含有"窝里反"的贬义。而英国《经济学家》在一篇文章里则指"南方民主党温和派"或"共和党自由派"。再如 gypsy moths 舞毒蛾，《时代》周刊用来喻"东北部共和党温和派"，即共和党内的反主流派或反对派。而《经济学家》在一篇文章里则既指"东北部共和党温和派"，也指"民主党保守派"。编者认为，这两个都是美国政治俚语，还是以美刊的释义为准，英刊将 boll weevils 和 gypsy moths 用拧了。

先见《美国政府与政治词典》对这两个词语的释义：

boll weevils 1. A long-used term for southern Democrats in the U. S. House of Representatives who support conservative policies. 2. Southern Democrats in the U. S. House of Representatives who supported President Ronald Reagan's economic programs. Boll weevils are insects that feed on cotton. **gypsy moths** Those liberal and moderate Republicans in the U. S. House of Representatives who tended to deny support to President Ronald Reagan's domestic and foreign policies. They were called gypsy moths, in contrast to boll weevils, after a leaf-eating moth found in the north, because most of these House members represented congressional districts from the Northeast and Midwest.

再看《时代》周刊的释义：

The spring swarm of "**Boll Weevils**" Southern conservative Democrats willing to support Reagan's first round of spending curbs, may be replaced by an autumn flight of "**Gypsy moths**", moderate Republicans from the Northeast who are reluctant to reduce social spending further.

《经济学家》在这篇文章里对"gypsy moths"用对了：

These wonders are happening because a breed of lawmakers thought to be almost extinct has been reasserting itself. They are **Republican moderates** — "**gypsy moths**", as they used to be called... Republican moderates, mostly from **the northeast**, felt taken for granted and informally grouped together under the name of **gypsy moths**, after the insects that plague the trees of New England.

第七章　学习方法　　　　　　　　　　　　339

《经济学家》在另一文却都用错了，请看：
In America's experience, things are more likely to get done when approached in bipartisan — or nonpartisan — spirit. Progress comes from co-operation among **liberal Republicans** ("**boll weevils**") and **conservative Democrats** ("**gypsy moths**"), plus a small number of genuinely bipartisan souls. (1996/5/18 The *Economist*)

(2) Xie Jun ends hold on **Soviet** chess title (1991/10/30 The Reuters) 这个标题犯了遣词的错误，应改为：
Xie Jun ends **Soviet** hold on (world) chess title
谢军在 1991 年 10 月夺得的不是苏联棋王或苏联国际象棋冠军的称号，而是世界女子国际象棋棋王或冠军的称号，从而结束了当时的苏联独霸棋坛的局面。可比较我国 *China Daily* 在同日就此事发表的文章标题：
Birthday girl takes world chess crown

3. 网络粗心错字多

我是 computer illiterate，本来无权对网络说三道四，但《美英报刊文章选读》（上下册）（第四版）送给我看的稿子里还有不少错字，有的字不纠正过来会闹出笑话，如有一课 "Colombia Crisis Is Settled, But Which Side Wins?"（2008/3/9 *International Herald Tribune*）第三段里第一句：
Latin America's largest rebel group, **the Revolutionary Armed Forces of Colombia**, or **FARC**, lost two senior commanders in a week.
其后全用的这个拼错首字母缩略词"FARC"，而不是"RAFC"。再如在 Stealing a Nation（2006 年 11 月号 *New African*）这课里错字竟达 10 来个。

4. 美英词典要区分

词典查字有美英之分，查美国的文章里的字查美语词典，如 official's time-out，*The New Oxford Dictionary of English* 没有 official 作"裁判（员）"（暂停）讲之义，而 20 世纪 80 年代出版的 *American Heritage* 都有 a referee or umpire 的意义。

5. 行话专业词典来当家

专业词语查综合词典不如看专业词典，如下例中的 effete snobs，有的综合词典甚至释义有误。
1969 年 10 月 19 日，时任尼克松政府的副总统阿根纽（Spiro Agnew）在 New Orleans 市晚宴上发表该话，抨击某些知识分子时说：
A spirit of national masochism prevails, encouraged by an **effete** corps of impudent **snobs** who characterize themselves as intellectuals.
后登在上报上作标题的是"effete snobs"而略去"corps of impudent"，这就是现在看到的词语。经查 1995 年由外研社和 Longman 联合出版的 Longman Dictionary of Contemporary English，effete 的第一义是：weak and powerless in

a way that you dislike：an attack against effete intellectuals. 这就是 effete snobs 中 effete 的意思，即人们不喜欢的那种软绵绵的、有气无力的知识分子。此处的释义似乎不对，因为阿氏不可能因为知识分子仅仅有气无力而加以抨击，网上和其他词典关于 effete snobs/intellectuals 的释义也大同小异。最后查到 *New Political Dictionary*，其义是：a derogation of the arrogance of pseudo-intellectuals，而且该词典还纠正读者的误解说：One reason the phrase caused such a fierce reaction was that many readers interpreted "effete" to mean "effeminate,"（a man who is effeminate looks or behaves like a woman——编者根据 Longman 注释），which is not its meaning—"enervated," "wrung out," "intellectually barren" defines the term and fit the context of his remark. 这本权威政治词典的释义是说"effete"在上下文里既非"手无缚鸡之力的"，也非"娇滴滴"或"没有男子气概的"，而是"草包"的意义。整句意思是："一股逆来顺受、以辱为荣之风席卷全国，是些冒牌知识分子、势利鬼在那里推波助澜。"

阿氏这里是对从政的知识分子（eggheads）如当年活跃于政坛的民主党人 Adlai Stevenion 等人的反击，他们常抨击共和党的尼克松政府（Administration）及阿氏的言行。

即使是美国公认的政治语言专家、前《纽约时报》专栏作家和总统撰稿人 William Safire，在 2008 年总统选举年由 Orford University Press 出版的 *Safire's Political Dictionary* 也有前后矛盾的疏忽之处。如他在 Prolegomenon（序，前言）里（p. Xii）写道："The Political language is constantly changing：*gutter flyer* replaces *roorback*,... *barnack* for *hanger-on*..." 可在 **obsolete political terms** 里却将 barnacle 列在其中，被 hanger-on 所替代（p. 487）。

第二节　词语学习记忆法

一、学习法

掌握一定数量的新闻词语相当重要,报刊文章在写作和用词等方面与我国学生在大学低年级学的规范语言不尽相同,课文大多是关于学习人生哲理的一些小故事,新闻语言罕见,词义面偏窄。这一点在前面已作了说明。

不少人都埋怨生字多。这是因为英国在历史上曾遭到多次外族入侵,占领时期有的长达几百年。这样,有的外来词就在英语中生根发芽,直接进入或融合到英语里,这也是英语生词多而难记的一个重要原因。读了《基督教科学箴言报》2001年1月2日一篇题为"If you speak English, you're a master of many tongues(语言)"的文章就明白了。前四段是这么写的：

How many languages do you speak? One, maybe two, you say? Wrong! If you speak English, you use words from at least 35 foreign languages. Want proof? Read the next two sentences out loud:

"Jane saw a baby squirrel eating ketchup(番茄酱) left out after yesterday's barbeque(烧烤). Although she was still wearing her cotton pajamas, she hurried outside to chase the creature away."

There. You just spoke seven languages—counting English!

"Baby" comes from a Dutch word spelled the same way. "Squirrel" is French. "Ketchup" originated in Malay(马来语). "Barbeque" was borrowed from Caribbean Indians(印第安人). "Cotton" was first an Arabic word. And "Pajamas" was taken right from the Urdu language (乌尔都语) of India. Surprised?

尽管如此,刚起步时一定要记忆一定数量的基本词汇,犹如盖房子必须夯实地基一样。掌握两三千词汇后,就可以通过上下文大体猜出某些生词的意思。英文忌重复,跟汉语有时爱重复不大相同。开头遇到生词,不必马上查字典,接下来或许会出现你学过的同义词或近义词,茅塞顿开,再查词典印证,看猜错没有,这样学到的词语就更加牢靠,慢慢举一反三,能力就愈来愈大,语感也随之增强了。这方面,在前面的章节上已举了数例,为深入阐明此法,此处再举几例：

In two others, they must share power with coalition partners. Distressing as this is for them, the picture could further darken in local and state elections slated for 1987. The next nationwide elections are not scheduled until 1990.

在上面前后两个句子中,"slated"或许是个生字而不知何义,可看到第三句中的"scheduled"就明白了。此处这两个字可视为同义或近义词。

再如:报刊文选有课文的标题"Lobbyists Out Of Shadow Into The Spotlight"(1985/2/25 *U. S. News & World Report*)(院外活动人员从阴暗处走到聚光灯照耀下,即从幕后走向前台)里出现的"out of shadow into spotlight",进而在副标题出现"shady" operators(幕后或不公开露面的说客),继而在文末倒数第二段出现 work "behind the scenes"(幕后活动)和 the Watergate era put a stop to all the "underground games"(地下把戏或秘密活动)being played, so they "came out of the closet(从隐蔽转为公开)",最后在末段又出现 Whether they "work offstage" or "in the spotlight"(是幕后或公开活动),这些都应联系起来对照,看哪些是同义或近义词语,哪些是反义词。

又如:另一篇课文"The Great Superpower Spy War KGB vs. CIA"中同义词也很多,如 arrest, nab, apprehend, capture 等为一组同义词,reveal, compromise, burn, expose 等为另一组同义词或近义词,intelligence officer, operative, plant, agent, double agent, triple agent, mole 和 spy 则又可将它们归入同义词或近义词来学习。

英语界前辈李赋宁先生在《英语学习经验谈》一书中对大家进行了这样的指导:在阅读时必须学会寻找同义词和反义词。这样做,对于加深理解有很大的好处。……把同义词联系起来,对照区别,对于理解上下文很有帮助。但有时同义词和反义词的对照比较隐晦,在这种情况下就必须细心找出同义词和反义词的对照,以便更加透彻地理解上下文的意思。

另一个用词特点是,词同义异,如上面提到的课文中有"shady" operators 和 "shady" reputation(不诚实的声誉),其中 shady 就不同义,前者指"behind-the-scenes",后者指"dishonest or unsavory"。

避免用字重复是个特点,也是个优点。但是在新闻语言里,往往过火,牵强附会,弄巧成拙。如此文竟将 outfits, operations 和 hitters 都用来指 lobby(ing) firms,虽说 operations 还算可以,outfit 和 hitters 就未必合适。

二、名师指点记忆法

对入门者而言,报刊里陌生词语随处可见,是一大拦路虎。如何记忆词汇?英语界前辈李赋宁先生在《英语学习经验谈》一书中作了如下的指导:

"语法知识固然重要,但是词汇知识也同样重要,因为思想和概念首先要通过词来表达。……首先要弄清楚词义,同学们查英汉字典时,往往发现一个词有好几个解释,有时多到十几个解释。如何选择一条最恰当的解释,就是我们在阅读中首先要解决的问题。我们一定要开动脑筋，紧密地结合上下文的意思来寻找一条最合适的解释，这样才能真正培养我们的阅读能力，这样才能把生词透彻理解，牢固地记住。词汇表对初学外语的人是有帮助的，但是我们不应依赖词汇表，我们应该尽早地多利用字典，尽早地结合上下文来寻找词的恰当的意思和正确的解释，也就是说我们应该尽早地培养我们的独立阅读能力。

"同学们还应该学会逐渐使用以英语解释词义的英语字典。为什么？因为阅读科学文献一定要概念明确。英汉字典往往只给一个汉语译名，这个汉语译名本身的含义可能并不完全相当于原来那个英语单词的词义。因此有时查了英汉字典，仍然感到理解得模模糊糊。至于以英语解释词义的英语字典，所用的方法是给每个词都下一个明确的定义，所以查了这种字典往往理解得更加清楚。

"在查字典时，除了要寻找合适的解释外，还应该注意一下所查的那个词的词源意义。例如，向日葵在英语中俗名是 sunflower（太阳花），但学名是 heliotrope，为希腊文 helios（太阳）+希腊文 tropos（转动）所组成。经常注意词源意义就会增加、扩大我们对于构词法的知识，培养我们分析词义的能力。

"除了词源意义外，在查字典时，我们还应该注意词的搭配，尤其要注意动词和名词的搭配、形容词和名词的搭配、动词和副词的搭配等。例如，meet requirements（满足需要），close attention（密切的注意），talk freely（信口开河）。在阅读时还应该把表示相同的或类似的概念的词和短语都搜集在一起，加以比较，又把表示相反的概念的词和短语搜集在一起，加以对照。这样来理解内容，这样来记生词，效果一定更好。例如，以前学的"The Story of Fire"课文中第一句：Fire could be harnessed and made to work for man. 在这里，动词 harnessed 和短语 made to work 就是表示相同或类似概念的同义词或同义现象，应该搜集在一起，加以比较。同一课也有不少表示相反概念的词和短语：combustible 和 incombustible，materials which burn 和 materials which will not burn 等都应联系起来记。用这样的方法来记单词，才记得多，记得牢。我不赞成同学们把单词抄在生字本或卡片上，孤立地、机械地死背硬记，而是应该把几个词联系起来记。当然在开始的阶段，记单词必须花很大的劳力。每课书上词汇表中有用的词都应有意识地记住。要做到眼到、口到、手到、心到。那就是说把每一个要记住的单词看上几遍，念上几遍，写上几遍，记上几遍。这样机械的死功夫在初学阶段十分必要，到了一年以后就用不着费这样大的气力来死记了。就应该用我上面说的那些办法来更有效地扩大词汇，培养独立阅读的能力。但是即使达到比较熟练的阶段也不能放弃某些较费力的活动，以便达到进一步的准确和熟练程度。例如每日清晨朗读半小时，每日抄写半页课文或资料，每日记住一、两个写得好的句子。基本功要经常地练，不断地练，才能保证外语学得又快又好。

三、词根的重要性

要多快好省学习生词,学了一定数量的词汇后,就应该学点构词法。这里有个公式:Modern English＝Old English＋Middle French,英语与低地德语同属西日耳曼语支,基本词汇相似之处甚多。初学英语时大都比较熟悉,讲法语的诺曼人统治英国几百年(Norman Conquest),英语报刊里大约 70％以上词汇都是希腊、拉丁词根加词缀构成的,一度通过法语大量引进,学了构词法可以成百上千记忆猜词,一本万利。这类构词专著出了一大批,不妨翻翻复旦大学陆国强先生在《现代英语表达与理解》一书对词根以图表形式作了如下有益的研究:

"英语中不少词是由词根加词缀构成的。词根是词中表示主要意义的成分,而词缀则是表示附加意义或语法意义的成分。如 unacceptable 这一词,其词根是 accept,而 un-和-able 是词缀。英语中词根有不同形式,有的是完整的词,在句中可作为一个独立的单位使用,如 working 中的 work。有的并不是完整的词,而与其他构词成分结合起来构成一个词,如 audience 中 audi 是词根,表示"听"的意思,-ence是名词性词缀。通过语源分析,掌握词根的意义对整个词的理解具有决定性作用。"见其所列图表:

词根	意义	实例	
agr	farm	agronomy	(农艺学)
aqua	water	aquarium	(水族馆)
anthrop	man	anthropology	(人类学)
astron	star	astronomy	(天文学)
bio	life	biology	(生物学)
capit	head	capitation	(人头税)
celer	speed	celerity	(迅速)
chrome	color	chromosome	(染色体)
chron	time	chronology	(年代学)
crat	rule	autocrat	(专制君主)
dent	tooth	dentist	(牙科医生)
dict	say	diction	(措词)
eu	well, happy	eugenics	(优生学)
frac	break	fracture	(骨折)
gamos	marriage	monogamous	(一夫一妻制的)
ge	earth	geology	(地质学)
greg	group	gregarious	(好群居的)
gress	move forward	progress	(进展)
gyn	women	gynecologist	(妇科医生)
homo	same	homogeneous	(同类的)

hydr	water	dehydrate	（脱水）
ject	throw	eject	（逐出）
junct	join	conjunction	（连接）
loq	speak	loquacious	（饶舌的）
mar	sea	maritime	（海上的）
med	middle	intermediary	（中间的）
meter	measure	thermometer	（温度表）
mit	send	remit	（汇寄）
mono	one	monotony	（单调）
pater	father	paternal	（父方的）
pathos	feeling	pathology	（病理学）
ped	foot	pedal	（踏板）
phobia	fear	hydrophobia	（恐水病）
phone	sound	telephone	（电话）
port	carry	portable	（手提的）
pseudo	false	pseudonym	（假名）
psych	mind	psychic	（心理的）
rect	rule	direct	（指导）
scope	see	telescope	（望远镜）
scrib	write	inscribe	（刻写）
sec	cut	dissect	（解剖）
sequ	follow	sequence	（连续）
spect	look	inspect	（检查）
spir	breathe	respiration	（呼吸）
tact	touch	tactile	（触觉的）
term	end	terminal	（终点）
vid	see	video	（电视的）
voc	call	convocation	（召开）

　　理解词根的含义固然十分重要，但对词缀的意义也不能忽视，特别是一些衍生出新义的词缀必须注意。如 anticulture 反正统或传统文化的/antihero 反对以传统手法塑造主角的；**-Aid**（后缀）救助，赞助：尤指义赛或义演性的，与其构成的词有：Fashion-Aid 慈善时装表演。Kurd-Aid 为救济库尔德难民而进行的如音乐会等的义演；**-friendly**（后缀）有助于……的；有利于……的；对……无污染或保护的；支持或同情的：customer-friendly 考虑客户需要的/environment-friendly(有利于)环保的(译成"环保的"比"环境友好的"达意,环境还能友好？)/Labor-friendly 支持工党的/Thatcher-friendly 支持撒切尔（夫人）的。

　　顺便提一句，近十年来出版了好几部谈英汉两种语言对比的专著，找一些读读会大有好处。

第三节　词义之确定及辨析

一、词义之确定举例

尽管各种网络和词典为我们提供了确定词义的极好工具,但一个词往往有多个意义,有的词义,只要看了上下文的对应同义词或近义词及反义词便较容易定义,如前面章节提到的 culture, interest 和 resources 等有些实例便是明证,所谓"no context, no understanding"是也。但有些词义在词典里找不到适合上下文的确切词义。除有的词义辗转引申外(如 It's the Economy, **Stupid!**),可能意随人生也是一个重要原因。这就要求我们多动脑筋才能捉摸出确切意义来。当然这种说法也难免笼统,这里面还有逻辑、对比法、上下呼应、词源意义、文化背景知识等许多具体方法和因素要考虑在内。另一个重要问题是,我们不能只靠网络词典,它们只能用作参考,主要还得自己思考。下面采取先易后难的原则,略举几例加以说明:

1. 从文内阐释求解 Decommissioning

虽然词典定义不合适,文章本身已作了阐释。这种情况很普遍。因此紧扣上下文还是不二法门。如 decommissioning 就是一个例子。在网络与大词典里至今只有"解除军官职务"、"武器退役"等义。可是在下列例句不靠谱。

In the context of escalating violence, **decommissioning** is no more than a fashionable buzzword, and will lead to the guerrillas laying down their arms.

有人译为:"在暴力不断升级的情况下,**解除军官军职**只不过是时髦的空话,游击队不会因此而放下武器。"

其实 decommissioning 在原文中已作了解释,即"laying down one's arms",或 decommissioning of arms,说得通俗一些,即 disarming。作为委婉词,即"缴械投降"。如果再看其他报刊的同类文章,就知道英国保守党政府 1996 年就同意谈判解决北爱尔兰问题,让爱尔兰共和军(IRA)政治组织新芬党参加。先决条件是 decommissioning (of arms),即爱尔兰共和军首先要放下武器,decommissioning 就成了"时髦词"(时髦的空话是此义的误译)。再看下面释义性的例句:

Then Major's government, reacting to Unionist defiance, demanded that the I. R. A. pledge a "permanent" cease-fire rather than a "complete" one. At the same time London declared that before peace talks could begin, the I. R. A. must disarm — "**decommissioning of arms**" is the euphemism chosen to avoid overtones of surrender. (*Time*)

同时通过这两例还可以看出,此字当时既是时髦词,也是委婉用词。

2. 靠同位语帮忙 Wheels Within Wheels

通过看同位语定义。例如"wheels within wheels"在这里该怎么讲？ *The New Oxford Dictionary of English* 唯一词义是"used to indicate that a situation is complicated and affected by secret or indirect influence"; *Longman Dictionary*: used to say that a situation is complicated and difficult to understand and because it involves processes and decisions that you know nothing about.《英汉大词典》(第二版)错综复杂的情况(或动机、影响、力量等);复杂的机构。

上述词典的释义可概括两个字"complicated situation"。可是,这一词义是否适合下例的意思呢？见例句:

The President's desk is cluttered and his mind distracted by his concern with the **wheels within wheels**, the foremen and the subforemen of our gigantic Federal machine. (Wendell Willkie)

批评 F. 罗斯福总统的 Wendell Willkie 原是 businessman and lawyer,与罗同属民主党人,但反对罗的 New Deal(新政),后来因政见不合,投奔共和党,成为 1940 年大选中的共和党总统候选人,但被罗击败。此例引自 1943 年他在 *Reader's Digest* 发表的文章,题为"Better Management, Please, Mr. President!"从语法上分析,"the foremen... machine"是"the wheels within wheels"的同位语,可"foremen and subforemen"显然与"complicated situation"的意思看来似乎不搭界。再则,Willkie 干吗要说"the foremen... machine"呢？

从上下文看,"the foremen and subforemen"都不是大事,而 Willkie 批评的正是政府不抓国家大事,显然总统是小事缠身了。这样,语言逻辑就通了。换言之,罗氏应该改进政府管理。不应抓小放大(govern at the margins),捡芝麻,丢西瓜,浪费时间,关注那些鸡毛蒜皮小事,像"小额索赔法庭"(small claims court)似的。但我们也可将"wheels within wheels"不作"复杂的情况"而作"鸡毛蒜皮"讲,与"commercial business/industry"一样,只能视为作者个人杜撰。因为"Words do not have meanings; people have meanings for words."何况至今尚未被网络和词典认可。这么一分析,此句的意思是:总统办公桌上乱七八糟堆着的文件,其满脑子想的都不是庞大的联邦机关的大事,而是那些鸡毛蒜皮的事,什么工头啦,小工头啦这类琐事。

若我们了解 F. 罗斯福执政时的历史背景或此处的文本语境,还可进一步分析。共和党头面人物 Willkie 为何批评民主党总统罗斯福用"foreman"和

"gigantic"及 Federal machine 这些字眼呢？这里要结合"读报知识"里的"政党"介绍加以探讨。罗氏执政于 1933 年，正值美国经济大萧条（Great Depression），推出了 New Deal 的施政纲领，应付危局，搞了经济复兴法案，设立许多应急机构，名目繁多，不胜枚举，只有用首字母缩略字来标识，如 NRA，AAA，PWA 等等，简直成了一锅字母汤（alphabet soup）。难怪 Willkie 用"gigantic"（extremely big）了。再则，联邦尽量扩大开支，以刺激经济复苏。酷似 2008 年大爆发的金融危机和经济危机，政府也放手干预经济。民主党的"大政府"（big government）是罗斯福开的头，工会是支持民主党的铁杆组织，选举时的票仓。他连续四次当选，除了对付经济危机有方、指挥反法西斯战争得力外，与工会大力支持是分不开的，共和党有意角逐总统职位者无不对工会及 foremen 和 subforemen 为罗氏助选愤愤不平。新政干将 Harry Hopkins 还说："spend and spend, tax and tax, elect and elect."意为只要扩大政府开支，刺激经济，多花钱来支持联邦政府的工程项目上马，减少失业大军，就可以获得选票而连选连任。这就又成为共和党攻击"大政府"的把柄。为什么不用 government 而用 machine？这是因为政府和政党组织（party machine）一样错综复杂，犹如机器，machine 是比喻用法。

3. 用对比法索义 Commercial Business/Industry

近几年一提到 Commercial，在翻译杂志上不断有作者举例说明学生只知道此字有"商业"、"商务"、"营利"等作形容词的词义，而不知晓作名词还有"an advertisement on TV or radio"的意义。那让我们来看作形容词用的"commercial"在下例是否还有其他意思：

(1) That, however, constantly reminds companies that their defense work is less profitable than their **commercial business**—and encourages them to steer their investment dollars elsewhere. (*Newsweek*)

如果说(1)例费解，下面(2)例的意思就很清楚了。

(2) Promoting flexible manufacturing would also strengthen defense manufacturing. This isn't a novel idea: **commercial industry** has long since moved away from single-purpose machine tools and toward computerized systems that can turn out dozens of different products on a single assembly line. (*Newsweek*)

从上下文看，(1)例中的 commercial business 与 defense work 对比；(2)例中的 commercial industry 与 defense manufacturing 对比。所谓防务企业和防务制造业，即军工企业。美国前总统艾森豪威尔在 1961 年的告别演说中曾提到"military-industrial complex"（军工联合集团或联合体）。这里采用对比法来理解就较容易。军工企业或制造业也要赚钱,也是商业,不过为军事服务;而 commercial business 也是商用企业,但为民用。这样一对比,指的当然是"民用企业"或"民用制造业"了。作"民用的"讲,恐怕网上和词典里都未收录。这与上例的"wheels within wheels"一样,除上下文外,也是作者在玩弄辞藻,"义随人生"。不然,为什么不用"civilian business/industry 呢?"用 commercial,难道国防工业就不是"商业或营利企业"?

当然还有另外一种可能性,那就是 *Newsweek* 喜欢追求新奇。不妨再看一例出于该杂志的另一篇文章:

(3) Demanding a "peace dividend" is easy in principle. But legislators look at the matter quite differently when they consider that two in five of the nation's 1.5 million defense-manufacturing workers will lose their jobs over the next decade—and that few blue-collar workers can match their defense-industry wages in the **commercial sector.** (1991/7/15 *Newsweek*)

此例中"the commercial sector"与"the defense industry"作对比,意思也是与上两例一样。

4. 向背景知识问路 Anti-Government 等

根据文化背景知识,何谓"anti-government"? 在一些国家常听说有"anti-government rebels/forces"。可美国居然也有"anti-government rebels",是怎么回事? 难道也有与美国政府闹分裂的集团? 见例句:

(1) Many of the president's admirers came to Washington, like Mr Reagan himself, as **anti-government rebels**; trapped in the bureaucracy, they have watched the government, now spending more than ever, win too many of the battles. (*The Economist*)

这里"anti-government rebels",我们学过美国两党理念不同,此处就不能理解为"反政府叛乱分子",因为里根及其 admirers 不可能是"反政府的"。说他们是反对政府政策的,什么政府? 什么政策? 里根是共和党保守派,一贯反对民主党自由派的"大政府政策"(big government),抨击政府开支和税收过于庞大,权力过于集中,对自由企业的干预过多。这是美国保守派和自由派的一个重要区别。里根是打着批判民主党总统卡特"大政府政策"的旗号上台的。他执政八年,可是却斗不过盘根错节、坚持大政府那帮人,结果里根政府比前任民主党政府花钱更多(当然,这只是英国《经济学家》的看法,事实并非如此)。了解这一情况后,"anti-government rebels"就不难理解了。整句的意思是:许多里根总统的追随者像总统本人一样,过去都是作为强烈的反对大政府政策者而到华盛顿做官的。可是,他们落入了庞大的官僚机关后,在与那帮坚持大政府政策者的多次较量中败多胜少,所以只能眼睁睁看着政府现在的开支比以往更大。

此例句中的另外一个字是"government",这个字在文中又指的是何政府?美国政府是三权分立,"Administration"虽也译为"××政府",但只代表行政部门,总统施政要经过立法部门(即国会)批准(见**读报知识**)。所以,双方的关系可以一言蔽之:"总统出主意,国会做决定。"总统花钱要经众议院立案审批,三审通过总统签署后才能如愿,偏偏里根执政时国会抓在民主党手里。里根想在与当时的苏联进行军事竞赛,要多花钱于军备;民主党又坚持"新政"的一套,希望多花钱于民生。这一来开支庞大。但里根却怪罪力主"大政府"的国会。所以例句中的"government"也指的是"大政府"。事实上,里根在军备上实行的是"hope and pray, borrow and borrow and spend and spend"(1985/3/27 *The New York Times*)(著名专栏作家 James Reston 语)(由于其举债太多,还曾出台了一项以三位国会议员之名,限制举债数额的立法,叫 the Gramm-Rudman-Hollings Act)。

(2) The Macedonian argument has a Greek dimension too.

句子看似简单易懂,不知背景,就要出错。马其顿1991年脱离当时的南斯拉夫联盟而独立,定国名为"马其顿共和国",遭到希腊反对,因希腊北部有个区叫 Macedonia region。当地马其顿族人有的主张跟新独立的国家归并,希腊吸取南联盟分裂的教训,才防患于未然。所以马至今在联合国的正式国名仍用希建议的"Former Yugoslavia Republic of Macedonia"。

此后,两国又闹起"认祖归宗"之争来。双方都认为亚历山大大帝(Alexander the Great 356—323 BC)属于本国。马视之为民族英雄,理当命名一些建筑物和道路,以资纪念,又遭到反对。希腊认为按出生地讲,这位昔日横跨亚非欧三洲的大帝国君主也是本国祖先。

马其顿国内还有阿尔巴尼亚族和希腊族的冲突,曾面临内战边缘。了解这些背景后,此句可理解为:马其顿内争还跟希腊沾边。如果同学们不问马为何争?与希又有何关系?就会按字面理解为马其顿之争也有希腊方面的因素,似懂非懂。如果说单凭一句无上下文,不能令人信服,请见下例。

(3)《国际先驱论坛报》在2000年12月14日发表的一篇题为"Decision:It's Bush"的文章中有这么一段:

Republicans narrowly retained control of the House in November. The new Senate will be split 50-50, and will include Mr. Lieberman. **But any ties will be broken by the new vice president, Mr. Cheney.**

此处,有的读者一定要问,为什么副总统能打破这种相持不下的局面?他不是参议员,有投票权吗?这就要求读者具有文本以外的知识才能解题。美国宪法规定,参议院议长(President/Chairman of the Senate)一职由副总统兼任,在表决出现相持不下的局面时,他才有投票权。全句的意思是:在十一月份大选后组成的新一届国会里,共和党仍勉强控制着众议院。在参议院,两党平分秋色,各占 50 席,而且民主党议员中还包括落选的民主党副总统候选人利伯曼。然而,如果在表决中票数相等而出现相持不下的局面时,新任副总统切尼先生会打破这种僵局。(见美国"**读报知识**""**国会**")

5. 紧跟形势解 Madonna 跟 Mogadishu 之对比

1993 年 10 月 18 日,克林顿任总统不久,《时代》周刊发表了一篇"It's All Foreign to Clinton"的文章,开头两句是:

Like most people, Bill Clinton is uncomfortable with what he doesn't know and avoids dealing with it. Fortunately for him, the nation he leads usually cares more about **Madonna** than **Mogadishu**; its turn inward following the cold war's end coincides neatly with the President's passion for domestic affairs.

有的学生曾问道:"怎么将歌星与地名作比较呢?"还有的学生说:"克林顿是不是对麦当娜感兴趣? 真摸不着头脑。"众所周知,"Madonna"是美国性感艳星,"Mogadishu"是索马里首都。克林顿上台时正值索马里内战,美派兵干涉,结果吃了大亏。了解这一情况后,再联系此段谈到克林顿的"passion for domestic affairs",有经验的读者就知道,此处 Madonna 指 domestic affairs, Mogadishu 指 foreign affairs。记者在这里不过是玩了点文字游戏,因为这两个字都是"M"开头,押头韵。句意是:像许多人一样,比尔·克林顿总统对不熟悉的事处理起来感到为难,所以总是避开。幸运的是他所领导的国家通常关注内政胜过外交。随着冷战的结束,重点转向国内,正好与他热衷于内政巧合。

二、报刊用词辨析

报刊词语辨析,重点放在一般同义词词典不收录的同义和近义词,包括少量反义词和个别易混淆的词。

1. Above politics 与 Nonpartisan

above politics 政治上超脱的,不参与党派之争:在西方,有所谓军不问政一说。商人只顾赚钱,也不问政。他们都标榜中立,是为了获得两党的支持。这与 nonpartisan 意同。nonpartisan 含有无党派斗争或无政治上分歧的意思,而 above politics 则暗含虽有党派斗争而不参与之意。

It is human nature to require a leader at the helm. In our century we have looked to our heads of state for this role. Apart from carrying out ceremonial duties, a head of state should foster the notion of political accountability, while remaining **above politics.** (*Newsweek*)

nonpartisan(尤指在非政治问题上)两党或多党派合作或支持的,无党派的,不偏袒任何党派的:

Lenny Skutnik was a bit unnerved when Nancy Reagan sat down next to him in the House gallery. But it was not until the President began talking about the "terrible tragedy on the Potomac" that Skutnik had an inkling that something was up. "Oh, oh," he thought, "here it comes." Suddenly the leaders of the land were on their feet and waves of heartfelt, **nonpartisan** applause rolled through the House chamber. (*Time*)

2. Avalanche 与 Clean Sweep, Landslide (Victory), Tidal Wave 和 Tide

avalanche 雪崩,山崩:喻候选人获得压倒性的多数选票;landslide 山崩,塌方;喻候选人个人或政党获得取得一面倒的胜利;clean sweep 指党在选举中获得大胜,该党的许多候选人当选;官员的大换班。源于谚语:"A new broom sweeps clean."(新官上任三把火。) tidal wave 或 tide 强调候选人在竞选中的胜利像潮水一般势不可挡的胜利。例如:

(1) The Reagan **avalanche** that buried Democratic challenger Walter Mondale fell short of gathering the strength needed in Congress to carry out the President's hopes of staging a "second revolution" in Washington. (*U.S. News & World Report*)

(2) Ronald Reagan's 49-state **landslide** on November 6 put him in commanding position to kick off the nation's third two-term Presidency in 28 years. (*U.S. News & World Report*)

(3) Despite Ronald Reagan's **landslide victory** in November, he will begin his second term without a mandate from the American people—or even from his own administration—on how to define and defend America's interests abroad. (*Newsweek*)

(4) We as Democrats will have an obligation to forestall the Republican **tidal wave** that could take place in November, absent a Clinton withdrawal. (*The Wall Street Journal*)

(5) In 1994, the Republicans had won a majority in the House for the first time in 40 years; in the 1996 election they suffered some slippage, principally within the 71-member "freshman class" that had been swept into office in the nationwide GOP **tide** of 1994. (*The World Almanac 1997*)

3. Nonperson 与 Unperson

nonperson 无足轻重或无权利之人；被忽视或遗忘的人；unperson 因政治失误或因政见不同等原因在政治失势、失宠或故意被抹杀的人，尽管他们在历史上有过贡献，但在政治上有意不再提，如前苏联对待布哈林就是如此。

4. Jail 与 Prison

《美英报刊文章阅读》（精选本）（第二版）第 8 课 "Judge See Politics in Los Alamos Case" 的课文是关于美籍华人李文和被拘押待审的报道，记者只用 jail，而不用 prison，有无不同？举例说明如下：

Judge Park agreed that last December that Mr. Lee should remain in **jail**, but said he was concerned "about the condition under which Dr. Lee is presently held". (*International Herald Tribune*)

美语中，此处的 jail/gaol 能否改为 prison？不行，先看美国 The *World Book Dictionary* 对 **jail** 的释义：a prison, especially one for people awaiting trial or being punished for some small offense. 再看美国法学专家 James A. Inciardi 的解说：A **jail** is not a prison. **Prisons** are correctional institutions maintained by the federal and state governments for the confinement of convicted felons. **Jails** are facilities of local authority for the temporary detention of defendants awaiting trial or disposition on federal or state charges, and of convicted offenders sentenced to short-term imprisonment for minor crimes.

英国 The *New Oxford Dictionary of English* 对 **jail** 的释义是：a place for the confinement of people accused or convicted of a crime: he spent 15 years in **jail**.

美国词典和法学家对 jail 的释义与英国词典不同，美语指的是关押待审者和临时拘留之地和轻刑犯的服刑之所，即"看守所"、"拘留所"；而《新牛津词典》的释义既可作"看守所"、"拘留所"[因为有 people accused（被告的人，被告人）]讲，也可作"监狱"（people convicted[已决犯]）讲。但据英国 Peter Colin Publishing 出版的 *Dictionary of Law* 的释义：prison or place where criminals are kept. 这里 jail 只作"监狱"讲。prison 在美语中尤指关押服刑期长犯人的"监狱"；据英国 *Dictionary of Law* 的词义是：(a) safe place where criminals are kept locked up after they have been convicted or while they await trial。英国英语则可指"监狱"，也可指"看守所"和"拘留所"。jail 和 prison 在美国的正式法律用语和文件中词义不同，但因报刊用语较随意，无视其差异，如：

Convicted of conspiracy and mail fraud, Jim Tucker faces 10 years in **jail**.

(*Time*)

此例与 Oxford 词典释义后所举例子相同。

5. Elector 与 Voter 和 Presidential Elector

elector 合格的选举人，与 voter 同义；在美国，指选举团（electoral college）成员，与 presidential elector 同义；voter 合格的选举人，选民；presidential elector 总统选举人，即选举团成员。

6. Rome Correspondent 与 Roman Correspondent

Rome correspondent 驻罗马通讯员或记者；Roman correspondent 罗马人担任的通讯员或记者。

7. Prime Minister, Premier 和 Chancellor

这三个字均可译为"总理"，Prime Minister 还曾译为"首席部长"，但 Chancellor 仅指德国总理。在加拿大，Premier 指省长。为避免用字重复，在报刊中，Prime minister 和 Premier 常交替使用。按一般习惯，有"王"就有"相"，因此王国行政首脑译作"首相"，不是王国的译作"总理"。但也有例外，例如朝鲜不是王国，却称"首相"，如以前称金日成为"首相"。泰国是王国，仍称"总理"。

8. Law Lord 与 Law Lords

law lord（英国议会）上院法官议员；Law Lords [the ~s]（英国）最高法院：由五人组成，包括大法官（Law Chancellor）在内。

9. Lord Commissioner 与 Lords Commissioners

Lord Commissioner 驻苏格兰教会最高立法机构的王室代表；Lords Commissioners 英国政府各部门委员会委员。

10. Armed Force 与 Armed forces

armed force 武力；armed forces 武装部队，海陆空三军。

11. National Emblem 与 National Symbol

national emblem 国徽；national symbol 国家或国民的象征，如 John Bull 约翰牛象征英国或英国人。

12. Confidential 与 Secret, Top Secret 和 Royal

confidential 机密的，秘密的：最低一级机密；secret 比 confidential 要高一级的机密；top secret 最高机密，绝密；royal（美）皇家密级：1980年9月确立、超过绝密的保密等级。

13. Ticket 与 Slate

ticket（美）竞选候选人名单；slate 候选人提名或任命名单：如作为候选人名单，就像小学生用的石板，名字容易写上去或换掉，而 ticket 上的名单较稳定，不能随意删除。

14. Tax Credit 与 Tax Deduction

tax credit 税额抵免，纳税额的扣除：美国允许纳税人从其应纳税额中扣除某些税金额的法律规定。tax deduction 税额抵免与课税扣减。tax credit 是从应纳税额中扣除一定金额，而 tax deduction 是从应纳税额收入中减免一定金额。一般而言，税额抵免要比课税扣减多交纳税款。

15. Neutral Nation 与 Neutralist Nation, Nonaligned Country 和 Uncommitted Nation

neutral nation 中立国：指在国际战争中不与任何一方交战的国家，如二次大战时的瑞士；neutralist nation 中立主义国家：在美语中含有贬义，如指在冷战时期不了解苏联的威胁和不与美国合作，从而对苏有利的国家。nonaligned country 不结盟国家；uncommitted nation 不表态结盟的国家。

16. Solicitor 与 Barrister 和 Sergeant-at-Law

solicitor（英）小律师，普通律师：他们不具有在高等法院为当事人辩护的资格。barrister（英）大律师：指可在高等法院出庭辩护的律师；sergeant-at-law 英国旧时最高等级的大律师。

17. Informer 与 Informant

informer 常为金钱驱使而向安全部门提供情报的职业告密者，关系，眼线；informant 有意或无意向特工或安全部门提供情报或消息者。

18. Limdis 与 Exdis 和 Nodis

limdis（limited distribution）小范围分发传阅：打在保密情报卷宗上的印记，这类密件分发的范围至多不超过 50 人。exdis（exclusive distribution）小范围密件专发，排他性专发：文件的绿色封面上盖有的特别印记，只供美国内阁成员阅读，最多不超过 12 人。nodis（no distribution）严禁分发传阅，只供一人专阅。

19. Need-To-Know 与 Eyes Only 和 Compartmentalization

need-to-know 按需阅读，即不该知道的不看，根据工作需要确定接触机密的范围；对机密限制在需要知道的人的范围内，不准传给不需要了解的人。eyes only 最高机密，绝密文件；compartmentalization 政府部门间的保密制度；部门分隔限密法：本部门的情况，尤其是军事和科研进展等情况不能让其他各部知道，本部门的人也只限于了解他必须了解的情况。

20. Spree Killer 与 Serial Killer

spree killer 杀人狂：指无预谋、无动机的突然随意杀人者，尤指在某一地点大量杀人。犯罪学家确立了两种大量杀人的罪犯，即系列杀人狂和在同一地点大量杀人的杀人狂。serial killer 系列杀人狂。

21. Preference Poll 与 Trial heat

preference poll 在同党中选出呼声高的候选人的民意测验；trial heat 模拟选举，部分选民对几位对立政党候选人进行意向投票的民意测验。

22. Police agent 与 Police officer

police agent（美）警官，指大学毕业的警察；police officer（美）高中毕业的警察。（见"**社会用语**""四、多元文化运动"＝policeman/lawman）

23. Disinformation 与 Misinformation 和 Black Propaganda

disinformation 为误导对方，通过媒体、情报机关等故意散布或泄露的假情报，假消息，假报道；misinformation（常婉称）尤指故意被用做欺骗的假情报或消息，失实情报，失实报道或消息；black propaganda 假冒敌方的宣传，冒充敌方散布的谎言和谣言。

24. Chairman 和 Leader

chairman 政党主席，与领袖相比，并无多大实权，主要负责竞选事务；leader 政党领袖，党魁，指执政党或反对党领袖，执政党领袖在英国为首相，主要反对党领袖则起影子内阁首相的作用。在美国，总统被视为当然的执政党领袖，反对党无领袖。

第四节　读报经验教训谈

一、文章和期刊的难易决定阅读的先后顺序

在看大报时,读者应先看"Inside"(导读框)再看"News Summary",然后浏览,犹如看书先看目录(Contents)一样。消息报道,尤其是通讯社稿件较易看懂。文字浅显,记者往往显示客观公正,只叙不论。大家常听广播、看电视和网上新闻,情况明,读报易。新闻有连贯性,可以温故知新。因此,建议先看消息报道文章,尤其要多看专题报道,文章虽长,但语言重复率高,背景交代清楚,可获得语言、知识双丰收。社论和评论要亮明观点,用词讲究,引经据典,卖弄炫耀,往往不再交代事件背景,不常看报者就较难。美国有位叫李普曼(Walter Lippmann,1889—1974)的,他是美国历史上成就和名气最大的专栏作家,在《纽约先驱论坛报》"Today and Tomorrow"专栏上发表的评论富有思想和哲理,深受高级知识分子青睐,具有很大的舆论影响力。他博学多才,有的词句不易读懂。一位北大知名英语教授曾经说,这些专栏文章,没有广博知识,欣赏不了,有些典故我们也不知道出处。

新闻期刊的难易程度,美英有别。英国报刊引经据典,咬文嚼字,怀旧情绪重。美国报刊追求新奇,俚语方言多些,各有难点,不过现在美语占上风,不论英美报刊都在往简明方向走,入门易,深造也不难。

美国是超级大国,英国是二流国家,我国及世界各国对美国的关注程度远胜于英国,对美国当然更了解。这样,读美国报章杂志自然就容易懂透些。如对这方面研究有兴趣者,不妨看看"English Out to Conquer the World"(1985/2/8 U. S. News & World Report)的文章(《上下册》四版课文)。另一方面,读者群体不同,美国的三大新闻周刊,普通知识分子是订户,英国的《经济学家》和《旁观者》是高级知识分子的读物。

美国三大新闻期刊在语言上的难易程度也不尽相同。普遍看法是,在文字上,《美国新闻与世界报道》较容易,其次是《新闻周刊》,《时代》周刊则最难。看《经济学家》要避开头几篇要文或社论[leader(s)],从后往前看就容易多了,后文有时解释前文,社论则是总结性表态。

看美国期刊也应遵循先报道后评论的顺序。与《经济学家》不同的是,以往《新闻周刊》和《时代》周刊的评论文章有时不登在开头,放在有关文章或专题报道之后。举1999年5月17日《新闻周刊》就美机炸我驻南斯拉夫使馆,先登题为"What Do We Do Now?"的文章,提要是:OFF TARGET: The tragic inadvertent attack on China's embassy in Belgrade is only the most recent illustration of what's wrong with the campaign against Yugoslavia. A Newsweek contributing editor analyzes NATO's misguided adventure—and the tricky road ahead. 接着再登题为"In China, Fury and Fallout"的评论文章。不过这种格式时常变,2009年《新闻周刊》的"目录"和报道形式就作了较大变动。

改革开放以来,国内英汉对照报刊越办越多,一般人看了可以消遣和了解世事,英语、新闻和涉外专业学生看多了就不合适,易产生懒惰和依赖性,还是先学报刊文选好,将它作为学会独自看懂报刊的渡桥,资深编者善于指点读报迷津,除注释外,还根据各课实际,或指出重点疑难新闻词语,作"语言解说",或根据背景知识,作"读报知识"介绍。这种语言与知识结合讲解,同学们看了就能学会举一反三,增强了理解力和语感。

二、泛读、精读和"死读"

看报是先精读还是先泛读?这也是常提出的问题。我认为应该先浏览,看自己爱看又能看懂大意的文章。要大量读就不能像在大学低年级学"精读"一样,想将每个字或每句话都弄懂。有的教员在上报刊选读课时两节课只讲了两段,是否抠过头了。在美英,教学很讲究量中求质。

有人或许会说,读报如雾里看花,压根儿读不懂。1958年,著名俄语翻译家曹靖华在北大向我们外语系新生介绍其翻译生涯时说,刚开始译不了,就"死译",一本书译几遍就行了,俄语也就学好了。季羡林先生在2002年9月接受香港《明报月刊》记者采访时,介绍他在德国读书学语言的经历,很有参考价值。下面选该刊几段供大家借鉴:

先生认为……"方法很简单,让学生尽快接触原文,不要慢吞吞地给他们讲","不要"在黑板上写动词变化什么的,要接触实际"。先生以自己学俄文和梵文的经历为例。说那时他在德国,俄文课每周只有4个小时,共20个星期。老师开头就把字母讲了一讲,原以为可以慢慢来的,没想到第三堂课时老师就拿了一本果戈理的短篇小说,让学生念!结果一星期4小时的课,学生起码得花上3天时间来准备:查语法、查生词……生词还只能查到前半个,后半个至词尾部分查不着,苦得很。先生说,不过20个星期下来,学原文、弄语法、念完了整本小说。

先生学梵文的情形也基本相同,也是20个星期,一本书,自己查语法、查生词。先生记得学梵文时的课本编得很好,前边是语法,中间是课文和练习,最后是像小词典一样的词汇表。学生在上课以前要好好准备。

"老师不讲,就你讲,讲不对的地方,他就给补充,他自己不讲的。"对于这个方法,先生引了18世纪一位语言学家的话来总结:"学外语啊,就像把学生带到游泳池旁边,推到池子里边去。有两个可能,一个是淹死,一个就是……淹死的可能呢,1％都没有。"

看来采用这种教学法的教师,一定得具备这种"置之死地而后生"的气魄才行。

从季老等先辈们的读书方法可以看出,坚持"死读"也会硬啃出很好的效果来。本人在上世纪60年代初刚大学毕业接触报刊时也经过这个如雾里看花的阶段,勉强往下读,仍似懂非懂,不知所云。当时我国书市上找不到一本像报刊文选、《当代美英报刊词典》或《美英报刊导读》这样集外文报刊词汇与国际知识于一体的文选,也无列出同义词、近义词及反义词能随时备查的工具书,更无因特网可言,比现在的条件差多了。但由于工作需要,不得不硬着头皮读,逐渐就能读懂了。我的一个朋友,学看日、俄、法、德等报刊,听广播,也用的这个办法,两三个月上路,效果还可以,不过重点得放在多读多听上,说写就谈不上了,作为多种外语,要求无妨些,当当哑巴,或会讲些日常用语,不当瞎子聋子就行了。

浏览了一年半载,阅读速度加快后,就可以回过来总结一下,选几篇文字较难或背景知识面要求较广的文章作精读。先泛读后精读,几个回合下来,掌握的新闻词语多了,文化背景知识也丰富了,读报水平会大大提高。日子久了,就能无师自通。要不然,哪怕现在工具书再多再好,因特网上答疑再方便,看报也不会理解得很深。要从游泳中学游泳,不怕呛水。有些文章要反复地阅读,细嚼慢咽,这是培养独立思考、逐渐掌握语言逻辑、将书报读懂读通的一个好的自学方法。简言之,语言、背景、逻辑乃读通报刊三要素,是我们大家都必须为掌握这学习语言三要素而终生奋斗的。

在学习中,语言上要注意扩大词汇量和常用词词义面及掌握报刊语言主要特点;本文所谈读报知识是我们必须要了解和掌握的。所谓"扩大词汇量",真正的新词比不上旧词新义多,而且也不如后者难。词义面尤指常用词词义面,已有章节用实例说明。读报知识,可以在阅读过程中积累,也可以从百科全书等工具书和因特网中获得,不过通过前者获得的知识更易记牢。现在市面上的"探索"等大量电视光盘,更是上等学习帮手。

三、带着问题读书看报

看不懂的词语或背景知识不要轻易放过。我初学翻译时,knowingly这个词表达不出来,英汉词典上也无释义。有一天,在家边干活边听广播时,忽然听到《洪湖赤卫队》电影广播中的一句话:"韩英会意地笑了",我也笑了。为什么?knowingly不正是"会意地"这个意思吗?当然,它还有"有意识地"或"故意地"

之义。再如我刚开始不明白为什么有的美国国会多数或少数党"督导"不用"whip",而用"assistant majority/minority leader"副领袖这个名称。经多年看报后发现,只有共和党喜欢用这个头衔,民主党则不用。为什么?在看了一本政治词典后方知,这是由于共和党与民主党的理念不同,英文词语的表达有时也不一样(见美国"**党语和竞争用语**")。又如 take-home pay 如只定义"拿回家的工资"就未说透,"税后实得工资或薪金"才是其真正意思。

有时刚出现的新词语,这份报刊上没讲清楚,另一份会令你满意。如一家周刊谈及"Contract with America"时,只说明它是"conservative Republican programs",并未交代是什么计划。U.S. News & World Report 却图文并茂,Time 更详析了一番。

又如:《上下册》一版里面选用了《外交》(Foreign Affairs)双月刊题为"Reagan Ⅱ:A Foreign Policy Consensus?"的文章,有两个词语较难理解和注释:

In perspective, the Reagan Administration's difficulties in dealing with the Soviet Union are familiar, almost traditional. From the outset, the Administration had trouble coping with the **yes-but formula** advanced for the last three decades by just about every specialist in the field:Yes, we must be strong, but at the same time flexible. Yes, we must understand that the Russians are relentless foes, but at the same time we must seek ways of coexisting. And so forth. Almost every new Administration comes into office paying lip service to the principle, while actually believing that a fresh start, a new approach—softer or harder—will permit escape from the painful, laborious **double track**.

何谓"yes-but formula"和"double track"?并不难猜测,要透懂则较难。几位外教也说不清楚。"double track"原是铁路的双线或复线,此处作"yes-but principle 或 formula"讲。原来我在一本书里注释的是"模棱两可或不置可否的方案",经过再三琢磨,或许这样理解更确切些:"两种并存的矛盾政策方案",因而成了"难以执行的政策原则"。也就是说,从背景看,里根对苏与 Catch-22(《第 22 条军规》,"两难")近似。既要强硬,又要灵活,既要将苏看成敌人,又要与之和平共处。两手政策,一手硬,一手软,时硬时软,软硬兼施,掌握火候、分寸并不太容易。

四、带着问号读书看报

过了理解关后,就要带着问号去读书看报。本书在前面已经指出英汉词典和外国报刊及词典的错误,事实上原文词典对词语的定位有高低之分,也不是所有用词释义、举例都正确,我国学者就指出过英英词典的某些错误。就是语言网站也各有特色,应货比三家多查才行,尽信书不如无书嘛。例如本人在看商务印书馆国际有限公司 1996 年出版的《最新英语新词语词典》中"Demopublican"条目时,觉得其词义——民主共和党人(指在政策上难以区分的共和党人或民主党人)——模棱两可。接着又看到吉林大学出版社 1996 年出版的《英语新词词典》中这个条目双解词义——Republican or Democrat, viewed as indistinguishable in policy; Repubocrat 民主党共和党的,在政策上难以区别的。不管其释义是从哪本外国书上抄来的,只说对了一半。这时,我想从其他工具书中找到答案,可都未收录该词条,于是,我脑子里老带着这个问号,终于有一天在《华盛顿邮报》上看到了下面这段文字:

'Tis true. Joined on stage by NOW leader Patricia Ireland and a dozen politicians and activists, Jackson did a number on Lieberman, accusing him of joining with Republicans to dismantle affirmative action programs. Jackson also drew a big laugh from the crowd when he branded Lieberman "a Demopublican" who had more in common with Republicans than Democrats.

看了 Demopublican 后的说明,结合自己在这方面掌握的知识,终于得出结论,应理解为"民主党内的保守派"。也就是说,像 Lieberman 这样的人,你说他是民主党人和共和党人都行,因为他名义上是民主党党员,但骨子里是共和党人。这种人的两面性令人难以辨别。

再如:我 1981 年刚到美国读书的第二年,正逢中期选举,听到有的候选人在电视竞选说:"I'm a family man."查了所有的词典都只说"family man"是"有妻室的人"。后来发现这些人都是共和党保守派,反对性自由和堕胎,认为传统道德观的沦丧是社会的万恶之源。一个国家、一个州和一个市要治好,必须要回归传统道德观。于是就明白了这句话的言外之意,即他们在吹嘘自己"齐家有方,治国有道"的理念。

又如:我国的新闻界和国际问题研究者都将"Reagan Doctrine"和"Reaganism"译为"里根主义",应该说,并非误译,但从报上看到具体内容各异,前者指里根的对外尤其是当时的对苏政策或主张,后者指他的内政,尤其经济政策或主张。再看 Truman/Nixon Doctrine 等后发现,它们也都是指美国的对外政策或主张。而 Thatcherism 等主要指内政或经济政策。于是得出结论,Reagan Doctrine 不完全等于 Reaganism。然而,我仍有所疑惑,直至见到 2008 年 Safire 的政治词典对 doctrine 的释义为 foreign policy 后,才觉得找到了依据。

又如：我国英语报刊多用 hegemonism, regionalization, multipolarization, 西方更多用 hegemony, regionalism 和 multipolarity，就发现我们从汉语翻过去的东西，别人不一定习惯。我申请恢复 WTO 资格时，最初把商品经济译为 commodity economy，西方不认，后来改译 market economy（与 planned economy 对应），才谈通了，白白耽误几年时间。

五、有关科研的几点看法

所谓"科研"，不要看得太神秘。带着问号读书看报就是科研的开始。

刚起步，题目不宜太大。有人说他在从事跨文化研究，记得钱钟书先生在北大比较文学研究所成立会上发表的洋洋万言字的讲话中，对中英在修辞学方面作了全面的比较，但他并没有说他在进行跨文化研究。如果说研究，也只能称之为其中的某一点。要搞跨文化研究，必须集综合大学各系，尤其是哲学、历史、语言、社会等学系大师级水平教授的智慧，进行既分散又综合的研究，仅靠英文专业的师资力量无论如何是不够的。但如果某人说他在进行汤显祖和莎士比亚的比较研究，那么他是在从事比较文学的某方面研究，方向明确而具体，可操作性强，很可能作出成绩来。

科研不能亦步亦趋，必须与自己的专长、志趣和社会需要相结合。如果已到不惑之年，中外名著又读得不多，古汉语又无多深功底，最好不要从事文学、翻译或汉英对比研究。对外开放，英语系学生渴望了解外部世界，自认为长处是知识面较广，对时事和国际问题评论感兴趣。本人就走上了一条普及阅读英语报刊的研究道路。对我而言，"Stick to my last"（意为"Stick to what I'm good at."）这句谚语再恰当不过了。

研究方向或题目确定后，首先要知道有哪些重要论著和参考书，尽量备齐。现在是电脑时代，要充分利用 Internet 为研究服务。不仅如此，要做有心人，随时收集和积累材料。要敏感，能随时将看到、听到的有用新词语和知识设法记录下来，并随手分类归档。例如 VOA 介绍美国在海湾战争后在伊拉克南部建立了"no-fly zone"（禁飞区），据报道在空袭南斯拉夫时美国在南也想照例行事。如不了解这些情况，还误认为是由于像百慕大三角区那样的危险区所以才禁飞。再如 1977 年 8 月 15 日，《泰晤士报》载文论及"ironically"的词义已扩大到能作任何意思的开头词，并举例说明。如不马上收集下来，时间一长，忘了该词词义在报刊用语中的引申和扩大，或许对有些句子难以理解。其实 ironically 当"讽刺"讲只指言语，其他方面还有"事与愿违"等意思，现在译文里，讽刺满天飞，也不管上下文合不合适。鲁迅先生教导我们说："无论什么事，如果继续收集材料，积十年，总可成一学者。"可见鲁迅是多么重视知识的积累。当然，这是讲的网络发明前的情况。

　　学问，学问，学和问两方面缺一不可，当然主要是自己探索。例如我在1987年编报刊文选时，所选的材料内容新，大多是那时近一两年发生的事，对有的情况和词语不是国内老先生能答出来的，又无网络为己服务，怎么办？办法只能是，如果是美国问题，遇上美国客座教授就向他们请教，有时还打电话到大使馆。如有篇课文中遇到印度议会选举用语之一的"three-round parliamentary elections"，一般理解为三轮议会选举，第一和第二轮选举无候选人得票过半数，第三轮选举只剩下两位候选人，为决胜选举。后来经向印度大使馆文化处请教，方才明白印度议会选举与多数国家不同，它是分"三个地区、三段时间举行选举"，其中时间间隔约一周。另一篇课文"Splendor on the Grass"中的Les Bleus（蓝队，法国一足球队名）就请教的是法国大使馆。

　　一个人不可能具有包罗万象的知识，不求教于他人是不可能的。如编者初学翻译时，最头痛的一个问题是，虽然知其义，却脱不开英文的束缚，也就是说，两种文字不能忠实地对应表达出来。其次，译文西化严重，"因为"、"所以"、"之一"、"对……来说"等等一大堆。但我有个好朋友，此君中英文俱佳，曾翻译过外交部某副部长的不少讲话，几次主动帮助改译文和释疑解难。这种帮助使本人对词义的理解和汉语的表达能力大大提高了一步。现在我审校英译汉的稿子，只要看译文就知道译者英文哪个词语理解错了，这也是当初得益于朋友的帮助。晚上有时与中文系、哲学系、经济系的教授一面散步，一面探讨问题，受益匪浅。现在有的年轻人，写上几篇文章，便自视清高，就怕人家指出不足之处或错误而有失面子。自己的文章不愿意请教他人或与人切磋，实在不是明智之举。

　　研究外国情况不能想当然就下笔，认为外国的情况也像中国的情况那样的划一。如我国在中央有人大和政协，各省市也都一律设有与此对应的机构。美国情况有别，国会有参众两院，其他各州也有此对应机构，唯独内布拉斯加州议会例外，只有一院（见"**读报知识**"美国"州议会英文名称种种"）。再如美国各州总统选举人（presidential electors）均由各州普选产生，但缅因州和内布拉斯州并非完全如此（见"**读报知识**"美国"总统选举"）。又如美国州议会（state legislature）英文名称也不尽相同（见"**读报知识**""美国州议会英文名称种种"）。又如美国各州的县都用的是county，唯有Louisiana州相当于县行政单位都用的是parish。美国在大选的初选阶级时，有的州举行primary，有的州举行caucus，全国并不统一。美英国情有别，更不能相互套用。如parish作行政单位就字同义异。（见"**美英政治比较**"）

有人问我新闻（或报刊）语言和翻译的特点，要研究其特点，首先要把报刊看懂，这是必要的功课，而不是相反。

凡是取得一些成绩的学人都有一个共同的体会，老师真正教会自己的并不是很多，学问主要还是靠自己静下心来钻研，读硕读博也是自己在读书写论文。史学泰斗陈寅恪虽曾游学美国，但并非博士，但他在历史方面的学问当时又有何人能出其左右。老师与学生的关系是好比"师傅领进门，修行在本人"。切忌浮躁，潜心读书才是正道。

中山大学知名教授王宗炎在他所著《汉英语文研究纵横谈》一书的"前言"中说："我的习惯是暗中摸索，独立思考。我是天生的怀疑者，从不囿于一家一派，觉得语言学界不应该有个教皇。"这些话值得任何研究工作者的深思，即使将他最后一句话作为座右铭也不为过。

六、教训

以前由于国内外环境所限，与外界尤其与英美等西方大国交流中断，所以英美报刊基本上看不到，工具书少得可怜，更说不上网络了。所以读外刊基本不可能，我在涉外单位呆了几年，能接触些外刊，但研究外刊语言不是任务，只是速读和搜集资料，对某一问题而非对语言进行研究。好在此时获得了一些难得的背景知识。改革开放教书后，只是教英语基本功，后主动要求开报刊文选课，因与时俱进，深受学生欢迎。自己无师承，受教育时间也不长和系统，只读了两年正规初中，自修上了大学。大学是五年制，可当时正赶上大跃进极左时代，上山下乡，教改成了只学中译英的政治文章，如高年级还学"Long Live Leninism"的译文。又因1962年中印边境事件而外出工作了近10个月，大概总共只有二三年的学习时间，李赋宁老先生为我们感到十分惋惜。基本功不如师兄师弟扎实。到工作岗位后，大量阅读外刊，全靠勤奋硬啃，直到1987年自认为积累的资料足以编两本报刊文选，后来又开始编报刊词典和导读，但水平不高，比较粗糙，未能精雕细琢。

遗憾的是，虽从1987年编书和工具书至今，并未写出一个师生都能接受的《英文报刊教学大纲》来，虽然本人对《高等学校英语专业英语教学大纲》中关于报刊语言方面的一些规定和要求并不满意。可本人年于古稀，怕完不成这个任务了。

第五节 编 书 谈

写"编书谈"这一节,一是应英文外刊课青年教员的要求,他们有时也要从网上选一些时文,作为报刊文选教材的补充。二是报刊文选之编注或编著要传承下去,让年轻人能迅速成长起来,编出更多更好适应学生需要的课本来。说来惭愧,在世的外刊编者中,我是年龄最大、读报时间持续最长的一个了。既编过 20 本课本,又编过《报刊导读》和《报刊词典》(两本),是至今英语报刊系统教材和参考书的唯一编者了,把自己的经验教训写出来或许对有志于此道者有益,少走弯路。这与"读报经验教训谈"一样,我也是跌跌撞撞一步步走过来的,所经历的甘苦只有自知。编者认为,下列三点值得参考:

1. <u>立场和动机</u>。我认为编书者首先要事事替读者着想,自己是渐渐摸索过来的,深知这一点的重要性,可说这是编书的首要宗旨。站在这种<u>立场</u>上,许多在编书过程中遇到的难题都可以通过学和问逐一解决。

2. 具有驾驭编书的能力。要了解中学和大学低年级学生学过哪些课文,课文中有哪些词语和文化知识。这样就知道他的读报时要补充什么,我们编书授课时就要在选材、注释、语言解说、读报知识介绍及新闻写作分析等方面基本功上下工夫,学生基础打好了,读报就不再犯愁。现在的问题是编委自己也未打好基础,往往主次不分,哪些语言要作重点解说,哪些作一般诠释,哪些一笔带过,哪些不注。读报知识等介绍也是如此。选择重点掌握词语更要根据学生的具体情况而定。但有编者却与此相反。例如在《精选本学习辅导》四版有一项 "Words to Know"(本课要掌握的重点词语),一编委不看该书"前言"说明,在一篇经济和竞选情势的课文里,列着"byproduct, contact, prolong"等学生已学过的词,反而弃"Goldman Sachs, Goldilocks economy, business cycle, farm belt, tech bubble, "It's the economy, Stupid", exit poll"等真正重点词语。当然取舍笼统与具体,拿捏好分寸也非一日之功,本人也犯这方面毛病。

另一个问题是,现在网络发达固然给我们提供了便利,但有的编者在注释时将网上的词语释义下载了事,一本书岂不成了三四本。

3. 厚积薄发。编文选者不必急于求成。英文报刊涉及内容广泛,涵盖当今美英国内外大事及各个领域,要具备这方面语言和知识,是有一个较长过程的。为此首先要通过文选、参考书和上网作桥梁,看懂报刊上的文章,再经历教书和读书积累较丰富的语言和读报核心知识,比较各种现有文选的优劣后,再审视自己能否编出比他们更好的读本。真正懂透美英报刊并不易,连英美教授也有犯难时,何况我们。记得有一次报纸广告登着日本出的收录机,上有 ambience(背景杂音)一字,在场七八个美国人纷纷马上查词典,又讨论了一会儿,才回答我,这种认真精神给人印象极深。

本人在1987年编的第一套文选为什么广受欢迎,而1993年的《新编美英报刊文章选读》却认为最差,都与上述两点有关。新编本以所以差,是因为当时觉得1987年版已太陈旧,跟不上形势,为"与时共进",除自己外,出版社催我速编,结果就产生欲速则不达之效果。出版后的社会效益和出版社的经济效益都未达到。这是一个很好的经验教训。

下面将简单谈谈自己编文选的几项原则和细则,这是在2006年我主编的高校报刊教材系列被定"普通高等教育'十一五'国家级规划教材"后,北大出版社召开的一个小型庆祝会上的发言稿经修改后写成的,所引例子大多是编委的缺点和优劣的对比,或许教训更能引以为戒和对比更能见孰优孰劣吧。

此外,除网络外,有志者要具备必要的工具书,如我认为 *Safire's Political Dictionary* 是有助于提高自己读报水平的一本重要词典,尽管其释义用字深奥。西方大词典隔几年就出新版,附录里有最新词语,不妨复印下来备查。英美历史书也是应该读几本的,否则说话论事感觉无根,更不用谈研究了。

一、选材与课文

课本是一课之本,课本优劣,对学生能否在一年半载学到一些读报的基础知识关系重大。好课本的一个重要前提是选材,选材大概占编书时间的三分之一。我认为选材有下列几方面的要求:

1. 趣味性和知识性是选材的首要标准

报刊在于紧跟形势,为了吸引读者,还故弄玄虚、耸人听闻。构成新闻的要素是及时性、重要性、显著性、相关性、奇异性和趣味性。但这些要素不全是选材的标准,课文应以各类时文为主,内容必须具有趣味性和知识性(语言知识和各种文化知识),两者紧密相关,缺一不可。例如在《上下册》三版第13课"A Plan Under Attack"(2003/4/7 *Newsweek*)里,不但文化知识方面有如伊拉克战争、反恐战、中东问题及美国在中东的图谋、人物、组织介绍等,这些知识对读者今后独自看懂有关中东问题的文章会大有裨益,情况明,读报易;语言方面也有不少值得学习的军语,如 shock and awe, decapitation strike, rules of engagement, cavalry, Kornet antitank missile, Abrams MIAI tank, the 101st Air Assault Division, the Fourth Infantry Division, death squad, elite army, CENTCOM, smart bomb, Black Hawk, the Marines, friendly fire, Apache helicopter, Operation Desert Storm 等等,还有诸如 embeded reporter, Rumsfeld war/Doctrine 等新军语。在修辞手段上,值得学习的俯拾即是,委婉语如 regime change，collateral damage；比喻如 hawk，micromanage；借代如 Capitol Hill，Pentagon，Vietnam 及新的以年月或年代作借代法，如本文里的"'91"指以美国为首发动的第一次伊拉克战争。这是一篇 cover story，课文长，没有将其分为两课是个不足之处。

凡是有教学经验的老师都深知，学生对课文没有兴趣，学习效果差；没有知识点或没有一定的难度和长度的课文，学生的学习目的落空。这就要求老师得多花时间备课。几年前，我和两位美国新闻学教授应《21世纪英文报》邀请去黄山作报告时，一位美国教授说："In teaching newspapers, teachers learn more than students do."这大概就是我们所说的"教学相长"吧。这里顺便加一句，其实读者也是我的老师，有人曾来函纠正书里错误或指点不解之处。有的文章虽然作为新闻的时效性不强了，但知识极其丰富，这类文章是非学不可的，不能完全迁就兴趣。例如：Why the Monarchy Must Stay(1996/3/11 Newsweek)，The Great Superpower Spy War KGB vs. CIA(1984/10/29 U. S. News & World Report)，English Out to Conquer the world(1985/2/18 U. S. News & World Report)等文章里，第一篇读报必备知识多；第二篇是读间谍书刊必备的词语多和对今后去国外进修和从事工作提高警惕有益。例如在法国、美国等国留学生一再发生所谓"间谍"事件，这也要求我们具有这方的知识；最后一篇说明英语如何一步步成为世界性语言的。这种选材的标准不是文选独有。读文学的学生普遍不愿念 Jane Austin 的 *Pride and Prejudice* 等小说，但文学专业却将此书列为必读书。这也就是说，并不是课文内容一定是越新越好，虽然弃旧换新是原则。不过话又说来，有的我在第四版里还忍痛割爱了。为帮读者打好报刊知识基本功，我想保留些质量好的旧课文，却不知哪家出版社愿做这赔钱的买卖。

2. 题材新颖多样，信息量大，覆盖面广

《上下册》课文多，能容纳多种题材，政治、军事、外交、法律、间谍、社会、文化、教育、经贸、科技、娱乐、体育、自然灾害、名人介绍等都有。面广，学生就能学习各种语言，知识面就越广，今后判断语义的能力就越强。我所选材的课本中最满意的是1987年出版的《上下册》一版，题材面较广，是在当时既无读报参考书，又无有读报经验老师的指导，更无网络可言的情况下编注的，其艰辛可想而知。连北大资深教授杨周翰先生见书后对我说："谢谢你做了件好事。我们早就说编报刊文选，不但书没有编出来，连课都没有上过。"另一位看了我全书稿子、懂得多门外语、一辈子持低调的老先生王岷源说："我看了全稿后，学到了许多新词语和表达法。"尽管从现在看来，仍有许多不足之处，不过稍年长的编文选者，或许都读过和教过此书。

3. 课文要有种种体裁

消息报道、特写、社评。这在87年首版中都有。我主张以报道性体裁为重点,兼顾其他。这在前面已经进过,此处不再赘言。

4. 选材内容配合国策,与时共进

随着改革开放的深入,为贯彻"以经济建设为中心"和"科教兴国"的国策,《上下册》三版与二版相比,增加了经济、科技、人才等方面内容的课文。第四版与第三版相比,内容更加丰富,增加了"社会"题材、"名人介绍"青年人喜爱的NBA和football的体育课文。

其次,与时俱进也体现在《精选本》二版至四版里增加"China Watch"(中国观察)一个单元的几篇文章。随着对外开放后,我国实力增强,关于"China"的文章在美英报刊里逐渐增多。有的文章还有建议和善意的批评,可以学到一些老外译汉语的方法。一位外交部高翻说,看了外刊对我国汉语新词语的译法,自己大有长进。回头来看,英国分量应该减轻一些,金砖四国以及全球化、信息化、金融和经济危机、新能源、气候变化等热门话题应该增加。

最后,与时俱进还表现在上述两套(现为三套,增加了一套非英语专业用书)课本一版一版往下编,《上下册》和《精选本》均已编到第四版,这是同类课本少见或不见的。

5. 选材内容等要平衡

除以中美英为主外,欧洲亚非拉等地区的题材也要收一些。人们最关注时政新闻,外刊上最多,选材比例上可稍大一些;选自报刊和杂志的文章数量要尽量平衡。

6. 课文尽量配有图表或漫画

课文配有照片、图表或漫画,可吸引读者,既可给人一种真实感,又节省篇幅,解疑释惑。图表、漫画等语言简炼、生动、形象、幽默(见**报刊用语主要特点**)。此外,它们还能使学生读起来轻松些。

据《新闻写作与报道训练教程》一书在"图表的重要性"这一节里说:

"报道配照片或图表非常重要。佛罗里达州圣彼得斯堡的波恩特传媒研究所(Poynter Institute for Media Studies)的研究表明,媒体对图表和色彩越来越重视。在一项名为"新闻报道与眼球"的研究中,研究人员观测了人们读报时眼球转动情况。这项研究名为眼球轨迹(Eye Track)。结果表明,读者首先被彩色照片所吸引,然后依次转向标题、图片说明、简讯(压缩到一至三段话的简短报道)以及其他一些视觉元素。读者首先注意到、引导他读下去的点称为切入点。抢眼点也包括报道中用大字号的副标题或引文。

"这项研究还表明,大多数人在读报时只是浏览整张报纸,看看标题和图片,很少通读某一篇报道。一般而言,读者大概平均会浏览报纸内容的四分之一,精读的部分只浏览内容的一半左右,即整张报纸的12%。"*

---

* [美]卡罗尔·里奇著,钟新译,中国人民大学出版社,2004,第28页。

7. 编排合理

课文编排涉及语言的难易程度、题材分类、国别分类等等多种因素。既然人们首先关注的是当今世界上第一超级大国的美国,又因英国毕竟是英语的发源地,所以这两国大事的课文置前,这有助于读懂报刊,世上许多大事都与这两国尤其美国有关。自从"China Watch"课文出现后,为贯彻先易后难的原则,将外国对华报道评论的文章置于最前面。学生对国内情况熟,较易读懂。

8. 讲政治

讲政治。如《上下册》第四版有一课"Big Maoist wins could reshape Napal's politics"(2008/4/15 *The Christian Science Monitor*)第一段就看到(武装起义)使一万多人丧生(见例句黑体)的内容就删掉了。见此段:

Barely two years after ending an armed insurgency **that killed more than 13,000 people**, Nepal's former Maoists rebels have stunned themselves, the Nepalese people, and the world with a landslide win in constituent assembly elections that could profoundly change Nepali politics.

二、词汇

"语言"知识章里已经花了许多篇幅,谈到了初读报者扩大常见词词义面和词汇量的重要性,并作了大量解说。

1. New Words 的范畴

对初读报者来说,新词新义多是首先遇到的一大拦路虎,哪些是新词新语,现在的英语教学大纲里没有规定,四六级词汇表倒在书市上随手可得,不妨用作参考。我主张单词一般均可列入词汇表,短语成语等列入 Notes 里。单词包括地名,但地名在课文作借喻、提喻或隐语用时则另当别论,应入 Notes 里。如 Washington 是地名,它既可作借喻、提喻也可作隐语,Brussels 是地名,还可指代 EU 和 NATO。

2. 以英文定义为主

New Words 应尽量用英文的 definition,annotation 亦然。因为学英文的最终目的还是为了使读者能看懂原文的书刊或资料。编委不能偷懒图快,而"省时省力",要查词典和上网,不然一天就可以编上好几课书。这样,虽然编者编书、学生学习和教员备课都不用动脑了,可吃亏的是学生。当然,英文注释应尽量用 *Longman Dictionary of English Language & Culture* 或 *The Advanced Oxford Learner's Dictionary of Current English* 等这样的释义用字简明的词典。此外,还要看你编的书读者群,如是给一类大学英文和国际新闻专业用的,英文定义后不必加注汉语;如是给自学者用书,就照二三类学校的,且对我国学生来说,词义较难阐明清楚的,得多加汉语注;如是给自学者用书,就照二三类学校的词汇注释办。如(精选本)便是。再如常用词 interest 作"organization 或 company"讲时,最好列入 Notes 里,或将这类词作"语言解说"。

3. 看懂全文再下定义

用上述这两本词典下定义的另一个优点是便于主编副主编审校,网上的定义往往太长,要经过压缩,不如词典定义精炼。但问题是有的编者不看这个字在上下文中究竟是何义,不管错对教条式地从这两本词典里找定义。例如《文选》(第四版)有一课是"The Economic Sucks. But Is It '92 Redex"(2008/1/21 Newsweek),这个标题里的 suck 被错误定义为"to take liquid, air, etc.(吸入)",其实其义应在其他大词典里查,是"to be very bad"之义。还有一种注解,读者看了也不懂,如 jittery 从原文词典一抄:having or feeling the jitters。jitters 是何意? 还不是与 jittery 一样让读者不懂。如其后加上(anxiety before an event)或最好这样注:feeling anxious before an event,这便一目了然。作为编者一定要看懂全文再下笔,要逐字校对,一个一个字地抠。作为主编,我在稿子里一再发现这类 definition 和 annotation 之误。英语一词多义,要找到与上下文合适的词义,有的可能词典和网上的所有词义都不合适,那就只有根据上下文或请教有经验的外教来确定其义。注解也是要下工夫的。有的词义即使词典上解释很清楚,不联系背景仍旧似懂非懂。1987 年我在第一次编文选时见到下列例句中的一个字,千思万想,不得其解:

McDonnell Douglas Corporation, for instance, gives employees a **laminated** code based on the Boy Scouts creed. (U. S. News & World Report)

何谓"laminated"? 我和老教授都不懂,因为当时的中国人还没有见过用透明塑料层封上的(如身份证之类的东西),更不用说以童子军信条为基准的公司职业规范也能用塑料层封上了。可见扩大知识面对读懂英文报刊很有帮助。

4. 拓展学生的词汇面和词义面

扩大学生的词汇量和词义面有多种手段,其中有:

(1) 词汇定义后加上同义词、近义词和反义词。符号既可用 Ant. Syn., 也用 cf.(意为"compare")。如 hawk(鹰派、强硬派)定义后加(cf. dove"鸽派", dawk"中间派")(当然 hawk 是用英文注释的,为节省篇幅此处用汉语) cold war (cf. hot war"实战"shooting war"真刀真枪的战争"), Hispanic (cf. Latino) title(标题;头衔)(cf. 书目;一种书;产权书;房地契如 title company"房地产权公司"), party line(合用电话线)(cf. party wall"伙墙")等等,这就使学生的词汇面和词义面都扩大了。

(2) 提醒学生注意易混淆的报刊常用词。如 Capitol(美国会大厦,喻国会)

(Don't get it consfused with the word"capital"),the Hill（美国会大厦所在地的小丘,称国会山庄。喻"国会"）(hill), Speaker（议长）(speaker"发言者",spokesman"发言人"), Administration（往往是某政党领导人的"政府",具有临时性)(government), ethnic(ethic) 等。尽管一再提醒学生,我教书时的考试说明,学生还是常犯这方面犯错。一般的地名如 California,只要注音后＋n.＋state of W US on the Pacific 即可。(见 *American Heritage Dictionary* 附录)

5. 注音一致,拼写有异

(1) 全书注音统一,或用国际音标,或用韦氏音标,两种音标各有所长。地名、人民也应注音。

(2) 拼写在课文里难以统一,因文章取自英美报刊,拼写必然各异。编者在注释中则可以统一。

6. 用通用的缩略词表明词性等

为节省篇幅,definition 和 annotation 里应尽可用下列一些较通用的缩略词或缩短词（见《精选本学习辅导》"前言"后、目录前的"Short Forms"）：如：*abbrev.*,*adj.*,*adv.*,*AmE*,*BrE* 和 *apprec.*,等等。

三、注释原则

注释是使学生读懂课文最重要的一环,他们能读懂课文,才能学到知识。要读懂课文基本功有三：语言、知识和逻辑,这三者密不可分。如果有人说对这句话或这一段这样理解不合情理,说明还没有弄懂,也就是说不合语言逻辑,定有误解之处。那么应该怎样注释才好呢？只要细读外国课本就会发现,一课书的难点如生词、新语和背景知识的注释,不是一揽子都放在 Notes 里,而是在 New Words,Notes,Vocabulary Building 里,有的甚至在个别 Questions 里既是问,又是释义(我称之为阐释性提问),若不从头至尾预习全文,教员上课提问时,便会抓瞎。说实在的,即使我自己编注的这么多文选课本,也达不到这个水平,其他国人编的课本,也大体如此。

注释要读透全文再下笔,不然问题必然多。这方面有许多经验教训。下列几点都与此有关。

1. 当注必注,不避难题

当注必注,不回避或删掉疑难词语。如 1997 年编《上下册》二版时,面临课文中几十个诸如 Unabomber,"It's the Economy, Stupid!" the West Lothian question, three-round parliamentary elections, eat one's children, the back alleys of the world,等等难题,当时网络尚不发达,老先生和外教也一时解答不了,我或查阅美英的议会记录、年鉴、政治和历史书籍,或直接打电话或写信给美英印等国使馆的文化官员求助,直到弄明白为止。做到对读者负责,决不敷衍了事。

所谓当注必注,还体现在不要注释那些与中国概念一致、学生易懂的语言及在中学和大学低年级已学过的一般构词法,更不要一般词典上都能查到或已学过的词语,注个没完没了,而真正的报刊语言的变化发展、用语特点和背景知识的难点都却有意或无意地回避。如《上下册》三版下册第21课"Labour begins fight for its heartland"(2004/5/4 *The Times*)第二段原本未注,我在最后一稿再加上了两个注释。见此例:

(1) Tony Blair and Gordon Brown will today prepare for the Labour Party's biggest electoral test of the Parliament by claiming that Michael Howard would ruin the economy if the Tories regained power.

The two men will attempt to **prevent** the party's local election campaign launch in Leeds **being overshadowed** by questions about Mr Blair's future and renewed **speculation about a handover deal between them.**

第二段有两个问题:一是字法。"prevent...being overshadowed",是创新省略了"from",还是记者、编辑的粗心大意漏字了?说明编委对字法不敏锐;二是背景。"speculation about a handover deal between them"。当时Blair任Prime Minister,而Brown是Chancellor of the Exchequer(财政大臣)。据报道,布莱尔之所以能连续三次赢得大选,主要是英国当时经济由布朗担纲搞得好,所以布莱尔曾与布朗达成默契,某年将首相一职交给党内强势人物Brown。

再如该书四版第三课"An American in Beijing"(2008/4/4 *Time*)

(2) Asia has played a huge role in shaping U.S. history and foreign policy. **Korea, Vietnam,** the World Wars—even **the Spanish-American war** was concerned with U.S. presence in Asia.

Korea, Vietnam, the Spanish American War 压根儿不注,说明编委对报刊语言特点不熟悉和背景知识不重视。好在《精选本》四版初稿送审时我发现了这一问题。此处Korea和Vietnam分别指Korean War和Vietnam War,这是报刊文章中常用的借代法。另外,说Spanish-American War与亚洲有关,是因为这场战争是1898年美国为夺取西班牙属地古巴、波多黎各和菲律宾而发动的战争。美西战争是列强重新瓜分殖民地的第一次帝国主义战争。

又如该书四版第20课"He's just like you and me, except for the £31bn fortune"(2008/3/9 *The Sunday Times*)第18—19段:

(3) After a first degree at the University of Nebraska Lincoln, he went to Columbia Business School in New York, where he fell under the spell of

第七章　学习方法　　　　　　　　　373

Benjamin Graham, an investment **guru** who awarded Buffett the only A⁺ grade he ever bestowed.

　　Buffett worked for his **mentor** after graduation but outgrew him, according to Roger Lowenstein, Buffett's biographer: "Graham would amaze the staff with his ability to scan a page with columns of figures and pick out an error. But Buffett was faster at it."

　　编注不注明此处的 guru 和 mentor 是同义词，guru 原为印度教、锡克教老师或领袖，在此处作"大师"讲。更不知道说明，guru 是现在的时髦词（buzzword），常作"顾问"、"大师"、"恩师"、"师爷"讲，mentor 是过时的时髦词，已被 guru 替代，如报刊报道 Carl Rove 是 Bush's guru，在 Bush 任期的政治文章里常见报，因 Rove 助小布什两次赢得大选，功不可没。还有此课的第 16 段里的"on a platform described as to the right of God"压根儿不注。

　　(4) He was born in 1930 in a house in Omaha on the banks of the Missouri River, the son of Leila and Howard, a Republican stockbroker elected to Congress **on a platform described as "to the right of God"**. His grandfather ran the family's grocery store dating from 1869, where Buffett's fortune began.

　　这里指的保守派或右翼观点的党纲，因为共和党保守派 God 不离嘴。又如"Path of the Storm"（2006/4/17 *Newsweek*）这一课最后一段最后一句中"Conrad Burns can no longer afford to phone it in"也避注，问编委也不知是何意，其实只要查"phone in"即可。见此段：

　　(5) Wary Republicans are waiting to hear what Burns has to say. The last place he wants to be seen is Washington D.C. When the Senate finished up business last Friday and closed up for a two-week recess, the senator rushed back home. There are endless speeches and fund-raisers ahead, and **Conrad Burns can no longer afford to phone it in.**

　　意为：超级游说者阿布拉莫夫出事使他胆战心惊，连电话铃声都怕听到，他在电话里对那些同党的 Wary Republicans 就阿氏闹出的丑闻不好表态。以上几例是当注不注、避难之典型。如主编只是挂名而不严格把关（事实上在《上下册》四版第一次印刷里就出现了若干明显的错误，当时由于我全力编著此书，审稿不严，没有把好关，亏对读者。第二次印刷才作了改正），这些问题如蒙混过关就苦了读者。又如此书第 17 课第 8 段：

　　(6) In early 2003, Mr Rumsfeld mused on what might be the cost of the war to come: $50bn (£25bn) or $60bn, he and White House planners thought. Five years on, the bill is already 10 times that, while here the

Commons Defence Committee has just warned of a "surprising" 52 per cent increase in the cost of operations in Iraq to nearly £1.45bn in the current financial year, despite the reductions in troop levels. An unprecedented amount has been funnelled to the private sector. The big winners have been the **money men**.(见四版课文:Iraq: Who won the war? 2008/3/16 *The Independent*)

出乎我意外的是,money men 不但不用英文注,而且不联系下文指的究竟是那些人或企业,就笼统而"简洁"地泛指"银行家,金融家,大亨,大老板"了事。其实本段已提到"the private sector"了。凡赚大钱者都与官方勾结或有瓜葛的公司,如美国发战争财的最大公司是 Halliburton(副总统切尼是发动伊战的一个主谋和该公司前任总裁),从 2004 年至 2008 年就赚了 160 亿美元,其分公司 KBR 获利 80 亿,Dyncorp18 亿,Blackwater 近 40 亿;英国的 Aegis 获利 2.93 亿,Global Strategies 和 ArmorGroup 等公司也都赚了个盆满钵满。当然它们对执政党也得投桃报李,在竞选捐款上助其一臂之力。

此例的这位编委不但没有吃透全文,认真负责,而是敷衍了事。

以上六例说明,编委必须掌握报刊语言特点和要有对读者认真负责的态度。

2. 注释精当,不画蛇添足

注释应精当,不画蛇添足。然而注释烦琐、用字不简约是通病。现在 IT 行业发达,上网找各种释义如囊中取物,比以往仅靠词典和百种全书及收听 VOA 和 BBC 容易得无可比拟,但我发现编委把从网上下载下来的如 cold war 或所谓 nuclear threats from the likes of North Korea 等分别占半页和大半页的注释全部用上,而不去精简。所以我要求他们如不精简删节,cold war 就用词典上的定义。一般而言,词典的释义比网络上的精炼。当然,如主题谈的是 cold war,就要追溯其源。关于朝鲜核问题,由于编委缺乏国际知识,不能三言两语就能说清楚,最后主编只用几句话就概括了事。(见 Iraq: Who won the war? 2008/3/16 *The Independent* 这一课第 8 段)

再如:在"Obama Makes History"(2008/11/5 *The Washington Post*)一课第 13 段:He is the fifth-youngest man elected to a first presidential term, after Theodore Roosevelt, John F. Kennedy, Bill Clinton and Ulysses S. Grant.

为省篇幅,只举对其中一位年轻总统的注释:John F. Kennedy—[1917—1963, often referred to by his initials JFK, was the thirty-fifth President of the United States, serving from 1961 until his assassination in 1963. He was] the second-youngest President, and the youngest elected to the office, at the age of 43.

其他三位也都是这么注的。我将上面框里的字全删了,其实还可改得更简单些。如"T. Roosevelt became President at the age of ..., Kennedy at 54, Clinton at... and Grant at ..."就行了。

注释精当可以用对比法而使学生一目了然。例如 the State of the Union (message/report)不但学生,有的老师也问我是何义。只要说明美国总统一年一度所作的国情咨文报告类似我国总理每年向全国人大所的工作报告。此处的 the Union 指的是美国。这就使读者或听者明白了。

注释不精当的例句不少。如《上下册》三版草稿里还引用朗文第三版里有篇文章报道说新加坡是 city-state,竟将该词定义为旧时代出现的"城邦国",应改为"无农村的城市国家",词义扩展了。再如第三版第 18 课"In a Sprawling Memoir, Clinton Cites Storms and Settles Scores"(2004/6/19 *The New York Times*)第 9 个注释是 the Whitewater affair,英文注释竟占了一页半纸(pp. 325—327)。这说明概括能力不强。此外,还有错误,如在第 7 课 Hollywood demons(1996/8/5 *Financial Times*)这电影分级搞成了六级,多了一个 M 级 (pp. 185—187)。作为主编,对这些错误,我应担全责。

3. 具有启发性、指导性和研究性

有的注释应具有启发性、指导性和研究性:例如在语言方面,本人对 family man, defining moment, Demopublican, Repubocrat, wheels within wheels 等词的定义,见解独到,发人所未发。读报结合实际,发现-ism 与 Doctrine 之不同。在读报知识方面,如 checks and balances 不只简单写出英英或英汉词典的"制衡"意义,还加上被美国视为政治制度重要的万全机制。美国宪法规定的三权鼎立,为的是防止滥用权利。再如 American dream,除了其词义外,如能加上:"人们普遍认为,美国体制被视为骨架,而美国梦则是其灵魂。"这样对美国梦的认识更清楚了(见《文选》第四版上册课文"The New Dream Isn't American")。对美英两国国情做了研究性介绍对比,对 All politics is local/personal 等名言释疑。在"A Plan Under Attack"文里对美国为何攻打伊克拉的说法有三:报复说;石油说;改造中东说。这对读此课及有关文章大有裨益。

对修辞格,"新闻用语的主要特点"及所编四种教科书里,处处举例说明。如 November 和 Washington 等作借喻、提喻和隐语等都注明。这里既有对报刊英语表达法特点的了解,也有对语言语法变化发展是否敏锐的问题。《文选》一版上下册具有启发性、指导性和研究性,是北大一位教授的评论。后来编的课本事实上还有一些注释够不上此评价,如在"A Plan Under Attack"这课的第 52 个注'91,当时只点出指 1991 年美国老布什总统发动的第一次伊拉克战争或海湾战争(*p.*230),并未指出这个省略数词如 November 一样,是报刊用语中借喻法新的表达形式。本书第四版的标题里还有用'92 表达 2008 年的经济和大选形

势与1992年的类似或是其翻版。

4. 扩大学生语汇量和语义面

扩大学生语汇量和语义面。如在本章"选材与课文"、"讲政治"的例子里有一个 landslide win,注释不应仅释其义,还应列出选举文章中常用的同义词 avalanche, clean sweep, tidal wave 等并辨义(见"**词义之确定及辨义**""**报刊用词辨析**")。再如 nagative campaign(ing)也是竞选文章的常用词语,那就要加上(*cf* attack/negative/slash-and-burn politics, mudslinging, slimesling, low road; positive campaign(ing), high road)。必要时在课文练习后的"语言解说"里连 go negative/positive 等都一并加以比较说明。

5. 讲政治

注释也要讲政治。有的西方政界领袖讲的对我不利的话,有的删,有的则不删。记得在《上下册》一版上册一课里有时任总统里根说的一句话:"Capitalism will defeat/prevail over Communism."我只是说明:"We should take what Reagan said critically."再如《精选本》三版第12课"The Spy Game"(2005/3/19 *The Economist*)第一段有"From Moses and Caezar to Churchill and Stalin"四个人物,据西方网络和工具书介绍,除摩西在《旧约》中称 prophet 和 lawgiver 外,其余两人介绍都分别用的是 statesman 和其他职位,而 Stalin 都却用的是 politician。严格地讲,此处的 politician 与 statesman 相比是贬义词,相当于"政治家"与"政客"之比。我们所用介绍材料80%以上来自英文资料库,西方对共产党领导人的态度一般都持否定态度,好在最后一稿检查出这个政治错误。这一点要特别清醒,切不可马虎。(见"**报刊的政治倾向性**")此外,对重要人物一定要说明出生或生卒年份,重要经历等。释义里如遇 industrial relation, whistle blower, political donation, obstruction of justice 等要在括号里加注"(劳资关系)、(敢于揭露上司谎言和丑闻者)、(竞选捐款)、(妨碍司法执行)"等,美国有的教科书也如此释义的。

6. 标志清楚,体例统一

标志清楚,体例统一。如编委人数多,这是一件要很细心的工作。各课在注明出处时,应顺便对其排名、座右铭、特色、立场、影响力、发行量、读者群、业主等作一介绍。美英报纸的编排与我国的不尽相同。纸张最多、分量最大的非《纽约时报》莫属,指出其编排特点(不过它现在的编排与以前不同了),看其他报纸就容易多了。此外,编委最好用一本释义简明,集语言与知识于一体的字典,便于体例统一。

四、注释与语言解说和读报知识介绍相辅相成

编者心中要有全局,哪些语言和背景知识必须在书中注释,哪些语言要结合

课文,对前面章节提到的那些类的核心"**语言**"作重点"**语言解说**"。如 presence, community, challenge, establishment 等常见多义词及其他选举用语、法律用语、社会用语、科技用语等。那些拟用作"报刊语言主要特点"进行讲解。背景知识以前面章节提到的那些核心"**读报知识**"结合课文介绍。如共和党和民主党、保守党和工党、大选、国会等作"读报知识"。这些"语言解说"和"读报知识"介绍,应与课文里出现的语言和知识尽量相结合,不搞为介绍而介绍。

1. 语言解说举例

"语言解说":如有的课文里既出现如今在政治用语中作"大师、恩师、顾问"讲的时髦词 guru,又出现已被其替代的过时时髦词 mentor,那么"语言解说"里加上其他一些时髦词,以"常见时髦词"加以举例说明;有的课文里上下两段分别出现两个 presence 和 challenge,除在注释中要联系内容确定其定义外,有的字同义异,如《上下册》一版第一课课文里两个 shady 就是如此。然而再决定是否分别用作"语言解说"。这方面《上下册》四版和《大英》都是如此讲解的。

2. 读报知识举例

"读报知识":如《上下册》四版有一课"Path of the Storm",讲的是国会议员与游说人员的关系,这课既可用作国会、政党介绍,也可用来专论 lobbyists 与议员的关系,说明为什么几个高官被 lobbyist 拉下水的原因。再如,"Obama Makes History"这课,就他如何入主白宫,就以美国大选作"读报知识"介绍。(见本人主编的三种文选)

总之,无论是"语言解说""读报知识"介绍都要有的放矢,不能与课文脱节。事实表明,许多编委缺乏经验,两者往往不衔接。这两方面介绍对开拓学生视野极其有益。但如编者本身没有下功夫研究过,是写不好的。

五、设计 Pre-Reading Questions 的要求和目的

在《大英》里增加了"Pre-Reading Questions"这一外国有的课本的项目,拟结合中国实际,不能如第一语言学习的外国课本一样,所提问题既要结合课文主题,又不拘泥于课文具体内容。这就是说,问题要简单上口,结合实际,使学生能说上几句,旨在引导学生对课文题材的兴趣,进入境界后,再学就容易多了。此外,还要避免与课文后的 Question 内容重复。见题:

该书的第一课是 A Race We can All Win(2007/12/31 *Newsweek*)其中心内容是中国经济发展不是威胁而是机遇。原来最后一稿的问题是:

1. What do you think of China's role on the world stage?

2. Do you think China's economic development is a threat or opportunity to other countries of the world?

这两题,尤其是第二题,学生不读几遍、了解全书课文内容,是很难回答的。我改为结合中国改革开放 30 年实际提问:

1. What place does China rank in the world economies?
2. Are your parents and uncles better off than they were thirty years ago?

孰优孰劣,由教师和学生去评论。

第 19 课 "Nanospheres leave cancer no place to hide" (2007/6/21 *New Scientist*)是题提得好的典范。见题:

1. How much do you know about cancer? Is it curable or incurable?
2. Do you have any relatives or friends who have suffered or are suffering from the disease? How about them now?

六、提 Questions 的要求及技巧

课文词汇表和注释后往往提出"Questions"。Question 必须抓住各段的中心思想和全课的主题,但往往 Questions 是编书者弱项或不愿费力去研究提问的技巧,难怪还有专门研究提问题的专家和博士学位,可见是门学问。问题必须用 Plain English 提问,这样学生才能不用书面语言答题。本人在前面已讲过,会提问者能将个别的语言难点融入解释性提问里。所以我要求《上下册》四版(因《精选本学习辅导》里有答题)里,编委一定要有答案供主编参考,否则,有人连自己的设题都不知是否切合文章内容。这样,他们才会有所进步而提高编书质量。

七、设计 Vocabulary Building 之技巧

《大英》里增加了"Vocabulary Building",对学生扩大词汇量和词义面有益。本人认为,在这项测试里出现过的词语,就不要再在 New words 和 Notes 重复解释。最好能参考 *Reader's Digest* 里 "Word Power" 栏目做法,以提高自己在这面的技巧。

八、课文导读

1. 写导读三要素

《上下册》和《精选本》一至三版都将"课文导读"放在第一个注释里,第四版改为"课文导读",置于课文前。导读有三要素构成:一是课文内容提要。标题、副标题是一课的灵魂,小标题是各段或几段的重点。看了这些,老手就能写出提要。有的无小标题,既然在定义词语时已熟读了全文,应该说就能写出来。从我作主编多年经验来看,事实并如此。汉语水平是关键。二是评论。不会写评论是通病,有的则是从网上下载一大堆不太切题的评论。评论应是一针见血。三

是学习此课的意义：或是能学到一些语言知识，或是学到了一些读报知识，或具有其他意义。

2. 不当的典型

凡是会写导读的，最长不要超过一页，最好以半页或大半页为限。下面举一些实例来说明优劣之分：

《上下册》四版和《大英》都有一课"An American in Beijing"（2008/4/4，*Time*），"导读"是这样写的：

"随着全球化的进一步推进，国际交往和交流的广度和深度日增。国际留学生作为各国文化交流的重要组成部分，数量也在不断增长。本文介绍了一名美国大学生在中国的留学生活，通过这一个体，可以管窥不同文化间交流的目的、益处及前景。"

缺点是写得太笼统马虎，没根据小标题将内容提写得具体一点。其中小标题有 **So why did they go**?（其中说明出国学习的两大好处："better way to improve language skills" 和 "excellent benefits for future employment opportunities"）**So why Asia**? **Why China matters** 和 **Making textbook a reality** 等共 9 个。内容清楚，提要较易写。我要求编委在一校清样时根据小标题重写。除评论外，还要联系随着我国经济的迅速发展，中国也有越来越多的学生以不同的形式出国深造、研究或游学。《精选本》四版写得稍好些。

3. 好范例

这两套书写得好的"导读"有"Obama Makes History"（2008/11/5 *The Washington Post*）这一课，不但说明他靠 on-line Obama 筹得巨款，说明金钱主导竞选。最后一段还加上奥氏上台前后出现的一些新词（见**改朝换代产生和流行的词语**）。

另一课写得较满意的是"Nanospheres leave cancer no place to hide"的"导读"：

"人们谈癌色变，它夺去了太多人的亲朋好友。为战胜它，国内中医有以毒攻毒的保守疗法，国外以外科手术为主。然而，手术后的化疗使患者痛苦不堪，可见这不是一个理想的好疗法。哈佛大学医学院曾有一份调查报告称，70%的患者都是吓死的。可见患者在治疗中的精神和心理因素也极为重要。

本文所谈治癌之法可说是另辟蹊径，纳米弹或粒子可以发光，光可产生热能，这样不用 CT 等仪器就能发现癌的位置，又能用产生的热能射线将癌细胞杀死，扩散未及的细胞毫发无损。不过，美国赖斯大学以 West 女士为首的实验团队仍处于实验阶段，从《新科学家》杂志的报道来看，前景光明，但愿它能成功，为人类添福。

"这篇"纳米球使癌细胞无藏身处"的课文中代词多，编者尽可能帮读者进行语法分析。有的词无论在网上或词典里，都不可能找到适合上下文的意义，这是常有的事，就只能根据本文上下文和文外的其他背景知识来确定词义。还有的词，如"control"，或许我们只知道广义，但在本文"control mice"却由泛指到特指，词义变化了，不能理解为"控制的鼠"。词义变窄后成了"对照实验或实验的对照物"的意思，即"用来作对比实验之鼠"。所以，我们在读报时对理解不透的词语，应多在网上或工具书中查出合适的词义，切不可望文生义。"

  这篇导读短小精悍，既道出全文的主题，指出了标题的意思，又联系国内外治癌的种种方法和弊病。最后还说明词义从泛指到特指的变化。对学生具启发性和指导性。

  若是换一种写法，将癌症病例的起因及各种治疗方法按时间顺序一年年的写下去，起码要占三页纸的篇幅。须知学生不是病史研究专业的。这就是说，这种"导读"写法不看对象，从网上下载一些资料乱塞给读者，果如此，是不会写"导读"的典型，决不可取。

  《文选》（第三版）第 13 课"A Plan Under Attack"的"导读"也是写得较满意的。见写法：

    A Plan Under Attack —— 2003 年 3 月 20 日，美国以伊拉克拥有大规模杀伤性武器和生化武器为借口，发动军事进攻，代号为"伊拉克自由计划"，第二次海湾战争爆发！

    战争伊始，美国的先进武器占尽优势，Abrams 作战坦克和精确制导武器发挥了决定性的作用，美军几乎没有遇到什么强硬的抵抗，直逼巴格达。

    然而就美伊战争的战略战术问题，五角大楼并非众口一词。多数军事指挥官倾向于传统的美国作战方式，即用压倒一切的猛烈轰炸摧毁敌军及军事设施。国防部长拉姆斯菲尔德另有想法，他要指挥官在战争中发挥更富有创造性的战略战术，即利用高科技、更灵活的作战方式迅速消灭敌军并占领巴格达。据报道，拉氏战术不仅仅是战略战术上的创新，更重要的是尽最大可能减少平民的伤亡和民用设施的破坏。他深知，伤及平民对于美军意味着什么。随着美军逼近巴格达，五角大楼对以后的作战方法以及其他问题的分歧达到白热化程度。如如何解决伊拉克精锐部队在巴格达周围的抵抗、如何进行进入巴格达后的巷战、战争能否尽快结束等等。这次"伊拉克自由计划"不仅周密地布置了美军作战的战略战术，还计划了美军进入巴格达以及其他城市后会遇到的巷战，甚至还包括美军占领巴格达后伊拉克的重建问题。当然，美国官方把对伊的重建大肆宣传，目的是取悦在伊拉克占多数的反对萨达姆统治的伊斯兰什叶派教徒，进而扶持一个亲美政府。他们甚至设想美军进入巴格达时，大街上会出现什叶派教徒夹道欢迎美军来解放他们的景象。当然,这只是一厢情愿。

美对伊拉克开战伊始,就备受抨击,因为不但国际社会对美英发动伊拉克战争进行指责,就连国内一些民众也强烈反战,而且伊拉克占领区自杀性爆炸和突然袭击所造成的美军士兵伤亡人数也不断上升。尽管该文作者所谓的"作战计划受抨击"是指布什政府针对伊拉克的作战计划,不无讽刺意味的是,该标题预言了战争结束后,美军在伊驻扎期间的整个计划也会备受鞭挞,正所谓"通往巴格达(以及占领巴格达以后)之路是一条漫长而危险的道路。"(部分副标题)

美国小布什政府为什么要借口伊拉克拥有大规模杀伤性武器和生化武器而发动这场战争呢?说法大致有三:(1) 报复说。老布什政府1991年发动第一次伊拉克战争未能把萨达姆推翻,在老布什访问中东时,萨达姆曾策划暗杀,从此双方结怨。(2) 石油说。伊拉克拥有大量石油,布什和副总统切尼都是石油家族成员或其家族与石油有关,发动战争是为独占伊拉克石油。(3) 改造大中东民主计划(Greater Middle East Initiative)说。伊拉克不但有丰富的石油资源,而且水资源也十分丰富,这是其他中东国家所不可比拟的。所以美国拿伊开刀,试图将伊建成以美国价值观为准则的"民主国家"的榜样,以它来推动其他中东国家的改革,最后使之都成为美式的民主国家。

从这一课可以学到一些当今常用的军事用语和新闻语言表达法的一些特点,并对美国和阿拉伯国家的关系、伊拉克国情等也有所了解。这对今后读类似内容的文章会有裨益。

导读不但点出了全文的中心思想,评论中提到美发动伊战的三个原因有研究性。最后说明学生学习此课的意义。此课课文相当于两课的长度,内容又相当丰富,"导读"也写得长了些。回头看来,语言还可精炼些(个别地方作了些修改)。

九、报刊课考试的若干建议

由高等学校外语专业教学指导委员会英语组2000年制定的《高等学校英语专业英语教学大纲》,只将外国报刊选读作为选修课,而六级考试的要求却是"能读懂难度相当于英国[The] *Times* 或[美国][The] *New York Times* 的社论和政论文章",对八级要求"能读懂一般英文报章杂志上的社论和书评"。这么高的要求表明,大纲制定者并未征求报刊教学第一线老师的意见,因而也没有多少学生能达到那么高的水平。

1985年,编者根据以前出考试题的经验,订出这个外刊选读课考试提纲,供读者参考。

1. 考试的目的和要求

考试的目的是使学生通过学习,了解美英的政治、外交、军事、经济、社会、文教和科技概况及当今世界大事,牢牢掌握好有关这方面的核心词语和报刊语言主要特点及读报的核心知识。对美英几大报刊的背景、立场、影响等情况也应有所了解。此外,还要求在阅读理解考试中分析外刊的政治倾向,提高判断能力。

通过 15 或 30 课报刊文选的学习、复习和考试,要求学生大大提高英语报刊阅读理解能力,初步掌握阅读美英报刊必备基本知识,从而为独立阅读打下基础。

2. 考试范围

考试以语言和读报知识基本功为主。具体讲,以课文中出现的政治、经济、外交、军事、文教、宗教、科技、国名、地名等词语为主,如 community, interest, story, the White House, Whitehall, Capitol, Speaker, spokesman, G. N. P., recession, Patriot missile, the House of Windsor, Protestant, launch window, Black Africa 等,并了解其中有些词的喻义。只要学生将《精选本》课文后的注释(Notes)、《学习辅导》书里第三部分"**Words to Know**"及"语言解说"、"读报知识"和"新闻写作"介绍中的词语和知识掌握好,及格应不成问题。不要求学生去记忆应该在中学或大学一二年级掌握的基本词语,如 byproduct, contract, prolong 等,更不能作为考试范围。阅读理解试题应结合课文中的上述内容,不宜太难。

3. 题型

考试题分三大部分:一是词语翻译:尤其要课文中各种题材如政治、经济、社会、宗教、科技等内容的词语,特别是一讲再讲,仍会混淆的词语。例如:the Capitol(美国国会大厦,喻"国会")与 capital 和小写的 capitol(州议会大厦,喻"州议会")不同;the Hill(国会山,也喻"国会")与 hill 不同;Speaker(议长)与 speaker 和 spokesman(发言人,不用 speaker)不同,combat fatigue 与 combat fatigues 不同,democracy 与 a democracy 不同等。此外,学生尚需掌握一些习惯性翻译,如 Secretary of State 译为(美国)"国务卿",Foreign Secretary(英国)"外交大臣",Foreign Minister(我国)"外交部长"等。再如 Prime Minister,是王国政府的如英国、荷兰和挪威等按惯例都译为"首相"。但也有例外,如泰国虽为王国,却称"总理"。又如英国外交(和联邦事务)部的"部",既不是"Ministry"也不是"Department",而是"Office"。翻译党派也应注意,如德国 Christian Democratic Union 是"**基督教**民主联盟",而意大利的 Christian Democratic Party 则指"**天主教**民主党"。此外,还应掌握其他一些用作借喻法、提喻法和隐语等的词语。二是选择题:要测试根据上下文判断词义及掌握同义词和反义词等词汇量；三是阅读 passage 或 article 后回答若干问题。passage 或 article 可考虑用要求学生自学的课文。如是课外的，文字应比课文容易些。试题内容与所学课文尽可能有联系。自考生和专科生试题应比在校本科生要浅显些，但第一部分的试题基本相同。

4. 时限

考试时间限定为两小时。考试第一部分的 20—35 个词语翻译需约 20 分钟，第二部分约 40 分钟，第三部分约一小时。

5. 复习方法和建议

复习时一定要读懂课文内容，结合有关文化背景知识重点讲解，使学生掌握上述有关方面的词语，尤其要学会辨析易混淆的词和掌握报刊语言中常见的多义词和喻词。使学生语言和知识双丰收。

以上所言，可参考我主编那三套文选"附录"里一所大学所出的"考试样题"。

十、学会校对

记得我在美国作 Special Student 时，英文系请出版社编辑上课，给博士班学生讲专业知识，有一节课单讲 Proofreaders' Marks（见 *American Heritage Dictionary* 附录）美国编辑用的符号。那些符号与我国编辑用的标识不完全相同。我们如写书，得学一些这方面的符号。如横线上＋号表明是英文连字符，♯表明是英文破折号，‖表明另起一段，ＶＶ表明退两个字格，等等。

十一、建议开设报刊语言班

为适应人才市场的需要，现在各所大学纷纷开设"外语学院"和"外语系"。有的教授问我如何定位他校的学院和系。如北大英文系以文学为主，北京外国语大学原来是为培养合格的外交语言人才为重点，还有的学校以语言学或翻译人才为中心，却没有一所学校开设新闻英语专业，与那些已是精耕细作专业相比，至今仍是待开垦的处女地。有的学校很重视报刊文选课，一学期作必修课，还有一学期作选修课；还有的将其定为一学年的必修课。北京联合大学英语系主任黄宗英博士说得好："我们学校与北大不一样，学生要多学一些实用性强的英语和知识，所以应该为学生多开一些报刊课。"

曾在延安教学后在北外奉献终身的已故英国老先生 David Crook 曾经说，如果只有两门课——文学选读和报刊选读让我选，我会选择后者。莎士比亚语言固然漂亮，但现在用不上。十年前，我去南京讲学时，时任南师大外语学院院长的程爱民教授对我说："周老师，你编的书很好，但我们学校没有一位老师真正够格教报刊文选的，因为涉及的知识面太广。"我认为要是哪个学校能培养出研究新闻语言、胜任报刊文选课的硕士生,他们找工作会容易些,这方面人才实在太稀缺了。

随着网络的普及,各类知识都可以上网求助,这对读报懂报刊如添一个无声为己服务的帮手和老师,可为什么还有一些年轻教师一提报刊就生畏呢?一些参与我编报刊文选的老师是文学或语言学教授和副教授,为什么好几年还不成熟呢?一是他们各自的教学和科研任务都忙,没有一位是专门从事这个专业的。"隔行如隔山",报刊语言和读报知识要积累,不能一蹴而就。二是高校英语教学大纲只将报刊课列为选修,要求却十分高,学生望而却步。三是缺乏合格或爱授此课的师资。有的老师觉得吃力不讨好。于是有的请老外应付,可外教不知中国学生究竟缺什么,往往选如克林顿的性丑闻之类文章,不注意学生能否从中学到语言和文化背景知识。结果学习目的落空,学生一反映,外刊课就砍了。再则,外教的英文水平普遍不高,有的编者编词典时问外教的不少英语词语都注释错了。如 put one's wallet where one's mouth is 竟错误地定义为"invest in what you believe in"。其实只要将"wallet"视为"money"就会在英英和英汉词典找定义。为了与时俱进,高校英语系拟增加一个研究生班,专门从事新闻或报刊语言研究。否则难以改变现状。现在的问题是,往往新闻系专业毕业的研究生语言水平不如英语系毕业生高,而英语系的又常缺乏读报知识,至今还是两张皮,一些国内出版的英语报刊便可见一斑。

十二、教训

本人双语水平不高,又因病不能上网,此书第一版较粗糙和缺乏系统性理论性,在写此书时发现《英汉美英报刊词典》和《当代英汉美英报刊词典》就犯了一些小儿科错误。看到错误,感到汗颜,作为主编得负全责。第二版本人力求加强系统性,总结出一些规律,但也没有把握,权当抛砖引玉,以待来者。

附　录

Ⅰ. 报刊从业人员常用术语

下列有些专业用语值得我注意。一是常见诸报端。二是我们翻译时不在行,如报纸的 page 应译为"版",staff writer 译为"本报撰稿人或记者"为好。

ace reporter 名记者
advertising edition 广告版
advocacy journalism 倾向性新闻报道
agony column(寻人、寻物、丧事、离婚等令人痛苦的)私事栏;读者问答栏
anecdotal lead 轶事式导语
assignment 采访任务
associate editor 副主编/主笔
attribution/speech tag 消息来源
back alley news 小道消息
back issue/number/dead magazine 过期期刊
banner heading 通栏标题
bizarreness 奇异性
body 正文
book page 书评版
box news 花边新闻
breaking news 突发性新闻
broadsheet paper 大开张报纸
budget 当日要闻一览
bulletin 通报;新闻简报
byline story 署名文章
by staff writer 本报讯;本报记者或撰稿人
cable editor 电讯编辑
caption 图片(文字)说明
carry 刊载
chief editor 主/总编;责任编辑
chronicle news 记事报
city editor 财经/(美)本地新闻编辑

city news 本市新闻,地方新闻
cliché 陈俗语,陈词滥调
(press)clipping 剪贴报
combined lead 复合式导语
comic news 滑稽新闻
comic strip 漫画栏
contrast lead 对比式导语
contributor 投稿人
copy reader 阅稿人
correspondent 驻外记者
criticism 评论
cub 初出茅庐的见习记者
deck/subtitle/subhead 副标题
delayed lead 延缓式导语
depth interview 深入访谈/采访
descriptive lead 描写式导语
desk ……部
direct address lead/personal lead 人称式导语
economic edition 经济版
editor's notes 编者按,编者的话
Eds=editor's notes
end 结尾
entertainment edition 娱乐版
exclusive 独家报道
exclusive news 独家新闻
express paper 快报
fashions 时装(广告)
feature editor 特写编辑

flash 快讯,新闻急电
follow-up(story) 补充/连续报道
free information 公开园地
freelancer 自由撰稿人
freshness 新鲜感
gatekeeper 新闻把关者
gazette 公报;……报
hard news 硬新闻
headline news 头条新闻
headlinese (带有新闻题特色的)标题语汇
hearsay news 传说新闻
human interest 人情味
inside dope 内幕新闻
interest 趣味性
It's said news 马路新闻
joint publication 联合版
journalist 报人,新闻工作者,记者
kicker 引题,眉题
label/no-news/empty lead 标签式导语
leaderette 短评
legend news 过时新闻
legman 外勤;采访记者
local news 本地/地方新闻
local press 当地报
locality feature 风光特写,当地风土人情特写
logo 报名
mail edition 通讯版
main fact lead 要点式导语
main head 主标题
managing director 总经理;社长
managing editor 主/总编
memorial 纪念刊
midget word 小字/词
miscellanies 杂感
monograph 专论
mosquito paper 刺人小报;黄色报
news editor 新闻编辑
news release 新闻稿
news vendor 报贩
newsy 报童
opinion page 言论/评论版
organ 机关报
periodical 定期刊
personal column 人事栏
personal/lonely hearts ad 征婚广告
picture editor 图画编辑
positions vacant 招聘(广告)
positions wanted 求职(广告)
press correspondent 摄影记者
press notice 报载小通告/宣传稿
press office 报社;(政府部门等的)新闻处
profile 人物特写
proximity 相关性,亲近性
publisher 发行人
question lead 提问式导语
quotation lead 引语式导语
rag 无聊小报;报纸的戏称
readers' corner 读者园地
resident correspondent 常驻记者
review news 评论报
right to inform 知情权
round-up/wrapup 综述;综合报道
route 订户
running stories 滚动报道
scandal news 黄色新闻,艳闻
scoop 特稿;独家新闻;抢新闻
screamer 耸人听闻大标题
sensational 有轰动效应的,煽情的,耸人听闻的
serial 连载
shield law 新闻来源保障法
situationer 时局报道
slot man 理稿编辑
slug line 提示行
social event feature 社会新闻特写

soft news 软新闻
special correspondent 特派记者
special dispatch 专电,专讯
special publicity 特宣稿
special report 专题报道
sporting editor 体育编辑
sports edition 体育版
spot news 现场报道新闻;突发性新闻
staff writer 本报撰稿人
stereotyped phrases 陈词滥调
subeditor 副/助理编辑;副主笔
subscription charge 订阅费
summary lead 概括式导语
sunday(news) 星期日报
supplement 副刊;增刊
suspense lead 悬念式导语
tab(loid) 小报
taster 审稿人
the editorial "we" 本报、本刊、我们等：社论式用语
the fourth estate （讽）报刊;新闻界/业
the heavies （英）态度严肃的大报

the opening number 创刊号
the yellow press 低级报刊,故作耸人听闻的报道以哗众取宠的报章杂志,与黄色新闻有别
thumbnail 小而短的文章,袖珍文章
tip＝inside dope
titbit（news） 花絮,趣闻
title 标题;（书刊等）一种
Today's Contents/Section 今日各版/要闻/要目
topic A 近来变为优先报道的连续/滚动报道;众人的话题
trade paper 行业报
training newsman 见习记者
uncrowned king 无冕之王
urgent dispatch 急电,急讯
wanted column 招聘栏
wire service/news agency 通讯社
wooden head 无味的标题
worn-out figures of speech 陈词滥调
yellow journalism 低级报刊/新闻,故作耸人听闻的报道以哗众取宠的办报作风

Ⅱ．美国选举常用词语

众所周知,美国政界人物成天热衷于党派斗争,迷恋于竞选做官,于是竞选词语层出不穷,若不掌握基本的和新造的这类词语,有关文章难以看懂。

As goes Maine, so goes the union 见缅因而知全国;缅因所之,举国响之：系美国共和党前身辉格党在1840年第一次大选中获胜后说的一句话。因预选于9月首先在该州开仗,它被获胜的政党认为是11月份举行全国选举的晴雨表。现在有人改用"As Maine goes, so goes the nation.",这样说大概是较合乎现在英语语法规则的缘故。1936年的大选之夜还出现了"As Maine goes, so goes Vermont"之说。

baby kisser 笼络人心的政客：在竞选中候选人亲吻选民的孩子,以示亲善,实为拉票。

beer track candidate 教育程度低、少数民族及蓝领工人联合支持的候选人

bundling 捆绑资金,竞选集资：为逃避公司对竞选捐款数额限制和讨好候选人,而将公司雇员的个人捐款合成一笔可观的竞选捐款交给某位候选人。这样,其上台后就会对该公司加以"照顾"。

(convention) acceptance speech 接受党代会提名致辞：党代会上接受提名为总统候选人者发表的致谢演说。

campaign message/theme 竞选的重大主题
coattails 燕尾;（喻）沾光,中国叫附骥(尾)：

美国竞选中,指担任公职的候选人常指在任总统助选的能力,牵着"他的燕尾"乘势走向胜利。当然,如他拉不了几个人,就说:"His coattail is very short."如他自身难保,就说:"His coattail has no tails."常用 ride on sb's coattails。

convention(政党)代表大会:由党代表参与的州或全国性大会,投票选出总统候选人和通过政纲,每四年一度各州的代表则于事前选出。

convention bounce 总统候选人获党代会提名后,在民调中有声望上升的现象。

Delaware Plan 特拉华方案:为纠正 Super Tuesday 和 front loading 的做法,2000 年特拉华州国会议员首先提出,选举人票(electoral vote)多的州,如加州和纽约州,压后举行预选。让小州先于大州初选,可避免出现过早决定候选人的局面,使其他州的选举变得可有可无。该建议由特拉华州共和党人首先提出而得名。

Federal Election Commission 联邦选举委员会、负责监督执行联邦竞选财务法的独立机构。

front loading 前期吃重或头重脚轻的预选:指在美国 2000 年的大选中,初选日程将人口众多的州的初选安排得过早,离决定总统候选人的党代会召开时间很早就使两党的候选人确定了下来,使其他州的选举变得可有可无。

front runner 领先者:指选举或提名进程中呼声高或最有希望当选的候选人。犹如跑在前面的赛马,易遭到落后者的攻击。

gender gap 性别差异:美国女选民偏向民主党或有自由色彩的人士。报界称之"性别差异"。在美国,女性选民比男性选民多,民主党和共和党候选人竞相争取。

give'em hell 竭力贬毁对手

hard/soft money"硬钱"/"软钱":这两个名词用来区分接受与不受联邦竞选财务法律约束的竞选资金。"硬钱"捐款数目受法律规定约束,虽然个人或竞选活动委员会(Political Action Committees)均可向政党或候选人捐款,只限 2 万元,但可影响选举结果,可用来为特定候选人摇旗呐喊。可译为"给候选人的竞选捐款";而"软钱"是捐给政党的,故可译为"给政党的竞选捐款"。2002 年 3 月,小布什签署了竞选资金改革法,废除了 soft money。2004 年大选,又出现了从事"秘密捐款战"(Secret money war)的 527 组织,比 soft money 的做法只有过之而无不及。

high road(竞选的)正道:指在竞选中不感情用事,不进行人身攻击,而是高瞻远瞩,采取摆事实讲道理的态度,大谈治国、治州、治市等大政方针,让选民自行得出孰优孰劣的结论。

low road(竞选的)歪道:指竞选作风不正,人身攻击,如杜鲁门把共和党总统候选人杜威(Thomas Dewey)蓄须比作希特勒的胡须。

majority minority district 少数民族占多数的选区

matching funds 对等资金:指总统候选人所得的公共资金,与私人赞助"对等"。初选期间,候选人每得一笔个人捐款均可获上限为 250 美元的对等资金。

money primary 竞选筹款起步阶段或初次筹款

national convention 见 convention

one-issue brothers and sisters 抓住一个问题如人工流产便决定支持某一候选人的信徒

platform(竞选)政纲:电视上候选人形象、人品和已露的领导能力一览无余,现在此种官样文章的分量显得轻多了。

plurality rule 简单多数原则:指选举中按多数票决定胜出的办法,票数最多,但不要求过半。
plural vote 一人多次投票
positive campaigning 积极的正面竞选：指候选人只在大政方针上辩论的竞选活动，给人好感。但时下这种正派作风并不吃香。
position paper 竞选中对有争议的问题发表的正式主张或政策声明
protest vote 投抗议票泄愤
public funding 公共资助：历年来此类捐款机构如 PAC 的数目与影响显著增加。（见 Political Action Committee）
redistricting 选区重划：众议院根据人口多寡决定名额，一个选区选一名议员。民主党和共和党都力争掌握州立法机构，以有利于本党的方式划分选区。
sewer money 赃钱，原指 hard money
single-member district 单一席位选区
Soccer Moms （住郊区、陪孩子去踢球的）足球妈妈集团：成员多，中上阶层，各为一方竞选助威。现在已类比造出这妈那妈的选举集团。
sound bite 反复播放某候选人说过的片言只语
spin doctor/spin 竞选班子雇用的媒体或竞选顾问，专事吹喇叭抬轿子，以使候选人获得最佳宣传效果。
stay-at-home 不在选举日出来投票的选民
Stupid Tuesday 愚蠢的超级星期二：对 Super Tuesday 的贬称。Super Tuesday 和 front loading 使政党过早选定总统候选人，尔后在其他州的选举和全国党代会（national convention）变得可有可无。
Super Tuesday（**primary**）超级星期二：此词从 1988 年以来一直被广泛使用。美国南部几个州于 1988 年 3 月 9 日同时举行候选人初选造势，以抵消早些时候在新罕布什尔州（New Hampshire）primary 和衣阿华州（Iowa）caucus 所产生的影响。1992 年，克林顿出师不利，靠"超级星期二"囊括了南部大部分州选票翻盘赢。后来，随着泰坦尼克号电影的上演，又造出 **Titanic Tuesday**；还不过瘾，2004 年印度洋发生海啸（tsunami），2008 年 2 月 5 日，民主党共有 21 个州举行初选。媒体改称为 **Tsunami Tuesday**（海啸星期二）。虽然有的总统选举年在这一天并没有那么多州参加预选，但仍称 Super Tuesday，有时也称 **Minor Tuesday**（小超级星期二）。仿 Super Bowl（美国职业橄榄球锦标赛超霸杯赛）而造。
superdelegate 超级代表：出席政党全国代表大会、非经初选党员挑选的代表，而是某党的政界大佬。
ticket splitting 选票分散：票是投给代表不同政党的候选人
tracking survey （候选人进行的）跟踪民意调查
wine track candidate 受过高等教育和白领选民精英支持的候选人

Ⅲ. 外事人员常用词语

除在"语言"解说里的"外交用语"外，下面列出更多的外交通常用语，部分外语和新闻专业毕业生将走上外事岗位，学了对他们有益。

air attaché 空军武官
ambassador without destination 无任所大使
approach 商洽
beyond containment 超越遏制
boycott 经济抵制
chancellor（使领馆）一等秘书
chargé d'affaires ad interim 临时代办
clash of civilizations 文明冲突
close breach 弥缝裂痕
closed/gag rule 封闭规则
conference report 统一文本
consular jurisdiction 领事裁判权

co-sponsor 共同提案人
counsellor 参赞
credentials 国书
cultural ambassador 文化使节
debase 降格
denial of justice 拒绝谈判
diplomatic corps 外交使团
Dominion 自治领
emissary 密使
envoy 使节
equerry 侍从武官
exchange of notes 换文
extraterritoriality 治外法权
follower 随从
franchise 特权
good offices 斡旋
high commissioner 高级专员
legate 教皇使节
legation 公使馆
letter of recall 辞任国书
line-item veto 逐项否决
mandatory administration 委任统治
military advisory group 军事顾问团
military attaché 陆军武官
military mission 军事代表团
minister 公使
mission 使节团

modified rule 限制规则
national treatment 国民待遇
naval attaché 海军武官
NCND (no confirmation and no denial) 既不确认,也不否认
note 照会
offer 提出条件
open lands/skies proposal 开放陆地/天空建议
pourparlers 预备性谈判或交涉
privileges 外交人员待遇
Proliferation Security Initiative 防扩散安全倡议
raising status 升格
resume trade relations 恢复通商
roving ambassador 巡回大使
secret clauses 秘密协定
sever diplomatic relations 断绝邦交
speaking notes (英) 说帖
special diplomatic envoy 外交特使
strike the last word 删去前一发言者的最后一个字
text of treaty 条约全文
treaty of amity and commerce 通商条约
verbal agreement 口头协定
verbal note 普通照会

Ⅳ. 宗教词语

英美信教人多,上教堂做礼拜犹如我们进行政治学习一样,是生活的一部分。美国人大多是基督教新教徒,信天主教者占少数。英国国王是英国基督教的保护者(Defender of the Faith),如坎特伯雷大主教等高级教士都是上院议员。由于移民的增多,英国也有其他宗教。

在报刊的宗教用语中,只要提及中东或以色列和巴勒斯坦冲突必提 Jerusalem (耶路撒冷),The Holy City,如无定冠词,也可指罗马或麦加圣都或圣城。而 The Holy Land 指巴勒斯坦。当今的以色列和巴勒斯坦,古称迦南(Canaan),后被称为"上帝应许之地",《圣经》称之为圣地、神秘之城。圣地上的耶路撒冷更具魅力。犹太人视其为历史、精神和民族中心,基督教视其为耶稣早年求学、中年布道、晚年罹难之所,伊斯兰教视其为穆罕默德登天之地。耶路

撒冷是举世闻名的文明古城。它位于约旦河西岸,东临死海,西濒地中海,群山环抱,地势优越,兵家必争之地,历经五千年沧桑,也是今后以巴问题最后解决的死结,双方均视其为"首都"。见例句:

During the ensuing struggle, Rabin was given a number of difficult missions. Early in the war he was ordered to break the Arab blockade of **Jerusalem** and keep the road open to Tel Aviv.(*Time*)

此外,还有 Jerusalem syndrome,圣城宗教气氛引发幻觉,受折磨者都是朝圣者。这类宗教词语(religious word),如 Mass, Jesus Christ, father, pastor, rabbi, chapel, synagogue, Lord's Day, confession, Easter 常见诸报端。对英美等西方人来说,这些都是常用词。

believer 信徒
born again 再生,重生
christening 洗礼式
confession 忏悔
creed 信条,教义(见 dogma)
dogma 教义,教条(见 creed, religious doctrine)
Easter 复活节
Epiphany 主显节
Father 圣父:三位一体之一位
fetishism 拜物教
founder of a religion 教主
God/the Deity/the Lord 上帝
Good Friday (耶稣)受难节
Jesus Christ 耶稣基督
Kingdom of God/Kingdom in Heaven 天国,上帝之国
Mass 弥撒
Mecca 麦加
Mormon 摩门教徒
Mormonism 摩门教
people in religious conscience 宗教界人士
Pope/Pontiff/the Holy Father/the Sovereign Pontiff 教皇
preach 讲道
preacher/missionary 传教士
prostrate oneself in worship 顶礼膜拜
Protestant 基督教新教教徒
Protestantism 新教,耶稣教
providence/God's will 天命
Puritan 清教徒
Quakerism 贵格会
read out of the party 逐出教门
religious doctrine 教义(见 creed, dogma)
religious service 礼拜
resurrection 复活
revelation/apocalypse 启示
ritual 宗教仪式
Satan 撒旦,即"魔鬼",又称 666
Society of Friends 公谊会
Society of Jesus 耶稣会
soul/spirit 灵魂
Sunday School 主日学校
Supreme Being 上帝(=God)
Ten Commandments 十诫
the City of God (基督教)天堂
the Holy Ghost/the Holy Spirit 圣灵
the Lord's Day 主日:即"礼拜日"
the Savior/the Redeemer 救世主
the Son of God 圣子:指耶稣,三位一体之一位
thearchy 神权统治
theism 有神论
theocracy 神权政治
totem 图腾
totemism 图腾崇拜
Whitsunday/Pentecost 圣灵降临节
World Council of Churches 世界基督教协进会

YMCA (Young Men's Christian Association) 基督教青年会

YWCA (Young Women's Christian Association) 基督教女青年会

V. 间谍行话

间谍用语大多是从泛指到特指而词同义异的一些俚语行话,其中有不少是 CIAese,KGBese 等 spookspeak(间谍行话),一般词典多语焉不详。

agent of influence 旨在影响舆论(而不是从事破坏、暗杀等间谍活动)的特工;散布假情报、反宣传等活动的人员;在美收买权势人物的日本特工

agent provocateur (鼓励涉嫌者从事非法活动而加以逮捕的)坐探,密探

asset (尤指美国中央情报局在搜集情报的国家所建立的)关系,眼线

bagman 从事收买拉拢的特工

biographical intelligence 人物情报

black bag (job) 黑袋(活计):指警察或特工人员为获取证据而"非法入室秘密搜查"。黑袋子是从事非法秘密搜查的象征,里面装着搜查用具。

blown (间谍)被发现的

boxed 被测谎过的

brainwashed (谍报人员的)心理经过调试的:如用测谎器就不一定能测准

burnt 身份暴露的,活动曝光的

cobbler 伪造者

code-name 化名

comint (*abbrev.* **communications intelligence**) 通讯情报:指通过卫星等监听外国的电台和其他广播、窃听外国密码通讯和电话等而获得的情报

compromised = burnt; 可能死了

country team 见 U.S. country team

cut-off man (地方情报站的)联络员,交通

cut-out (情报联络或交易的)中间人

desk man (情报总局负责间谍活动部门的)总管,主管

destabilize 颠覆

double = double agent

double agent 双重间谍:有的为敌对双方或一方两个相互竞争的情报机构服务;有的假装不忠实于一方而与另一方合作(见 **triple agent**)

drop (间谍用于传递情报、转交赏金等的)"信箱":如树根、古庙等均可用作这样的地点;如"无人情报交接处"则为 **dead (letter) drop** (见 **dubok**);(为获取情报而进行的)成功讹诈

dubok (俄语)无人情报交接处,无人材料、信息交换处:一方将"信"放在隐蔽之处,另一方然后再去取,两方不见面。

elint (**electronic intelligence**) (通过窃听器或类似的电子监视或侦察系统而获得的)电子情报

Farm (中央情报局设在弗吉尼亚的)培训学校

field agent/man 外调特工,派遣特工

flaps and seals (美国中央情报局给学员开设的)邮检)启封课:a ~ man 邮检专家

front (为非法活动、间谍活动而装的)门面,(作)掩护者

G-men 联邦调查局特工;美国特工处:源于一同名电影和美国特工处设在华盛顿 G Street 之故。

honey trap 美人计:以靓男俊女为诱饵而设的反间圈套

humint (**human intelligence**)(利用特情或间谍等获得的)人工情报

illegals (无外交身份和豁免权的)间谍(网)

legals (具有外交官身份的)间谍(网)

legend 间谍的化名和伪造的履历

mole 鼹鼠,(打入敌对情报机关而)长期潜伏的间谍(见 sleeper)

naked 无掩护和支援的

nash 我们的一个人,我方的一员

onetime pad 简单的、只能用一次的编码法

paroles (未见过面的间谍接头时确认双方身份的)主要暗号

playback (被捕间谍)被迫继续向己方发送(情报)

plumbing (为进行颠覆等重大活动前而设的)秘密机构

resident director (驻在某国的)情报站站长,间谍网头头

safe house (接待或安排特情或投靠者用的)密点,秘密招待所,秘密旅馆,(旅馆的)秘密套间

sanitize (从要公之于众的文件或档案中)删掉,修改(会使情报机关或其他政府机关尴尬的材料),(如会使水门事件曝光的录音带等)洗掉

secret secret service officer 秘密机关从事秘密工作的官员或人员,情报机关的情报人员或特工,保卫机关的安全人员。例句中的 Peter Wright 就曾在英国的情报机关MI5(军情五处)工作,后来他曾著书 Spycatcher (《抓间谍者》),揭露该机关的非法活动和策划反对首相的阴谋。

... and it is likely that the former **secret secret service officer** [Peter Wright] with a Government pension of £ 2,000 a year (or $3,200) is already a millionaire. (The Guardian)

sigint (signals intelligence) (通过电子和通讯信号而获得的)电讯情报,信号情报

sleeper (随时待机活动的)潜伏间谍(见 mole)

spook 间谍,特务

stringer (非情报机关的)兼职间谍

swim (间谍的)外出活动,旅行

take (因间谍活动而取得的)情报成果

terminate with extreme prejudice (婉)暗杀,干掉:指美国中央情报局常选择"暗杀"政界要人甚至国家元首,原指其在越南战争期间"暗杀"北越村长

triple agent (为三方或三个情报机构服务的)三重间谍

turned 被说服(而倒向另一方)或收买的

U.S. country team 由驻某国大使和情报站长组成的美在驻在国的情报班子

walk-in 主动提供情报或支持的志愿人员

watcher 主管监视怀疑对象的情报人员

wet job (间谍进行的)流血行动,暗杀行动

Ⅵ. 美国历任总统一览

顺序	姓名	任期	届别	政党
1	George Washington 乔治·华盛顿	1789—1797	1—2	联邦党
2	John Adams 约翰·亚当斯	1797—1801	3	联邦党
3	Thomas Jefferson 托马斯·杰斐逊	1801—1809	4—5	民主共和党

续表

4	James Madison 詹姆斯·麦迪逊	1809—1817	6—7	民主共和党
5	James Monroe 詹姆斯·门罗	1817—1825	8—9	民主共和党
6	John Quincy Adams 约翰·昆西·亚当斯	1825—1829	10	先"无党派"后"民主共和党"
7	Andrew Jackson 安德鲁·杰克逊	1829—1837	11—12	民主党
8	Martin Van Buren 马丁·范布伦	1837—1841	13	民主党
9	William Harrison 威廉·哈里森	1841	14	辉格党(任内病逝)
10	John Tyler 约翰·泰勒	1841—1845	14	辉格党
11	James Knox Polk 詹姆斯·K·波尔克	1845—1849	15	民主党
12	Zachary Taylor 扎卡里·泰勒	1849—1850	16	辉格党(任内病逝)
13	Millard Fillmore 米拉德·菲尔莫	1850—1853	16	辉格党
14	Franklin Pierce 富兰克林·皮尔斯	1853—1857	17	民主党
15	James Buchanan 詹姆斯·布坎南	1857—1861	18	民主党
16	Abraham Lincoln 亚伯拉罕·林肯	1861—1865	19—20	共和党(任内遇刺)
17	Andrew Johnson 安德鲁·约翰逊①	1865—1869	20	共和党
18	Ulysses Grant 尤利西斯·格兰特	1869—1877	21—22	共和党
19	Rutherford Hayes 卢瑟福·海斯	1877—1881	23	共和党
20	James Abram Garfield 詹姆斯·A·加斐尔德	1881	24	共和党(任内遇刺)
21	Chester Arthur 切斯特·亚瑟	1881—1885	24	共和党
22	Grover Cleveland 格洛弗·克利夫兰	1885—1889	25	民主党

续表

23	Benjamin Harrison 本杰明·哈里森	1889—1893	26	共和党
24	Grover Cleveland 格洛弗·克利夫兰	1893—1897	27	民主党
25	William McKinley 威廉·麦金利	1897—1901	28—29	共和党(任内遇刺)
26	Theodore Roosevelt 西奥多·罗斯福	1901—1909	29—30	共和党
27	William Taft 威廉·塔夫脱	1909—1913	31	共和党
28	Woodrow Wilson 伍德罗·威尔逊	1913—1921	32—33	民主党
29	Warren Harding 沃伦·哈定	1921—1923	34	共和党(任内病逝)
30	Calvin Coolidge 卡尔文·柯立芝	1923—1929	34—35	共和党
31	Hubert Hoover 赫伯特·胡佛	1929—1933	36	共和党
32	Franklin Roosevelt 富兰克林·罗斯福	1933—1945	37—40	民主党(任内病逝)
33	Harry Truman 哈里·杜鲁门	1945—1953	40—41	民主党
34	Dwight Eisenhower 德怀特·艾森豪威尔	1953—1961	42—43	共和党
35	John Kennedy 约翰·肯尼迪	1961—1963	44	民主党(任内遇刺)
36	Lyndon Johnson 林登·约翰逊	1963—1969	44—45	民主党
37	Richard Nixon 理查德·尼克松	1969—1974	46—47	共和党
38	Gerald Ford 杰拉尔德·福特	1974—1977	47	共和党
39	James Carter 詹姆斯·卡特	1977—1981	48	民主党
40	Ronald Reagan 罗纳德·里根	1981—1989	49—50	共和党
41	George Bush 乔治·布什	1989—1993	51	共和党

续表

42	William Clinton 威廉·克林顿	1993—2001	52—53	民主党
43	George Walker Bush 乔治·W·布什	2001—2009	54—55	共和党
44	Barack Obama 贝拉克·奥巴马①	2009—	56	民主党

Ⅶ. 英国历朝国王一览

顺序	国王	译名	执政期
1	William Ⅰ	威廉一世	1066—1087
2	William Ⅱ	威廉二世	1087—1100
3	Henry Ⅰ	亨利一世	1100—1135
4	Stephen	斯蒂芬	1135—1154
5	Henry Ⅱ	亨利二世	1154—1189
6	Richard Ⅰ	理查德一世	1189—1199
7	John	约翰	1199—1216
8	Henry Ⅲ	亨利三世	1216—1272
9	Edward Ⅰ	爱德华一世	1272—1307
10	Edward Ⅱ	爱德华二世	1307—1326
11	Edward Ⅲ	爱德华三世	1326—1377
12	Richard Ⅱ	理查德二世	1377—1399
13	Henry Ⅳ	亨利四世	1399—1413
14	Henry Ⅴ	亨利五世	1413—1422
15	Henry Ⅵ	亨利六世	1422—1461
16	Edward Ⅳ	爱德华四世	1461—1483
17	Edward Ⅴ	爱德华五世	1483.4—1483.6
18	Richard Ⅲ	理查德三世	1483—1485
19	Henry Ⅶ	亨利七世	1485—1509
20	Henry Ⅷ	亨利八世	1509—1547
21	Edward Ⅵ	爱德华六世	1547—1553
22	Mary	玛丽	1553—1558
23	Elizabeth	伊丽莎白	1558—1603
24	James Ⅰ	詹姆斯一世	1603—1625
25	Charles Ⅰ	查尔斯一世	1625—1649

---

① 奥巴马是第44任、第55届美国总统，但不是第44位而是第43位美国总统，因为Grover Cleveland曾分别担任过第22任和24任不接续的总统。

续表

26	The Commonwealth	共和政体	1649—1660
27	Charles Ⅱ	查尔斯二世	1660—1685
28	James Ⅱ	詹姆斯二世	1685—1689
29	William and Mary	威廉姆和玛丽	1689—1702
30	Anne	安妮	1702—1714
31	George Ⅰ	乔治一世	1714—1727
32	George Ⅱ	乔治二世	1727—1760
33	George Ⅲ	乔治三世	1760—1820
34	George Ⅳ	乔治四世	1820—1830
35	William Ⅳ	威廉四世	1830—1837
36	Victoria	维多利亚	1837—1901
37	Edward Ⅶ	爱德华七世	1901—1910
38	George Ⅴ	乔治五世	1910—1936
39	Edward Ⅷ	爱德华八世	1936—1936
40	George Ⅵ	乔治六世	1936—1952
41	Elizabeth Ⅱ	伊丽莎白二世	1952—

Ⅷ. 英国历任首相一览

顺序	姓名	译名	任期	政党
1	Sir Robert Walpole	罗伯特·沃波尔爵士	[1721]—1742	辉格党
2	Earl of Wilmington	威尔明顿伯爵	1742—1743	辉格党
3	Henry Pelham	亨利·佩尔汉姆	1743—1754	辉格党
4	Duke of Newcastle	纽卡斯尔公爵	1754—1756	辉格党
5	Duke of Devonshire	德文郡公爵	1756—1757	辉格党
6	Duke of Newcastle	纽卡斯尔公爵	1757—1762	辉格党
7	Earl of Bute	比特伯爵	1762—1763	托利党
8	George Grenville	乔治·格兰维尔	1763—1765	辉格党
9	Marquis of Rockingham	罗金厄姆侯爵	1765—1766	辉格党
10	Earl of Chatham	查塔姆伯爵	1766—1768	辉格党
11	Duke of Grafton	格拉夫顿公爵	1768—1770	辉格党
12	Lord North	诺斯勋爵	1770—1782	托利党
13	Marquis of Rockingham	罗金厄姆侯爵	1782—1782	辉格党
14	Earl of Shelburne	谢尔本伯爵	1782—1783	辉格党
15	Duke of Portland	波特兰公爵	1783—1783	联合内阁
16	William Pitt	威廉·皮特	1783—1801	托利党
17	Henry Addington	亨利·埃丁顿	1801—1804	托利党
18	William Pitt	威廉·皮特	1804—1806	托利党

续表

19	Lord William Grenville	威廉·格伦维尔勋爵	1806—1807	辉格党
20	Duke of Portland	波特兰公爵	1807—1809	托利党
21	Spencer Perceval	斯潘塞·帕西瓦尔	1809—1812	托利党
22	Earl of Liverpool	利物浦伯爵	1812—1827	托利党
23	George Canning	乔治·坎宁	1827	托利党
24	Viscount Goderich	戈德里奇子爵	1827—1828	托利党
25	Duke of Wellington	威灵顿公爵	1828—1830	托利党
26	Earl Grey	格雷伯爵	1830—1834	辉格党
27	Viscount Melbourne	墨尔本子爵	1834—1834	辉格党
28	Duke of Wellington	威灵顿公爵	1834—1834	托利党
29	Sir Robert Peel	罗伯特·皮尔爵士	1834—1835	保守党
30	Viscount Melbourne	墨尔本子爵	1835—1841	辉格党
31	Sir Robert Peel	罗伯特·皮尔爵士	1841—1846	保守党
32	Lord John Russell	约翰·罗素勋爵	1846—1852	辉格党
33	Earl of Derby	德比伯爵	1852	保守党
34	Earl of Aberdeen	阿伯丁伯爵	1852—1855	联合内阁
35	Viscount Palmerston	帕尔姆斯顿子爵	1855—1858	自由党
36	Earl of Derby	德比伯爵	1858—1859	保守党
37	Viscount Palmerston	帕尔姆斯顿子爵	1859—1865	自由党
38	Earl Russell	罗素伯爵	1865—1866	自由党
39	Earl of Derby	德比伯爵	1866—1868	保守党
40	Benjamin Disraeli	本杰明·迪斯雷利	1868—1868	保守党
41	William Ewart Gladstone	威廉·E·格莱斯顿	1868—1874	自由党
42	Benjamin Disraeli	本杰明·迪斯雷利	1874—1880	保守党
43	William Ewart Gladstone	威廉·E·格莱斯顿	1880—1885	自由党
44	Marquess of Salisbury	索尔兹伯里侯爵	1885—1886	保守党
45	William Ewart Gladstone	威廉·E·格莱斯顿	1886—1886	自由党
46	Marquess of Salisbury	索尔兹伯里侯爵	1886—1892	保守党
47	William Ewart Gladstone	威廉·E·格莱斯顿	1892—1894	自由党
48	Earl of Rosebery	罗斯贝利伯爵	1894—1895	自由党
49	Marquess of Salisbury	索尔兹伯里侯爵	1895—1902	保守党
50	Arthur James Balfour	亚瑟·J·贝尔福	1902—1905	保守党
51	Sir Henry Campbell-Bannerman	H·坎贝尔—班内南爵士	1905—1908	自由党
52	Herbert Henry Asquith	赫伯特·H·阿斯奎斯	1908—1916	自由党
53	David Lloyd George	大卫·L·乔治	1916—1922	联合内阁
54	Andrew Bonar Law	安德鲁·B·劳	1922—1923	保守党
55	Stanley Baldwin	斯坦利·鲍德温	1923—1924	保守党
56	James Ramsay MacDonald	詹姆斯·R·麦克唐纳	1924	工党

续表

57	Stanley Baldwin	斯坦利·鲍德温	1924—1929	保守党
58	James Ramsay MacDonald	詹姆斯·R·麦克唐纳	1929—1935	联合内阁
59	Stanley Baldwin	斯坦利·鲍德温	1935—1937	联合内阁
60	Neville Chamberlain	尼维尔·张伯伦	1937—1940	联合内阁
61	Winston Churchill	温斯顿·丘吉尔	1940—1945	联合内阁
62	Clement Attlee	克莱门特·艾德礼	1945—1951	工党
63	Sir Winston Churchill	温斯顿·丘吉尔爵士	1951—1955	保守党
64	Sir Anthony Eden	安东尼·艾登爵士	1955—1957	保守党
65	Harold Macmillan	哈罗德·麦克米伦	1957—1963	保守党
66	Sir Alec Douglas-Home	亚历克·道格拉斯—霍姆爵士	1963—1964	保守党
67	Harold Wilson	哈罗德·威尔逊	1964—1970	工党
68	Edward Heath	爱德华·希思	1970—1974	保守党
69	Harold Wilson	哈罗德·威尔逊	1974—1976	工党
70	James Callaghan	詹姆斯·卡拉汉	1976—1979	工党
71	Margaret Thatcher	玛格丽特·撒切尔	1979—1990	保守党
72	John Major	约翰·梅杰	1990—1997	保守党
73	Tony Blair	托尼·布莱尔	1997—2007	工党
74	Gordon Brown	戈登·布朗	2007—2009	工党
75	David Cameron	戴维·卡梅伦*	2009/5—	联合内阁

* 从 Robert Walpole 至 David Cameron，共有 53 位首相。从这份表中可以看出，有的首相如 Winston Churchill 担任过不连续的两任首相，还有的担任过三任甚至四任。

Ⅸ. 美英司法系统一览
U. S. & British Judicial Systems

1. Organization of the Federal Courts & Judicial System in U. S.
   美国联邦法院和司法系统

(1) Organization of the Federal Courts
   联邦法院系统

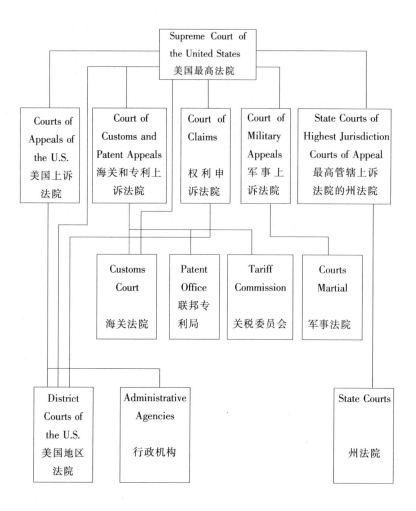

(2) **Federal Judicial System**
联邦司法系统

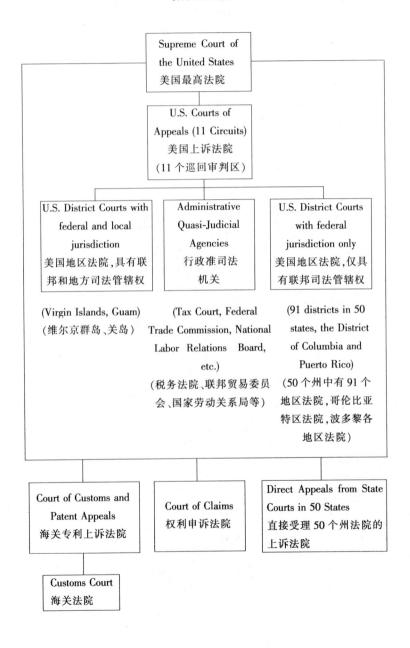

2. Organization of the Courts in Britain
英国法院组织系统

House of Lords
贵族院或上议院

Court of Appeal
上诉法院

- Criminal Division 刑事上诉庭
- Civil Division 民事上诉庭

The High Court of Justice
高等法院

- Queen's Bench Division (王座庭)
- Chancery Division (大法官庭)
- Family Division (家事庭)

Assizes 巡回法庭
- Crown Court at Liverpool and Manchester Assize Courts for South Lancaster 利物浦和曼彻斯特刑事法庭南兰开斯特巡回法庭
- Central Criminal Court at Old Bailey in the City of London 伦敦老贝来刑事法庭

Special Courts
专门法院

Quarter Sessions 四季法庭

County Courts 郡法院

- Central Criminal Court 中央刑事法院
- Restrictive Practices Court 限制开业法院
- National Industrial Relations Court 全国工业关系法院
- Coroners' Court 验尸法院
- Divorce Court 离婚法院

Administrative Courts
行政法院

Magistrate's Courts-Juvenile Courts 治安法院-少年法院

- National Insurance 国家保险
- Industrial Tribunals 工业法庭
- Rent Tribunals 租金裁定法庭
- Domestic Tribunals 内部事务法庭

Miscellaneous Courts
混合法院

Criminal Law 刑法

- The Mayor's and City of London Court 市长法庭和伦敦城法庭

Civil Law 民法

X. 美英军衔一览
U.S. & British Military Ranks

1. 美军

Army 陆军	Air Force 空军	Navy 海军	Marine Corps 海军陆战队	Chinese Translation 汉译
General of the Army	General of the Air Force	Fleet Admiral		五星上将
General	General	Admiral	General	上将
Lieutenant General	Lieutenant General	Vice Admiral	Lieutenant General	中将
Major General	Major General	Rear Admiral	Major General	少将
Brigadier General	Brigadier General	Commodore	Brigadier General	准将
Colonel	Colonel	Captain	Colonel	上校
Lieutenant Colonel	Lieutenant Colonel	Commander	Lieutenant Colonel	中校
Major	Major	Lieutenant Commander	Major	少校
Captain	Captain	Lieutenant	Captain	上尉
First Lieutenant	First Lieutenant	Lieutenant Junior Grade	First Lieutenant	中尉
Second Lieutenant	Second Lieutenant	Ensign	Second Lieutenant	少尉
Chief Warrant Officer	Chief Warrant Officer	Commissioned Warrant Officer	Commissioned Warrant Officer	一级准尉
Warrant Officer, Junior Grade	Warrant Officer, Junior Grade	Warrant Officer	Warrant Officer	二级准尉
Master Sergeant	Master Sergeant	Chief Petty Officer	Master Sergeant	军士长
Sergeant First Class	Technical Sergeant (技术军士)	Petty Officer First Class	Technical Sergeant (技术军士) Staff Sergeant (参谋军士)	上士
Sergeant	Staff Sergeant (参谋军士)	Petty Officer Second Class	Sergeant	中士
Corporal		Petty Officer Third Class	Corporal	下士
Private First Class	Airman First Class	Seaman First Class	Private First Class	一等兵

				续表
Private	Airman Second Class	Seaman Second Class	Private	二等兵
Basic Private	Airman Third Class	Apprentice Seaman		三等兵

2. 英军

Army 陆军	Air Force 空军	Navy 海军	Marine Corps 海军陆战队	Chinese Translation 汉译
Field Marshal	Marshal of the Royal Air Force	Admiral of the Fleet		元帅
General	Air Chief Marshal	Admiral	General	上将
Lieutenant General	Air Marshal	Vice Admiral	Lieutenant General	中将
Major General	Air Vice Marshal	Rear Admiral	Major General	少将
Brigadier	Air Commodore	Commodore	Brigadier	准将
Colonel	Group Captain	Captain	Colonel	上校
Lieutenant Colonel	Wing Commander	Commander	Lieutenant Colonel	中校
Major	Squadron Leader	Lieutenant Commander	Major	少校
Captain	Flight Lieutenant	Lieutenant	Captain	上尉
Lieutenant	Flying Officer	Sublieutenant (Senior Commissioned Branch Officer)	Lieutenant	中尉
Second Lieutenant	Pilot Officer	Acting Sublieutenant	Second Lieutenant	少尉
Warrant Officer (Class I)	Warrant Officer (Class I)	Warrant Officer (Class I)	Warrant Officer (Class I)	一级准尉
Warrant Officer (Class II)	Warrant Officer (Class II)	Warrant Officer (Class II)	Warrant Officer (Class II)	二级准尉
Staff Sergeant	Flight Sergeant	Chief Petty Officer	Colour Sergeant	上士
Sergeant	Sergeant	Petty Officer First Class	Sergeant	中士
Corporal	Corporal	Petty Officer Second Class	Corporal	下士
Lance Corporal	Senior Aircraftman	Leading Seaman	Marine First Class	一等兵
Private	Leading Aircraftman	Able Seaman	Marine Second Class	二等兵
Recruit	Aircraftman	Ordinary Seaman	Recruit	新兵

XI. 美国地图
A Map of U.S.

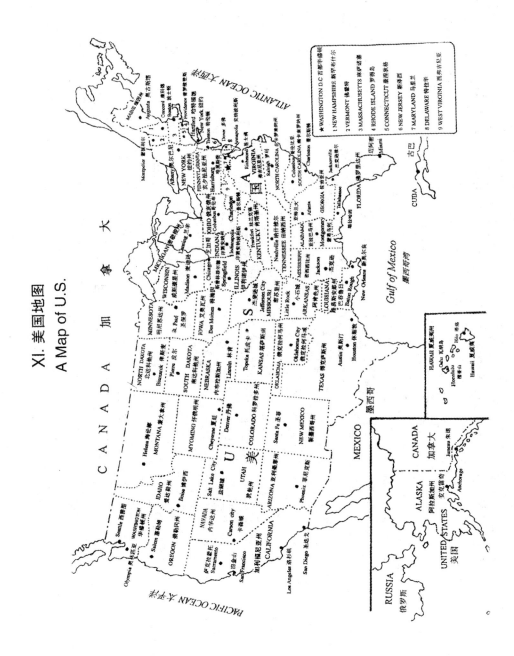

XII. 英国地图

A Map of Britain

MAP OF Britain 英国地图

参 考 书 目

Bibliography

Janice Abbott, *Meet the Press*, Cambridge University Press, 1981

Stephen K. Bailey, *American Politics and Government*, World Today Press, 1975

Rene J. Cappon, The *Word An Associated Press Guide to Good News Writing*, The Associated Press, 1982

Central Office of Information, *Britain* 1996, HMSO, 1995

Cultural Section of the Embassy of the United States, *An Outline of American Government*, 1982

Christopher Dobson & Ronald Paye, The *Dictionary of Espionage*, Grafton Books, 1986

Nils E. Enkvist, "Context" in Literature and New Interdisciplinery: Poetics, Linguistics, History. Roger D. Sell and Ptter Verdont, Amsterdam-Atlanta, 1994

Terry L. Fredrickson & Paul F. Wedel, *English by Newspaper*, Newbury House Publishers, Inc., 1984

International Communication Agency: *An Outline of American History*, World Today Press, 1979

Frank Luntz, *Work That Work*, Hyperion, New York, 2007

William A. McGeveran, Jr., Lori P. Wiesenfeld & Elizabeth J. Lazzara, The *World Almanac 2000/2002*, World Almanac Books, 2001

Iain Mclean and Alistair McMillan, *The Concise Oxford Dictionary of Politics*, Oxford University Press, 2003

Melvin Mencher, News Reporting & Writing, McGraw Hill Education（Asia）Co. & Tsinghua University Press, 2003

Adrian Room, *Dictionary of Britain*, Oxford University Press, 1986

William Safire, *Safire's Political Dictionary*, Oxford University Press, 2008

Jay M. Shafritz, American Government & Politics Harper Perennial, 1993

Alan Warner, *A Short Guide to English Style*, Oxford University Press, 1961

韩加明："试论语境的不同层次"，1997 年英国文学学会首届研讨会论文

卡罗尔·里奇：《新闻写作与报道训练教程》（第三版），中国人民大学出版社，2004

可非："美国：最有宗教情怀的世俗国家"，《世界知识》2006 年第 9 期

李赋宁：《英语学习经验谈》，北京大学出版社，1993

刘世生，朱瑞青：《文体学概论》，北京大学出版社，2006

李长栓：《非文学翻译理论与实践》，中国对外翻译出版公司，2004

刘宓庆:《文体与翻译》,中国对外翻译出版公司,1998
陆国强:《现代英语表达与理解》,上海译文出版社,1984
陆国强:《现代英语词汇学》,上海外语教育出版社,1983
马祖毅:《英译汉技巧浅谈》,江苏人民出版社,1979
潘维洛:《美英报刊的阅读与理解》,中国对外翻译出版公司,1984
钱歌川:《英文疑难详解续篇》,中外出版社,1974
王克勤等:《世界知识大辞典》,世界知识出版社,1988
王宗炎:《汉英语文研究纵横谈》,北京大学出版社,1997
谢荣镇:《新闻写作》,北京大学出版社,1987
新华社国际部资料编辑室:《各国国家机构手册》,中国对外翻译出版公司,1993
张健:《报刊英语研究》,上海外语教育出版社,2007
张今:《英汉翻译教程》,商务印书馆,1997
周学艺:《当代英汉美英报刊词典》,北京外语与教学出版社,2007
周学艺:《美英报刊导读》(第一版),北京大学出版社,2003

索 引

Index

a democracy　382
A Farewell to Arms　152
A fish rots from the head first　306
a general's never-die optimism　91
a socialist market economy　86
a super-national reserve currency　98
A Tale of Two Cities　152
a Uniter　75
a war to end all wars　306
A woman's place is in the home　287,306
A(HINI)　129
A/One Picture is worth a thousand word　158
ABB(anything but Bush)　57
ABC(anything but Clinton)　57
Abidjan　292
ABM　106
abortion　94,177,228,244
above politics　351
Abrams MIAI tank　366
abstentionist party　162
academics　219
accord　139
according to　181
accounting scandal　99
Achilles' heel　290
Act of Union　251
action　101
adjust the front　177
Administration　56,350,371
administrative assistant　119
adult fantasy service　177
advise and consent　309
adviser　150
affirmative action　76,212
affirmative action program　76
Africa Command(AFRICOM)　87
African American　150
African Union (AU)　302
African-American politics　227,229
ageism　99
agenda　36
aging　176
agreed departure　177
aid　86,170
aide-mémoire　86
air presence　48
Al　299
Al Qaeda　65
Albanianization　148
All politics is local　199, 274, 280, 305,306,375
All politics is personal　278,305
All politics isn't local　305,307

All the News That's Fit to Print　27
all thing to all men　155
Alliance for Progress　60
all-Democratic　199,235
all-democratic Congress　235
all-Republican　79,199,207
all-Republican Congress　79,207
alphabet agencies　59
alphabet soup　348
Alphonse-and-Gaston routine to end all Alphonse-and-Gaston routines　306
ambassadors of trade　268
ambience　365
ambulance chasers　78
amen corner　64,155
America Coming Together　196
American Civil War　184
American Dictator　219
American Enterprise Institute　300, 301
American Enterprise Institute for Public Policy Research　301
amiable dunce　64
amigo diplomacy　82
Amsterdam Treaty　303
analysts　181
and National Defense system　89
Anglican Church　238,239
Anglicanism　238
Anglo-American special relationship　271,272
angry young men　119
Animal Farm　112
ankle-biters　157
annotation　369,370
another Yalta　117
anticulture　345
antihero　345
antimachine Republican　119
antimissile defense system　90
anti-abortion　76,177
Anti-Ballistic Missile Treaty　89
anti-European　67
Anti-Federalist Party　218
anti-foreignism　30
anti-government　349
anti-government rebels　349
anti-Maastrichtian　67
anti-war movement　325
anything but beef　69
AP reports　181
Apache helicopter　366
apology　170
apology fatigue　86
appeal　103

apprehend　342
April 15　295
Arab Lobby　233
archbishop　238
Archbishop of Canterbury　239
Archbishops　239
Are you any better off　63
Are You better off than You Were Four Years Ago?　74
arena　155
Arlington　290
armed force　354
armed forces　354
ArmorGroup　374
Army-Mccarthy hearing　325
arrest warrant　101
arrest warrants　24
arrest without a warrant of flagrante delicto　101
arsenal of democracy　320
artificial satellite　105
as safe as Fort Knox　290
Asia-Pacific Economic Cooperation (Group) (APEC)　302
ask not what your country can do for you, ask what you can do for your country　60
ask what you can do for your concubine　307
asked not to be ID'd　161
Assembly　215,264,284
assembly line method　286
Assistant Floor Leader　200
Assistant Majority Leader　200
Assistant Majority/Minority Leader　276
assistant majority/minority leader　360
Assistant Minority Leader　200
Assistant Secretary (of State for East Asian and Pacific Affairs)　187
Assistant Whips　261,276
Associate Justice　213
Association of Southeast Asian Nations (ASEAN)　302
astronaut　105
asymmetric(al) warfare　90
at this/that point in time　62
atheist　237
attack dog　157
attack politics　376
attorney　101
Australia　291
Austria　291
authoritative sources　181
available　317
avalanche　352,376

ayatollah 118
B & Q 286
Babyboom 95
back alleys of the world 371
back channel 62
back to basics 69
Back to the Future 289
backbench revolution 67
backbencher 256
background 180
backgrounder 180
backlash 94,119
Bailey Memoradum 60
bailouts 96,99
Bakke case 77
bald eagle 155
bamboo curtain 67
Bapist Church 238
Baptism 238
barefoot boy from Wall Street 75
bargaining chip 62
barnacle 340
barrister 355
Barry Goldwater 285
battle 336
battleground states 170
Bay of Pigs 60
BBC 374
be selected out 177
Beat 95
beatnik 94
beatniks 106
beauty contest 57
Beijing 172,175
Beijing Consensus 85,86
Beltway bandit 64
benchmarks 66
benign neglect 154
best-looking candidate 230
between a rock and a hard place 118
between Scylla and Charybdis 118
between the devil and the deep blue sea 118
Beverly Hills 290
Bible belt 155
Bible reading at public school 240
bicameral 198,215
Big Bang 107
Big Brother 112
big daddyism 61
big enchilada 62
big government 58,65,217,348,349
big mo 58,332
big shot/wheel 119
big small company 154
bigger bang for a buck 60
Bill Gates 284
Billygate 63
bipartisan politics 281
biracial 195
bird dog 157
bishop 238
Bishops 239
bitten by the presidential bug 191
Black Africa 291,382
black capitalism 61
Black Friday 265
Black Hawk 366

black hole 103,105,178
Black Power 92
black propaganda 356
Blackwater 374
blame game 325
blame-America-first crowd 73
Blarism 289
bleeding heart 224
bleeding hearts 155
Bling 150
blitzkrieg 88
blocking back 156
Bloemfontein 292
blog 106
blogger 106
blogging 106
blogosphere 66
blooper 66
blue state 169,170
blue chip 156
blue dog Dems 155
blue helmet 175
blue helmets 175
Blue States 170
blue-chip team 156
board of commissioners 216
Board of Film Censors 248
Board of Governors 187
board of selectmen 217
boiler 223
Bolivia 292
boll weevils 119,155,338
Boll Weevils 162,338
bolt 72
bolter 119
bomb 106
Bonesmen 230,231
Bonies 230
boondoggle 59
Bootylicious 150
booze and broads 232
bork 211
born again 120,155
borough 216
Borough 290
Bosnia 145,173,294
Bosnia and Herzegovina 145
Bosnian 145
botax 106
bottom line 73
box 102
boycott 284
Bradley effect 230
brain cell 107
brain dead 107
brain trust 300
brainwashing 29
brand extension 99
BRIC 98
bridge to nowhere 66
Brief 20
brief 103
brinkmanship 60
British 155
British Commonwealth 269
British Commonwealth (of Nations) 251
British Council 121

British Empire 251,269,270
British Judiciary 262
British Secret Service 299
Bro 150
Broadly speaking, the short words are the best, and the old words best of all. 139
Broadway 174
Bronx 290
Brookings Institution 300,301
brothel 177
Brotherhood of Death 230
Brown Power 92
browse 106
browser 106
Brussels 172,175,369
brute creation 19
Bubba 284
bubba factor 65
bubba ticket 65
bubba vote 65
Buckingham Palace 174
budgetspeak 113
budget-sensitive 80
buffer 147
Building a Bridge to the Twenty-first Century 75
bully pulpit 155
bummer 93
Bundestag 284
bundling 65
bureaucratic empire 202
Burma 163,292
burn 342
bursting of the (high) tech bubble 100
Bush 178,289
Bush administration 146
BUSH-CHENEY 04 125
Bush Doctrine 66,82,84,289
Bush Fatigue 57
Bush fatigue 170,178
Bush junior 285
Bushisms 38,66,178
Bush's Doctrine of pre-emption 82
Bush terror 178
business cycle 365
business PACs 236
bust 93
button man 336
buy American 58
buy American 99
Buy American 126
Buy one, give one free 57
buzzword 85,168
buzz-word 373
By uniting we stand, by dividing we fall. 319
byline 16
by-election 202
cabinet 257
cabinet government 273
cabinet ministers 277
Cabinet Secretaries 256
California State Assembly 215
call 177
call-girl ring 177
Cambodia 292

索　引　411

Camelot　61
campaign manager　226
campaign message　65
campaign theme/message　74
campaign-finance scandal　70
campus race preferences　77
candidate　192
can't-do Congress　204
Cape Town　292
capital punishment　102
Capitol　215,232,370,382
capitol　215,382
Capitol Hill　174,367
captive　103
captives　178
CARA　247
cardinal　238
Caretaker Government　257
Caribbean Community and Common Market(CARICOM)　302
carpetbagger　229
case the joint　104
cash-for peerage affair　70
Catch-22　360
catch-all party　264
Catholic Church　238
Catholicism　238
Cato Institute　302
caucus　193,279,363
cavalry　366
censure　286
CENTCOM　366
Center for Responsible Politics　195
Central Command(CENTCOM)　87
CEPA (Closer Economic Partnership Arrangement　100
Cetinje　292
Ceylon　292
chad　107
chair　102
chairman　102,356
Chairman of the Standing Committee of appropriations/Armed Forces/Banking, Housing (Finance) and Urban Affair…200
chairperson　92
challenge　34,38,377
challenged　176
chamber　198
Chancellor　354
Chancellor of Exchequer　256
Chancellor of the Duchy of Lancaster　255
chaplain　239
character assassination　75
checks and balances　190, 210, 274, 375
check-out system　290
chemistry　107
Chief Directorate of Intelligence of the General Staff　299
chief Judge　211
chief justice　102
Chief Justice　211,213
chief procurator　101
Chief Secretary to the Treasury　256
Chief Whip　260
Chief Whip in the Commons　261
Chief Whip of the majority party　261

Chief whip of the minority party　261
Chimerica　58,85,99
China card　86
China Watch　368,369
China+India+ME(Middle East)+Africa　99
China-free　85
Chindia　99
Chinese development mode/model　86
Chinese intellectual community　40
Chinese model　86
Chinese/China model　86
Chiwan　100
choices　91
Christian Democratic Party　382
Christian Democratic Union　382
Christian science　5
Christianity　238
christmas-tree bill　274
chronic campaigner　192
Chronological Order Form　18
Chronology of Events　293
Chronology of Scientific Development　293
Chronology of World Events　293
Church　238
church elders　155
Church of English　239
Churchillian resistance　287
CIA　139,288,297－299,367
CIA camps　178
CIA Director　288
CIAese　72
CIA president　288
cigar-chewing veteran　227
circumlocation　56
circumlocution syndrome　178
Circus　299
city on a hill　63
City-Manager form/system　216
city-state　375
civil rights activist Al Sharpton　76
civil service reformers　119
Civil war　294
civilian casualties and deaths　80
civilian casualties/death　178
civilian death　78
claim　140
class action　101,103
Clause Four　70－72,264
clean sweep　352,376
Cleggeron　71
Cleopatra　290
clergyman　239
client　101
climate change　78
Clinton　84,289
Clinton Doctrine　65,84,289
Clinton Republican　57,147,225
clone　106
close the window　112
closed　193
closed primary　193
clout　37,73
club　177
Coalition Government　258
coalition government　71,281
cold　157
cold peace　91

Cold War　287
cold war　67,117,157,370,374
collateral damage　78,80,178,367
collective responsibility　257
color　118
color/flower revolution　84
columbianization　148
combantant command　87
combat　336
combat fatigue　88,116,336,382
combat fatigues　116,382
Come home with that "coonskin on the wall.　61
Come now, and let us reason together.　243
come-to-Jesus meeting　243
comfort factor　289
commercial business　348,349
commercial business/industry　347
commercial industry　348
commercial quarters　181
commercial sector　349
Commission form/system　215
Commission on Human Rights　302
commissioners　216
commissioning　176
commission-manger system　216
committee　275
Committee/Commission for/of State Security　299
committology　71
commodity economy　362
common good　57
common law　251
Commonwealth　269,270
Commonwealth of Nations　269
Commonwealth(of Nations)　251
community　39,382
community charge　40
community council　263
compartmentalization　355
compassion　86,170
Compassionate Conservatism　75
compassionate conservative　65
comperation　85
complainant　101
compromise　342
compromised　296
computernik　106
condemn　102
condone　132
Confederation　283
conference　72
confidential　354
congagement　84
Congo　291,292
Congo Republic　291,292
Congregationalism　238
Congregationalist Church　239
Congress　189,199,283
Congress of Industrial Organization　236
Congressional　278
Congressional Election　200
consciousness-raising　92
conservative　225,240
conservative Democrat,Demopublican　119
Conservative Party　265
conservatives　73,223

Constitution Party   223
constitutional crisis   75
constitutional monarchy   251
consultant   177
contain communism   294
Contract with America   79,360
contras   64
control mice   105,380
convention rebounce   164
conventional phrases   161
conventional wisdom   329
conventions   252
convergence thesis   71
conviction   102
cook the books   99
cooker   336
coonskin on the wall   88
corporate   73
corporate welfare   337
Corporation of the City of London   263
cosmic   93
couch potato   95
council   217,263
Council of Ministers   303
Council of the European Union   68, 303
council tax   68
council-manager system   216
counsel   101
count   102
countdown   107
counterclaim   101
counterculture   92,240,244
Counterintelligence Field Activity (CFA)   298
county   263,363
county board   216
county council   263
county legislators   216
coup   140
Court of Appeals   214
court reporter   337
covenanted relationship   177
cover story   33,51,52,367
cover-up   62
cowboy   114
Crawford cowboy   114,115
credit   105,106
CREEP   62
creeping socialism   58,59,96
crime against nature   177
Criminal Investigation Department   299
cross-over voters   193
Crown   172
crowdsourcing   100
CRR   62
crusade   155
CT   106
cult of the robe   104
cultural   328
cultural cleaning   329
cultural handicap   329
cultural presence   47
culture   324,328,330
culture of fear   329
culture of mind   330
curate   239
currency persuasion   178

customer-friendly   345
cut and run   66,148,169
cutthroat   173
cut-and-run Democrat   78
cut-and-run Democrats   66
Côte d'Ivoire   163,292
dampish persuasion   68
dark horse   155
dawk   370
dawks   88
Dayton   172
deacon   239
deal   140
Deans   239
death sentence   102
death squad   366
death tax   77,79,217
decapitation strike   366
Declaration of Independence   184
declined to be named   161
decommissioning   346
decommissioning of arms   346
deep background   180,181
Deep Throat   62,117
deep-six   62
Defeatocrat   78
defence procurement   186
defendant   101
defendant's agent   101
defender of the Faith   239
defense   101
defense in lawsuit   101
defense industry   349
Defense Intelligence Agency (DIA)   297
Defense Intelligence Staff (DIS)   299
defense lawyer   101
defense manufacturing   348
defense work   348
defining event/achievement/hour   111
defining moment   109—111,375
definition   369,370
defuse   107
delayed lead   18
democracy   382
democracy deficit   71
Democratic Party   217
Democratic Republican Party   218
Democrat-turned-Republican mayor   280
Demopublican   223,225,239,361,375
denominations   238
Department   382
Department of Defense   186
Department of Homeland Security   298
Department of the Army   186
Department of War   186
dependency   269
dependent culture   329
depleted uranium shell   106
Depression   59
depressionista   99
Deputy Assistant Secretary   187
Deputy Assistant Secretary for Acquisition Management   186
Deputy Chief Whip   261,276
Deputy Secretary   186
Deputy Secretary of State   187

Deputy Speaker   260,276
Deputy whip   276
derecruit   177
desert cat   88
desert cherry   88
Desert Saber   88
Desert Shield   88
Desert Storm   88
Desert Sweep   88
designated heir   243
detainee   102,103
DGSE (Direction Generale de la Securite Exterieure)   299
did not   161
Diet   284
dimension   41
dinosaur wing   73
diplomatic presence   50
diplomatic sources   181
direct lead   18
Dirty Harry   309
dirty tricks   313
disinformation   356
dismiss   177
Disney World   290
display ad   125
Diss   150
dissolve Parliament   279
district attorney   101,103
district council   263
divided government   198,199,206
DNA   106
Doctrine   63,65,84,289,361,375
dogcatcher   216
dollar diplomacy   82
domino theory   60
Donkey   154,174,221
Don't swap horses in the middle of the stream   307
don't-work Congress   204,258
Doro   98
dotcom   107
dotcom crash   100,107
double agent   342
double track   360
doublespeak   114
doubletalk   114
dove   68,155,225,370
doves   88
down   93
Downing Street   174
downsize   177
Dow-Jones & Company, Inc.   5
do-gooders   224
do-nothing Congress   60,206
draft   317
drive   106
drug   330
drug culture   93
dry   68,157
dry peace   91
Dubya   284,285
D'Amato Act   285
détente   62
E Pluribus Unum   183
E.D./erectile dysfunction   119
earmarks   96
ease out   177

East 291
East end 290
Eastern Orthodox 238
Eastphalian 98
eastward enlargement 304
eastward enlargement/extension 91
eat crow 155
eat one's children 371
eat/live on high hog 157
eat-in 92
eavesdropping 79
eavesdropping affair 79
ecclesiastic 239
ECFA (Economic Cooperation Framework Agreement 100
economic convergence 71
Eduskunta 284
effete snobs 339
Eisenhower Doctrine 60,84,289
elected board 217
election 278
election dictatorship 260
elector 354
Electoral College 193,354
electors 194
electricity 107
electronic intercepts 79
elephant 154
Elephant 174,221
elite army 366
Elysée Palace 175
Emancipation Proclamation 184
embedded reporters 29
embedded reporter 366
emerging economies 98
Emirates 283
Emperor Club 177
ends of Pennsyl-vania Street 174
enemies list 62
engage in personalities 60
enough and in time 319
Enron 99
enron 100
enronesque 100
enronish 100
enronism 100
enronista 100
enronite 100
enronitis 100
enronlike 100
enterprise culture 34,329
entitlement 116
entitlements 116
environmental correctness 94
environment-conscious/friendly 80
environment-friendly 345
equal opportunity 77
equal opportunity in education 76,79
escalate 91
escalation 169
escort 177
escort service 177
Established Church 239
established company 99
establishment 43
Establishment 43
estate manager 119
estate tax 77,217

ethic 371
ethnic 371
ethnic cleansing 65,178
EU 138,369
Eullar 98
euphemism 72,80,176
euro 69
eurocrat 68
Eurodoubt 67
Eurofanatic 68
European Command(EUCOM) 87
European Commission 71,303
European Community 39,67
European Council 303
European Court of Auditors 303
European Court of Justice 303
European Parliament 68,303
European Treaty institutions 303
European Union (EU) 303
Europhile 68
Europhobe 68
Europhobia 68
Europhoria 68
Euroskeptic 67
Evan 175
Evangelicalism 240
evangelicals 219,240
Everyman a King, but No Man Wears a Crown 308
Everything but arms 100
exdis (exclusive distribution) 355
executive 216,255,278
executive agreements 205,208
executive privilege 190
expanded simple sentence 148
expat 121
expensegate 71
extortion charges 229
eyeball to eyeball 86,158
eyes only 355
E-bomb 106
Facebook 106
fair advantage 77
Fair Deal 59,96,157,206
faith-based 66,76
Falklands factor 69
Falklands venture 69,277
family 229
family machine 227
family man 246,361,375
family political machine 230
family values 244,246,247
Fannie Mae 96
far out 93
farm belt 365
Fashion-Aid 345
fast track 78
fast track trade authority 78,79
fat cat 155
father 238
fatigue 86,170,178
fatigues 336
fault lines 107
FBI 298,299
FBI 297
feature 20
Federal Assembly 284
federal judge 102

Federal machine 348
federal presence 50
federal prosecutor 101
Federal Republic 273
Federal Reserve Note 131
Federal Security Service 299
Federal Service of Security(FSS) 299
Federalist Party 218
feeding frenzy 99
feeling one's age 177
feminazi 92
feminism 92
feminist 92
fengshui 161
fetus 76
fever 191
fi 139
Fifth (Amendment) 101
fifth estate 301
figurehead 254
final solution 178
financial crisis/meltdown/storm/tsunami 96
financial presence 48
financial quarters 181
financial resources 331
Finlandization 117
fire 177
fire in the belly 191
fireside chat 59
firestorm 62,107
First Lord 256
First Lord of the Admiralty 256
first lord of the admiralty 257
First Lord of the Treasury 256
first reading 204
First Sea Lord 256
first-past-the-post electoral system 259
first-past-the-post system 266
flagship 154
flash memory 106
flasher 106
flay 141
Fleet Street 8,174
flexible response strategy 89
flight attendant 119
flip-flopper 195
floo-floo bird 73,155,224
Flower Power 92
flower revolution 118
fluid South '117
fly ineffective sorties 88
Foggy Bottom 173
foil 141
Folketing 284
follknik 106
food pyramid 133
for health reasons 86
for the reason of health 86
forced busing 242
Ford 286
Ford Motor Company 286
foreclosure 96
Foreign and Commonwealth Office 255
foreign community 40
Foreign Minister 382

Foreign Office 255
foreign secretary 335
Foreign Secretary 256,382
foreman 347
foremen 348
forgive and forget 309
form 86
Former Yugoslavia Republic of Macedonia 350
formula 360
Fort Knox 290
four freedoms 59
Fourth Infantry Division 366
Fourth Lord 256
four-line whip 262
foxhole 88
Fo'shizzle 150
Franklin Deficit 219
Freddie Mac 96
free market health care 77
freedom agenda 65
freeholders 216
Free-Soil Party 218
French Empire 294
friendly fire 366
fulcrum 107
full-court press 155
functional responsibilities 87
fundamentalism 226
fundamentalist 76,247
fundamentalists 240,241
future unpleasantness 178
G category 247,248
G.I. 95
G.N.P. 382
G2 99
G2(Group of Two) 85
G20 98,99
G8 99
Gallant Leader 219
game plan 61,155
Gang of Four 157
garbage removal 118
gategate 163
gatenik 163
Gaul 293
gay 94
gay community 40
gay marriage 118,150
gay partner/companion 177
Gay Power 92
GCHQ (Government Communications Headquarters) 298
GDP 96
geek 106
gems 139
General Assembly 215
General Court 215
general doctor 337
general election 260
general elections 192,278
Generals never die 313
Generation Jones 95
Generation O(bama) 95
Generation X 94
Generation XXL 95
genetic code 106
Geneva Convention on the Treatment of

Prisoners of War 103
genocide 178
geopolitical powers 98
George McGovern 285
Georgia 291
Georgia Mafia 156,157
Georgian conflict 145
gerrymander 155
get going 321
get the walking ticket/papers 177
getting on in years 177
Ghetto 150
ghost 72
ghostwriter 72
Gideon(英雄) of Democracy 219
gig 93
Gingrich Congress 286
Gingrich contract 286
Gingrich revolution 79,286
Gipper 63,289
girl 177
girlcott 92
give them hell 206
given 116
give'em hell, Harry 59
Global Strategies 374
global warming 78
globalization3.0 152
go fishing 72
go negative 376
go to Korea 75
go to the country 279
go to the well 99
goals and timetables 76
goal-line 156
goal-line stand 156
gobbledegook 72
God bless America 239
God bless you 239
gold 105,106
gold collar 99
gold window 112
golden handcuffs/cuffs 99
golden handshake 99
golden hello 99
golden parachute 99
Goldilocks and the Three Bears 100
Goldilocks economy 58,100,365
Goldman Sachs 365
Goldwaterize 285
Good Friday Agreement 336
good neighbor policy 59
good ole boy 227
goof on 93
Google 106,108
GOP 228,295
Got game 150
Gourmet 128
govern at the margins 347
governator 147,194
government 56,255,257,258,350,371
Government Chief Whip 261
Government is best which governs least 97
government of the people, by the people, for the people 309
government party 281

Government Whip 262
Government Whips 261
Governor 214
go-to 117
Gramm-Rudman-Hollings Act 350
grand 101
Grand Assembly 283
Grand Duchy 283
graphite 106
Great Communicator 63,288
Great Depression 59,75,219,221,318,348
Great Society 61
Greater Middle East Initiative 381
green berets 174
Green Party of the United State 222
Green Party USA 222
green power 92
greenmail 99
groove on 93
gross political product 195
ground zero 107
Group of Eight (G8) 303
Group of Twenty(G20) 303
Group of Two(G2) 58
GRU 299
guidelines 79
guillotine 284
Gulag 175
gunboat diplomacy 82
gunship 335
gunships 24
guru 22,74,150,170,373,377
gut 141
gutter flyer 119
gypsy moth 155
Gypsy Moths 162
gypsy moths 338
Gypsy moths 338
hack it 61
Haigspeak 113
Halliburton 374
hanger-on 119,340
hard power 85
hardball 62,155
hardware 107
Harlem 290
hat in the ring 155
haul 141
hawk 155,225,367,370
hawks 88
He is not even qualified to be elected a dogcatcher. 217
He is the only man able to walk under a bed without hitting his head 75
head hunters 99
hearing 103
hearing officer 103
Hearsay is no evidence 104
hearts and minds 88
heavy 93
heavy defeat 177
hecker 106
hegemonism 362
hegemony 362
Helicopter Ben 96
helicopter gunship 336
Hella 150

索　引　　　　　　　　　　　　　　　　　　415

Helms-Burton Act　285
Helms-Hyde Bill　285
hemorrhage　107
henchman　119
Heritage Foundation　300,301
heroic failure　154
high commissioner　269
high road　376
high/highest court　104
Hill　371,382
Hillary Factor　287
Hillarycare　65
hippie language　93
hippies　92－94
Hispanic　370
hit the road　152
holier hands　243
holier than thou　104,155
Holla　150
Hollywood　174
holy warrior　66
Homer　290
homo sexuality　177
honeymoon period　257
Hoover Institution　302
Hoover Institution on War, Revolution, and Peace　302
hope and pray, borrow and borrow and spend and spend for more weapons　220
hope and pray, borrow and borrow and spend and spend　350
Horn of Africa　175
hospitalities　116
hospitality　116
hostilities　116
hostility　116
hot　157
hot peace　91
hot pursuit　90
hot war　91,157,370
House　200
house arrest　102
House of Commons　259
house of ill repute　177
House of Lords　205,259
House of Representatives　198
House of Windsor　382
House Speaker　189,199
hidden agenda　36
human embryos　106
human genome　106
Human Rights Council　302
Human Right's Committee　302
humanitarian crisis/relief　84
humanitarian intervention　84
humanitarianism　84
human-rights abuse　84
human-rights policy　84
Hungary　172
hypotaxis　305
Hytrel　128
I know the price of every man in this House　308
I Like Ike　75,79
I shall go to Korea　60,75
I will not accept if nominated and will not serve if elected　317
ICBM　111

ICE(involuntry career event)　177
ideological PACs　236
If nominated, I will not run. If elected, I will not serve.　318
If working hard, even a cowboy can be president　196
If you can't convince them, confuse them.　81
illegal immigrants　26
illegal prisons　103
IMF　139
impeach　62
impeachment　189
imperial presidency　190
imperial president/presidency　189
imperial uniform　189
importance　16
In God We Trust　101,239
In politics a man must learn to rise above principle.　209
In teaching newspapers, teachers learn more than students do　367
in the spotlight　342
INA (involuntary normal attrition)　177
incorrect　94
incursion　177
independent　217
Independent　222
independent candidate　280
independent counsel　103,178
independent special prosecutor　103
indictment　101
indigenous community　40
indirect lead　18
industrial quarters　181
industrial relation　376
industrial relations　337
ineffective sorties　88
informant　355
informative sources　181
informer　355
inheritance tax　77
initial public offer　116
ink　141
inoperative statement　62
Inside　2,357
inside the Beltway　64
inside the Beltway stuff　64
inside the Beltwayer　64
inside-the-Beltway politics　63
Institution for Intelligence and Special Duties　299
institutions　204
insurgent　66,103
Insurgent　136
insurgents　178
integration　68
intelligence community　43
intelligence design　76
Intelligence establishment　43
intelligence officer　342
Intelligence Service　298,299
intelligencegate　70
intelligent design　134,240
interceptor missiles　90
interest　16,45,370,382
interests　34,336

international community　31,40
International Criminal Court　84
International Criminal Police Organization (ICPO—Interpol)　303
International Institute for Strategic Studies　302
Internet　106,362
internment　102
Interpretative Reporting Form　18
into　93
invasion　177
Inverted Pyramid Form　18
invisible government　297
invisible hand　96
in-depth interrogation　178
IRA　70,296
Iran-Contra affair/scandal　63
Iraqification　148
iron curtain　67,287
Iron Lady　68
ironically　46,164,362
Islam　239
Islamic Establishment　44
Israel Lobby　233
It affords no small surprise to find that...　179
It can be safely said that...　179
It cannot be denied that...　179
It has been calculated that...　179
It has been illustrated that...　179
It has recently been brought home to us that...　179
It is alleged that...　179
It is arranged that...　179
It is asserted that...　179
It is claimed that...　179
It is demonstrated that...　179
It is enumerated that...　179
It is established that...　179
It is generally agreed that...　179
It is generally recognized that...　179
It is hypothesized that...　179
It is incontestable that...　179
It is learned that...　179
It is mentioned that...　180
It is noted that...　180
It is noticed that...　180
It is outlined that...　180
It is preferred that...　180
It is quite contrary to our expectation.　180
It is reputed that...　180
It is striking to note that...　180
It is taken that...　180
It is undeniable that...　180
It is universally accepted that...　180
It is usually considered that...　180
It is weighed that...　180
It may be argued that...　180
It was described that...　180
It was first intended that...　180
It was noted above that...　180
itch to run (for the White House/presidency)　191
itching　191
It's the Economy, Stupid　58,79,109, 136,171,306,346,371
It's the economy,Stupid,exit poll　365

Ivory Coast 292
I'm a family man 244,361
J Street 174
J. P. Morgan 286
Jai Ho! 151
jail 353
jaw-breaking euphemism 81
Jerusalem 293
Jesse 285
Jewish 239
jihardist 66
jittery 370
Joe makes no joke 59
John 174
John Bull 354
Johnson Treatment 61
Joint Forces Command (JFCOM) 87
Joint Intelligence Committee 299
Jonesing 150
Joseph McCarthy 285
Judaism 239
Judeo-Christian 237
judge 102
judges 216
Judicial Panel on Multi-district 214
judicial restraint 211
jujitsu politics 156
Julius Caesar 293
junior Bush 285
junior citizen 176
junior ministers 256
juror 101
jurors 216
jury 102
jury box 101
jury deliberation 102
justice 102
justices 104
K Street 174,233
Kampuchea 292
Katrina 90,117
KBR 374
Kennel dog 157
Keynesian 219
KGB(Komitet Gosudarstvennoi Bezopastnosti) 139,299,367
KGB President 288
Kidnapping,Stabbing,Raping 125
kinder and gentler nation 64
King Arthur and his Camelot 290
Kingdom 283
King's Secretary of State 255
Kiss Me, Stupid 312
kiss-of-death 243
kitchen cabinet 275,278
Knesset 284
knowingly 359
knowledgable worker 337
knowledge management 337
knowledge of culture 333
knowledge of the language 333
knowledge worker 337
Korea 292
Kornet antitank missile 366
Kosovo War 65,70,90
Kremlin 173,175
Kremlinology 173

Kurd-Aid 345
La Paz 292
labor PACs 236
Labor-friendly 345
Labour 264,265
Labour Party 264
lace curtain 67
lady of pleasure the night/evening 177
laissez-faire 97
lame duck 155
laminated 370
land wad 89
landslide 147,352
landslide win 376
Langley 174,297
Las Vegas 290
lasséz-faire 309
last hurrah 191
last resort 87
Latino 370
launch 141
launch window 105,106,111,382
Law Chancellor 354
law lord 354
Law Lords 354
lawsuit 101
lawsuit abuse reform 78
lay off 177
lazy Susan 337
lead story 51
leader 356
Leaders 260
League of Arab States (Arab League) 303
League of Nations 304
lean federation 154
learning experience 163
left wing 282
leftist 282
legislative 278
legislative agenda 37
Legislative Assembly 215
legislative election 259
legislature 215
Legislature 215
Les Bleus 363
lesser of two evils 228
Let's win this one for the Gipper 289
level playing field 64
leverage 332
Lib Dems 266
liberal 225,227,280
Liberal Democrat Party 266
Liberal Democrats 266
liberal Eastern Establishment 44
liberals 73,223
Liberia 291
Libertarian Party 223
Liberty Is the True Mother of Invention 152
Liberty Party 218
Libya 260
Lieutenant Governor 214
lie-in 92
life imprisonment 102
lightening rod 107
like Fort Knox 290
limdis (limited distribution) 355

Lindley Rule 181
line 141
line in the sand 64
Line Item Veto Act 203,204
Lion 155,175
liquidity 116
Litigation 214
lobby 231
lobby group 231,235
lobby groups 233
lobby scandal 71
lobby(ing) firms 233
lobbying 232
lobbyist 204
lobbyists 232,233
local councils 265
local election 295
Local Governmnent 262
local justice 102
lodge/file/submit a complaint 103
logistical 336
logistics 117,336
logrolling 280
London 173,175
London boroughs 263
loom 141
Lord Chancellor 259
Lord Chief Justice 255
Lord Commissioner 354
Lord (High) Chancellor 260
Lords Commissioners 354
Lords Commissioners of the Treasury 261
Lost 95
Loved for the enemies he made. 319
low road 376
Lower Court 213
Lower House 259
lower house/chamber 198,214
Loya Jirga 283
lunar module 105
Lunar rover 105
Lutheran Church 238
Lutheranism 238
M 247
Maastricht 117
Maastricht Treaty 69
Mac Daddy 150
machine 229,348
Madison Avenue 174
Madonna 351
mad-cow disease 69,265
Mafia 157
mafia family 104
magistrate 102
maglev train 106
Magnolia Mafia 63
major international organizations 302
Major Literary Events of the English-Speaking Nations 293
majority 259
Majority 260
Majority Leader 200,276
majority party 199
Majority Whip 200
make a comeback 143,152
male chauvinist 92
Malmab 299

man 140
man on the wedding cake 75
manage down 177
manager 216
man-of-war 336
March on Washington 325
market economy 362
marriage penalty 77
marriage tax 77
Marshall Plan 60
mass murder 178
massive retaliation 60,89
Mass-State 283
Mauritania 291
Mauritius 291
maximize 91
Mayor 217
mayor 217
Mayor-Council form system 215
McCain-Fingold campaign-reform law 196
McCarthyism 285,325
McGovern 285
Media Fund 196
Mediaid System 63
Medicare 65
memo 137
memo(randum) 86
mentally 176
mentor 22,150,170,373,377
Men's Lib 92
merchant of death 99
merchants of debt 99
message of the President 210
metaphor 154,173
Methodism 238
Methodist Church 238
metonymy 172
metropolitan district council 263
MI5 299
MI5 (Military Intelligence, Section Five) 298
MI6 296,299
MI6 (Military Intelligence, Section 6) 298
Micawber 284
micromanage 367
Middle American 62
Middle French 344
midterm (election) 201
military 336
military presence 34,48
military quagmire 78
military sources 181
military-industrial complex 348
Millennial Generation 95
miniministers 256
ministers in the Cabinet 256
ministers of Cabinet rank 256
ministers of state 256
Ministry 382
Minority 260
Minority Leader 200,276
minority party 199
Minority Whip 200
Minority whip 276
minster 239
Minuteman 111
Miranda rights 101

Miranda rule 101
Miranda warning 101
MIRV 106
misdemeanor/felony 102
misinformation 356
missile silo 159
mission accomplished 66
Missionary 95
MIT 139
moderate 225,240
moderate/middle/more/most conservative 247
Modern English 344
Mogadishu 351
mole 342
Monaco 291
monarches of the wilds 19
monetarist financial policies 265
Money counts 58
money men 374
Monicagate 65
Monroe Doctrine 83
Montenegro 292
moonfall 105
moonman 105
moonwalk 105
Moore's Law 106
moral equivalent of war 63
Moral Majority 241,242
morally 94
Morgan Stanley 286
morning in America 63
morning-after pill 106
Morocco 291
Moscow 175
Mossad 296,299
mossback 120
Motion Picture Ratings System 247
Motion Pictures Association of America 247
mount a goal-line stand 156
MOVABLE TYPE 133
Move On Org. (Voter Fund) 196
move the goalposts 64
MP(member of Parliament) 259
MRI 106
mudslinging 75,376
multinational 116,147
multipolarity 362
multipolarization 362
municipality 216
muscle 157
must-win states 194
My daddy told me that if I didn't want to get shot at, I should stay off the firing line. This is politics. 310
Myanmar 163,292
Myspace 106
nab 141,342
nadir 83
nagative campaign(ing) 376
nanny state 266
nanoparticle 106
nanoshell 106
nanosphere 107
Nanospheres 106
nano(technology) 106
National Assembly 283

National Assembly for Wales 263
National Cemetery 291
national convention 193
National Council 284
National Counterterrorism Center (NCC) 298
national diplomacy 83
national emblem 354
National Geospatial-Intelligence Agency (NGIA) 297
National Intelligence Council (NIC) 298
National Intelligence Director 297
National Reconnaissance Organization/Office(NRO) 298
National Security Agency 297
National Security Council (NSC) 298
National Security Strategy 87
national symbol 354
National People's Congress 284
Nations of the world 294
nation's credit window 99
nation's gold window 99,112
NATO 91,139,369
Natural Law Party 222
Naypyidaw 293
NBA 368
NC-17 category 248
Neanderthal wing 73
nearshoring 100
Necessity is the mother of invention 152
need-to-know 355
negative 376
negative campaign 327
negative campaigning 75,327
negative politics 327
neocon 65,225
neocons 190
neoconservatism 84,225
neoconservative 225
neoliberalism 86
net 141
netpreneur 107
netroots 66,107
neutral nation 355
neutral sources 181
neutralist nation 355
neutron star 105
new collar 99
New Covenant 64
New Deal 58-60,65,157,219,220, 314,347,348
new face 57
New Federalism 61
New Frontier 60
New Labour 70,72,264
new look 60,89
new McCarthyism 94
New New Deal 58,157
new world order 64
News Summary 357
newspeak 72,113
Niger 291
Nigeria 291
night-vision goggles 106
nikgate 163

nine old men　211
Nineteen Eighty-four　112
Nixon　84,289,361
Nixon Doctrine　84,289
no 3rd term　219
no context, no understanding　346
No matter whether th' Constitution follow th' flag or not, the Supreme Court follows the election returns.　213
No news is good news　16
No such Agency　297
Noah's Ark　290
nobody drowned at Watergate　62
nobody shoots at Santa Claus　155
nodis (no distribution)　355
nomination stage　193
nonaligned country　355
nonmarital cohabitation　177
nonpartisan　351
NonPC Word　93
nonperson　337,353
non-cabinet members　278
non-cabinet ministers　277
non-paper　86
non-unitary authorities　263
Norman Conquest　344
North Atlantic Treaty Organization (NATO)　304
Northern Command (NORTHCOM)　87
Northern Ireland Assembly　263
North Korea　292
Not a Divider　75
not for attribution　181
not to be ID'd　181
notable personalities　284
nothing to fear but fear itself　59,318
November　173,294,295,375
no-fly zone　362
NSA　297
nuanced approach　73
nudity　116
nutritionally correct　94
Obamabot　57
Obamacan　56,57,225
Obamacize　58
Obamacon　56,58
Obamacons　147
Obamafy　58
Obamania　58
Obamanomics　58
Obamatum　58
Obama-Biden ticket　193
Obamican　58
observers　181
obstruction of justice　102,376
October　294,295
October Surprise　63
October surprise　295
off　93
off the record　181
office　141
Office　382
Office seeks the man　56
official　339
official diplomacy　82
official sources　181

officialese　72
official's time-out　339
offshore outsoucing　100
offshoring　100
(offshore)outsourcing　171
offstage　342
off-message　65
off-off year　201
off-year　201
off-year election　201
Oh, you're a lefty.　154
Old English　344
Old Guard　224
Old Labour　70
Old soldiers never die　91
old time religion　99
on lobby terms　181
on the record　181
On the Tuesday following the first Monday of November　295
One and a half war　90
one hundred first Air Assault Division　366
one man/person, one vote, one value　260
one-chamber　214
one-line whip　262
one-o-one　135
one-self action　103
one-term President　62
online presence　50
only a heartbeat away　189
on-line Obama　379
on-message　65
OPEC　139
open　193
open covenants　64
open primary　193
open the window　112
Operation Desert Storm　366
OPERATION LOST CAUSE　131
operative　342
operative statement　62
opportunist　119
opportunity scholarship　76
Opposition Assistant Whips　261
Opposition Chief Whip　261
Opposition Chief Whips　261
opposition party　281
Opposition Whip　262
Oprahbate　286
Oprahfication　287
opt　141
options　91
opt-out　69
Op-Ed　25,146
ordeal　141
Order of Skull and Bones　230
ordinary mortals　104
organic　93
organization　336
Organization for Security and Cooperation in Europe (OSCE)　304
Organization of African Unity (OAU)　304
Organization of American States (OAS)　304
Organization of Petroleum Exporting

Countries (OPEC)　304
organized crime　104
Orthodox　238
Orwellian　112—114
other fellow blinked　158
Other Local Governments　216
out of the loop　64
out of shadow into spotlight　342
out of the closet　342
outasight　93
outplace　177
outsider　63
outsourcing　100
Oval Office　174
overblown　96
overstatement　82,177
PAC　195,235,236
Pacific Command(PACOM)　87
pacification　178
pact　141
Page three girl　11
palm　191
panda hugger　85
pandahugger　151,155
Pandora's box　152
Pantagonese　72
Papal States　283
paper curtain　67
paper tiger　155
parataxis　305
parent choice　76
(Party) Whip　262
parish　216,263,363
Parliament　258,264,283,284
parliamentarianism　258
parliamentary constituency　260
parliamentary democracy　273
parliamentary election　259,278
parliamentary government　258
Parliamentary private secretary　256
Parliamentary question　258
parliamentary secretaries　256
Parliamentary Secretary　256
Parliamentary Secretary to the Treasury　261
parliamentary system of government　273
parliamentary system (of government)　258
Parliamentary Undersecretary　256
partially sighted　176
partisan newspaperman　119
partisanspeak　73,81
party government　254
party in/out of the white House　281
Party Leaders　260
party line　370
party machine　259,348
party national convention　279
party of big business　218
Party of Depression　221
party of God　241
party of privilege and private monpoly　218
party of the people　218
party of the poor/havenots　218
party of the rich/haves　218
Party of War　221
party wall　370

索　引

Party Whip　200
partyspeak　81
party-line Democrat　230
pass the buck　316
past one's prime　177
pastor　239
Patriot missile　382
patriotically　94
patronage Secretary　261
Paula Jones affidavit　103
Paula Jones disease　103
Pax America　98
Pax Dollarium　98
PC　94
PC language　94
PC Word　93
peace　157
peacenik　106
peaceniks　94
peanut　63
peanut politician　63
peanut politics　63
peanut President　62
Pentagon　172,174,367
Pentagon Papers　2
Pentagonese　91
people convicted　353
people with mental retardation/disabilities　176
people-to-people diplomacy　83
perennial　192
perestroika　161
perjury　102
Permanent Secretary　256
Permanent Under Secretary　256
permissive era　245
perpetual　192
personal　375
personal accounts　77
personal diplomacy　83
personal injury lawyer　78
personalization　77
personalize health care　79
personalize Social Security　77
Personals　128
pet dog　271
petty jury　101
Pew Research Center　302
PG category　248
PG-13 category　248
phased withdrawal　177
Phat　150
Philadelphia lawyer　102
Philippic　120
phony votes　119
phrasemaker　72
Physical culture　330
physical persuasion　103,178
physically　176
physically challenged　39
physically inconvenienced　176
pig　93
PIGS　98
PIIGS　98
pit　141
plain English campaign　178
plaintiff　101
planned economy　362

plant　342
plantation　330
plausible deniability　64
play politics　328
Player/playa　150
plea bargain/bargaining　102
plea bargaining agreement　102
PLO　138
plum　119
plural vote　260
plurality　193,259
pocket veto　204
podcast　106
Podgorica　292
poised　141
police action　178
police agent　356
Police Launch Anti-crime Drive　141
police officer　356
policy agenda　36
policy bank　337
policy of appeasement　67
political　229
political accountability　268
Political Action Committee　204,235,326
political ad　124
political advance man　326
political base　71
political campaign　324,328
political contribution/donations　326
political correctness　93
political dead end　189
political donation　376
political fault-line　107
political football　155
political manager　326
political participation　205
political zoo　154
politically correct　93
politician　376
politics　324,327,376
Politics is like football If you see daylight, go through the hole.　324
Politics is the truth of somersault　324
politics of fear　124
poll　141
poll tax　265
Pope　238
popular culture　329
popular election　193
popular vote　193
pork barrel　280,315
pork-barrel legislations　307
position paper　86
positive　376
positive campaign(ing)　376
post-family customers　177
Post-Soviet　172
post-Watergate　190
Potomac　191
Potsdam Conference　294
pour oil on trouble waters　337
POW　78,103,213
Powell　84
Powell Doctrine/principle　90
power corridor　231
Power tends to corrupt; absolute power

corrupts absolutely　187
POWs　178
powwow　157
prance-in　92
prayer　244
predator　125
preemptive action　178
preemptive strike　66,87
preference poll　356
Premier　354
Presbyterian Church　239
Presbyterianism　238
presence　34,47,116,377
President　276
President of the Senate　199
President Pro Tempore　276
President Pro Tempore (of the Senate)　199
President Pro Tempore of the Senate　189
President/Chairman of the Senate　351
presidential　191,194
presidential (form of) government　189
presidential election　192,278
presidential elector　354
presidential electors　193,363
presidential primary　193
presidential system　189
Presidential system/government　274
presidential timber　56,192,196,278
President's cabinet　274
presiding judge　102
press book　337
press the flesh　61
pressure groups　231
Pretoria　292
prevatize Social Security　77
preventive strike/war　178
pre-owned car　119
Pride and Prejudice　152,367
primary　279,363
primary (election)　193
Prime Minister　354,382
Prince of Wales　268
Principality　283
prison　353
private accounts　77
private agenda　36
private health care　77
private sector　374
privatization　77
privatize Social Security　81
Progress for America (Voter Fund)　196
Progressive Party　217
progressives　73
prominence　16
proportional representation　193
proportional represention　260
protective reaction　178
Protestanism　238
Protestant　238,382
Protestant Establishment　45
Protestant Church　238
Protestanten　238
Protestantism　238
proximity　16
prozac　106
pro-china/chinese　85

pro-choice   73,76,177,228
Pro-European   68
pro-life   73,76,79,177
public prosecutor   101
pulsar   105
pundit   170
pure hard news   20
purple state   169
purple America   170
purple states   170
purse strings   208
put down   93
put on   93
put one's cards on the table   157
put one's money where one's mouth is   33
put one's wallet where one's mouth is   384
Quai d'Orsay   175
quatoes   73
Queen's Speech   254
quiet diplomacy   62,83
quotas   76
quotas/goals and timetables   74
R   247
R category   248
rabbi   170
race-sensitive admission   80
race-sensitive admissions   76
racial charlatan Al Sharpton   76
Rand (Corp)   301
Rand Corp   300
Rangoon   293
rap   93,141
rattle his cage   190
Read my lips. No new taxes   64,306
read out of the party   72
Read Their Lips: No New Internet Tax   306
Reagan   84,289
Reagan Democrat   57,147
Reagan Democrats   64
Reagan Doctrine   63,84,289,361
Reagan Revolution   76,241
Reaganism   148,361
Reaganomics   63,64,220
real conservative   228
Real Estate   128
Real stars never die or retire   91
real/solid/true/compassionate conservative   247
rebounce   164
recession   382
recessionista   99
recovery   105
recruit   280
rector/vicar   239
red state   169,170
red baiting   325
red herring   60
red pickup truck   227
red plaid shirt   227
Red Power   92
Red States   170
redeployment   177
redistribution of wealth   220
referendum   207
reflexive response   91

Reform Party   222
refusenik   106
regime change   66,118,178,366
regional responsibilities   87
regionalism   362
regionalization   362
regular election   279
reliable sources   181
relief pitcher   156
reluctant candidate   317
rendezvous with destiny   59
rendition   66,73,78,80
representational government   258
representations   86
representative   199,258
reprieve   102
reprimand   102
Republic   283
Republic of Serbia   292
REPUBLICAN NATIONAL COMMITTEE   125
Republican Party   217
Republika Srpska   292
Repubocrat   223,225,361,375
resource center   163
resources   324,330,332
resources—both emotional and financial   331
responsible government   255,257
responsible stakeholder   85
retail   327
retail fund-raising dinner/party   58
retrograde maneuver   177
revenue enhancement   178
Reverend   242
Revlon President   64
revolution of rising expectations   66
revolving-door lobbyists   233
rich man's club   205
rif   177
Right to Life   228
right wing   225
right wingers   73
rightroots   107
rightsize   177
Riksdag   284
rip off   93
rising tide lifts all the boats   60
rocket science   107
rogue state   30
Roman Catholic Church   238
Roman correspondent   354
Rome correspondent   354
rout   141,177
row   141
royal   354
royal family   266
rubber-chicken circuit   155
rugged individual   97
rugged individualism   97
rules and practices   252
rules of engagement   366
rumpled, martini-drinking   226
Rumsfeld Doctrine   84,90
Rumsfeld war/Doctrine   366
Rumsfeld war/strategy   90
Rumsfeld's strategy   66
run against Washington   63

running mate   193
runningmate   280
Russel Trust Association   230
Russia   294
sack   141,177
same   94
same-sex marriage   118,119,150,244
Samoa   292
sand curtain   67
sandwich   284
sanitation services   118,119
sartorially   94
Saturday Night Massacre   62
sawdust Caesar   19
school choice   76,79
school prayer   76,94,240
SCHOOL SHOOTING   132
school voucher   76
SchwarzKopf boot   88
Sci   139
Scotland Yard   175,299
Scottish Parliament   263
Screen shopping   151
Sea Lord   256
second channel   83
second Gulf/Iraq war   78
Second Life   106
Second Lord   256
second reading   203,204
secret   354
secret CIA prison camps   103
Secret Intelligence Service(SIS)   298
Secret Money War   196
Secret Service   298,299
Secretary of State   186,187,382
Secretary of State for Foreign and Commonwealth Affairs   256
Secretary of State For Foreign and Commonwealth Affairs   335
Section 527 of the U. S. Tax code   196
secular   236
Secular head   239
self-incrimination   101
self-made man   58
self-sacrifice bomber   178
semiofficial diplomacy   83
semi-diplomacy   83
semi-official sources   181
Senate   198,200
Senate confirmation   208
Senator   199
senior citizen   176
sensitivity training   80
sentence   102
Seoul   293
separation of church and state   240
separation of the three (constitutional) powers   187
Serbs   294
sergeant-at-law   355
serial killer   356
server   119
sex marriage   94
sex worker   177
sexism   92
sexual harassment   92
shadow cabinet   278
Shadow Cabinet   257,279

索引

Shadow Chancellor 335
Shadow Chancellor of the Exchequer 335
shadow government 297
Shadow Minister 279
Shadow Minister/Secretary 335
shady 377
shady operators 342
Shanghai Mafia 157
shellshock 88
Sherman statement 317
Shiite community 40
Shin Bet 299
Shin Bet/Beth 299
shipping captives out for torture 80
shipping captives out for toture 78
shock and awe 366
shooting war 370
Shout out 151
showing the flag 48,116
shuck 93
shutdown 204,208,286
shuttle diplomacy 62,83
siege economics 99
Silent 95
silent majority 61,241
Silicon Valley 174
simple majority system of voting 259
simple,barefoot Wall Street lawyer 75
Sina 106
single 330
Single European Act 68
single European currency 69
single-issue politics 327
single-stick 156
sing-in 92
sing-song 177
SIPRI 302
SIS (Secret Intelligence Service) 299
sit it out 72
situational awareness 91
sit-in 92
Skull and Bones 230,231
Skype 106
slam dunk 56,65,156
slash-and-burn 376
slate 342,354
sleaze factor 63
sleeping policeman 337
sleep-in 92
slim 177
slimesling 376
sloshed 73
slowly in the wind 158
slumdog 152
slush fund 196,326
small government 219
small-time political manager 119
smart 106
smart bomb 366
Smart power 58
smart power 85,168
smell of magnolias 61
snag 142
snollygoster 120
snub 142
social agendas 38
Social and Liberal Democrats 266

Social Security 65,77,219,323
Socialist Party 217
socially liberal 224
soft bigotry of low expectations 66
soft landing 107
soft money 196
soft power 85
software 73,79,107
solicitor 355
solid conservative 228
Solid South 117
solid-state drive 106
solitary confinement 102
solon 142
Sonnenfeldt Doctrine 84
sources 180
South 292
South Africa 292
southern Africa 292
Southern Command (SOUTHCOM) 87
southern strategy 170
Soviet Union 292
space suit 105
spaced 93
spasm 91
Speaker 199,260,276,371,382
Speaker of the House 199
Special 301 99
Special Court 214
special election 201,202
Special election 295
Special Election Commission 212
Special Operations Command(SOCOM) 87
special relationship 67,270
special relationship between the British Commonwealth and Empire and the United States of America 270
special-interest groups 220
speechwriter 72
speed 93
spend and spend, tax and tax, elect and elect 219,348
spin doctor/master 73
splendid misery 154
spoils system 319
spokesman 382
spree killer 355
sputnik 89,105,106
Spycatcher affair 70
Squidgy 267
Sri LanKa 292
stakeholder 85
stakes run high 157
stalking horse 155
stand-in 92
star wars 153
Star Wars 89,158
State Council 186
State Duma 284
State Government 214,215
state legislature 214,363
state minister 256
State of the Sudan 283
State of the Union address/speech/report 210
State of the Union message 254

State of the Union (message/report) 375
state trial 337
state trooper 337
statesman 376
state's attorney 101
statue law 251
stay the course 64,66,169
stay-at-home mom 119,150
stealth auto bra 106
steel Magnolia 63
stepping-stone 189
step-by-step diplomacy 62
Stick to my last 362
Stockholm International Peace Research Institute 302
Stone of Scone 70
stoned 93
Stops Here 305
Storting 284
story 35,51,382
strange bedfellows 280
Strategic Arms Reduction Treaty 90
Strategic Command(STRATCOM) 87
Strategic Defense Initiative 89
strategic withdrawal 177
street walker 177
stricken in years 177
strife 142
strike three 104
strong mayor system 215
strung out 93
student power 92
student-driven car 337
stupid 33, 109, 120, 121, 164, 171, 312
Sub 139
subcommittee 275
subforemen 348
submerged in a bowl of alphabet soup 59,219
subprime mortgage crisis 96
subsidiarity 68
Subsidiarity 69
sub-Saharan Africa/countries 291
Success has many fathers, but failure is an orphan 60,370,320
success stories 53
success story 58
suck 370
Sucre 292
Sudden Impact 309
suitor 99
Sun reader 11
Sunday driver 337
Sunday Night Massacre 62
sunset years 176
Super 301 99
Super Tuesday 117
supervisors 216
super-sovereign currency 98
supply-side economics 63,220
support magnet 106
Supreme Court 104
Supreme Court of the United States 213
Supreme Governor 239
supreme ruler 254

surge 163,164,168,169
suspect 101
Suspended Interest Form 18
suspended interest form 22
Swaziland 292
sweeps clean 352
swift boat 196
swift boat spot 108
Swift Boat Veterans for Truth 108,
 116,147,196
swift-boat 108
Swift-Boat 147
swift-boating 108
swim-in 92
swine flu 129
swing voter 119
Switzerland 292
swoop 142
symbolic head of the Commonwealth 269
synagogue 239
synecdoche 173
system 257
(system of) proportional representation
 266
Taft-Hartley Bill 206
taikon 105
taikonaut 105
take a walk 72
take action against sb 103
take our case to the people 207
Talk Show 286,287
talking points 86
talk-show campaign 287
talk-show debate 286
Tammany Tiger 155
target process error 178
tax and spend 217
tax credit 355
tax deduction 355
tax reform 79
tax relief 77
tax simplification 77,79
tech bubble 365
technical 53
technical changes 54
technical defeat 54
technical(ly) 86
technically 54,55
teflon(-coated) President 64
Tel Aviv 293
term limits 192
term of imprisonment 102
Terri Schiavo Case 213
terror fatigue 66,170
terror fear 170,318
Terrorist Threat Integration Center
 (TTIC) 298
testify 101
testimony 102
test-tube baby 106
Texans for Truth 196
that Man in the White House 219
Thatcherism 148,361
Thatcher-friendly 345
Thatherism 289
the Achilles' heel 152
The Adventures of Tom Sawyer 152

the aged 176
The ball is in sb's/the other court 86
the big white jail 190
the blue helmets 172
the Bones 230
The Bug 305
the capitol 174
the Capitol 174
The City (of London) 174
the city on the hill 184
the city on/upon a hill 183
the Commons 259
the Congo 292
the Conservatives 265
the Democrats(Dems) 218
the Department of State 186
The duty of an Opposition is to oppose.
 206
The era of big government is over 65
the Federal Circuit 214
the first reading 203
The Foreword Was the Mideast,
 Stupid 306
the freedom agenda 84
the golden-agers 176
The government is best which governs
 least
 218
the gray hair 176
the graying Army 176
the Greens 222
the Gulf 172
The Hague 292
The Hill 174
the Hoover Institution 300
the ides of March 152
the international community 41
The jury is (still)out 156
The jury is still out 102
the left 281
the less fortunate,special-needs pupils
 176
the longer living 177
the Lords 259
the majority party 37
the Marines 366
the mature men 177
the Ministry of Foreign Affairs 186
The monarch reigns but does not
 rule 254
the mother of all battles 88,89
the mother of all bombs 89
the mother of all Bushes 89
the mother of all... 88
the nation of nations 183
The Netherlands 292
the old words best of all 151
The only thing we have to use is fear itself 124,170
The only thing we have to use is fear itself. 318
the other person 94
the otherly abled 176
the party in the White House 37
The phone is ringing off the hook 337
the plumbers 62
the Primate of All England 239
the Republicans(Repubs) 218

the right 281
The Rise and Fall of Conservatism 97
The rubber meets the road 107
the seasoned men 177
the second childhood 177
the shining city on the hill 183
the sources close to the White
 House 181
the special Olympics 176
the spokesman/spokeswoman 181
the State Department 186
the state of art 91
the States 183
The Supreme Court follows the election
 returns. 213
the Swifties 196
The Terminator 147,194
The Terminator II: Judgment Day 147,
 194
the third way 70
the Tories 265,282
the Treasury 112
the Treaty of Wesphalian 98
the U.S. presence 49
the Union 210,375
the upper house 198
the veterans 177
the well-preserved persons 177
the west end 290
the Whigs 218,282
the writing on the wall 152
the "tax-and-spends Democrats 219
The London Times 10
There the adversaries stood, eyeball to
 eyeball. 320
There you go again. 63
thermobaric 106
these two bozos 75
They never go back to Pocatello 322
think tank 300
Third House 233
Third Lord 256
third party 222
third reading 203,204
third way 264
third-party 280
third-party movement 223
Thirteenth 95
Those by death are few; by resignation
 none
 308
thousand points of light 64
Three strikes and you're in—for life
 without parole 104
three-headed monster 187
three-line whip 262
three-martini lunch 63
three-round parliamentary
 elections 363,371
three-strikes law 104
three-strikes-and-you-are-out law 104
Throttlebottom 189
ticket 354
tidal wave 352,376
tide 352
Tight 151
Time for a change 57
Timeliness 16

索 引

title 370
title company 370
to be identified 161
to begin 141
to safeguard the independence and integrity of news service 27
together 93
Tom sb 147
top secret 354
top story 51
tort abuse 81
tort reform 74,78
Tory Party 265
toss/throw one's hat in the ring 156
totalitarian state 30
touchdown 156
tough guy 321
tour the country 119
town 263
Town and Village Government 217
Track One diplomacy 82
Track Two diplomacy 83
Trade follows Her Majesty's visit 268
trade agenda 37
Trade follows Her Majesty's visit. 319
Trade follows the flag 82
trade promotion authority 79
trade promotion authority(TPA) 78
tradeoffs 91
traditional tax-and-spend president 58
transexual operation 106
transformational diplomacy 85
transitional government 257
Translating means translating the meaning 305
Transportation Command (TRANSCOM) 87
trial attorney 103
trial heat 356
trial lawyer 77,103
trickle-down theory 220
trip 93
triple agent 342
Trippin' 151
triumvirate 187
troika 187
Trojan horse 270
troop "surge" 85
Troubles 70
true believer 117
true-blue conservative 223,225
true-blue Republican 225
true-red Democrat 225
true-red liberal 223,225
Truman 84,361
Truman Doctrine 60,84
truth drug 337
turf fight 190
TV Parental Guidelines 248
TV-14 249
TV-G 249
TV-MA 250
TV-PG 249
TV-Y 249
TV-Y7 249
TWEET 133
twist slowly 158

twisting slowly, slowly in the wind 62
twitter 106
TWITTER 133
two-chamber Congress 198
two-chamber legislature 215
two-house 198
two-line whip 262
two-party system 217,222
two-term President 63,64,191,197
type of cultural conditioning 328
type of news reporting 146
types/forms of news writing 20
U. S. Judiciary 211
U. N. presence 48
U.S. Arms 136
U. S. Gold Bullion Depository 290
U. S. presence 48
U. S. attorney 103
U. S. district attorney 103
U. S. (district) attorney 101
Ulster 175
ultraconservative 240,247
Ultramontanism 238
UN mission 50
Unabomber 371
Uncle Sam 174
uncle Tom 284
uncommitted nation 355
unconstitutional 212
uncrowned King 27
under oath 102
Under Secretary 186
Under Secretary (of State for Political Affairs) 187
underground games 342
understatement 82,177
undocumented immigrant 80
undocumented immigrant/worker/alien 78
undocumented immigrants 26
ungood 72
unholy terrorist 66
unicameral 214
unilateral action 84,114
unilateralism 87,190
unitary authorities 263
unitary council 263
unitary county administration 216
unitary county borough council 263
unitary government 273
United Kingdom of Great Britain and Ireland 251
United Nations 294,304
United States 283
United States Claims Court 214
United States Court of Appeals 214
United States Court of Appeals for 214
United States District Court 214
United States Secret Service 298
United States Temporary Emergency Court of Appeals 214
unofficial diplowacy 82
unperson 337,353
unusualness 16
unwelcome visit 178
unwritten constitution 251

up 93
Upper House 259
upper house/chamber 214
uprising 178
urban cowboy 114,115
urban resources 331
USSR 294
usually reliable sources 181
uterine contents 76
values 244,246
values voter 57,241,246
values voters 66
Veep 189
Velcro President 64
Velvet Revolution 84
verbal note 86
verdict 103
verdict of guilty or not guilty 101
vertically 176
very low food security 177
vested interests 75,205
Vet 139
viagra 106
vibrations 93
Victory has a hundred fathers, but defeat·ia an orphan 60
vie 142
Vietnam 172,367
Vietnam syndrome 88
Vietnam War 92
Vietnam War syndrome 60
Vietnamization 88,178
Vietnik 106
visible hand 96
vision thing 64
visually 176
visually impaired 176
VOA 362,374
Vocabulary Building 378
void 142
voodoo economics 64,220
vote of nonconfidence/no-confidence 257
voter 354
voting 262
vulnerability 105
W 284,285
Wacked/Whack 151
wage peace 84
walk back the cat 86
Wall Street 174
Wal-Mart 286
War Department 186
war horse 155
War on Poverty 61
war on terror 66
war room 65
Warsaw Pact 294
Washington 194,375
Washington Belt 194
Washington Beltway 64
Washington Consensus 85
Washington consensus 220
Washington insider 229,230
Washington mafia 173
Washington pol 63
Washington politics 227
WASP 195
waterboarding 66,103

Watergate 4,62,99,117,267,342
Watergate Affair 297
Waterloo 294
We elect a leader, not a lover 246
We must be the arsenal of democracy 59
weak mayor system 215
weapons of mass destruction 56,65
weasel word 72
weaseling 73
Web 2.0 152
webonomics 107
webzine 107
weekend pass 125
weighted votes 69
well-informed sources 181
(the) West 291
West Lothian question 70,371
Western Samoa 292
Westminster 263
Westminster 175
Westminster Abbey 70
Westphalia 98
wet 68,225
What's good for General Motors (...is good for the country.) 321
wheel horse 155
wheels within wheels 117,347,349, 375
when going gets tough, the tough gets going. 305
When the going gets tough, these cops get going. The other way. 305
Where we are going, we don't need roads. 289
Whig Party 218
Whip 200,276
whip 360
whipper-in 200
Whips 260
Whistle blower 337
whistle blower 376
whistle-stop 206
white backlash 76
White House 174,382
white paper 86
Whitehall 175,382
Whitewater 65
Whitewater affair 375
whiz kids 61
WHO 145
Who Lost China? 325
wholesale fund-raising 58
wholsale 327
Wiener Form 18
wikiality 107
wikinomics 107

wikinovel 107
Wikipedia 106
wikiproject 107
wikiworld 107
Willie Hortorn ad 125
wimp factor 64
Win one for the Gipper 289
window 105,106
window of opportunity 105,111
window of opportunity/vulnerability 106
window of vulnerability 111
Windsor 175
winner-take-all 194
wiretapping 79
witkey 106
witness order 102
witnesses/eyewitnesses 181
WMD 65
wolf-pack robbery 104
women's lib 62
Women's Lib 92
Woodrow Wilson Doctrine 84
Word Power 378
Words do not have meanings; people have meanings for words 347
Words That Work 113
wordsmith 72
work behind the scenes 342
World Almanac 293
World Com 99
World Trade Center 291
written Constitution 184
wrong detention 102
WTO 100,362
WWW 106
X 247
xenophobia 30
xerocracy 162
Xerox 99,162
XXX category 248
Yahoo 106
Yalta Agreement 117
Yalta Conference 117,294
Yamoussoukro 292
Yangon 293
yardsticks 79
yeepies 94
yellow press 337
yes-but formula 360
yes-but principle 360
You blinked 86
You can't have your cake and eat it too 323
You can't win 69
You don't run for second. 154
You Never had It So Good 74

Youth International Party 94
YouthTube 108
YouTube 106
Yugoslavia 292
yuppies 93
Zaire 292
zero out 99
zip(per)gate 65
"ABB"(anybody but Bush) 57
"anything goes" philosophy 149
"BIT" (bilateral investment treaties) 100
"BTA"(border tax adjustments) 100
"don't ask, don't tell" 90
"gotcha" story 51
"NAMA"(nonagricultural market access) 100
"NTB"(nontariff barriers) 100
"TRAIPS"(trade related aspects of intellectual property) 100
(extraordinary)rendition 178
(Government/Opposition)Chief Whip 276
(independent)special prosecutor 178
(Party) Whip 276
(political) system 258
(special) rendition 103
(white)backlash 118
Animal Spirit 100
China's Megatrends 86
Megatrends 86
One Nation 69
swift-boat 73
The Daily Telegraphy is read by the people who remember the country as it used to be. 28
The Financial Times is read by the people who own the country. 28
The Guardian is read by the people who like to run the country. 28
The London Times 10
The Times is read by the people who run the country. 28
The Thunderer 10
-Aid 345
-friendly 345
-ism 375
101 117,237
1600 Pennsylvania Street 174
1994 Republican revolution 79,286
301(the 301st provision of the U.S. Trade Act) 99
527 116
527 group 108
527 groups 106
527 organizations/groups 196